A READER'S GUIDE TO THE CANADIAN NOVEL

Second Edition

A READER'S GUIDE TO THE CANADIAN NOVEL

Second Edition

JOHN MOSS

McClelland and Stewart

Canadian Cataloguing in Publication Data

Moss, John, 1940-
  A reader's guide to the Canadian novel

Includes index.
ISBN 0-7710-6547-7
1. Canadian fiction – History and criticism.
I. Title

PS8187.M67 1987   C813'.009   C86-094754-8
PR9192.2.M67 1987

McClelland and Stewart
The Canadian Publishers
481 University Avenue
Toronto, Ontario
M5G 2E9

For Ginny

CONTENTS

CONTENTS

viii

CONTENTS

CONTENTS

PREFACE TO THE SECOND EDITION

In the six years since the original *Reader's Guide* was published, the Canadian novel has matured in spectacular and diverse ways. Some fine new writers have appeared on the scene, and many established writers have continued to flourish, some in quite unexpected directions. In this edition, I have added essays on sixty more novels, most of them published since 1980. Revisions have been made to update earlier entries and, occasionally, to reflect a change of critical stance on my part or new work in the field. More than a dozen novels written before 1980, but for one reason or another left out of the first edition, have been added. Also included are new entries on Québécois Novels in Translation and Canadian Novels for Young Readers. A detailed explanation for the criteria of selection, as well as omission, follows in the reprinted "Preface to the First Edition," which also contains information on how best to use the *Reader's Guide*. My pleasure in working on this new edition has been sustained by the quality of the literature, the forbearance of my family, and, as before, the drive and patience of my editor, Charis Wahl.

J.M.
Bellrock, Ontario, 1987

PREFACE TO THE
FIRST EDITION

A Reader's Guide to the Canadian Novel is a critical reference
work, consisting of separate commentaries on over two hundred
Canadian novels. Each essay was written expressly to be included
here. They are arranged alphabetically by author, chronologically
where an author is represented by more than one novel. There is
no argument to the book as a whole. Novels from 1769 to 1980
have been selected on the basis of their significance within the
Canadian literary tradition, as seen from a present perspective.
The treatment of each novel makes the case for its inclusion and
attempts a critical explication of its salient features. I have tried
in this book to provide the fullest possible access, for the general
reader and specialist alike, into the rich and diverse achievement of
Canadian writing.

Each critical commentary is a complete essay in itself, although
when there are several entries for an author they should be considered cumulative. The commentaries are not written to a for-
mula; they vary according to the novel under consideration, each
being a specific critical response to a particular work. If form is
the dominant feature of the novel, then form dominates the discussion; if theme, then theme; if content, content. At the same
time, I have tried to provide in each commentary a comprehensive critical description, including information on plot, character,
setting, motifs and themes, structure, language, voice, and moral,
social, or aesthetic vision. Only where especially relevant have I
suggested the relationships of a work to an author's canon, or to
genre, literature, culture, history, or society.

Critical theories and cultural generalizations have been kept
at bay. The essence of a novel is unique; no single approach, no

one system or construct or hypothetical argument could accommodate the diversity of an authentic national literature. Every essay here represents an attempt at functional criticism, that is, criticism that seeks to illuminate its subject, not itself and not another thing. Since the subject of each is a separate work, each commentary endeavours to be autonomous and unique, its intent defined by the perceived significance of that work alone.

Significance is an elusive concept on which to base the selection of novels for an encyclopaedic study, but it is also an eclectic concept, elastic and tolerant enough to abide *The Man from Glengarry* and *Surfacing* in the same company, each for its own merits. Significance, in fact, is utterly mercurial: one novel might be found significant for its historical importance, and another for its thematic complexity; another, as a representative of its author's work, or of its type; another for some aspect of its narrative content, or for its excellent use of language, its innovative form, its exhilarating or alarming vision; some, simply because they are superb works of art in their own right. Thus it has been possible to examine the novels of Margaret Laurence alongside those of May Agnes Fleming and Arthur Stringer, without demeaning Laurence or elevating Fleming and Stringer. I have been able to applaud the talent of Robertson Davies, and more or less ignore the singular failure of his novel, *The Manticore*. Lily Dougall has been recovered from obscurity; Mavis Gallant's inexplicably neglected novels are celebrated; the genius of Elizabeth Smart extolled. The challenge in writing this book has been to avoid predetermined or inflexible criteria of significance. The criteria for selection and critical treatment vary from novel to novel; the standards of evaluation and analysis remain, as much as possible, constant throughout.

Apart from significance, the factors determining selection were practical and arbitrary. The practical factors relate quite simply to the physical limits of space on the one hand and the finite resources of the literature on the other. Given that I wanted to discuss only novels that I felt merited discussion, and in sufficient detail according to their individual needs, the number of selections was largely determined for me. The boundaries within which they were made, however, were arbitrarily established as matters of critical judgement. These are certainly open to contention and demand an explanation.

To be considered, a work had to be a novel or a closely related form. Several unified collections of short fiction have been included, where the work as a whole seemed clearly to be more than the sum of its parts: George Elliott's *The Kissing Man* is a cumulative surreal portrait of a town and its times; in *Who Do You Think You Are?* Alice Munro translates the intricate phases of a woman's life into the complex rhetoric of a whole personality; Thomas McCulloch's *The Stepsure Letters* rises beyond its origins in the columns of a newspaper to offer a coherent comic vision of early Canadian experience from a decidedly Presbyterian perspective. Full-length works of narrative prose that fall outside the purview of the novel form were considered for their importance to the development and appreciation of the Canadian novel, and several have been included. Susanna Moodie's *Roughing It in the Bush*, arguably a novel in any case, plays a significant role in the evolving tradition and is represented; her sister's book, *The Backwoods of Canada*, while delightful in its own right, remains a document of the past and is left out. Frederick Philip Grove's *Over Prairie Trails* employs the techniques of fiction to create tremendous narrative power out of incident and description, even though, like Moodie's work, it is more or less a factual account. It is included. John Glassco's *Memoirs of Montparnasse*, however, was reluctantly omitted: although the author may have been a great fictionalizer about himself, the object of Glassco's narrative is the elucidation of Glassco, not his re-creation in art. Similarly, the haunting and very beautiful book by J. Michael Yates, *The Great Bear Lake Meditations*, struggles with conviction to make the author's consciousness into art, without quite separating it from the man himself. It was left out. Autobiography is only represented here when it is in a fictional mode; non-fiction, only when it transcends its factual sources. The novel is an extremely elastic form, but not infinitely so.

To be considered, a work had to be "Canadian." This was probably the most contentious boundary to determine, and now to defend. I tried to be as flexible as possible, drawing criteria from consensus and common sense. Novels were not to be selected according to a preconceived notion of their internal Canadianness: that would perpetuate the critical fallacy of so-called thematic criticism, or systems criticism, which has dominated the popular perception of our literature for a generation. The advantage of an encyclopaedic format was that all generalizations—critical, cultural, historical–could be abandoned. A literature is defined by the works within it, not by someone's idea of what it should accommodate. No selection in this book is *more* Canadian or *less* Canadian than any other; in the same way that no person is more, nor less Canadian by virtue of personal characteristics.

Although authorial nationality was the most obvious determinant, even that admits ambiguities. I have no idea, for example, whether John Metcalf holds Canadian citizenship, or whether Mavis Gallant has abandoned hers. Both are included–while Elizabeth Spencer and Joyce Carol Oates, although quite possibly citizens, are not. In the final analysis, novels, not authors, participate in a literary tradition. Where the author's nationality proved an unreliable measure, form and content became the determining factors in judging a work Canadian: each work was considered, however, entirely on its own merits. In several instances, novels empirically not Canadian have been included in deference to popular acceptance (*Maria Chapdelaine*), or critical fiat (*Under the Volcano*), or a particular author's bent (Brian Moore insists on what his fiction will not entirely affirm, that he is a Canadian novelist). It is quite possible, of course, for a novel to participate in several literatures simultaneously, and have utterly different significance in each. Canadian literature as a cultural concept is very accommodating in this regard. Quite a number of works represented here were published before Canada existed: *The History of Emily Montague* (1769), *St. Ursula's Convent* (1824), and *Wacousta* (1832) are Canadian only in retrospect and their authors, two of whom were born in what is now Canada, were not Canadian at all.

Except for the section of this book devoted to Québécois novels in translation, only novels originally published in English were considered. Québécois literature, including the relatively few Canadian novels written in French outside Quebec, is a separable phenomenon from the literature of English Canada, although closely associated with it on a number of counts: its treatment here reflects its sovereignty. Canadian fiction written in languages other than English or French is not represented. It has been my feeling that while Josef Škvorecký, Jacob Zipper, Eva Sarvari, and the many others in Canada who write in a variety of languages may all make important contributions to the cultural mosaic of Canada, their impact on or within the national literature is slight. (A novel by Škvorecký has been included in the *Second Edition*, along with an explanation for the change of heart.) Similarly, the little aboriginal literature that has been translated into English has been of limited consequence (apart from *Harpoon of the Hunter* by Markoosie, which has also been included in the *Second Edition*). Ironically, immigrant, Indian, and Inuit experience provide major subjects for the Canadian novel in English.

For the most part I have selected novels from among those readily available. In order to be comprehensive, however, I have occasionally included works that are somewhat less accessible. I have tried to avoid undue emphasis on any particular period, region, type of novel, or group of authors. However, I have also attempted to reflect in my selections and in their critical treatment the preoccupations of the literature itself.

While selections make their own case for inclusion, omissions are acknowledged primarily by their absence. Ideally, an explanation would appear for each Canadian novel left out. While that is a practical impossibility, a few of the omissions deserve special notice. Such promising novels as *Middlewatch* by Susan Kerslake and *Family* by Jean-Guy Carrier were reluctantly excluded. Recent first novels by established writers such as W.D. Valgardson and Leon Rooke were left out, with regret similar to that felt in omitting the later works of such genuine fixtures in the Canadian firmament as Morley Callaghan, Ethel Wilson, Hugh MacLennan, and Adele Wiseman. (Rooke's *Fat Woman* and a recent novel by Callaghan have been added to the *Second Edition*.)

A significant number of novels by poets were omitted, although I appreciate their authors' poetry: among these, *King of Egypt, King of Dreams* by Gwendolyn MacEwen, *Various Persons Named Kevin O'Brien* by Alden Nowlan, and *The Charcoal Burners* by Susan Musgrave, as well as the fiction of Tom Marshall, Elizabeth Brewster, Barbara Seachel, P.K. Page, and, especially, Don Gutteridge. People I admire for a variety of reasons not related to their novels were left out if their work did not meet criteria: these include historian Donald Creighton, surgeon Wilder Penfield, critic Ronald Sutherland, actor Gordon Pinsent, journalist-provocateur Silver Donald Cameron, and dramatist George Ryga.

Novels were omitted by authors to whom I am personally predisposed, if their work seemed inappropriate: thus, Jessie L.

Beattie, Roy MacGregor, Bharati Mukherjee, Stan Dragland, Ken Mitchell, Kent Thompson, and Katherine Govier are absent, each for different reasons. There are certain works of special interest I particularly regret leaving out, although their inclusion would have stretched the standards of selection intolerably: for example, *The Awful Disclosures of Maria Monk (The Hôtel-Dieu Nunnery Unveiled)*, a delightfully scurrilous exposé originally published in the 1830s, and a prolix but innovative mystery by James De Mille called *The Cryptogram*, published in 1871, and the evocative *Narrative* of explorer David Thompson, as well as Glassco's *Memoirs of Montparnasse*, and such singular oddities as *Inglorious Milton* by Victor Lauristan and *Consider Her Ways* by Grove. Nor could I yield to a fascination for the sociology of potboilers by including more than a representative few: omitted are the works of such prodigious talents as William Lacey Amy (aka Luke Allen), who wrote more than fifty novels, and Dan Ross, who has published scores of romances under pseudonyms too numerous to mention.

In several cases the secondary work of an author was so overwhelmed by his or her primary work, and had no specific claim on its own for inclusion, that it was reluctantly omitted. Thus, the anomaly of *The Cruelest Month* by Ernest Buckler, *Sawbones Memorial* by Sinclair Ross, and *The Assumption of Rogues and Rascals* by Elizabeth Smart not being represented, although novels clearly their inferior are included for reasons other than aesthetic achievement. Other anomalies will undoubtedly be discovered. I would strongly encourage anyone reading this book to bear in mind that novels of quality and worth might have been omitted due to oversight or, even more regrettably, to authorial bias. I have attempted a fair and thorough consideration of Canadian novels, but this is by no means their definitive assessment.

The bibliographical descriptions at the head of each commentary are based on entries in the card catalogue of the National Library of Canada in Ottawa, as of January 1981 (1987, for the *Second Edition*). Information is provided according to the resources of the national repository on the original publication of a work and on the most recent edition available (Canadian wherever possible). When both editions are from the same publisher, I have simply added the date of the subsequent edition to the information on the first. (When a paperback edition is available, this is indicated in the description.) The selections of Québécois novels in English translation include in their bibliographic notes the name of the translator and information on the work's original publication in French (I have prudently not attempted to assess the quality of the translations). Appended in brackets to the bibliographical notes on the Canadian novels for Young Readers is the suggested age range for each work. No bibliography is given for secondary works mentioned in my text – all such information is readily accessible through standard reference procedures. Nor have I indicated abridgment or revision or other textual aberrations except when these might be of special concern. The reader should bear in mind that although I have tried to be thorough and accurate in the bibliographical descriptions of each selection, this is a critical study, not a bibliographical document.

The incentive to create this book came from the literature itself and from the apprehended need for such a work. There have been so many Canadian novels published over the last two centuries that standard reference books, with a mandate to be inclusive, not selective, can do little more than skim the surface. Critical overviews, by comparison, are exceedingly selective, in pursuit of rhetorical coherence rather than illumination of the novels extant. Reviews in the popular and periodic press evaluate but seldom analyse or explicate. Scholarly research and serious critical essays are necessarily restricted in scope and often available only to the specialist. The result of critical procedures to this point is a general awareness, on the part of teachers, critics, and the literate public at large, of many novels in the Canadian tradition, but practical familiarity with only a very few.

Canadian literature courses taught at all levels tend to treat the same novels again and again, without reference to the rich variety of other worthwhile works available. Critical systems and cultural generalizations are often based on the few key works that will accommodate them. CanLit and Canadian literature have come to mean different things, which only incidentally overlap. Recently, great strides have been made in scholarly approaches to Canadian literature; texts are scrutinized, compared, annotated, and evaluated. The art and its impact, however, are largely ignored. Scholarship and appreciation seem presently at odds with each other, as were criticism and appreciation in the immediate past. This book does not presume to resolve such disparities, but it is in response to conditions like these that it was written. If a broader base has been established for the appreciation of Canadian writing, if more novels have been made accessible or more accessible, if the tradition has been exposed in a state of excitement, if interest or even antipathy has been aroused; then, the objectives of this book will in good part have been realized.

As the work of an individual author, *A Reader's Guide to the Canadian Novel* bears the recognizable imprint of a single personality. I have tried to restrain my own presence throughout; however, objectivity born of impersonality I find particularly suspect. I have made no effort to hide my enthusiasms, nor to conceal what I dislike, but I have tried in each commentary to validate my responses through critical discussion, to objectify them in fair and responsible argument. This book has been a formidable undertaking, calling for a discomfiting combination of arrogance and humility. It has been an undertaking through which the demands of perseverance were continually offset by the pleasures they yielded. In reading and re-reading well over a thousand novels for this project, I discovered as much about myself as about the literature. The reader, however, is spared anything more than subliminal confession, and is, rather, invited to share in the vast resources of the Canadian novel. The extent to which this book succeeds in attaining its objectives is a tribute to Canadian writing. Its limitations are my own responsibility entirely.

Bellrock, Ontario, 1981

A READER'S GUIDE TO THE CANADIAN NOVEL

MARGARET ATWOOD

The Edible Woman. Toronto: McClelland and Stewart,
1969. Toronto: McClelland and Stewart, New Canadian
Library, 1973. Toronto: Seal, 1978. Pages: 294. Paperback.

Margaret Atwood is a ubiquitous presence in recent Canadian
literature. Atwood made her reputation as a poet during the 1960s
and has since developed an avid following as a writer of fiction.
During the past quarter century she has also published literary
criticism, cartoons, interviews, children's books, and numerous
letters to the editor. She is an international celebrity, especially
among feminists. A thorough professional, Atwood continues to
create works of exceptionally high quality. Until *The Handmaid's
Tale*, however, her novels seem to have been increasingly less satisfactory to the critics, particularly within Canada, than to the literate public. She lost none of the intellectual precision or acerbic
wit she showed in her earliest work, and her prose continued to
be commanding; but her sensibility is very much of her own times.
As these inevitably pass, her vision seems dated, even though it
is reassuring to those who mature with her.

In her fiction as well as her poetry, Atwood is a writer of themes
and style. Her peculiar astringent blending of these two elements
links her separate works, which display such technical and intellectual versatility that they often seem unrelated. Through a
narrative voice that slyly draws her readers into its confidence
on the side of her protagonists, we become allied with her against
the more obvious evils of contemporary society (Atwood is by no

1

means a radical dissident). In *The Edible Woman*, the voice complements Marian MacAlpine's character; but even in the first and third sections, which are related from a first-person point of view, the voice suggests a consciousness far more knowing than Marian's own. In *Surfacing*, the voice is perfectly in keeping with the narrative point of view as it slips deeper and deeper into subconscious realities. In *Lady Oracle*, voice and character seem somewhat out of sync; in *Life Before Man*, where the point of view is split into several parts, the voice often seems out of control. While in *Bodily Harm* voice is simply an aspect of atmosphere, in *The Handmaid's Tale* there is a tension between the principal narrator's voice and the presence of the author within language itself that creates a sophisticated pattern of emphasis and ironic counterpoint, which is one of the novel's most arresting characteristics.

Atwood's first novel describes the travails of a young woman just out of university and adrift in Toronto. Like her friends, she has no real past and only a nebulous future: all attention is focused on the present. Marian MacAlpine is overwhelmed by an awareness of options. She can marry Peter, the smooth young lawyer who needs a wife to complement his collection of knives, guns, and cameras. Or she can align herself with the irrepressibly self-indulgent Duncan. In looking for role models, she hovers between Ainsley, the flip, feminist manipulator, and Clara, the old friend immersed in diapers and drudgery. The office virgins and the graduate English students, in counterbalance, provide choral comic relief. Atwood allows her reader the smug satisfaction of finding them all rather feckless and absurd – all except Marian, who is our consciousness in the midst of this ménage.

Marian works for Seymour Surveys. Her job provides Atwood with an ideal point from which to jibe at consumerism, at corporate manipulation of public appetites, and at the voraciousness of the indiscriminate masses. There are no surprises in the objects of Atwood's derision. Instead, we feel reassured that someone else has noticed the problems in society that we have noticed, and has written about them.

The Edible Woman is striking because of the fusion of its two modes: the confessional and the satiric. Marian discovers that she is being plastic-wrapped, consumed. Her knowledge nearly destroys her. What might have been a conventional story of self-discovery is, instead, the frightening vision of a struggle for survival or for sanity. Marian's integrity carries her through–but to what? We are not given enough insight to know. Marian's survival depends on what the world will bring upon her–and therein lies the novel's biggest problem. Atwood rails at the effects of the plastic world but does not examine their root causes. As those effects change, the novel seems more a document of the sixties than a vision.

When *The Edible Woman* first appeared, enthusiasts of Atwood's poetry had high expectations, and they were not disappointed. Here are images that seem so precise and simple they are almost clichés; yet they contain sudden, often cruel, twists that transform even the most ordinary into the bizarre. Here is wit, not quite concealing a cry of despair or a supercilious hiss. Here, too, are situations, characters, and conditions the reader can immediately recognize; Marian's responses to them are compatible with the reader's own. *The Edible Woman* confirmed the intimations in Atwood's poetry that here was a Canadian writer of major significance.

Surfacing. Toronto: McClelland and Stewart, 1972.
Don Mills: General; New Press Canadian Classics, 1983.
Pages: 192. Paperback.

In *Surfacing*, Atwood gets everything–words, images, themes, and story–together into a form that extends from surface patterns in the beginning down into the very depths of being and then surges, at the end, to the surface once again. It is a more difficult and demanding novel to read than her others, and proportionately better. *Surfacing* stands comfortably among the best novels in our literature.

The narrator of *Surfacing* is a nameless woman in her late twenties. With her lover and two companions, she travels to the island cabin in northern Quebec where she had spent childhood summers. The woman is searching for her father, who is reported missing. Her friends, whom she hardly knows, are diverted by the rustic novelty of the setting. The woman begins to feel increasingly isolated. She is haunted by her missing father, by her dead mother, by childhood memories, by a marriage that never occurred, by the child she aborted. As time passes she turns increasingly inward and begins to view the external world from a new perspective. This process has the appearance almost of madness, though from her point of view, where appearance and reality are one, she is quite sane.

Memory apparitions of her father and mother act as guides as she approaches prenatal, primeval consciousness. Her three companions leave. She reverts to an animal consciousness – her mother's legacy, her link with the natural process. She grows human again – her father's gift, the ability to confront the beast within. Pregnant once more, she is ready to leave when her lover returns for her.

During her time on the island, Atwood's narrator experiences a return to her sources as a human being. She discovers that words and word-consciousness seal off our heads from our bodies, thus dichotomizing our experience of self. With this recognition, she begins to take responsibility for what she has and has not been and for the person she has become. In the process, she discovers much about the contemporary world of facile communications and mindless consumption. She has explored the world beneath the surface of her experience, but she must return to the surface – she cannot survive anywhere else – and she does so with determination.

The narrator's search for her father is combined with her interior quest, providing a complex story-line of intriguing subtlety. Atwood's biting wit is always present, keeping us at a safe distance from the narrator's madness. At the same time, Atwood makes us see reality from the narrator's perspective. We see vividly what the narrator, even at her most irrational, experiences.

Atwood has a perfect command of images and words as poetic determinants of reality. That is, image and word not only describe something, they become that something, as it is perceived or conceived. Thus, the *idea* of a fish jumping is the reality; an owl's voice has claws and feathers. The word "tree" joins speaker to object; they become one. Atwood offers us the reality her narrator perceives/conceives, and appearance and reality merge. Where they do not, as in photographs and mirrors, there is only surface. In all, *Surfacing* is a formidable achievement, brilliantly accomplished.

Lady Oracle. Toronto: McClelland and Stewart, 1976.
Toronto: Seal, 1977. Pages: 345. Paperback.

Atwood's third novel, *Lady Oracle*, manages to be shallow and deep at the same time, like an image in a mirror, which is both two-dimensional and three-dimensional. Joan Foster is a thoroughly bland protagonist, and yet the novel, a gothic comedy, fascinates. Certainly, Joan's experiences are interesting enough. It is the self-indulgent passivity of her responses to them that, in the comic tradition, is so inept, so uninspired, as to be ludicrous and moving. Whatever meaning we are to draw from Joan comes from outside her own recognition of things. She is more a part of the satire than the heroines of Atwood's earlier fiction were.

The novel opens in Italy, after Joan has faked a suicide. The various personae of her life were converging, and she, typically, took the course of least resistance. A celebrated poet, Joan left behind a hopelessly radical husband, a far-out lover, and an inept blackmailer. She also left two friends, who had to account for her disappearance to the police. And she left the reputable publishing firm of Morton and Sturgess to reap the financial benefits of her tragic demise. She brought away with her the fat little girl she was (whom she can never quite escape) and her alter-identity, Louisa K. Delacourt. Louisa is presently at work on her sixteenth sentimental historical romance, appropriately entitled *Stalked by Love*. Everything about Joan is fake or superficial. Even her poetry, which, under the title *Lady Oracle*, thrust her into literary stardom, was automatic writing.

Atwood's account of Joan's life is choppily chronological. Incidents and relationships emerge and disappear. Some are hilarious, others quite touching. At seven, Joan plays the role of a mothball in a dance-school pageant; she learns to accept what cannot be altered. Years later, in London, she takes up with a Polish count; to divert herself from his chauvinistic demands, she starts writing her historical romances and discovers herself at home in the manipulation of surface realities – another devastating lesson. Innocent, innocuous Joan: all around her, people are hurt without her even being aware of it. Somehow, cruelly, Atwood allows those people to deserve what they get.

The novel ridicules romance, philosophy, spiritualism, creativity, literature, physicality, parenthood, heroism, sexuality. Atwood attacks not the thing itself, but its distortion. And her bite is worse than her bark. By making Joan Foster as romantic a heroine as those Joan creates, Atwood parodies romance. Yet Joan lives in a real world, which is realistically conveyed. There she is, a sad, absurd person of epic dimension – with no substance. She is the satiric embodiment of our present times.

In her critical work, *Survival*, Atwood has aligned women in fiction with three major motifs – maidenhood (Diana), fertility (Venus), and death/the oracular (Hecate). The protagonists of her first three novels coincide rather neatly with one or another of these categories; thus it became a matter of critical interest where she would go in her next novel. *Life Before Man* features a whole cluster of protagonists (perhaps inevitably, given the above), with a compound narrative voice that seems, at times, out of control, related neither to the separate characters nor to their collective reality. The effect is a novel that seems curiously sluggish, a vehicle for predictable swipes at all that is fashionably open to attack. The characters are conventionally off-beat; the situations, called relationships, are tired and trivial. *Life Before Man* is not a very good novel by objective critical standards, yet it appears to have sold exceptionally well, a tribute to the author's reputation more than to the novel's achievement. It has fared better with the critics outside Canada than at home; perhaps their expectations are lower.

The same could be said about her penultimate novel, *Bodily Harm*. It has sold well and has been generally praised by foreign critics. While it has the expected dimensions of significance, conveyed through the clever use of cancer and a Caribbean setting, it is clearly Atwood's most concerted attempt at capturing the popular market, albeit with dignity. It is quite successful in achieving its limited ambition.

The Handmaid's Tale. Toronto: McClelland and Stewart, 1985. Pages: 324. Toronto: Seal, 1986. Paperback.

What a wicked, sad, and witty rendering of nightmare – Atwood at her best! This novel is a striking achievement on a number of counts. After faltering somewhat in *Bodily Harm*, Atwood hits her stride again with this mordant fantasy of the world gone awry. *The Handmaid's Tale* is a gut-wrenching novel of ideas, a future projection set in a past that has not yet happened. It is the first major feminist novel to come out in Canada since Audrey Thomas's *Blown Figures* (1974)–feminist in form and not just in content (story as rhetoric). It is postmodern, though only by default since Atwood seems to work intuitively rather than intellectually beyond the strictures and illusions of modernism. While as indisputably Canadian as its author, Atwood's dystopia is set in Massachusetts and its cultural, intellectual, and historical referents are determinedly American, or else drawn broadly from the Western, Judeo-Christian heritage as a whole. It is a cautionary tale, evoking angst and outrage rather than pity or fear. It leaves the reader with a somewhat unspecific vision, but nonetheless chilled to the bone.

Imagine: the world of Jerry Falwell's Moral Majority made explicit in images by Hieronymus Bosch; imagine a world with the power to retaliate against Boy George. Think of the consequences of negative population growth in a society committed, like Amway and Mary Kay Cosmetics, to perpetual expansion. Think of America imploding and the land of Gilead displacing New England. And think of a future world where legislation rests not on interpretation of the Constitution but on literal and selected readings of the Old Testament. This is the closed world Atwood dreams for us.

Imagine: the patriarchal hegemonies of Jacob or of Abraham, the misery, mysogyny, lack of personal freedom (there is no antonym for freedom in English, only examples of its absence); combine with what Nazi Germany has taught us in this century, and history in others, of the human will to rule through terror, and of our capacity to suffer and endure; sanction all of this with the insidious power of contemporary technology; call such a world Gilead. This is the world Atwood offers, floating on the surface of our own only a decade or so away.

The grotesque distortions there of social and environmental conditions, of politics and sexuality, and, encircling all, of religion, are implied by the way things are in the present. This is the dream vision of a strange future that seems inevitable in retrospect. Perhaps the most disconcerting twist is that in the closing pages of the novel Atwood reveals this future to be the partially obscured past of an even more distant future–which, ironically, is oddly akin to "now." Time, ultimately, becomes the only sanctuary from Atwood's nightmare.

The details of her dystopian vision, while at times alarming, are relatively unimportant. Their narrative function is to enliven rather than elucidate: they are an extension of the narrator's life and mind. Her presence, however, is not the novel's centre but its perimeter, its circumference. Offred's story opens up to us in a series of discontinuous revelations that eventually provide a panoramic view of her experienced world, without the author either defining that world apart from her protagonist or drawing Offred through it in a linear sequence of episodes toward completion. In other words, the main character is neither the sum of her experiences nor an extension of her context. That would be modernism in the male mode.

The Handmaid's Tale is very much a postmodern venture. The primary activity of the novel is within the reader's mind–not reacting but acting; putting together the contrary, confusing, and incomplete elements of the narrator's account. The reader extrapolates a coherent if terrible world from Offred's pathetically narrowed vision, projects beyond the severe emotional constraints of her conditioning, and literally shares with Offred the dilemma of how to construct narrative. Atwood's own presence in the narrative is paradoxical. She is quite separable from her narrator, yet her style and Offred's intersect. The cockeyed commas, inverted syntax, distended clichés, startling and enigmatic metaphors, cumulative extended analogies–Atwood and her narrator share a fondness for these, in prose that comes simultaneously from both. Yet the same words, language, and style have different meanings, depending on which of the two is ascendant. Atwood's mordant wit, for example, may powerfully drive a point home while, from the very same turn of phrase, Offred might offer only meagre defiance, barely secure within the confines of her constricted mind.

When Gilead came to be, Offred lost her husband and daughter, and, as a fertile woman, her rights to individuality and self-determination. Designated a "Handmaid," her sole function became to bear children. To this end, her name and identity and all personal freedoms are taken from her (she is reduced to a prepositional phrase, "of Fred," modifying her current liege). After appropriate training, she is assigned to a barren household, her future determined by the function of her womb. She lives the cloistered life of a nun with no God. Dressed in red habits, she and the other Handmaids move about in Atwood's wry rendering of Cambridge, Mass., in stifled terror. Fragmented memories from "the other time" still lacerate her mind, yet give her strength to endure. She meets secretly with her Commander for illicit Scrabble; then with Carl the chauffeur for sex – an affair first arranged by her Commander's wife, the Wife, who desperately wants the status of a household pregnancy. She witnesses torture and execution by manual dismemberment. Being a woman she cannot, must not, ever read.

As a Handmaid, Offred follows literally the example from Genesis of Bilhah with Rachel and Jacob. She lies between the Wife's legs to receive her Commander's periodic insemination. She has three years to conceive; thirty-six encounters. If not, then off to the Colonies, a vague and frightening place on the edge of Gilead. But also on the edge of Gilead is Canada, much the same as now, and beyond is the world we know, a little older but apparently much the same. This we discover in an epilogue wherein Offred's text is the subject of a Learned Conference in the twenty-second century. At her story's close, Offred escapes to reconstruct her "life." The academics who place her in historical context, however, cannot be certain what became of her. Within her own story, in a lovely solipsism, she struggled to create narrative, to write herself into being. In reducing her account to facts, to documentary artifact, they empty it of personality and meaning. Offred becomes historical and therefore unreal – for history, it seems, is the procedure, academic or otherwise, by which we absolve ourselves of the past. Even when it has not happened yet.

In this novel Atwood affirms her reputation as one of our very best and most versatile novelists. Along with a few of her contemporaries such as Matt Cohen and Timothy Findley, she proves the inadequacy of such limiting critical appreciation as she herself popularized in *Survival*, in which writers are clustered thematically according to their contribution to national identity. The disturbing themes of this novel, the radical structuring, and the speculative vision relate more to our essential humanity, or lack thereof, than to matters of self-doubt and self-indulgence. *The Handmaid's Tale* is a brilliantly conceived and executed work of art, taken from almost any perspective, seen in almost any context.

JOAN BARFOOT

Abra. Toronto: McGraw-Hill Ryerson, 1978. Pages: 199.
Scarborough: New American Library, 1979. Paperback.

Joan Barfoot's three published novels establish her as one of the most accomplished young writers in Canada. Her second, *Dancing in the Dark*, is a tour de force – its brilliance and audacity are exhilarating. *Abra* pales a little in comparison, but it is lucid, fresh, and moving, a singular achievement. It is a rare first novel in which striking maturity of insight is conveyed with remarkably disciplined and yet lyrical style. Her third, *Duet for Three*, is a sound novel, but conservative. A study of the relationships among women, especially of different generations, it represents more a consolidation than an extension of Barfoot's talent.

In *Abra*, what might have been a rather enigmatic little story is, in fact, far-reaching, complex, and powerful. Not that a woman leaving her husband and two children to live by herself on the edge of wilderness is of little consequence. This woman, like Melville's Bartleby the scrivener, neither understands what she does nor feels called upon to account for herself, yet she acts with intransigent determination. Such a story might easily have foundered had it not been for Barfoot's deft handling of narrative to make us care.

We do care about Abra Phillips. Barfoot has a special talent for drawing us deep into the lives of characters who take no responsibility for those enormous actions in their lives that inexorably alter the world around them, who seem uninterested in the consequences of what they do and only vaguely interested in why. Abra becomes important to us from her opening words. She contemplates her name. She seems nearly to have forgotten it. There is no urgency about the memories that move through her, into consciousness, over the next few months and chapters. They seem to rise from within her, neatly and coherently, as if they belonged to someone else and she were considering them for the first time. We are far more involved with her memories than she is. And why? Well, precisely because she is not. To her, they are of only passing concern. Her life, the enormity of what she has done in coming to this isolated stone cabin nine years ago, mean little to her. We cannot resist the fascination of a character who lives so wholly within herself that nothing else matters – not past or future, but only the present; not children or identity, but only being; not life, but living.

Much of the credit for this is philosophical. As with Bartleby, we are forced to evaluate the relationships between action and inaction, self and other, motivation and behaviour, responsibility and being. But much else is due to the quality of Barfoot's writing. With only the rarest lapse, the style of her prose slips by in haunting counterpoint to the emotional condition of her narrator. When Abra is least in command of herself, the words, syntax, and imagery are most under control; when her sense of self is diffuse or opaque, the language is precise. Only as she regards the world immediately surrounding her cabin and performs the essential tasks for comfortable survival (she burns much wood, but has electric heat throughout) do consciousness and the prose used to express it fall into harmony. Then, there is a discontinuous intensity that is disturbing and, curiously, reassuring – suggesting obsession but also stability.

Abra has lived on her own for nearly a decade when the novel opens. She is an eccentric, a recluse, a subsistence gardener, and apparently quite at ease with herself and her way of life. That, in fact, is of utmost importance: self and way of life for Abra are one and the same. In the unity of doing and being she has found peace. The arrival of her daughter Kate, now eighteen, changes things. Not dramatically, for Abra seldom allows anything to touch her beyond the moment. Kate arouses neither self-recrimination nor regret, but only a self-consciousness that is mildly disconcerting as it draws Abra first to survey the conditions of her present life and then, as Kate's visit stretches through the summer season (its purpose, to repossess her, undeclared but affecting), to survey the past. She remembers in a disconnected sort of way her marriage to Stephen Phillips, a kind and successful man, and she remembers their children, Elliott and Kate. She recalls only a little of her childhood, but her wedding is clear in her mind. And so are working to support Stephen through university, and labour, childbirth, mothering, and keeping house. She remembers feeling empty, numb, blank, tired, directionless – and guilty. She remembers Stephen's success, a big house, dinner parties, the dog, keeping house; waiting for the others to come home; and waiting, to be someone. And then she remembers seeing an ad, buying her place with a small inheritance, and simply leaving. No second thoughts, no remorse. An escape from time, from words, from responsibility; an escape from identity, from people, perhaps from self.

The remainder of her story consists of a detailed description of her life in apparent harmony with the natural world, the seasons, the primal demands of her existence. This account is interspersed with brief and muted encounters in the ongoing present with Kate, who wants to know – to know something, anything, that will help her understand. But Abra herself does not understand why she left, why she lives the way she does, what might have been, who might have been affected (the nine-year-old loving daughter, now a young woman wanting to connect). None of this interests Abra very much. Briefly she thinks of going back with Kate to Toronto (it is only one hundred and thirty miles away; and another world), but in the end she stays. Kate leaves. Abra remains content.

Is that enough? To be content, to be at peace – or is Abra mad? It does cross her mind that she has had a breakdown, but has her cabin refuge been the evidence of this or the cure? Is her dissociated condition and consequent sense of peace insanity, a safe environment she has made for herself, such as R.D. Laing might provide for one of his psychotics in a more clinical setting? Is this what would have happened to Atwood's narrator in *Surfacing* had she not surfaced, this living in relation to time as an animal, in relation to nature as a survivor, in relation to society as a recluse? We strangely admire Abra for her determination to remain dispassionate, disengaged, beyond the pale of responsibility or affection. At the same time, surely, we are appalled.

As always with the best of writing, the content in Barfoot's fiction cannot be separated from form and style. Each is an expression and a reflection of the other. The words in Abra Phillips' mind and the words of Barfoot's prose, Abra's account of herself and Barfoot's narrative, are often at ironic odds although they are the same words, the same story. They come simultaneously from two directions, from within, from Abra's experience of reality on the one hand, and from the text, from the author's vision of reality. The resulting indeterminacy is what makes our own experience as we read simultaneously acute and opaque, sympathetic and yet disconcerting. It is, in good part, what elevates this quiet, sad, and beautiful novel to the highest level of art.

Dancing in the Dark. Toronto: Macmillan, 1982, 1986.
Pages: 183. Paperback.

It's enough to take your breath away, the sheer brilliance of her writing! As you read you want to applaud. You want to take Edna aside, to whisper through the impermeability of her isolation, to say, "My God, you say it right." You want to shout, "Leave her be. Let her write. She does it perfectly." Poor Edna. They do leave her be: they protect her, clean and feed her, try to make her talk and be who she was before the murder. Only you and she know both sides, before and after. You see inside Edna's world, which she writes for you with such astonishing lucidity you reel at times from the force of her eloquence, and outside Edna's world, the outside *of* Edna's world, the hospital, nurses, doctors, windows, walls. You see who she was and is, and what she has done and does. To do and be are not the same. Edna explains herself. You listen.

(It is interesting to compare Edna with Abra, in Barfoot's first novel. For Abra doing and being become virtually the same thing, and, as a consequence, she lives in what is either a state of near-grace or of benign insanity.)

Edna's story is a woman's story. This is a woman's novel. That does not mean it is accessible only to women. It is a feminist novel, and that does not mean it is one-sided rhetoric. *Dancing in the Dark* dramatically illuminates experience familiar to all of us but to which the female reader may relate directly in ways the male can only guess at and imagine. It is a work of the imagination, so genders meet in sharing Edna's story – but it is not, perhaps, the same story for both.

Joan Barfoot is a fine writer. *Dancing in the Dark* is a major novel. It is not a classic in the sense that people will turn to it for years to come in search of vital ambiguities that will reaffirm their own precarious existence. In that sense, *As for Me and My House* and *The Double Hook* are classics. Nor is it a large work, spanning generations, continents, or philosophical systems. It is a major novel in the way of something written by Mavis Gallant or Alice Munro. The beauty of the prose, the perspicacity of insight, the quite remarkable elevation of fictional reality to a particularized intensity that sears indelibly into the reader's mind, the apparent rightness of every word, tone, and detail, of shape, movement, rhythm, of every aspect of the novel as it contributes to the impact and integrity of the whole–these make this novel a major achievement. It is a haunting novel, both while being read and to hold in the mind, afterwards. It is not the story, though, nor even the character of Edna, that will do the haunting. Confinement in a mental hospital, murder of her beloved husband, revelations of personality, these are important elements of the fiction. But what invades the consciousness while reading and takes command is the reality of Edna's world. Her world is more real than our own: it is fiction and made of language, but words and images and insights work so wholly toward the singular end of making Edna's world real for us that our own while reading is to some extent displaced. This is a curious thing to happen, given that Edna is, by all external measures, quite insane.

Edna Cormick in the hospital writes in perfectly neat small script, keeping carefully within the lines, about her life as a perfect housewife. Her notebooks accumulate rapidly; they are her only form of expression, for she speaks to no one and stays locked inside herself beyond the reach of therapy, or of contrition or despair. She is calm and curious. Had she done something wrong, left some corner of her house undusted, some need of her husband unfilled? Was it something she did not do that made him unfaithful, that made it necessary for her to carve him up with the tomato knife? She tried so hard to please him: never serving two white vegetables in the same meal, never putting him in the awkward position of having to ask for a clean shirt, changing the beds daily and vacuuming the entire house twice a week.

From early girlhood Edna acknowledged her own limitations by taking magazine articles to heart, articles on how to look your best, be popular, decorate your room, please your man. She had no ambition, growing up, but to be twenty–at which point things would turn around, she was sure, and she would be somebody's. And at twenty, at university where she lives alone, she meets Harry and becomes his. They make love and marry. For more than twenty years she lives in his reflected light. She does not live vicariously through Harry, through his ambitions, achievements, and modest demands in the consumer world. She lives for him. Her life is his, to serve him, care for him, anticipate his needs. She wants nothing for herself but to be needed, to be his. Oh, there are small perks. Her domestic ritual includes soaking in the tub, with cigarettes and magazines close at hand, and lying down in the afternoon, listening to music, eyes closed, dancing in the darkness of her dream-illuminated mind. For twenty years she is the perfect housewife, the perfect wife. She is not a mother–that hurts, if she lets it. She is proud of her perfection. Afterwards, she searches vainly for the flaw. Why would Harry do such a thing? (She does not query the necessity of murder, but rather, why he made it so.)

Edna almost always maintains control. Small insults or unintended slights she lets slide off her slick, well-groomed, magazine-designed exterior/interior (with Edna, there is little difference, or so it seems, even to her). Now, in the narrative present, in the hospital, as she writes all this down of who she was, her apparent control is nearly absolute. But inside, in her writing and her written self, she admits vulnerability, admits worries, fears, the anxiety of knowing how limited were her desires. She admits, but does not comprehend. She was perhaps not happy, but she was content, resting her life on Harry the way she did. Recognition that all was not always well leads, now, only to a new appreciation of just how committed she had been to making things work. At the novel's end, her account of herself catches up to the present, and her story is complete–but having told it makes no difference. She has not reached an understanding; she has not purged herself of imperfection; she has merely drawn herself together and, whole in herself, she might now perhaps become someone else. But who?

Edna's narrative retrospective is delicately interwoven with brief passages describing her ongoing life in the hospital. In a feat of writing accomplishment to marvel at, Barfoot conveys Edna's radically limited perspective and her demented manner with vivid, almost lyrical, intensity. We share her experience of the hospital but we also share her consciousness, her experience of herself, and the two seem irreconcilable. From outside, she appears dumbfounded and clearly mad. Inside, she is cool and articulate. The few times she speaks we simultaneously recognize how reasonable it is, what she says, and how insanely absurd it must seem. She tells us what her psychiatrist asks, she writes his questions meticulously in her notebooks as he asks them. And we see, as well, what he sees–an expressionless, demented woman busily scribbling as he talks, apparently not even aware of her surroundings.

And shot through the fabric of these two simultaneous narratives, her life story and her hospital life, are sporadic flashes of another narrative, of the day she murdered Harry. These flashes

15

are at first opaque, ambiguous, elusive, but they are sufficiently sinister to cast an ominous aura over everything else she recalls and observes. By the end they coalesce into a direct and pitiless account of Harry's death: Edna, waiting at home for Harry, perfectly groomed, looking younger still than forty-three (says Harry: but what happens when she does look forty-three!), waiting as she always does from the moment he leaves in the morning, waiting, and cleaning her house, taking care of her body, for Harry, cleaning up, cleaning, vacuuming–but she never finishes. There is a telephone call and all her suppressed fears of aging, of losing her appeal to Harry, suddenly converge with an utter absence of feeling as she learns of his betrayal. Edna waiting for Harry. And then the murder. The feel of the knife in flesh, on bone. Harry dead. And briefly, the end of Edna's story.

We know from the beginning, from the first pages of her account, what she has done. We are fascinated by its lack of consequence: she does not avoid or evade; she simply does not allow the act significance. It happened. We know to the end what she has done. It is this knowledge, as we read, that makes Edna, plastic as she is, superficial, self-serving, unimaginative as she is, a character at once pathetic and powerful. She is the woman in the supermarket at eleven in the morning wearing full makeup and dressed by a magazine, slick and cool, getting the best lettuce before it wilts. She is the woman on the small white bed, unmoving, ice cold, waiting. We do care for her.

The sheer brilliance of Barfoot's writing is enough to take your breath away. She is among the best prose stylists of her generation–and yet her prose invariably serves the fiction, brings her character's reality alive in the reader's mind. *Dancing in the Dark* is a singular achievement by a very important writer.

ROBERT BARR

The Measure of the Rule. New York: Appleton, 1908.
Toronto: University of Toronto Press; Reprint Library,
1973. Pages: 308.

As time passes, works of literature often experience shifts in relative importance. A book that at one time seemed negligible assumes great significance; another work, once seen as seminal, seems now to be peripheral. From the perspective of a moving present, nothing in the past is fixed. Almost nothing: there are a few works that, while they continue to excite a certain curious interest, are indisputably, intransigently second-rate. *The Measure of the Rule* is one such work. If one were to write a paper in praise of the second-rate, no better example could be found upon which to build a thesis than this novel by Robert Barr.

The Measure of the Rule is an episodic account of Thomas Prentiss's life and times at the Toronto Normal School before the turn of the century. Tom and his friend Sam McKurdy are the brightest in their class, except for the heroically consistent bounder John Henceforth, with whom the two friends sustain a running battle of invective. The thrust and parry of verbal wit provides much of the novel's vitality. There are romances between Tom and Aline, and Sam and Sally, who, under the prudent dispensation of the school, are forbidden to exchange so much as a glance. There is Tom's arch-enemy, John Brent, the dazzling head of the Model School. The head of the Normal School is the kindly Dr. Cardiff; the powerful and righteous Dr. Darnell is an instructor. Stock characters, stock situations. Add to these an excruciating prose style, sexism, racism, and narrative contrivance of the most arbitrary and presumptuous sort. In the end, Tom quite suddenly decides to leave Normal School to become an artist; he submits a painting of his true love, Aline Arbuthnot, to the Salon in Paris and, of course, takes the prize.

The novel is determinedly second-rate but not tenth-, and it is of importance in our literary tradition. Its saving grace lies in the insistent portrait it provides of time, place, and, most significantly, popular taste. From the opening pages, Toronto springs to life with colourful vigour unmatched until Hugh Garner's *Cabbagetown* appeared half a century later. The broad humour, caustic wit, and sarcasm raised to a fine art contribute to the reader's clear impression of contemporary sensibility; but it is in the details of locale that Barr's novel excels. *The Measure of the Rule* is convincing even when it is not at all believable.

CONSTANCE BERESFORD-HOWE

The Book of Eve. Toronto: Macmillan, 1973. New York: Avon, 1975. Toronto: McClelland and Stewart; New Canadian Library, 1984. Pages: 191. Paperback.

That old woman dragging a tattered shopping bag through the snow, wearing boys' running shoes and a stained coat with a frazzled fur collar, a yellow muffler wrapped imperiously about her head and huge sunglasses perched against her face, muttering aloud as she picks a treasure out of the gutter – she may have been somebody once. In this delightful novel we discover she was, indeed, somebody: a middle-class matron from NDG in Montreal. She was grandmother, mother, wife, daughter of parents now deceased, nursemaid to a cranky husband, MA, former teacher, hardly different from anyone else in the safe, smug world she left behind. We also discover that she is far more a somebody now. She is an eccentric refugee from Eden; she is her own person, damned with the knowledge of her separate existence in the world and proud of it; content, finally, to be so.

One day, in the autumn of her sixty-sixth year, Eva Carroll walks out on her husband of forty years and takes a taxi and her pension cheque across Montreal to a different life. She moves into the basement apartment of a dingy rooming house and contemplates her own audacity with both triumph and foreboding. Beresford-Howe's novel is a warm, humane, and often very funny account. She generally writes polished fiction for a broad market. This novel certainly has wide appeal, but it also has that special quality of fine literature in which narrative and narrative voice are in perfect harmony. Eva is a truly memorable literary creation.

Although Eva relates her account in the conventional past tense, there is a powerful immediacy to her words; it is as if she were recording what had just happened to her, moments before. As she ruminates we discover in this unassuming woman a vital personality that has been all but extinguished, throughout her long life, by middle-class restraints. Yet she has managed this one great act of defiance; she has renounced responsibility and respectability; and she now struggles to come into possession of the sensitive, anarchic personality that has always been inside her. Her first months of freedom find her coping with the enormity of her act. She composes letters to God, to an old friend who died years before, and to herself; she adjusts to poverty, to winter; she learns to accept practical eccentricities, like the running shoes and the muffler, as conditions of her free state; she develops her most profitable habit, scavenging; she survives. And she survives with wilful high spirits, with humour. Only occasionally do the grave depths to which she sinks remind us she was not always this vital personality.

Gradually, Eva becomes involved with others in the house. Johnny Horvath, a forty-eight-year-old Hungarian roughneck-intellectual, becomes her lover—much to her bewilderment. But eventually, despite his fine meals, wild talk, and tender affection, she rejects him for his infidelity with a young waitress. Then, recognizing such a response belongs to the world she left behind, she takes charge of her own existence and opens herself to Johnny again. She is the new Eve, as the title and numerous allusions imply. But has she left the Garden, or returned to it? In the end, she accepts her fallen state and the gifts of knowledge and independence that go along with it.

The enormous appeal of the main character tends to determine the reader's response to the whole novel. Yet there are formal weaknesses that ultimately undermine the story's impact. Some of the flashbacks seem too realistic to be memories of a ruminative mind; some seem arbitrary, and others too obviously provide thematic reinforcement. Despite the originality of the characters, the romance between Eva and Johnny follows a predictable, conventional format. But any structural flaws are forgiven. Eva's cultivated mind exonerates her grubby appearance with an entirely unexpected obscenity. When she befriends silverfish and cockroaches but leaves poor suffering husband Burt to wallow in his arthritic misery, she is heroic beyond any flaw in her context.

Though she would roundly deny it, she is as strident a voice for feminism and for personal freedom as any character in Canadian literature. And she speaks for what she calls the third sex, the old, with an unfaltering voice. By the example of her actions, she restores to them the difficult benefits of gender. She is Eve. She is – a rare achievement – her own woman.

EARLE BIRNEY

Turvey. Toronto: McClelland and Stewart, 1949. Toronto: McClelland and Stewart; New Canadian Library, 1963. Pages: 288. Paperback.

To think of *Turvey* as a conventional comic novel is like remembering Marilyn Monroe for her smile. Comic fiction is not an inferior genre; nor does *Turvey* lack humour. But the generic description does not begin to do the novel justice. *Turvey* is a vision of modern war; a huge, impersonal social disruption beyond comprehension or meaning. It is the picaresque account of a truly innocent scoundrel in a fallen world, echoing Dante and Cervantes and Dostoevsky. *Turvey* is an existential parable in which reality is defined by the actions of those struggling to endure it. It is theatre of the absurd, Genet with pink cheeks; it anticipates *Catch-22* and *M*A*S*H*, but without their pitiless smirk. It is also quite beautifully written, and as profound a comedy as Canadian literature has ever produced. There is definitely more to Marilyn's smile than meets the eye.

Turvey is a slow-reading novel. Birney shares his fascination for the details of military life with his readers: there is a no more thorough account anywhere of the day-to-day drudgery of the ordinary soldier, nor of the tedium during that four-year-long wait by Allied troops in England before the invasion of Europe. Birney revels in the absurdities of enervating passivity, and his protagonist seems to encounter every possible absurdity. *Turvey* is also slow because the author has an acute ear for regional dialect and a nearly obsessive need to render it into dialogue. Thus there are long conversations in which each word must virtually be sounded aloud to capture its meaning. Only by careful attention does the sense of the whole fall into place. Birney is, by nature, a poet, and the aural impact of words is a prime consideration.

The author of *Turvey* is a major Canadian poet. Several of his works, most notably "David" and "Canada: A Case History," are widely known. He has also published another novel, *Down the Long Table*, which mixes social outrage with caustic wit to provide a disturbing commentary on both the McCarthy era and the Depression. *Turvey*, though, stands with his best poetry as enduring art, and is a superb document of its times.

The novel is episodic. Thomas Leadbeater Turvey, otherwise known as "Tops" or "Topsy," of Skookum Falls, B.C., enlists in the Canadian Army in Toronto in the spring of 1942. He is determined to become an infantryman with the Kootenay Highlanders. By late 1944 he is in Belgium, wearing the Highlanders' insignia. But the Highlanders were disbanded in Halifax before he joined, so he is attached to the Royal Bogshires as a driver. The next year he is home, demobilized, adrift in the Horse Palace at the CNE grounds in Toronto. He is thousands of miles from his beloved Peggy, in England, and is weighed down by the death of his best friend, Mac. He is also as free and absurdly innocent as a man could be.

Turvey is dumb, hapless, well-meaning, loyal, and irrepressibly optimistic. He scores abysmally in the tests the Army keeps attacking him with, yet there is always a clear-eyed logic to his answers. There is the definite possibility that the rest of the world is simply not up to his level of inspired incompetence. Eventually, after the eleventh turn at one particular intelligence test, he scores as a genius. But by then it is too late: the war is over. During his military career, however, Turvey cannot seem to avoid being appraised–by psychometrists and psychiatrists, by Officers' Training School, by several courts martial. He is goosed by a stereosophagoscope, hospitalized on separate occasions for a fractured ankle, dysentery, a nervous dysfunction (smiling), diphtheria, palatal paralysis, and indeterminate disorders. Turvey endures. When Mac is killed and Turvey sees terrible sights on the road to Nijmegan, he is thrown, but still his innocence prevails: he makes the most of himself and endures. The war is not comic, it is an awesome absurdity. But Turvey is a comic hero nonetheless.

CLARK BLAISE

Lunar Attractions. New York: Doubleday, 1979.
Toronto: Seal, 1980. Pages: 264. Paperback.

The primary difference between *Lunar Attractions* and a Blaise short story is that the novel is longer. It meets the same exacting standards of technical excellence; it similarly evades structural or narrative coherence as if they were anathema to art. It is built on the same assumptions of innate interest in the autobiographical mode, and it features much the same protagonist. Unlike the narrators of his short story collections, *A North American Education* and *Tribal Justice*, the narrator of *Lunar Attractions* maintains the same name from segment to segment. There is, perhaps, more attention paid to chronological continuity in *Lunar Attractions* but little else that qualifies it as a novel – least of all, form. It does, however, contain brilliant fragments of writing in a plausible context and holds up as a coherent organism somewhat better than the more recent *Lusts*.

Readers of Blaise's stories will have met David Greenwood before, although perhaps under a different name. Blaise seems to have a special affinity for the young protagonist who is overweight and awkward, intellectually precocious if undisciplined, socially and sexually inept, morbidly self-absorbed, blithely amoral, and indifferent to the emotional lives of others except occasionally his parents. He has a streak of perversity that manifests itself variously in voyeurism, in a fascination with the mindlessly trivial and the grotesque, or in the insufferable arrogance of the unaccomplished. The protagonist invariably does his early growing up in humiliating conditions in Florida and moves, in early adolescence, into the northern sector of middle America, in this case to a city called Palestra. There is always a Canadian connection – usually dual citizenship provided by one or both parents – a father in the furniture trade who has anglicized his name from the Québécois, and a mother of more refinement who endures the demeaning consequences of her marital choice with a bitchy display of forbearance.

The best parts of *Lunar Attractions* occur when both David and the author forget themselves and plunge through grotesque thickets of plot in a way that parodies lesser types of fiction. One part of the novel in particular stands on its own as a fifty-page novella. It is in the middle of David's story and is at the same time a weird confessional of sexual initiation and a wild burlesque of adolescent sexual fantasies. David, at thirteen, makes love to a beautiful classmate who turns out to be the girl's own hoodlum brother. This discovery does not deter either from consummation, and for the next while David ponders the fascinating possibilities of androgeny. In the real world of Palestra, of course, he can be only one sex and must suppress his female side. Almost inevitably, his erstwhile lover, Laurel/Larry, dies, disembowelled. David suffers virtually no grief or remorse beyond his initial horror at witnessing the putrescent corpse. He plays private games with the news reports of the murder, then gets on with his growing up. Only through a casual reminder, four years later, does he give the affair a second thought.

The first third of the novel covers the most familiar territory, David's Florida childhood. Early adolescence and the Laurel/Larry adventure make up the middle section of the book. The final section erratically chronicles David's last few months in high school. He appears among friends of his own kind, smug but not overly ambitious, awaiting the onslaught of maturity. In this section, there seems little attempt to establish narrative coherence of any sort. A bizarre, Mafia-type shakedown simply dissipates; several fascinating characters enter the narrative and disappear; David discovers that sex is something to be watched or grabbed at; there is no emotional complexity, no commitment, no development, no sympathetic awareness.

Throughout, David tells his story from an elusive future perspective. Yet nothing is gained from such arbitrary distancing. What holds the novel together, apart from a haphazard consistency of facts and chronology, is Blaise's prose. There is not a single word out of place in the whole novel, not an inappropriate phrase, an indelicate clause, or an awkward sentence. Blaise exhibits remarkable command of the language. His is not eloquent prose or stylized prose, but English used with precision and clarity, competence raised to high art.

PATRICIA BLONDAL

A Candle to Light the Sun. Toronto: McClelland and
Stewart, 1960. Toronto: McClelland and Stewart; New
Canadian Library, 1976. Pages: 316. Paperback.

Patricia Blondal died of cancer in her early thirties. *A Candle to
Light the Sun* was her life's work. Another novel, published posthumously as *From Heaven with a Shout*, was printed in serial
form before she died. *A Candle to Light the Sun*, however, marks
her death an awesome tragedy, and yet redeems her passing. Long
after the resentment has subsided in Souris, Manitoba, her apparent betrayal of the town forgotten, Blondal's novel will continue
to hold a mirror to our past. Her vision will remain as vital and
immediate as fictional reality can be.

Towns large and small play an important part in Canadian
fiction. Blondal's Mouse Bluffs (a play on the word *mousse*, suggested by the turbulence of the river, and on Souris, French for
mouse) is the definitive rendering. Nowhere else in our literature, not in Duncan's Elgin, Leacock's Mariposa, Ross's Horizon,
Laurence's Manawaka, or Munro's Jubilee, has a writer managed
to capture the complexity and the organic unity of the Canadian
community with such unerring authenticity. Mouse Bluffs remains
alive in the imagination long after the novel is read.

The town dominates the first of the novel's two books. The point
of view slips casually through a variety of lives, with young David
Newman almost incidentally the primary character. The personality of the town and David's growing awareness of himself are
revealed simultaneously. Mouse Bluffs is a living context, and
David is only one of its inhabitants. As readers, we learn much
that is beyond his knowledge. We experience the community as
an organism inseparable from David's experience of himself. In
the second book, Blondal shifts the narrative centre to Winnipeg
and adjusts the novel's vision: Mouse Bluffs becomes an ambivalent source in the backgrounds of several people's lives. It is a
place to be from, a place to become reconciled with. For David,
the town has been internalized, inseparable from the personality
it helped so much to form. Blondal is on less sure ground in the
second half, and the novel tends towards melodrama. In the first

part, a murder grows inevitably out of the reality of Mouse Bluffs; murder and execution in the Winnipeg episode seem contrived.

A Candle to Light the Sun is a portrait of the artist as a young man/woman–Blondal clearly identifies with David's growing sensibility, the better, perhaps, to understand her own. It is also a quest for identity: David's search for a father equal to his emotional needs leads him into complex relationships with the Ross family. It is also a story of romantic love, although the romance, while haunting, is overwhelmed by David's strange and compulsive friendship with Darcy Rushforth. The details of various interpenetrating lives, told through apparently random vignettes and obliquely described episodes, gradually coalesce into a love story that imposes form on all that preceded it. The novel is also a fascinating exploration of the complexity of human relationships, as well as of the psyche of one individual in particular. But *A Candle to Light the Sun* functions best as a portrait of society. Blondal gives Mouse Bluffs an urgent immediacy, as if it were slipping out of reach; at the same time she establishes its immutability, fixing it forever in the imagination.

In language that varies subtly with the shifting perspective of her vision, Blondal creates a town full of memorable characters. Some we become quite familiar with, while others are kept at a suitable distance. Lilja, whom David loves, and Roselee, who loves him, are never known to us with quite the same intimacy as the townspeople whom David hardly knows, but whose personalities are inseparable from the town's own personality. The Souris Valley setting grows indelibly in the reader's mind, associated, as it is, so closely with the characters' experiences. Time is handled spatially in the first book: it provides the context in which Mouse Bluffs and David's early awareness of it take shape in the reader's consciousness. In the second, time becomes linear, stretching away from the town. In the first book, childhood memories are clustered in random patterns; in the second, memories of young adulthood race one after another in a cause-and-effect sequence. Blondal conveys magnificently a bittersweet sense of possession and loss. *A Candle to Light the Sun* is a triumph, flaws and all.

FRED BODSWORTH

The Last of the Curlews. New York: Dodd, Mead, 1955.
Toronto: McClelland and Stewart; New Canadian Library,
1963. Pages: 127. Paperback.

No other Canadian writer can match Bodsworth's ability to bring
alive details of the natural world. In all his novels, he imbues
biologically authentic descriptions of nature with tremendous narrative power, not merely as settings or metaphors but as inseparable parts of the dramatic action. Nowhere is this more evident
than in *The Last of the Curlews*, in which the main character is a
bird hovering on the verge of extinction. Man and the natural
world are integrated both dramatically and philosophically in his
brilliant narrative, *The Sparrow's Fall*. In his other novels, competent by any standard, the human element seems a bit romantic
and contrived, deployed to argue a theme rather than to illustrate it. *The Atonement of Ashley Morden* is an enthralling novel,
which insistently argues that man's weaponry has developed
beyond his evolutionary ability to control it: natural morality, born
out of the instinct to survive, has been subverted by technological
progress. It is a clear thesis, told in an intricate and sophisticated
romance that lacks only the simple eloquence of *The Sparrow's
Fall* to make it truly memorable. Another novel, *The Strange One*,
is less successful, although equally intelligent, compassionate,
concerned, and entertaining; proof that Bodsworth at his least is
still perhaps our most neglected serious writer.

The Last of the Curlews* is a classic of its genre. Canada has a
fine tradition of animal stories, by writers as different as Sir
Charles G.D. Roberts and Farley Mowat, Ernest Seton and Sheila
Burnford. No writer, though, surpasses Bodsworth in the knack
of balancing scientific objectivity with narrative excitement. Determinedly careful not to anthropomorphize, the author conveys the
full force of tragedy through dispassionate observation. The male
curlew of the story is both a unique tragic protagonist and a
representative of his species. Never does Bodsworth sink into
bathos or pathetic fallacy; never is the bird conscious of himself
or his precarious condition. He is one of the last of his kind, an
Eskimo curlew (now extinct). In Bodsworth's novel, the curlews
have been so decimated by the wanton slaughter of hunters that

natural habits, which once allowed them to thrive, now guarantee their demise. Unable to adapt, they die.

Bodsworth details the inexorable progress of their destruction with fond attention to detail. The story itself is heroically simple. The curlew arrives at his Arctic breeding ground and awaits a mate, but none comes. He vehemently protects his territory but does not explore beyond its limits. Gradually, the sex drive fades into a migratory impulse; the curlew moves down and across the continent to Labrador. There he gorges himself on crowberries, fuel for the flight ahead. He joins a flock of golden plovers and leads them on the long, non-stop run to Venezuela and then on to Patagonia, where he again goes on his own and waits for a mate. A female appears. Together the two curlews fly north. They are shot on the Canadian prairie and the female is killed. The male waits. Then, driven by instinct, he proceeds north. A solitary figure in the Arctic, he once again awaits the arrival of a mate.

The breeding patterns of the curlews have been broken down by depletion of their numbers, and the fate of the curlews is determined even while a few such as this one still remain. Interspersed throughout his story, Bodsworth provides reportorial passages in "The Gauntlet," from a variety of sources, detailing the slaughter of the curlews, who were often killed by the wagon load and ploughed under as fertilizer. These documentary pieces work in horrific counterpoint to the spare, restrained prose in the narrative account, elevating the simple story of the curlew to the level of high art and giving it moral dimensions of disturbing proportion.

The Sparrow's Fall. Toronto: Doubleday, 1967.
Scarborough: New American Library, 1971.
Pages: 176. Paperback.

The spare and disciplined prose style that serves Bodsworth so well in *The Last of the Curlews* is equally effective in *The Sparrow's Fall*. This novel, like all of Bodsworth's writing, contains a blend of intelligent humane insight and passionate conviction. The narrative flow is linear and uncomplicated: Jacob Atook is forced to leave his wife, Niska, who is in the last stage of pregnancy, alone in their tent in the harsh northern Ontario winter, to travel farther north through the land of the little sticks in search of food.

His quest has the quality of an epic about it. Jacob endures terrible hardships: hunger and cold and fear for his wife and unborn child. He also fears the young man, Taka, who was meant by the tribe to be Niska's husband and who is pursuing him. But most disturbing to Jacob are the philosophical implications of his solitary quest.

Jacob's life depends on the resolution of abstractions. He and his wife are in exile from their people for having fallen into Christianity, which sanctions their union based on love rather than tribal necessity. Normally, marriage was a way of allotting essential hunting territory to ensure that everyone had enough. Now he must hunt on his own. But faith in the white man's God has undermined his determination to kill. The procedures for survival, codified in ancestral religion, have been subverted. He persists in the hunt, but at the same time, with painful determination, he struggles to fathom the mysteries of an alien God who loves each sparrow yet allows the existence of a predatory world. Eventually, Jacob perceives a balance between life and death in the natural world. He kills a caribou giving birth and saves his own family. He left his people and overcame a religion that did not fulfil his needs; he has become a new Adam, an uncomprehending epic symbol of renewal.

Reinforcing the argument of the novel, and at the same time adding immensely to its drama, Bodsworth periodically shifts the narrative focus to the fleeing caribou; with a naturalist's objectivity, he makes hunter and hunted parts of the same inexorable process of nature. *The Sparrow's Fall* is a novel at once simple and complex, as the best epics and folk myths are, and is as moving a defence of the natural universe as has been written. It is fine art and a classic argument that should not go unread.

GEORGE BOWERING

Mirror on the Floor. Toronto: McClelland and Stewart, 1967. Pages: 160.

Bowering has caught perfectly an era that teeters between the beat and boozing cynicism of the fifties and the righteous amorality of the sixties. It is exciting to rediscover this novel more than a decade after it first appeared. I found its potent qualities still intact, reaffirmed and consolidated by the discriminating passage of time. The style is free-flowing and intuitive; the form is highly structured, even arbitrary. There is self-conscious allusiveness, symbolic and literary, and, on the part of the characters, morbid self-absorption. Bowering defines the sensibility of the sixties, before the sixties really got into gear. *Mirror on the Floor* should not be read as a document of an era, however, but as a fine novel in its own right.

The plot brings together two realities. One concerns Bob Small, a UBC student in his early twenties. There is nothing at all outstanding about him; he is likeable enough, reasonably sensitive, relatively defiant towards authority (or else indifferent), and overly reliant on his friend Delsing. He is a first-person narrator. The other reality is associated with Andrea Harrison: hers is a third-person world. The narrative alternates between their two realities: Bob's inept confessional struggle to grow up and be himself, or at least get by; Andrea's deep and troubled moods and memories. His exuberance, her stillness, his yearning, her haunting. Strangely, the reader feels better acquainted with her than him.

The story is hers, the context his. Bob kills time through a spring and summer in Vancouver. He falls in love, kibitzes with Delsing, does university chores, works, and drinks. Andrea's life, when she is not with Bob Small, remains largely unknown. Yet many facets of her past and interior life emerge. We feel the misery of a childhood spent with parents who hated each other–her father was intimidated by all things; her mother was mean and grossly insensitive. Andrea remembers happiness and a drowned lover; she remembers the sweet, modest incest shared with her father; she lives with the knowledge that she is her mother's accident. She is forever associated with death and the sea; she seems doomed in her mind and in the symbols Bowering gives to her. Bob Small is an observer, in love, a mesmerized outsider. Andrea's father kills himself and she murders her mother, with the terrible conviction of inevitability. Small is freed of her.

Mirror on the Floor manipulates mood with striking ease. Bowering fuses words with things to create uncannily tactile or palpable impressions. He is afraid of neither subtlety nor flamboyance. The language is almost always appropriate to intent, although a certain mawkish bravado creeps into the conversations between Bob and Delsing, and there is occasional awkwardness in the terms of endearment between the two lovers–perhaps this, too, is appropriate. Ingenuously, Bowering blends idea with emotion in a story of young love and passing tragedy. The novel is original and moving. It should be more widely known. Perhaps now that Bowering has won a Governor General's award for fiction as well as poetry, it will be.

A Short Sad Book. Vancouver: Talonbooks, 1977.
Pages: 191 (including Index). Paperback.

I barely resisted opening a discussion of this novel by writing a sentence with my name in it. Reading *A Short Sad Book*, I enjoyed myself: italics are necessary to make the point. I enjoyed *myself* reading. This is a brilliant and ridiculous novel about me, writing this. Bowering plays weird games, but the reader is not left on the margin to observe the author at play, as in most postmodern writing, for instance in Kroetsch's *Gone Indian*. Rather, you are invited in. And yet, reading *A Short Sad Book* you are always aware of yourself reading. You are aware of holding a book in your hands, of having fun. And of the author having fun. And, as with all really good games, immensely serious things are going on, sometimes on the surface and sometimes deep beneath the surface; and as with really good games you keep the pleasures and the highlights wrapped together within you, forever it seems, to be relived some other time, just by thinking about the form.

This novel is liberating to read, and probably quite damaging to sensibilities conditioned to assume utter humility in the face of art–freedom *to be* is a heavy burden for readers accustomed to being refined out of existence or kept in place at a distance, looking through keyholes and over shoulders. I suspect many will be unsettled to find that their own pleasure in reading is part of the text; in fact, to find the text a context, and the fiction itself a stimulant. Now reading Dostoevsky I secretly watch myself reading, and Dostoevsky does too.

Yes he does.

This gift of postmodernism, and that's a term no one is very comfortable with, is from the conventional point of view almost a breach of trust. It is also an invitation to exist as a reader, and that is an exciting prospect. To achieve this phenomenal effect, Bowering writes of writing, of himself writing, of his novel being written, of his novel writing. The novel writes, and Bowering keeps up with it, writing. The novel is not *about* writing; it is writing. What it is *about* is staking peonies, the Black Mountain influence, Canadian history and Canadian literature, smoking cigars, Evangeline and Sir John A. Macdonald, postmodernism, British Columbia, the West Coast experience, alienation, the Bowering experience, pursuit of the Pretty Good Canadian novel, the *Tercentenary History of Canada*, Volume III, from Laurier to King, MCMVIV–MCMXLV, rootless cosmopolites, feckless nationalists, baseball, Americans, underwater discoveries, Tom Thom(p)son's body, other things, motifs, word-combinations, images, and a plethora of allusions. *A Short Sad Book* does not make allusions; it consumes them. It is a novel filled with its own sense of being a novel.

The quips, gibes, jokes, and asides that make up the text of *A Short Sad Book* cohere in a condition of breathless excitation. They define the nature and limits of the whole, as an organism; but they seem of little substance or directional coherence in themselves. Everything in the novel yields to critical scrutiny, yet there is no point in searching for meaning in the tortured syntax, or trying to discover in the author's whimsically indulgent references to his friends, enemies, and relatives insights into the novel's structural design or its ontological aspirations. Nevertheless, someday someone will undoubtedly do an annotated edition of this novel, much like *The Annotated Alice*, and then everything will be understood; then it will no longer be a postmodern novel, but it will be a cultural artifact and people will remember that it was once great to read. At that point, *A Short Sad Book* will collapse into a single dimension, a theoretical point in George Bowering's career, a spot in the development of the Canadian novel.

Burning Water. Toronto: Musson, 1980. Don Mills: General; New Press Canadian Classics, 1983. Pages: 258.
Paperback.

Burning Water deserves more attention than the casual reader is likely to give it. Despite earning a Governor General's Award, it is not a novel that reassures sensibilities conditioned by a millenium of historicity, centuries of print as a linear medium, and decades of realism and literary modernism. In fact, this novel evades conventional analysis and appreciation with such élan that the reader may hardly realize the extent of its achievement. Most, myself included, took it more as an affront when it first appeared than as the modestly outrageous embodiment of a revolution. Yet on reconsideration it seems to me that *Burning Water* irrevocably changes things: having read it, I no longer find history, time, and the nature of reality quite the same. Reading, being, and the text are realigned. Were Bowering's revolution to have universal impact, the world would be a different place.

In the first edition of this book, I wrote a fair acknowledgement of what happens within the text of *Burning Water*, without showing much awareness of its significance. That was five years ago. My essay was analytic and descriptive. My attention was directed somewhat myopically toward the fictional reality, as if it existed apart from the surrounding world and took precedence over it. This, in spite of Bowering's insistence, within the novel, that I as a reader do otherwise! The whole thrust of his work, at this stage, is against barriers between life and art. *Burning Water* insists there is a world beyond the text. It does so, perhaps paradoxically, by repeatedly collapsing the illusion of reality within the text, so that we are thrown, again and again, back upon ourselves, reading. In attending to the collapse, I seem to have ignored myself– although my presence is crucial to Bowering's achievement. *Mea culpa.*

Burning Water makes a presence of the past. It is not, as the original cover copy ludicrously asserts and the cataloguing data affirm, a solemn exercise in historical revisionism. If anything, it forces a revision of our very concepts of history and historicity. There are two spheres of time in the novel, the past in which Captain George Vancouver occupies the centre, and the present, in which the writer writing within the text, George Bowering as a textual persona, is at the centre. These two spheres interpenetrate through zany manipulations of language, narrative loop-the-loops, logical absurdities. At the close of the novel, as the Georges merge and the spheres become a single sphere, we curiously find ourselves as much on the inside looking out as on the outside looking in–we and the novel have likewise merged; it has become inseparable from our knowledge and experience of ourselves.

History, in such a context, ceases to be linear. It ceases to be a text. As George Vancouver struggles valiantly to become a story, to become a word, Bowering the author as determinedly insists that reality shaped and sanctioned by language is illusion until vitalized by present consciousness. Vancouver dies into language: Bowering resurrects him, through language. History, like fiction, is isolated from the lived-in world only because we have made it so. Historical authenticity and fictional verisimilitude are grotesque illusions fostered by the obsessive linearity of the Western mind: in *Burning Water*, the author, Bowering, collapses both in the present experience of the reader reading.

His story of George Vancouver begins on June 10, 1792, off the west coast of North America, and ends on the penultimate leg of Vancouver's four-and-a-half-year voyage in search of the Northwest Passage, with Vancouver's death by madness and misadventure. Time as a matrix moves ineluctably forward, yet the narrative fragments swarm within it in temporal and stylistic confusion of apparently stunning pointlessness. The confusion of the past is set against the present narrative in which a third-person Bowering tries to cope with writing a novel. What threatens to become a hackneyed postmodern device, fraught with the dangers of self-conscious irony, is here singularly appropriate: the novel's anachronisms and apocrypha seem inevitable in such a context.

As the textual Bowering moves around the world in one time frame, in another the protagonist of his novel sails up and down the coast, surveying and searching for treasure and/or a short passage home. Bowering's Vancouver deals fairly with the Indians, nurses a pathological hatred for his botanist-surgeon, and has a series of gay encounters with Senor Don Juan Francisco de la Bodega y Quadra, the Peruvian-born commander of the Spanish coastal possessions. This is not the historical Vancouver (who is an accumulation of data and artifacts), nor the actual Vancouver (who is dead). This is the *real* Vancouver who lives and dies in Bowering's fiction. Continues to live and die.

Vancouver in the text is by terms fey and tyrannical. He is a devoted servant of the crown and equally devoted to his crew. The latter, he forces to eat massive quantities of sauerkraut and inflicts other such cruelties, including liberal use of the lash, as the expression of his love for them. Vancouver seems at times a mighty mythic figure, and then, suddenly, a comic-book caricature. He is transformed from buffoon to gentleman-explorer with the flick of a phrase, the twist of a whim. He is a disconcerting creation, inseparable from his text.

George Vancouver and George Bowering together occupy a narrative world in which bathos reigns supreme. Sundry officers, seamen (including one called Delsing), and Indians do and say things that lead nowhere and apparently mean nothing. To some extent the bathos arises out of character and situation, but more often it derives from the flamboyant use of utterly inappropriate language, especially in dialogue. Thus, for example, an Indian discussing the white men asserts to his companion, "There you go, speaking out of some habitual framework of guilt." An Indian woman is described as being so excited her blood turns to Drambuie. A sailor exclaims, about the surgeon who has just slaughtered an albatross, "I fear him and his glittering eye." And so on. The only rule, it seems, is that there are no rules.

Throughout *Burning Water*, Bowering plays syntax against meaning, forcing us to see, again and again, how ready we are to accept anything, so long as it is said well, so long as the grammar makes sense. He plays intellect against emotion: no matter how acutely we recognize improbabilities, violations, logical disjunctions, we still cannot disengage ourselves from the text or cease to care about the characters and respond to their precarious condition within the weird world of words their author gives them. Bowering confounds our expectations in regard to the nature of fiction, especially historical fiction, and our assumptions about history, especially history conceived as if it were a text.

Perhaps *Burning Water* has not quite the biting wit of *A Short Sad Book*, and not the ingenuous sincerity of his first novel, *Mirror on the Floor* or the brash and enthusiastic self-absorption of *Autobiology*, his second. Nor has it the casual authority and precise imaginative originality of his best poetry (for which he won a Governor General's Award in 1969, making him one of only three creative writers to achieve such recognition in two genres, the others being Douglas LePan and Margaret Atwood). But for its assault on the conventions of historicity and literary modernism, for its demand that we reconsider the relationships between text, reality, and consciousness (and its example of what happens when we do), and for the freedom it offers us from the tyrannies of narrative, intellectual, and temporal linearity, for this and more it is a major work.

Burning Water is of itself a revolution. When the dust settles and the debris is cleared it will still be with us, its manic fury subdued, perhaps, but its significance more evident, its achievement more apparent in retrospect. That is the way it often is with revolutions.

FRANCES BROOKE

The History of Emily Montague. London: Dodsley, 1769. 4 volumes. Toronto: McClelland and Stewart; New Canadian Library, 1961. Pages: 319. Paperback. Scholarly Edition: Centre for Editing Early Canadian Texts. Ottawa: Carleton University Press, 1985. Pages: 459. Ed. M.J. Edwards. Paperback.

The first Canadian novel was not written by a Canadian. Confederation was still nearly a century away when this epistolary romance appeared in the salons of London. The author had just returned to England after spending five years with the British garrison at Quebec City, where her husband was chaplain, to take up her modest place in the eighteenth-century world of British letters. What makes this novel seminal to the Canadian literary tradition and sets it well above her other work is that Brooke holds two realities, Old World and New, in direct confrontation. Out of this dynamic meeting her fiction draws shape and energy: diction, mood, imagery, story, and thematic complexity are derived from the dichotomy of consciousness that the Canadian experience engendered. In addition to its historical significance, *The History of Emily Montague* is pleasantly diverting to read. From our perspective it is a rare treasure, although from that of the British it remains perhaps merely an interesting document.

With a fine eye for detail, Brooke brings to life the garrison world and its surroundings, both social and natural. Country sleigh rides and gala balls; casual flirtations and complex liaisons; the Indians, the Canadian peasantry, the French elite, and the occupying British; such natural phenomena as the falls at Montmorency and the great St. Lawrence River – all are treated in the letters that, for a pleasing variety of reasons, pass among the principal characters. Brooke takes full advantage of the epistolary mode, which provides immediate responses from a number of clearly defined viewpoints: William Fermor, for example, sends prosaic reports to a nobleman at home, while Arabella Fermor, his daughter, assesses everything that comes her way with delightful insouciance according to her flighty shifts in mood. What emerges is a world as strange and real as any the imagination could create, where beauty and the sublime, right reason and natural passion, the Enlightenment and the Wilderness, vie for prominence.

There are three affairs of the heart in the novel; two take place in Canada – or, rather, in what had newly become an extension of British North America. The rituals of courtship are all quite English, independent of the New World setting. However, the relationships themselves develop almost entirely according to the dictates of their alien context. A rather insipid Emily Montague and the excessively noble Colonel Rivers test their love through the travails of their garrison exile and marry in England. The mutual attraction between Arabella and her fickle Captain Fitzgerald is nurtured to fruition by the Canadian milieu. The facts of the affairs belong in the New World; the sentiments are from abroad. Subplots and subsidiary affairs are enriched by the Canadian context while remaining consistent with the demands of the genre and Brooke's readership in England.

The romantic stories are amusing but not outstanding either in themselves or in what they represent. They are redeemed from mediocrity, however, by Brooke's sophisticated use of Canadian dichotomies. In a context of wit and incisive perception, she sets society against nature, the urbane against the rustic, civilization against savagery, male against female. Reality becomes the principal subject of her fiction. With ingenious command of language and with casual authority, she explores the structures and assumptions of society, the nature of mankind, and the meaning of life, as if her vehicle were much more than a diverting amusement, which it is.

BERTRAM BROOKER

Think of the Earth. Toronto: Nelson & Sons, 1936.
Pages: 288.

Were it not that this novel won the first Governor General's Award
for fiction, there would be nothing outstanding about it at all. It
survives on the periphery of academic interest today as a curiosity on three distinctly separate counts. Having won the highest
literary prize Canada has to offer, it commands most attention
now for the precedent it set of distributing awards with cavalier
idiosyncrasy. As one of two novels by an important painter and
cultural critic, it illuminates the author's aesthetic through what,
in his hands, is a decidedly inferior medium. Perhaps of most
interest, *Think of the Earth* is an example, all too rare in our
literature, of writing that aspires to be visionary – writing that
not only reaches towards the reader's soul, but tries to change
and shape it.

Think of the Earth is set in Poplar Plains, Manitoba, in 1907.
Brooker has a good eye for evocative details, if a tin ear for the
language with which to describe them. Occasional nostalgia, born
of his 1930s perspective, intrudes awkwardly into the narrative;
but for the most part the mood is sombre, the atmosphere authentic. Into what Brooker offers as a typical small Canadian town,
he introduces a rather unlikely Englishman. Geoff Tavistock is a
man utterly committed to what he takes to be a divinely inspired
mission – to reconcile man with God once and for all. As Brooker's
protagonist sees it, there is a unity to everything, within God,
and therefore evil is an impossibility. God cannot contain evil;
but man will bear the misery of judgement in the fallen world
until redeemed by one who can sin without guilt, the new and
true messiah. Tavistock accepts himself as a son of God above
Christ, whose suffering was incomplete, in that He did not know
guilt, never having sinned, and therefore could transcend death
but not carry with Him the burden of evil and good that man
endures as his legacy of the Fall. Convinced that death is irrelevant and that evil and good are non-existent, Tavistock prepares
himself to commit an innocent murder, thereby taking on the guilt
of the world and freeing man forever of judgement. The theology
may be naïve and confused, but it is offered with conviction. And

somehow, it seems less bizarre in a small Manitoba town than it might have appeared in a more worldly setting.

Tavistock is presented as an eccentric, but without a trace of irony. Brooker tries to lighten the weight on his protagonist in such a realistic context by keeping him at a distance during much of the novel. He is seen through Canon Macaulay's eyes, through Dr. Bundy who runs the Home for Incurables, through Gawthorp, the editor-publisher of the town's weekly, through old Pitts, who had known Tavistock in South Africa, and most significantly, through Laura Macaulay, the minister's daughter, with whom Tavistock falls in love. As perceived by others, Tavistock is a strange and intriguing man. When the author allows him the narrative centre, he seems ludicrous–a man of soaring conviction and no passion, a man whose only transcendent characteristic lies in the premise he shares with his author that he is a superior being. As a character in fiction, Tavistock is improbable; as a messiah, a man living a miracle, he is pathetic; as an authorial voice, he is profoundly inept.

The biggest problem with Brooker's novel is that it is not well written. No amount of sincerity can counter the effects of awkward language and poor technique. The plot seems pushed from behind; characters move and think like puppets; events dissipate between poles of verbiage and intellectuality. Brooker uses a lot of description; seeing perhaps with the painter's eye, he does not catch the instant as it happens or the scene as it is, but turns the most vivid places and events into still-life arrangements. There is no movement in the novel: in the resolution of contraries, there is no progression. *Think of the Earth* attempts to be visionary, and, had Brooker been more in control of the art of fiction it might have been. As it is, it is a novel about visionary experience, not a visionary experience itself.

MARGARET A. BROWN

My Lady of the Snows. Toronto: Wm. Briggs, 1908.
Toronto: University of Toronto Press; Reprint Library,
1973. Pages: 518.

Margaret Brown passionately believes in *noblesse oblige* and the divine right of the ruling class. She believes in the innate inferiority of the masses and the moral slovenliness of everyone not born to wealth, good manners, and position. *My Lady of the Snows* is a romantic story set in what Brown believes to be the best of all possible worlds, a world that is slowly slipping away into history. It is as if, by the eloquence and conviction of her novel, Brown could stop its passing.

Canadian society in the 1880s was never quite like Brown's portrayal of it. The author, in a prolix preface, scorns realism as the restricted aesthetic of democratic materialism and vows to favour the reader with a loftier entertainment. She is a reactionary idealist, and her ideal is a Tory Camelot where the best people rule the lesser and accumulate vast wealth and power in the best interests of all. Brown claims that her novel is political, and that is how it is generally described in bibliographies. But although it is set in the political climate of Ottawa amidst the ruling class, it devotes only a subordinate clause to the passage of a general election. Brown does not bother to specify which election.

The whole novel is an ornately rendered exaggeration of society, and it contains fascinating insights into the principles upon which that society is based. Sometimes these insights seem almost inadvertent, as when an injured husband says to the wife he abhors: " 'If any other person should say such a thing she would publicly retract it or prove it, or I should shoot her nearest male relative like a dog.' " There is a great deal of information, too, about lifestyles and social events, all given with fond attention to detail. It is in her attempt to capture the discourse of elegant society, however, that Brown most disconcerts the modern reader. Sometimes on a single page she or her characters will drop more than a dozen names–philosophers, poets, people of letters. They are sometimes quoted at excruciating length and at other times represented by trivial phrases wrenched out of context. Lucretius, Talleyrand, and Ruskin all pop up in conversations about the weather.

The novel is related from delightful Olympian heights. This allows the author to move, in a sentence, halfway across the fledgling capital and back, in and out of carriages and conservatories and private thoughts, always with a plethora of appropriate quotations and solemn wit. The plot itself is fascinating, based squarely on Brown's conception of ruling-class values and modes of behaviour. Modena Wellington, the première hostess of Ottawa, and Keith Kenyon, the youngest member of Macdonald's cabinet and a man whose future is as promising as the nation he was born to lead, are in love. Two things stand in their way: the Tory party and personal honour. Keith marries someone else, Modena waits, Keith and Modena pine, the wife is killed, and love conquers all, without a jot of honour sacrificed. In Brown's novel, reason is more important than passion; yet, because the novel is a romance, passion wins in the end.

The reader of today will feel a touch of pride at getting through this novel, and the effort is rewarded in several ways. It makes an interesting contrast with Sara Jeannette Duncan's *The Imperialist*, which looks as much ahead in style and content as this novel looks back, though both are ostensibly social-political novels, written at about the same time. Brown's ephemeral novel makes a fascinating contrast with the detailed political analysis of another contemporary novel, *The Curé of St. Philippe*. In itself, *My Lady of the Snows* contains a pleasing amount of very good writing and elevates cleverness almost to art. It sheds light on society of the time and inadvertently casts great shadows, which outline a welter of social injustice. Finally, it is virtually in a class by itself as an intellectual romance in which the author's convictions weld an age-old love story to her vision of the ideal Canadian society.

CHARLES BRUCE

The Channel Shore. Toronto: Macmillan, 1954. Toronto:
McClelland and Stewart; New Canadian Library, 1984.
Pages: 398. Paperback.

Charles Bruce published two novels. His first, *The Channel Shore*,
is a beautifully evocative novel of times and a place that no longer
exist. The Channel Shore of Nova Scotia has not disappeared, but
it can never again be as Bruce captures it in his fiction. Bruce
describes a landscape that, in its farms and bushlands that slope
to the sea, contains the imprint of generations. In his second novel,
The Township of Time, Bruce describes these generations, showing something of the life of each from first settlement to the present.
The story is sensitively told, but it lacks narrative cohesion; beyond
the passage of time and the stability of place, there is nothing to
bind the separate episodes together. Lives echo without gathering substance. In comparison, *The Channel Shore* builds in a
sequence of repetition and change. The landscape sets the perimeters and provides a substantial part of the story itself. Three generations of the people around Currie Head are described in ways
that evoke the life of a place so authentically, the lives of its people so convincingly, that their loss in the passages of time haunts
the reader as a personal tragedy. *The Channel Shore* is a fine
regional novel.

There are three sections in the novel, with roughly thirteen years
between each. As a boy, Bill Graham, from Toronto, visits his ancestral home on the Shore. He returns after the Second World War,
some twenty-seven years later. Graham provides a link with the
outside world, a bridge across time, but Bruce does not use him as
narrator. In fact, much of the action occurs beyond Graham's
awareness, and he does not appear in the middle section at all.
He is a sympathetic visitor, an authorial persona who holds the
story together, but is not a significant participant.

It is the families–the Marshalls and Gordons and McKees–and
the places–Kilfyle's Hole, Katen's Store, the Channel Shore Road,
Currie Head–that provide the context for an intricate story. Bruce
follows the patterns of love and misfortune in one generation; the
pattern is repeated, with variations, in the next. Threads of pride,

affection, recklessness are woven through, and ultimately, a grand design emerges, a story that shows the resilience and integrity of the people of the Shore.

Bruce is more than a chronicler who defines complex genealogies or describes the spirit of a particular locale. He creates a continuity that can leap whole generations with a gesture, that defies the passing of decades with a chance remark. His men, Anse and Grant and Alan, and his women, Hazel, Anna, Josie, Margaret, these and all the others, live not in a continuum in spatial time, but time that is shaped by the powerful presence of the land and by the sometimes difficult insistence of their forceful personalities. Charles Bruce writes fine, straightforward prose, but it is for the world of imagination, the Channel Shore itself, that he will best be remembered.

ERNEST BUCKLER

The Mountain and the Valley. New York: Holt, 1952. Toronto: McClelland and Stewart; New Canadian Library, 1961. Pages: 302. Paperback.

David Canaan is sensitive and articulate. He grows up in the Annapolis Valley of Nova Scotia immediately before the Second World War and bears his sensitivity as a mortal wound, which, indeed, is what it proves to be. Buckler has written one of the finest portraits of the artist as a young man that the language has known. It has a singular sardonic difference from others of the kind, however: the protagonist, with his vision of the perfect writer still in his head, dies at the novel's close. For David, death is an end of things. For the novel his death is inevitable. The potential of art to redeem time, to absolve the past and translate it into perpetual present, is unequivocally affirmed as an ideal, while simultaneously denied as a practical possibility.

While related chronologically, *The Mountain and the Valley* expands in a rich and complex design, much like the rag rug

David's grandmother creates which acts as the novel's main unifying image. The story is contained within parenthetical chapters describing David's last day alive. The intervening sections
present, in flashback, the times of his growing up, each section
built around a particular incident or event, almost a story in itself.

The novel celebrates rural family life while showing how tenuous and painful the evolving relationships in such a context must
inevitably be. The gulf between David, his brother, and his parents widens as he grows increasingly more self-aware. He resents
his family's special regard for him. But the dynamics of his relationship with his twin sister, Anna, and his friend Toby, whom
Anna eventually marries, generate David's greatest anxieties and
the novel's richest interest on both narrative and thematic levels.
The ambiguous presence of Ellen, the grandmother, with her locket
keepsake and her memories of a renegade young sailor, lends
David's story a special dimension and marks him an adventurer
of the soul as well as the mind.

The novel shows great depths of psychological perception.
Buckler delves more deeply into relationships than into the growth
of the creative sensibility, but it is as an artist that David develops.
He is increasingly troubled by the problems between time and
consciousness within his own experience, problems that only creativity can resolve.

The novel is a *tour de force* of regionalism, not a rural idyll but
an almost perfect fusion of regions of the imagination with regions
of actuality. The prose is lush, intricate, precise; Buckler mixes
the concrete and abstract with munificent ease. The tendency of
the novel to be too rich, too sensitive, too warmly nostalgic, is
offset by the unrelenting accuracy of Buckler's language. As well,
the author creates an ironic distance through his use of the third-
person voice and retrospective structure. Some readers might be
bothered by apparent excesses in the novel. Few, however, fail to
be irrevocably moved by it.

Buckler's other fiction has not met with the popular or critical
success of *The Mountain and the Valley*; neither does it offer the
same satisfaction. His second novel, *The Cruelest Month*, reads
too much like the work of someone determined to measure up to
an earlier achievement: the language is rather turgid, with an
effusive "literary" self-consciousness; the plot, although slow and

meandering, seems forced. *Oxbells and Fireflies*, a collection of essays, contains some of his finest writing, but the context is shaped by the reminiscing mind and does not satisfy the needs of art. *The Rebellion of Young David* contains stories that provide insight into *The Mountain and the Valley* and into Buckler's aesthetic, but the collection is of interest more as a document than in its own right. Buckler's first novel remains the pinnacle of his achievement as a writer and a powerful testament, now that he is gone, to the validity of his own vision at the novel's close. The ultimate impossibility of David's vision, of what perfect art should be and do, is finally brought home. There is no perfection in the mortal world beyond what we glimpse in reaching for it. That seems to be the meaning at the heart of Buckler's novel, and of his life.

JOHN BUELL

Four Days. New York: Farrar, Straus & Cudahy, 1962. Toronto: Popular Library, 1962. Pages: 232. Paperback.

Each of John Buell's novels is built around the suspenseful resolution of a problem. The mystery, however, is in the protagonist's psyche or soul, as much as in his or her adventures as a spy or detective or suffering hero. In *The Pyx*, a prostitute's suicide declares the author's essential optimism; she has chosen death over the absolute degradation of a satanic mass. *The Shrewsdale Exit* chronicles Joe Grant's progress from rage (he vows to avenge the rape-killings of his wife and young daughter) to the grace of acceptance, not as defeat but in defiance of death and depravity. *Playground* turns the somewhat hackneyed plot of a downed flier in the northern bush into a solitary man's struggle to endure – and to find meaning for doing so. In *Four Days*, a boy tries to deny his brother's death and then, in affirmation of his own life, murders a molester and lets himself die.

In each case, the struggle of Buell's protagonist is more important than either its origin or its outcome. Each novel explores a moral dilemma in terms that verge on the sensational; each suggests the spiritual implications of the story without insisting on them. Each follows a rather single-minded thread of plot and theme: there is little room in such fiction for aesthetic or formal complexity, although the story-line itself can take enthralling twists and loops along the way, and characters can surprise – perhaps not with sophisticated motivation, but with the determined conviction of their responses.

Buell explores the narrative possibilities of good and evil, fear and guilt, loneliness and acceptance rather than using his narrative to explore the spiritual, moral, or psychological implications of such concepts. His novels are certainly not great literature, but they are high-minded and gripping entertainment.

Four Days is possibly the most low-key and thoughtful of Buell's works. It is less self-consciously concerned with the battle between the sinister and the sacred than either *The Pyx* or *The Shrewsdale Exit*. It shows more depth of compassion than *Playground*, although superficially it is more negative. It has a specificity of detail, essential to the best realistic fiction, that Buell's other works lack. Val Laurent (a ringer for Ste. Agathe, a resort town in the Laurentians) and St. Henri (one of the most depressed areas of Montreal) are persuasively real as Buell depicts them. City and country, slum and resort are key factors in *Four Days*; they are poles in the brief life of "the kid" and in Buell's vision of contemporary society. There may be no best among Buell's novels, but for its easy integration of time, place, plot, and theme *Four Days* is probably his most enduring.

The story begins at the beginning. The kid, who is never named, is thirteen and street-wise. He is used as an accomplice in a bank robbery in which his brother Milt is gunned down by police. Before he dies, Milt passes the money to the kid, who takes a bus to their rendezvous point in the Laurentians. He is befriended by a male homosexual, whom he eventually kills, and pursued by police, by bad guys after the cash, and by his own loneliness in this unfamiliar world away from the city centre. Buell shifts the point of view a good deal; he often leaves the kid aside, for example, while he details the police search, which is eventually successful. The police find the kid hours after he flees from a priest and swims out into a lake to drown. The pace of the story never lets up; the foreboding atmosphere builds to an intolerable density; almost with relief we accept the kid's death and the novel's end.

SHEILA BURNFORD

The Incredible Journey. Boston: Little, Brown, 1961. Toronto: Paperjacks, 1973. Pages: 127. Paperback.

An internationally celebrated best-seller is not necessarily a flawless masterpiece. From an objective literary point of view, there is much wrong with Burnford's novel. Yet so appealing is it that only the hardest heart could fault her for falling short of perfection. From first to last, the reader is thoroughly absorbed with Champion Boroughcastle Brigadier of Doune, an irascible and homely old bull terrier otherwise known as Bodger, with his close ally, Tao, a lithe Siamese cat, and with Luath, the proud young golden Lab. Luath leads the trio three hundred miles through the northern Ontario bush in an attempt to reach home before winter sets in. There are no complications or distractions; the plot unfolds with striking simplicity as one episode follows the next from the beginning of their treacherous journey to its inevitably happy conclusion. It hardly seems to matter that the writing is awkward in places and the plot somewhat forced.

Burnford's prose, with its uncomplicated syntax and lack of ornamentation, is entirely appropriate to the animal sequences. It has an allusive purity that is almost scriptural at times. Yet in the episodes where humans predominate, the same style creates an atmosphere of awkward sentimentality. Burnford successfully uses words associated with human responses–"disgust" or "humiliation" or "joy"–to describe the behaviour of her inarticulate protagonists, while never suggesting that they are in any way "human." They remain, throughout, two dogs and a cat. However, the humans in the story appear simplistic throughout, like caricatures in a Disney film.

As the novel opens, the animals are in the keeping of a family friend while their owners are in England for a lengthy holiday. Through a most improbable coincidence and because of the young Lab's overpowering urge to lead his compatriots towards the Lakehead and home, the three animals set out and are not missed for several weeks. By the time their absence is discovered, they have adapted to their ordeal, endured incredible hardship, had some grand good times, and covered more than two hundred miles. The cat supplies the old terrier with food; the Lab overcomes his conditioning and kills frogs and the occasional rabbit for himself. Along the way the animals encounter several encampments of humans: an Indian band harvesting wild rice; a Finnish girl whose immigrant parents help her to save the Siamese cat from a most unlikely river calamity; a dotty old man who tips his hat to them and treats them like passing guests; a kindly old farm couple who fortify the trio with food for the last barrier before the animals reach their frantic owners.

Improbable coincidences (as opposed to those that appear inevitable) are native to adventure stories, but occasionally Burnford stretches credulity a bit too far. Despite improbabilities, however, bathos and sentimentality are balanced by Burnford's regard for natural justice. The animals kill to survive; when a lynx nearly catches Tao, Burnford increases the horror by withholding judgement. She describes the cat's terror and the lynx's viciousness quite dispassionately.

Burnford has a great affection for animals and a meticulous eye for the behavioural nuances that set one species apart from another; she is even more meticulous in describing the nuances that make each individual separate from his fellows. Thus, when Tao scatters dirt across the lynx's carcass, it is both an instinctive act of the species, covering his tracks, and the haughty expression of a distinct personality. Time and again, Burnford brings the reader to that fine edge between tears and laughter. There is a lot of humour in her novel, much warmth, and a great deal of humanity.

MORLEY CALLAGHAN

Such Is My Beloved. Toronto: Macmillan, 1934. Toronto: McClelland and Stewart; New Canadian Library, 1957. Pages: 144. Paperback.

Morley Callaghan has become his own favourite celebrity. A recent novel, *A Fine and Private Place*, transparently pleads his unappreciated greatness. It is a pity because while he maintained authorial detachment in his craft he wrote some remarkably good fiction, the proof being a brief and brilliant reversion to earlier discipline, without the austerity, in his 1983 novel, *A Time for Judas*.

It took several novels before Callaghan learned what he seemed to have known intuitively in his short stories: that his métier was idea wedded to character rather than the dramatic revelation of plot. With *Such Is My Beloved* he found his stride. It is a novel of love and grace, charity and redemption; but it is also a novel about people. Father Dowling is a robust young priest and a compassionate idealist who befriends two streetwalkers, Ronnie and Midge, and tries desperately to save them. Dowling is spiritually innocent and socially naïve. Unable to cope with an imperfect world, he is left at the novel's end a patient in a mental hospital; there, in moments of clarity, he works on a commentary about spiritual love in the lusty passages of *The Song of Songs*.

Father Dowling could not cope with the reality of a Church built on absolute love but sustained by dispassionate compromise. The bishop of his Toronto cathedral is a fund-raising administrator. One of the major benefactors of the Church is a hypocrite who considers Midge and Ronnie feeble-minded liabilities, while his wife holds them in contempt. Dowling's friend Charlie Stewart, an idealistic socialist, sees the two women as economic factors; Lou, their pimp, obviously has an interest in Dowling's failure. Nowhere can the priest get help. Alone, he does not have the resources to absolve them except at the price of his own sanity. They are not reformed in the end, but they are saved by the grace of Dowling's sacrifice.

It is a bittersweet story, set in an amorphous context, related in prose that is strikingly unpretentious. Peripheral accounts give the story dimension: Mrs. Schwartz, for example, fusses frantically about dying, then dies in peace and beauty. There is no character development and the plot is elemental, but the characters do come alive in the reader's imagination – not fully created but half formed, struggling towards definition. It is a novel informed by an underlying faith, not submissive but questioning, lamenting, and ultimately affirming. Neither parable nor vision, it is a rather ordinary story with resounding spiritual and moral implications.

They Shall Inherit the Earth. Toronto: Macmillan, 1935. Toronto: McClelland and Stewart; New Canadian Library, 1969. Pages: 256. Paperback.

This novel has much of the moral intensity and the austere prose style of *Such Is My Beloved*, but there is greater social realism, a more intricate and dramatic plot, and a less pontifical tone. It is arguably Callaghan's best novel. *They Shall Inherit the Earth* explores guilt and responsibility, remorse and absolution, and in the process offers a compelling story. The author's tendencies towards moral generalization and dramatic excess are curbed by a story that is restrained yet intriguing, a point of view more humane and less condescending than usual in his writing. There is an uncharacteristic humility about this novel that sets it apart from Callaghan's other works.

The potential for melodrama in the novel's opening sequence is adroitly offset by the moral problems it evokes and the psycho-moral narrative it sets in motion. Michael Aikenhead, the protagonist, commits an act of criminal passivity when he allows his step-brother, David Choate, to drown. Michael lets his father, Andrew, bear the blame for the drowning and carry the guilt for it. Then, throughout the novel, Michael searches for self-justification. Unable to escape moral responsibility through religion or revolution, cynicism or indifference, he attempts to cope. He shares love with Anna Prychoda. The evasion breaks down when their child is born. Life created is an unbearable reminder of the life he helped to destroy. Remorse overwhelms Michael, and after confessing to his wife, he asks forgiveness from his father. He becomes a son again, a part of something extending beyond himself, and is absolved of his crime, or at least of the guilt that followed upon it.

There are two important digressions in the novel. One tells of a wolf hunt; in witnessing the hunt, Michael learns the harsh, just order of nature. The other, "The Parable of the Misshapen Shoes," tells of the vanity of superficial compassion. The wolf hunt is fully integrated with the plot, its message inseparable from the narrative drama. The parable is more arbitrarily delivered, a structural aberration; while thematically effective, it is an awkward irregularity of form. Structurally, the novel falters somewhat: the moral dynamics are not sustained by the plot dynamics. The mood sinks deeper and deeper towards despair, then surges upward towards a resolution that seems externally imposed. Nonetheless, Callaghan has concerned himself, and the reader, with vital matters. His themes are important and visible, and the art of his novel supports them admirably.

More Joy in Heaven. New York: Random House, 1937. Toronto: McClelland and Stewart; New Canadian Library, 1969. Pages: 159. Paperback.

In this novel, Callaghan returns to a theological anomaly that haunts him: there is more joy in heaven for the repentance of a single sinner than for virtue maintained by a multitude of just men. The criminal holds a fascination for Callaghan; the reformed criminal especially captivates him. The fallen man who has been redeemed is beloved of God and his fellow men; he is subject, therefore, to the enticements of pride and vainglory, subject to fall even farther than others because he has been elevated from such depths. Kip Caley is one such man, based on the real-life hoodlum Red Ryan, who was paroled from the penitentiary a hero and died ten months later while robbing a liquor store. Callaghan is concerned with more than the obvious drama inherent in such a story; he is concerned with the social and moral implications and, more important, with the spiritual drama the story represents.

One of Callaghan's main contributions as a novelist is the sustained impression he creates that people have spiritual as well as social and psychological dimensions to their lives, and that their moral and spiritual aspects are inseparable. He is not always ready with answers to the weightier problems of human existence, but he provokes intriguing and essential questions. Events and personalities seem constantly to be evading his grasp as he reaches for something deeper, more significant in his characters' experience. He displays minds rather than mannerisms, internal responses rather than overt behaviour. His concern is with life rather than with living. But Callaghan clearly envisions the writer as a popular entertainer as well as a moral seer, whose aim must be to excite the reader's imagination as much as to vitalize his soul. In a novel like *More Joy in Heaven*, the two impulses collide. The popular story and its profound moral base seem at odds with one another. As a result, the novel seems ambitious yet superficial. *More Joy in Heaven* is an admirable failure.

Through the good offices of a senator, a priest, and a pressure group of well-wishers, a reformed Kip Caley is given early parole from Kingston Penitentiary. He returns to Toronto as the fêted prodigal son. But his absolution is mundane, founded on false charity. Of those who help him, some want to prove their own worth; others, like the owner of the Coronet Hotel where he is hired as a "greeter," have an economic interest in him; the senator's daughter wants to be his friend for thrills; the convicting judge uses Caley to confirm his own sense of self-righteousness; Whispering Joe uses Kip as a challenge and entices him back into crime to confirm the rightness of Joe's own fallen state. Joe acts as the insidious voice of Caley's past, an expression, almost, of original sin. In contrast, there is Julie Evans, whose love is too spiritual, too compassionate, to survive an intimate encounter with reality. Caley is a giant, exciting man who does not have the humility to see that he has been absolved of his crimes without being redeemed. He cannot see that his reform has been social, not spiritual, not absolute. In the end, he and Julie are killed, the bodies forming a bullet-riddled cross.

This novel, as much as any, shows why Callaghan is a significant writer in the Canadian tradition without necessarily being an accomplished artist. The prose is awkwardly simplistic, but forceful and direct. It reads almost like a parody of a certain American style, though he has sustained a moral dimension not found in his American counterparts, who were generally more concerned with society and personality than with psyche and the soul. Callaghan stands out among Canadians writing in the thirties for his determined cosmopolitanism, which from a present perspective appears somewhat provincial. He is probably the best example we have of the serious artist as entertainer. *More Joy in Heaven*, while not his best novel, is the best example of this impulse.

Luke Baldwin's Vow. *See* Canadian Novels For Young Readers.

The Loved and the Lost. Toronto: Macmillan, 1951. Laurentian Library, 1970. Pages: 234. Paperback.

This novel deserves attention – for its weaknesses as much as for its strengths. It is the least overtly religious of Callaghan's earlier novels, but it has spiritual depths and complexities not found elsewhere in the Callaghan canon. It contains some of his least successful writing – and at his worst, Callaghan is capable of atrocious prose, violently forced symbolism, and turgid dramatics. It shows only a superficial understanding of its subject materials: of women, blacks, Montreal society, and the nuances of human personality. Through all this, however, it displays the ambiguities, anomalies, and ironies of real life without cloying explanation – indeed, with a compassion and tolerance his other fiction lacks.

Callaghan's intentional cosmopolitanism dominated the Canadian literary scene for more than a decade. Several of his earlier novels, along with a few of his short stories, are part of his enduring legacy. *The Loved and the Lost* marks the end of his most creative and successful period. While not great by any measure, it is of singular importance; it illuminates the novels that came before and those that followed. It shows both the best and the worst of one of our most significant writers.

Jim McAlpine, a former University of Toronto history professor who has moved to Montreal to write a newspaper column, provides the story's point of view. Through Jim, Callaghan explores the debilitating bondage that love can sometimes impose, the corruption that innocence can sometimes engender. The focal character is Peggy Sanderson, a perennial outsider who thrills with middle-class shock at being a factory worker, at being on intimate terms with the "Montreal negro community," at being socially engaged in an alien world. Structured as carefully as a formal argument, the novel describes McAlpine, caught between Peggy and his publisher's aristocratic daughter, between his tavern cronies and the publisher's lofty Westmount world. No cliché is left unturned. Blacks are caricatures, each with the soul of a jazz musician; Peggy's unusual aggressive naïveté is the legacy of her preacher father and the Indian family who welcomed her among them. Ultimately, Peggy, the corrupting innocent, is murdered:

the moral enigma she embodies is not resolved but intensified–her haunting of McAlpine begins in earnest.

Callaghan is far too sophisticated to explain himself. His novel explores the tensions between pride and humility, innocence and corruption, without drawing conclusions. There are ways of reading each aspect of character, situation, and motive. McAlpine sees an incident at a hockey game, by analogy, as evidence of Peggy's innocence; the reader as readily sees it as proof of her guilt. The strength of the novel rests in the idea that both conclusions are correct.

Callaghan's writing tends to seem naïve to contemporary readers. It has simplicity and directness without resonance. Meaning in his fiction does not arise inevitably from the narrative: rather, plots and characters seem to be arranged to illustrate themes. For a time, however, Callaghan dominated the Canadian tradition, and it cannot fully be appreciated without considering his importance to its development.

A Time for Judas. Toronto: Macmillan, 1983. Scarborough: Avon, 1984. Pages: 247. Paperback.

In this novel, Callaghan takes the best-known story of the Western world and tells it as if it had never been told before. He makes an account of Christ's passion seem unexpected and immediate. He commands our renewed attention to the spiritual, moral, and psychological enigma at the heart of our whole civilization. In prose of lucid beauty, he overwhelms secular indifference with the sheer power of his story.

That a writer of eighty should find a new voice, as Callaghan has in *A Time for Judas*, is something of a marvel. That this voice speaks with vigour and a casual authority not found in his fiction for over a generation is virtually a miracle. Callaghan's recent novels have seemed rather mean and even demeaning. *A Fine and Private Place* is an exercise in self-aggrandizement and *Close to the Sun Again* is an over-wrought attempt to prove the juggler has not lost his balls. *A Time for Judas*, however, takes the reader back to early Callaghan, while showing a contemplative and disciplined maturity his work then lacked. *Strange Fugitive* (1927), *It's Never Over* (1930), and *A Broken Journey* (1932) seem thin and forced in comparison. Yet this novel shares their remarkable vitality and narrative clarity (which, paradoxically, give rise to haunting ambiguities, especially moral ambiguities) and their delight in the power and the beauty of the English language.

It is difficult to know from his text whether Callaghan is familiar with the Nikos Kazantzakis novel, *The Last Temptation*, in which Judas is likewise the favoured disciple in the conspiracy of Jesus to achieve secular immortality. Both novels suggest that only Judas loved his Messiah enough to betray him, in fulfilment of scriptural prophecy and to make the story good. Only him could Jesus trust to play the part of villain–though ultimately he is crushed by the role assigned him. Whether Callaghan picked up such radical revisionism from Kazantzakis or devised it on his own is irrelevant, though, since each works to such different ends. The Judas of Callaghan's version dies as a consequence of betraying his Lord's trust to the narrator and not for his compliance in the suicide of the man-god whom he served. And likewise, if the literal body of Jesus remains earthbound, bones into dust, Callaghan owes nothing to Charles Templeton, whose novel, *The Third Temptation*, explored in pop-fiction fashion the liturgical implications of an unrisen Christ. It is a plausible conceit in a secular age–and, in any case, Callaghan covers himself with an "envisioned" resurrection that renders bodily ascension of no consequence.

Callaghan adheres to convention in devising a multiple framing structure that simultaneously distances us from the central narrative, to make it seem more authentic, and draws us in, to make it seem more immediate. The present writer receives the word from a dying writer who gets it from an old professor who received it, through the Church, from a sealed jar where it was deposited by Philo of Crete, who wrote as a witness from memory, including parts related to him directly by Judas himself. Callaghan misses a fine chance to compound the formal and thematic complexity of his narrative by closing his account with the sealing of the jar, rather than returning (with it) to contemporary times and the presence of the present narrator, and us, reading. This is a curious dereliction, given the importance he places on "story," its transcendent capacity to establish truth beyond the strictures of time and factuality. Perhaps, though, he is even more taken up with the spiritual implications of his account and does not want such essentially postmodern considerations to interfere.

In any case, Philo provides both the centre and the perimeters of Callaghan's narrative. The story of Jesus is narrated obliquely and in selective fragments determined by Philo's personality and Callaghan's narrative ingenuity. As a scribe who sometimes works for Pilate, Philo has a privileged vantage on events in Jerusalem—yet, for the most part, events surrounding the Galilean seem insignificant. Philo is embroiled in the murderous treacheries of the thief Simon who, as it comes to pass, shares the agony of Golgotha with Jesus and certain words that Philo cannot hear. He keeps a young whore called Mary who, for the sake of the story, lends her function to Mary of Magdalene, the lover of Jesus—because story demands that the woman closest to him be redeemed. And so it goes: for the sake of story. Everyone plays a part. Some play according to the covert directions of their Lord; and some, according to the impress of history. And in the end only Philo knows the difference between what was acted and what was enacted. This knowledge he seals in a jar for a posterity that will be sufficiently sophisticated/jaded/indifferent to cope.

Callaghan does not create a scholarly reconstruction but writes with complete ease about a world as immediate and real as in the most contemporary of fiction. That, in good part, is the genius of this novel–it is contemporary. Then and now interpenetrate, are one. His language is more opulent than we are used to in his writing; his imagery more detailed and luxuriant. Structure is multidimensional, more contrived and yet seemingly less arbitrary. However, it all hangs together quite beautifully. This is a vital new venture from an old writer, and living proof that he is still among the best.

PHILIP CHILD

God's Sparrows. London: Thornton Butterworth, 1937. Toronto: McClelland and Stewart; New Canadian Library, 1978. Pages: 325. Paperback.

Nearly two decades after the First World War and two years before the Second, Philip Child published *God's Sparrows*. It is the quint-

essential Canadian war novel. Child puts war in perspective; he
places it against the structures and alliances of family, friends,
and community, against the values of the individual, society, and
civilization. Yet he shows how war overwhelms all other realities,
how at the Front only death is reality. The novel evokes sadness–
not quite bitter but not melancholy, either. It sustains the feeling
of loss–time lost, life lost, meaning lost, faith lost. There is only
sadness, until we forget. And Child does not want us to forget.
This novel is a chronicle of shattered lives, social chaos, moral
absurdity; an eyewitness history; a memoir. But it is many things,
more things than can be borne by a single work of fiction. If the
soul of art is unity, as ambiguity is its wit and eloquence its form,
then Child's novel bears an injured soul.

The primary centre of consciousness in the novel is Dan That-
cher; but intersecting, like the rings from a handful of pebbles
thrown into a pool, are the lives of his family and friends. The
narrative begins with Dan's birth in the closing hours of the nineteenth century, and the novel tells the story of his growing up
and coming to terms with himself. A portrait of the artist whose
mettle is tempered in a terrible inferno, the novel is also the story
of Dan's descent into an underworld. He has his own Beatrice,
whom he loves in a great, impetuous romance. The novel is also a
family saga; it describes, in fine detail, the colourful relationships of Thatchers and Burnets, centred around the family home
"Ardentinny" in Wellington, Ontario; it follows four of the family to France, where two die.

Child is concerned with the moral and existential questions
raised by the war. His novel is a dramatic inquiry, which examines the pathetic death of Dan's father for his belief in humanity;
the life and death of Dan's cousin, a poet and thinking man; the
life and death of Dolughoff, a maniacal prophet and misanthrope.
There is a moving dream sequence in which God, in a court martial,
conducts inquiries into souls, and finds Himself wanting. *God's
Sparrows* is the story, also, of men at war; of men under unimag-
inable pressure, where death is more immediate and real than
the mud and torn bodies and deafening shrill guns; of the relations among men under duress, in extremity; of valour and duty
and fear.

Not least, *God's Sparrows* is a memoir of the war, a history
related from the perspective of an artillery officer in France, at

the Salient, at the battles of Ypres, which consumed hundreds of thousands of lives for a few miles of ungodly broken earth. The dates and facts are not given as an historian's account, however, but as a soldier's experience. The narrative voice sometimes rises out of the fiction to declare authenticity (unnecessarily, for Child's fiction has the truth of actuality about it).

Most of the novel takes place at the Front. Child describes conditions awesome beyond brutality or meaning; he writes with unparallelled immediacy. *God's Sparrows* suffers occasionally from an awkwardness of style, primarily in dialogue and in scenes away from the Front. It is the war, in fact, that elevates the novel from the merely competent to a unique achievement as a strange medley of chronicle, memoir, and romance. It is a vision of civilization gone berserk, but with the nobility of man somehow left intact.

AUSTIN CLARKE

Storm of Fortune. Toronto: Little, Brown, 1973.
Pages: 312.

Storm of Fortune is the key work in a trilogy about Barbadians in Toronto, although it also stands complete on its own as the best writing Clarke has done. The novel moves with boisterous *élan* between two realities, almost indistinguishable from one another in some ways yet as different as old and new. It opens with a loose cluster of expatriates from Barbados and closes with the same group (one less in number) a year or so later. The expatriates have become immigrant Canadians. The change occurs fragmentally. None of the characters is particularly aware of it, nor is the reader; yet the change is profound. Clarke has written as dynamic an immigrant saga as any in Canadian literature. But the story does not end in the triumph of assimilation, for Clarke writes of black people in a white land. He chronicles the phases of change in the nation's complexion. *Storm of Fortune* and the other books in the trilogy, *The Meeting Point* and *The Bigger Light*, will disturb many readers, even as they entertain them, with revelations of the inequities and anomalies of the complacent Canadian society.

Clarke is first and foremost an artist, a creator of good fiction. It is a disservice to suppose him a mouthpiece for the black community, an arbiter between blacks and whites. But so good is he at capturing the experience of these two groups in conflict that, inevitably, his fiction has value as a social document. It will shock the white Canadian reader on several counts. Clarke shows a polite society riddled, beneath the surface, with bigotry and ignorance. Also, his portrait of Barbadians in Canada, which seems authentic, appears to confirm every prejudice held about them. The men are loud, ignorant, amoral, shiftless; the women bossy, bitterly obsequious, and amoral. Gradually, though, these characteristics are placed in the perspective of the Canadian context. Here are people who have grown up proud and free; they are poor, uneducated, and naïve. They are not "black," they are Barbadian. Harlem, Africa, Trinidad have little to do with them. They are people with a strong sense of their own identity. In Canada, more precisely in Toronto, they are forced into roles of defiance. The language and behaviour of Barbados become exaggerated out of pride. Their language, especially, which only roughly approximates Canadian English, is both shield and weapon against the brutality of their Canadian experience. By the end of the novel, Clarke's Barbadians speak an English that is distinctive, yet close to the Canadian norm.

The narrative moves almost at random among the characters–Bernice and Estelle, sisters; Boysie and Dots, husband and wife; Henry and his rich, clever, Jewish woman, Agatha. There is little in the way of a plot, although the characters always have much to talk about. A good portion of the novel, in fact, is dialogue, and Clarke is a master of dialect, particularly the mellifluous English spoken by his expatriate Barbadians. Clarke's own use of language is precise. It is a wonder he managed to render his characters' speech with such humour and yet avoid the appearance of condescension.

As the novel progresses, each character moves separately towards the dignity that his experience in Canada has undermined. Bernice is summarily fired from her work as a domestic by her Jewish employer; but she discovers that even Jews in Forest Hill, from the perspective of Rosedale or The Bridal Path, live in a ghetto, and by turning racism in her favour, she rises above it. Her sister, Estelle, carries her half-black baby proudly. Boysie begins working, after more than a year of smarting from battered pride and having some wild good times on the side. Dots quits her job as a domestic, trains to be a nurse's aid, and pays the rent. Agatha marries Henry and becomes black, temporarily. Of the six characters, Henry alone cannot cope. A poet, an outsider to all worlds, he kills himself.

Clarke focuses more attention on the women in this novel than on the men. It is the women who are down to earth, strong, wilful, independent; the women lead the way into this alien world and force a working compromise with it. The men talk and brag, gamble and drink, and eventually, somewhat sadly, fall into line. Clarke has not written a novel of triumph; instead, with profound understanding and a good measure of sardonic humour, he has created a story of reconciliation with the fallen world.

LEONARD COHEN

Beautiful Losers. Toronto: McClelland and Stewart, 1966. Toronto: McClelland and Stewart; New Canadian Library, 1981. Pages: 260. Paperback.

The strength of Leonard Cohen's first novel, *The Favorite Game*, comes from its directness of language and emotion. Sometimes the imagery is flashy; sometimes sentiment becomes sentimentality. But such indulgences are appropriate to the romantic and indulgent sensibility of the protagonist. Cohen has never been afraid to overextend himself: witness *Beautiful Losers*, his experimental monument to the sixties. Few novels have suffered wider divergence of critical opinion (few decades have engendered such extreme responses to reality). *Beautiful Losers* is extravagant, obscene, bizarre. It wrenches narrative coherence and historical authenticity wildly askew. At the same time it celebrates the wholeness of life, the diversity of experience, the triumph of body over mind, and freedom over slavish convention. It is a book filled with love and depravity; its style is ingenious, energetic, outrageous; it sings of its own defiance. Ultimately it fails, because much of what it defies was a passing thing; much of what it celebrates is obscured by its lavishly inventive rhetoric.

One of the main characters is a Mohawk girl, a popular saint who died in Quebec in 1680. This girl, Catherine Tekakwitha, becomes a martyr to her own fervour. Devotion, instilled in her by the Jesuit fathers, leads to the scourging of her body until, in self-mortification, she dies. The other characters are a contemporary triangle: the nameless narrator; his wife, who is an Indian of the A–tribe (losers all); and F., who is either dead or in an asylum through most of the novel. All together, they make a strange and curiously engaging foursome.

Skits, quips, aphorisms, and a broad array of allusions to pop culture and the contemporary scene are scattered throughout the novel. Occasionally, the sheer poetry of Cohen's language creates the illusion of beauty where there is none, of sensitivity where there is only eccentricity, of passion where there are only orgasms ingeniously achieved. *Beautiful Losers* was one of the most aggressively experimental Canadian novels of the 1960s, and certainly one of the best known. It was meant to shock, and there was a time when it did. Less shocking today, it remains a fascinating document.

MATT COHEN

The Disinherited. Toronto: McClelland and Stewart, 1974. Toronto: McClelland and Stewart; New Canadian Library, 1976. Pages: 240. Paperback.

The Disinherited is one of the best Canadian novels of this generation. Technical and aesthetic accomplishments coincide exactly with the novel's thematic intent: what is said and how it is said are inseparable. Everything Cohen published before this novel promised such an achievement, without at all anticipating what manner of work it would be. Everything he has published since – and he is a prolific professional writer – has helped to consolidate his achievement.

Three subsequent novels have been set in the same area of southeastern Ontario as *The Disinherited*, and include many of the same people. Yet, due to Cohen's versatility with form and language and a maturing sensibility, which allows increasingly more scope for the adventures of ordinary lives, there is no sense of a saga developing. Instead, Cohen seems to define a region not only with facts and events but from different perspectives, seeing it in different ways, in different dimensions of narrative reality, with each work in what have come to be known as the Salem novels. (As well as *The Disinherited*, these include *The Colours of War, The Sweet Second Summer of Kitty Malone,* and *Flowers of Darkness.*)

The Disinherited employs a radical distribution of time and discovers narrative continuity in the discontinuous fragments of intersecting lives. Yet it is still, in many ways, a very traditional novel. Or, more correctly, it turns a major Canadian tradition back upon itself to expose the literary and social assumptions on which that tradition is based. The focal and narrative centre of *The Disinherited* is a family farm. Cohen displays a full awareness of the dramatic possibilities of the Canadian farm environment. Beneath the surface of the Thomas family's separate lives there seethes a raw, violent sexuality, which occasionally erupts and is quelled for the common good; life on the farm goes on. But the irony is that, with each succeeding eruption and the passing of each generation, the farm changes. At the novel's close it no longer belongs to the family but is bequeathed to the adopted son, Brian; it remains in the family's shadow.

Cohen's story concerns four generations of the Thomas family. They carve their farm out of the wilderness and see it prosper; its gradual fall into disrepair is parallelled by the disintegration of the Thomas family itself. Cohen does not relate the story as a chronicle. He begins with the present. Richard Thomas is dying in the Kingston General Hospital; Erik Thomas, his son, refuses the farm life for a post at the University of Alberta. From their perspectives, Cohen fills in the details of the family's past. He illuminates fragments of their mingled lives, then lets them slip away, gradually shading and highlighting their common design until the picture is complete. Time, as Cohen arranges it, has a spatial quality; it becomes linear again only when Richard dies.

The separate pieces of the story are stitched together with recurring motifs and with the tantalizingly gradual revelation of details that coalesce in the reader's mind. Thus the affairs between Katherine Malone and two generations of Thomas men come slowly into focus, not merely as a network of events but as a dimension of their separate lives. Similarly, physical details accumulate across time. We see the canopy formed by the rows of mature maples along the farm driveway, but we see the trees also as saplings. There is no sequential pattern of growth; we see saplings and trees simultaneously as the past and present merge. From the beginning there is a sense of luxuriant density. A genealogical table would ease the reader through the intricacies of the Thomas family – yet Cohen makes no attempt to describe each character as the limb of a family tree. Some figures in each generation emerge in strength; others remain vague or incomplete. The language Cohen uses ranges from the regional vernacular to a timeless, somewhat elevated prose. It moves easily from one extreme to the other as the narrative leaps generations in a single paragraph, in a memory, or in pursuit of an elusive motif.

The Disinherited deals with great themes, but it does so with humour and a refined sense of the absurd. Still, it is the serious that predominates. Genealogies of blood and spirit are etched through the narrative, so that the conflict and continuity between generations have seemingly limitless dimensions. Themes of personal identity multiply with each narrative revelation. Themes of man's relationship with the land, with time, and with himself are explored with resounding irony. Time wins, yet the end of the novel is ambiguous. With Richard's death, the family farm cycle is completed. Erik becomes part of a "new beginning" – but in a city world removed from the natural world that Cohen celebrates. It is a questionable affirmation at best. Only the lost past remains; in the pages of this fine and memorable fiction, the past transcends time itself.

Wooden Hunters. Toronto: McClelland and Stewart, 1975. Toronto: McClelland and Stewart; New Canadian Library, 1977. Pages: 219. Paperback.

In one way, *Wooden Hunters* serves as a mirror-image sequel to *The Disinherited*: the novel's characters have already lost their pasts. They are prisoners of the present tense, cut off yet haunted by their lost histories. Their lives are filled with quiet, inarticulate despair and incipient brutality. On the surface, nothing much happens. Yet there is tension, bearable only through drink, dope, sex, or sporadic violence. This is Cohen's existential vision. Ironically, it ends on a positive note.

Set on an island off the coast of British Columbia, *Wooden Hunters* has all the elements of contemporary escape literature – and much more besides. The central protagonist is Laurel Hobson, a strangely beautiful and eccentric young woman. Her first (and former) lover and closest friend, Johnny Tulip, is an island Indian with whom she shares an almost mystical bond; Laurel bears an uncanny resemblance to Johnny's dead sister. Her present lover, Calvin, is a counter-culture drifter. The three are surrounded by the magnificent beauty of the natural world, which is threatened: the lumber interests are gearing up for a new assault on the environment. But Laurel dominates the novel. She is the centre of consciousness – and conscience; she suffers and she endures. By the novel's end she is reconciled to the present, has assimilated her past, and has tentatively discovered the future open before her.

In *Wooden Hunters*, Cohen fuses the extravagant and the subtle, the grotesque and the commonplace. His prose arrests the imagination with graphic detail, striking imagery, and just the right shade of ambiguity and allusive resonance. His fiction is essentially realistic – his perception of reality is sometimes bizarre, but what he sees is invariably plausible enough in its own right. *Wooden Hunters* sets character against theme: they do not develop together but reveal one another. Cohen's vision is ultimately both an indictment and a wary celebration of its time.

The Sweet Second Summer of Kitty Malone. Toronto: McClelland and Stewart, 1979. Toronto: McClelland and Stewart; New Canadian Library, 1982. Pages: 217.

Paperback

This is a fine novel, and it confirms Cohen as a major writer. His special knack as a story-teller – his particular genius for blending the bizarre and the trivial – takes a fresh turn with *Kitty Malone*. Here is the region of southeastern Ontario he approached tentatively in *Johnny Crackle Sings* and to which he gave resounding depth in *The Disinherited*, the region to which he returned somewhat obliquely in *The Colours of War*, given now the dimensions of lived-in reality. We are continually surprised by what we read, and are utterly convinced by it.

Cohen describes with uncanny fidelity the hard, undisciplined beauty of marginal farmland north of Kingston. What makes him the best regional writer Canada has yet produced is the conviction with which he populates that region: through the interaction of his characters with each other and with the environment, over generations of time, he brings the region alive as a part of our own experience. The novel describes the events of Kitty Malone's life; the carryings-on of Pat Frank, her lover and, at forty-nine, her second husband; his hard-drinking, glass-eyed twin brother, Mark; the weird eccentricities of Kitty's mother, Ellen; the nervous innocence of her daughter, Lynn; and the careless truculence of her son, Randy. In the earthy particularities of Kitty's world, Cohen has created drama that is honest and unique. It is as universal as love and death, and as moving.

Regional does not mean provincial. Cohen is an urbane and sophisticated prose stylist. He seems to meet language as a challenge: syntax bends and even breaks to serve clarity and mood; diction creates a sub-text of tonalities. The narrative voice speaks from a perspective outside the novel, yet the words and phrasing create a delicate discord with the characters, sometimes underscoring, sometimes counter-pointing, to create resonance in our perception of their lives. Words and phrasing and images are always appropriate to the particular centre of consciousness at any given time, yet they are under control enough to sustain the ironic viewpoint of the reader/narrator outside of context.

Cohen's imagery has a surreal quality, quite apart from the surrealism of situation that he has always found attractive. In the imagery of *Kitty Malone*, physical and mental conditions extend into the real and abstract world: a stomach cramp, for instance, can cause spasms to explode across the morning fields, or dissipate to emptiness. Animate and inanimate, natural and man-shaped worlds all continually converge, merge, separate, and rejoin. Existence becomes so complex and excited that the often primal methods of coping with life adopted by his characters seem both appropriate and inevitable.

Characters dominate. Cohen manipulates time, collapsing it and expanding it seemingly at random, to bring Kitty and her intimate community alive. Plot is revealed rather than developed. It turns out to be nothing more, and nothing less, than a cluster of lifetimes held together by proximity of body and soul.

The Spanish Doctor. Toronto: McClelland and Stewart, 1983. Pages: 344. Markham: Penguin, 1985. Paperback.

The Spanish Doctor is a remarkable departure for Cohen from all that he has done before. There is nothing in this versatile writer's canon to anticipate an historical novel set during the cataclysmic dawning of the Renaissance, in which the main character is a lesser messiah, a secular Jewish prophet of the new age (patterned somewhat, perhaps, on Paracelsus), and the plot, his life story. While each of the Salem novels is written in a different mode, from prophetic to gothic, and provides a different dimension to Cohen's regional vision of southeastern Ontario, and while, especially in his short stories, Cohen romps almost recklessly through an eclectic variety of styles, voices, forms, and attitudes, *The Spanish Doctor* is still a remarkable shift in venue.

It is the first novel by a prolific Jewish writer to deal with the Jewishness of characters as more than an incidental and somewhat esoteric accident of birth. The protagonist is born a Jew; at seven he is baptized a Christian under threat of the sword; and for the rest of his life, as a Marrano, he is neither Christian nor Jew, and yet both. This crucial ambiguity provides the shape to his story. The parallels with the experience of North American Jewry are a haunting echo throughout the novel, just as the Inquisitional extermination of medieval Jews invokes a sustaining awareness of the Holocaust. Yet Cohen is much too sophisticated a writer to deploy the past in his fiction merely as a commentary on the present by turning medieval Europe into an ironic counterpart of the twentieth century. He strives at every turn for authenticity of mood and detail and leaves the parallels to evolve (as they surely must) in the reader's mind. To do otherwise, where despite historical intervention so much seems unchanged, would have surely meant bathos in the extreme, or an exceedingly ponderous anachronism.

The Spanish Doctor is a fine example of those qualities that distinguish the best historical fiction from second-rate historical romance. The characters live within history; they are not superimposed on it. In a broad sweep that extends his narrative from Spain to the Ukraine through the course of a generation that came to maturity around 1400, Cohen deftly integrates the most intimate details of his characters' lives into the vast panoply of European history. Brutality, during this most crucial turning point in the development of Western civilization when medievalism gave way to the Renaissance, coincided in a perverse balance with reason. Avram Halevi is born and lives at the fulcrum. He is a man of the new age, a doctor devoted to science and the humane arts. But he is a man of his times, and these are unconscionably brutal and demeaning. As Europe tortuously subdivides and the arts and sciences flourish, Avram pursues his destiny in response to, and in some small ways responsible for, the violent rebirth of civilization after a millenium of apparent darkness.

In six sections, or Books as he calls them, Cohen's narrative details the life of Avram from conception in Toledo to his death seventy-six years later in Kiev. Born from the multiple fatherhood of his mother's rape when Christian soldiers ravage the Jewish sector of Toledo, Avram leaves Spain as a young man to study medicine in Montpelier. His skill in the arcane practice of surgery leads him into close contact with the Velasquez family, one brother of which becomes the patron of Avram's first love, Gabriela, while the other, who would be Pope, falls victim to his dagger after having been responsible for the deaths of his wife and daughter in France. In Montpelier, precariously denying both Christianity and Judaism, Avram becomes Dean of the Medical School— until a circumstantial allegiance brings havoc upon him and those around him. Then, in Bologna, where Gabriela has become Italian lieutenant in Juan Velasquez's commercial empire, Avram becomes virtually a dybuk, avenging his family, avenging the Jews who died by the thousands under Catholicism, avenging his boyhood friend, Antonio, by the murder of Cardinal Roderigo Velasquez, who is on the verge of resolving the great schism in the Church by becoming Pope. After almost a decade in prison, Avram escapes with Gabriela and with his son and her daughter, who marry en route to Kiev, where after a brief stint at abject poverty they prosper with pride and a new/renewed faith in their Jewish heritage.

The Spanish Doctor has all the ingredients of a best-seller. While *Flowers of Darkness*, the last of the Salem novels, anticipated the strong narrative line and a greater commitment to gothic conflict, this novel is Cohen's first attempt at what might be called intentional popularity. It does not pander, but for the reader who wants action vivid, passions powerful, and an atmosphere seething with violence and significance, it will surely satisfy. At the same time, it explores, or perhaps more accurately, it exposes themes of such moral complexity that the reader is perpetually left strung out between poles of understanding and outrage, comprehension and disbelief, acceptance and revulsion. While the best-seller readily allows the reader a comfortable position on the moral sidelines, however, in that we share the victim's suffering and know the villain's shame, in this novel suffering does not relieve us of responsibility, nor does acknowledgement of guilt absolve us from pain. Such ambivalence lifts *The Spanish Doctor* from disturbing and provocative entertainment to the level of art – a lasting achievement and signal turning point in the canon of an important writer.

Nadine. Markham: Penguin, 1986. Pages: 294.

In *Nadine* both the author and his protagonist struggle successfully toward self-acceptance in the larger world. Whether the history and the cultural geography of Western civilization, especially through the middle of our present century, are amenable or even comprehensible is not nearly so relevant to our survival as whether we can accept ourselves in such a context. From Hitler's war and the Holocaust we have wrung out the conditions of our precarious life on this planet. As individuals we watch the grotesque dance of science and politics from the wings or in the darkened theatre – and with the house-lights down it is frighteningly easy to believe we are not substantially a presence. During breaks in the performance we hurry off to exercise our individuality, oftentimes in bed, but when history takes the stage again we are immediately returned to the dark, hardly ourselves at all. Only by stepping forward into the light of history can we see ourselves and be seen. This is what Cohen does with *Nadine*, and what Nadine does within her novel.

The point is not that after Auschwitz there can be no poetry. It is that after Auschwitz and the fifty million brutal deaths that we are heir to, there can *still* be poetry. A full generation later, we still make love, make art, drink tea, and chatter aimlessly or with excessive purpose. The point is, we still get by, those of us chosen by the indifference of history to be survivors. But how to endure survival, how to cope with individual presence in a world poised on the brink of annihilation, following deadly practice under the aegis of Adolf Hitler? How, especially for a Jew?

Cohen deals here with great themes, not so much as theme but as philosophical inquiry. Each of his novels has a serious underlying purpose, of course. Sometimes, as with *The Spanish Doctor*, it is inseparable from a world view of history. In other novels, especially the Salem works, it has more to do with universal problems of love, death, time, and continuity. In *Nadine* we have the subtle and dramatic confluence of both extremes – the interpenetration of life lived and history happening. It is a compelling *tour de force*.

Matt Cohen, along with Margaret Atwood and Timothy Findley, has in the last decade or so risen to the fore by virtue of his ability to surprise. The talent of these writers is so freewheeling they provide wondrous dimension to our literature, unlike anything gleaned or given by their more conventional and predictable confreres. Much as I admire Munro, Kroetsch, and Davies (and I cannot think of three writers more different from one another to provide an example), none have taken such remarkable shifts in direction as Atwood in *The Handmaid's Tale*, Findley in *Not Wanted on the Voyage*, and Cohen in *Nadine* – and these, not from some created norm but following on the unexpectedness of *Bodily Harm*, *Famous Last Words*, and *The Spanish Doctor*. No one else writing in Canada today disturbs and delights with each new work as do these three. Although Munro's style may approach perfection, though Kroetsch may tease us brilliantly and Davies continue to astound us, none of them, nor Bowering, Thomas, Hodgins, Richards, or any other so utterly disarms us with such a play of diverse instruments. In retrospect, each new Atwood, Findley, and Cohen novel may seem inevitable within its canon, yet none could have been anticipated, none is simply another volume in the larger work. It is this, and of course the talent with which they write, that makes these three stand out from all others writing in Canada at present.

The title character of *Nadine*, the ostensible narrator who moves somewhat unsurely in and away from the centre of her story, is strong and yet her deference to history and to the stories of lives that touch hers makes her at times opaque. Hers is an account of self obliquely told. Yet the fiction she inhabits is vital and distinct; the voice, which includes Nadine's as one of its dimensions, is acerbic, precise, engaging, poignant, and urbane. That is the formal paradox of the narrative – it is diffuse and yet highly accessible. That is the paradox of Nadine's presence within the world – she intersects with history the way most characters in fiction intersect with narrative events. What happens to her happens to others; happened; is happening. It is the novel as a whole that conveys to us her story. It is the novel's voice and vision, not Nadine's, with which we as readers become intrigued, entangled, and in a most rare and moving experience, engulfed.

Nadine is divided into five Books and a prologue, each given over to a particular time and place in the life story of a woman born in Paris, raised in Toronto, educated in England, maimed in Israel, and, finally, celebrated in Paris for being the victim of impulse and the arbitrary whim of history. Nadine is Jewish, but as with virtually all of Cohen's Jewish characters, she is a secular Jew, a Jew culturally and ethnically – not by conviction or commitment but merely through genetic circumstance. Nonetheless, she is a Jew, and therefore as an infant in Paris during the German occupation she is liable to the horrors of Hitler's "final solution," as liable as her parents and those millions of others who disappear in the clouds of human smoke that smothered Europe during the Third Reich. As an orphaned refugee in Toronto, Nadine endures the pity of the privileged and the lascivious attentions of her uncle, a brilliant and pathetically perverse scientist. At Cambridge she discovers the curiously English habit of ineffectual social commitment. Back at the University of Toronto, Nadine prospers professionally but her personal life hardly breathes, except for relatively innocuous encounters with Miller, her childhood friend, who abandons her for the excitement of California. In a return match with Miller in Israel, she is wounded by a terrorist grenade and ends up in Paris, where she started, as she was at the novel's beginning, recuperating.

Science and humanism, technological evolution and the morality of survival, commitment and indifference, love and sex, Europe and the New World, these are a few of the paired polarities explored in *Nadine.* Yet this beautifully written and intricately plotted novel is, more than anything, an inquiry and a vision rather than a debate. It is a vision, related from the perspective of an individ-ual life, of our present brutal and absurd times; and it is an inquiry from an historical perspective into the life of a particular woman, contemporary, bright, deeply alienated, and yet somehow not disaffected, a woman we neither admire especially nor dislike but whose life we intimately, forcefully, even radically share.

Nadine is a major work, typical of the new confidence in Cana-dian fiction pioneered perhaps by Robertson Davies, which dares to explore highly particularized content, much of it Canadian, in an international, cosmopolitan, and urbane context. No less concerned with universals than earlier writing in Canada by Laurence, Munro, Hodgins, and their predecessors, this new mode acknowledges an intellectual and historical milieu beyond the boundaries of regionalism. With *Not Wanted on the Voyage* and *The Handmaid's Tale*, *Nadine* offers Canadian reality as a point of departure rather than as a limitation. Behind such works as these the garrison mentality lies wasted and irrelevant, and ahead the world opens to us.

ROBERT G. COLLINS

Tolerable Levels of Violence. Toronto: Lester & Orpen Dennys, 1983. Pages: 241. Don Mills: Totem, 1985. Paperback.

This is the kind of novel, like *1984*, that one does not really enjoy reading but, having read it, remembers vividly. Collins mixes rhetoric with violence in such extremes that the reader feels con-tinually under assault–from words in a variety of quasi-academic contexts, and from images of such ominous and horrific content the sensibility reels. *Tolerable Levels of Violence* is the dystopian vision of a future that may not be inevitable but is surely a possibility, given where we have been and what we have become. Collins builds his fiction from the cultural implications of West-ern civilization rather than from politics or science. In this, his novel differs significantly from other works in the prophetic and the speculative fiction genres. Within the moral and aesthetic traditions of our cultural history, Collins founds his version, his vision, of the future. In his world of 1999, politics and science, as well as religion, commerce, and communications, have deteriorated to the point of being nearly irrelevant, both to the narrative and to those within it.

John and Anne Cobbitt and their young son, Andrew, live in Braeside, just west of Arnprior, west of Ottawa. They live within an exact geography. Collins meticulously details the setting; he provides numerous place names and highway numbers, brief histories of the substantial world, brief descriptions of the landscape and the people who have lived within it. This is in marked ironic contrast to the overwhelming sense, conveyed throughout the novel, of human experience being almost entirely removed from the environment. Setting, in the lives of people in 1999, has become largely a matter of context. Only on their own property at Braeside does Cobbitt's experience seem integrated with his surroundings. Otherwise, the world is a strange and alien place.

As the narrative opens, Cobbitt is burying a Wanderer, killed by Anne when she found him raping their son. The Wanderers, like Hell's Angels run amok, are only one of the worst aspects of a society overwhelmed by violence. They will return, despite elaborate and rather makeshift defences, and in the end Andrew will die. In an act of absolute sacrifice, he will give his life to save his father's. In this, Cobbitt finds solace, and compensation enough to face the future. There is no alternative; and Anne, in any case, is pregnant.

The Braeside story works as a sort of parenthesis to contain the account of Cobbitt's journey into Ottawa where, since the barometer of public violence has fallen to a tolerable level, he delivers a lecture at the National University. He works there, when violence permits. His office is on the University of Ottawa campus, a recognizable reshaped remnant of the present institution. His students, the few of them there are, seem as desultory and uninspired as some professors now regard them in the present. Cobbitt's academic duties are dangerous but not onerous. Our heritage is violence, and literature, which Cobbitt teaches, while offering diversions, does not provide a refuge. There is no safety, even in books.

Cobbitt's time in the commuter convoy to work and home again provides Collins a chance for esoteric dialogue, mixed with splashes of violence. The worlds of intellect and brutal actuality run parallel. On the way to Ottawa, the commuters discuss such things as whether or not the artist can neutralize brutality, render it a matter of indifference. Discussion is followed by a reading, a tale written by one of the car's occupants, about the satisfactions of serial murder. On the return trip, ideals and actuality collide: talk about situational ethics is abbreviated by the sudden violence of a shell tearing through the limousine. After a masturbatorial nightmare episode in which Anne, a writer, grapples with her fictional characters, Toby and Tim, who have become monstrous parodies of themselves, kid-characters through whom to make elusive concepts accessible to simple minds, the narrative returns to Cobbitt's dilemma and finds him alive, among the dead, and brings him home.

There is little sense of pain in all of this, as there is little sense of urgency in the rhetorical discussions, but there is a genuine sense of "home" conveyed, of the importance of place and a centre of being, of primary relationships and a centre of commitment. Against a world gone bad, Collins envisions as the only consolation the ongoing act of love. If the present is built on the corpses of the past, and the future on the corpses of the present, then the only option for the humane and free-willed person is to accept with courage and grace one's place in the continuum: to love, and to hope. In conveying this, *Tolerable Levels of Violence* is more visionary than it is prophetic. The future, dreadful though it may be, as Collins sees it, is merely a context. His novel is about the present.

RALPH CONNOR
(CHARLES WILLIAM GORDON)

The Man from Glengarry. Toronto: Revell, 1901.
Toronto: McClelland and Stewart; New Canadian Library, 1967. Pages: 288. Paperback.

This novel is too banal to be an adolescent adventure yarn, yet too adolescent to be a novel for adults. Connor's prose style is cloying, forced, and extravagant. His characters are not defined well enough to be caricatures; instead, each is a cluster of clichés built around a simplistic concept of ethnicity, age, sex, or moral "type." The narrative voice (and the author behind it) is pretentious, patronizing, chauvinistic, racist, and rigidly self-righteous. *The Man from Glengarry* is as easy to read as a comic book, and no more satisfying. Why, then, it may be asked with considerable justification, why read it? Why not let it sink to its own level in the abyss of past pulp, where it rightfully belongs?

Aesthetically and morally, Connor's novel is a travesty. Yet it is arguably the best of the more than a score he produced. Historically and culturally, it is of primary importance. The year it appeared, *The Man from Glengarry* was outsold by only a few other titles in the Canadian market. The following year, according to literary historian Mary Vipond, it topped the list. Connor, a populist proselytizer, had already made the bestseller list with a prairie saga, *The Sky Pilot*. He was to continue to be a bestselling author for a generation. He wrote a sequence of socio-evangelical novels in which the quasi-religious message was simple and direct: God is on the side of good, right is might, and the bad shall fall to waste and perdition. Connor shifted his concentration from the Glengarry region in his later novels, to accommodate a world war and western Canada, but he never lost the determined righteousness of his calling as a Presbyterian minister.

The Man from Glengarry provides a sentimental picture of the Ottawa Valley, where Connor grew up in the 1860s, and includes idealized portraits of motherhood and life in a manse. It effectively recognizes the powerful relationship of Glengarry to the Dominion and God; it acknowledges their common aspirations, each for the other. In ways Connor could not have anticipated, *The Man from Glengarry* is a revealing document, illustrating attitudes and assumptions often in direct contradiction to the apparent values propounded by the text.

ROBERTSON DAVIES

Tempest-Tost. Toronto: Clarke, Irwin, 1951. Markham: Penguin, 1980. Pages: 284. Paperback.

This is the first and the best of Davies's Salterton novels, a threesome linked by common setting, common characters, and common attitudes but distinctly separate from one another in mood, voice, and achievement. Broadly described by the term "satirical romance," these works provide an intriguing balance to the dark and murky depths of Davies's later Deptford novels. In Salterton he keeps to the surface: with a sure sense of comic timing, he weaves intricate, amusing plots that provide opportunity for witty commentary on a marvellous variety of human foibles and conceits. There is something very eighteenth-century about twentieth-century Salterton society and the way he writes of it.

Salterton is the literary embodiment of those elements of Kingston, Ontario, that are conducive to social satire with a Tory bent. The university, the military college, the fine lakefront situation, the architecture, and the local history are retained; church, journalism, the law, and old money are prominent. Industry, tourism, the working class, and students are ignored. Davies does not attempt a balanced social portrait; his strength is wit, not sociology. He is quick and sure to judge, an arbiter more of values than of virtues. He is moved to instruct amusingly rather than to inspire or elevate.

Tempest-Tost is built around a Little Theatre production of Shakespeare's *The Tempest*. The play echoes through Davies's complicated plot on several levels. The dominant echo is the most superficial: who plays what, why, and how well. As the production takes shape, characters form alliances, manipulate one another, fall in all manner of love, and move inevitably through occasional pathos to a happy conclusion. The reader remains aware, throughout, of how cleverly the characters are being manipulated. The characters are, in fact, a cast. A number of them are caricatures: the rich beauty, the enamoured high-school teacher, the pneumatically endowed young woman who has risen above her station, the eccentric musician, the foolish professor, the pushy club president. The characters are all delightful, but most are presented with such a facile wit that they have no souls nor even personalities, no lives beyond those Davies explicitly assigns to them. A few do manage to rise prominently above their narrative function. Among these are Solly Bridgetower and his eventual wife, Pearl Vambrace, who reappear in the other two Salterton novels, *Leaven of Malice* and *A Mixture of Frailties*.

Davies writes in a manner suggesting Leacock; but showing less warmth and a sharper, more austere sensibility, a more restrained sense of fun and of anger, and an infinitely more developed aptitude for disdain. If there is a single dominant flaw in the Salterton novels, it is that Davies implicitly upholds the very pretentiousness he lampoons: he ridicules what he most admires. Nevertheless, they are fine, clever, amusing novels; immensely diverting, if somewhat ephemeral and a little dated. Whereas Leacock's Mariposa is still very much with us, Davies's Tory voice manages to make Salterton, from a present perspective, appear faded and gaudy at the same time, like an aging courtesan.

Fifth Business. Toronto: Macmillan, 1970. Markham: Penguin, 1977. Pages: 266. Paperback.

Maturity can be fascinating, in ways that youth can only marvel at. As if he had crossed over some private threshold that turned his wit and sense of theatrical contrivance inwards, in *Fifth Business* Davies shifts from the intellectual surfaces that informed his earlier work to the worlds of wonder within the human mind. This novel is a stunning achievement. It is the first of three Deptford novels, named after the town in which the sequence originates. *Fifth Business*, one of the best Canadian novels ever written, dominates; *The Manticore* provides an elaborate gloss on the Jungian principles at work in *Fifth Business*; and of the three linked novels (they are not a trilogy, but a triptych) it is least able to stand on its own merit. *World of Wonders* provides a gloss on devils, illusion, and magic in the primary text. Each work complements the others, but each is entirely self-contained.

The story begins when young Percy Boyd Staunton throws a snowball at Dunstable Ramsay. The snowball, which has a stone inside it, misses Dunstable and stuns Mary Dempster, precipitating the early birth of her son, Paul. Paul eventually becomes Magnus Eisengrim, possibly the best magician alive. Mary becomes a personal saint for Dunstable (who has become Dunstan) and dies in an asylum. On the eve of being named lieutenant governor of Ontario, Boy Staunton is found dead in Toronto harbour with the fateful stone clenched in his mouth.

This is a novel of becoming. Identity is something encountered in the procedures of living, although it is not always recognized or possessed. With a good push from Liesl, his grotesque seductress and the protégé of Eisengrim, Dunstan succeeds in reconciling the various interior conditions of life into a whole and amenable personality. The story of *Fifth Business* is the story of this process told from the ironic perspective of being virtually completed.

With theatrical audacity and a double vision that admits two sides to all things, Davies draws us into the depths of the human personality. He explores good and evil; appearance and illusion, illusion and reality; the dark shadows and genteel surfaces of personal behaviour and of social alliances. He explores the anomalies of secular sainthood, of the psyche as soul, of magic as truth. For all the presence of saints and devils, there is little theology in the book but a lot of psychology. In search of himself, Dunstan spends his life pursuing saints and overtakes his quarry only after sleeping with the devil. He displays a fascination for myth and for magic, in defiance of an apparently dessicated personality– actually, in search of balance within. Davies has made him memorable, not only as fifth business in the drama of other lives but as a principal actor in his own.

Fifth Business works on many levels at once, setting them one against the other, while still managing to entertain on a purely narrative level. Its language is nothing short of elegant, entirely appropriate for the voice of Dunstan Ramsay. Davies's theatricality, harnessed to a vision deep into the heart and source of things where magic and mystery hold sway, becomes profound drama, moving us towards wonder rather than enlightenment, towards passion, enthusiasm, eccentricity, and away from ordinary conceptions of reality. Coincidence, improbability, and contrivance abound, but the logic of symbolism and synchronicity rules supreme. At some level or another, all things are plausible.

World of Wonders. Toronto: Macmillan, 1975. New York: Penguin, 1977. Pages: 315. Paperback.

Sandwiched between this novel and *Fifth Business* is *The Manticore*, a clever illustrated lecture on Jungian analysis, suggesting the cure comes when the client understands the theory. Fortunately, *World of Wonders* is more sophisticated. It presents Magnus Eisengrim's side of things. It is an engrossing tale, though not as compelling or resonant as Dunstan's account of himself in *Fifth Business*.

Magnus relates his story in preparation for a film role: he is to play the great illusionist, Robert-Houdin. He, Ramsay, and Liesl live together at her estate, Sorgenfrei, in Switzerland. Magnus explains how he came to be there while Ramsay writes it all down, in academic penance for the fanciful history he gave Eisengrim in *Fifth Business*. In the final section, Ramsay completes the account, telling again of Boy Staunton and of the fateful stone that brought about Eisengrim's premature birth as Paul Dempster.

Paul's progress occurs in stages, and at each stage he participates in an illusion. As a boy, he is raped and abducted by Willard the Wizard, and he joins Willard's travelling carnival: he works inside a dummy that tells fortunes. Later he becomes the stand-in for Sir John Tresize, a swashbuckling old actor past coping with exotic feats of derring-do. He moves on to Switzerland, where he repairs a badly damaged collection of mechanical toys—illusion again—and there he meets Liesl; they force each other to make love and he becomes Magnus Eisengrim. As *World of Wonders* begins, he is to be Robert-Houdin. He has already been Paul Dempster, Cass, Jules Legrand, and Mungo Fetch; and always, the animator of illusion.

In *Fifth Business*, saints have a peculiarly Protestant representation. They are aspects in a psychological, specifically Jungian narrative, not a spiritual one. *World of Wonders* thrives on a similar anomaly. Purporting to plead for the necessity of wonder, it in fact rather effectively displays the sordid machinery behind the things we wonder at. Davies is clearly more concerned with the procedures of creation than he is with cause or effect. He describes events preceding Magnus's metamorphosis into the greatest illusionist in the world, but he shows us nothing of his talent, none of his illusions. In *World of Wonders*, Davies has created a portrait of the artist from a Jungian perspective. He shows not the sources of personality but the variety of its parts. When these parts come together, what Jung calls "individuation" is achieved. After the mutual rape with Liesl at Sorgenfrei, Magnus the artist has been reborn whole, a mature person. How he actually comes to be great is unimportant.

The violent structural shift in the book, when the narrative centre moves abruptly from Magnus to Dunstan, is from a psychological vantage quite justified. The portrait must ultimately be put into context. Magnus the artist, who in his story has re-created himself, is ultimately a creation of Ramsay, the recording consciousness, who must restore him to the larger world.

The Rebel Angels. Toronto: Macmillan, 1981. Pages: 326. Markham: Penguin, 1982. Paperback.

This novel draws to a close around such a sordid little episode that all its brilliance, ultimately, is locked inside, like treasure in a brocade purse tied with a broken shoelace. For the most part, *The Rebel Angels* is superb entertainment. It sadly falters in the final pages, probably because Davies attempts the transformation of his rich discursive narrative into something it was never meant to be–a closed form. Quite arbitrarily and with a grotesque flourish he tries to shape all the loose ends and esoteric strains of his fiction into a single coherent whole. It is somewhat akin to making a sow's ear out of a silk purse–neat feat, but why bother?

The essential problem of *The Rebel Angels* derives more from its success than from the author's failure to sustain its form. Were it not so brilliant an accomplishment, its squalid collapse would matter little, except to pedants and critics. Until Davies decides to force his meandering intellectual discourse through the tiny sphincter of an episode involving a most peculiar form of buggery, preceded by acts of humiliation and followed by murder, his fiction is exhilarating to read and contemplate. While insisting on the primacy of otherworldly and super-rational experience, he writes as an intellectual with an eclectic taste for a wide variety of knowledge. His delight is in sharing anecdotes from intellectual history, dropping names and off-beat concepts amid the *bons mots* of a born aphorist.

His characters all speak like Robertson Davies in his erstwhile role as Master of Massey College. The twenty-three-year-old half-Gypsy graduate student, Maria Magdalena Theotoky (there is only one student at this university), Professor Ozias Froats, former football star and award-winning examiner of excrement, the paleopsychologist Hollier, the vicious Urquhart McVarish, the gentle

Father Simon Darcourt, the Gypsies of Rosedale, the sceptic demon, Brother John Parlabane, the financial wizard, young Arthur Cornish–no matter what the name, age, gender, educational background, or vocation, they all speak like Robertson Davies expounding over a glass of sherry in the Senior Common Room. This is great fun–and a long way from modernist realism, which demands narrative continuity followed by closure.

Davies loves to expound. His characters in this novel speak for themselves through one of his two narrators, Maria Theotoky and Father Darcourt. Narrators and the characters narrated, however, draw from a central pool of knowledge filled to overflowing by the splendidly undisciplined and self-indulgent mind of their common author. They all seem to know names from the biblical Apocrypha and from medieval theology; they all seem familiar with Tarot and Cabala and alchemy. Each can quote verbatim from a variety of texts, from ancient Greek to modern Canadian. They all share their author's rapture over the writings of Rabelais and Paracelsus. They all know the meaning of such words as "incunabula" and "vagarious"; and all speak knowledgeably, though not always accurately, one might suppose, about angels, devils, saints, and a variety of lesser sorts. Davies loves to share what he knows. His novel at its best is shaped to accommodate his gleanings about penis-bones of the raccoon and how virgins may carry water in a sieve, and he muses briefly on such topics as the uses of filth, the nature of evil, the foibles of his fellow mortals, and the impact on their lives of supra-mortal patterns of behaviour. The university as a repository of trivia and the arcane provides him an amenable context; plot gives him the occasion to speak; characters allow him an apparent variety of perspectives. And his readings of, or perhaps about, Paracelsus, the late-medieval/ early Renaissance renegade scientist, and Rabelais, the post-medieval monk who wrote scurrilous satire, give him motivational coherence.

While the plot of this novel is intricate, the story is simple. Maria works as Hollier's graduate assistant. Parlabane, a reprobate philosopher, comes between them. Darcourt is the friend of them all, Urquhart the enemy. Parlabane is a devil of a nuisance, a demon incarnate and relatively harmless, for the most part. Cornish is the nephew of the late Francis Cornish (for more about whom, read the enthralling *What's Bred in the Bone*), whose estate is a mess to be sorted out by Hollier, Darcourt, and Urquhart. Darcourt, the middle-aged Anglican priest, loves Maria. Maria loves Hollier. Cornish and Maria (eventually) love one another. Parlabane writes a novel. Many of the principals and a few extraneous types gather in the Senior Common Room and discuss things. Urquhart steals a rare manuscript. Froats, on the periphery, ponders the significance of excrement. Maria's Gypsy mother mixes potions and fixes fiddles. In the rarefied university atmosphere, as conceived by Davies, these habitués of what we are told Paracelsus called "The Second Paradise of Learning" (the first being Eden) interact with sound and a fury signifying very little–were it not for the labels and demi-myths and arcane roles the author drapes upon them with the abandon of an excruciatingly well-read dilettante.

The differences between this world and the university setting of the Salterton novels (based on Queen's) are significant. In the earlier works, mockery, word-play, and wit are paramount. The Salterton novels are mannered entertainments. The community and the university hang together in a kind of elitist symbiosis: there are only token students, token representatives of the working class, and no one but no one plays hockey or passes wind. The university is a pretty place and life in a university town is provincial. Davies has good fun there, with us, in his pleasing guise of narrator as pompous ass. The university world of Toronto, a generation later (in the author's life, the university's, and the world's), is utterly transformed. It is almost entirely dissociated from the community at large. It is a haven for brilliant eccentrics, a warren of magnificent esotericism and obsessive scholarship, a refuge from technology, modernity, and crass material concerns. There are still no students (except for the all-beloved Maria Theotoky) and the closest we come to the working class is a porter at the college gate. But there are depths everywhere. Beneath the Salterton-like surface, Davies has discovered, uncovered, invented such a load of quasi-mystical paraphernalia, his novel seems alternately to stumble beneath the weight and soar with haunted eloquence. Darcourt and Hollier, for instance, and possibly Parlabane (the poor devil), are taken by Maria to be Rebel Angels, after those thrown out of Heaven for betraying its secrets to Solomon. Maria is accepted by Simon Darcourt as Sophia, whom the Gnostics saw as "the feminine personification of God's wisdom."

And Mamusia, her mother, is a *phuri dai* (and all the characters seem to know without explanation what that is!). *Etcetera.*

The depths in a Davies novel are not necessarily deep. He thrives on discourse about what lies beneath the surface of things and his university setting in this novel gives him the opportunity to range about with abandon among various spheres of knowledge. But he is not a learned man, though he is quite wise, and very opinionated. He does not really explore depths – he comments on them. And always in the same voice. Who else but Robertson Davies could put in the mouths of Canadian characters such a phrase as "tipped the wink," and expressions about rum-types and "grass" on you? Who else could have a twenty-three-year-old virgin describe herself being "tumbled" on the sofa? The voice, the point of view, the opinions, are always Davies. In the end such lack of discipline betrays him, and a fine sequence of set-pieces, brief essays, and exotic trivia collapses under its own weight.

What's Bred in the Bone. Toronto: Macmillan, 1985. Markham: Penguin, 1986. Pages: 525. Paperback.

There is no question where the voice is coming from in this novel. Davies is the oldest living Victorian novelist in the world, if voice is the measure, and in *What's Bred in the Bone* the voice is indisputably his own. This is one of the great charms of the novel, although ultimately charm alone is not sustaining and it is one of the novel's principal weaknesses as well.

The voice of *What's Bred in the Bone* (notice I say "of" rather than "in," for I am talking not of the voice speaking within the novel but of the voice of the novel, speaking) is its most striking characteristic and utterly inseparable from the off-beat and exotic predilections of the narrative itself. The novel speaks to us in aphorisms, or at least aphoristically, and in esoteric homilies, pronouncing on everything from the nature of women according to pseudo-psychological classification, to innate characteristics of the Aristocracy, to exact methods of forging old paintings. Davies may not always know what he is talking about, but he always sounds as if he does. And nothing, it seems, is beyond his reach: theories of art, of culture, of religion, of deportment; conceptions of morality, reality, and the mythological; all fall obliquely across the page, in discussion, debate, or soliloquy. His characters quote literary and philosophical texts to one another and instantly recognize quotations made to them by others. He uses the word "chthonic" twice in two pages. At his most outrageously pompous, he is often at his best: from an Olympian perspective (patrician, Protestant, highly educated, neo-British, elderly, completely self-assured), he weaves a world of words in which no one, especially those of his own kind, is left unscathed. He is part the eighteenth-century wit and man of letters, part an elitist Victorian social reformer, and part the postmodern anarchist and pedant. But his voice, his novel's voice, is Victorian. Diction is rich, expansive, and dated. Its reach is marvellously broad and inclusive. It animates a world entirely of his own making and utterly fascinating.

One must be careful not to take a Davies plot too seriously. What it conveys may be serious, indeed, but the plot itself, especially in this novel, has so much in common with those fat American novels sold in special display cases to coincide with TV mini-series of the same name that a high-serious response would be quite misplaced. In *What's Bred in the Bone*, knighthoods are dispersed as a matter of narrative convenience, and one is likewise withdrawn; a bad liaison breeds a bastard idiot; people with titles start up a cosmetics empire; people are the greatest or the worst or the best (Tancred Saraceni is the greatest picture-restorer and faker, just as Magnus Eisengrim in *World of Wonders* is the greatest magician in the world); a lumber baron starts up a financial empire because he wants to; an art critic is offered the directorship of The National Gallery because he wants it; Frances Cornish, the protagonist (rescued from death in *The Rebel Angels* where his function is to be a benefactor), is a renowned art expert, an undistinguished spy, a Cambridge graduate, a cuckold, ponderously wealthy and bleatingly cheap, both Protestant and Catholic, a brilliant forger of fine art, a bit of a misanthrope, and a great benefactor of his culturally beleaguered Canadian homeland. If that isn't enough – and here we leave *Princess Daisy* and its ilk far behind – his story is mostly related through a personal daimon, Maimas, and an Angel of Biography called The Lesser Zadkiel, both of whom in the end concede to being merely metaphor. And there is also, for balance, a mortal biographer who understands little of the man at the novel's centre.

What's Bred in the Bone is romance, of course, not realism. It is a curious hybrid of contrived romance and personal commentary: whether plot and characters provide a vehicle for Davies's splenetic and often amusing pronouncements or the other way around, wherein wit and bombast animate the narrative, it is difficult to say. The public story of Francis Cornish is quite unexceptional, as indicated by his death notice in the opening pages. The episodes of his life in themselves, however, hold a dramatic fascination quite out of proportion to his rather meagre personality.

The reader never participates in the action. We are told of it. Characters are introduced with brief descriptive sketches; likewise, key locations. Cornish's early life at Blairlogie in the Ottawa Valley is preceded by sweeping biographical summaries of his forebears' lives. His childhood is likewise delivered to us episodically, as in fact is the whole of his life, but all is described in such a way that the voice dominates, and nearly smothers, the vision. Even when Cornish as a boy develops his talent by sketching corpses, we are kept at an emotional distance. We are not ever allowed to feel or to share his feelings: when Cornish's father dies, although his early story had a major function in the narrative, his death is mentioned parenthetically, literally within parentheses, in passing. We eventually learn much of how Cornish goes about restoring/faking art and duping Hitler and helping in his modest way to win The War, but we are never involved. Eventually, we witness his death as dispassionately as he does himself.

It is not Francis Cornish but Robertson Davies, his mentor and maker, who elevates this novel to the level of a near-classic. Just as *Fifth Business* is the expression of Dunstan Ramsay's whole life, so this novel is the expression of the whole of Robertson Davies, animated by his personality, informed by his wit and world view, shaped by his obsessions. As might be expected, Davies plays here with concepts of duality, with the relationships between illusion and reality, good and the devil, reason and passion, psycho-theology and a variety of uncreditable cosmologies, and much else besides. This novel is the culmination of a great writer's life. If there is more to come, we are blessed, or if not, then this novel works well in bringing closure to a fine canon and laudable career. What's bred in the bone, indeed.

FRANK PARKER DAY

Rockbound. Garden City: Doubleday, 1928. Toronto:
University of Toronto Press; Reprint Library, 1973.
Pages: 292.

Let us admit from the start there are unconscionable awkwardnesses about this novel that might put off less adventurous souls
than those of us looking for enlightenment in small, unlikely
places. *Rockbound* is a far from perfect work of art; it is not even
a particularly good exemplar of its type. It is naïve, almost primitive, in its apparent indifference to literary convention. It is
regional to the point of insularity, as if culture, society, and commerce were irrelevant beyond the narrow confines of these few
lives described with such passionate conviction. This is a Maritimes equivalent to the fiction of Erskine Caldwell, which is set
in a pocket of the American South quite discontinuous with the
larger world. Here we have a small enclave of fishermen, so isolated on islands off the southern coast of Nova Scotia that they
seem, within the narrative and from our perspective outside, to
be entirely removed from the real world. Yet – and herein lies the
value of the novel, its power and charm – *Rockbound* is a fiction
surging with experience so palpably rendered the reader can feel
the ocean air and taste the bitterness of these harsh and haunted
lives. Like Caldwell, Frank Parker Day has portioned off a brutish remnant of the world and made it a world on its own.

The irony of it all is that Day was an intellectual and apparently somewhat of an aesthete. According to the excellent introduction by Alan Bevan in the University of Toronto Press reprint,
Day paid only one rather brief visit to Ironbound, the island prototype for Rockbound, and was otherwise familiar with the sea, it
seems, mainly as a sports fisherman and from a safe and distant
vantage among the groves of academe. His written work includes
an autobiography and a collection of scholarly addresses, as well
as two other novels. (One of these, *John Paul's Rock*, has mis-
takenly been accounted a novel of the sea by bibliographers and
critics who have written of it without reading – it is about a Micmac
Indian and set well inland.) His life work kept him on campuses
in Canada, Britain, and the United States. Yet this novel fairly
throbs with a sense of the sea, the salt sea air and the gutted fish,

the battered boats and the flotsam shanties, the rotting kelp, the bone-numbing flesh-wracking life among inshore fishermen. It is not a novel of their families but of their work. It does not document their ways but conveys their experience. It is a novel so authentic in its impact the reader marvels that words can bridge the gulf between their reality and ours in such a visceral fashion. It may not be Day's own world he articulates for us, but it is one he has observed carefully and renders with a superb command of idiomatic language.

Language is the source of greatest pleasure in reading *Rockbound*. There is the language of fishing, ships, and the sea; and there is the dialect of the people. The first is complex, intricate, exact. The second, while exactly rendered, is awkward and haphazard – the voice of an inarticulate, isolated people, constrained by ignorance and superstition. There is precision in language of the sea that Day clearly loves: and to his credit he has such command of it that even the most esoteric terminology springs alive in context and conveys meaning to us. And in the mouths of his characters the coarse and tortured syntax seems entirely appropriate. Their dialect is thick, and far from trying to smooth it out for the reader Day delights in capturing every elision and reversal apparently in the name of authenticity. In fact, the two languages merge throughout the narrative, for it is their life shaped by the sea that has made these people speak and be as they are, and the sea is the one world they talk about in knowing detail.

The plot of *Rockbound* is simple, linear, and a bit fragmented. We follow the life of David Jung from age eighteen, when he lands on the island, to a point roughly ten years later when, despite hardships, loneliness, and tragic loss, all works out for the best. David is something of a picaresque hero. He is the poor cousin, a foundling, disliked by his kin for the quality of his character. Through hard work he becomes the best among them, the highline fisherman, year after year; he attains relative prosperity and becomes owner of his own island.

Rockbound itself is ruled by two clans who share a common ancestry. The overlord of the Jungs is Uriah, and of the Krauses, old Anapest, midwife to all the island for over forty years. David occupies a nether point between the family factions, and it is his isolated life there, as he struggles towards self-fulfilment to complement the self-reliance forced upon him by circumstance, that gives the novel its backbone. Still, Day does not develop his novel episodically. While the author does detail David's friendship with the giant Gershom, his comfortable marriage to Tamar Jung and subsequent loss, his survival of a shipwreck, and his love for Mary Dauphiny, all such episodes are secondary to the atmosphere that, it seems, is his novel's chief purpose to convey. This is a tale of the sea, of fishing, and of human life stripped to its basic elements by the struggle to prevail in a brutal world. And while there is little room for an appreciation of beauty and virtue in such a world, Day shows them, nonetheless, to be there.

MAZO DE LA ROCHE

Jalna. Toronto: Macmillan, 1927. Toronto: Pan, 1971.
Pages: 268. Paperback.

Jalna is one of the most widely read Canadian novels, and Mazo de la Roche is probably the most critically abused and misunderstood of Canada's writers. *Jalna* is romance. It does not pretend to be anything else. Its intent is clearly proclaimed in the first chapter, told as it is from nine-year-old Wakefield's ingenuous perspective. This perspective provides an ideal entry into the romantic world de la Roche creates and perpetuates through another fifteen books. Some are admittedly pulpy, while others, such as *The Master of Jalna, Mary Wakefield,* and *Whiteoaks of Jalna*, invite rereading with the same engaging insistence as the first. In all, romance is the governing principle. The characters loom large. Society is simplified; social relevance is negligible; manners and customs are of great importance; nature, human and otherwise, predominates.

To measure *Jalna* in terms of realism or relevance is to miss the novel's moving power and lasting charm. *Jalna*'s characters are memorable not for struggle or achievement or meaning in their lives, but for themselves. In the Whiteoak family, de la Roche has devised a wonderfully intricate genealogy. Through the hundred years and more of the saga, every family member holds the centre stage for a while, and thereafter refuses to fade from memory. Each is thoroughly individual, yet it is the family, ultimately, that is de la Roche's greatest creation. The novels together form an unparallelled family chronicle.

In *Jalna* itself, the family overwhelms any single character. Yet several individuals come vividly to life: old Adeline, an imperious centenarian, the matriarch surrounded by her kin, proud and unforgiving; Renny, dashing, stern, and responsible, master of the Jalna estate; Eden, the poet; Alayne, Eden's wife, who falls in love with Renny, as he with her; stolid Piers; Meg and Finch and young Wakefield. The family is its members, and each is graphically portrayed. Convenient idiosyncrasies are well articulated, as befits the genre. The family is also a place, Jalna. The reader comes to know the house intimately, from newel post to farmland setting (near Lake Ontario, just west of Toronto) to basement kitchen. Like everything else in the novel, place is a little larger, a little more vivid, a little more intriguing, than life. Against this background, inseparable from it, de la Roche offers compelling situations, shifting alliances, and complicated affairs of the heart with affectionate sincerity.

Jalna is not de la Roche's first novel. Both *Delight* and *Possession* are worth looking at. *Delight* perhaps forces romance into breathless contrivance; but *Possession*, with its brooding sensuality and close relationship between characters and the land, reads very well. It does not affect the reader's heart as easily as *Jalna*, perhaps because it tries too hard to have significance. *Jalna*, having none, delights.

JAMES DE MILLE

The Lady of the Ice. New York: Appleton, 1870. Toronto: University of Toronto Press; Reprint Library, 1973.
Pages: 146.

One of the delights of an academic symposium is the shared delight by a colleague of something genuinely original to which we have access that we had previously overlooked. This is exactly what happened at "Future Indicative: A Symposium on Literary Theory and Canadian Literature," which I organized at the University of Ottawa, in the spring of 1986. Among the papers delivered, and since gathered as a book, was one by Richard Cavell in which he reintroduced us to the genius of James De Mille. Many were familiar with De Mille's fine speculative novel that was published posthumously as *A Strange Manuscript Found in a Copper Cylinder* (see below). As most of us at the symposium were of a postmodern bent, De Mille's achievement seemed largely due to this work's intellectual dexterity and its historical situation in an esoteric tradition. But Cavell reminded us of *The Dodge Club* (1869) and its pyrotechnical brilliance. On looking back at it, I realized just how exuberant and eccentric this travelogue-cum-novel really is. Compared to, for instance, *A Social Departure: How Orthodicia and I Went Round the World by Ourselves* (1890) by Sara Jeannette Duncan, or Mark Twain's earlier account, *Innocents Abroad*, published in the same year as De Mille's book, the latter is the very soul of wit – not for story but for textual innovation. De Mille's playfulness with language and typography, his compendious lists and outrageous authorial asides, mark his work as unusual, to say the least. While the narrative might drag a bit for the contemporary reader, to see the author freely at play in his art is well worth the price.

I have no such reservations with the work immediately following in De Mille's canon. *The Lady of the Ice* moves at a dizzying pace. What do you do, however, with a novel that defies literary conventions with such enthusiastic abandon as this, and yet relates a story so ordinary at times that conventions are stretched to cliché. *The Lady of the Ice* is great fun, but it would seem appropriate to celebrate its eccentricities judiciously, for I would be negligent to allow the misconception that this novel is of substantial literary worth. The tangled web of narrative intrigue and romance is unexceptional: young English soldiers, officers in Her Majesty's 129th Bobtails posted to Quebec early in Victoria's reign, pursue a variety of liaisons among the Canadian ladies. Their adventures are comic and mannered, and all works out well in the end. But how De Mille relates their tale, that is another story – quite literally another story. At the textual level, his novel is an hilarious compendium of recklessness, inventiveness, and daring quite marvellous to experience.

The voice of Alexander Macrorie, who relates the narrative, is surprisingly individuated and conversational. As the leading man in his own account, Macrorie jokes with the reader, teasing, lampooning, at times drawing belly laughs and at others exercising a fine and cutting wit. His description of Jack Randolph as "an intimate friend of mine, and of everybody else who had the pleasure of his acquaintance," is a classic of affectionate bitchiness. But the author within his text, and not his narrator, is the most striking feature of the novel–not as voice or point of view but quite literally as a textual presence. If this sounds postmodern, it should be remembered that Sterne's *Tristram Shandy* offers a brilliant precedent from the century before. And yet in some respects both Sterne and De Mille can be considered postmodern, for it is only now that their radical innovations are appreciated as more than aberrations, the shenanigans of irrepressible authorial enthusiasm.

The reader is used to chapter headings, for instance, providing continuity in eighteenth- and nineteenth-century fiction, especially nineteenth-century romance. Often quite lengthy, they serve as prologue and program for what is to come–a tantalizing link between stages of narrative development. But here De Mille parodies such conventions: his headings in this novel are offered as both précis and puzzle, for they are remarkably detailed and yet make little sense in themselves–except for the heading to the final chapter which, the narrator decides, can stand in place of the chapter itself, and therefore he follows it only with a note of congratulations to the reader for having persisted to the novel's conclusion. Often, in fact, while set typographically on their own, the headings are wholly inseparable from the text, the heading of one chapter being formulated from the closing remarks of the one preceding it, paradoxically confounding their function as a textual link by their presence as narrative interruption. Thus, they break the narrative apart rather than hold it together, forcing the reader to confront the fictionality of the fiction.

Other such antics abound. De Mille has Macrorie offer us his calling card in the opening pages; and later quite absurdly lists the accoutrements of his bachelor quarters, numbering them one to twelve, the sofa being number three and sugar, number seven. Later he lists the esoteric topics of his various conversations with O'Halloran, the charming Fenian anarchist (or visionary, depending on one's perspective) and father of his beloved (or her husband, depending on one's progress through the narrative). And he ultimately catalogues the reasons for the rapid swing in his beloved's

affections from Jack to himself, reasons which include (I) The muta-
bility of humanity, and (VI) The uniform of the Bobtails (neglecting
to note that his rival wears the same costume!). Furthermore, he
proclaims that this untoward shift, such that a novelist would
never countenance, he must, perforce, relate as his own true
account and therefore we should be happy with it.

   Ah, there is so much good fun in this brief novel–its obscurity
is a wonder and a shame. Apart from formal and textual innovation, it is a fine parody of literary romance, especially the Canadian version, with Quebec as an exotic context. It is a clever and
sometimes hilarious satire on a society adrift from its origins and
not yet anchored in its new place in the world. It is a burlesque of
the manners and pretensions of class and type and race familiar
to readers of nineteenth-century romance. *The Lady of the Ice* is a
delightful pastiche, and yet the novel is coherent. Macrorie finally
does win his lady of the ice; his friend Randolph does receive come-
uppance for his coquetry (for he is a male coquette, rather than a
satyr) and is happily wed. All, as it must, works out in the end.

A Strange Manuscript Found in a Copper Cylinder.
(Anonymous). New York: Harper, 1888. Toronto:
McClelland and Stewart; New Canadian Library, 1969.
Pages: 255. Paperback. Scholarly Edition: Centre for
Editing Early Canadian Texts. Ottawa: Carleton
University Press, 1985. Ed. M.G. Parks. Paperback.

Rare in Canadian literature, this novel is a superior example of a
type that was rather common and quite popular in the latter part
of the last century. De Mille himself was somewhat of a Jekyll
and Hyde, an academic at Acadia and Dalhousie universities but
also an author of popular fiction. *Strange Manuscript*, published
posthumously, seems to fuse his two sides, for it is both a fantastical adventure yarn and a seriously conceived satire, each aspect
admirably serving the other's purpose. It invites comparative scrutiny with Plato's *Republic* and Haggard's *She*, with Darwin,
Fraser, and the *Boy's Own Annual*. Not that De Mille's work is
esoteric: rather, it is exuberantly inclusive. Today it reads as a
marvellous document of the Victorian mind and as a thoroughly
engaging work of speculative fiction.

In the adventure narrative, Adam More tells of being lost at sea, of how he found his way to the incredible land of the Kosekin in the south polar region, and of what happened to him there. The Kosekin, surrounded by prehistoric animals, are in a stage of social development apparently more primitive than More's own. More lives among them and, in his manuscript, records their remarkable ways. Among the Kosekin, darkness is admired above light, poverty above wealth, weakness above power. Their world is a grotesque distortion of our own. According to their own dictates, the Kosekin are civilized.

Adam More is called Atamor by his captors/hosts. But his English names are aggressively allusive, suggesting he represents, or is a parody of, both the first man and renaissance man. His adventures and romance among the Kosekin eventually lead him to assume wealth and power on their behalf as a prelude to either the Fall or their reformation. And that is the end of his story – or, rather, the end of the interest of the men within the novel who are reading More's story. De Mille has devised a curious foursome and placed them between us and More in a becalmed boat; their function is to read the manuscript they retrieved from the sea and to discuss it. They occupy what can loosely be called the frame story, although their presence is apparent throughout the entire novel and functions reciprocally with More's.

De Mille's four men in a boat do more than analyse and interpret. In providing scientific and cultural veracity to More's tale, science and society are themselves satirized. Through them, De Mille distances us from the more fantastical elements of More's story. Thus the bizarre is made more acceptable, and the seemingly ordinary is made to seem bizarre. The scholar, the doctor, the man of letters, and the effete aristocrat become as much the butt of De Mille's satire as are the values of their world, which the Kosekin so dreadfully distort.

Precisely what is being satirized is marvellously ambiguous. Much thought is aroused, but De Mille does not feel called upon to provide a systematic resolution. The novel can be taken as a satire on Christianity, British society, the aristocracy, the new age of science, Darwinism, or all of these – or something else entirely.

De Mille's contemporaries were fascinated with the imaginative possibilities thrust upon them by the new age of science.

A novel that combined social vision with social satire and the fantastical with an apparently serious debate could not help but provoke and appeal. Whether, as critics argue, it is utopian, anti-utopian, or some other type of speculative form entirely, it remains a well-crafted and exceedingly readable work, a trove of allusions and an inviting enigma.

LILY DOUGALL

What Necessity Knows. New York: Longmans, Green, 1893. Pages: 445.

Take time to read this remarkable novel. After you search it out from an obscure corner of the library, you will need leisure to peruse its three books uninterrupted. It is a complex and demanding novel, filled with intricate gyrations of plot, fulsome descriptions of society and wilderness in the Eastern Townships of 1873, more than a little sophisticated theology of the day, the determined polemics of a social revolutionary, a great deal of fun and wit, and numerous righteous homilies. It is not a novel to be hurried through or distracted from; it is a work of singular intensity and intelligence. If Dougall takes her role as the readers' instructor in life a little too seriously, she also shares with her readers the warmth and wisdom of her personality. Occasionally her descriptions seem turgid, particularly those of the natural world, but she was writing in response to the tastes of another era. Sometimes the contemporary reader might prefer judgement of motivation and behaviour to be left more open. But Dougall wrote when such things were attributed not to the ambiguities of unconsciousness but to the moral conditions of mind and soul. In all, no livelier and more accomplished account of Canadian pioneer society was ever written, or one of such literary and intellectual excellence.

Dougall wrote at least fifteen books, nine of which were novels. The other six were anonymously published theological inquiries—she was far too imaginative and clever to have written mere religious tracts—and she contributed inspirational expositions to half a dozen other books and to various periodicals. Her first novel,

Beggars All, was published in 1891. It was appraised by critics as a work of serious literary merit, displaying great scope of subject matter and depth of treatment. *What Necessity Knows* came next, in 1893; in this book, her concern for the reconciliation of Christianity and the social realities of the modern world became abundantly apparent. By 1908, she seems to have put aside fiction as a mode of inquiry and turned to more direct methods of theological consideration. *What Necessity Knows* remains her most inspired work. It is a happy blend of provocation, inspiration, and entertainment.

In a brief preface, Dougall disparages realism as "degrading ... by ... superficial truth." But it is as a realistic writer that she excels. Admittedly, there is a strong measure of conventional romance in her novel, and there are occasional but striking elements of the gothic. The incisive descriptions of manners and affectations are in the best romantic mode. But her clear-headed rendering of society itself is realistic; her sardonic analysis of the social machinery in provincial Anglo-Quebec retains an aura of arresting authenticity even today.

The plot of *What Necessity Knows* is exceedingly intricate. It opens with Sissy, a rebellious girl of seventeen who refuses the well-meant advances of Bates, her late father's partner, and escapes their wilderness clearing in her father's coffin, having buried him herself on his own land. Sissy makes her way to a train, where she joins the Rexfords, a family of breeding from England who have fallen on hard times. Disguised as Eliza White, Sissy does well for herself in the village of Chellaston, where the Rexfords settle. Eventually she returns to the clearing to marry Bates and to reform him – and there is no doubt she will succeed.

Earlier Sissy was seen rising from her father's casket by Alec Trenholme, and a rumour is spread that her father rose from the dead. The rumour is encouraged by one Cyril Harkness, an upstart young American dentist in Chellaston who suspects Eliza's real identity and wants to blackmail her into marriage. Meanwhile, Alec Trenholme arrives in town and threatens to reveal his true vocation as a butcher and thereby ruin his brother, a clergyman and the principal of a promising new private school. By hiding his humble origins, Robert (the brother) has managed to be accepted by polite society. And Alec's revelations might destroy Robert's chances with Sophia Rexford, whom Robert has loved for nearly a decade. In the end, it is young Alec to whom Sophia gives herself; Robert learns Christian humility and forbearance.

In the midst of all this, a possibly resurrected and surely demented old man is mistaken for Eliza's father. The old man leads a group of adventist zealots to a mountain top, there to be taken by God. But the prophet is murdered by a jealous husband. There is much more: intrigue, assignations, romance, arguments, good times, and laughter. Holding the various plots and subplots together are the strong personalities of two women, Sissy/Eliza and Sophia, both of whom resolutely buck convention. Eliza is desperately ambitious; she wants to break through the barriers of a rigid class society, but eventually settles – at least temporarily – for an unlikely marriage. Sophia refuses to be bound by social strictures and happily marries beneath her station. Both women embody strong elements of social and feminist revolution; both challenge what Dougall clearly feels is a repressive inheritance from Britain, dangerously inappropriate to the ideal Canadian world she envisions. (And she as surely rejects the vulgar and acquisitive American alternative.)

Dougall has written a fine novel. She is an excellent if somewhat prolix prose stylist, a writer of fire and compassion, of great intelligence and imagination. She is filled with affection and concern for her subject matter; she is a reformer and entertainer, a thinking Christian, a feminist, a radical, a Canadian nationalist, an artist of the first rank. She should be read.

SARA JEANNETTE DUNCAN (SARA JEANNETTE COTES; MRS. EVERARD COTES)

The Imperialist. Toronto: Copp Clark, 1904. Toronto: McClelland and Stewart; New Canadian Library, 1971. Pages: 269. Paperback.

In *The Imperialist*, Sara Duncan has limned a clear vision of where we come from, historically and culturally. Duncan's strength is social realism. She steers her fiction between poles of sophisticated political analysis and conventionally sentimental romance towards a coherent definition of society, of which the town of Elgin just before the turn of the century occupies the centre.

The plot of *The Imperialist* moves upon the configurations of courtship, while themes crystallize in the expressions of love. The principal liaison is between Advena Murchison and the Reverend Hugh Finlay, both martyrs of forbearance, who prove the quality of their love by refusing to give in to it. Finlay was betrothed, in a loveless match, before he left Scotland, and he and Advena both take exquisite pains to honour his commitment. Not until the senior clergyman, Dr. Drummond, steals Hugh's fiancée away from him, are Finlay and Advena free to wed. The other liaison is purposefully insipid and inept by comparison: Lorne Murchison, Advena's brother, loves Dora Milburn with more passion than sense, and loses her to a thoroughly shallow Englishman, Hesketh, who is Lorne's friend. Advena's affair embodies the novel's political ideals; Lorne's illustrates why those ideals are untenable.

Lorne is the novel's protagonist. Through him, the Canadian experience is rhetorically and dramatically dissected. He is not a representative Canadian, however, but a young idealist championing one extreme of political possibility. Lorne is dedicated to the Imperialist cause. He sees mutual moral and economic advantages in reinforcing close ties between Canada and England and fears for both countries should the Empire drift apart. Lorne fights the insidious forces of Annexation, which draw Canada's destiny ever closer to the United States and annihilation. There is no question where Duncan's sympathies lie, but she is astute and realistic. Lorne runs as a Liberal candidate in the South Fox riding on an Imperialist platform. He wins, but is then unseated by his own party. His idealism prevents him from seeing what Duncan knows so well: the community survives on ambivalence, a balance between the two extremes. That is the Canadian way.

Duncan has created an image of the times that extends from the family to the community of Elgin, to Canada, and to the Empire. She renders the town with affectionate authenticity. Elgin is more than an accumulation of people and their statistics: it is the customs, manners, memories, and dreams of a whole organism, where place and people merge—the quintessential Canadian town. The church, which Duncan describes with authority, assures a continuity of social values and structures in the community, a continuity that history has not provided. Presbyterianism in this context is not stultifying (as the cliché would have it) but life-sustaining.

Elgin is modelled on Brantford, Ontario, Duncan's childhood home. After she left, she worked as a journalist and political commentator, then married and went to India. There, she wrote *The Imperialist* as well as a number of novels very important in the Anglo-Indian tradition but hardly known and quite unavailable in Canada. Her Indian fiction includes *His Honour and a Lady, A Burnt Offering*, and the stylish *Memoirs of a Memsahib*. Duncan lived outside Canada for the rest of her life. Something of her remains, however, in her warmly convincing portrait of the world she left behind. As an example of social realism at the turn of the century, it is superb.

DOUGLAS DURKIN

The Magpie. Toronto: Hodder and Stoughton, 1923. Toronto: University of Toronto Press; Reprint Library, 1974. Pages: 330.

The Magpie is a novel of theoretical analysis, a true novel of ideas. Its purpose is to provide responsible discourse on political and economic conditions in an aesthetically palatable context. Durkin explores the implications of irreconcilably opposed social philosophies around the time of the Winnipeg General Strike of 1919, when labour and the ruling class met head-on. Despite its intellectual intentions, *The Magpie* is a passionate novel; despite its rational consideration of all sides in the argument, it is a novel of deep commitment.

Durkin's protagonist, Craig Forrester (known to his friends as "The Magpie"), returns home from the Front in France at the end of the First World War. He takes up a place in the Winnipeg Grain Exchange that was secured for him before he went overseas by his late father. Four years of war have had their effect on Craig, and while others of his class resume their place in society, he impatiently awaits the promised changes that so many men and women had suffered to bring about. But instead of reform he sees the workers sink bitterly under the exploitation of the owners; he sees speculators reap unearned rewards. He is confused, outraged, frustrated, as he struggles to understand. He is disturbed by the tyrannical Blount, determined to crush the rebellious workers at any cost. He is equally appalled by the demagoguery of Tuttle, who would reduce the leisure class to destitution, or exterminate them if he could. At painful cost to himself, Craig rages against Blount, just as his leftist friend Amer denounces the fanatical side of revolutionary labour. Both men want social justice and a new order; instead, there is a brief clash in the streets, and things continue as they were. Nothing has been resolved. Amer is deported to England; Craig Forrester retreats to the family farm. It is a curiously peaceful ending for a book so filled with outrage and the sense of an ominous future.

Durkin introduces three striking women into the story who embody the tortuous geometry of Craig's moral life. They serve as points of reference. Durkin gives them lives of their own, however, and personalities that do not always submit easily to their ideological function. The result is a pleasing tension that involves the reader emotionally as well as intellectually – an uncommon response in this type of novel, and one that Durkin admirably exploits. He purposely sets emotional and intellectual dimensions at odds with one another and attains an effect beyond the reach of rational language alone.

In his determined quest to understand, to reconcile opposing philosophies for the sake of an unnameable "ideal" that so many suffered or died for, The Magpie sometimes displays an intellectual ferocity that marks him a madman to both sides and leads to his utter rejection. Much of the novel consists of his theoretical debate with himself; the loss of rational understanding that overwhelms him at the time of the street-fighting seems appropriate, even inevitable. If beauty, love, and goodness are gone, then sanity must go as well. But as the mind is restored, those things, too, will return. On an idealistic and a romantic level, such affirmation is possible; it provides hope for a society that, rationally considered, is beyond hope.

Durkin writes clearly but with no great aesthetic gift. While he may have co-written *Wild Geese* and other novels with Martha

Ostenso, it was clearly her part to contribute the art; his contribution was the polish. In this novel, where plot and character are entirely subservient to idea, where little actually happens directly in the reader's line of vision, there is none of that dramatic flair one associates with his lover's fiction. But Durkin was far more the strident feminist than Ostenso. *The Magpie* is filled with examples of masculine condescension, but it also acclaims "the new woman" and gives her a voice. There are several speeches delivered by women in these pages that read like a feminist call to revolution–for social justice, not only for abortion on demand.

Realism intrudes in *The Magpie*, and effectively so, only in the scenes in the Grain Exchange. Durkin returns again and again to the trading floor, each time reeling off numbers and fractions in a frenzied flurry that is as mesmerizing as it is meaningless. There could be no more fitting chorus to a debate on the economic survival of Canada and the world.

GEORGE ELLIOTT

The Kissing Man. Toronto: Macmillan, 1962. Don Mills: General, 1984. Pages: 136. Paperback.

Imagine a painting by Grandma Moses in three dimensions, the third dimension given by the shape of time, and you have a sense of George Elliott's remarkable work. It is primitive, naïve, and formless; at the same time, it is sophisticated and strangely unified. One might hesitate to call it a novel, but one would assuredly not call it anything else. The separate chapters–or stories, or segments–are not linked so much as they are interpenetrating. As in a Moses painting, or a Breughel painting (for Elliott has the morose wit of the latter as well as the nostalgic innocence of the former), numerous distinct tableaux are formed on a single canvas. These relate to each other through tone and texture and design, through theme, through narrative control. Elements dominating one scene may fill a peripheral function in several of the other scenes. A river or a street or a mood might run among them, tying them together, separating them. The whole picture does not emerge gradually: it is there from the beginning. Nor do the parts somehow contribute to a larger whole: they *are* the whole. Elliott, like Grandma Moses and Pieter Breughel the Younger, has created an unworldly dream vision of the real world.

Most of the chapters deal with death, yet they are strangely life-affirming: through many runs a strain of the supernatural; in several segments, it becomes the dominant reality. In "The kissing man" and "A leaf for everything good" in particular, the unearthly aspect offers solace for sadness and isolation. Even in the chapters where the commonplace prevails, and the small western Ontario town looms into actuality, the mode is not realism or naturalism. As soon as verisimilitude begins to take hold, Elliott upsets everything by leaping ahead fifty years, or back fifty years, or by changing voice or narrative perspective. He refuses to let his fiction become merely a document.

The town in which the stories are set is small, about the size of Beeton or Minto or Hope. Its only referents are Lake Huron, a railway line, and a city some distance away–possibly London. The time period is, for the most part, early in this century. But time is not stable here; a character might be a youth and, in the same context, an old person, or unborn. The book opens with a young couple in the middle of the last century; it leaps a lifetime into the thoughts of a grandchild tending their graves. A beautiful account in the middle of the book, "A room, a light for love," makes an equally dramatic leap forward into the second half of the twentieth century. The eerily enigmatic and moving segment "What do the children mean" could be anytime, yet names tie it to the 1920s. Glimpses of lives lived fill these pages. Linear time disintegrates. Doc Fletcher dies, then is there, later, and later again. Young Honey Salkald appears as a youth, a boy, a man, a youth again. Doug Framingham, his family name given on the opening page, bursts through later in the first-person voice, retreats immediately into the passive third, ages, fades. The buildings at times seem constant; the Queen's Hotel, the train station, the barber shop. But the stability is illusion. They, too, are passing things.

The Kissing Man is written in curiously conventional prose. There is a hint of muted lyric in the style, but it uses mostly simple, direct syntax with almost no ornamentation and few literary devices. Sometimes the language is so clear it is ambiguous, like glass that reflects what is behind you, even while allowing a vision of what lies ahead. Occasionally, Elliott's prose becomes so enigmatic that its impact is lost; sometimes the shift in voice and perspective is so ingeniously extreme that we wonder if the writer is in control at all. Yet, *The Kissing Man*, on the whole, is a unique and disquieting work, one to be enjoyed and greatly admired.

MARIAN ENGEL

Bear. Toronto: McClelland and Stewart, 1976.
Toronto: Seal, 1982. Pages: 141. Toronto: McClelland and Stewart; New Canadian Library, 1983. Paperback.

This is not a great novel, in some ways not even a very good one, yet there is something entirely engrossing about Engel's story of love and explicit sexuality between a mole of a woman and a pathetic, stupid-eyed old bear. The novel deals in careless subtleties, with a bland sort of extravagance. Lou, the protagonist, is "reborn," licensed to exist, "healed of guilt," the way characters in other novels eat breakfast. Engel does not build mood or character or theme. She simply tells a rather unusual story, which manages to be spontaneous and timeless at once. It is a fitting transition work connecting her earlier writing and her superb novels, *The Glassy Sea* and *Lunatic Villas*, which follow.

The Historical Institute for which Lou works is bequeathed an island estate known as Penarth, in northern Ontario, with an octagonal house and an eccentric history. Lou arrives to take inventory. There is a bear. There is a library. Lou reads. Soon Trelawney, Beau Brummell, and Colonel Cary, who founded the island estate and brought the books with him, begin to populate her isolation. Homer Campbell, a local character versatile in the ways of the north, occasionally visits. Lou becomes close to the bear and to the dead Carys, particularly to the last of them, a woman by the name of Colonel Jocelyn Cary. Lou makes love with the bear–that is, she uses the bear to be made love to. She loves the bear. Rejected as animal, Lou returns home, perhaps to a better life.

Lou emerges fragmentally to become a whole, if somewhat hollow, person. She has always been used, always unsatisfied by her own sexuality. Through the bear she takes possession of herself. It may be questionable whether such exploitive affection as she holds for the great, indifferent beast can possibly be liberating, yet it can be seen to jar Lou out of the complacent frustration that has marked her life up until now. Through acceptance of herself in such a bizarre affair, Lou comes to accept herself as a woman.

Engel writes about the legacy of women's past and how it affects Lou in the present. The female Colonel Jocelyn is described to her by Homer as an imitation man. The male bear is described several times as an old woman. Lou both identifies with romantic male figures of the past and desires them. There is a terrible, debilitating ambivalence in being a woman today, as Engel portrays life; only entire self-acceptance can overcome such ambivalence. On another level, closer to myth, or that dreamtime area where myth and psychoanalytics merge, Lou confronts the beast within as a separate creature, makes love with it, offers herself over to it totally, and learns that she can live comfortably with the knowledge of its presence – and therefore live without it.

In some ways, *Bear* is a radical departure for Engel; in some ways it is quite consistent. In *The Honeyman Festival*, which is the best of her earlier writing, the protagonist suffers the role of drudge while entertaining memories of an extravagant affair in Europe. There are emotional echoes of this in *Bear*, along with the same perverse sense of the romantic. *Bear*, however, dares far more, abjuring the domestic altogether in favour of the exotic; focusing not on problems but on their resolutions. Language is more carelessly applied and takes on unexpected vitality. The whining tone is gone, replaced by a knowing shrug.

The Glassy Sea. Toronto: McClelland and Stewart, 1978. Toronto: Seal, 1979. Pages: 164. Paperback.

Engel grows in daring leaps with each new book. *The Glassy Sea* is a triumph of art and conviction. The cycle of squalid pessimism in her first novels (which she endeavoured to break from, through erotic perversity, in *Bear*) has here been entirely subsumed by the lyric resonance of her prose and by the defiant affirmation of her vision. Her other works end on a tentative, upbeat note; here, she sings "The Hallelujah Chorus." With this novel, Engel moves to the very front rank of Canadian writers, a solid and respectable body of work behind her, and a work of courage and beauty to her lasting credit.

The Glassy Sea enthralls with its delight in language. The narrator says that she says: " 'Oh?' Small o." There could be no better way of expressing her response – utter simplicity, with a wealth of ambiguous implications. Engel's words show wit in their striking brevity, particularly when the narrator is judging herself, which she is prone to do. Yet sometimes Engel's imagery caresses a scene until it takes on a life of its own and returns the affection. Occasionally, Engel will fuse allusions to Hopkins or Donne, Eliot or Yeats or the Scriptures, with flights of her own poetic imagination, to enrich a description with moving intensity. Never does her prose falter, although it ranges from the colloquial to the elegant.

Humour abounds: Engel is a master of the unexpected tagline, which turns the whole paragraph it ends in a new and delightfully unexpected direction. Dialogue, especially, is effective. Even in discussions of ecclesiastical matters, speech is invariably delivered directly from the character's mouth, making what might have been a dull discourse a complex expression of individual personality. Characters speak for themselves yet are entirely contained within the narrator's account of her own life. Despite the sophistication of Engel's prose, however, there is an ingenuous quality of shared innocence in her writing; it perfectly suits the relationship she allows us to have with her narrator. We cannot help but like Rita Heber/Bowen, Sister Mary Pelagia – she has a way with words.

Much of her story is in the telling. After a purposely confusing Prologue, in which all the main aspects of her account are anticipated in oblique allusions, she writes an impossibly long letter to her friend Philip, bishop of Huron, turning down his offer to assume responsibility for the Sisters of Eglantine, an Anglican Order on the verge of extinction. She herself was a sister but left the Order a decade earlier and married disastrously. At the time of writing, in the late 1970s, she lives in exile on Prince Edward Island, kept there by her former husband, an Ontario Tory politician who is now married to a flower of youth. Gradually, the pieces of the Prologue gather into a coherent – shape: even as Rita concludes her letter, declaring her loss of faith and detailing her present abusive lifestyle, we realize she will ultimately accept Philip's offer. The whole of her letter answers the question why and carries the force of a lifetime confession. At forty-two, faithless and world weary, she is absolved. In the Envoie, or epilogue, she returns to the Order. Having fled responsibility for herself all her life, she now, with passionate if secular conviction, determines to make Eglantine House a hostel for women abused by a hostile society.

Rita's story is told without arbitrary chapter breaks; it falls naturally into three phases. The first describes her childhood in a small and inbred southwestern Ontario village. Here, as throughout her account, there is an engaging mixture of warmth and wit. Inevitably, her abbreviated vision of family life is dominated by loss and disappointment, change and death, but the retrospective point of view allows compassion to keep bitterness in check. She joins the Eglantines, nine Sisters all called Mary who live in harmless ease in London, Ontario. The transition to the cloistered life is handled well, both in terms of plot and psychologically, as is Rita's change from nun to Toronto chatelaine. And so is the final metamorphosis, violent though it is, that brings her back to Eglantine House.

The closing pages of the novel resound with passionate rhetoric about the battle between men and women. It is a clarion call not to arms, but to a just peace; the rhetorical delivery is entirely justified by the nature of the woman who utters it, who rises like a phoenix before us out of the ashes of her own life. It is a powerful and yet curiously temperate statement of conviction, in all senses of the word. Its context is a fine novel. Engel's range includes the comic and the tragic, the earthy and the transcendent, the soul and sexuality. She writes of the whole woman in a society still determined to sever her into pieces, and discard those pieces when used.

Lunatic Villas. Toronto: McClelland and Stewart, 1981.
Pages: 251. Toronto: McClelland and Stewart; New
Canadian Library, 1983. Paperback.

This is a very human book. I can think of no better tribute to Engel's achievement with *Lunatic Villas* than to acknowledge it as a living presence within my own experience as a reader, one imbued with and radiating personality, vulnerability, and aspiration. It is not just that she has brought alive a centre-city cul-de-sac called Rathbone Place as if it were a vital organism. She has done that, no question, with one sprawling family at the heart and one most precious and eccentric woman at the heart of hearts, the core of this heartland of the whole nation. But more than this, what she has done is to make the novel itself a living thing, and in a way so very rare I do not know of another accomplishment quite like it in our literature.

Marian Engel died in 1984, at the height of her career as a writer. She was forty-eight years old, the age her character Harriet Ross would be if she were real. But of course she is real, the living proof of fiction's capacity to transcend the page, to endure outside of time and disarm death. Harriet is the pliant and enduring matrix for all those intersecting lives, fictional and actual, including my own, touched by the gift of Marian Engel's creative imagination.

The novel's loose-knit structure and casually haphazard point of view seem at first, like Harriet herself, undisciplined, even indulgent. Gradually, though, the narrative accumulates within the reader's memory and takes on what is virtually a spatial form. As Engel opens Harriet's life to us, time may be linear but personality and experience are not; so with the novel's structure – print demands linearity but narrative reality accumulates, expands, fills in, not according to the measured sequence of a clock but in a curious, furious, fragmented mélange of thought, feeling, memory, event, and dream that all hang together somehow in an almost tranquil, and certainly comprehensible, state of excitement.

Becoming more and more evident in recent years is what might be called a feminist form in certain works of fiction. *Lunatic Villas* offers a prime example, although similar structural characteristics are apparent, for example, in Audrey Thomas's *Blown Figures*, Margaret Atwood's *The Handmaid's Tale*, and Janette Turner Hospital's *Borderline*. In these fictions, the narrative does not develop episodically or sequentially. It is not linear as we are taught good narrative should be. It is spatial. It is visionary without, necessarily, a vision. As it expands, paradoxically, it becomes more dense. It reaches completion (rather than conclusion) when these two tendencies are brought into harmony or balance. There is only balance, never resolution.

Engel seems relatively unconcerned about conventional narrative coherence. Voice and perspective shift repeatedly away from

Harriet, although both always return to her as a sort of touch-stone when alternate realities threaten to overwhelm or obscure her presence as the focal centre. Sometimes Engel seems merely to catalogue what has already occurred in her characters' lives. We get almost facile précis of situations and personalities appar-ently beyond the normal flow of narrative events; yet these, in effect, are what make the narrative happen. The domestic trivia of ordinary lives, in the ongoing sequence of interaction that occu-pies the novel's present tense, provide a context, but the brief accounts of personal history, the passages of genuine reflection, the documentary episodes from city life, the grand colloquy of Harriet's friend Marshallene on marriage, the epithets coined on love and death, the relationships defined, the lives glimpsed but unexplored, the quips, the wisdom, the articulated hopes and fears, these make the novel live in the imagination as a whole world, inseparable from our own.

Harriet Ross lives in Rathbone Place, Toronto. So do a number of others, in other houses on the same street. Some we get to know as well as Harriet does. Of others, we don't even know their names. Harriet has a variety of children, some of them her own. Some we get to know intimately, others only at a distance. Harriet is single. She had two husbands, one of whom died. She has two sisters, one of whom dies. She writes for a living – not real writing, only for a magazine. Her alter ego, "Depressed Housewife," sustains her financially for fifteen years. She has a house guest, an ancient lady who ultimately, in a lovely parody of existential adventure, runs off with Harriet's mid-teen son to win, the two of them, a bicycle race extending across the nation, from sea to sea.

From a house on a street in Toronto, Engel's vision extends out-ward to encompass the whole of Canada, while reaching within to explore the private depths of one lonely, frightened, loving, and joyfully defiant woman. This novel does not have the eloquence of *The Glassy Sea*, but sometimes a phrase or a sentence will take the breath away, so beautifully is it turned. At other times the syntax and word choice display the genuine uncertainty of spon-taneous emotion. Similarly, it does not have the steady and con-trolled focus of Engel's earlier fiction, especially the domestic monodramas. Here the narrative reality shifts and slides, for a while as solid as brass and then as elliptical as the love for a diffi-cult child. There is less the sense of real life rendered into art in this novel and more the quality of actual experience. *Lunatic Villas* does not convey a particular reality so much as share it. From inside the narrative, we as readers see the world in an ever-expanding series of concentric and intersecting circles—as if someone has thrown a handful of pebbles in the glassiest of seas, and our perspective on the scene is from the biggest piece as it gradually submerges.

There is no purpose served to describe plot and sub-plots or to detail principal relationships. That would render Engel's achievement in terms of conventional analysis, when adjectives are more appropriate. It is a warm and moving novel, funny and at times brutal, alive with love and with fear and frustration, with rage at times but never merely with anger. It is an exuberant and yet melancholy novel; it is frenetic and yet contemplative, and as satisfying to read as it is disturbing. It provides a perfect fusion of the universal and particular in a world given us to experience as if it were our own. As, indeed, it is.

HUBERT EVANS

Mist on the River. Toronto: Copp Clark, 1954.
Toronto: McClelland and Stewart; New Canadian Library, 1973. Pages: 282. Paperback.

More than half a century passed between Hubert Evans's early fiction and his most recent. *The New Front Line*, published in 1927, is very much a work of its times—self-consciously so, perhaps. It explores a theme common to many North American novels in the wake of the First World War: a soldier's difficult return to civilian life. The prose is tight and intense, the mood serious, and the purpose didactic. *O Time in Your Flight* was published in 1979; it is the chronicle of a boy's year in Galt at the close of the last century. It is so obviously written from personal memory that giving the young protagonist another name seems little more than obedience to convention. It is a stunning and unique achievement, without being of particular literary significance. There is no story, only a marvellous accumulation of the trivia of an elderly gentleman's fecund memory. There is no narrative development, only the exquisitely slow passage of time. Evans writes from a nine-year-old's point of view, but it is the octogenarian who sets it all down: each item of daily life has become a storied artifact, seen from a perspective eighty years in the future.

Mist on the River, published in 1954, has much more in common with Evans's didactic work of the twenties than with his work of the seventies and eighties, which includes several recently published books of poetry. It is a compassionate and daring attempt to portray the reality of contemporary west coast Indian life from an Indian perspective. Since Evans's novel first appeared, numerous such accounts have been written by whites; there had also been a few before it. Earlier works almost invariably romanticized or mythologized the Indian experience, however; or, like *Tay John*, they did both. But Evans writes a determinedly realistic account. Despite certain awkwardnesses of style, it seems uncannily authentic. He shows a deep sympathy for his native protagonists (he uses the term "native" as a colloquialism for Indian), and a profound understanding of the bewildering effects, often tragic, of their running confrontation with white society. It is a novel that does not lay blame so much as it compels pity and fear for these Indian refugees from another dimension of time.

The Skeena River in British Columbia during the early 1950s provides the setting. The river runs inland from the coast for several hundred miles, past Prince Rupert, past the Junction, to a small Gitshan village in the interior. This is the limit of Cy Pitt's world. Like most of his people in the village, Cy's life blends old ways and white ways in uneasy alliance. At eighteen, he travels by train to the coast with his mother and sister to work in the canneries. But before autumn comes, they return upriver with all the others to their village to bring in the potatoes, gather berries, and cure salmon for the winter. They live in small houses, but the old people still remember the shared lodges. Around the village are totem poles, weathered but erect; one man, Old Paul, is determined to raise a new one to himself before he dies, and to have a great potlatch at which he will give away thousands of dollars in gifts, even though the traditional festivity has been outlawed by the whites.

Gitshan is still spoken in the village, although the young speak English as well. The older people see their language as the storehouse of their culture; as it passes from use, they see the old ways die. Downriver, when they hear Gitshan or Kitamaat or Haida or Tsimpshean, they feel pride. But in Rupert, or even in the Junction, they listen to their people speaking only English and they are ashamed. Evans evokes their loss beautifully. Even though the reader may be struck by the ungainly formality of their dialogue, it gradually becomes apparent that this is Evans's representation of the Gitshan voice or personality rendered into English. He has risked art for authenticity.

Cy Pitt is the central character, the structural and thematic centre of the novel. His mother, Melissa, and his uncle Matt, who have lived together since his father died, provide a reinforcing context for him in the village, but everyone else seems to represent a pull on his loyalty or conscience from a different direction. Old Paul and his granddaughter Miriam, whom Cy marries, demand obedience to the old ways, some of which Cy recognizes are bad and some essential for him to survive. On the outside, there is his cousin Dot, a prostitute, but there is also his young sister June, proud of her Indian blood, who is making it in the white world. There are the Hanleys, a white couple who come to the village and befriend Cy. They are accepted by the community, then leave. Everywhere, Cy is assaulted by the difference between white and Indian realities. Evans creates a series of situations–at the cannery, in the white hospital, at a wedding feast–where Cy's knowledge of both worlds tears him apart. His ambivalence embodies Evans's own. Evans does not naïvely assume all things white are evil, nor that all things Indian are noble and pure. He acknowledges that the white disease, TB, is fifteen times more deadly to Indians, but he also sets white medicine against Indian superstition, which he abhors. He provides no simple solutions where there are none, but offers moving insight into the problem.

TIMOTHY FINDLEY

The Wars. Toronto: Clarke, Irwin, 1977. Markham: Penguin, 1978. Pages: 190. Paperback.

There are things wrong with Findley's third novel, *The Wars*; but it is powerfully affecting. Not as tightly knit as *Famous Last Words* (nor as contrived), and falling somewhat short of the brilliant play of language and imagination in *Not Wanted on the Voyage*, this is one of the best war novels ever written by a Canadian. Other novelists have conveyed the terrors of the battlefield with more authority, but none has so vividly portrayed the sheer carnage and waste, the desolation and depravity of corpse piled upon corpse upon corpse, the mutilations and putrefaction of flesh, and always the mud, and the shifting earth, the flames, the gas.

Findley describes the breakdown of a soldier in the First World War. Young Robert Ross does not finally yield to emotional strain, however; in the dehumanizing crucible of war, he succumbs to spiritual deprivation. Not psyche but soul bears the wounds that finally destroy him in a mad, redeeming, humane, and futile act.

Findley deals with great and complex moral themes. His perspective is so diffuse, however, that the themes never resolve into a coherent structure on their own. Rather than providing form and direction, they are somehow reduced to a sequence of responses. We are moved to revulsion and dismay, not horror; anger, rather than pity and fear. We are not taken into the fiction, but follow the themes, as we do the characters and events, from outside and at a distance. This quality may give the novel its spiritual power, but it dissipates the narrative energy. The drama falters, in spite of the dramatics.

Much of the novel's problem lies in the narrative perspective. With an unusual twist, Findley uses the second-person voice – not for the protagonist, but for the narrator. This "you," unidentified, researches and recreates the war experiences of Second Lieutenant Ross, while accounting, in sporadic detail, for Ross's family context (wealthy Torontonian) and his social life overseas among the privileged English. This "you" writes from a 1970s point of view and sustains the haunting impression that everything being recorded is also irretrievably lost. But "you" also goes on the troopship and into the trenches; "you" becomes the unseen accomplice in Ross's experience. And "you" is the implied reader: "you" speaks in tones of the imperative conditional, as in, "you would do that, then." If Findley's intent was to hold us near to, yet far from, the narrative vision, then he has succeeded. Whether such an effect serves the aspirations of the novel is questionable. The novel explores great themes through the dehumanizing nightmare of our past; in distancing us from the events in order to make their significance more immediate and relevant, he risks turning his fiction into a graphically illustrated polemic.

Findley's novel shows a morbid fascination with male homosexuality: it seems intimately related to depravity or death. And it shows a naïve fascination with wealth, although curiously not with power. It displays an alarming and contextually appropriate interest in mutilation and brutality. Animals are, at times, the only worthy object of human affection–this attitude reflects despair, however, more than misanthropy. The prose in the novel remains clear and precise throughout, although it often lacks subtlety, linguistic or dramatic, and is sometimes awkward, almost to the point of being trite. *The Wars* is an uneven achievement. Yet as a rendering of conflict and the human spirit, it is superbly moving.

Findley's first novel, *The Last of the Crazy People*, is in some ways more successful, primarily because it attempted so much less. With lucid, unassuming style, Findley draws out of an Ontario family's eccentricities a singular tale of pathos and horror. The main character, Hooker Winslow, is eleven, a secretive boy given to burial ceremonies for the birds his cats kill. In the end, with psychotic aplomb, he kills his family, or what remains of it. Findley has created a terrifying story of the Winslows' disintegration and demise without obscuring the narrative by attending too much to its broader implications, psychological, moral, or social. *The Wars*, by contrast, falls short in exactly that, in trying to say–and mean–too much.

Famous Last Words. Toronto: Clarke, Irwin, 1981. Pages: 396. Markham: Penguin, 1982. Paperback.

Famous Last Words is a snuff novel. A woman is cut in half by bullets: her wounds sigh. The protagonist-narrator's corpse is a grisly presence in his own story: through a clever bit of artifice, he is dead as he tells it. People burn and drown; people expire in a variety of scenarios. Many of these deaths are gratuitous. Findley seems fascinated by the narrative impact of death, even when it is not a narrative necessity. People die in this novel simply, at times, because their author decides to kill them off.

It is, of course, much more than this. *Famous Last Words* is a big, complex, and impressive fiction. Nothing if not ambitious, it tries to rewrite the history of the twentieth century. This is not, however, a novel built on alternate realities: What if Hitler had won the war? What if Edward VIII had been a celibate? The large events of history are left intact. Instead, Findley provides an alternate account of why things happened the way they did. To this end, he weaves in and out of known events a strong thread of fantasy, of might-have-been. He invents characters and situations and deploys both in ways to cast recent history into a whole new light. Edward, as the Duke of Windsor, and his experienced bride, the Duchess, assume disconcerting importance in the narrative, then fade, and the Third Reich comes to seem merely a nasty episode, an aberration, in a larger project that ultimately collapses under the force of its own evil weight. Things turn out, in the end, as they did.

Given the chaotic and then cataclysmic events of the 1930s and 1940s, it is not implausible that a cabal should have existed, a ruthless clique of the world's military, political, social, and industrial elite, and that this cabal, with influence extending deep into the power structures of opposing forces, should have manipulated world events toward their known outcome (although their intentions were quite different). Particularly in retrospect, as malevolence and movements seem personified, as Hitler, Mussolini, the Duke of Windsor, and Ezra Pound embody discrete aspects of a complex historical process, it is easy to believe, almost desirable to believe, that history is a consequence of intentional manipulation. How else could the world have fallen so utterly into such a desperate state?

Findley brings leading personnel of the times to his task. From Hitler's henchmen to the residue of European aristocracy to American malcontents, familiar faces populate his narrative and mix with purely fictional characters. The most interesting and important of the latter is the artist manqué, Hugh Selwyn Mauberley, who tells the tale. There is a grand irony, of course, to Mauberley as narrator. Mauberley leaves the story after he dies as a monument to himself. He has been a promising writer in his time. He wrote fiction. His story, Findley allows, is the legacy of a professional and accomplished liar, a writer of novels. Furthermore, HSM is himself a twofold fiction, for he exists as a created character in Findley's account but, beyond that, he originates in a poem bearing his name written by the real-life Ezra Pound. Pound, however, is also a character in Findley's fiction. Pound and Mauberley are friends!

How to find the truth in such a pack of lies? It is everywhere. The greater truth is in effect the lie that can subsume even history–and give it back remade. Such exploits with the truth of fiction, upon which the narrative is based, are much more interesting than those occupying the surface of Findley's novel. What really went on in Nassau during the Windsors' tenure there? Who really killed Sir Harry Oakes? Why? Will the cabal succeed? How? In doing what? Will the world change? This kind of thing comes closer to Ian Fleming than to art. And when the intricacy of relationships between poor Edward and his mother, Queen Mary, or among the literati and the floundering aristocracy takes over, the novel approaches the level of a gossip piece (albeit imaginative gossip), more in the order of popular historical romance than speculative fiction in an historical context.

The novel's form lends such doings among the rich and powerful an element of depth. The plot to control the world is not really of much account. But the way we come to know about it is fascinating. What significance there is to the narrative is not drawn from history itself. That most apocalyptic war, in fact, seems reduced to near inconsequence, an excuse to keep the plot in motion. But Mauberley's account of it, etched literally into the walls of a hotel in Austria–why does he do it? Is it the truth, or fiction? Is it an explanation, a document, an apology? Do the men who read it determine its value by virtue of their perspective, their personalities, their dispositions and predispositions? Is worth determined by perception? Is truth? Are truth and fiction separable? Is history what we know–that is, is history that which we know or that which is past? What if a different set of causes leads to the exact same end: is history what we do not know? Are we, as readers, witnesses, part of the plot? As witnesses, are we merely readers?

Hugh Selwyn Mauberley, erstwhile protégé of Ezra Pound, carves his version of history on sixteen walls of the Grand Elysium Hotel, using a silver pencil given him by his father moments before he killed himself, when Hugh was a youth. American soldiers discover Mauberley's writings, with his mutilated frozen corpse at the centre. Quinn reads sympathetically; Freyberg, with contempt. Lesser soldiers, enlisted men, look on with indifference. Quinn and Freyberg quarrel. We learn how Mauberley died, with an ice-pick through an eye, at the will of the cabal. His notes were destroyed, but the walls left intact. The Americans leave: the walls will fall. We are left with history as we know it, the revisionist version lost forever, but for the telling of it here.

With great finesse, Findley violates the rules of verisimilitude. Mauberley tells the story yet tells of situations he could not possibly have witnessed. Findley tells of Mauberley, his last days and death, in a narrative that contains Mauberley's, and contains Quinn's as well. Findley creates fiction; within the fiction, Mauberley insists that what he says is true; within his truth, he describes what he could not possibly know, except through fiction – that is, by invention. Findley's violations are clearly an intentional affront to the principles of realism, which insist that fiction and factuality are mutually exclusive, and external reality is irrelevant.

Famous Last Words is an ambitious and curiously unsatisfying novel. It is important within the canon of Findley's work, following the strident power of *The Wars*, anticipating the exhilarating extravagance of *Not Wanted on the Voyage*. It poses great questions – somewhat awkwardly. And mercifully, it does not condescend to give the answers.

Not Wanted on the Voyage. Markham: Penguin, 1984.
Pages: 352. Paperback.

I know, now, why there are no gryphons anymore. Many things not wanted on the voyage have been cast aside and the ark floats on precariously without them, over the dream-remembered earth. Findley hardly mentions gryphons, but I know from my experience of his novel and of a world without them what must have happened – and if the voyage lasts forever they will never come back.

Not Wanted on the Voyage is a thing of wonder, one of the truly great books. So different from Findley's other novels, yet filled like them with wit and terror, with wisdom and despair, this novel elevates Findley to a place at the forefront of Canadian writers. For the scope and diversity of his fiction, for the power of his prose

and the precision and clarity of his vision, he is at present without peer. I wished so much while reading *Not Wanted on the Voyage* for the proper eloquence to complement his fine achievement,
but in this novel Findley has pushed language and imagination
so close to the edge of possibility that it is presently beyond criticism to articulate a full appreciation.

The world of *Not Wanted on the Voyage* is discontinuous with
our own. It draws from what we know and have imagined to
re-create our world in an awesome, awful void. Findley's vision is
of unicorns and gryphons and sheep that sing "I'll take you home
again, Kathleen." People ride about before the Flood in democrats
and the antedeluvian God is a tyrant with food in his beard, who
appears as Noah's house-guest in a monstrous great carriage with
a motley retinue, including the wickedly eccentric Archangel
Michael. Lucifer is good, and of indeterminate, or rather, inexact
gender. Noah's wife, the gin-swilling Mrs. Noyes, is the unlikely
major protagonist. Her friend Mottyl, a personality as round as
one could hope to find in fiction, is a cat. And so it goes, through
mounting horror dramatically offset by occasional high humour,
towards the shock of the last line, when Mrs. Noyes aboard the
floating ark prays for the rains to continue.

Despite opulent contrivance, reminiscent of the classics of children's literature, this is definitely not a child's book. And despite
its fabulous conceits and casual fusion of the beautiful and grotesque, it is neither adult fairy tale nor revisionist fable. It is not
allegory, for it has no single pattern of meaning; nor is it satire,
for death here is deadly grievous and warmth is warm, joy is
genuine, and good, rare and lovely. And evil, loathsome.

Not Wanted on the Voyage transcends genre, as it transcends
time, to relate the great and terrible story of an angry God who
exterminates all the creatures of his creation, save those few unfor-
tunates that endure with Noah and his family aboard the ark.
God does not die in this novel, but he is out of touch and embittered
as he consigns the world to man's dominion. In abjuring responsibility, he becomes irrelevant – fate, for a god, surely worse than
death. Yet Findley's vision is not of abject despair. Throughout
the narrative there are gestures of affection and devotion: they
may not compensate for our condition on the ark, but at least
they offer consolation for our being there. The final call of Mrs.
Noyes for rain is a plea, after all, to keep the ark afloat.

This is not a re-telling of God's own holocaust as described in

Genesis. It is a highly original response to it. Findley invents with almost desperate abandon, discarding conventions of genre, defying the rules of history and chronology. Realism, fantasy, myth, and romance are not offered in some curious postmodern medley of divergent realities. Rather, they are present simultaneously – merged in a marvel of possibilities, limited only by the reach of an apparently boundless imagination. The story itself is sequential, but historical time is so utterly conflated that all that ever has been still *is* in the narrative present. There is a veritable flood of anachronisms. God has a pair of cats called Abraham and Sarah; Mozart, Whitman, and Einstein are casually mentioned, as are pirates and pagodas, the Resurrection and the Reformation. This is a fiction set in the present, and the past collapses helter-skelter on the immediate moment.

The reader views with wonder the esoteric exotica scattered through the text. Findley, for example, plays on the medieval association of the unicorn with the wounded Christ on the one hand, and the marriage bed, on the other, and grotesquely inverts the lore that only a virgin can tame it, by having the gentle unicorn's horn used savagely to deflower a virgin. This is re-invention, the very stuff of fiction – but how, one wonders, does Findley know that unicorns, contrary to medieval tapestries, are the size of lap dogs? How does he know of their woeful timidity? Or that angels have webbed fingers? Such things are born entirely of his imagination, as are the stories of Japeth, turned blue in a marinade, and of the many battles and outrages aboard the ark.

Findley writes in apparent delight, or with grief, or in horror, at what his fiction reveals. It is as if the narrative voice learns what happens only as it happens. He writes in language at once timeless and colloquial; in a style that suggests authority and yet sustains the sense of intimacy between reader and the text throughout. *Not Wanted on the Voyage* is a deeply moving and beautifully written novel, in which the reader can grow and grow without ever being aware of a circumference!

The Telling of Lies. Toronto: Macmillan, 1986.
Pages: 359.

The Telling of Lies is like a seance with a dead medium: your guide has crossed over so successfully into the other world that you cannot hope to follow. In this case, the other world is not death, though death is a presence throughout the novel in the person of the blue-skinned frozen corpse of Calder Maddox, but a hermetically sealed enclave of the rich and powerful. The entire narrative is set in the environs of a gracious old New England hotel, the Aurora Sands (called ASH by its life-long habitués), except for sporadic forays in the narrator's mind to her internment during World War II. This was in a Japanese concentration camp in Java, a horrific interlude in her years of growing up amidst the kind of privilege and indulgence that only old money can buy. These are memories, though, not narrative episodes. They are discontinuous with place and time; mind images, not mental reconstructions. Only the present setting along the coast of Maine has any substance in the novel, and it is meticulously and affectionately described. This brief segment of geography is also disembodied from the larger world. Like a ship of fools, it floats free of the amorphous world *out there*, and its confrontation with an iceberg face to face through much of the novel seems Findley's only concession to the possibility of external realities.

Findley is enthralled by class. His fascination for Old and New World aristocracies is well exercised in *The Wars* and *Famous Last Words*, but always with a measure of irony engendered by the certain knowledge, shared with the reader, that there are other ways to be. Here, class is not a matter of status and decorum but the principal condition of being. No greater accolade befalls the narrator than to be accepted in the end by the most imperious resident of the hotel, albeit they dislike one another intensely. Only class can measure class: there is no irony in this. So taken is Findley with high society, in this novel, that his narrative leaves the reader on the outside looking in. Despite his attempt to separate the narrator somewhat from her context, she is too much a part of it to act as a mediator on our behalf. He gives her the terrible experience of internment to provide dimension; he gives her a profession as a landscape architect to provide perspective (she is a career woman, although we see nothing of her work). And she is unmarried, and apparently devoid of sexuality, to provide detachment. However, Vanessa Van Horne is to the manor/ manner born: she may know otherwise, but she accepts the reality of the denizens of ASH as absolute. Both she and her author fail to distance themselves sufficiently from this world to make it matter very much.

Since *The Telling of Lies* is offered as a mystery, this might seem to be a virtue rather than a particularly significant flaw. After all, especially in the Agatha Christie tradition of British who-done-its, of which this novel seems an offbeat variant, the reader should not be allowed too much familiarity with characters or corpse, lest empathy displace the delicious illusion of objectivity by which the genre titillates the mind while leaving sensibilities largely undisturbed. There is no room for sentiment or familiarity, except in relation to the sleuth–and the sleuth, while being a wonderful mélange of idiosyncrasies, must have no complexity. As personalities, Hercule Poirot and Miss Marple do not distract from progressive revelations of the mystery at hand. Miss Van Horne is much too complicated, without being particularly engaging.

The Telling of Lies is not really a mystery at all. It is a puzzle. It does not offer clues from which the nimble reader might resolve the problem of the narrative in advance. At the close, one does not think: "I should have seen that! Of course; it was there all along!" Rather than clues, there are plot complications, sometimes of little apparent consequence, that only in the end make sense. The novel is a puzzle that must be resolved by reading it through to the dénouement. Whether it is worth doing so is a moot point. The conclusion is so contrived and portentous that many readers might decide there could have been a better way to get there. Committed Findley fans will, of course, disagree.

Nessa Van Horne witnesses a murder quite by accident, while taking photographs along the beach. The victim is Calder Maddox, who had been one of the richest and therefore most powerful men alive. His mistress, Lily, is one of Nessa's oldest friends (Vanessa is fifty-nine). Her other oldest friends, from a childhood shared at the ASH, are Meg and Mercedes. They are as involved in the plot as she and Lily. One of them is abducted, one does the deed, one resolves the puzzle, and one is very very rich. Ultimately, the murderer gets off; the CIA is exposed as evil; power is shown to corrupt; the president of the U.S.A, were he not so bland, would seem to be a villain. There are several Canadians involved, one of them an utter twit.

Does it all really matter? No, I think not. But the novel is worth reading because it is so well written, because it consolidates major themes and motifs running through Findley's work relating to class, power, corruption, illusion, death. *The Telling of Lies* tries to be much more than a mystery. It is a good read, by a fine writer. It would have been much better had he tried to do less.

MAY AGNES FLEMING

Kate Danton: or The Captain's Daughters. New York: Street and Street, 1876. 1904. Pages: 285.

May Agnes Fleming leaves no cliché unturned. It is surprising that she was able to write more than one book, so thoroughly does she exhaust every stock possibility of pulp romance in *Kate Danton*. Surprising, that is, until the last page, when an abrupt cessation of the action is followed by a publisher's note explaining that a sequel, *Proud as a Queen*, will complete the story. The reader is left with no choice but to want more of the same. Is the pallid little seamstress really the wife of the profligate son of the household, now hidden in the remote upper chambers of Danton Hall, a fugitive for the murder of his wife's lover? Will his new friend, Reginald Stanford, youngest son of a titled British family, marry the divine Kate, eldest Danton daughter? Or will he succumb to his own baser nature and the earthy charms of Rose, the coquettish younger sister? Will Captain Danton, still in his forties and master of Danton Hall, finally marry his trusted housekeeper and poor third cousin, the gracious Grace Danton? And will Grace's brother, Doctor Frank, eventually marry Eeny, the Captain's youngest daughter? Or will he marry Kate, for whom he is neither handsome enough nor rich enough to be worthy? Who knows, until the sequel is read? Many obviously cared. Fleming sold exceedingly well in her day. She was a master of the pulp romance. Consider some of her other titles: *Silent and True, Carried by Storm*, and the tantalizing *Wedded, Yet No Wife*. She knew her market and wrote to it with flair and without literary pretensions of any sort.

From a present perspective, Fleming's work is of interest only as documentary, although it must be admitted that the simplistic emotional appeal of her writing can be intriguing. The reader's interest, however, is engaged by curiosity alone. There is no development of character or thought, only of action and sentiment. There is no depth or complexity, and ambiguity is always a matter of "what will happen next?" and never a matter of "why?"

Fleming's writing style is appropriate to the genre. Her prose is the kind of pseudo-literary English appropriate to bad romances, heavily ornamented with breathless clichés and formalized expressions of sentimentality. The story line wanders about, picking up bits and pieces of the narrative from a variety of perspectives–enough to arouse curiosity, hint at things yet to come, affairs yet to be resolved–then moving on. Descriptions are minimal–except descriptions of characters' complexions. The great house, the St. Lawrence scenery through the winter, the nearby village of St. Croix, and Montreal itself; the parties, gatherings, balls, the sleigh rides; the sumptuous meals, the beautiful clothes–none of this is given more than an adjective or two. Yet the beating of Rose's heart, the pallor of Kate's cheek, the beauty of Reginald Stanford–these are rendered over and over in excruciating detail.

Fleming's Canada is exotic. As a good Harlequin writer of the present day will use Sri Lanka for the same effect, Fleming does not dwell too closely on the local scene, lest it obtrude with annoying life of its own. It is the *idea* of an exotic setting, not the place itself, that serves her purpose. Its foreignness allows for a touch of the gothic and abundant scope for unfettered romance. But what now comes through with alarming clarity is a devastating chiaroscuro portrait of the times and place. In Canada it was once possible to be very rich yet middle-class. It was possible to have servants and finery, to ride horses for pleasure, to hold celebrations in houses big enough to have ballrooms while maids skulked efficiently in the background, quaint, impoverished souls prepared to stay up all night to comb out their mistresses' hair. Sometimes there is a hint that Fleming recognizes the injustices–yet the last thing her readers wanted to read was a social document. It is as a social document alone, however, that *Kate Danton* might still be read.

SYLVIA FRASER

The Candy Factory. Toronto: McClelland and Stewart,
1975. Scarborough: New American Library, 1977. Pages:
294. Paperback.

Fraser is a prolific and intelligent professional whose novels hover
in the murky abyss between popular writing and serious literature.
Fraser is nothing if not versatile; she has published an exploration of German culpability in the Second World War, a somewhat
garish historical melodrama, a curiously unsettling modern fairy
tale, a thoroughly competent novel of childhood called *Pandora*,
and *The Candy Factory*, which is her most polished and ambitious work to date – a strange and determinedly obscene ghost story
set in contemporary Toronto. Unlike her other works, *The Candy
Factory* has depths of ambiguity associated more with inspiration than with technique. Fraser is an excellent technician; her
prose is crisp, clear, dynamic, aggressively correct. But somehow
her imagination seems generally too constrained – except in this
one novel. Perhaps the obscenity itself overwhelms good sense;
perhaps the ambiguity inherent in such an elusive subject as
"modest miracles" frees the imagination. While it will certainly
not be to everyone's liking, *The Candy Factory* is a significant novel
by an author who commands both public and critical attention.

There are eleven main characters in *The Candy Factory*; they
are related to each other by their association with The Hunter
Confectionary Company. They are all recognizable types, avoid-
ing stereotype only by Fraser's skill at defining their separate
realities. Each character dominates a segment of the novel and is
present as a peripheral personality throughout. There is Sam
Ryan, the loud, foul-mouthed salesman; Irma Burbank, the Pla-
tinum Pussycat from Soft Centres; Laurie Temple of Quality
Control; Eve Martin, Senior Executive Secretary; Charles X.
Hunter, the reluctant boss; his wife, Celeste, of Bishop Strachan
School, Toronto, and Muskoka, and a year in Neuchatel. Each of
the main characters can be itemized by a thumbnail sketch, all
except Mary Moon, who lives alone in a loft of the Old Factory,
and the tramp, a derelict artist who lives in a dry sewer under it.
These two defy simple analysis; together, they invade the lives of
the others. They bring practical resolutions to their problems, and,
in the process, unify the novel.

Mary Moon is an anonymous and aging virgin, seemingly transparent, who haunts the factory at night and discovers, in her co-workers' personal effects, their innermost secrets. In her Special Accounts Book, she rewrites their lives, and laments their loss of wonder, the sterility of their imaginations. The tramp, meanwhile, dabbles in his own excrement, lures stray dogs to their deaths on the highway in order to claim benefits from guilt-stricken motorists who think the animals are his; sometimes he eats the remains. He is utterly depraved. When Mary and the tramp – fey charity and gleeful depravity – get together, something special happens: an act of rape-murder is suspended, without completion, and the miracles begin. The miracles are elusive accomplishments, marked only by a hint of the rose perfume Mary always used, or a flash of white, like the dress she wore the night she invited the tramp to her loft to fill in the face of a portrait she had once had commissioned, long ago, in Paris.

Miracles: for one, the romance between Danny and Daphne is resolved. Danny emulates the *Playboy* life; Daphne is the girl next door, and pregnant. It takes an overturned canoe and the impetus of unrestrained anguish to bring them together. Or: Laurie Temple escapes from the clutches of the lascivious Sam Ryan in the storeroom when a fire alarm is mysteriously triggered; Sam returns for a diabolical assignation, arranged by his co-workers, which ends in his appalling humiliation. Celeste Hunter takes over the company, as she is by temperament fitted to do, and Charles retires. Others are taken down somewhat or elevated, as they deserve. And so on. In the end, Charles Hunter climbs the stairs to Mary's loft, and before her body, or ghost, or whatever, is found, the novel fades – while the scent of roses lingers on awhile.

Fraser has created an intriguing contemporary allegory. The separate stories illuminate not morals but psycho-social conditions. She uses scenes of depravity to shock readers into an awareness of how depraved our world is, how obscenely deprived it is of mystery and meaning. There are episodes, however, in which metaphors for social conditions seem so grotesque that the reader's sensibility is not opened but offended. Sometimes, sexuality is so perversely explicit or obscenely rendered that it seems to undermine the essentially positive intention of the novel. Yet there are scenes of touching beauty, and of high humour. There is also some fine writing. Fraser adjusts her prose to accommodate the central consciousness of each episode; syntax and idiom are appropriately

altered to suit character. Unfortunately, there is never any doubt
that the author herself is in control. The fictional reality never
wholly takes over. However, as a realistic fable, *The Candy Factory* is very effective fiction.

STANLEY K. FREIBERG

Nightmare Tales. Ottawa: Borealis Press, 1980.
Pages: 93. Paperback.

These tales are as uniquely disquieting as a confrontation with
death. They nonetheless display a fine sensibility, rare in even
the most lyrical prose. In Kings County, Nova Scotia–below
Wolfville, around Canning and Kingsport–Freiberg has found a
region of the imagination in which the bizarre and the unreal
infuse every detail of the ordinary life of the people with dimensions of terror. Whether offering up murder or myth, fear on a
bad night or a grotesque rape, the gruesome or the supernatural,
these tales remain rooted firmly in a specific time and place; they
are entirely convincing.

Death and violence are, for the most part, treated obliquely, while
day-to-day life in the region is presented directly, fully integrated
with the land and the sea and the seasons; the procedures of life
seem almost eternal. Some of the tales rise directly out of social
and natural conditions of the locale. But even as that locale is
affectionately rendered, with superb authenticity, it is transformed
into a world of nightmare. None of the tales is entirely separable
from the region; each depends on local activities and customs,
superstitions, value structures, ways of seeing and doing. The tales
are regional in the most positive sense. In their specificity and
substance lies the source of their affective power, their means of
conveying the ineffable.

Our literature has many instances of the gothic, particularly in
romance. Québécois writing has dramatically wedded the more
unsettling qualities of the folk story with the aesthetic intent of
the postmodern novel. Freiberg, however, has created a world
that echoes both the folk tale and the horror story, yet portrays a

community with realistic conviction and the characters with affection, at times even tenderness. It is a singular achievement, the creation of a world.

It is for this world that I have included Freiberg here. His book is in no conventional sense a novel. It is, however, a whole, bound together by mood, vision, and subject matter, in a structure that lends the separate tales collective coherence and impact. They are not really short stories; their individual movement comes closer to that of the yarn, although they are highly polished, told in prose that is poetic and precise rather than in the vernacular of the region. The first of the ten tales contains haunting allusions to Indian mythology; the myths are bled into the landscape and the working lives of twentieth-century people. The last tale, "Death and Dr. Landrin," brings an American cottager back to the community, a perennial outsider whose observations of the external world affirm his innermost terrors. The other stories build from the beautiful and elusive "Apple Autumn" to the nerve-shattering "The Building of the Ship." As the stories accumulate, the community takes on more and more substance; characters and details recur in different contexts until the unearthly and the ordinary are both as substantial as the sea and the seasons.

The prose throughout is a curiously engaging blend of the graphic and the opaque, the prosaic and the poetic. The syntax is contemporary to the point of being experimental, yet the words and the images have a timeless quality. Freiberg's imagery has a visceral appeal, appropriate to stories of horror. Occasionally, his choppy paragraphing is awkward, although usually effective in the way stanza breaks are in narrative poetry. The author's voice remains benign and somewhat removed, yet paradoxically the point of view is intimate, bringing the reader close to the strange and ominous realities created out of authentic regional materials and a haunted imagination. While the form is somewhat reminiscent of George Elliott's *The Kissing Man*, *Nightmare Tales* is unique in our literature, and no less a masterpiece for being so.

MAVIS GALLANT

"Its Image in the Mirror," in *My Heart Is Broken*. New York: Random House, 1957. Don Mills: General; New Press Canadian Classics, 1981. Pages: 100 (of 273). Paperback.

Although she has an international reputation, Mavis Gallant is far less known in her own country. This may be due in part to her affinity for the short-story form, which the public deems somehow more ephemeral than the novel, and in part to the fact that she has lived abroad for nearly three decades. Unlike one-time expatriates such as Mordecai Richler and Margaret Laurence, Gallant seems determined to stay away. Perhaps, too, it is because she lives in France, isolated and insulated from the English-speaking world. Her origins, however, as well as her estrangement from them, breathe through her work, even when there is no overt Canadian content. Her two novels, several novellas, and numerous short stories are extremely important to Canadian literature, and it is we, not Gallant, who lose by continuing to ignore her.

The Pegnitz Junction includes a fine novella of the same title, which seems to insist that its context, the whole book, is a single entity, a most unusually structured near-novel. Possibly even better, among her shorter works, is "Its Image on the Mirror," published in *My Heart Is Broken*. This novella displays a genius in Gallant's use of language, her insight into personality and her deft ways of conveying it, her subtle revelations of society, which is nothing short of breathtaking. She approaches perfection in creating character from the inside out; her use of language elevates ordinary consciousness to the highest art.

The narrative is related by Jean Price, who is ironically conscious of her own voice: occasionally she stumbles over a word, or retracts one, for greater emphasis or precision. Although she is a self-conscious narrator, however, her reason for speaking is never apparent. She recounts her life in a motival pattern, in response to her creator's sense of narrative propriety.

What Gallant does with narrative time inspires awe. Jean speaks, then remembers; then there is a flashback within the flashback, then the centre of consciousness skips forward and around and perhaps back again and forward until eventually, now and then, it returns, as if for assurance or a reprieve from the past, to Jean in the present tense, in 1955. Gallant does not attempt to tie things together, except as they contribute to Jean's experience of herself. Characters–such as Jean's orphaned niece Poppy– drift into the action for brief periods and then fade away, seemingly forgotten or misplaced. Whatever Jean does focus on, whether her life with her husband and four children in the fifties, or her time in Montreal alone during the war when her husband was overseas, or a period of her childhood in Allenton, the interest Gallant creates lies in Jean's perception of things, not in characters or events in themselves.

Here, as in all of Mavis Gallant's fiction, there is a purity of language and an unpretentiousness of design that has striking appeal. With devastating precision, Gallant shares her fascination with the petty anomalies and foibles and ambiguities out of which personality is made. There is a translucent quality to her writing, as if it is all happening within the reader's mind, that makes what she has to say in this novella an immediate experience, yet strangely elusive.

Green Water, Green Sky. Boston: Houghton Mifflin, 1959. Toronto: Macmillan; Laurentian Library, 1983.
Pages: 154. Paperback.

The first thing a reader notices about this novel, and its lasting impression after one leaves it, is its style–not just the prose style, which is diaphanously precise (like silk draped casually across a handful of diamonds); not the lifestyle (exquisitely rendered expatriate decadence and ennui); but the style of perception, the special, haunting, dissociated way the author sees reality. This is Gallant's first full-length novel, one of only two. She is one of the finest short-story writers around; it would be unjust to criticize her for slighting the novel form. Yet Green Water, Green Sky, with its echoes of Henry James, Thomas Mann, Jean Rhys, and many others, makes the reader yearn for more from Gallant in the same mode.

In spite of the idiosyncrasies of style in this novel, there is absolutely no authorial persona, not a whisper in the narrative of its origin. The crisp, clear language has a life of its own, related to nothing except the reality it conveys. The point of view is meticulously orchestrated, completely impersonal. The reader seems to be inside the fiction, like a ghost inside other lives–lives that continually threaten to vanish, leaving the reader nowhere.

The novel is in four sections, which relate like the sides of a square. When all the sections are in place, and their common points and opposing relations are fixed, an unanticipated shape is revealed, another dimension. Contained in the square is a picture of Flor McCarthy: a sad and moving portrait of a squandered soul. The first section seems more about her cousin Georgie, who, at seven to her fourteen, earns Flor's lasting indifference one afternoon in France. The narrative then skips ahead ten years to Flor's unpromising wedding, at which Georgie finds himself still an outsider in her life. The second part begins with Flor's mother, Bonnie, in Paris, where she lives with Flor and her husband. Gradually the emphasis shifts to Flor, whose dissociation with the world, originating years ago when she and her mother began an endless cycle of wandering in penance for Bonnie's meaningless infidelity, takes over completely, and Flor slips into quiet madness. The third section takes us back two years and follows Wishart, an androgynous fake, as he visits Bonnie in Cannes and observes with distaste the courtship of Flor and Bob Harris, the wealthy young American Jew she marries. Finally, the fourth side closes in: Georgie is in Paris for a brief visit to Bonnie and Bob Harris; Flor is institutionalized.

Flor emerges as a pathetically insubstantial personality. Yet she is somehow tragic, the victim of her mother's vanity and love; she lives without a centre; her life has only arbitrary perimeters. She is the ultimate expatriate and, in many ways, the personification of postwar society. Most of all, she is a child who never really grows up to become a woman. Yet she ages and passes out of the world's way. Her life is described in the uncannily precise and continually surprising behavioural imagery that is Gallant's trademark–a gift that has seldom been put to better use. *Green Water, Green Sky* is a disturbing, subtle, and elusive novel, a truly fine work of fiction.

A Fairly Good Time. New York: Random House, 1970.
Toronto: Macmillan; Laurentian Library, 1983.
Pages: 308. Paperback.

This is an easy novel to like, although difficult, at first, to admire. The prose is less intense than that which we are used to from Gallant. The pace is slow, the structure digressive, the narrative vision strangely opaque; and the voice is elusive, as if the author were not quite sure how much reality to reveal and how much to obscure. But the reticence and imprecision that seem to characterize the novel's formal elements also characterize the protagonist's sense of reality. In other words, form and content are exactly appropriate to each other. Shirley Higgins's experience of the world and of herself is conveyed with a manic detachment that makes even the most tragic aspects of her life a comic mockery and, inevitably, lends to the pleasanter parts of her life an element of tragedy. Gallant has not erred in technique: so effectively has she made technique the substance of her novel that we are apt to overlook it entirely and, in our pleasure upon reading the work, miss the quality of her achievement.

Set almost entirely in Paris, the narrative follows Shirley from June of 1963 until April of the following year. During the year, she adjusts to the desertion of her second husband and to the casual abuse she suffers from friends. In the end, she accepts whatever befalls her as her due. With bitter poignancy, Gallant describes middle-class reality – it languishes rather squalidly between the poles of despair and ennui – and defines the struggle to endure it by an ordinary woman (a Canadian expatriate, an outsider in France) in whom others take refuge. Resilient herself, Shirley lends resilience to others' lives; once restored, the others move on. Shirley Higgins's condition of exile provides a centre, in the novel, between the sardonic humour and the suppressed rage that give it its ambivalent power. Despite its close chronicling of Shirley's experience, *A Fairly Good Time* is not a novel of psychological realism. Gallant keeps to the surface; she shows us what her character *thinks* she feels, and why she *thinks* she feels it, but never delves into the complexities of motivation or of feeling, itself. She does not explore the hidden recesses of Shirley's psyche or past: the surface is far too ambiguous for comfort, as it is. And, on the surface, Gallant's protagonist's engaging cynicism becomes, at times, provocatively funny. Telegrams, for instance, are irresistible because "They may contain bad news about someone else." In films, nobody ever "has to look for parking space," or "When a girl is leaving her husband she never has to go down to the basement to look for a suitcase. There will be a brand new one right there." But, also on the surface, evidence of the author's anger is fused with her character's presence. Shirley has been married twice. She is twenty-six. Her first husband, Pete Higgins, died on their honeymoon. Her second husband, Philippe Perrigny, has used her as a lever to break free of his mother. Shirley identifies herself as "somebody's wife." She is a feminist protagonist, not because she endures, or prevails, or even coherently recognizes her condition, but because Gallant sees her as a victim of the sexual privilege of males. All the women she knows are victims. "They are all happy," says the overbearing father of her free-spirited young friend, Claudie Maurel, whom he has reduced to simpering servility. "All the women. You will be happy too one day. As happy as any of them." It is, in Gallant's view, an outrageous prospect.

This is a novel about women and about the middle class, about marriage, about aging, about Europe and the New World, about personal isolation, freedom, responsibility to and for one's self. Paradoxically, it is thematically the richest of Gallant's work. Yet the themes are so much a part of form and style that they seem relatively obscure. *A Fairly Good Time* is a cry of hurt and rage, muffled nearly to the point of suffocation behind a mask of cynical good humour. It is a discomforting novel but well worth the experience.

The Pegnitz Junction. New York: Random House, 1973. Toronto: Macmillan; Laurentian Library, 1982. Pages: 193. Paperback.

Rather than call *The Pegnitz Junction* a novel, which invites debate as to both form and authorial purpose, I would describe it as a work of fiction, with the emphasis on "work," on wholeness or completeness or unity. Within this work are separable fictions that have been separately published. A novella, "The Pegnitz Junction," is followed by five short stories, each of which stands entirely on its own. These are not linked stories as in *A Bird in the House* or *Who Do You Think You Are?* They do not share characters or events, although all are set in postwar Europe, mostly in Germany. Only a common context, as parts of the same book, and the revelation of common attitudes through exquisitely rendered detail, hold them together. Yet, the opening novella is mostly about the incidental coincidence of lives, the unaffecting intersection of life stories, the discrete and arbitrary nature of stories gathered by artifice or happenstance – the form of the whole work effectively embodies this principal thematic intent.

This is probably the most bleak of all Gallant's writing. There is little room in the lives of these characters for intimacy or joy. They are filled with the emptiness of a past they either cannot or do not wish to remember, and they are caught up in a present that neither redeems nor offers more than superficial consolation. Events on a large scale provide them a context – not historical or psychological but rather a sociological context, the conditions within which they live their limited existence. These are people of the German postwar generation, for the most part too young to have been activists in the National Socialist cause yet old enough to be haunted by it. Collective guilt and shame, plus private images of deprivation and suffering, fill them with an emptiness, a void. In place of childhood memories, they carry within them a spiritual and moral fatigue that makes their lives seem trivial, relationships fatuous, achievements unimportant.

While circumstances and personalities vary tremendously from character to character, story to story, it is people rather than situations that occupy Gallant's attention. Narrative consists of character delineation, not the development of plot. In the title story a young woman, her lover, and his son travel across Europe by train from Paris, where an attempt at romance is ingenuously thwarted by the boy, home to Germany, where they are temporarily stranded at Pegnitz until the trains get sorted out. Christine, Herbert, and little Bert (accompanied by a bathroom sponge called Bruno) seem stationary as the world slips by and away. The only break in their journey's narrative comes in stories that Christine intercepts, drawing them as it were out of the air. Fragmented accounts from other people's lives simply enter her consciousness, as if she could hear their minds, witness and comprehend their private realities. This does not surprise her. Nor her author: Gallant appears to make nothing of such perception, neither ascribing it to Christine's paranormal imagination nor exploiting it as an off-beat structural device. The fragments accumulate and intersect with Christine's own story, told by a voice separate from her and from her struggle to account for herself. The effect is strange and enigmatic: a story tumbling with meaning and feeling, yet going nowhere, signifying virtually nothing. Despite the story's obsessive linearity, there is no plot. Despite the intersection of lives, they seem not to touch one another. This is a fine and detailed character study – but of whom? We cannot be sure.

The five shorter fictions are somewhat less bewildering, but no less disturbing. "The Old Friends" seems like another of the stories crowding into Christine's mind, though in fact the web of meaning and meaninglessness in a relationship between old lovers has nothing at all to do with her. Tensions between the miseries of the past and comfort in the present create an aura of sadness in this and the following stories, a sadness less apparent in Christine's narrative, possibly because she is only twenty-one and the war, for her, is borrowed memories, not her own.

The best of the stories is "An Autobiography." It is a lovely, sad, and discontinuous account of a woman's life. Erika is presented in a sequence of bold narrative strokes. Like a Picasso portrait, the whole is a distortion, yet the parts work together to create a unified effect. Much of her story is about the need to tell about herself, and about the pointlessness of doing so. Almost as disturbing is the final story, "An Alien Flower." In this character study, once again the reader cannot be sure who is the main character being studied – the passive wife who narrates, the arrogant and dynamic husband, or the displaced Bibi, who commits suicide – and yet the story's impact is one of overwhelming emptiness, as if all three are no more than reflections of an empty world.

In this book, Gallant's talent for precise images and biting mordant twists of phrase is used superbly to involve her readers in a kind of modern purgatory that we so easily mistake for a life of relative ease. After the inferno of Hitler's Reich, there can be no paradiso. Purgatory, it seems, is the best we can expect. These pathetic, embittered, or complacent lives being lived in Gallant's fiction, these are the dimensions of our present world as she envisions it.

JOHN GALT

Bogle Corbet. London: Colburn & Bentley, 1831.
3 Volumes. Vol. III reprint; Toronto: McClelland and
Stewart; New Canadian Library, 1977. Pages: 209.
Paperback.

As a work of literature, *Bogle Corbet* certainly has its limitations. As a rousing document of immigrant experience and sensibility in the early part of the nineteenth century, it is unsurpassed. Galt sets out to write a useful account of conditions in Upper Canada; his didactic commitment is so strong that the modern reader often forgets the book is fiction. Fiction, however, allows Galt to circumvent the required reticence of the documentary genre; it allows him to describe the emotional responses the New World inspires. Only occasionally do the sentimental demands of romance intrude, although there is a complex romantic subplot that adds nothing to the value of the narrative and actually works at cross-purposes to it.

Bogle Corbet suffers for trying to represent two of its author's quite separate careers at once. As a romantic novelist, Galt was a well-known contemporary of Walter Scott. His most widely acclaimed fiction was *Annals of the Parish*. He also wrote a companion piece to *Bogle Corbet* entitled *Laurie Todd*, which describes the immigrant experience in New York State and is much less given to reportage and editorializing than its Canadian counterpart. But Galt was also an adventuresome Scottish entrepreneur. In the 1820s, he made several trips across the Atlantic as an agent of the Canada Company and founded the town of Guelph. He appears to have been a man of great industry, definite ideas, and intemperate habits. And, according to Elizabeth Waterston (in the reprint edition of *Bogle Corbet*), he completed his North American novels from the solitude of a London debtor's prison.

The business of immigration concerned Galt immensely, and the third volume of *Bogle Corbet*, which stands quite apart from the other two and appears in the New Canadian Library as a work in itself, provides him with both a case history and a platform. Quite unlike his Presbyterian contemporary in the Maritimes, Thomas McCulloch, Galt believed in the absolute efficacy of community. From the newly established town, Galt believed, agriculture would spread through a district; within the town, commerce and culture would necessarily thrive. He also believed firmly in the division of society by class. The higher class was responsible for the well-being of the lower, who voluntarily gave their betters allegiance and labour. Thus, a town built around the magisterial beneficence and organizational abilities of a gentleman such as Bogle Corbet was not merely an ideal but, as Galt saw it, the only practical mode of developing Britain's far-flung colonies. Galt extolls the virtues of Canada as a place for labourer and gentry, though the United States, he admits, would prove more amenable to the tradesman. He acknowledges the hardships in immigrant experience, and bemoans the ineptitude of the British Colonial Office, offering innumerable suggestions for the improvement of immigration procedures.

The narrative voice of Bogle Corbet is disarmingly intimate. He assumes that his readers are of his class, and that they share his interest in bettering their circumstances in order to be more worthy of their station. He also ingenuously discusses the book itself even as he writes it. His wife proclaims it to be "as common as an old newspaper," and he readily admits that certain passages are included for the express purpose of giving information to potential immigrants; he denies that any of it is fiction. The descriptions of town-building and congress with the working families under his patronage is direct, and no more condescending than realities of the time demanded. The rather bizarre and contrived account of illegitimate births and discovered birthrights contained in the romantic subplot is worked into the narrative as if it were of an equal truth with the first-person account of settling a new land and building a nation. Measured by the standards of any particular genre, *Bogle Corbet* is an awkward misfit. Yet by itself it is a commendable achievement, very readable, and one of a distinctively Canadian literary type.

HUGH GARNER

Storm Below. Toronto: Collins, 1949. Markham:
Paperjacks, 1983. Pages: 208. Paperback.

Hugh Garner's name is intimately associated with inner-city
Toronto. In recent years he has been identified with such potboil-
ers as *The Sin Sniper* and *Murder in Don Mills*. His reputation as
a serious writer, however, rests more with *Cabbagetown* and
Silence on the Shore, and his enormously successful short stories.
Garner is also the author of an excellent Canadian war novel,
Storm Below. This novel does not wrestle with great moral questions, as do Colin McDougall's *Execution* and Douglas LePan's
The Deserter. Nor does it offer an immediate view of the horrors
of combat, as do C.Y. Harrison's *Generals Die in Bed* and Timothy
Findley's *The Wars*. It is a naval story rather than a sea story, an
artlessly unpretentious document. It describes the lives of the men
aboard the Canadian Flower Class corvette, H.M.C.S. *Riverford*,
in mid-March, 1943, on convoy escort duty in the North Atlantic.
The characters seem isolated by, rather than occupied with, the
vast ocean that surrounds them and the battle that rages just
beyond their reach and extends around the world. This is a novel
of civilians at war, of lives suddenly drawn together in an arbitrary hierarchy by conditions beyond their control.

There is no single character who dominates, unless it is the corpse
of Knobby Clark, who fell down a ladder from the wheel-house on
his first trip out. With death at the core of the story, and ships of
the convoy on the narrative horizon, Garner moves omnisciently
among the ship's company, focusing on characters almost at
random, providing brief accounts of their pasts and insights into
their personalities. There are glimpses into the captain's marital
strife and into the problems of command, into the terror felt by
Clark's friend, into Frenchy's isolation and quiet pride, into the
sub-lieutenant's pusillanimity, into the first lieutenant's Semitic
burden. Garner weaves more than a dozen private lives into an
improbable corporate personality. What these diverse Canadian
men share is the war and their presence together on the *Riverford*;
they are isolated on the North Atlantic with the corpse of a young
Ordinary Seaman – the death of innocence – in their midst.

In this matrix of history, Garner has created an intriguing metaphor that encompasses the complexity of Canadian society, the human community in conflict, and relations between the quick and the dead. The few days he describes are relatively uneventful. Clark dies; the captain decides to keep his body on board for burial in St. John's. The *Riverford* nearly engages in battle with a German submarine. There are minor mishaps; the men grow restless. Ashore, they get drunk. The ship sails, leaving Clark's friend behind to watch from Signal Hill.

Garner writes with compassion about each individual, but he shows disciplined restraint in dealing with them together. He does not romanticize their war experience, and dwells neither on minor heroics nor on grand passions. These men do not cease to be the men they were; instead they subdue those aspects of themselves that cannot be readily adapted to the corporate purpose. Garner writes with the eye and ear of one who has been there. He visualizes ordinary shipboard details for the reader, using the special language of the sea to make his story seem authentic and immediate. At the same time, his frequent sallies into the minds and lives of individual characters provide a slightly disconcerting perspective beyond narrative reality. This is a minor flaw in a novel that strives steadfastly for realism and is the result, it seems, of Garner's attempt to relate his deftly rendered smaller world to the larger one surrounding it.

Cabbagetown. Toronto: Collins, 1950. Toronto: McGraw-Hill Ryerson, 1978. Pages: 415. Paperback.

Cabbagetown is about the pride of a survivor. It is an intriguing popular document of life during the Depression in the largest Anglo-Saxon slum in North America, as Garner describes it, a region of Toronto now riddled with chic outsiders that was once the preserve of the proletariat. Cabbagetown is the neighbourhood about which Garner wrote best. Although some of his potboilers were set in Don Mills and he even took an excursion into small-town Ontario in *A Nice Place to Visit*, a transitional novel between his literary and his commercial work, the inner city was the source he turned to in his most serious fiction. While Callaghan was still disguising his Canadian cities and MacLennan was defining them, Garner wrote about Toronto as if it were a real place of the imagination. Long before Margaret Atwood elevated the Royal Ontario Museum and the Park Plaza in her fiction, Garner gave literary presence to Cabbagetown. He did so without the coy evasiveness afflicting so many of his successors. In *Cabbagetown*, Toronto is not merely a setting: it represents the hard conditions of his protagonist's life.

The novel opens the day Ken Tilling quits school; the Depression gapes ahead of him. We follow Ken and a handful of his contemporaries over the next few years; at the novel's close, Ken goes off with the Mackenzie-Papineau Brigade to fight (as Garner did) in the Spanish Civil War. While Ken is very much the dominant figure in the narrative – he appears to be an autobiographical persona – the plot is structured around his protracted love for Myrla Patson, whom he meets at a party while they are still in their mid-teens. He meets her again two years later when he is on probation for stealing a toilet. She is pregnant, the occupational hazard of working as a maid. Ken's strength of character is already strained by poverty, unemployment, an alcoholic mother; his pride is nearly broken. When he discovers Myrla's condition, he leaves; he acquires cynicism, socialism, independence, and, ultimately, self-respect during his travels. Myrla waitresses, mistresses, and then whores. Meanwhile, of Ken's old friends, Billy Addington drowns in a vat of chocolate, Bob McIsaacs dies in a shoot-out with the police, and Theodore East rises above himself.

Abstracted, *Cabbagetown* seems more flamboyant than it is. Melodrama is defused by the low-key presentation. Garner shows restraint in even the most garish events and balances a tolerant warmth for people with his sense of outrage for their social condition. His prose is prosaic. It might have benefited from a few curves and flourishes to match the action. Also countering the novel's dramatic excesses are Garner's naturalistic descriptions – of the city, of the Depression, of the tone and temper of the times. The author's point of view parallels Ken Tilling's own perspective on the world: involved without being committed, concerned without being overwhelmed, intimately familiar with life yet detached, although never to the point of indifference. In his subject and its treatment, Garner is on his own, in a class by himself.

Silence on the Shore. Toronto: McClelland and Stewart,
1962. Markham: Paperjacks, 1983. Pages: 352.
Paperback.

This novel draws together an arbitrary cluster of people under
the single roof of a boarding house in downtown Toronto, and
explores facets of their various lives until, ultimately, the many
facets cohere as a luminous if somewhat rough-cut gem. Garner
has never been remarkable as a prose stylist; he has always been
concerned more with the story than the telling, with the characters more than characterization. In this novel, nevertheless, he
has drawn a fine portrait of the Canadian community that is a
convincing cross-section yet convincingly idiosyncratic. There are
nine subplots in the novel; there is no main plot. No story-line;
but a rich variety of stories.

Garner's Toronto is palpably recognizable, and his attempts at
disguise are a minor annoyance. Adford Road is Bedford Road
north of Bloor Street, above the University of Toronto. The Park-
lawn Hotel is clearly the Park Plaza. Beaver Gardens is Maple
Leaf Gardens. Matheson-Corbett, the publisher, is Maclean-
Hunter, and so on. What might serve as clues in a roman à clef
are, in naturalistic fiction, a distraction. They do indicate, however,
the close attention Garner pays to setting: Toronto is not merely
a background, it is an intricate geography, inseparable from the
lives of the people living there. Garner's greatest achievement is
to invest Toronto with a soul. In a literature with an impoverished urban tradition, Garner's work stands out for the easy familiarity it shows with the city as a way of life and not merely as a
conveniently complicated place to be.

Silence on the Shore takes place in six months in 1959. In a
sequential pattern, it weaves together the stories of Grace Hill
and her boarders at 120 Adford Road. Characters reminisce and
ruminate on the past, but the forward action of the novel does not
use flashbacks. Drama arises from the arbitrary or coincidental
intersection of the boarders' lives. Grace Hill is a superb character,
at once an archetype and a singular creation. She is a middle-
aged snoop, an overweight nudist whose sexual release comes
through watching wrestling matches at the Gardens, a severe,
vulnerable, and compassionate woman whose personality permeates the house. There is an alcoholic, George Lightfoot, with whom

Garner clearly empathizes; but the authorial persona seems to be Walter Fowler, commercial editor, aspiring writer, life-long Torontonian adrift from an old and awkward marriage. Garner allows each consciousness to be convincing, to dominate in its turn its portions of the narrative. Old Jim Martin, in the basement, gradually comes into his own. Clark Cronin aggressively enters the narrative, then draws back into nervous near-obscurity. Aline Garfield's reality is obliquely presented as she wrestles with fundamentalism and a lascivious mentor. Sophia Karpluk, a Polish refugee, pathetically struggles to cope with her loneliness, her vulnerable, low-class position in an apparently classless world. The Laramées, a family, draw the affection of the rest, yet seem inviolate, a unit separate from the others. Some of these lives become intimately involved–Cronin has a torrid session with Sophia in a darkened cinema; Cronin and Aline are married–and some go their own ways. In the end, Grace Hill dies and the house disperses the lives it has held together into the Toronto air.

Garner has described himself as a careless writer, yet clearly this novel demanded a great deal of attention to detail. In consequence, his prose is somewhat more polished than in his other long fiction. (His short stories tend to be highly polished, with a casual authority not found in most of his novels.) He has made subtle but appropriate adjustments in language as the omniscient point of view shifts from character to character. Yet, typical of Garner's work, this novel is unpretentious. It is meant to be an entertainment, not merely a diversion but an involving encounter with imaginative reality. If it is also the best realistic novel of Canadian city life yet written, that is an added benefit for the reader. Garner had too much integrity, too much personal arrogance, and too much creative humility, to have attempted such heights consciously. Lofty aspirations he left to lesser writers than himself.

GRAEME GIBSON

Five Legs. Toronto: Anansi, 1969. Pages:194.
Communion. Toronto: Anansi, 1971. Pages: 119. "*Five
Legs* and *Communion*." Toronto: Anansi, 1979. *Five
Legs*; *Communion*. Toronto: McClelland and Stewart;
New Canadian Library, 1982. Pages: 333. Paperback.

Graeme Gibson is probably our most celebrated minor author. *Five
Legs* was a notable experimental work in its time, and *Communion*
a laudable sequel. Together they spoke for a new, post-centenary
Canadian nationalism. Form and style and content were largely
indigenous, but the standards to which the two novels aspired
were international. Gibson was the heralded leader of a new wave.
But while others (like Matt Cohen and Marian Engel, who came
out of that same surge) have developed as major Canadian writers,
Gibson energetically devoted himself to cultural politics. The passage of time inevitably deflated his modernist, *avant garde* aesthetic, yet Gibson remains before the public eye. Thus, we have a
curious anomaly: a novelist acclaimed more for himself as a writer
than for his art. His most recent work, *Perpetual Motion*, while a
valiant attempt at epic, did little to change this status.

Five Legs still reads remarkably well. The innovative stylistics
no longer surprise, but they remain effective equivalents of narrative consciousness: style and content in *Five Legs* are virtually
inseparable. Through fractured syntax, aggressively unorthodox
punctuation, unfinished thoughts, fragmented language, Gibson
re-creates his characters' consciousnesses within the minds of his
readers. It is not a novel that can be read aloud. In the halthing,
inarticulate reality of his characters' awareness of themselves,
we perceive Gibson's larger vision. It is one beyond words; a grey
world by false morality and limited imagination, a world without
beauty or honour but with a smattering of hope. In *Communion*,
the same anarchic vision leads to despair, then to nothing, to a
void. Perhaps there is nothing left for Gibson to write about.

Five Legs is divided into six parts. Three are from the vantage
of Dr. Lucan Crackell, an ambitious, emotionally stifled professor of
English at the University of Western Ontario; three belong to
Felix Oswald, a confused and sullen graduate student. Together,
the two men journey from London, Ontario, to Stratford for the
funeral of Martin Baillee, Crackell's former student and Oswald's
roommate. Baillee died in a car accident after forsaking his dreams

of writing and adventure to marry Susan, his hometown sweet-heart, and to teach high school – a compromise that killed him. These three men dominate the narrative.

On the way to Stratford, Crackell ruminates fitfully about himself, his faculty wife, Rose, and his lover of long ago who refused an abortion and him at the same time, a humiliation that forced him to flee Stratford for the safety of academe. He reflects, too, on his attraction to Baillee's fiancée and his dislike for Oswald. He takes shape, in the reader's mind, as a rather pathetic, dreary, and pompous person, yet Gibson's manner of presenting him is lively enough. Then, at the funeral, Oswald's reality takes over. He, also, ruminates fitfully – about Crackell, whom he dislikes; about Baillee, whom he comes to realize he never did like; about his parents, whom he torments with threats of turning either Catholic or Communist; about himself, his anxieties, frustrations, fantasies, about himself especially.

Everyone in *Five Legs* is an emotional cripple. In *Communion*, the implications of such a dark vision are pursued. Felix Oswald is out of school, working in Toronto for a veterinarian. In the central incident of the novel, Felix forcibly frees a dying husky from its cage. That is the best Felix can do – commit another being to unwanted freedom. Felix himself perishes in flames in Detroit.

Gibson is a writer of themes, with style. On the surface, *Communion* is radically different from *Five Legs*. The language is more coherent. The narrative moves through time in fits and starts, forward, back upon itself, forward again, struggling painfully towards completion. The overall form, however, is quite conventional. The stylistic aberrations still tend to be of language rather than of design – of style rather than structure. In both novels, themes are explored, echoed, resolved through extensive symbolism and ingenious metaphors. What the novels mean, however, cannot ultimately be separated from what they are: tentative experiments in frustration and despair.

The long-awaited appearance of *Perpetual Motion* in 1982 was disappointing. The stolid complexity of Gibson's prose combined with a forced exuberance suggests massive over-writing. The principal situations seem designed to illustrate themes rather than illuminate them. There are superb evocations of nineteenth-century Ontario, and a number of macabre set-pieces (a hanging, for example) that stand well on their own. But on the whole, this is not the novel Gibson's reputation led us to anticipate.

JOHN GLASSCO

Harriet Marwood, Governess. Don Mills: General,
1976. Pages: 232. (According to an author's preface, this
edition is the first authorized, complete, and final version,
but ***The English Governess***, as it was originally called,
has had a confusing history of withheld editions, pirated
and pornographic editions, and a variety of reprints since
it was originally completed in 1954.) Paperback.

Glassco was one of the great eccentrics in Canadian letters. Why
someone would put so much talent into such drivel as this particular novel is hard to fathom. I include the work here for its rarity,
its single-minded perversity, and its example of squandered genius.
Glassco's novel suggests not the silly obscenities of Henry Miller,
but the lush eloquence of a *fin de siècle* romance combined with
the burbling eroticism of a Fellini film. *Harriet Marwood, Governess* seems a grotesque cliché from beginning to end, yet it is well
written; the reader clings to the idea that it will suddenly reveal
itself a clever parody of sado-masochistic literature. Instead, it
remains a polished example of the genre. Unfortunately, it is a
rather sordid and humourless book; readers not attuned to whips
and leather will not find much to keep them reading except the
consistently sophisticated prose style and the contrived but convincing atmosphere of late-nineteenth-century British decadence.

In his prefatory note, Glassco entreats those of his readers "who
are in sympathy with the obsession it celebrates" to share in the
novel's delights. For the rest of us, the novelty quickly palls. I
was left with the feeling of having walked in upon two gentlemen
of distinction sharing a toilet cubicle in a public lavatory – or perhaps upon one, in a furious release of importunate longings. It is
not the subject matter of the novel that creates problems of impropriety but rather the leering way the story is handled. No
subject is beyond the legitimate consideration of art. But when
all the techniques at an author's command are brought forth
merely to titillate a particular deviant taste, then art itself is
demeaned. This is the sort of masturbatorial writing one generally
associates with hard-core pornography, although Glassco is a
brilliant stylist and an artist of refined, if exotic, sensibility and
commanding intelligence.

The plot is simplicity itself. Harriet Marwood takes over the education of Richard Lovel, who is fourteen when his mother dies. For the next half a dozen years, Harriet beats the lad, demeans him, tortures him, enslaves him, and, finally, after receiving all his worldly goods in her name, marries him. That's all. But each and every episode of Richard's humiliation is offered up in intimate, though decorous, detail. Devices of restraint and abuse are fondly described. Pain and sensuality invariably command the scene; they are inseparable. A deep hatred of women and a fascination for the terrors they embody define the general atmosphere. In all, whatever his readers are after in this novel, Glassco gives them more than enough.

For those who want perversity in a more literary caste, less redolent of the commercial and more representative of the serious artist at play, three Glassco novellas were published in 1974 by The House of Anansi under the collective title, *The Fatal Woman.* These works, while very different from each other, are all quite dissociated from reality and the conventions of realistic fiction. "The Black Helmet" (1936-1944) is a fascinating, highly stylized confessional. A young writer eventually overcomes chronic auto-eroticism, ennui, obsession with a former governess (called, inevitably it seems, Miss Marwood), and his fear of women, all in an atmosphere suggesting nothing so much as an ironic adult fairy tale. "The Fulfilled Destiny of Electra" (1934-46) describes incest and the fatal impact of familial devotion with placid innocence. "Lust in Action" (1964) is the most unusual – a surreal future-fantasy of female dominance, a world where men have been emasculated by a puritanical lesbian society and where an obscene flurry of adolescent male rebellion is quickly squashed. These works are sophisticated trivia in a tradition of erotic literature that has been little cultivated in Canada – perhaps because it seems more a literature of creative exhaustion than of cultivated decadence, when imagination, passion, and sensibility are used for such an ephemeral purpose.

Glassco is also the author of a fine literary memoir. *Memoirs of Montparnasse* was written between 1928 and 1933 but not published until 1970. Much of the book was supposedly written within weeks of the experiences it chronicles, giving it the immediacy of a diary or journal. And yet its tone is one of insouciant detachment. It was completed in hospital in Montreal while the author, a weary twenty-two, awaited major surgery from which he rather amiably anticipated not recovering. This book is refulgent with incisive trivia about the great and the soon-to-be-celebrated in Paris during the late twenties; it is informed by his own joyfully amoral dissipation, awash in a sea of lust and indolence. One cannot help but wonder what a splendid set of curiosities we might now have if Glassco had contrived to consume the rest of his life with the same flair. As it is, he retired to the Eastern Townships to write refined erotica and good poetry, and to create worthy translations from the Québécois.

DAVE GODFREY

The New Ancestors. Toronto: New Press, 1970. 1972. Toronto: McClelland and Stewart; New Canadian Library, 1984. Pages: 392. Paperback.

Few Canadian novels are more complex; few demand more of the reader in perseverance, intelligence, and arcane or esoteric knowledge. The question immediately arises: is it worth it? The answer is a loud but qualified yes. *The New Ancestors* is monumental fiction by an author whose work otherwise consists of finely crafted short stories gathered under the titles *Death Goes Better with Coca Cola* and *Dark Must Yield*. The more one reads–or rereads, for this novel cannot possibly be comprehended or fully appreciated on first reading–the more complex and obscure the novel becomes, and yet the more is revealed of form, story, and theme. That is the novel's special genius. But the reader must be willing to work in earnest, at a taxing level of analysis and synthesis, in order to uncover the profound and moving truths within the tangled luxuriance of Godfrey's formal design, linguistic pyrotechnics, and striking discontinuities.

The New Ancestors is set in a fictionalized West African country called Lost Coast, in which the historical processes that have taken centuries in Canada are endured in a decade. Godfrey probes the relationships between reality and human consciousness reaching from deep within the tortured psyches of several related characters outwards to encompass the political and moral upheaval of the whole nation. Always, there are many levels and dimensions of experience present simultaneously. The individual and the state, in Godfrey's vision, exist in troubled symbiosis.

Time is both the medium of erratic consciousness in the novel and the source of narrative form. Each of the four main sections is told through a different set of voices associated with a major character. In the first, Michael Burdener, born an Englishman, provides an account of himself he believes he can live with. The second is related by Burdener's African wife, Ama, in rueful, masturbatory self-analysis. Burdener's associate, a devious rogue named First Samuels, dominates the third part. The hallucinatory fourth part is the product of Burdener's fevered mind, something not clarified until the brief, final section, which ends several weeks before the opening prologue begins.

All this talk of complexity should not dissuade the reader who feels up to the challenge. The rewards are most satisfying, for *The New Ancestors* is a work of power, insight, sophistication, and great sensitivity. In the nature of a truly great aesthetic experience, the novel yields more and more as the reader progresses deeper and deeper into it.

PHYLLIS GOTLIEB

Sunburst. Greenwich: Fawcett, 1964. Toronto: Fitzhenry
& Whiteside, 1977. Pages: 171. Paperback.

Science fiction – or, as it is more properly known, speculative fiction – enjoys immense popularity among a limited segment of the reading public. The rest of us remain relatively indifferent to its curiously insistent mixture of the simplistic and the ominously sophisticated. A number of Canadians are outstanding in the field of speculative fiction, although little known outside it. Phyllis Gotlieb and Judith Merrill, in particular, are notable for the quality of their writing. Merrill's forte is short fiction, but Gotlieb is at her best working within the longer format of the novel.

Sunburst was published in 1964 and, prophetically, is more topical today than when it first appeared. Somewhere in the middle of "America," circa 1994, there is a thermonuclear blow-up in a power plant. From this, Gotlieb develops a compelling story of mutations and supermen. The moral implications of genetic distortion vie in the narrative for preeminence with horrific accounts of telepathy, psychokinesis, and teleportation. The prevailing mood is oppressive; an aura of foreboding permeates the story. Yet it is ultimately a story of triumph, an account, against a background of panic and brutality, of a modest leap forward in the evolution of the human species.

Thirteen-year-old Shandy Johnson is born in the year 2011 in Sorrel Park, a town isolated from the world to suppress the news of its exploded reactor. Shandy is alarmingly precocious and uniquely impervious to the mind-probing psi powers of the mutant children (who were a consequence of the reactor accident). The novel is told from Shandy's perspective. She becomes involved with the benevolent keepers of the Dump, the compound where the mutants have been isolated since the night they spontaneously gathered into a destructive organism and rampaged through the streets. It is Shandy who realizes the bizarre power of the mutants is a throwback to an animal state of being rather than an ominous advance. It is she, along with her friend Jason Hemmer (and several others who combine psi with a refined sense of moral responsibility), who quells the revolt of the Dumplings. And it is she, at the novel's close, who stands alone at the dawn of a new era in the human story.

Sunburst is Gotlieb's best. It is the most realistic: its prophetic aspects are particularly chilling. It is psychologically acute: at one level it is a sensitive portrayal of Shandy's transition from childhood into the world of adult experience – with the science fiction merely providing a metaphor for the process of maturation. The relationships, especially between Shandy and eighteen-year-old Jason, are developed with a subtle beauty not common to the genre. The writing itself is unpretentious, occasionally quite lyrical, and always precise. Consistent with the demands of speculative fiction, Gotlieb tries to sustain an illusion of verisimilitude by grounding even the most bizarre elements of her story in an apparently logical base. This attempt leads occasionally to some rather inane chatter about ectomorphs and endomorphs, stable moral equilibrium, force fields, and psychodynamics. On the whole, though – given the requisite willing suspension of disbelief on the part of the reader – her novel is as convincing as it needs to be, and an engaging, provocative entertainment.

GWETHALYN GRAHAM

Earth and High Heaven. London: Cape, 1944. Toronto:
McClelland and Stewart; New Canadian Library, 1960.
Pages: 254. Paperback.

This novel caused a stir among the literati for its apparently forthright treatment of anti-Semitism in Montreal; at the same time,
Germany was perfecting death camps to resolve the Jewish question, and Anne Frank was writing her sad and valiant diary in
Amsterdam. Graham's novel is an important work now only
because it was thought to be important then, and not for any intrinsic value. It is a social document so lacking in depth that it suggests illusions of depth. Were it not for the "timeliness" of the
topic, this novel would more properly belong in the company of
drug-store romances. For writing about a relationship between a
Jew and a Gentile, however, Graham's courage was applauded
by her contemporaries, and her talent endorsed. From a present
perspective, her novel tells much about her contemporaries and
virtually nothing about love or bigotry, or the function of art in
the service of democratic ideals.

Jews are just like everybody else, this novel insists, every bit as
good as *we* are. The point of view is resolutely Westmount, with
overtones of well-bred compassion, charity, and understanding.
In making her case for universal equality, Graham denies people
their essential differences, ignores Jewish heritage, ignores the
transcendent identity of the Jewish people born of persecution
and endurance over millennia. It is not that she forgives Jews
their Jewishness so much as that she seems unaware of it. The
inadvertent condescension of the novel makes it still worth reading. The realization that it was considered controversial, humane,
and even deep is far more relevant to the contemporary reader
than is the story itself.

The forbidden love affair is between Marc Reiser, perfect in every
respect, a handsome, intelligent lawyer, polished as only the self-
made can be, presently in the service of his country at war as a
captain in the Canadian Army, and Erica Drake, of Westmount –
with all that that, in bad fiction, implies. The impediment between
them is her otherwise intelligent and sophisticated father's bigotry.
Marc is a Jew. The conflict and the drama are not so much between
Marc and the Drakes as within the Drake family itself, between

father and daughter, among siblings, between generations. It is an intriguing dynamic context within which to explore relationships and values, anatomize society, plumb the depths of neurotic behaviour. Instead, Graham manipulates the surface drama to illustrate theme and arouse generalized emotion, much in the manner of a soap opera. The novel's resolution is consistent with this baleful genre: the Drakes of Westmount, their assumptions shattered by the loss of the family scion overseas, accept Marc Reiser among them. A patronizing conclusion, but, in the pulp-romantic context of the plot, an inevitable one.

Graham's prose is serviceable. Her characterization is shallow: there is little awareness of motivation, none of psychological complexity. The plot moves because she tells it to. As a rather sardonic voice for the limited world of the Drakes, Graham is superb. But her insight into other worlds is lamentable. Her novel is important, ultimately, for its failure, worth reading to understand the benign context in which bigotry can grow.

FRANCIS W. GREY

The Curé of St. Philippe. London: Digby, Long, 1899. Toronto: McClelland and Stewart; New Canadian Library, 1970. Pages: 313. Paperback.

The title of this novel is inappropriate. Grey was obviously searching for a unifying character or unifying motif, and the curé, Abbé Francois Xavier Lalonde, must have seemed convenient on both counts. The novel is, in fact, a careful chronicle of Québécois society from 1894 to 1897; it is not a personal account of the cleric, whose church inevitably dominates parish life. The parish of St. Philippe does provide the perimeters of the community under analysis, but not the limits to Grey's astute perception. With pleasantly benign cynicism, he moves from descriptions of individual political and social behaviour to explications of the national scene. But he never loses sight of the community of St. Philippe, his focal centre. Increasingly, as the novel develops, Grey examines the implications of parish politics on a larger scale; by the end, there are individuals in the town who have attained positions of great power in the nation. Indeed, it is difficult to know how Grey avoided libel suits since his book was published less than two years after his Machiavellian scoundrel, Alphonse Bilodeau, was named lieutenant governor of Quebec (a reward for political chicanery of the lowest order, according to Grey's fiction). Did the real people involved in the election of 1896 not object to such aspersions? Or were they silenced by complicity? Or by Grey's family connections with the Earls Grey, among others? In any case, his novel is a most thorough and thoughtful socio-political document of early Canadian life.

Sara Jeannette Duncan's *The Imperialist* might be better written; it might show a more sophisticated comprehension of the political scene as a whole. But for his understanding of Québécois society and his detailed analysis of one election in particular, Grey's achievement is monumental. Sometimes, unfortunately, it is also as unmoving as a monument. Not that Grey has no wit or warmth about him, for he does, in good measure. But he is, as he explains from time to time without any qualms over such intrusions, anxious to make his chronicle complete. He leaves no detail of intrigue or self-interest in doubt, no idea or theory or scheme unexplained. To his credit, he does try to work his explanations into the narrative situations, but often he is left with two characters in rhetorical discourse; often an event occurs, the sole purpose of which is to illustrate a particular point.

Grey does his best to bring the parish of St. Philippe alive. He populates it with such intrinsically fascinating people as Fitzgerald, the real-estate agent, and Toussaint Charette, possessed of a prime chunk of land in the middle of the new parish and a beautiful daughter who is coveted by an absurdly unamatory trio. There are the politician Bilodeau and his obnoxious understudy, M. le Maire, Charles Fisher. And there are literally dozens of minor characters, most of them French-speaking, minions in the work of church and state. There are intrigues and romances and church bazaars and denunciations from the pulpit. There is much gossip, and much to gossip about. The affairs of the church are illuminated with a fine understanding of ecclesiastical machinery. But everything ultimately contributes to the political aspect of the novel, and it is politics, most of all, that makes this novel a major work. Through fiction, Grey has found the best avenue for truly comprehensive social analysis.

The first half of the novel attempts to explain the French Canadian personality. It is a sly and cynical but affectionate and knowing social document. All sides are given a voice, including one strident plea for Québécois separatism: "This, in a few words, is the race-problem of the Dominion; two nations—no other word is adequate—separated, not only by race and creed, but by language as well."

Having established an understanding of French-Canadian "sensibility," Grey delves deeper into the issues of the 1896 election. Quebec had been steadfastly Tory; the bishops supported the Conservatives; the major issue, the Manitoba Schools question, showed the Tories on the side of Catholic control. But the Liberals were running a French Canadian for prime minister (the Liberals promised more restraint of Catholicism in the West, but, wisely, in Quebec argued otherwise). As history shows, Quebec voted overwhelmingly in support of Laurier and the Grits. In this novel, Grey goes a long way towards showing us why.

FREDERICK PHILIP GROVE

Over Prairie Trails. Toronto: McClelland and Stewart, 1922. Toronto: McClelland and Stewart; New Canadian Library, 1969. Pages: 146. Paperback.

Among cultural pundits, a popular ploy is to denigrate Grove. Those who do so betray indiscriminate and uninformed critical intelligence. Grove is a writer of singular importance in the Canadian literary tradition. Aesthetically, he has certainly been bettered; for depth and originality of thought, he is not without peers. Other writers show greater talent for dramatic intensity, for narrative structure, for realism, for character development. But Canada has yet to host another writer of the same creative magnitude: among the work of his contemporaries, Grove's varied canon stands like an awkward and imposing edifice. His mind was large, his ambition colossal, his achievement an enduring legacy even to those Canadian writers and critics who presume to despise him.

The first of Grove's books to be published in Canada was *Over Prairie Trails*. It is an account of seven weekend journeys, of thirty-four miles each, through rural Manitoba. The journeys happened one winter during the First World War as the author travelled from the school at which he taught to his home, where his wife and child waited, or back again. Not a novel, nor fiction, it nonetheless uses many of the creative writer's techniques to engage the reader's interest and to sustain the narrative flow. This work provides a foundation, as well, in its investigation of relations between man and nature, for his major works that followed.

The seven journeys are the distillation of thirty-six trips in all. Each is built around a single dominant motif–a snow storm, a family emergency, a contemplative mood. Tying them together is the narrator's insistent personality: he is a man whose fascination with expository detail approaches pedantry, but whose solemn affection for the natural world provides compensatory warmth and humility. Nature does not provide the book with its informing principles; rather, the author's perception of nature and his attitudes towards it unify the work and lend it a power rarely found in the contemplative memoir. The presence of Grove's personality is reinforced by the book's narrative vigour. It is not Grove's purpose to relate seven personal adventures, but to provide drama and momentum to seven sequences of experience, in which the lyric and the thoughtful are combined. Six of the seven journeys take Grove homewards; he moves from sombre isolation through refining solitude towards the community of his small family.

Grove's prose is rich and formal and anything but relaxed. Yet there is an oddly colloquial air about it. Intimacy is conveyed by lucid image, confessional tone, and insistent authenticity of detail, despite the formal syntax and occasionally pontifical erudition. The diction, as much as the content, establishes the presence of a rather austere sensibility struggling to perceive his own place in a world of overwhelming power and complexity. *Over Prairie Trails* is still eminently readable, if only for the touching naïveté of the author's elevated posturing in the face of awesome nature and his own pedestrian condition.

Settlers of the Marsh. Toronto: Ryerson, 1925. Toronto: McClelland and Stewart; New Canadian Library, 1966.
Pages: 222. Paperback.

This is the first of Grove's farm novels and quite possibly the best–certainly it is the most psychologically powerful. *Settlers of*

149

the Marsh created a minor sensation when it originally appeared—and sold poorly. The brooding naturalism of its vision and the perversity of its plot consolidate earlier Canadian attempts to relate man's destiny to the land and the natural order of things; it anticipates Grove's own major themes and many of the motifs that came to dominate Canadian prairie fiction for the next fifty years. With this novel, Grove was in the vanguard of the Canadian literary revolution that followed the First World War, when fiction turned away from saccharine didacticism and preachy contrivance. Here was a novel that incorporated a complex, gloomily deterministic world view far beyond the scope of Connor's sophistries or Roberts's solemn revels in the woods.

Neils Lindstedt's pioneer dream to build a dynasty out of the primeval land and his own labours illuminates the relationships between fate and free will, between man's endeavours and the passing of time, between the natural world and man's effort to make it yield. These are among the themes this novel explores against a background of tortuous sexuality and brooding emotions that erupt into righteous violence. Ultimately, the themes and the plot and the sombre, roiling mood are inseparable.

For a man who aspires to build a dynasty, Neils's utter ignorance about human sexuality is virtually a fatal flaw. Neils envisions Ellen Amundsen as the chatelaine of his "white-line" house. But Ellen has been witness to her father's sexual brutality, which led to her mother's sordid death, and she has promised her mother to avoid men. Neils is left to his own devices. His farm grows prosperous. The hopelessness of his love for Ellen and his own naïveté lead him to marry a woman of elastic virtue whom he eventually, pitiably, murders. The novel closes as Neils arrives home from prison; he is met by Ellen, and their future is left ambiguous.

What redeems this plot from seamy melodrama are the psychological realism of Grove's characterizations and the naturalistic description of the farms laid precariously upon the northern Manitoba landscape. Grove is a master of evocative details: the reader does not necessarily see and sense what Grove envisions, but seems to experience it from within. Grove's prose is clear and controlled, never indulgent and yet rich with specifics. Images tend to be documentary rather than "literary." The plot moves in a direct linear progression, with references to the past but without flashbacks. Events gradually take on an aura of the inevitable, so that

Neils seems more the centre of pathos than of tragedy; given the tentative affirmation of the novel's closing scenes, this seems appropriate.

Throughout, Grove maintains a rather formal and sometimes arch or patronizing view of things, as evidenced by the tone of the narrative voice and the subtle, elevated perspective from which the narrative is related, both of which suggest experience of worlds far different from those described. Grove, the European, self-consciously shapes provincial Canadian reality into a story of universal dimension. He shows that it can be done.

A Search for America. Ottawa: Graphic Press, 1927.
Toronto: McClelland and Stewart; New Canadian Library,
1971. Pages: 392. Paperback.

A Search for America is a literary curiosity. It remains one of Grove's most popular works, yet in many respects it is the most inept. There is an irritating quality about the voice of the novel, an air of smug condescension, that makes it an easy book to dislike. Yet it cannot be easily dismissed. It is a large, insistent social vision of a continent–in effect, an anatomy of the New World–combined with the epic quest of a picaresque hero in search of a place to belong, a place where enlightened social expectations may be personally fulfilled. "America," here, is a place or condition discontinuous with the Old World. In America the potential of Western civilization, released from the suffocating strictures of history, has been realized–and found wanting. Without the ethical foundations of tradition, the revolutionary ideal provides little more than a context for deceit and scope for new dreams.

Using the name Phil Branden, Grove writes with such conviction in an insistently autobiographical mode that the narrator's name seems little more than a pseudonym. Because the voice of Branden is so convincing, and because it alludes to facts from Grove's life outside the narrative, many took this novel to be Grove's own story in light disguise, a misconception he did nothing to correct. Curiously, his supposed autobiography, *In Search of Myself*, for which he won the Governor General's Award for non-fiction, draws heavily on *A Search for America* for the "facts" of his fantasy account of himself.

Phil Branden is an immigrant of Swedish-Scots extraction. After arriving in Toronto before the turn of the century, he works and wanders, explaining himself to his readers, advising us on all manner of things that attract his eclectic mind. After discovering graft as an omnibus-waiter in Toronto he travels south. In New York, where he becomes a book salesman, he uncovers rampant hustling and becomes involved in fraud. For someone of such insufferable worldliness, his naïveté is sometimes alarming, although never portrayed with enough humour to make him endearing. He tramps westward; works in a factory; lives the life of a hobo; works at farm labour for a young millionaire, to whom he explains socialism; travels north, back to Canada, to teach, to explain life to others less gifted than himself, and to write.

The guise of social philosopher is not unusual for Grove. In *The Master of the Mill*, his social vision is apocalyptic. In *Consider Her Ways*, it is satiric and somewhat prophetic. In his earliest writings, it is largely implicit, reflected in his declared personal values and habits. In the farm novels, his social vision is codified and structured by the conditions of agrarian society. Only in *A Search for America* does social commentary run through the novel in parallel with the narrative flow, reinforcing the novel's epic intent and enlarging the narrator's experience. It is not Grove's quasi-determinism (man has free will but ultimately what befalls him is beyond his control) that makes this the brooding, powerful novel it is: all of Grove's writing explores such paradoxes, most in an equally sombre fashion. Nor is it his rather simplistic notions of socialism. Nor is it the prose: in this novel are some of Grove's most awkward dialogue and stilted diction. Rather, the enduring success of *A Search for America* grows out of the search itself and the epic vision it conveys: the fusion of personality, place, and event encompasses a whole society.

Fruits of the Earth. Toronto: Dent, 1933. Toronto: McClelland and Stewart; New Canadian Library, 1965. Pages: 271. Paperback.

Abe Spalding, Grove's most Promethean hero, is almost as much an entrepreneur as he is a pioneer settler, despite his close association with the land. In this chronicle of a district in Manitoba from 1900 until shortly after the First World War, Grove focuses on the man at the epic centre. Through shrewd judgement and obsessive devotion to the task, Abe Spalding amasses wealth and power. He eventually owns a huge tract of land, the most prosperous spread in the district. In the process, he becomes increasingly out of touch with time and nature, and with his wife and children. Eventually rejected even by the voters of the district, the myth once again becomes a man. At the novel's close, Abe Spalding is a benign remnant of a time before machines, when man and nature were protagonists worthy of each other.

Novels of the family farm are the Canadian version of Greek tragedy. In a context where territory and personality are interdependent, where social and natural orders merge or clash, where genealogy determines continuity, where enforced intimacy provokes perverse and passionate responses, the family farm provides Canadian writers with tremendous possibilities for weighty drama. In Matt Cohen's contemporary rural worlds, this potential is richly realized, as it was in Grove's novels. Between these two, there have been dozens of writers in the genre, including de la Roche, Stead, Ostenso, Ross, McCourt, Bruce, Buckler, and Wiebe. It is primarily a male preserve: it deals emphatically with a system of patrilinear primogeniture. In the most significant exception, Ostenso's *Wild Geese*, a female character in fact destroys the tyranny inherent in such a system.

Fruits of the Earth anticipates other concerns central to Canadian literature. It is now popular in Canada to discover our indigenous mythologies but also to de-mythologize our past in order to repossess and/or exorcise it. Grove does both, particularly in this novel. Abe Spalding is the prototypical pioneer of the Canadian West; he is larger than life and more believable than history (the name Abe is appropriate). He is also brought down, brought into a more human perspective, in the end. He is not tragically destroyed, but sadly reconciled to the loss that time and pride have brought upon him.

Fruits of the Earth is a chronicle and inevitably follows a historical, sequential structure. Grove is concerned with cause and effect, with the progress of the human struggle through time, with the process. The character of Abe Spalding does not develop; it enlarges and then collapses. Other characters are extensions of Spalding's personality; they are opaque or fragmentally intense, according to their relationship with him (not his perception of them, which tends to be diffuse). (Of all Grove's novels, only in *Two Generations* and *The Master of the Mill* do a variety of characters come into sharp dramatic focus. Even in *Our Daily Bread*, where John Elliott's relationship with his children dominate the narrative, it is the old man himself who remains always the strong central presence.)

Fruits of the Earth has about it an unmistakable epic quality. Always ambitious, Grove deliberately attempts to bridge specific history and universal truth. The grandeur of effect is occasionally off-putting, and is flawed, in places, by awkward prose. But it is as powerfully moving today as it was when the novel first appeared.

The Master of the Mill. Toronto: Macmillan, 1944.
Toronto: McClelland and Stewart; New Canadian Library, 1961. Pages: 332. Paperback.

This is Grove's most intellectually pretentious novel and, curiously, his most naïve. *Consider Her Ways* is more intellectual: it brims with scientific details about ants, details worthy of the most ardent myrmecologist, all to provide the subtle substance of a satire on human nature. But *The Master of the Mill* is a sombre attempt to blend, in a narrative context, a deterministic social philosophy (which Grove does not entirely understand) with a prophetic vision (about which he is ambivalent). The effect is monumental: this novel is huge, sedentary, and largely irrelevant, like a statue of a horse-soldier in a modern urban park.

By far the most complicated of Grove's novels, it is also the most aesthetically ambitious. The plot includes the lives of three generations and is presented in an apparently random, discontinuous fashion. Senator Sam Clark, near the end of his long life, is the epic centre. The narrative voice is always in the third person and invariably, no matter what the focal perspective, that of the self-conscious author. Sam Clark is the middle generation of a family that controls an agro-industrial colossus. He seems to represent the family's conscience; Rudyard, his father, contributed ambition and the unscrupulous opportunism upon which the mill is

Nova Scotian. Sam Slick is a clever, vulgar, and conniving demo-
crat, an American chauvinist, a huckster, and a folk philosopher.
The narrator is an innocent abroad, a bit of a gull, a bit pompous,
and an eager pupil; he is anxious to learn about the natives of
this vaguely familiar place so far from the centre of the world.

Like so many satirists, Haliburton is a social reactionary. He
wants to reform society by returning to an ideal that never existed.
In Sam, Haliburton has created the perfect voice to air his causes
and ridicule the peccadilloes of his times. It would be intolerable,
though, for Sam to aim his wit and cunning directly at the folk he
so easily manipulates and carelessly passes judgement on, and
equally intolerable for him to address the reader with such impertinence. It was therefore necessary for Haliburton to provide
an intermediary – the unnamed English gentleman to whom the
Yankee clockmaker extols his vulgar democratic principles and
expounds upon deficiencies in the Bluenose personality.

The bland Englishman is ridiculed for his naïve assumptions of
superiority. And Sam is a figure of ridicule for his appropriation
of all things good and beautiful to the American way and for his
utter lack of refinement. It is the Nova Scotians, however, upon
whom Haliburton lets loose his most vigorous barbs. He speaks
for thrift and industry and against greed and indolence, sometimes intruding, in his own voice, to urge his countrymen towards improvement. Through Sam, he argues for such causes as
a Halifax-to-Minas Basin railway and predicts that Saint John
will be the eventual rival of New York City. More accurately, he
anticipates a bloody American Civil War.

As with the best work of this sort, the satire remains effective
even when its apparent object is no longer of importance. Human
nature is a lamentably stable commodity, and it invites instructive
ridicule as much now as then. The verbal play in *The Clockmaker* –
the punning and double-entendres and insolent colloquialisms – no
longer amuses as perhaps it once did. However, the aphoristic pronouncements on everything from government to domestic relations, while somewhat antiquated in their utterance, remain
astute. Sam's indelicacies and deceits are appalling; his sense of
humour remains ribald, coarse, and caustic. The serious themes,
concerned with social stability, social progress, slavery, economic
development, and the precarious future of unbridled democracy,
remain as sobering as ever, if somewhat wrongheaded by present

standards. What dates the Sam Slick stories most, it seems to me, is the burden of expectation placed upon them.

The Old Judge. London: Colburn, 1849. 2 volumes.
Ottawa: Tecumseh Press, 1978. Pages: 358. Paperback.

The Old Judge is a different work entirely from *The Clockmaker*. There is humane warmth and gentle humour throughout these stories. There is no less wit, no less versatility of language or sense of ridicule; nor is there diminished social conscience or assumption of Tory rectitude. The prose is less frenetic; the insistent aphorisms are largely dispensed with; the abrasive Yankee presence has been discarded. Some of these pieces were originally published in magazines (as opposed to newspapers) and their pace is drawn-out and leisurely. Their different purpose, too, is quite evident. Haliburton temporarily divests himself of the reformer's mantle and takes on the role of benevolent public scribe. Satire is the dominant mode of *The Clockmaker*, while humour characterizes *The Old Judge*. The former is scathing; the latter, tolerant, benevolent, affectionately amusing and amused.

   The Old Judge, otherwise titled "Life in a Colony," describes Nova Scotia society in the early-to-middle nineteenth century. As a record of its time it is without peer. It provides copious information and insight into the legal, political, theological, and commercial institutions of the day, into various trades and professions, into relations between classes and sexes and among peers at every level. Although it is not a travelogue, it describes, with meticulous care, certain homes, buildings, towns, bits of countryside, and social events. As Haliburton notes in his Preface, his observations might be applicable to almost any part of the Maritimes, but they would not extend to Upper and Lower Canada. His book is an account of a particular people, the Blue Noses or Bluenosers (people, he notes, aptly named after a superior type of potato). His purpose, he proclaims, is to define their peculiarities. The effect, through the imaginative quality of his art, is to make them universal. In *The Clockmaker*, on the other hand, characters tend never to rise above the level of generalization.

   There are several voices in the narrative. Haliburton's is there, of course. He shows no desire whatsoever to refine himself out of existence: the Conservatism, the tolerant condescension, the acute social awareness are his. The author is also represented by a persona within the fiction, a visitor from England who stops off to tour the colony on his way to New York. He is a gentleman–decent, inquisitive, well-informed, pliant, and bland, and both the observer and the receiver of offered information and anecdotes. There are actually two principal narrators: Mr. Barclay, an acquaintance of the traveller and a member of the provincial Bar, and the Old Judge, Mr. Justice Sandford, retired from the Superior Court of Judicature to Elmsdale, his country home. The only other significant voice is that of Miss Sandford, the Judge's attractive niece and companion. There are, as well, all the voices within the various stories of characters who speak for themselves in the dialects of their place and trade and class. Haliburton has a grand talent for relaying the qualities of speech that distinguish one character from another, yet making each a representative of his type.

Humour predominates, but each story is unique in mood and purpose. Some are affectionate descriptions of people and places, with just enough curmudgeonly cynicism to prevent them from being sentimental. Some, like the Old Judge's rollicking anecdote of a court case early in his career, "How Many Fins Has a Cod?", indirectly illuminate complex social procedures. Others ridicule them: "Asking a Governor to Dine" parodies the pretensions of society and exposes, in caricature, the types that inhabit its upper reaches. In "The Keeping Room of an Inn," Haliburton spins out tales, from haunting to ribald. "The Witch of Inky Dell" has that same ominous wit found in some of Washington Irving's stories, while "The Seasons" seems as poignant and precise as a Breughel painting.

Haliburton describes a callow man's face as looking like the inside of a spoon; he parodies a learned man's discourse, and captures the awkward compassion in a decent man's address. He uses irony to elevate ordinary description, and he descends to slapstick or farce. In all, he exercises an uncommon versatility. Perhaps *The Old Judge* is more self-consciously Canadian than *The Clockmaker*, more honest to a particular time and place, as the best art is. It is written less to instruct and admonish with satire than to reflect what the author saw of his own home ground and record for the general good the humour it invoked in him.

ROBERT HARLOW

Scann. Port Clements: Sono Nis Press, 1972. McCelland
and Stewart; New Canadian Library, 1977. Pages: 307.
Paperback.

Harlow is a first-rate craftsman whose novels seem to plummet
into the abyss of obscurity between popular acceptance and critical acclaim. Only *Scann* shows resistance to the fall, but it survives more as an esoteric hybrid than as a literary masterpiece.
Harlow's main problem seems to be his love of words, his passionate appetite for a hundred words where one will do. Even the most
grisly or exciting scene suffers from a density of verbal obfusca-
tion that makes it merely interesting. And he knows too much
about the art of fiction. *Scann* reads like an exercise in form and
technique; it is invested not with conviction but with the writer's
commitment to craft; there is no passion except for Harlow's obvious desire to do things well. Yet *Scann* is an important novel,
well worth the effort required to read it.

In *Scann*, Harlow illustrates the elasticity of the so-called realistic mode. Forty-eight-year-old Amory Scann, editor of the twice-
weekly *Chronicle*, is ensconced for the long Easter weekend in
1969 at the Linden Hotel in Linden, British Columbia. Through
Scann, the author creates a welter of different, interpenetrating
realities. The novel envisions an ideal unity of consciousness in
which dream, memory, myth, allegory, invention, history, and actuality come together in Scann's rather feckless personality. Each
is a dimension of reality on its own; yet not only do they share
characters and locale, there is also movement among them. They
all, ultimately, exist only as extensions of the perceiving mind–in
this case, Scann's.

Out of Scann's allegory of Canada and creativity, which is set
in a context of bizarre rituals and told to the chambermaid as a
questionable prelude to seducing her, issues the second wife of
Thrain, who dominates the realistic novel Scann is writing about
the town's mythic origins. Thrain's first wife, Erica, who ran the
very hotel where Scann is writing, comes to life, in Scann's imagination, as she might have been in 1919 while her husband was
off in the bush with trapper Linden. The struggle for survival
between Linden and Thrain that winter is vividly told–their story

is Scann's novel in quest of a communal identity that he can co-opt for his own. The transition between fiction born of history and the fictional character who is creating what has already happened is effectively accomplished; Harlow repeatedly traces the genealogy of events from writer to pen to words on paper to narrative inevitability to occurrence – and back again, to the hotel room where Scann sweats his way through the created worlds and the real ones enclosing him.

Harlow also offers a novel within the novel, a real-life documentary. Scann accounts for his war experience in England, out of which his interest in the town of Linden originates. During the Second World War, he became enthralled, according to this account, with Wing Commander David Thrain; he later travelled to British Columbia as a reporter to cover David's trial for the murder of his stepmother, Amantha (Thrain's second wife, from the allegory), with whom he and his foster brother, Ro Linden, were lovers. David was acquitted and became the MP for the area. As Scann writes about him, in 1969, he is still a member of Parliament.

There is much going on. Everything is neatly compartmentalized, yet distorted by the interpenetration of realities; no critical description could convey the real achievement of the novel, which is one of form rather than content. What the stories are about is wildly imaginative but less important, despite their graphic, bizarre, erotic hyper-realism, than how they relate to the solitary Scann, the man at their centre. Harlow uses Scann's consciousness as a context within which to break down the structures of linear time, of historical continuity, and of rational sequence. All things, his novel insists, can happen at once – the past can be present, and the present can also be past. There are no separate realities, the novel argues, only perceptions of reality, and no barriers between what is imagined and what is.

There is some very grisly writing in this novel, as in the sequences in which Thrain amputates parts of Linden's putrescent flesh, or when the dead wolverine's head, impaled on Thrain's arm, glowers up at him with rotting eyes. There are grotesque scenes: Philippa Morton's dog emasculates her lover during orgasm; the priest baptizes an Indian infant while it is still descending from its dying mother's womb. There are poignant moments associated with Erica Thrain, whom Scann seems to create in tender response to the needs of his own inadequate personality. There is humour, some of it wildly absurd, some touchingly humane. There are moments of inventiveness that leave the reader breathless, and there is an understanding of invention, of creative function, that draws our admiration. There is a joy in articulation that, even when it distracts from the narrative flow and diminishes Harlow's achievement, provides ancillary pleasures of considerable magnitude. In all, *Scann* is a rare accomplishment–not so much a good novel as a novel that aspires to greatness and dazzles, even as it fails.

CHARLES YALE HARRISON

Generals Die in Bed. New York: Morrow, 1930.
Hamilton: Potlatch, 1975. Pages: 269. Paperback.

The title expresses a soldier's cynicism, but it is one of the few places in this powerful war novel where such judgement is evident. Harrison presents combat with a disarmingly bland directness that precludes moral reflection. Few novels match this one's grim austerity of passion as it describes the most appalling horrors of war. It is an eyewitness account too terrible to allow the embellishment of sentiment and moral purpose.

Quite possibly the best novel in English to have come out of the First World War, *Generals Die in Bed* enjoyed brief celebrity in the early thirties and then faded into obscurity. It had none of the romance of Hemingway's combat sagas, which could sustain the imagination of people sickened by war. Only indirectly did it challenge readers to consider the moral implications of strategic slaughter. It permitted no cathartic release through heroism and tragedy; its readers could not rise above the degradation it described. It is written in prose so spare that it reads like a précis of the Apocalypse, so dispassionate that it could be an officer's dispatch from the front (instead of a soldier's memoir issued out of the mud and blood and putrefaction of the trenches). The style is simple, direct, unpretentious: words are concrete, sentences brief, paragraphs so short they follow a staccato rhythm down the page, echoing the inexorable onslaught of the war they describe. Ambiguity rises out of what is left unsaid, from the spaces and the silence. Invention and imagination seem irrelevant in a world so bizarre and overwhelming.

The action is described with the authority and tentative immediacy of a first-person account related entirely in the present tense. Authenticity is paradoxically reinforced by the anonymity of the narrator. In style and form, Harrison was far ahead of his time; now, when the sensibility of the reading public would be more open to the hyper-realism of his vision, he is virtually unknown.

Unlike so much of the Canadian fiction to come out of war, Harrison's novel is not built around either a complex moral question or a picaresque hero. Rather, it is a straightforward chronicle of the narrator's experience at the Front. The story starts when the narrator and other Army recruits are shipped out from Montreal and ends when he is transported away from the Front, wounded, after the battle of Amiens in 1918. He is an ordinary man, brutally dehumanized and yet as human, in the end, as he was when it all began. He and his cohorts kill thoughtlessly and die ignominiously. They follow orders. There is no alternative, no better option. More emotion is expended on lice infestation than on a comrade's death. Conscience is aroused more by a corpse floating in the clean water of a river than by the wanton slaughter of surrendering prisoners.

Harrison's novel is so restrained in judgement that it is impossible to tell the allies from the enemy – except that some are shot at and some shoot. The officers, and the imperial powers they serve, seem the ultimate enemy, for they have the power of choice, and they choose death. The sacrifices they make so magisterially are not their own lives but the lives of the young men who die at their command. Harrison's novel is an indictment of war and of those who make it happen. It is a disturbing testament, and a terrible reminder.

JULIA CATHERINE (BECKWITH) HART

St. Ursula's Convent: or The Nun of Canada.
Kingston (Upper Canada): Thomson, 1824. Sackville:
Mount Allison University, 1978. Pages: 208.

This is the first novel published in what is now Canada by a native-born Canadian. According to the author's preface, Hart was seventeen when she wrote it. After a careful reading, there is no reason to doubt the sincerity of her claim. *St. Ursula's Convent* is an awkward and unpolished romance; its sprightliness and its lurid inventiveness suggest adolescent naïveté more than adult abandon. While it is by no means a good novel, even by the tolerant standards of melodramatic romance, it holds the reader's attention; amazingly enough, it manages an ingeniously contrived and complex plot with relative aplomb. Do not expect much insight into the author's times, or the period fifty years earlier about which she writes, for her novel is clearly conceived as an entertainment with moral highlights and nothing more. Surprisingly, it is still good fun to read, a modest but not unworthy beginning to our fledgling tradition – one of several.

The contrivances of Hart's plot are sometimes inadvertently hilarious, so determined is the author to work in every cliché of the genre. There are not one but two accounts of exchanged infants; innumerable false reports of death; various accounts of piracy and peril at sea; a most unlikely confinement underground in a Mexican silver mine; switchings of names and identities; and so many conferrings of titles and estates by inheritance that even the writer seems at times confused and has to restate lengthy genealogies to sort it all out. Hart is fascinated by titles, and in her pursuit of them she is necessarily forced to carry much of her plot across the Atlantic to curiously unpopulated romantic versions of France and England. The shift makes little difference to her account of polite society, but it does provide time-lags in communication to enhance her plot; as well, there is a large body of water to be traversed, in which all manner of splendid and terrible things can happen – and do.

Despite the title, Adelaide de St. Louis is the dominant character. She is introduced after her family history has been sufficiently given and sent almost immediately off to a convent school in Quebec at the age of twelve. There she meets Mother St. Catherine, who tells her a melancholy tale of the loss of her husband and children. Adelaide also meets Charlotte Turner. In her late teens, she returns with the Turners, who have just received an inheritance, to England for a visit. There Adelaide is betrothed to Lord Dudley, who has a perverse admiration for his own sister, Lady Louisa, while Adelaide, in turn, actually prefers Lord Grenville. Some French visitors arrive, among them the Count de Bordeaux, whose story occupies the middle section of the novel. Then, in the third section, a Canadian wet-nurse reveals her sordid story and all falls into place. Briefly: the French count is Mother St. Catherine's lost husband, and several of her children (one she did not even know she had!) are restored to her; Adelaide turns out to be the real Lady Louisa, and vice versa; thus can each marry her preferred lord, and incest and other unpleasantries are neatly avoided; Adelaide/Louisa's father comes into an estate, which allows him to leave Quebec for resettlement at his ancestral home in France. In the end, everyone in this Canadian fable leaves the New World for the Old, there to find enduring happiness.

Hart takes great delight in relating her tale and makes up, with youthful charm and enthusiasm, what she lacks in art. In fact, the artlessness of the novel is perhaps its most endearing quality. From Hart's perspective, true happiness could only be found in the make-believe worlds of England and France. That was an inviolable part of her colonial conditioning. *St. Ursula's Convent* was published by subscription; ten copies were assigned to A.J. Beckwith of Fredericton, surely her father, while only one or occasionally two were committed to others on the published list. It was a modest undertaking, and it is rather pleasing to know how pleased she might have been that there are a few who still know of her work.

DAVID HELWIG

The Glass Knight. Ottawa: Oberon, 1976. Don Mills: General; New Press Canadian Classics, 1983. Pages: 192. Paperback.

The Glass Knight slipped into print almost unnoticed, but it will not slip as easily into obscurity. It is a fine and quiet novel about self-consciousness and sexuality; Helwig uses language beautifully, as a poet might, to expand the emotional lives of his characters rather than to define them. Helwig writes with disarming simplicity and a poet's confidence in the power of plain words and clear syntax. He communicates far more than meaning or emotion: he communicates actual experience, with all its baffling ambiguities, its subtle intensities, its poignant absurdities. He is unafraid of silences. The vast spaces of possibility that lie between words and the phrases or images that startle, yet seem inevitably right, he moulds to his characters' lives with unerring precision.

Perhaps anticipating the impressionistic indulgences such a poetic use of language invites, Helwig maintains a third-person voice for both major protagonists. Yet he attains a rare immediacy. Robert Mallen is a divorced man of about forty who lives in Kingston, Ontario, where he works as an editor for the university press. Elizabeth Ross is one year past being a student; she is on a curiously private sabbatical that allows her to read, think, and keep a wary distance from involvement with the world, men, and reality. Robert and Elizabeth meet, and an affair slowly takes shape despite the various impediments: their age difference; her frigidity (born of an ugly abortion); his ex-wife and children; the occasional merging of their identities; his inability to see her, or anyone, as whole outside himself; her fear of being overwhelmed, subsumed. Yet there are rare moments of joy and intimacy, almost love, between them. In the end, she flees, perhaps to the unthreatening comfort of lesbian affection, and he, perhaps, to his former wife – allowing their love to grow unencumbered by actual presences.

No other novel has so well captured the tender and the terrible subtleties of sexual politics from both sides. Occasionally, the dialogue is awkward, but that is because it is so lifelike, so authentic. There are clichés, as in the opening sequence of photographs, but they are always turned in upon themselves. The drama of the affair, caught in the nuances of language, is amplified by the recurrent references to the FLQ crisis and the Trudeau debacle in the autumn of 1970 and made substantial by the vivid presence of the Kingston setting. *The Glass Knight* is unassuming; but then so is the cry, from underwater, of someone drowning.

Helwig's next novel, *Jennifer*, picks up the story of Robert's wife: the two works relate like obverse sides of a coin. *Jennifer* is not a sequel or complement; it is simply another side of things, Jennifer's story. Robert appears only as a secondary character; Elizabeth does not appear at all. Helwig is a versatile professional, adept at radio and television scripts, at popular fiction, documentary, poetry, and the short story; as in all of his writing, more happens here than at first appears. The calm, deliberate prose and pared precision of his observations of behaviour give the protagonist's involvement with a mental patient, with her lover, her daughter, mother, and estranged husband, a muted drama of moving intensity. *Jennifer* is perhaps a more complete novel in terms of character and plot development, but it shows somewhat less subtlety and wry intelligence than *The Glass Knight*. It is nonetheless a worthy successor.

Since 1981, Helwig has come out with such a plethora of fiction, the mind reels. Two more works, *A Sound Like Laughter* and *It Is Always Summer*, have been added to the Kingston novels to form a casually linked quartet. Others, including *The King's Evil* and *The Only Son*, have also appeared. The former is a tightly knit and intricate yarn, the latter rather a careless novel about the presence of the past. Helwig has the capacity to be one of our best writers, but his recent work betrays such urgency to see print that quality suffers. When a cigarette is described in the opening pages of *The Only Son* as a "slim white tube" through which a character "sucks fire greedily to make it burn," there is evidence enough that Helwig should slow down a bit and attend to his talent with the care and integrity it deserves.

PAUL HIEBERT

Sarah Binks. Toronto: Oxford, 1947. Toronto:
McClelland and Stewart; New Canadian Library, 1971.
Pages: 155. Paperback.

Humour is more subject to the vagaries of individual taste than
are most types of literary expression. This work is an excellent
case in point. It will move some readers to tears of laughter, others to a tight grimace of dismay. Can there be humour in names
like Professor Marrowfat, Miss Drool, or Dr. Taj Mahal? Certainly
there is little wit to them, but possibly, as verbal equivalents of a
pratfall, they are comic. Is the inflated appreciation of a bad poet
amusing for only a paragraph or two? Is bathos redeemed by
Hiebert's remarkably droll examples of the poet's work? Is the
fictional biography of the "sweet songstress of Saskatchewan"
informed by academic condescension? Or is it delightful and
insightful parodic nonsense of the first order?

In the form of a critical biography, Hiebert offers the life and
poetical works of Sarah Binks. The "life" is an inventive parody
of the academic critical biography. Binks is a ludicrous figure; so
are her previous biographers, and so are her friends and family –
and her readers. Preposterous are the idyllic antecedents of her
childhood on the farm, which Hiebert traces through motif, image,
and symbol in Binks's poetic works. Incongruous and bizarre are
the critical controversies and inflated trivialities through which
the poet's story is unravelled. Hiebert knows intimately the nature
of pedantry and of prairie chauvinism; he exposes them with mali-
cious glee. His work is not subtle in style or detail, nor is it meant
to be.

But there is genius in *Sarah Binks* – in the poetry itself. Hiebert
has written some of the world's best bad poetry. Only consummate skill with language and a thorough understanding of poetic
principles could deliver up such gems:

> Horse, I would conjecture
> Thoughts that spring in thee;
> Do, in contemplative hour,
> Teeming doubts thy soul devour,
> As in me?

or

> Oh, it's time for this and it's time for that,
> For mending unending and tending the brat . . .

or

> Should maddened pterodactyl chance to meet
> With raging crocodile,
> Then crocodile the pterodactyl eat
> Or pterodactyl eat the crocodile.

The poems are spread through the "life," and they draw wit and irony from their context. Some are related to the poet's childhood in North Willows, Saskatchewan; some to her dog, Rover; some to the hired hand, Ole; some to her Grandfather Thurnow, around whom a critical controversy has arisen. (The extent of his influence on – or possibly authorship of – certain of Binks's poems is open to question.) Each poem is accompanied by scholarly apparatus, bibliographic notations, evidence of academic infighting. Ultimately, Sarah's story is ephemeral: pedantry suffocates the parody of pedantry. But the poetry will endure.

JACK HODGINS

The Invention of the World. Toronto: Macmillan, 1977.
Scarborough: New American Library, 1978. Pages: 357.
Paperback.

Hodgins's fiction is regional in the very best sense of the word. With two fine books of short stories, *Spit Delaney's Island* and *The Barclay Family Theatre*, with *The Invention of the World*, and with *The Resurrection of Joseph Bourne*, Hodgins has given Vancouver Island a dimension of universal proportions. He re-invented the Island as a world of the imagination, made it accessible in a way that only fiction can. His Vancouver Island becomes as known to us as Buckler's Annapolis Valley or Ross's prairies. More so, perhaps, because Hodgins is a more ambitious writer.

The Invention of the World is an attempt to expose the fallacies of world laid upon world upon world by the conscious invention of its various inhabitants. At the same time, paradoxically, it tries to show reality as the sum of these various distortions. Moving easily from myth to history, documentary, fantasy, comedy, romance, and narrative realism, Hodgins adjusts his prose style to every perspective and every voice. He shapes a marvellous new world in the reader's mind, one not easily forgotten.

Strabo Becker frames the whole with his notes, tapes, and eccentric assumptions of intimacy. He addresses the reader in the second-person voice. Within this frame, Maggie Kyle occupies the novel's centre, along with her boarders in the former Revelations Colony of Truth. Donal Keneally, sired by a bull, started the colony some eighty years earlier, when he imported an entire village from Ireland. The pioneers of the Island, who speak their memories into Becker's tapes, illuminate the formidable struggle of history to fill in the gaps and discrepancies between mythic origins and present conditions. Meanwhile, Wade Powers with his fake fort reshapes the past to attract tourists. The people of the present–wild Danny Holland, sad, officious Cora Manson, and doughty old Madmother Thomas–bring loggers and town into continual, rambunctious conflict. Through it all, Maggie dominates–Maggie and Donal Keneally. And Strabo.

Hodgins creates memorable characters by shrewd definition of detail. Maggie Kyle and Donal Keneally exist in different dimensions of the world at different times. Yet they are ultimately aspects of the same reality. She is as earthy a character as we have in our literature–many times married, fiery, proud. He is beautifully unreal, born of a myth, swaggering, staggering into the Island's history and Maggie's life. The language surrounding him is rich with Irish brogue. Maggie's word-milieu has a realistic Island twang to it, evoking the setting rather than invoking it. Hodgins is an accomplished master of the shades and nuances that make language inseparable from his characters' lives. It is language, ultimately, that binds them all into the same compelling vision.

The Invention of the World has a certain indefinable looseness to it, which judicious editing might have eliminated. But there is such a febrile torrent of words, images, personalities, and modes of reality that such a job would have been formidable. It is not a perfect novel, but it is certainly one of the finest around. The invention of worlds is an imperfect art, God knows, but Hodgins has given us a fine approximation; he has provided all the ambiguities, raw vitality, and enthralling personalities of the real thing. Having been to his Island, we can never quite leave.

The Resurrection of Joseph Bourne: or, A Word or Two on Those Port Annie Miracles. Toronto: Macmillan, 1979. Scarborough: New American Library, 1980. Pages: 263. Paperback.

Despite the title, *The Resurrection of Joseph Bourne* does not have a featured protagonist. Rather, the north island town of Port Annie has a whole array of characters. They are certified as individuals by their unusual names, their behavioural idiosyncrasies, and their overwhelming influence on the narrative voice. In the beginning, the town has just suffered a sea change, the victim of a curiously benign tidal wave; in the end, Port Annie slips on a mud-slide into the sea. But it doesn't seem to matter much – Port Annie was only known to the reader at third hand, and its demise, even the death of one of the more important inhabitants, seems relatively trivial.

In this novel, Hodgins exaggerates some aspects of his early achievement and sacrifices others. His refined sense of the absurd, of different realities in sometimes hilarious and occasionally pathetic conflict, is exercised in abundance, but it is almost exhausted, at times, by snippets of rational explanation. Hodgins never makes his readers care about Fat Annie Fartenburg, or the Chamber-Potts, or Baldheaded Pete, or the Peruvian seabird, or Joseph Bourne, the world-famous poet in hiding; neither their personalities nor their situations are developed beyond the level of protracted sketches. Hodgins attempts to capture each character's consciousness in turn – but he does so from the outside, through a few verbal mannerisms repeated without variation. As well, the point of view flits nervously in search of coherence. The effect is inevitably splotchy. The voice changes paragraph by paragraph, yet maintains an incongruent third-person omniscience and brings the narrative perilously close to bathos. This tendency is counteracted by the story: little happens directly before the reader's eyes, everything is told obliquely in the past tense. The reader seems at several removes from reality, without the benefit of a mediating narrative voice or perspective.

Gone is the intensely vivid realism that made details of time and place leap into the imagination in the earlier books, and in its place is not some other form of hyper-realism, but a world of words and voices quite removed from reality of any sort. There is still the torrent of words, though, and of variant images piled atop one another, and of endearing improbabilities. But *The Resurrection of Joseph Bourne*, despite a Governor General's Award to its credit, must ultimately be counted a likeable exercise in authorial ingenuity. Hodgins's considerable reputation rests primarily on his short stories in *Spit Delaney's Island*, and with his brilliant first novel, *The Invention of the World*.

ABRAHAM S. HOLMES (A.S.H.)

Belinda: or The Rivals. Bagg and Harmon, 1843. Toronto: Anansi, 1975. Pages: 122. Paperback.

This cheerfully trivial sentimental romance cannot quite make up its mind whether it wants to be taken seriously or whether it is a parody of its type. It is, in short, a novelistic equivalent of its title character – a coquette. Not that *Belinda* ever risks undue solemnity; instead, it pontificates often and at length on virtue and vice, until the reader is almost convinced of its sincerity. Then mirth takes hold again and restores the titillating ambiance. Reading Holmes's novel is a disconcertingly pleasant occupation, although one feels a certain vague gullibility for being amused by such a bit of fluff.

Set in the Kent County region of southwestern Ontario, with many references to Chatham, the Thames, and Lake Erie, *Belinda* will surprise many readers of today with its presentation of genteel society in the 1830s. The area is not a backwoods enclave: Holmes describes a world of fine dwellings, carriages, commerce, and elevated company. Bearing in mind that his novel appeared only a year after *Wacousta* and nearly ten before *Roughing It in the Bush*, the reader cannot help but applaud its rare view of Upper

Canada, one that does not depend on the hardships of life for its effect, but instead celebrates social pleasures. Neither the refinement of manners nor the practice of virtue is subjected to the author's ridicule. Instead, his wit is directed at those who abuse the more civilized restraints. His novel is, at heart, conservative, even if its title character is a delightful wanton.

In a deathbed confession, Belinda decides that her fall occurred a decade earlier on the fifth of June, 1833, when she was still in her teens. She dies not because her conscience demands it, but because it is appropriate to the genre to do so, and the event gives rise to some fine maudlin prose. Between her fall and her demise lie the events of a wilful and wasted life, told with a mix of moral indignation and excited affection by a bachelor narrator who has no purpose in relating her story other than the pleasure of gossiping.

Belinda comes of good family and lives elegantly at Clifton Hall with her father, who is a wealthy landholder, her mother, a noble brother, Brock, and an exceedingly virtuous sister, Sophia. She is attended by numerous suitors, and in their attentions lies her downfall: she so relishes their lovemaking that she encourages them all, until, one by one, they discover her duplicity. Even the one Belinda truly wants marries another in the end. Publicly shamed, Belinda takes to offering popular lectures on morality and other methods of raising the spirit. Eventually, she falls in with the lascivious Bickerstaff; shortly before meeting her husband, she conceives little Ichabod. Her husband, Theodore Unwin, is somewhat nonplussed when the baby arrives not two months after their wedding.

Holmes's prose is ideally suited to sentimental romance and contains just a twist of irony to suggest parody. The spoof itself comes not so much from language or sentiment, however, as from plot. Despite her repentance and death, Belinda seems quite triumphant throughout. No sooner do the tears of humiliation dry than she is back to acting the coquette again. In a different age, she might have been a nymphomaniac–or, more likely, an anarchist. If she is a loser, she is a thoroughly audacious and charming loser. She is perhaps less significant than her narrative context, from a present perspective, yet she is a genuinely effective literary creation. *Belinda* is a first-rate minor work of Canadian art.

HUGH HOOD

White Figure, White Ground. Toronto: Ryerson, 1964.
Don Mills: General; New Press Canadian Classics, 1983.
Pages: 246.

It is difficult to evaluate Hood's contribution to literature, partly because his own public estimation of himself is so overwhelmingly and disarmingly inflated that normal procedures of critical judgement are thrown askew. However, the real problem lies with the writing, not the man. *White Figure, White Ground*, his first novel, is an excellent example of Hood's strengths and weaknesses in uneasy alliance.

As fictional realism, *White Figure, White Ground* is conventional and rather awkward. The characters seem motivated from outside and tend to be stereotypes. There is the questing artist, Alexander MacDonald, in search of himself and the meaning of life; his wife, Madeleine, a worldly, aggressive, and well-born Québécois; Ellen, a demure ingénue and MacDonald's affectionate second cousin; Claire and Blanche, his elderly aunts; Abe Shumsky, his Jewish agent; his father, who died too young, an underachiever. The use of setting is similarly uninspired: a small town in Nova Scotia, MacDonald's ancestral home, to which he returns on his quest; Toronto; then Montreal; and then, by implication, New York, Paris, Planet X. The relationships around which the narrative is structured, and the plot, which follows Alex through the therapeutic creation of a special pair of paintings, are not particularly engaging. Hood's prose is, at best, serviceable. Voice and point of view self-consciously swing from first person to third in the service of rhetoric. Syntax is direct and simple; the language conversational. His imagery avoids the ornate and extravagant; symbolism arises casually out of the context.

In some ways, the context seems to be an insufficient foundation for the metaphysical epic adventure, which is the novel's real goal and purpose. Most novels ultimately reveal the author's vision of life, or what is often called his "world view." But Hood's novel bursts at the seams with an entire philosophical system, as he struggles with art to subdue the ineffable. He is not looking for answers: he is in no doubt, as the rest of us are, about the nature of absolute truths. His problem is how to convey them.

Worked carefully through the novel are a number of key motifs. Numerology—and particularly variants on the number three—informs the novel's structure and its underlying message. The traditional and liturgical values of colours are clearly enunciated. Light, with all its symbolic and literal implications, is exploited through all levels of the novel—narrative, aesthetic, theoretical, and spiritual. Motifs of incest, of Catholic doctrine, of geography, are used in Hood's epic quest.

Alex is in retreat at Barringford, Nova Scotia; he paints a picture called *Light Source No. 1*, layers and layers of white on white. It is recognized by his wife as a major painting and a turning point in the artist's life. But Alex is compelled to paint *Light Source No. 2*, in which tones of black are relieved by a hint of "comical" green, which only he and his cousin Ellen can see. It is in this vision of hope, signified by the green, that Alex redeems his own state in a fallen world. Beyond the darkness, there is hope—despair, even death, are only phases in the divine comedy. Life, then, is a relative affair: it is what we make of it. That which on the literal level is compromise is, on the level of doctrinaire Catholic theology, an affirmation.

The allegorical intent and the narrative realism in this novel do not always seem compatible. Madeleine and Ellen, for example, are demiurge and inspiration on one level, wife and temptress on another, lover and confidante on a third. And Hood is not entirely in command of who is what, when. Still, for its ambitious attempt to reach beyond the conventional domain of contemporary fiction, Hood's novel must be commended. With one exception, *You Can't Get There From Here*, the rest of his longer fiction suffers from the problem of integrating idea with art until, in his cycle-in-progress, *The New Age*, aesthetic proprieties seem virtually abandoned.

You Can't Get There From Here. Ottawa: Oberon,
1972. Don Mills: General; New Press Canadian Classics,
1984. Pages: 202. Paperback.

As if to expunge from his system all the enticements of literary invention before setting out on his twelve-book cycle, *The New Age*, Hood wrote *You Can't Get There From Here*. This novel quite brilliantly fuses horror and humour. The perversely sinister is wedded to satire and to occasional high comedy, providing a sardonic vision in which the absence of moral authority leads to anarchy – a nightmare inversion of how the world should ideally be. It is a clever novel of ideas that avoids the usual pitfalls of linear argument. Hood creates a spatial structure in which a dozen subplots expand towards completion and the characters interrelate as individuals caught up in affairs larger than themselves rather than as ciphers in a dialectic presentation.

Capitalizing on the apparent proclivity of Canadian writers to write about Africa, Hood sets his novel in the fictional West African country of Leofrica, where biculturalism runs rampant. In his rendering of Leofrica, much depends on popular Canadian misconceptions about such countries. Hood's purpose is not the revelation of political affairs or the African experience, but illumination of a perverse moral vision.

The novel is divided into three sections. The first is related in a documentary style, but with covert irony and overtones of the absurd. Anthony Jadeb, whose regime in the newly independent state is chronicled from inception to dissolution, is the focal centre of the entire narrative. In this section, his country and his cabinet are formally introduced. In the second part, the terrible treacheries of his closest colleagues, of his lover, and of the international powers – Russia, the United States, and the Chinese/ Albanians – become apparent. The narrative perspective, the voice, seems increasingly subject to the developing chaos. In part three, events seem to overtake narrative control; they tumble over themselves until, in an ending at once bathetic and appropriate, Jadeb dives into the mud on the bottom of the river that separates his country from the rest of the world.

Jadeb is a good man, too innocent to cope with a fallen world. The Albanian ambassador shows equal integrity, as a representative of anarchy, and he eventually wins out. All else is duplicity. Russians and Americans, for example, vie rather nastily with each other for the fealty of Leofrica, but covertly they brutally undermine their own efforts, each hoping to saddle the other with responsibility for the pathetic little nation. Three dominant motifs of the novel sardonically affirm the corruption of the world: money – the Leofrican ruble-dollar commands $0.00 on the American exchange; excrement – the natural element of the moral Yahoos who betray Jadeb's trust; perverse sexuality–consummation is related intimately to treachery. These motifs draw the narrative fragments together into a vision of moral anarchy that profoundly illuminates, by implication, a truly moral universe.

You Can't Get There From Here provides ample evidence that Hood is quite capable of complex narrative design and of the creative fusion of idea with aesthetics. It displays his command of language and style, his wit, the range of his imagination, and the depth of his emotional insight. It illuminates his sense of the absurd, of the sublime, of the outrageous. It is a fascinating novel. But it never rises far beyond the level of prelude–it is a sophisticated five-finger exercise.

The New Age/Le nouveau siècle (to date consisting of: **The Swing in the Garden**. Ottawa: Oberon, 1975. Pages: 210. Don Mills: General; New Press Canadian Classics, 1984. Paperback. **A New Athens**. Ottawa: Oberon, 1977. Pages: 226. Don Mills: General; New Press Canadian Classics, 1984. Paperback. **Reservoir Ravine**. Ottawa: Oberon, 1979. Pages: 238. Don Mills: General; New Press Canadian Classics, 1985. Paperback. **Black and White Keys**. Downsview: ECW, 1982. Pages: 298. Don Mills: General; New Press Canadian Classics, 1985. Paperback. **The Scenic Art**. Toronto: Stoddart, 1984. Pages: 284. Paperback. **The Motor Boys in Ottawa**. Toronto: Stoddart, 1986.)

Only the title of this novel sequence is bilingual. Hood's proposed cycle of twelve interlocking works insists on defining for us our time and place in twentieth-century Canada. How it turns out as a work of art depends in good part, then, on what events befall the author and the world, as seen from his perspective, over the next two decades. The first six novels in the series are out; the others are due, inexorably, at regular intervals until the series and the century are simultaneously complete. *The Swing in the Garden* (1975), *A New Athens* (1977), *Reservoir Ravine* (1979), *Black and White Keys* (1982), *The Scenic Art* (1984), and *The Motor Boys in Ottawa* (1986) are worth consideration individually and as a group: the appalling arrogance their separate visions convey reveals also a marvellous talent struggling to emerge. They have such promise that the completion of the sequence may yet justify their impertinence.

Hood has abjured the formal elements of the novel entirely. None of these novels has a very coherent narrative shape or structure. There are numerous motifs, but these are reference points; they provide the perimeters of each work, but are not elements in an organic system. The philosophical basis of Hood's vision is given as axiomatic: he does not question reality or explore it, he defines it. The narrative voice is not merely omniscient; it is omnipotent and omnicentric. Loosely threaded along a linear sequence of time are the observations of minutiae, past and present, that attract the author's attention, and which he meticulously renders for the reader's appreciation. There is no discernible motive for the accrued details: they are not present to generate mood, nor to further action, to develop character, or to illuminate idea. Perhaps an overall shape will emerge. Hood declares the cycle is a work of genius: perhaps, when it is complete, we can better evaluate his judgement of his own achievement.

The recording persona in the sequence is Matt Goderich, although his father, Andrew Goderich, dominates half the novels, to date. In *A New Athens*, the second novel of the cycle (to pick one as representative of the rest), Hood records Matt's post-adolescence as an architectural history student during the early fifties. Matt specializes in the Canadian vernacular tradition, seen from the carelessly rendered perspective of 1966. Primary focus has shifted from Toronto to Brockville, which Hood persists in calling Stoverville despite nearly obsessive verisimilitude and his disconcerting habit of naming all other places in the immediate area by their actual names. Matt marries into the Codrington family and proclaims to us, his readers, the joys of young love and innocence, of marriage, of in-laws, of eccentricity, and so on. Through this litany, Hood piles fact upon fact upon fact – about the landscape (giving Latin names of common flowers), about the society and history of a small segment of eastern Ontario, from Brockville north to Westport. The novel closes with a curiously contrived account of Matt's mother-in-law's apotheosis as a visionary artist.

As in the other novels in *The New Age*, there is a scattering of first-rate set-pieces in *A New Athens*. Yet, on the whole, it is strangely unevocative of the times and places it records. This is perhaps due to the suffocating presence of Matt Goderich. Since he provides the reader's perspective on the world, it would help if he were somewhat more self-critical and self-analytic, more aware of himself as a person rather than a persona whose greatest fan is his own creator. Matt's father, Andrew, is a more appealing and dynamic presence. The project they animate, on the whole, is speculative in conception, but with an obsessive archival intent. At the very least, it will be a curiously intimate documentary account of one man's eclectic experience of himself.

HAROLD HORWOOD

White Eskimo. Toronto: Doubleday, 1972. Markham: Paperjacks, 1973. Pages: 278. Paperback.

Horwood spins tales for purposes that are never obscured by narrative subtlety, yet are admirably sustained by the manner of their telling. This novel recounts a legend. The style is sometimes stilted; characters converse in rhetorical debate; the author's conscience is disruptive. The message is clear: into the ways of the Eskimo and the North, white Christian society has introduced destructive ideas and customs, values and laws; as a result, natural society will fall into extinction. It is not an original thesis, and it has been treated with greater authority and far more literary sophistication by writers like Bodsworth and Theriault, Houston and Roy. Yet in spite of the rhetoric, Horwood is devastatingly convincing. *White Eskimo* overwhelms the reader with seductive intensity, with vigour and conviction. As a novel, it has severe limitations; as a document, a protracted fictionalized essay, it is highly effective.

Esau Gillingham dominates the novel. He is a great, noble visionary, a revolutionary-reactionary who is determined to save the peoples of the Arctic east coast. His story is told on board a northbound ship. Gillingham is described as a great man, in sympathy with all humanity, and a great hunter. With his song-brother Abel Shiwak, he leaves the acquisitive whites in Nain and their vicious preacher, Reverend Manfred Koch; they travel deeper into the north and at Okak Bay they found a fur-trading empire. Gillingham makes legendary forays northwards, marries an Eskimo girl, adopts a half-breed girl, and prospers, until Abel is shot dead. Gillingham is tried for his murder in St. John's. He is acquitted, but serves three months for selling liquor to "natives." The half-breed girl, meanwhile, is taken from her mother by a self-righteous do-gooder. She flees the mission school and ultimately dies of exhaustion. In the end, Gillingham's wife conceives and the hero heads for the Land of the Dividing Waters and vanishes into his own mythology.

Gillingham's life is a quest, a "journey in pursuit of itself." He seeks nothing on his own account. He is a great seeker of truth for those, the Eskimos and Indians, who are still within its reach. His story is large, but it is not epic, for while he comes to the North as a saviour, a Messiah-figure, his story does not merge with the story of the people he would save. He becomes like them, but not of them. In the end, his apparent transcendence does nothing for those left behind.

The author is realistic, even though his fiction leans heavily towards romance. He accepts that there is no turning back, no redemption. His novel is more an indictment than a lament. It is an argument for the prosecution rather than a plea for the victim. As Horwood allows it, there is no defence.

JANETTE TURNER HOSPITAL

The Ivory Swing. Toronto: McClelland and Stewart, 1982. Pages: 252. Toronto: Seal, 1983. Paperback.

The Ivory Swing is not at all what the reader might expect. Although set in India, it is far from being exotic and lush. In fact, the prose is taut, terse, and very precise; imagery and emotions are both handled with restraint. (While in India, I was told that Hospital did not understand India. Reading her novel after my Indian colleagues had read it, I discovered that the problem of understanding is a major concern in *The Ivory Swing*–India for the outsider is within reach in so many ways, and yet it remains beyond comprehension. It seems to me that the author has an excellent understanding of the barriers between what the Westerner experiences in India and what the Indian might know to be the truth. *The Ivory Swing* is certainly not the novel of a native Indian; it is quite unlike the work of Narayan or of Rushdie. Nor is it a novel of the Raj: this is not a variant of *The Jewel in the Crown*. Nor is it the work of an informed outsider like Forster, for whom India becomes metaphor.) *The Ivory Swing* describes India as the context for a confrontation between a woman who does not belong there and the veiled enigma of her innermost self. It is a novel of the spirit; it is a feminist novel, a novel of conflicting ideas debated at the level of the soul.

The plot is denominated by the central image of an ivory swing. This image, as a motif, is not simple: it suggests a pendulum, never at rest; it suggests ambivalence between polarities; it suggests poise and suspension, the maintaining of delicate balance over an abyss; it suggests art, the precarious and immutable condition of an aesthetic creation; it suggests, through antithesis and rhythm, human sexuality; it suggests, in the fusion of stasis and motion (ivory carved to exquisite beauty and the flow of its arc through the air), the confluence of an instant and eternity; and finally it suggests the illusions of choice, when antimonies are fixed to the same axle.

Juliet loves David and she loves their children. She cannot release the past (Jeremy); she envies the freedom of her sister (Annie); her spirit is nearly extinguished by life as an academic wife in Winston, Ontario. Sabbatical leave for David to do research in the south of India offers – what? Solace. Diversion. Escape. Perhaps a crucible to test the mettle of marriage, of personality, of self-worth.

Most of the novel is set near the South Indian town of Trivandrum on the estate of Shivaraman Nair, where the Canadians live in a well-appointed house in remote isolation from other Westerners. Juliet is very much the focal centre of the novel. The few people she meets become our principal contacts or points of intersection with India itself. There is the beautiful widow, Yashoda, who also lives on the estate, whose innocent sensuality draws others to her, especially men, until she is destroyed by them. There are Prabhakaran, the servant boy who becomes part of the family in violation of the rules of caste and custom; Matthew

Thomas, the prosperous low-caste Christian; Prem, the Marxist student; and Shivaraman Nair and his family, high-caste Hindus who are locked in timeless tradition and belief and whose privileged position depends on the maintenance of established order. Others are background, fragments of the surrounding five hundred million people, inseparable from the fetid climate, the luxuriant growth, the foulness of poverty and waste. In this world, this alien context, Juliet struggles against the impositions, the humiliations, the psychic mutilations committed upon herself by custom, tradition, moral righteousness. She rages against the evident perversities of India and struggles to understand. But she is too sensitive and intelligent, and too much the prisoner of her own cultural conditioning, to accommodate India any more than it will accommodate her. Ultimately, she participates in the murder that is the direct result of this clash between worlds, between old and new, East and West, male dominance and woman's defiance. She achieves a conditional release from the past in the end–sanction to be herself.

This is a thoughtful novel, bringing the reader into the midst of narrative meditations about the nature of being; about perception and reality, the relativity of absolutes, the intractability of the human spirit; about spiritual pride, the relations between men and women, the nature of power in relations between the sexes and in relationships between the sexes; and about the necessity of revolution, qualified by the fear of anarchy, the fear of loss. It is a love story, though between whom is indeterminate. It captures with exquisite precision the impact on sensibility and on common sense resulting from a sudden shift among worlds. From beginning to end, *The Ivory Swing* is captivating fiction, and well-deserving the major award it received as the third winner of the annual Seal Books prize of $50,000.

It is also a quite imperfect novel on a number of counts. There is a carelessness in the way Hospital arbitrarily changes voice and point of view–narrative integrity is violated, and we have the feeling, in suddenly perceiving reality from within a minor character's mind, that the author has lost control. There is a false quality of burlesque in some of the Winston segments (no doubt based on Kingston), yet quite remarkably she has a "Canadian" character at one point say she does not know where Kingston is! A faculty-wife episode is a dismal cliché, and a university party episode suggests neurotic self-importance on the part of the author rather than anything much at all about Juliet. Finally, and this is minor, perhaps, but not negligible – Juliet and David are not *from* anywhere. They are apparently Canadian but there is no sense of a specificity of origins in relation to either character. Not being "from" anywhere, they are not "real," not in the sense that narrative reality is otherwise sustained throughout the novel. Where in the West does Juliet speak from; she is candid, colloquial, intensely curious, but without an originating context her presence continually threatens to dissipate. The strongest character in the novel, she has the same elusive impact on us as the unmasked host at a masquerade.

Place, on the other hand, is brilliantly evoked. Place and time in India, if not in Canada, merge as a single entity. Place and time, Juliet's consciousness and her emotional condition, are all inseparable in India. There is a lugubrious quality to time there, as seasons pass without dates, only weather; instead of numbers and labels, there are descriptions of the heat and humidity. And curiously, the precise descriptions of this small opening in the Indian geography refuse any sense at all of their connection to the rest of the world or even the rest of India. This place is exact, remote, and immediate – like a nightmare.

Borderline. Toronto: McClelland and Stewart, 1985.
Toronto: Seal, 1987. Pages: 290. Paperback.

We have come a long way from Margaret Laurence. I do not mean that unkindly, or that Laurence has not been among the best writers of her time. But suddenly, reading *Borderline*, I realize how far that time has gone from us. Now we live in another world, one where *The Stone Angel*, like *Pride and Prejudice*, is a transcendent artifact. Transcendent, yes, a fine work of art; but an artifact nonetheless, a token of the past.

Borderline is the present. It is a representation to the future. It is a novel of such maturity, a novel exuding such literate confidence, the reader thrills to the fact that a fiction like this has become possible. Hospital is in command of her medium: she makes me think of Hubert Aquin and some of the brilliant things he was doing with narrative before his inevitable and untimely death.

She makes me think, as I observe myself entangled in her labyrinth of stress and expectation, of Jorg Luis Borges and, consequently, of how far literature has come, and how far it goes. That is enigmatic, I realize, but so is Borges, along with being a master of his craft; and so is Hospital.

Reading *Borderline*, I am aware of myself reading. But such knowledge in no way interferes with the intensity of the narrative, the fidelity of my response. Whether I as reader set limits to the text or am a cursor within it, moved about by a will more canny and determined than my own, it is hard to say. The narrator himself, after all, tells a story beyond the possibility of his knowing, and he is also a character within the story, subject to the conditions and limitations he as narrator allows himself. So, if he can both contain a narrative that is larger than himself and move within it, then why should not the reader do the same? The narrator is a piano-tuner who cannot resist occasionally taking a turn as conductor. Hospital is the composer, of course, but Jean-Marc Seymour seemingly usurps her role at times. Appropriating her authority, he invents her novel before our eyes, a conductor spontaneously re-creating the music for us that only he can hear.

With *Borderline*, Janette Turner Hospital has moved into the aesthetic and philosophical realm of postmodernism, and she has done so with such panache there is no one writing in the country to match her. Unlike Robert Kroetsch, for whom postmodernism is a literary device, albeit one superbly used, and unlike Audrey Thomas, who in *Blown Figures* uses it as a psychological correlative, or Margaret Atwood, who drifts into postmodernism in *The Handmaid's Tale* and as casually slips away, Hospital works with utter confidence and grace in the postmodern mode. This is quite incredible, given that her first two novels, good as they are, in no way anticipate the nature of her achievement here. *The Ivory Swing* occasionally suggests a lack of narrative discipline, as the point of view at times wanders quite erratically; and *The Tiger in the Tiger Pit*, while exploring different narrative perspectives with dazzling precision, lacks clarity of intent and betrays an uncertainty of narrative purpose. *Borderline*, however, is not in the least tentative or haphazard. Nor is it experimental (in the conventional sense of a testing, to see if something works). It shows confidence comparable to that of Borges, Calvino, Barth, in its refusal to separate the philosophical tenets of postmodernism from the formal or aesthetic. It is a vision of angst and anarchy – can the postmodern be otherwise? – conveyed in language, form, and narrative indeterminacy that are its inevitable embodiment. Form does not follow function: form *is* function, and function, form. The what and the how of the novel are virtually the same – can fiction be otherwise when the conventions of both life and art are apparently in chaos?

Jean-Marc Seymour tells the story. But his father's sometime model and former mistress, Felicity, lives it. And so, to a lesser degree, does Augustine Kelly, a philandering life-insurance salesman from small-town Ontario. At a border crossing, Augustine intersects with the cosmopolitan Felicity, who grew up motherless in India, parentless in Australia, misunderstood by maiden aunts in Boston, where she now lives, who has travelled widely, loved passionately, studied in depth, especially art, and more especially art of the fifteenth century, and is very beautiful, runs an art gallery, and never lets her lovers stay the night. Actually, she never brings her lovers home. In a chance encounter, these two unlikely conspirators spontaneously collaborate in the rescue of a Central American refugee, an illegal immigrant hidden inside a frozen carcass of beef who will otherwise be caught by the border authorities and disposed of, as the law determines. This is the beginning, only the beginning, of a strange and marvellous account.

Jean-Marc, a year later, after the disappearance of Felicity and Augustine and the refugee woman known as La Magdalena (named by Felicity after a picture by Perugino in the Pitti Palace), re-creates what happened. He describes the extraordinary and the usual with equal dispatch, deferring always to Felicity as a future reader of his narrative, sure she will reappear and confirm his version of her life, her reality. He presents the most enigmatic of occurrences, the weirdest convolutions of improbable coincidence, with the same earnest flair as he describes the innermost thoughts and memories and dreams of the lovely, troubled, terrified Felicity and of the pathetic Augustine.

Jean-Marc tells it, but it is really Felicity's story. *But* Felicity's story is really Jean-Marc's, for he invents it. He dreams her private world for us, for himself, for her. Again and again as the fiction progresses, he reminds us that what he says is fabrication. And this Felicity he creates, and her bizarre world of intrigue and terror and arbitrary connectedness, nonetheless, are authentic–more so, paradoxically, than Jean-Marc and his denials. Art supersedes life (but, of course, Jean-Marc is himself art, and he and his world in turn supersede our own: the fiction is more "real" than our world outside the text). This is one of the more impressive achievements of postmodernism: to set narrative reality against our own, and show our capacity to sustain it as the truth, despite our certain knowledge of its invention. No matter how explicit Jean-Marc may be in admitting the impossibility of knowing what could really have befallen Felicity or what could be within her mind, we still accept his version of her as "real," still plunge with her through the narrative despite his interruptions. We tolerate his lapses in decorum–because he is the necessary condition for her presence within the text.

He is, of course, a worthy presence in his own right. Hospital makes brilliant use of her piano-tuning narrator to convey the vision of a world where ethical determinism goes hand in hand with moral chaos: a world wherein there is no choice in what we do nor any measure of its worth. This is the world Felicity lives in, dreamed for us by a piano-tuner who knows just when to defy the exactitude of the tuning fork for the intuitive feel of truth, when to trust the inner ear of his imagination over the probabilities of fact and circumstance.

I have not been evading story or character in considering this novel, but rather trying to show the primary source of its astonishing impact. Characters, in fact, are superbly drawn. Some, like Felicity, are fully rounded, with rich interior lives, and some, her aunts Norwich and Ernestine, for example, are caricatures. Yet all work well, appropriate to the different depths or dimensions they occupy in the narrative. The story is complex, fast-paced, and exciting, much akin to a spy thriller or a murder mystery: there are bodies and beatings, trysts and travel, suspense and intrigue, though related on such a literate plane that habitual readers of such perversities might find themselves quite out of their element. And holding all together, the dreamed, the dreaming, the dreamer who writes it down, is what might be called the "textual consciousness," the personality of the text.

This personality originates with the author, but is quite independent of her as a person. It is highly articulate, and shows no hesitation in grounding the narrative, for all its postmodern élan, firmly upon literary tradition. This is a very literate novel. And this personality is evident in the prose of the novel, which is beautifully wrought and filled with startling metaphors and provocative analogies. It is there in the horror and the warmth and the hurt of its vision, and in the sophistication and the cosmopolitan breadth of experience, which inform the novel from first word to last.

Borderline, in my estimation, is among the best novels in English of a new age, one barely upon us but infinitely promising. Hospital writes so well, here, that as a critic I am disconcerted by admiration, even while, as a reader, my sensibilities are enthralled by the power of her achievement. *Borderline* is a novel of exceptional quality, offering the reader exceptional worth.

JAMES HOUSTON

The White Dawn. Don Mills: Longman, 1971.
Scarborough: New American Library, 1972. Pages: 267.
Paperback.

No one writes fiction about the far North with more authority and enthusiasm than James Houston. His adult novels, such as *The White Dawn*, *Ghost Fox*, and *Spirit Wrestler*, and his many novels for young readers teem with authentic details of Eskimo life. During the twelve years he spent in the Canadian Arctic, Houston lived with its native people. His fiction conveys his profound affection for them and his great respect for the old ways that are passing. Houston's juvenile novels take the form of tales, each recounting an adventure between man and the frozen wilderness. His adult novels are more like sagas, chronicling the lives of people who must struggle constantly to stay in harmony with the natural world merely to survive.

Houston's adult fiction uses plot mainly to provide a narrative context for the detailed documentary descriptions that are the outstanding feature of his work. The inherent drama of arctic life, as the author records it, takes precedence over aesthetic artifice. His most effective expository use of the Eskimo point of view appears in *The White Dawn*, in which the plot is related with intriguing subtlety. Three New England whalers gradually undermine the traditional values of a remote Eskimo camp. Ultimately, in a frenzy of self-preservation, the people of the camp violate their own codes and commit the terrible atrocity that anticipates their demise.

Until the climax, no single event stands out. The Eskimos pursue their precarious existence, changing camps and adapting their hunting patterns to each new season. Their way of life, meticulously described, dominates the narrative. In the background, however, Houston shows the outsiders inadvertently abusing Eskimo hospitality to the point of threatening their survival. Only when it is too late for the common good are the strangers eliminated.

The White Dawn is set on West Baffin Island, from May, 1896, through to July, 1897. The Eskimos have had little to do with white civilization, but as the title ominously implies, a new era is inevitably dawning. Apart from brief log entries, which establish the dramatic situation at the beginning and end of the novel, the narrative is recounted by a young Eskimo, Avinga. Being crippled and the adopted son of Sarkak, the proud and powerful chief, Avinga is privy to information and events normally outside a young male Eskimo's experience. His special status makes him an effective narrator. As the Eskimos struggle to accommodate the strangers, Avinga describes the subtle effects of their outlandish behaviour on camp life. At times the whites, one of them darkskinned, one fickle, and one well meaning, appear grotesquely stupid and barbarian. When they cook meat and fish, Avinga sickens at the stench. He is shocked to witness a kiss, although copulation is openly and frequently enjoyed in the communal beds. He is appalled at the outsiders' insensitivity to traditional ways. From the Eskimo perspective, they become increasingly offensive. With horror, Avinga accepts the necessity of their execution after they have violated not only hospitality but nature, as well.

Houston describes life among the Eskimos in dignified prose that rises occasionally in flights of epic exuberance and enthusiasm. He makes no attempt to simulate the Eskimo language in English, but creates authenticity through his superb command of subject materials. Occasionally the irony of his adopted perspective is a little heavy, for the reader obviously shares more with the "barbaric" outsiders than with their Eskimo hosts.

However, this is a minor flaw in a novel of passionate intelligence, a novel that moves unhurriedly through dense and beautiful descriptions towards a conclusion that speaks to and for whole civilizations as they clash in the elemental arctic barrens.

Frozen Fire (1977). *See* Canadian Novels for Young Readers.

PERCY JANES

House of Hate. Toronto: McClelland and Stewart, 1970. Toronto: McClelland and Stewart; New Canadian Library, 1976. Pages: 320. Paperback.

This novel is a chilling family portrait, an antidote to all the sentimentality the genre invites. Janes conveys the relentless oppression within the Stone family with single-minded determination. Vivid insights accumulate into impoverished Newfoundland life in a small mill town during the Depression, and into the rude prosperity of the same place a generation later. Always, the Stone family dominates the narrative; always, Saul Stone, mean, ignorant, despised, dominates the family.

The narrative voice captures well the vicious onslaught of the Newfoundland tongue on the English language; makes it ring with a crude delight all its own. Language provides one of the few bright aspects of the novel, for the author-narrator's memories are bleak. Yet, despite the bitterness and hostility, Janes captures a certain harsh vitality that makes his novel a perverse celebration of the family he describes.

The novel is effectively structured. In the first half, each of the six children dominates a chapter; the remaining three chapters in the first part belong to their parents, Saul and Gertrude. The chapters overlap: details accumulate as the same period presents itself from each new perspective, yet there is virtually no redundancy. Janes sustains firm control and creates a rich, allusive family context.

Each of the children is, inevitably, unique; and yet none is outstanding in any particular way. Ank, the oldest, is stolid and sullen.
Hilda (or Flinksy, as she is called) is the only girl. She suffers
least from their father's malice but bears a grudge as long as any.
Racer moves fast, as his nickname implies, and fights brutally
with Saul. Crawfie works hard to compensate for lack of imagination and becomes a teacher. Juju, the narrator, is sensitive and
articulate; he is the only one, ultimately, to escape, first to college
and then "away," to Canada. Fudge, the last born, is fat, frightened,
indolent.

In the second half, Juju returns home at the age of forty. Again,
a chapter is given to each of the children, though there is none for
him. There is no need. In the first part, Janes described their growing up: in the second, he evaluates what they have become. Or
rather Juju does the evaluation. He does not give much attention
to himself, an outsider now, although his judgements are often
self-revealing. Of all the children, only Hilda has achieved anything approaching happiness. Misery and bitterness rule the
others' lives. Old Saul dies, and the narrator leaves.

There is pride in the telling of this story. It is a family portrait.
And it is unique in our literature, both for its innovative form
and, curiously, for its artlessness.

SUSAN KERSLAKE

Penumbra. Toronto: Aya Press, 1984.
Pages: 144. Paperback.

This is prose of tortured genius: the prose is tortured, and in the
agony of its dismemberment there is genius. This is not poetry. It
is poetic, often, in that it sometimes makes no literal sense yet
holds together with a fierce intensity, coherent through the sheer
force of words fused in the furnace of the narrative mind, and
makes sense on many levels simultaneously but not on any one
alone. It is prose, not poetry. Kerslake makes the language sing,
but in the exercise of her imagination, not to serve the song. Her
words never reach for more than their context allows: significance

comes through limiting their meaning, deciphering their intent, not by opening to them or going with them. The language is strangled, not set free; cut up, served piecemeal, each word severed from the others, from its other meanings, other usage. We do not spin out from Kerslake's text into possibilities of response. We close in, centred on a vortex that ultimately contains her very private vision, one that we can only guess at.

In one of the silliest and most demeaning promotional gambits in some time, the Canadian Book Information Centre recently appointed three jurists to select the best young fiction writers in the country under the age of forty-five, as of 1986. I shudder to think what other criteria for selection there might have been—gender, perhaps; ethnicity or ethnic origin; region; height (in centimetres). One wonders that jurists Margaret Atwood, Robert Enright, and Beth Appeldoorn would lend themselves to such an enterprise. Their list is silly and does not bear repeating. But one name on it, sandwiched among such established writers as Matt Cohen and David Adams Richards (forgive them their youth) and neophytes like Paul Quarrington and Sarah Sheard (who may yet prove worthy, given time), is that of Susan Kerslake. On the basis of two novels, a handful of short stories, and a few slim volumes of poetry, she ranks with the best. The irony is, she really does. If "Forty Five Below" achieves nothing else, it provides Kerslake with deserved exposure on a national scale.

Her first novel, *Middlewatch*, is fine, for a first novel–the kind one attaches the word "promising" to–and files in the mind for future reference. It is sincere, overwhelmingly sincere. It tries so hard that language twists into tight knots of latent significance as the author works through her narrative toward the illumination of a vision that is touching, evocative, and ephemeral. Kerslake lives in the Maritimes and writes of rocks, trees, wind, and the sea. She writes of haunted souls and loneliness and tender gestures of defiance against the treacheries of being human. Reading *Middlewatch* is moving; you want it to be better than it is.

Penumbra is better. Readers of a particular bent will find it absolutely first-rate. Few novels written in Canada can match it for the diffuse beauty of its prose, for its stunning elliptical structure, its elusive brooding moodiness, and its sinuous imagery in which concrete and abstract, literal and figurative are bound in disconcerting harmonies. It is a novel to be savoured by readers who love the feel and taste of words, their sound and texture, their weight on the page and in the mind.

Set in a place called Lune, hard by the sea and close to an unnamed whaling town, some time deep in the last century when the chase for whales was paramount, *Penumbra* casts light on shadowed people at the edge of the world. The main character, who sometimes narrates and sometimes is eclipsed by episodes from other lives, is a girl-woman caught up in the sadness and the ecstasy of this strange and isolated place. She observes herself, observes her family, father, mother, young brother Colin, and observes the rest, her aunt, the people in town, the whalers, her lover, and the lunatics all around her. She lives in an "islanded" place (I borrow the word from the dust-jacket note, for one cannot be sure that Lune is an island rather than just a place accessible only by water, by a water-journey from another world). On Lune her father runs an asylum. One cannot be sure who are the inmates and who are not. Perhaps they all are: Hebel, who carries the sea within him; Serenna, Mercy, Coffin. There are grotesque deaths, the bleeding of a corpse, the hacking of ice to make graves, the shark-ripped agony of an old man at sea. The narrator's father perhaps murders Hebel, holding him close until the sea sets him free.

Much of the narrative attends so intimately to details of the moment that there is no movement, only a heightening of awareness. Sometimes, intruding upon the timelessness are episodes of utmost haunting beauty: the brief account of Hebel's childhood; the story of John and Sarah, the narrator's parents; her love affair with a young whaler, who inspires her devotion and ships out to sea; the washing down of an old woman's corpse. These are not narrative intrusions, for this novel does not develop as a progression. Rather, it moves towards wholeness, towards fulfilment of a vision, and these episodes are markers, like stars in a constellation. Within them, among them, lies the whole of what Kerslake has to offer us. Even without fully comprehending what it is she shares, it is enough. We are struck by her generosity, though we do not, perhaps, understand the gift.

W.P. KINSELLA

Shoeless Joe. New York: Houghton Mifflin, 1982. New
York: Ballantine Books, 1983. Pages: 224. Paperback.

It is a lovely irony that the Great American Novel of our times
should be written by a Canadian. It is ironic, and perhaps fitting,
for who else but a sympathetic outsider (from, say, Alberta) could
hold such a naïve, touching, and courageous vision of America. This
is not the United States, the U.S.A., that Kinsella writes about;
not the brawling obstreperous military-industrial brutish bully
the world has come to loathe as emblematic of all our ills in these
closing years of the millenium. This is the antidote, the other side.
Shoeless Joe is America the way *Huckleberry Finn* is America,
the way Hemingway's Nick Adams is America. *Shoeless Joe* is
about baseball and dreams and the will to believe, about love and
wonder and the power of imagination to transcend reason, time,
and yes, even death. *Shoeless Joe* is a sheer delight to read. It is
very weird, quite surreal; and yet the more improbable it gets,
the more eagerly do we reach to accept. It is very calming, yet
exhilarating. Like baseball. There is genuine magic in Kinsella's
vision of America, and baseball, and reality. I cannot think of a
novel I would rather live within; and I am utterly un-American
and have had little interest until now in baseball.

I am still not enthralled with baseball itself, but rather with
the author's astounding enthusiasm for the sport. Kinsella's obsession is not merely infectious, it is invasive. This is perhaps the
most obsessive novel I have ever read. It displays a single-minded
fascination with baseball that overwhelms the reader, reducing
even the most dour and jaded, I would imagine, into a sort of manic
submission, so that we relish every detail of the game, every
analogy drawn from it, every anecdote spun out from it, in spite
of the excesses. It would seem impossible for a game to mean and
be so much. Yet Kinsella achieves the fusion of baseball with life
itself, especially in America. He makes us love the game no matter how indifferent we may have been to it, or thought we were.
More accurately, so beautifully and wholly is Kinsella's novel committed to the sport that we love, perhaps, not baseball but the
splendid passion for being alive that his own love for it conveys.

Kinsella's obsession is inseparable from his narrator's; so much so, in fact, that they share the same surname. Ray Kinsella in the novel, who believes in baseball the way Moses believed in God, has an identical twin who is not among the chosen, who does not believe. It is as if the author subdivides himself and then lets imagination run free with the side that accepts baseball as a glorious absolute. Richard Kinsella is a carny faker, but Ray–Ray is *different*. One day on his Iowa farm Ray hears a voice, and the voice says: "If you build it, he will come." It is the voice of a ballpark announcer, and without further ado Ray knows what he has been called for, and who will come. He is to build a baseball stadium in his cornfield, and when everything is ready Shoeless Joe Jackson, possibly the best left fielder ever to play the game, will play on it.

It is 1979. Shoeless Joe and seven other White Sox players were banned from the game for life, for throwing the 1919 World Series. He died in 1951. But no matter, he will come. Ray builds his diamond with only a left field, and he builds bleachers in the left field, behind the place where Shoeless Joe will, and does, appear. Ray and his young daughter and his wife Annie watch games at night. Karin can see even more than Ray, and Annie accepts her husband's vision as if it were her own. Gradually, more players shift from spectral to substantial, at least for the course of the game. Through Ray's love for baseball, anything can happen. Before the end of the novel, old players become young again, dead players come to life, the course of baseball history changes. Dreamers get a chance to play with the greatest, to fulfil their potential, to play out their dreams. The oldest living Chicago Cub, who hardly had a chance in the big leagues, gets another crack at it. Moonlight Graham, who played a single inning for New York on June 29, 1905, after a full life as a doctor in Chisholm, Minnesota, where he died, returns to the field. Ray Kinsella's father, who never made it out of the minor leagues, appears as a young man, behind the plate, and holds his own. In due course, Ray talks to him, deeply moved.

Although it is only given to some to see–those with faith in the verities of baseball and the imagination to see what they believe– Ray eventually opens his vision to the larger world. Between the first annunciation and the arrival of the crowds, there is a baseball odyssey across the eastern half of America that both Kinsellas, Ray and his author, invite the reader to share. Imagine, then, travelling with an American Don Quixote, and think at the same time of a young James Stewart, as he was in *Harvey*. Annie, back home, is June Allison. J.D. Salinger is Sancho Panza. Or Harvey. It is only confusing if you think about it. The fact is, the reclusive author of *Catcher in the Rye* comes out of hiding in the real-life world to participate as a character in Kinsella's fabulous fiction. Ray hears a voice that commands him to "ease his pain." He knows that "he" is Salinger and thus treks from Iowa to northern New Hampshire, via all the major-league ballparks en route, to kidnap the famous realist and take him to a ball game at Fenway Park in Boston. At first understandably reluctant, J.D. Salinger soon gets caught up in the dream vision adventure, and before long he is seeing and understanding even more than Ray. Eventually, it is he, not Ray, who is privileged to cross over, to accompany the players on the Iowa field when they pass through the gate at the end of a game–into what? Maybe J.D. Salinger will someday write about it.

As well as being about America as a metaphor for baseball, rather than the other way around, *Shoeless Joe* is about nice people: Ray and Annie and Karin, and J.D. Salinger, Moonlight Graham, Joe and his ghostly teammates. They are decent, wholesome, well-meaning people, and they are anything but boring. Sure, they are neurotic, obsessive, reclusive; sure, some of them are fakes, some are naïve, and some are dead. But they all believe in baseball, and on this common ground their lives take on a magic that is quite enthralling.

W.P. Kinsella writes with such ingenuous cheerfulness, and with such a sure command of language as a lived-in medium, that even when he acknowledges the dark side of life it is with tolerance, even affection. And when he writes of mysterious voices, transcendent visions, inexplicable forces in the lives of men and women (especially in the lives of men, for women are generally not fans, not to the same degree or in the same number–though certainly he allows that women can, and do, share the vision), he does so with such apparent candour and conviction that we, too, are ready to believe. He is, paradoxically, a superb realist: what could be more real than baseball. Like his hero–that is, Ray's hero–J.D. Salinger, he works language to make us genuinely love his creation. Fictional reality becomes superimposed on our own experience of the world: Holden Caulfield, Franny, Zooey; Shoeless Joe,

Ray, Annie; they are part of our experience of ourselves. Did Shoeless Joe ever actually exist? I don't know, but he certainly does now.

W.P. Kinsella is an amazing writer, with an imagination as literally phenomenal as his narrator and namesake, within the text. He has a vision of America that is benevolent, of humanity that is profoundly affectionate, and of reality that seems irrepressibly optimistic. But it is baseball, in this novel, that contains all else: baseball is religion, art, philosophy; it is emotion, idea, memory, and dream. Each game is a repetition of every other game, something you can count on; yet like snowflakes and separate lives, no two are ever quite alike. The world changes, people live and die, wars and depressions and scandals come and go, landmarks crumble, statistics accumulate, and the game stays much the same. Baseball is everything – and the love of baseball as Kinsella lives it is a glorious thing, indeed.

WILLIAM KIRBY

The Golden Dog. Montreal: Lovell, Corywell, 1877. Toronto: McClelland and Stewart; New Canadian Library, 1969. Pages: 321. Paperback.

The Golden Dog is a potboiler of high order, intended to sustain the reader's interest, remain true to the historical evidence, and deliver a message, all at the same time. The plot is structured according to the complex rules of gothic romance. Characters are stock figures of the genre; they show little depth and less complexity, even when involved in the most intricate set of relationships. Yet there is an aura of authenticity about Kirby's fiction, the result of his extensive research into the historical setting.

Kirby's story is set in Quebec in 1748. He carefully weaves fictional reality with the historical, intensifying the history and lending even the most bizarre elements of the fiction a certain verisimilitude. Bigot (the Intendant) and his mistress, Caroline De St. Castin, are drawn from real life. So are the basic conflicts between Bigot and the Governor, between the Grand Company and the Honnêtes Gens, between Jansenists and Jesuits, between representatives of La Pompadour and the allies of Louis XV. France and England are at war, on both sides of the Atlantic, but New France is falling apart from within. Using moral and political instability as a context, Kirby unravels a tortuous plot of doomed love and the triumph of evil.

Amélie de Repentigny loves Pierre Philibert. Pierre's father is eventually killed by Pierre's friend and Amélie's brother, Le Gardeur Repentigny; the murder blights their troth forever. Amélie flees to a convent, where she dies; Pierre dies in battle. Forcing the action along this tragic course is the lovely Angélique, whose passion for Bigot – and thence for Le Gardeur – drives her to seek the help of La Corriveau, a truly gothic sister of Satan. Angélique uses Le Gardeur to get rid of Bigot's most respected opponent, Pierre's father. Le Gardeur is thus condemned to a miserable and solitary life. Caroline is murdered, at the behest of Angélique, by La Corriveau, who is executed for a different crime. Angélique lives out a full, if somewhat perverse, life in splendid sin.

Kirby's fiction is so well wedded to historical conditions that the impending fall of Quebec seems an inevitable consequence of the moral turbulence Kirby portrays. That is part of Kirby's message: the fall was inevitable. And, by historical implication, the British presence was a moral necessity. The other and more important point he seems to be making is that the corruption and decadence, the social anarchy, were due to specific individuals. Freed of their past, the Québécois have become a worthy partner in the new confederation of Canada.

The style of *The Golden Dog* is occasionally excessive and always rich. While the novel shows considerable cultural insight and compassion, it offers little insight into the characters themselves. This is appropriate to the genre, but at times the reader craves subtlety and an occasional touch of elegant simplicity amid the dark, exotic shadows of the *ancien régime*. *The Golden Dog* is the best novel in English about Old Quebec/New France, and the best of its type written by a Victorian Canadian. It embodies much of the Victorian sensibility in its excesses, its odd sentiments, and its high moral purpose; but it is still a novel worth reading for its entertainment value alone.

A.M. KLEIN

The Second Scroll. New York: Knopf, 1951. Toronto:
McClelland and Stewart; New Canadian Library, 1969.
Pages: 142. Paperback.

Even in a tradition as strongly enriched by Jewish writing as
ours, Klein's novel stands out as a singular achievement. It is a
universal vision of the relations between man and his God, God
and His people. Other Canadian writers portray Jewish sociology and the Jewish psyche with more clarity, more irony, more
ambiguity, more wit. But none so well depicts the Jewish soul
and draws from it the essence of our common humanity. None
elevates the English language to such refined and sonorous eloquence or to such inspired purpose. *The Second Scroll* is rare visionary fiction by one of our finest poets; alone among Canadian works,
it offers revelations of God as well as of human destiny. It is in no
sense a modest work.

   Form and structure in *The Second Scroll* are quite inseparable:
what it is, and what it says, are the same thing. It is divided into
two main sections, analogous to the Torah and Talmud. Thus, there
are five "books" and five "glosses." The books are entitled Genesis,
Exodus, Leviticus, Numbers, Deuteronomy; they correspond, in
the story of Melech Davidson, with the books of the first and sacred
scroll. The glosses are not meant to be interpretive annotation.
They are esoteric addenda in which particular aspects of the story
are pursued outside the narrative context, for their own aesthetic
and moral worth. Circumscribing the whole is the organizing consciousness of Melech's nephew, a Montreal journalist assigned in
1949 to cover the emergence of modern Israel as a sovereign state.
Together, the whole constitutes a vision in which historical, theological, and spiritual dimensions work in a moving harmony that
seems discordant only when the parts are separated.

   The Second Scroll must be read as a whole: while it provides
great and moving pleasure on first reading, it does not come
together as a vision until it can be held in the mind all at once.
The brilliance of the prose, spare yet exuberantly demanding, suggesting Old Testament, Joyce, Hopkins, and the depths of conviction, compels the reader's attention. Klein, the writer, moves us;
but it is Klein, the visionary, who subsumes our recalcitrant souls,
overwhelms us with the depth and power of his vision.

Melech Davidson, whose given name means king, *becomes* his people. He is a messiah, and he is everyman. In 1917, the horror of the Russian pogroms turns him away from God. He assumes the role of zealot for the Bolsheviks. During the Holocaust, he climbs miraculously out of a pit of death, his faith reborn. He wanders. In Rome, the spiritual destiny of mankind is revealed to him; in Morocco, the unity of the species; finally, in Israel, God's covenant. Through his story, he becomes progressively more generalized until the nephew who has never met him discovers, at his grave in Israel, his presence as the spirit of his people. The Jew, restored to his proper place in the world's geography and with God, is once again the mediator between fallen man and the Almighty. Klein affirms the divinity of the human spirit.

As the five books build the narrative shape of his vision, the glosses relate in poetry, a letter, a play, and prayers its spiritual form, which has no shape, but *is*. If that sounds mystical, it is because that is the nature of such a work: it conforms not to the conventions of literature or logic but to the needs of its own being. As with all visionary works, *The Second Scroll* is entirely a thing in itself, yet wholly accessible to those who will work to hold it in their minds and immerse themselves within it.

RAYMOND KNISTER

White Narcissus. New York: Harcourt, 1929. Toronto: McClelland and Stewart; New Canadian Library, 1962.
Pages: 135. Paperback.

White Narcissus is one of the few novels to be enshrined in our tradition because of the promise it shows rather than for its own achievement. When Knister died in his early thirties, he left behind six novels (only two of which were published), scores of poems and short stories, occasional criticism, and a lasting influence on other Canadian writers. *White Narcissus* has major flaws, though it is not as pretentious or contrived as *My Star Predominant*, his fictionalized life of John Keats. While essentially realistic, *White Narcissus* fails to create convincing characters, and the action is arranged in static sequence. The ruminations of the protagonist seem interminable, and the language bogs down periodically under its own weight: "Richard Milne had never ceased to admire the peripety of life, its myriad fugacious shadings like lake tints which become more intricate to the sight with care in scrutinizing them." Such prose neither expands the possibilities of language, nor provides a precise definition of actuality. Neither does it elevate verbal simplicity to high art – all of which Knister, the proselytizing imagist poet, believed good prose should do. His legacy is not in his use of language or in his development of character and plot. His lasting gift is the radical conversion, the metamorphosis, of ordinary Canadian experience into art in the realistic mode.

There is much emotion in the novel, and little feeling. The reader is left outside the action, a passive onlooker, ultimately a bit dubious about the whole thing, a bit relieved at not being too closely involved. The whole is a metaphor for failed communication and the depleting frustration of solitude. Richard Milne returns to the small Ontario farming community where he was brought up by the Burnstile family. Now a successful novelist, he has come one final time to convince his childhood sweetheart, Ada Lethen, to go off with him to the city. She, unfortunately, is locked into a disturbing ménage as mediator between her parents, who have not spoken a word to each other in years. Richard's determined attempt to free Ada from the bondage of responsibility and the tyranny of her parents' hatred coincides with the eruption of Frank Lethan's rage. Lethan demolishes his mute wife's jungle of white narcissi, the only living thing she has warmed to, and the spell between them is broken. The Lethans speak. Ada is set free. Love prevails. As their name implies, the Lethans were in a deadly spiritual sleep from which they have been awakened by the power of love.

Knister's plot seems slight. It draws considerable substance, however, from motifs of the farming life, the creative process, the natural world, and communal society. The symbolism is carefully deployed to make themes of isolation, alienation, and renewal seem the inevitable adjuncts of the narrative situation. Imagery of the rural world is beautifully realized in *White Narcissus*, and that, above all, is the source of the novel's lasting importance.

JOY KOGAWA

Obasan. Toronto: Lester & Orpen Dennys, 1981. Pages:
250. Markham: Penguin, 1983. Paperback.

You read *Obasan* with a mixture of curiosity, shame, and horror.
This must be what a German feels, reminded of Nazi atrocities.
Oh, I know, we did not systematically murder Canadians of Japanese descent; but we turned the system against them–Canadian
government and law, bureaucracy and the public will. We made
some among us outlaws and turned the full force of our self-righteousness against them. This happened in the 1940s, but
Kogawa's fiction makes such grievous wrong from the past a presence still. We may forgive ourselves for what we did; but she
reminds us that we cannot turn away from what we are.

Obasan is fiction, document, and truth. It is a novel, first and
foremost. As such, it provides its own context: it does not depend
for its effect on what you know outside the narrative, on knowledge of the war or wartime conditions or the tenor of the times in
Canada. It uses the resources and conventions of the storyteller's
art to create a sense of authenticity. So well does it succeed in
this, it assumes the didactic force of a documentary in our minds,
even as it moves us through impact on our sensibilities. It relates
what happened in ways accessible to the imagination that a mere
accumulation of facts could never do. It is not an artifact of history but a vision of the truth, a vision of what it must have been,
and must be, to be a Japanese Canadian in a country that has
held the sovereignty of citizenship in such contempt.

Obasan documents the effect, when Canada arbitrarily abrogated the civil rights of tens of thousands of our citizens, on the
imagination of one young Sansei woman, a third-generation
Canadian, Naomi Nakane. And inevitably, since Kogawa lived
through those times as her character's contemporary, and as this
novel is the work of her imagination, it documents their effect on
her. As an artist she has turned darkness into light, illuminating
a most dismal episode in our collective past with temperance,
compassion, and controlled rage. She is not Naomi. That is clear
from the beginning, for Naomi through the narrative only gradually becomes convinced that such things are not better left
unremembered. Not so Kogawa, who makes of Naomi's evasions,

in confrontation with various shards of memory, her own as a child and those of people close to her while growing up, the most discomfiting of art.

Obasan, for all its darkly lyric beauty, is sometimes a clumsy novel. But paradoxically its clumsiness is inseparable from its achievement: there is a disconcerting juxtaposition maintained throughout between the poetic quality of Kogawa's prose and the awkward, tentative development of the narrative. It is as if there is so much to say but uncertainty about how to say it–because of the enormity of events and the necessarily limited perspective of the narrator. Naomi tells her own story, opening with a touching description of the last time she visited her uncle, who raised her with his wife, Obasan. It is August, 1972, a month before he dies. The novel closes with an excerpt from the memorandum sent by the Co-Operative Committee on Japanese Canadians to the House and the Senate of Canada, April, 1946. Between, there are extracts from letters, research articles, newspaper reports, government directives, and a diary; all this is interspersed with narrative progression on two planes, both originating with Naomi. One narrative describes with calming affection Naomi's care for Obasan after Uncle's death. The other describes her childhood, from the good times before Pearl Harbor when her family prospered in Vancouver and along the Pacific Coast–the Issei, her grandparents' generation, born in Japan; the Nisei, her parents' generation, Canadian by birth; the Sansei, her own generation of Canadians, with little more than hearsay memories of an ancestral homeland. She is four years old when war with Japan is declared. This plane of the narrative follows the enforced transportation from the coastal area of all Japanese Canadians and Canadians of Japanese descent; it describes the incarceration of women and children in cattle stalls, the dispersal of men to work camps, the dispersal of families, the confiscation of assets. This plane details the indignity, the humiliation, the suffering. For Naomi and her aunt and uncle, this means removal to a hovel in the B.C. interior, and then to a one-room shack, little more than a packing case, near Lethbridge, Alberta. The first, Naomi remembers rather fondly; the second, with deep-felt anger, with profound sadness.

Slipped in between the two planes of the narrative are fragments of her life and of her Aunt Emily's crusade against the past. Whether Emily wants compensation, retribution, vengeance, or public acknowledgement of the wrongs done, it is difficult to know. Emily is the antithesis of Obasan. She is fiercely Canadian, and unforgiving. And she is determined it should not occur again. The past and future meet in the present fury of her ongoing mission. Obasan, in contrast, bears the burden of memory in enigmatic silence, as did her husband right to the grave. And Naomi, although reminded of the past by unending slights of prejudice she encounters as a schoolteacher in contemporary Canada, remains determinedly disengaged – until the death of her uncle collapses time for her and she has no choice but to face what happened. Naomi, Obasan, and Emily are foils for one another: three responses, each designed to draw the other out. They are parts of a cleverly didactic narrative design, three dimensions of a chilling story. It is a story that has not yet ended; nor, perhaps, ever will, so long as we remember it – which, as *Obasan* drives home, it is imperative we do.

HENRY KREISEL

The Betrayal. Toronto: McClelland and Stewart, 1964.
Toronto: McClelland and Stewart; New Canadian Library,
1971. Pages: 218. Paperback.

Kreisel is better known for his first novel, *The Rich Man*, yet *The Betrayal* is the more mature and accomplished work. *The Rich Man* is an account of an Austrian Jewish immigrant's return to Vienna from Toronto during the squalid years immediately prior to Hitler's *Anschluss*, which saw Austria and Germany united and the Jews under murderous siege. It is a sensitive novel, but in skimming over the historical details in its rendering of the personal, it misses being a major achievement. Kreisel does not have the command of prose or sufficient insight into personality to make such an account rise to the universal. In *The Betrayal*, however, he capitalizes on what he does best and turns his weaknesses into strengths, creating a rare discourse in a dramatic context on moral responsibility. It is a novel of "ideas," but it also shows a strong romantic impulse – it is, in fact, a curiously effective blend of romance and moral anatomy, realistic fiction and thriller. Not a great work of literature, perhaps, but a provocative and ambitiously engaging moral drama.

Canada is important in *The Betrayal*. The narrative is told from the perspective of Edmonton in 1952 by a second-generation Jewish Canadian, a young history professor who is a veteran of

the Sicilian campaign and as pompously innocent as his Canadian homeland. By fate or accident–the two are purposely difficult to distinguish–Max Lerner becomes involved as the pivotal
figure in a moral conundrum that defies resolution. Born in a
country where "it was possible without too much difficulty to be
a decent human being," he is drawn in as confessor and judge to
bear witness to behaviour that could only have occurred in a
morally absurd world, such as Vienna was under the Nazis when
Jews were being rounded up and transported to concentration
camps, when moral laws collapsed and human decency faded to
whispers and memory. Lerner, the history professor, must apply
the lessons of history to the lives of living people. From the safe
and austere vantage of Edmonton in winter (beyond the reach
of history, as it were), he must witness past betrayals brought
by circumstance before him now as a judge not of ideas but of
humanity.

Lerner's involvement is cleverly staged. An attractive student,
Katherine Held, becomes distraught; Lerner discovers that her
fear is due to her relations with Theodore Stappler, who tells Lerner his story, finding in him a kindred soul. Stappler has hunted
Katherine's father, Joseph Held, for betraying him in 1938. Held
was well paid to lead Stappler, his mother, and others out of Austria to safety in France. Instead, he turned them over to the Nazis.
Only Stappler escaped. Stappler's mother, a Jew, eventually died
in a camp. When Stappler finally confronts Held in Edmonton,
Stappler is disconcerted by the man's ordinariness. Yet there is
no forgiveness. Held, in turn, accuses Stappler of deserting his
mother–and explains that his own actions were necessary to save
his wife and daughter. Stappler determines to avenge himself
through the daughter, Katherine, now a young woman. Compli-
cating things, Katherine and Stappler become romantically involved. Lerner enters the scene: Stappler draws him in as a sort
of innocent alter ego. In the end, Held kills himself; Stappler flees;
Lerner courts Katherine and loses; Stappler eventually dies in
the Arctic on a mission of mercy.

This summation of the story suggests two things: one, that there
are strong elements of the melodramatic, which might better be
described as romantic, for they are handled with restraint; and
two, there are so many moral ambiguities contained within the
plot that there is no hope for a resolution. There is not meant to
be–Kreisel's purpose is clearly to provoke thought rather than to
provide answers. There is no character development and little

description in the novel. Although the discourse is thoroughly engaging, particularly when it deals with concepts of sin, free will, and moral responsibility, the dialogue itself is wooden. There is a great deal of wit in the novel, primarily associated with the narrator, and a great deal of compassion, coming directly, it seems, from the author. Thought invariably dominates action, character, and mood–not in the sense of themes being illustrated or illuminated, but rather as a philosophical conundrum, gradually revealed. Nowhere in our literature has a discourse on moral responsibility been so thoroughly and disturbingly enacted. The ideas remain with the reader at a gut level long after the narrative itself has faded out of mind.

ROBERT KROETSCH

The Studhorse Man. Toronto: Macmillan, 1969. Don Mills: General; New Press Canadian Classics, 1982. Pages: 175. Paperback.

Some say Kroetsch is an acquired taste. Those who endorse him are aggressively enthusiastic. Those who do not for the most part shrug him off. Generally, critics are positive. His novels are clever, irreverent, inventive, filled with ambiguities, word-games, puzzles, suggestive allusions, and intriguing illusions. His mode is fictional realism: realism that will not exist outside the narrative but has convincing vitality within. His first novel, *But We Are Exiles*, indicated coming predilections with improbable metamorphoses; disjointed sexuality; death as the source of life, and sex, therefore, as the source of transcendence; the search for self and identity in relation to place and time; and a whimsical fascination with morbidity and violence. What it lacked was the controlled humour that makes *The Studhorse Man* his most popular novel to date and *Badlands* his finest achievement.

Motifs in *The Studhorse Man* echo through the rest of Kroetsch's work: a seemingly puerile obsession with the male sex organ and all the improbable calamities to which it can fall heir, and all the resurrections it can sustain; the coffin or lying-in-state sequence, which gives rise to a different but associated resurrection; the picaresque journey, quest, escape, all of which are the same. Kroetsch's writing suggests no one so much as himself. Thus, while his best is very good indeed, the rest can seem derivative.

The Studhorse Man is narrated by Demeter Proudfoot, a temperate and articulate man who works naked in an empty bathtub, housed in an insane asylum (we are well on the way through the novel before his identity and perspective are revealed). Demeter's story, much of which he obviously must invent, chronicles the adventures of his rival for the affections of his cousin, Martha Proudfoot. The rival, Hazard Lepage, has been Martha's fiancé for thirteen years; he is Kroetsch's greatest creation.

Hazard lives in a derelict country mansion, with a gelding improbably named Girl in the dining room and Poseidon, a virgin stud, in the parlour. Hazard serves an overwhelming dream: to foster a new blood line through the great blue stallion. Hazard comes of an old family, Québécois and Acadian, but he has no base for his identity in Alberta, in the new West. Poseidon is the sixth generation bred from an anonymous sire Hazard once came upon by chance, but the line is not yet genetically established. Hazard's world is horses, his poetry and philosophy *The General Stud Book*. He owns a magnificent stallion, but he has not the twenty dollars needed to cover a mare and buy her offspring. It is 1945. To raise money, he collects bones for the war effort. But the war ends and Hazard finds himself and Poseidon, amidst a boxcar of bones, on their way to Edmonton.

The novel follows episodically from there. Hazard loses Poseidon, finds him, and treks halfway across Alberta to get back to where he started. His adventures are wildly bizarre: he makes love to a curator in the provincial museum, plays poker with the Sisters of Temperance, services a demanding young widow, picks up a backside of buckshot and is nursed back to health by a sexually imaginative woman rancher, is asphyxiated in a fire, and rises on ice, literally, to attend the conception of a daughter, who will also be called Demeter. Episodes ribald and picaresque tumble one over another. In the end, Hazard is killed by his stallion, who is raised to a frenzy of lust for Martha's mares, which the other mad Demeter provides in a jealous pique. With resounding irony, both tragic and comic, Poseidon establishes a line proficient in the production of PMU (Pregnant Mare's Urine), used in the manufacture of birth-control pills.

Potency, fertility, sex as the fulcrum between life and death – these are, in the manner of a picaresque novel, explored as motifs rather than themes. Other motifs proliferate – Hazard metamorphoses through identities as a studhorse man, murderer, milkman, Mountie, preacher, corpse, and lover. Diverse motifs are all worked together in an effort, largely successful, to merge individual identity with the community, through the immediacy and elasticity of contemporary myth. While there is still time, Kroetsch tries to give voice and vocabulary, but also personality and mythology, to a new place – new in the consciousness of its people.

Gone Indian. Toronto: New Press, 1973. Pages: 158.

In Notikeewin, Alberta, an American graduate student named Jeremy Bentham Sadness (after the British philosopher-jurist who transcended death by having his corpse stuffed) pursues his identity. Sadness has problems, not the least of which is to keep his genitals from freezing. He cannot finish his doctoral thesis or satisfy his wife back in Binghamton, New York. He is impotent, except while upright, and at a loss for a self he can live with. He dreams of dying, stealing the existence of another – a buffalo or Grey Owl, the celebrated fake Indian, or the comatose Roger Dorck. He dreams of becoming the departed, but not necessarily dead, Sunderman – while having vertical relations with Sunderman's daughter and then, on the horizontal, with his wife. In the end, Jeremy and Bea Sunderman soar off a railroad bridge, straddling a snowmobile. But they never land.

Kroetsch's fiction invariably attempts to accomplish many things at the same time. In *The Studhorse Man*, a determined forward momentum holds it all together. Its predecessor, *The Words of My Roaring*, hovers indecisively between documentary and parody. Perhaps *Badlands* alone brings everything together as it sorts through the pursuit of self, the transcendence of time, the welding of personality and place, all with exuberant Kroetschean flair. *What the Crow Said* is brilliantly inventive. The opening chapter is one of the finest set pieces of romantic fantasy that has ever been written: a lovely young woman is convincingly seduced and impregnated by a swarm of bees. Unfortunately, as inventive as the novel is, that is all it is. After a while the cleverness palls, the reader yearns for depth, emotional, metaphysical, even intellectual – but Kroetsch persists in skating his zany patterns on the surface. His most recent novel, *Alibi*, is a superbly ironic retreat from those aspects of postmodernism that most undermined the achievement of *What the Crow Said* (see below).

Gone Indian has much less emotional impact that either *The Studhorse Man* or *Badlands*, and more narrative control than *What the Crow Said*, but it is as flamboyant and bizarre as anything Kroetsch has done in prose or poetry.

Gone Indian is aggressively sophisticated, intricate and intellectual, an accomplished self-parody. The reader is kept at a distance from Jeremy Sadness – Kroetsch cannot allow us to get too close or absurdity becomes irrelevance. His deviously inventive use of narrative voice generates dimensions of ambiguity and significance that words and actions alone could not obtain. What we receive has been taped, then transcribed, edited, interrupted, and interpreted by Professor Mark Madham, Jeremy's faculty adviser back in Binghamton. Madham makes love to Jeremy's wife while Jeremy pursues himself. Madham's objectivity and disinterest, of course, are quite unreliable.

Kroetsch himself is readily visible throughout the novel – in subject, theme, and style, but more insistently in the wit and in the jokes that range from sophomoric to urbane. Such names as Roger Dorck, both halves of which are kids' slang for penis, and Madham, with its suggestions of Mad Adam, Mad Man, Madam, *et al.*, are rather obvious. The name Sunderman has more subtlety and resonance. The naming of Miss Kundt and Miss Petcock is silly – the context is not sufficiently a comedy of manners to sustain such trite whimsy. The playful merging of identities, by contrast, is both amusing and profound. The exploration of the symbolic possibilities of Jeremy's graduate-student status is devastating: after nine years in graduate school and six thesis attempts, Jeremy has almost managed to become no one. Kroetsch's creative ingenuity gives the novel its effervescent power, but his gamesmanship ultimately drags it down to the level of clever exercise – albeit the best of its kind.

Badlands. Toronto: New Press, 1975. Pages: 270.
Don Mills: General; New Press Canadian Classics, 1976.
Paperback.

It was not until a third or fourth attempt at reading *Badlands* that I got beyond the bias of my own expectations into what turned out to be one of the most exhilarating novels I have ever read. Decked out in the gleeful obscenities the reader has come to expect from Kroetsch, *Badlands* teems with ribald wit and pungent vulgarity. Brimming over with mind-games, word-games, games with symbols and allusions and telegraphed meanings, it is structured as carefully as an episodic quest through a labyrinth. *Badlands* delights in language that is aggressively regional – boldly, self-consciously, chauvinistically, universally regional. While it shares all these characteristics with his other novels, it also stands apart as a more unified work, one that is profoundly moving and humane. *Badlands* is a strange and splendid work of fiction.

The novel opens at a slow, meandering pace, building gradually like the Red Deer River, on which Dawe and his men drift towards the heart of the Alberta Badlands. Only after they arrive at the site where they are to dig for dinosaur bones does the narrative begin to tremble with excitement and drive forward in vigorous spurts, until suddenly it is over. But it is not over; the whole of Dawe's 1916 expedition is a reconstruction to account for the notes in his daughter's possession, some fifty-six years later. It is her story that contains his, as a clock contains time.

Dawe's story is not finished until Anna Dawe and Anna Yellowbird (an old Indian woman who as a girl had been with Dawe in 1916) throw away his notes and the photographic relics of his existence, proof that he had been in their lives, and turn themselves to the future. Anna Dawe's story is sparse, yet Dawe's is entirely enclosed within it. Anna's story insists that the obsessions of Dawe's masculine reality are locked in a struggle with her representation of feminine reality – history against dream, as it were, linear time against time that is spatial and without form. She allows Dawe's story to be told, then learns from Anna, who might have been her mother or her sister or even her other self, that she is sufficient *in* herself. This is something her father never knew of his own being; something men never know. Male reality, as Kroetsch conceives of it here, is an argument to be pursued; female reality is a case to be stated. *Badlands* puts such flesh to these bare ontological bones that they dance with the lewd and menacing vigour of an oversexed drunk in an understaffed brothel – an appropriate enough image in a Kroetschean world.

Inside the all-important frame story, Kroetsch describes the picaresque adventures of Dawe with Grizzly, his Chinese cook, and Web, and Tune. In the beginning, there is also McBride, who lights out for home and family after getting sprayed by a skunk and nearly drowned. In the end, young Tune is buried under tons of clay, along with the tail bones of a Daweosaurus. Web and Grizzly stay the whole way. Grizzly says little; he supplies the young Indian widow, Anna Yellowbird (who follows them downriver along the shore), with food and inscrutable affection. Web endures through utter indifference to the project, sustained only by a deep hatred for Dawe, which is indistinguishable from his dependence on him; and once, in the eye of a tornado, makes savage love to Anna, who has also been applying her favours to Dawe while Dawe is laid up with injuries.

On the slow journey down river, there are exotic encounters with sisters, one on the side of virtue and one given wholly to vice; with a demolition expert who lives deep underground in a mine, never surfacing; and with a mad, imperturbable photographer, stranded in the middle of the river, snapping pictures. Once at the site, the adventures become more and more sinister. The humour never leaves, in part because of the beautiful vulgarity of Web and his various splenetic expressions, and in part because of the manic presence of the author, who gleefully plays God with the language and syntax and punctuation and form. But the mood deepens. An almost feverish pace takes over as the men dig out and prepare three sets of bones, and Dawe sees immortality ever closer at hand. Then it is over; they emerge from the wilderness, and even the photographer leaves them – after having exchanged his documentary shots for a flash in the dark with the ubiquitous Anna Yellowbird.

Kroetsch has developed a wonderful story and context for the exploration of time and reality. Bones that are millions of years old, the object of a quest for lasting fame down a river cut eons ago through the earth, a quest for the random detritus of death while a world war rages far away – all provide the perfect grail for the humpbacked knight-errant, the field scientist, Dawe. And his notes and reputation, all that is left of him for his daughter, prove a worthy guide to her on her own quest, the end of which is that her father's legacy is irrelevant. Not only the narrative account but also the Badlands setting from a river perspective, which is rendered with exquisite detailed authenticity, participate in the complex explorations of reality, as do the bizarre and zany bits, the coarseness and the brief touching vignettes. All parts of this novel serve the whole vision with a coherence of form and meaning not found in Kroetsch's other works. I regret not having read it sooner, to the end.

Alibi. Toronto: Beaufort Books, 1983. Pages: 239. Don
Mills: General; New Press Canadian Classics, 1984.
Paperback.

This is a retreat from postmodernism – which may be the same as
saying it is an advance beyond postmodernism. *Alibi* abandons
the free-form and fabulist indulgences of *What the Crow Said*
(which some of Kroetsch's fans regard as his most serious novel,
but I do not) and takes up the ironic gamesmanship that rescues
Gone Indian from inconsequentiality and makes *The Studhorse
Man* such brilliant fun. But it is a move forward, not back. It is an
attempt to make everyday absurdity seem commonplace. It is a
novel in which irony reigns supreme. Nothing, in *Alibi*, is what it
seems, but only because nothing seems to be what it is. And if
that seems a tautology, it is. It is also solecism, solepsism, and a
paradox. Kroetsch inspires such evasions.

Alibi takes the reader over familiar territory. The expected motifs
and obsessions are there unapologetically and in profusion. The
protagonist's genitals seem almost to have a life of their own. They
are caressed and scalded, embraced by an octopus, slathered in
mud, stretched, squashed, and satiated. They/it are/is the centre
of his being. And there are panties – panties in all the colours of
the rainbow, panties everywhere. Men have sensate protrusions
between their legs; women have swatches of cloth. It might seem
in bad taste to inquire whether such a fetish belongs to Kroetsch
or to his narrating protagonist, Billy Billy Dorf, or William William Dorfendorf, or Dorf (as he and his author prefer). But it is a
pertinent question, since the success of the novel hangs on the
narrator's establishing a separate personality from his author,
for whom he is a personal representative within the text – not quite
persona and not quite self. Dorf at forty-six behaves and thinks
like a superannuated undergraduate from the halcyon days of
beer and vomit that most of his generation have long since left
behind. He is pathetic and heroic at the same time, a projection
by the author into fictional reality of the self he had otherwise
and mercifully left behind. The panty fetish, then, is not so much
Dorf's, nor even Kroetsch's, as it is the fiction's, where the author
and his character are parsed into separate personalities. Dorf and
Kroetsch provide alibis for each other, within and outside the text.

The fiction itself is what counts. Dorf animates it and Kroetsch

animates it–but, despite its being the expression both of authorial desire and of the narrator's will to re-create himself from journal notes, it is only as their mutual creation stands apart from
either of them that it stands at all. And it does. Quite beautifully.
Alibi opens to us like the petals of a budding flower, a rose, and
when it is fully open there is nothing there but the flower itself.
This may seem a strange analogy to convey the impact of a novel
that is ostensibly picaresque. But that, to me, is what most fascinates. *Alibi* seems to chronicle adventures in the life of its rogue-
hero, episode by episode, when in essence what enthralls the reader
is the revelation of design, as motifs unfold, fall open, fill out the
fiction. And even then, it is not the motifs that delight but the
patterns of their blooming.

Briefly: Dorf is a collector's agent, commissioned by the Howard Hughes-like Calgary recluse, Jack Deemer, to accumulate
whatsoever money can buy that he desires. Dorf is assigned to
acquire a spa. To this end, he travels from Banff, through Bath, to
Wales, Portugal, and Greece, with a side trip to Germany, then
back to Alberta–giving Kroetsch the opportunity for some splendid sardonic descriptions and Dorf the opportunity both for quasi-
erotic adventures and for pursuing the cure for which he has no
ailment, other than the angst and ineffectuality he shares with
much of his civilization. He is accompanied at times by Karen
Strike, who films what he sees, and he is met at times by Julie
Magnuson, Jack Deemer's female emanation, a killer, Dorf's lover,
eventually a corpse on ice. There are other characters encountered here and there–grotesques, for the most part. There are Dr.
Manuel de Medeiros, the beautiful and sinister dwarf, and Estuary,
she of the multi-hued underwear and withered hand. And Fish.
And the man with no name, given one by Billy Billy Dorf, who
has one to spare. And the seemingly ubiquitous Deemer (whom
we never actually meet, except as a skeletal spectre and a disembodied voice in the darkness). Motivation and response are aspects
of plot. The characters themselves have no depth, no emotional
complexity. They occupy time, so to speak, but not space–the
unfolding narrative gives them life, rather than they, the narrative. And yet nothing much of consequence occurs. When the right
spa is found, the depthless Dorf retires to benign oblivion. Everything is irony.

Wherein then lies the power of this novel to engage, to amuse
and move the reader? That it does so is itself an irony worth noting.
It is, curiously and paradoxically, a powerful novel of some consider-

able depth. Not Kroetsch's best, perhaps–but close. The pattern of motifs that contain Dorf, the way air contains sculpture, provides at least part of the answer. Dorf is defined by recurrent versions of the spa, by his function as an agent for another man's desire, another man's life, by alibis, by a whole unwinding skein of motifs related to the care and appeasement of male genitalia, to water and mud, cleansing and cures, to mortality, to death, to identity and being, self and otherness, names, naming and being named, to consolation and indulgence, time and the human condition. The spa, like a labyrinth, simultaneously embodies opposing principles. As the resolution is also the heart of containment, so, too, the cure is at the centre of decadence. And the concept of alibi is equally a paradox: everything we do provides a cover for what we do not do; as lives intersect, each of us offers an alibi for the other; what we are is the only excuse for what we have not become. In such a world of contradiction and anomaly, so intricately devised, Dorf's very lack of character and definition allow him to occupy the focal centre. He is the lens through which we see reality conceived entirely in the ironic mode–which is, essentially, what *Alibi* seems intent to convey.

MARGARET LAURENCE

The Stone Angel. Toronto: McClelland and Stewart, 1964. Toronto: McClelland and Stewart; New Canadian Library, 1968. Toronto: Seal, 1982. Pages: 308. Paperback.

Margaret Laurence died as this book was going to press. It is a grievous loss. She has dominated the last two decades of Canadian fiction as an almost overwhelming yet nurturing presence. In the public mind she has taken the place of MacLennan, Callaghan, or Grove as our premier novelist. Teachers and academics have elevated her work to institutional status, while critics generally laud it as the unassailable object of inquiries into the art of fiction. Laurence has come to embody the force and quality of the literary revolution that swept through Canada in the sixties, proclaiming with adolescent vigour our new-found maturity. Her novel *The Stone Angel* is the most celebrated Canadian novel of our time. It is certainly one of the best–though perhaps a little more vulnerable to criticism than is generally allowed.

Although Laurence was born and grew up in Manitoba, *The Stone Angel*, her first major Canadian work, came only after a flourishing African phase in her career, which yielded a travel book, a book of Somali translations, a book of literary criticism, a thoroughly competent apprentice novel called *This Side Jordan*, and a brilliant short-story collection published under the title *The Tomorrow Tamer*. *The Stone Angel* marked her triumphant return to Canada, where she could write at last from an inside perspective rather than as an observer. (It is worth noting, in this respect, that Laurence's Canadian protagonists are invariably female; in her African fiction, where she wrote as an outsider, they are often male.)

The Stone Angel is the first in a cycle of five works called, rather loosely, "the Manawaka novels" after the town in Manitoba (patterned on Laurence's birthplace, Neepawa) that figures so prominently in her fiction. Only two books, *A Jest of God* and *A Bird in the House*, are set entirely in the Manawaka area, while another, *The Fire-Dwellers*, is set almost entirely away. *The Diviners*, the most recent of her adult fiction (she writes children's books as well), is perhaps most truly a "Manawaka" work; in it, Laurence directly confronts the impact of small-town origins on her characters' lives. Manawaka is not merely a setting for Morag's story, but a condition of her being. Laurence has never been a regional writer–although she draws from a specific locale, she only incidentally transforms it into a realm of the imagination. But in *The Diviners*, she makes a conscious attempt to define the perimeters of a particular region that has influenced her and/or her characters on every level of personality and experience. Perhaps more than any other writer, Laurence has shown that the regions defining each of us in Canada are those we carry within us–and these regions are defined by the quality of our lives.

As an artist, Laurence has continually developed both her narrative technique and the capacity of her soul to encompass the larger and more intimate realities of her characters' lives. *The Stone Angel* is a fine early novel, but it does not have the creative or experiential maturity of *The Fire-Dwellers* or *The Diviners*. Yet it remains her most widely acclaimed and perhaps her most aesthetically coherent work; thematically and technically, it is the most unified.

The Stone Angel rewards thematic analysis with a complex yet coherent web of allusions, symbols, motifs, and related images.

For this reason, it is sometimes easy to overlook the rich, resonant quality of the language itself, or the accomplished manipulation of time and the narrative point of view in the novel. The
story of Hagar Shipley, in fact, plays two temporal sequences
against each other for a sustained ironic effect that culminates in
an episode of personal exoneration shortly before Hagar's death.
One sequence illuminates the besieged consciousness of Hagar at
ninety, living in Vancouver during the final season of her life:
memories of the past and domestic trivia of the present vie for
her attention, leaving her sometimes confused and at other times
touchingly lucid. There is a bifurcation of experience in this
sequence, a split of a different sort, as Hagar's consciousness often
seems to separate from her physical being: she observes this
present-tense, ungainly, ancient woman as something apart from
herself. In reality, Hagar is all that she has ever been: the other
time sequence, which takes place mostly in Manawaka, moves at
a much faster rate so that eventually it overtakes the present.
This second sequence begins with an awkward array of memory
fragments dating from when Hagar was about six, as she struggles to get a fix on her earliest years. Impending death, in the
present sequence, provides sufficient motivation for the chronological ordering of her account. As she gets more involved in her
story, the momentum and the narrative pattern build, until we,
too, accept her present self as reservoir and remnant of a whole,
dynamic life.

Such linguistic devices as alliteration – to reinforce the childish
aspect of Hagar's early memories – and the fusing of archaic and
colloquial words – to suggest the time span of her awareness –
effectively add to characterization. So, too, does sentence structure:
inverted syntax, in particular, echoes Hagar's Highland ancestry
while suggesting something of her truculent and unaccommodating nature. It is the imagery, though, that contributes most to
characterization. Laurence deftly applies metaphors to her characters in such abundance that their various likenesses provide
almost an allegorical parallel to the actual story.

In the present-tense sequence, Hagar lives with her surviving
son, Marvin, and his wife, Doris, who try to engineer Hagar out
of her house and into the Silverthreads Nursing Home. Enlisting
a minister and then a doctor in their cause, they close out Hagar's
options until, desperate, she runs away. At a deserted fish cannery she confesses her life to a failed insurance salesman in an

episode laden with allusions to liturgy and the mass. Reconciled to her past, she enters the nursing home and dies.

The account of Hagar's past, while it develops chronologically, is structured to explore certain key motifs in her life – in particular, her relationships with males and the suffocating roles these imposed upon her. Another key motif is the ambivalence of her pride, a pride that is the source of both her strength and her almost tragic isolation, as she rejects roles and relationships. Laurence vividly portrays Hagar's stormy marriage to Bram Shipley, following discordantly after an indulgent and wilful childhood with her austere, widower father, Jason Currie. In brief dramatic episodes, Laurence conveys Hagar's failure to communicate with her brothers, then with her sons. She does not allow self-pity to extinguish Hagar's pride, nor compassion to overcome the restraints of self-possession. When all of Hagar's hopes are pinned on her son John, and he dies, pointlessly, almost to spite her, her past rapidly collapses into the confessional at the fish cannery.

The Stone Angel opens in a cemetery and ends with Hagar's death. In between, it celebrates life while lamenting the limitations placed upon it by personality. Throughout, Laurence explores themes of freedom and responsibility, pride and humility, time and consciousness, reconciliation with the human condition, acceptance of self, retaliation against a sexist world, the impact of Protestant inhibitions, and much more. She weaves an intriguing pattern of images – flowers, insects, animals – and allusions – biblical, literary, cultural. She develops motifs involving mirrors and eyes, Indians and nature, sexuality and gender, almost to the point of excess. Some readers will prefer the more restrained and subtle sensibility of Laurence's later fiction, but few would deny the achievement of *The Stone Angel* as a work of power and beauty.

A Jest of God. Toronto: McClelland and Stewart, 1966. Toronto: McClelland and Stewart; New Canadian Library, 1974. Toronto: Seal, 1977. Pages: 246. Paperback.

At once more subtle and more intensely dramatic than *The Stone Angel*, this novel attempts somewhat less than its predecessor in both narrative technique and character development. Laurence makes brilliant use of interior monologue to convey Rachel Cameron's obsessive word-consciousness and to articulate the innermost desires and the fears that haunt her. Rachel is a thirty-four-year-old grade-school teacher in Manawaka; she lives with her mother over the funeral home her father operated until he died. Rachel is reticent and ruminative, a self-conscious virgin and, in her own estimation, a wallflower. Only in passing allusions does Laurence sketch in a picture of Rachel's whole life: the novel focuses on one particular summer, when Rachel commits herself to change and is changed.

Rachel's insistent sexuality appalls her, not in itself but because it implies an assault on her painfully nurtured inhibitions. She rejects her friend Calla's lesbian advances with more concern for her own impropriety than for Calla's actions. She fumes at her awareness of the principal's petty authoritarian masculinity. Most of all, she fears loss of self-control. After she breaks into glossolalia, burbling in voices, at Calla's tabernacle meeting, she accepts her lack of restraint as a public disgrace.

Overcoming the stiff and arid self-possession that has become a prison for her, Rachel rather determinedly has an affair. With school out for the year, so that even that limited outlet for emotions is gone, and with only her suffocating relationship with her mother to fall back on, Rachel turns to Nick Kazlik, an acquaintance from her own school days who has returned to Manawaka for the summer. Nick's family were immigrant Ukrainian farmers, and in having an affair with him, Rachel confronts not only her sexual inhibitions, but other social restraints and prejudices of her Presbyterian childhood as well.

Verbal confusion leads to the end of the relationship. Then Rachel discovers that she is pregnant; then, with heavy irony, she finds that she is carrying a benign tumour. Nonetheless, with mind and body, and interior and external selves united at last, she experiences a sense of modest triumph. Firmly in charge, with her mother in tow, Rachel leaves Manawaka as the novel closes. The movement from benighted passivity to such positive action has come about not through sex but through taking a risk, through willing herself to be vulnerable, to love and be hurt, through willing herself to live. Her departure is not flight, but affirmation.

Like Hagar in *The Stone Angel*, Rachel discovers freedom and responsibility are interdependent. But pride was Hagar's predominant characteristic; the lack of pride is Rachel's. She is not a character as inherently interesting as Hagar, but Laurence generates a surprising amount of empathy through narrative technique. Rachel's voice does not replicate the processes of consciousness, but it conveys an immediacy and authenticity of experience that makes the reader both a witness and participant in the fears, frustrations, and qualified triumphs of her life.

Appropriately, the imagery in this novel is more restrained than in *The Stone Angel*, and the symbolism is directed more to narrative unity than to depth or breadth of allusion. Time is less interesting in *A Jest of God* than it is in Laurence's other novels, providing as it does a relatively simple, linear context. Language is less pretentious, less ambitious – appropriate to Rachel's somewhat dessicated consciousness, where words and sex seem to represent the two opposing sides of her personality, words being on the side of inhibition and self-deprecation. In the ironic fusion of voice with narrative point of view, this novel represents an advance over Laurence's earlier fiction and anticipates her increasingly sophisticated attempts to make language embody her characters' personalities, not merely define them. *A Jest of God* is an important novel, more ironic than anything else Laurence has written, and a significant phase in the development of a major writer's growing body of work.

The Fire-Dwellers. Toronto: McClelland and Stewart, 1969. Toronto: McClelland and Stewart; New Canadian Library, 1973. Toronto: Seal, 1978. Pages: 277. Paperback.

The most underrated of Laurence's Canadian novels is *The Fire-Dwellers*. Here, the town of Manawaka is reduced to remnants of memory within Stacey MacAindra's mind and the lasting impression it has left on her personality. Stacey is the married sister of Rachel Cameron (the main character in *A Jest of God*); in some ways, she is Rachel's married counterpart and, in others, a mirror inversion. If Rachel's story was one of modest liberation, Stacey's is one of reconciliation – though both are stories of the attainment of self-possession.

Stacey speaks directly to the reader in several voices. By shifting from one voice to another, Laurence adroitly manages to convey boredom, drudgery, and the commonplace without being boring or banal. Much of the novel's drama comes from the interplay among Stacey's various selves, the roles imposed upon her by her lifestyle and her own personality. She daydreams and fantasizes; she has her current-affairs level where she monitors world events; she remembers Manawaka, when she was young and life was exciting and full of options; she copes with the domestic needs of her husband, Mac, and her children and deals with their urgent personal demands; she watches herself through all of this and provides commentary on her own life and behaviour.

Stacey is thirty-nine; the contours of her body are filling in with middle age; she is fading, aging, tiring. Panic strikes as she feels the world closing around her. In response, she has an affair. Following an abortive effort with her husband's friend, she falls into a relationship with a much younger man. After a time, she rejects him and turns to home – not so much renewed as restored. She has discovered the liberating power of choice. There are always options – by choice, she lives with Mac and the kids in their Bluejay Crescent world.

Like Laurence's other main characters, Stacey manages to be both ordinary and unique. The genius of this novel is that the former is stressed over the latter, and still the protagonist is a fascinating creation. Laurence's women suffer the roles forced upon them by society, by their Presbyterian small-town Canadian backgrounds, and by their own individual personalities; and yet they manage to cope; they even prevail. Laurence's characters suffer, reach out, risk humiliation, and endure. They are of the same world we are, and they do endure.

A Bird in the House. Toronto: McClelland and Stewart,
   1970. Toronto: McClelland and Stewart; New Canadian
Library, 1974. Toronto: Seal, 1978. Pages: 179. Paperback.

The Vanessa McCloud stories, as these linked works of short fiction are sometimes called, do not collectively add up to a novel: a novel is not a cumulative entity but an organic whole that begins to take shape right from the beginning. There are narrative and thematic connections among the stories, but no overriding design in which each segment somehow anticipates the ones to follow and illuminates the ones preceding. However, as an integral part of "The Manawaka World of Margaret Laurence," to borrow the title of Clara Thomas's study of the Laurence canon, the stories cannot be excluded from this context without leaving a critical gap. And certainly, in terms of their quality, they are among Laurence's best work.

Vanessa is more of an autobiographical persona than Laurence's other protagonists. Paradoxically, she is more elusive. The reader does not have the sense of knowing Vanessa, but rather is given glimpses into her complex and almost ephemeral personality during its formative stages. This book is the closest Laurence has come to writing a portrait of the artist as a young woman – she seems concerned less with giving a balanced account of Vanessa's childhood than with providing insight into her sensibility and the sources of her imaginative responses to the world at large.

Each story fills in details of Vanessa's Presbyterian and relatively affluent, relatively happy childhood in Manawaka, defining its limits and conditions. The people all exist as Vanessa perceives and remembers them. They do not occupy roles in a larger vision, but embody aspects of her experience of herself. Thus, the death of her father is more ironic and sad than tragic, and the death of Piquette Tonnerre is more an opportunity for solemn introspection than an event in itself. Each story is shaped towards some particular cluster of insights on Vanessa's part, which she intuitively responded to as a girl and young woman, and comments on from the vantage of maturity with a mixture of guarded warmth and ironic tolerance. The narrative voice throughout includes the past and present both, but the author makes no attempt to merge them. Nor does she attempt to link the stories: Laurence is satisfied that each story stands alone in the mosaic of Vanessa's early life, which itself remains an incomplete design.

The Diviners. Toronto: McClelland and Stewart, 1974. Toronto: McClelland and Stewart; New Canadian Library, 1978. Toronto: Seal, 1982. Pages: 465. Paperback.

The Diviners is a sweeping, sprawling novel, as moving, in parts, as anything Laurence has written. It is a novel of explicit themes, the mature work of a writer who has certain things she wants to say, and who knows how to say them effectively. At the same time, it is a curiously tentative exploration of the protagonist's personality set against a bold, confessional account of her earlier life. The two narrative sequences are interwoven, much in the manner of *The Stone Angel*, in order to illuminate Morag's past as well as her present. When past and present merge, the novel comes to a close. In *The Stone Angel*, this merging coincided with Hagar's death; here, the author leaves Morag's life unresolved. This is as it should be, for the forty-six-year-old Morag, a successful novelist, has finally come to accept herself as a woman, separate from the roles she has always balked at playing. Morag Gunn is a more elusive character than Laurence's earlier protagonists (with the possible exception of Vanessa McCloud) and correspondingly more realistic. *The Diviners* does not define Morag's life; rather it explores it and draws from it an enduring vision of the world Morag occupies.

There is a rhetorical openness to *The Diviners* that contributes tremendously to its thematic and dramatic power, yet this openness makes Morag seem occasionally more of a persona than a personality. Laurence provides inadequate justification for Morag's chronological review of her own life–even if the "memorybank movies" are a basis for the autobiographical novel she is, perhaps, in the process of writing (as has been suggested by several critics and the author herself). There is another problem associated with Morag: she is an acclaimed novelist, and yet we are given little insight into either the creative process or the problems of celebrity. Of course, Laurence is more concerned with her protagonist as a woman than as an artist–and perhaps it is only the occasional confusion of author and character that invites such a criticism.

The Diviners is powerful fiction. Morag's story takes her from a foundling child in Manawaka to a mature and successful woman, without her losing the burden of a self-conscious need for personal fulfilment. At times in her life she submits to or even invites a variety of "female" roles, but invariably she falls back upon her essential self, and finally she accepts that this is what her daughter, Pique, at eighteen, must do as well. This is a form of qualified liberation for Morag–to set her daughter free in some measure is an act of liberation for Morag, too. Whatever Morag has learned from Christie Logan, the keeper of the Manawaka dump who raised her on the lore of her father and forebears, whatever Jules

Tonnerre, Pique's Métis father, has told her about his storied heritage, whatever she has learned through an arid marriage, precarious independence, and professional success, can be offered–but ultimately Pique must learn her own truths for herself.

Morag lives alone among friends at McConnell's Landing near Toronto, where she worries about Pique, works on her novel, and struggles to attain some sort of peace after a life of reticent dissent. This perspective allows Laurence to consolidate the themes that provide her novel with its form as well as its meaning. What Morag learns is what we also are to learn. Morag comes to realize the vital truth of ambiguity: her fiction is and is not her own story. She discovers the truth of myth–that identity is in the imagination as much as in the blood. She learns that this is as true for countries as for individuals. She learns the essential ambivalence of consciousness; that time and the river flow both ways. She learns to accept herself, learns freedom, learns that life is a gift, that nothing lasts, and that we are each alone.

Laurence has the special gift of allowing us to share the complex emotional condition of her characters without insisting we understand them, or that the characters understand themselves. In this novel in particular, the language is direct, yet so rich and brimming with allusions and ambiguities that it gives the most casual observations an uncanny resonance and the most chaotic state of consciousness a coherence beyond words. *The Diviners* is by far her most ambitious novel, and it threatened to exhaust its author's resources–only temporarily, one hoped, for the knack of divining or of writing fine novels is not easily lost. Suddenly, with her death in January, 1987, however, we are forced to realize that *The Diviners* is indeed the culmination as well as the apex of her considerable achievement. Not only has Margaret Laurence shown us so much about ourselves that we are forever in her debt, she has helped to shape the way we are. She will be missed.

A.C. LAUT

Lords of the North. Toronto: Ryerson, 1900. Pages: 442.

Agnes Laut's novels and popular histories mark her as a writer with a clear mission to restore our heritage to us. In *Lords of the*

North, she combines dedication to make the past a living presence with determination to make it an entertainment. Skilfully, she blends historical documentary and conventional romantic fiction into a novel as rewarding today, but for a few awkwardnesses of style, as when it first appeared.

The narrative is related by Rufus Gillespie, a retired trader living in Winnipeg late in the nineteenth century; the action he recalls dates back to events in the month preceding the slaughter of June 9, 1816, at Seven Oaks near Fort Frances on the Red River. Through Gillespie, Laut describes the journey west from Quebec with the voyageurs and, in a panoply of detail, provides vivid impressions of life in trading outposts along the way. She draws from authentic accounts, which she has embellished with great fidelity. She describes the wild excitement of a buffalo hunt on the plains, with six hundred mounted hunters and fourteen hundred people following to claim their kill; she describes the Indian encampments, the life of the Bois-Brulés, the rowdy celebrations among traders when they gathered together, and the rough deprivations they endured on their own. With dramatic eloquence, she relates events in the running battle between the Hudson's Bay Company and the North-West Company for control of an empire that would dwarf Europe.

Laut chronicles the desperate struggle between corporate giants at the boardroom level and, more significantly, among the canoemen who carry the traders into the wilderness and the Indians who are their reluctant hosts. In the clash at Seven Oaks–which brought Selkirk's settlers, Indians, Bois-Brulés, and company men into bloody conflict and led to a lasting peace among the adversaries–Laut founds her vision of Canada and the new West. Adversity triumphs in her novel and welds opposites–savage and civilized, nature and man, French and English, Catholic and Protestant, past and present–into a new nation destined for greatness. This seems, in the novel, a likely prospect historically, and dramatically it is a most satisfying outcome to her romance.

The romantic narrative follows young Gillespie, who is pursuing a renegade band of Sioux. The Indians have kidnapped his friend's wife and son in Quebec and spirited them through the wilderness into the vastness of the prairie plains. The friend, Eric Hamilton, treks west with the Hudson's Bay Company; Gillespie travels with the Nor'-Westers. Both are desperately trying to effect a rescue and repeatedly meet with failure due to the conditions of the country, the savagery of the Indians, the feuding between the trading companies, the moral corruption of individuals, and the occasional ineptness of the rescuers. It is a fast and rousing tale, one that allows great scope for Laut's documentary imperative. It lets her move the narrative among historical adversaries, and to shift perspective radically, with only minor turns of plot.

Throughout, Laut develops an aura of the legendary, of the past being honoured. By occasionally using archaic language, and by including several complete songs of the Métis poet Pierre Falcon (who turns up in fiction again, nearly eighty years later, as the posthumous narrator of Rudy Wiebe's *The Scorched-Wood People*), she effectively bridges romance and history. In spite of potentially conflicting intentions, *Lords of the North* reads well as a wholly unified work of the imagination.

STEPHEN LEACOCK

Nonsense Novels. London: John Lane, 1911. Toronto: McClelland and Stewart; New Canadian Library, 1963. Pages: 155. Paperback.

Leacock was so prolific it is sometimes difficult to separate the droll and the dross. *Sunshine Sketches of a Little Town* is his acknowledged masterpiece, but he wrote a great deal more, and much of it was widely celebrated in its time. *Nonsense Novels* does not wear as well as *Sunshine Sketches*, in part because it is a literary parody, and the novels it ridicules are no longer read, and in part because the more enduring work seems to have been conceived, to some extent, as social commentary, a purpose that imposed needed restraints on Leacock's ebullient and undisciplined wit. To take an image from its own pages, *Nonsense Novels* rides off in all directions at once. It plays for laughs at any cost, and while it often elicits laughter, the reader is sometimes left to make his own way back into the narrative. The word-play is closer to Charlie Farquarson's mindless punning than to anything else, and the obvious satisfaction the author takes in his own cleverness is from the same school. Plots and characters are necessarily shallow in abbreviated parodies such as these. Were Leacock truly satirizing the works he ridicules, he might have developed greater depth. As it is, *Nonsense Novels*, along with *Frenzied Fiction*, *Literary Lapses, Short Circuits, et al.*, attempts little more than a bit of fun.

The book consists of ten small novels patterned after types of fiction popular at the turn of the century, which Leacock reduces to their distinctive characteristics and then burlesques with abandon. The Sherlock Holmes character in "Maddened by Mystery: or The Defective Detective" keeps half a bucket of cocaine close by, and a dipper for ladling it out. He deduces the obvious, or entirely disregards it, disguises himself as a dachshund and, after winning his case, is destroyed by the dog-catchers. "Soaked in Seaweed: or Upset in the Ocean (An Old Fashioned Sea-Story)" misuses nautical terms with gay aplomb as it follows Blowhard, the second mate of the *Saucy Sally*, through an adventure that inevitably includes Blowhard's being adrift on a raft, eating his companion, dying on a desert island after missing out on the buried treasure, and burying himself. Depending on the type of work being parodied, Leacock directs his extravagant humour at language or character or situation. In each, however, he captures the essence of the original and then exaggerates it to the point of absurdity.

Sometimes Leacock tries too hard and seems simply silly. But often, even the most cynical reader cannot help but laugh out loud. The parodies themselves suggest a fine grasp of the works they are based on – not a critical understanding of them so much as an intuitive grasp of the needs they played to in their readers' lives. Many people apparently enjoy the side of Leacock displayed in *Nonsense Novels*, just as many find Charlie Farquarson amusing. For those of more demanding taste, Leacock offers a fine alternative with *Sunshine Sketches of a Little Town*.

Sunshine Sketches of a Little Town. New York: John Lane, 1912. Toronto: McClelland and Stewart; New Canadian Library, 1960. Pages: 153. Paperback.

Leacock himself may have been somewhat of an irascible misanthrope – according to some accounts he was difficult to get along with and squandered his talent in pursuit of creature comforts–but this book alone elevates him to the status of beloved national institution. Of all the works by which Canadians are known, both to ourselves and to the world, none surpasses *Sunshine Sketches of a Little Town* as a document of how we would like to have been. It is an affectionate illusion of our common past, as specifically Canadian in detail, as universal in assumptions of value and in exposure of human nature, as any work could be. *Sunshine Sketches* is an idyll, but an idyll tempered with irony. Leacock's Mariposa is endearing and funny; his manner of presenting it shows warmth tinged with regret for its ephemerality. Leacock wrote many other books, but none so effectively balances affection and judgement in equal parts, all in a context of sparkling good spirits. *Arcadian Adventures with the Idle Rich*, in some ways an urban companion piece to *Sunshine Sketches*, seems by comparison bitter rather than biting, sardonic rather than witty, not loving enough of the world it so assiduously exposes. Other works–such as *Literary Lapses* and *Nonsense Novels*–are more gentle, ranging from parody to ridicule, but without the sharp edge that makes *Sunshine Sketches* seem, some seventy years after it first appeared, fresh and original.

Each sketch stands on its own, more anecdote than short story, in which the speaker's personality is an intrinsic part of the effect. The sketches are linked by common characters and, of course, the town of Mariposa. The voice, however, is what ties the sketches together into a unified whole. Leacock speaks directly to the reader, playing the role of mediator between Mariposa and the outside world. In the preface, he introduces himself and suggests that the subject of these sketches could be any one of seventy or eighty communities. In "L'envoi," he allows that Mariposa can only be reached by travelling back to where we have come from. It is a unique place, common to all of us; an idyllic source of the Canadian personality.

Mariposa is not a real place. The people at the centre of the sketches are caricatures, exaggerated generalizations. The situations are prototypical. There never was a Jos. Smith, Prop. of the local hotel, consummate sleazy politician; nor was there a love affair between Peter Pupkin, modest hero, and Zena Pepperleigh; nor a Rev. Mr. Drone. Nor did the *Mariposa Belle* nearly sink, nor did Jefferson Thorpe make and lose a fortune. But there are hundreds of people and events just like these, in every small town, everywhere. And Leacock makes us care about this world, even when he ridicules it. He does this through felicity of detail, on the one hand creating an engaging illusion of reality; on the other, through outrageous intrusions into the text, asserting his own affectionate familiarity with his creations.

Leacock never condescends, but he deflates pretension with relish; he never distorts facts in themselves, but he exaggerates or diminishes their significance with the ease of a born raconteur. He has been called a great satirist, yet there is no measure of reform in his vision, nor even of criticism in the sense that he would have things other than they are. He has been called a great humorist, yet the warmth and wit of *Sunshine Sketches* invokes smiles, not laughter, and a nostalgic sense of loss. The key to *Sunshine Sketches* seems to lie in Leacock's unusual combination of idyll and irony. With this combination he creates a unique vision of human nature: Mariposa is part of every reader's experience of himself.

DOUGLAS LePAN

The Deserter. Toronto: McClelland and Stewart, 1964. 1973. Pages: 298.

Douglas LePan's haunting and eloquent novel is set in London, immediately following the Second World War. Places and dates are not given, however. All things in the novel are anonymous and unlabelled; they seem more the elusive substance of a nightmare than of actuality. This is not the aftermath of one conflict but of all conflicts, perceived by a sensibility at once brutalized and refined by war. In some senses, *The Deserter* is the ultimate war novel, but it is also the archetypal story of fallen man who descends into the underworld in pursuit of nameless perfection. It is a moving, beautiful, and ambitious novel, quite unlike any other in Canadian literature: it echoes Kafka and Goethe and Dante and the Scriptures. The prose is precise yet opaque, ornamental but abstract, filled with metaphor and music, yet authentically, gut-wrenchingly specific. Not being in the realistic mode, *The Deserter* is largely ignored today, except by fans of the war-novel genre who come away from it disconcerted.

LePan is a poet, one of only three Canadians (the others being George Bowering and Margaret Atwood) to win a Governor General's Award for both poetry and fiction. Style and vision, form and content are inseparable. The story itself is a straightforward, episodic account of a deserter, Rusty, who after the war is over walks away from the army with money and a medal in his pocket and melts into the dark side of the capital city. He is uncertain why he deserted, except that it has something to do with a woman named Althea he once picked up on leave, with whom he shared total but brief ecstasy. He descends deeper and deeper into the postwar underworld, where he drinks, sleeps with prostitutes, maintains his independence, and refuses to be drawn into dishonour. Always, he is pursued: by the police from one side, by criminals, who feel his honesty betrays them, from the other. His world changes from glittering excitement to nightmare; he races and walks through the night streets and moves restlessly from room to room. He loses the girl with whom he had taken up because he cannot help her out of her madness, and a young refugee is murdered for trusting him. Finally, he surfaces.

The vision LePan creates is one of fascinating horror. The story is told in an intimate, third-person voice, as LePan presents Rusty's experiences of himself in a postwar world. The questions and mysteries that assail the young protagonist take on palpable force, more real than the city, which is busily rebuilding itself, yet these equations remain largely unnamed. All that Rusty endures, as he descends deeper into the dark, is punctuated by fragments of combat memory. The memories of men in extremity, and himself among them, are more vivid, more immediate than anything in the present. Despite the world's blindness to the horrors it has been through, and despite the deadly routine of reconstruction (essential to its practical survival), LePan envisions at least one man who will accept, however unknowingly, the burden of responsibility. He sinks under such weight to the very depths of possibility but then rises to create a new world. Existential despair builds and builds, and by an act of will dissolves in the end beneath the power of hope.

LePan's prose is intensely experimental and lovely to read. Adding to the dissociated quality of the setting, his language is an international English, rather than specifically British or Canadian English. He has a genius for flourishes of extended metaphor, which search out the image-equivalents of inexpressible emotions or ideas. He melds abstract and concrete in descriptions that convey precisely the physical world and the psychological world at the same time. Syntax is flawless – it is the allusive density of the words, not the grammar, that is unique. The prose is invariably polished, even in the dialogue. The characters all speak in the same smoothly oblique way; yet, curiously, each character comes across as a distinct personality.

The Deserter is not always an easy novel to read, but there are few works of fiction that can draw the reader so completely into another world and sustain him there at such a high level of excitement. It is a demanding experimental novel, unquestionably worth the effort it takes to read it.

ROSANNA LEPROHON

Antoinette de Mirecourt: or, Secret Marrying and Secret Sorrowing. Montreal: John Lovell, 1864. Toronto: McClelland and Stewart; New Canadian Library, 1973. Pages: 200. Paperback.

So much a part of the Québécois literary tradition is this novel that a contemporary reader might be quite surprised to discover it was originally written and published in English. It has been reprinted a number of times in French but was not reprinted in English until the New Canadian Library edition in 1973, more than a century after its original appearance; so the confusion about its history is understandable. As well, before her marriage into a prominent Québécois family, Leprohon published under her maiden name of Mullins. Afterwards, although always writing first in English, she was a familiar figure in the French-Canadian literary establishment and saw virtually all her major works appear in immediate translation to enthusiastic reception. Such marvellous cultural versatility led eventually to oblivion. Fortunately, with the reprinting of *Antoinette de Mirecourt*, a new interest has been sparked in her work in English, and renewed interest in the Québécois tradition has aroused more than passing curiosity about her unique contribution to French letters in Canada.

Many novels in English look to French Canada for the essential ingredients of romantic intrigue demanded by the nineteenth-century reader. Leprohon's fiction is exceptional, however, in that she wrote about Quebec with the profound sympathy and insight of a committed insider. In three thematically related works of romantic fiction, she struggled valiantly against the limitations of the genre to provide accurate, sympathetic, historical portraits of Québécois society. In only one, *Antoinette de Mirecourt*, do the English figure as a significant presence. They appear as a beneficent force of occupation following the Conquest. The other two novels, *The Manor House of de Villerai* and *Armand Durand*, examine society immediately before the Conquest and some time later. In all three novels, Leprohon portrays society in the manner of English social realism in all its stratified complexity, and devises a romantic tale of sentiment and manners that reflects society's virtues while exposing and exploiting its vices. Because *Antoinette de Mirecourt* introduces the English into French society, it retains an added dimension of relevance for the contemporary reader.

Set in the same period of Québécois history as Frances Brooke's *The History of Emily Montague*, which deals with the same social class and many of the same locations, Leprohon's novel curiously seems more authentic in detail and atmosphere. This, despite the fact that Brooke was an eyewitness, writing directly out of her own experience, and Leprohon wrote in historical retrospect, almost a hundred years later. Leprohon, however, does not have Brooke's fine gift for language, nor her biting wit. Keeping to the Victorian conventions of her day, she writes with an excess of sentiment that makes her work seem, at times, a parody of Brooke's social verisimilitude. Both writers incorporate the Canadian landscape and seasons into the narrative flow of their novels, and both intrude occasionally upon the action to ruminate over cultural or social concepts implied by their fiction. Brooke is unquestionably the better artist, but Leprohon provides far deeper insight into the Canadian historical process.

Antoinette, herself, is a modest heiress, a country innocent visiting her cousin, Lucille D'Aulnay, and Lucille's husband in Montreal. Lucille is a woman of worldly experience, an irrepressible and irresponsible teacher for the naïve and beautiful Antoinette. Immediately reconciled to the changes imposed on polite society by the occupation, Lucille entertains British officers at her home while her husband remains sequestered in his library. She plays matchmaker for her younger female friends. Two officers, Major Audley Sternfield and Captain Evelyn, are attracted to Antoinette. Sternfield, who is charming, mean, and an incorrigible flirt, covets Antoinette's wealth. Evelyn, appropriately a Catholic but as disenchanted with the Church as with women, remains aloof. With the blundering complicity of Lucille, Sternfield secretly marries Antoinette, who is then in a miserable state, but who is rescued by her hometown admirer, Louis Beauchesne. Beauchesne kills Sternfield in a duel, effectively annulling the disastrous clandestine marriage, and Antoinette is free to marry her beloved misanthrope, Captain Evelyn. Presumably, she elevates him to a life of altruistic enchantment after the novel closes.

The plot is melodramatic, and Leprohon handles it with extravagance of language and sentiment. The novel nevertheless speaks resoundingly to the social problems of romantic intemperance. Marriage not for moral worth and practical suitability but for love was a notion quite alarming to Leprohon and her peers. Her novel would make delightful light reading under any circumstances, but with its historical implications on the bicultural experience in Canada, its determined sense of social responsibility, and its historical authenticity—combined with its revelations of sensibility of its own mid-Victorian times—it is an important novel, fortunately now retrieved from the library archives.

NORMAN LEVINE

From a Seaside Town. Toronto: Macmillan, 1970.
Pages: 220. Markham: Deneau, 1980. Paperback.

If novels could be characterized the way humans are, I would call this one "morose." Perhaps "erratic." Certainly "indulgent." On the whole, like someone you might wish to spend a few hours with, but not a lifetime. And that explains its effectiveness, for this novel has the shape of a personality, rather than of a narrative in any conventional sense: it draws a whole life together through a brilliant pastiche of vignettes and episodes, within a few brief and easily read pages. It is not a novel of character so much as it is "novel as character." Joseph Grand, in the process of living, is at the narrative centre; but the novel provides dimensions to his personality and experience of which he is hardly aware. We know him, in other words, better than he knows himself–a lovely irony, considering he intends (from within the text) the book to be confessional. But, of course, it is Norman Levine's work, imbued with a character of its own, and Joseph is only a single facet, albeit the dominant one, of the novel as a whole.

Levine writes a simple colloquial English, colloquial although it is hard to tell just where exactly in the world the voice originates. Language and syntax are informal, as if he were talking the novel, and pared to the bone–less for economy, perhaps, than for the haunting ambiguities that come of precise and minimal accounts of things. When describing scenery and setting, the effect is almost lyrical. In descriptions of people and relationships, it seems enigmatic, sometimes to the point of being terse and a little arrogant. Nevertheless, it is a voice in keeping with the author's conception of his novel, apparently, as a personality in its own right.

Seemingly in counterpoint to his prose, the structure of Levine's narrative is elliptical, diffuse, fragmented (it depends on where you are–it is any and all of these). There is no plot as such. Joseph offers us what he describes as a sequence of confessions, and what is essentially the serial account of his life as a writer through nearly a decade of poverty, privation, and petty personal indulgences masquerading as strategies for artistic survival. Joseph is not particularly a likeable man, but he is convincingly and brutally honest. What he gives, in place of plot, is as much of himself as seems to him worth giving, and various accounts of friends, neighbours, and family as occur to him during the course of his writing. Levine allows Joseph to deliver himself and his world to us apparently at random. Yet, where structure might seem incidental, discipline is not. The author shows superb control in building an intricate, dense, and carefully modulated vision of life as a difficult but somehow worthwhile endeavour.

Not that anyone in *From a Seaside Town* enjoys life very much. There are small pleasures, small compensations, but they usually sour or prove false. Joseph Grand lives with his wife, Emily,

and their three daughters in the English seaside town of Carnbray,
patterned perhaps on St. Ives, where Levine lived for a number of
years. They are desperately broke and quite unhappy together, it
seems. Joseph is Canadian, Jewish, a writer, and fairly jaded.
Emily is English, not Jewish, not, she says, good at anything much,
and expects little from life, in her husband's estimation, beyond
the occasional diversion provided by visitors from London or a
cheque in the mail. Emily is *the wife*. (Sadly, it seems neither her
husband nor her author recognizes just how abused she really is
by the circumstances of her life.) Periodically, Joseph visits local
friends, or travels to nearby towns, or visits friends in London, or,
on one occasion sponsored by the income from an article, visits
family in Ottawa and old haunts from college days in Montreal.
All of this is done without Emily. She stays at home. All of this is
to help him cope with the burden of being a writer, being himself.

Some of Joseph's friends are interesting, in fact, more interesting than Joseph. They all have English names that sound exactly
alike to the mind's ear: Arthur, Albert, Charles, Walter. One is a
cuckold. One is a successful painter, two are homosexuals, one is
an inveterate traveller and womanizer. Several are womanizers.
One is a suicide. None are happy. These and others enter Joseph's
life in a series of narrative interludes. His rich and sleazy friend,
Jimmy Middleton, dies suddenly. He has an unrequited affair with
Anna Likely, who eventually becomes a sleazy movie star. His
father dies. Time passes. Visitors come and go. Time accumulates,
as one interlude bleeds into another. Life is a bleeding; in effect, a
blood-letting. After years of this, the novel ends. But, surprisingly,
it does not drag–it is interesting, engaging, and on the whole quite
moving.

Not until Chapter Five does the narrator acknowledge that he
is in the act of writing, that what we read is "in progress," even
though it is always related in the past tense, as having just
happened. The first few chapters seem evasive, as he focuses on
his friends, his wife, and on the town of Carnbray, on anything
but himself. But, of course, in these and other seemingly haphazard sketches we see much of Joseph's character indirectly revealed.
And such indirection, carefully controlled, is what makes the novel
so good. Each anecdote, sketch, episode, and aside (there is even a
sad confessional short story included, which Joseph claims to be
the summation of his first five years of marriage) are shadings in

the portrait of a life. As they accumulate and as we get to know so much about the narrator without really knowing him, we recognize that both Joseph and Norman Levine have been subsumed by the personality of the novel itself.

Joseph Grand comes a long way from Ottawa's Lower Town to brief internment in a derelict Jewish cemetery in Penzance and, ultimately, to completion of his confessional project. Levine, in creating him, comes farther. And the novel stands apart from them both, containing them, with a life of its own.

MALCOLM LOWRY

Under the Volcano. London: Cape, 1947. Scarborough: New American Library, 1984. Pages: 328. Paperback.

Under the Volcano is far more celebrated than read. Its author is an international legend among literati, only the most committed of whom have actually turned the novel's pages, one by one, and read the excruciatingly convoluted and allusive prose. Lowry was a tragic drunk. His writing is the plaintive, grasping, eloquent diary of that tragedy; most of his published work has appeared posthumously, and most stays close to the format of a personal journal, revealing in discontinuous fragments brilliant flashes of writing along with the tortured personality of the man who creates them. His work seems the random detritus of immense intellect and undisciplined talent up against an impoverished imagination. *Hear Us O Lord from Heaven Thy Dwelling Place, Dark Is the Grave Wherein My Friend Is Laid,* and *October Ferry to Gabriola* are unfinished; they contain aspects of a greater whole that was not, and perhaps could never have been, completed. Lowry's first novel, *Ultramarine,* is an apprentice novel, and the posthumous *Lunar Caustic* is a self-indulgent, surrealistic portrait of depravity. Only *Under the Volcano,* out of the thousands of pages Lowry wrote, stands as a finished and fine work of art.

Under the Volcano is set in and around the Mexican town of Quauhnahuac on the Day of the Dead in November, 1938. The novel actually begins exactly a year later, and an introductory chapter sets the three main characters and the events of that fatal day into a looming sort of perspective. Since the future is known, everything, including the death of Geoffrey Fermin, is inevitable. Lowry obliquely introduces Fermin, the ex-British consul, first through his friend Laruelle and then through the eyes of his ex-wife, Yvonne, who has just returned, compelled by fatal love, to attend his last day. Fermin finally comes into focus, and he is drunk, has been drunk for years, and will continue to drink throughout the long day ahead, which Lowry details with painstaking deliberation. The other main character is Hugh, Fermin's younger half-brother, a seeker of the full and active life. With Hugh and Yvonne sometimes leading, sometimes in tow, Geoffrey Fermin struggles through the hours, continuously feeding his raging thirst with beer, wine, tequila, and finally mescal. He fights with his companions, separately and together, parts with them bitterly, is shot to death in the street by the police; his body is dumped into a ravine. It is a brutal story, though neither pathetic nor tragic.

As Lowry allows each moment of the day to move fitfully into the past, he defines the worlds inhabited by each of the three main characters, in memory and dream, in knowledge and perception. Hugh's story is a simple narrative of a fickle boy who went to sea and who still yearns for adventure. Yvonne's life has seen greater heights (she was a movie actress) and greater depths (she has lived through three marriages, a miscarriage, and her proud, sad love for the consul). Geoffrey Fermin's life, however, contains these other two lives, contains worlds beyond their reckoning. He is the central reality. The others are merely presences in his mind, joined by fragments of memory from other times, knowledge of the vast political machinery of civilization, eclectic knowledge of literature, philosophy, languages, knowledge of the cabala, the occult, and the broad reaches of hell, as well as its depths. In Fermin's inebriation, as he struggles for and against meaning in the chaos of his perceptions, as Fermin fights drinking and loses, loves Yvonne and loses, Lowry creates a squalid, morbid, and almost obscenely intellectual vision of one man's descent into hell, the whole of Western civilization on his conscience. It is an overwhelming achievement.

Under the Volcano is a challenging novel to read. Lowry's erudition and his showing-off are difficult to separate. His words are invariably precise, but his sentence structure is awkward, and deliberately so, as he moves from chaos towards clarity. Words become artifacts: lists, schedules, menus, place-names become things in themselves–consciousness sometimes seems at their mercy. Each physical step of the day is described, as the narrative slowly moves towards completion, towards a vortex within the whirling fragments of meaning and allusion. Endless details within Fermin's experience–from the pavement rising up to meet him as he collapses to ominous birds flying overhead–all are described with meticulous care. Gradually, as the disciplined form within which Lowry is working imposes itself, everything takes on meaning–until, finally, style and form and meaning are fused, the dreams of Canada and the future collapse, and there is only the past, and then nothing.

HUGH MacLENNAN

Barometer Rising. Toronto: Collins, 1941. Toronto: Macmillan, 1969. Toronto: McClelland and Stewart; New Canadian Library, 1960. Pages: 219. Paperback.

Hugh MacLennan's name denotes quality, whether it be printed on a coffee-table art book, a collection of essays, or a novel. He is a writer of unique stature in Canada, as his receipt of five Governor General's Awards testifies. He comes the closest of our writers to being the artist as statesman. This stature, in part, is due to his personal demeanour, but much more to the careful, thoughtful, dignified, thoroughly intelligent quality of his writing. MacLennan's novels engage the reader's mind and heart, though seldom his imagination. He is not an artist inspired to create new worlds or new visions, but a craftsman, intent on relating stories that, in his judgement, are worth telling. There is much of the practical Presbyterian in MacLennan's approach to the art of fiction.

MacLennan's fiction was the perfect correlative for the age in Canada that he so much dominated. From the forties into the sixties, MacLennan was generally regarded as the premier Canadian novelist, and his fiction was considered definitive Canadian art. It was, perhaps, such conservatism that made people of literary sensibility so ready, in the mid-sixties, for the literary explosion in Canadian letters ignited by Margaret Laurence, the House of Anansi, the Canada Council, *Canadian Literature*, and like forces.

MacLennan purposely addressed himself to the middle-distance world on Canada's behalf, with varying degrees of success. *Each Man's Son* remains a classic, while *The Precipice* has slipped into oblivion. The first echoes Western cultural mythology, but tells a story unique to its own time and place, while the second tries too hard to be definitively Canadian and to explain American and Canadian cultures to each other. *The Return of the Sphinx* no longer seems relevant, while the more naïve *Two Solitudes* remains widely read, revealing less political sophistication but far more compassion, less generalization, and more of the particular. The rhetoric of trying to account for the failure of civilization from a Canadian perspective overwhelms narrative proprieties in *Voices in Time*, MacLennan's most recent novel. In the most enduring and ambitious of his novels, *The Watch That Ends the Night*, definition of the Canadian experience remains largely implicit in the adventurous inquiry into the conditions of mortality. Possibly his most popular work is still his first published novel, *Barometer Rising*, in which self-conscious Canadianism is so thoroughly integrated as to make the novel virtually a political allegory.

Barometer Rising reads well. It is a dramatic reworking of the Ulysses story in a Canadian setting during the First World War, told largely from the point of view of Penelope, who awaits the return of her lost warrior. Penelope Wain is a successful Halifax naval architect whose lover, her first cousin Neil MacRae, was disgraced and apparently killed while serving under her father at the Front. Major Angus Murray, a middle-aged medical officer and likeable drunk, acts as her confidant and foil. Murray wants to marry her even when she reveals that Jean, the daughter of her aunt and uncle, is really her child by Neil. Neil returns, incognito, determined to vindicate his name and lay the blame where it belongs–on Colonel Wain. To complicate things, Neil was brought up in the Wain household, so the colonel is not only a villainous blood relative and father-in-law figure, but a father-figure as well. Neil must find Big Alec MacKenzie, the only one who knows Wain is culpable. Complications ensue, but all is resolved by the devastating explosion of a French munitions ship

in the Halifax harbour. Murray's medical skills are brought back
into practice; Neil proves himself level-headed in a crisis; Colonel
Wain is killed, naked, with his mistress; Big Alec signs a sworn
statement of Neil's innocence, and authenticates it by dying;
Penny's aunt and uncle are killed, freeing Jean to be returned to
her rightful parents.

It is hard not to be cynical about so mechanistic a plot. However,
MacLennan has created an exciting account of lives in dramatic
conflict. He writes an articulate generous prose. His characters
are not psychologically realistic, but they are dramatically convincing. The allegorical underpinnings are well integrated: as a
story of the returning combatant claiming his rightful place, echoing conditions of colonialism and empire, relations between Canada and Britain, it is illuminating. First and foremost, the novel
is an intelligent entertainment.

Barometer Rising is in some ways a prototype for MacLennan.
Its themes, motifs, incidents, and dramatic devices recur, with
sometimes dismaying frequency, throughout his canon–dismaying
only in their cumulative effect and not, of course, in their separate occurrences. True and false parenthood, and the relationships
between fathers and sons, real or surrogate, repeatedly occupy
MacLennan's imagination. Women tend to display a sexuality
that transcends physical presence, and a grace that transcends
intellect. There is often a love triangle, in which the third party
is a rather weak, suffering male. Births or origins are often mysterious and tragic. Dead soldiers return to life, or soldiers return
from war with the shadow of death forever upon them. People are
stamped, though not stereotyped, by race and religion. Catastrophe resolves plot complications, moral conundrums, and character conflict. Always behind the narrative, there is the covert
presence of the warm and knowing author at work trying to make
us believe him.

Two Solitudes. Toronto: Collins, 1945. Toronto:
Macmillan; Laurentian Library, 1968. Pages: 412.
Paperback.

Two Solitudes is the most determinedly Canadian of MacLennan's
novels. Many regard it as his best, but this judgement seems more

for the novel's polemical intent than for its aesthetic achievement. In *Two Solitudes*, MacLennan creates several memorable characters; the most notable is Athanase Tallard. He also offers several of his shallowest, especially Tallard's wife, Kathleen, whose main function appears to be to provide Paul Tallard with an anglophone mother, the better to use Paul as a representative of the new Canada. Typical of MacLennan's work, and of good popular fiction at the time, *Two Solitudes* is straightforward in all matters of form; stylistically, it is without a flourish. The narrative voice is vaguely patronizing, very self-assured, and has not only an omniscient view of happenings but an all-knowing command of their implications, particularly on a socio-political plane. It is a highly engaging novel that seems, at the same time, to be of lofty purpose. Well-crafted, a pleasure to read, and good for you – a combination that is hard to beat.

MacLennan leaves little doubt as to his novel's political intent: characters represent aspects of the Canadian reality, which is analysed and defined through their various conversations, actions, and relationships, or by the authorial voice speaking directly to the reader. The first half of the novel is dominated by Athanase Tallard and his sad and inexorable fall from power. He represents the old Québécois aristocracy, which, in breaking faith with the ancestral past, seeks a reconciliation with English Canada, with capitalism, Protestantism, and parliamentary democracy, and is ultimately left with nothing. His "French" son, Marius, ends up in domestic squalor; his second wife, Kathleen, gives herself over to an American; his "English" son, Paul, leaves the ancestral fiefdom, St. Marc, and Quebec as well. In Part Two, after eight years of wandering the world's oceans, and after picking up an Oxford degree, Paul Tallard returns as an ambitious young writer to join forces with Heather Methuen, a Westmount rebel who proves her free spirit by studying in Lausanne and working in New York. Together at the novel's end, they will make the new Canada and make it work. But first, the war.

In retrospect it is a naïve vision and terribly paternalistic. The Québécois are diminished to the status of an ethnic group. The new elite is to be a laundered version of the old establishment. We, the people, will unite in a common purpose to vanquish our hatred and find tolerance for our differences. The Church, played by Father Beaubien, the really rich, played by Sir Rupert Irons, and the benevolent arbitrator, played by the sympathetic French-speaking anglophone, Captain Yardley, are strategically deployed to convey this message and to give it the stamp of truth.

Amid these procedures, MacLennan provides fine insights into the medieval Catholicism that dominated Quebec, and into the Norman character of the Québécois personality. He offers a sensitive and intelligent picture of social problems, but also offers solutions (which inevitably, with the passing of time, must prove to be simplistic, inadequate, or simply wrong-headed). Recognition is given to these limitations when, in *Return of the Sphinx*, the author rescinds some of his more benign assumptions. *Two Solitudes* is a prime example of how art, used for ends outside its own context, may be sorely diminished.

Each Man's Son. Toronto: Macmillan, 1951. Toronto: Macmillan; Laurentian Library, 1971. Pages: 244. Paperback.

MacLennan's highest achievement as an artist is represented by this, the least pretentious of his novels. *Each Man's Son* lacks the profound insights of *The Watch That Ends the Night*; it also lacks that book's awkward characterization and forced plot. Nor does it show the socio-political aspirations of his other fiction. *Each Man's Son* is a well-balanced and subtle novel; at the same time, it is graphic, dramatic, and highly moving. The cultural, historic, and geographic conditions of Cape Breton are fully integrated both into the plot and into the characters' lives–rather than being pressed upon them as their burden. The motifs of true and false parenthood, of origins in violence and mystery, of the suffering hero of mythic proportions, of the passive but involved observer, of ethereal or enigmatic women, are all here. They are so well worked into the narrative design that they seem strikingly original, yet also offer echoes of age-old tradition. In *Each Man's Son*, MacLennan's background as a classical scholar is most evident, yet paradoxically least obtrusive. It is the work that most surely guarantees his place at the very centre of the Canadian literary pantheon.

As with most MacLennan novels, there are two heroes; one is passive and one active. Eight-year-old Alan occupies the focal centre, yet it is Dr. David Ainslie who is the novel's dominant personality. Alan is the son of three "fathers." Pulling on him from one side is Ainslie, the Cape Breton Highlander. The embodiment of strength in individuality, Ainslie has no son of his own. On the other side is Archie, the husband of his mother, Molly MacNeill. Archie is a prize-fighter whose Highland instincts have long since been corrupted. Also serving as a father figure is Molly's friend, Louis Camire, a curiously effete representative of the masses. The plot turns around Archie's discovery of Molly's infidelity and his murder of that pathetic woman and her uninspired lover. The murder frees Alan to become Ainslie's charge and provides the culmination of Ainslie's story, told in parallel with that of Molly and her son.

Dr. Ainslie is one of MacLennan's "superior" people. As with all such heroes, there is much suffering in his background and much wilfulness in his character. He is a doctor in an area remote from the benefits of modern science; he is of deliberate and refined sensibility in a region given to rough amusements; he is a dedicated and compassionate professional. And he is doomed to suffer in isolation. MacLennan gives him immense strength of character, but at the cost of terrible solitude that even his wife, Margaret, cannot penetrate. Ainslie's mother died a martyr to his father's obsessive pride: much of Ainslie's personality, perhaps too conveniently, has its source in a grim Presbyterian childhood. He and Margaret cannot have children. Alan, then, is not only to be a surrogate son but a surrogate self. It is a complex connection, the implications of which are explained in *Return of the Sphinx*, which takes place a full generation later.

In *Each Man's Son*, MacLennan's prose shows an emotional dimension not apparent in his other fiction. Usually, his use of language suggests a Rockwell illustration more than a Wyeth painting. It is clear, direct, and unambiguous. Here, however, it is informed with a special quality, in the imagery, the diction, the fortuitous choice of words and phrases, that conveys not only heart and mind, but soul as well. Perhaps due to its autobiographical resonance, this novel rings with truth–not merely an inspired illustration but a genuine work of vision, of art.

HUGH MacLENNAN

The Watch That Ends the Night. Toronto: Macmillan, 1959. Toronto: Macmillan; Laurentian Library, 1975. Pages: 373. Paperback.

Despite its extravagant plot and characterization, something about this novel conveys a private hurt deep into the reader's sensibility. *The Watch That Ends the Night* is about death and coping with death. It is a masterpiece of spiritual reconciliation and acceptance, as mature an explication of middle age, and those conditions of mortality attendant upon it, as has yet been written.

In terms of form, this novel is by far the most complex MacLennan has written – as if he were searching for the means adequate to his loftier purpose. The plot depends, for much of its impact, upon the carefully wrought arrangement of temporally discontinuous episodes. Told in a linear pattern, the story would have lost the rich network of implication and significance that MacLennan builds from one set of events to another. His use of flashbacks and extended excursions into the past draws events from quite separate times into a complex, emotional structure. The reader's vantage point is outside the sweep of time, where the ironic implications of events are dramatically apparent, even while they seem to occur, within the novel's context, in an orderly, inevitable flow.

Jerome Martell is the dominant figure in the novel. Even more than Athanase Tallard in *Two Solitudes* or David Ainslie in *Each Man's Son*, he is of mythic proportions – "not like other men." Certainly on one level he is a Christ-figure, with all the allusive paraphernalia that that implies, including resurrection. He is a close replica of Dr. Norman Bethune; he is, as well, a returning Odysseus, and perhaps a Byronic prophet of Protestant theology. He comes, nameless, from the New Brunswick interior and is adopted by a clergyman; he eventually becomes a great but rebellious doctor in Montreal. He leaves his wife, Catherine, and their daughter to go off to the Spanish Civil War with his mistress; he returns, as the novel opens, in the 1950s, after being reported dead during the Second World War, to find his wife married to his old friend George Stewart. After helping Catherine and George both through the crisis of Catherine's death, he sets off for China, an ascension of sorts.

All this is seen from George Stewart's perspective. He and Catherine provide the context. The novel tells the story of their lives as shaped by Martell in the past and present. If Martell is somewhat overwhelming as a presence in realistic fiction, it is in part because the narrator is rather fey, and Catherine is too mindlessly compliant to be true. Their reality and Martell's do not always appear to be on the same plane. Yet, on the thematic level, this threesome forms a dynamic paradigm for the essential aspects of love, for reconciliation with mortality, and for spiritual transcendence. George is the novel's consciousness, so to speak, and working upon him is a powerful will to live, as represented by Jerome Martell, and an inspiring grace to accept, as represented by Catherine. Through their complicated three-way relationship, George takes possession of himself as a whole person, physical and spiritual. He is the weakest character in the novel; it is nevertheless his novel – he is a common man in a secular world – and MacLennan's only sustained attempt in fiction to rise above describing the social conditions that normally so fascinate him.

Much of the action in *The Watch That Ends the Night* occurs during the Depression in Montreal, and it is a first-rate document of those times, presented from the ironic retrospective view of the fifties. Characters in this novel, as in all MacLennan's fiction, do not develop. The circumstances around them change, but they remain relatively constant. They are not psychological creations but the dramatis personae in the drama of their own lives. MacLennan's prose style is more elevated in this novel than in his others, and more restrained and precise, except when Jerome Martell is present. Martell himself is most engaging and, paradoxically, distracting; he overwhelms the reality he is meant to redeem. *The Watch That Ends the Night* is a fine flawed novel, possibly the author's best, if the extent of its aspirations are a measure of its worth.

JOHN MARLYN

Under the Ribs of Death. Toronto: McClelland and Stewart, 1957. Toronto: McClelland and Stewart; New Canadian Library, 1964. Pages: 220. Paperback.

This novel pares the immigrant experience in Canada down to its bones. The skeleton is sound enough, even striking, but it cries out for flesh to warm it, to give it shape and character. It cries for the spark of life, for soul, to make it move. *Under the Ribs of Death* is a theme novel, a story told with single-minded determination in order to illustrate a structure of ideas. Other immigrant novels, from Wiseman's *The Sacrifice* to Salverson's *The Viking Heart*, build on the inevitable immigrant themes of alienation, dissociation, and assimilation, giving us complex dramas of human pride and passion. Marlyn provides a case history. It is for this reason that his novel has lasting significance in the Canadian tradition. *Under the Ribs of Death* endures as a typical account, of which the many other works of immigrant fiction seem variants.

The novel opens in May, 1913, in that fecund barrow of immigrant promise, the North End of Winnipeg; it closes with the Depression, a generation later, only a few blocks from where it all started. Sandor Hunyadi grows from a twelve-year-old boy, bitterly ashamed of his Hungarian parentage, into a broken man named Alex Hunter. The novel is in two parts. The first details Sandor's humiliation. He yearns to be English, to come naturally (as he imagines it) to wealth, power, and refinement. Marlyn details Sandor's bitterness with a certain nostalgic affection, tempered by a judicial severity of tone: the more Sandor denies his authentic self, the more clearly the author underlines his wrongheadedness. In his ingratiating relations with English boys his own age, in his contempt for his family, Sandor is judged harshly by the author. Yet, always, Sandor has enough compassion, enough humility, that we remain attached to him, concerned for his welfare. In the second part, Sandor becomes Alex Hunter, aggressively making his way in the world of business. He marries another immigrant, Mary, and they have a son. The bottom falls out of both the economy and his fortunes. He is disconsolate. But his family rallies to him: in the end, the continuity of generations so terribly threatened by the immigrant experience has been restored. Social progress has been slowed but not halted. Sandor/Alex, neither Hungarian nor English, becomes Canadian.

Sandor's father once tells him of the progress, in four generations, of their family from serf to peasant to worker to gentleman scholar. The father does not see that the largest gulf is between the last two phases, and that it will take Sandor's generation to bridge them. Sandor is a scheming wheeler-dealer, a Duddy Kravitz but without conviction or *élan*. He responds to the principles of democratic capitalism as if they were rungs on a ladder. Were he drawn by Marlyn with more depth or complexity, he might have been a tragic archetype. Were he imbued with irony, he might have provided sardonic commentary on the world or himself. As it is, he is often little more than a cipher in a context of sombre social realism.

Further limiting the dimension of Marlyn's novel are problems of wooden characterization and stagey dialogue. Only Sandor's Onkel Janos comes alive, and this happens through the sheer vitality emanating from the character himself. Despite the uninspired prose and the limitations already suggested, there is a certain forthright authenticity to Marlyn's novel. The ethnic details, the careful descriptions of the Winnipeg locale, the period details: all contribute to its static but convincing quality. It does not have the aura of art or even of truth: rather it seems to come out of personal experience, remembered with a mixture of fondness and cynicism from a comfortable vantage outside the novel's reality – as if Sandor's son had grown up to tell the tale.

NELLIE L. McCLUNG

Sowing Seeds in Danny. Toronto: Wm. Briggs, 1908.
Toronto: T. Allen, 1965. Pages: 313.

It is difficult to imagine anyone's not liking McClung's novels. Nellie McClung, the woman, is justly celebrated today by feminists, but her fiction, exemplified by *Sowing Seeds in Danny*, is now largely forgotten or ignored (or, worse yet, wrongly dismissed as "evangelical" writing). This is the first and probably the best of the three Pearl Watson novels. It is rather capriciously named after Pearl's four-year-old brother who, in one small segment of the book, is a beneficiary of the attentions of Mrs. Francis. This well-meaning woman is determined to sow in Danny the seeds of an enlightened life, when what he really needs are food in his stomach and clothes to shield him from the Manitoba winter. McClung writes with an acutely developed social consciousness – she deftly ridicules hypocrisy at every level of society, moving from one level to another without a trace of condescension (in itself a revolutionary achievement for her time). She displays a strong moral bent, but tempered always with an abundance of irony and wit. This novel deserves to be read – indeed, celebrated. It is a fine work of humour, with an irreverent charm and a guileless innocence about it that quite sensibly rewards virtue with money; a childlike book that only the jaded could not enjoy.

Sowing Seeds in Danny has few aesthetic pretensions: it is an entertainment. Yet every word is right, every sentiment, no matter how extravagant, completely appropriate, every contrivance justified. McClung shares with Mark Twain the rare ability to be sentimental without being soppy or silly – there is always just that touch of cynicism to keep things in order. She is a match for Twain, or any writer, at capturing dialect. You can tell what part of Ireland a speaker comes from, and how long he has been in Canada, or the origin of a child's parents, from the generous way McClung has with their words – she overdoes it just enough to make the manner of speaking amusing in itself. Another quality she shares with Twain is a special genius that allows a child's precocity to flourish without the child's seeming to be an obnoxious, saccharine twit. McClung's children can be selfless, pathetic, and brave, but they are also irascible avaricious schemers, sometimes cheeky and sometimes sullen. And the best of them, Pearl, is wildly imaginative as well.

Pearl is the central character in the novel, but the narrative line seems to meander at leisure, touring half the population of Millford, Manitoba, and the surrounding Souris River valley. McClung creates memorable characters in bold strokes, and then moves on, seemingly at random, to devote another chapter to another cluster of characters. Yet these are no mere sketches, for, as in a Kurelek painting, the details come together to make the whole a finished work. There is, in fact, a variety of plot-lines that are tied up rather neatly in the end. But character and vision dominate the novel.

The vision is of community, a record of its complex personality from a keen but benevolent perspective, and of the lives of the people who live there. Here are the young doctor and the alcoholic old doctor, the severe clergyman who is in love, the businessman, the farmer, their wives and daughters. There is no hint of feminism, yet McClung's clear view of woman's function in Millford society implies the necessity of the coming change. Perhaps, though, the feminist element in the novel is expressed in

Pearl Watson, for at twelve she is self-sufficient and capable, as appealing as Tom Sawyer ever was, and twice as smart.

McClung writes with fearless sentimentality and irresistible humour. Whether it is one of the Watson children begrudgingly awarding another a chew of his gum for going to bed in midday so that yet another can wear the only decent pair of pants among them; or whether it is a maliciously delightful description of character ("she was known to have a leaning towards canned goods"), or a play on words ("Mrs. Ducker considered it more serious to drop a final *g* than a dinner plate"), the humour abounds. The humour of situation and character and language, however, is balanced by a lyric beauty that creeps into the prose; there is a rich sprinkling of song, and a few moving, if maudlin, episodes of unadulterated pathos.

Pearl Watson should really be an integral part of the Canadian experience. Her origins are not lofty, her world is too bleak to allow her Anne Shirley's simple charm. Her creator was too beneficent to grant her Brian O'Connal's depths of experience. But she is a fine character, nonetheless.

EDWARD McCOURT

Music at the Close. Toronto: Ryerson, 1947. Toronto: McClelland and Stewart; New Canadian Library, 1966. Pages: 222. Paperback.

Edward McCourt's novels have a stolid thoroughness that puts them at the very centre of prairie realism. Probably no other writer has provided as complete a social record of an era: the prairies in the second generation of settlement. Social authenticity, however, is not matched by depth of characterization or subtleties of thematic development. McCourt's prose does not enhance his subject matter; it is serviceable but it does not provide an equivalent to the power of the prairie scene or the passion of his romantic plots.

It is for their strength as dramatic documents that McCourt's novels have been measured, and *Music at the Close* selected as a representative work. *Home Is the Stranger* is more dynamic in plot and characterization, as it relates the story of a war bride adjusting to the Canadian experience, albeit at the cost of a battered marriage and a child's death. *The Wooden Sword* attempts greater insight into behaviour, attempts greater profundity, primarily by generalizing. *Music at the Close*, however, is McCourt's most competent work in its use of prairie life and the prairie setting.

Story is important to McCourt. It can be readily extrapolated from context, but when that is done it seems mechanistic and arbitrary – and excessively romantic, although he is not writing romance. His characters are in the realistic mode, and the social setting and the prairie environment approach the naturalistic in the attention he gives to documentary authenticity. The consequence of mixing genres the way he does is that characters often appear uncomfortable within their context; personalities are out of place in their own lives. Only the prairie rings true – and therein lies McCourt's lasting strength as a novelist.

The story in *Music at the Close* moves chronologically through Neil Fraser's life, from the time he arrives, a twelve-year-old orphan, at his great-uncle Matt's farm in 1918, until his death on a Normandy beach in 1944. War provides the perimeters of the story, but the drama takes place on the prairie in the years between. Neil's life is encumbered by failure that seems imposed on him by a wilful world, but which, as McCourt makes clear, in fact comes from his own personality. His main problems are that he cannot seem to resolve the differences between dream and reality; he cannot fully commit himself to any ideal; he is an outsider. Neil is an *étranger*, isolated even from himself by a defect in his character – which is emblematic of the defect in his whole lost generation between the wars.

While he is still a child, there is room in his life for romantic illustions. He rides his pony, helps his uncle with the farm, and becomes a star of the baseball tournaments. But the older he gets, the more easily reality undermines his aspirations. He loses Moira Glenn to his friend Gil Reardon. Later, working as a strike-breaker in the Saskatchewan coal field, he becomes inspired by Gil, who is a labour organizer, and switches sides; when Gil dies for the cause, Neil marries his widow, Moira. This comes after Neil makes an entirely unsatisfactory attempt at university and after he loses most of his inherited farm through reckless overproduction. The

Depression and his own despair contribute to a brutalizing domestic life. Moira has an affair with a remittance man, in a close parallel to the affair Gil's sister had, years earlier, with another remittance man, whom Neil idolized, an affair that ended in murder. The war, then, comes as a relief for Neil, and his death brings him a sort of peace. His wife and son at home will be as well off without him. For once, he ceases to be an observer—imminent death forced him to accept himself. His death, as McCourt has it, justifies his life. Yet the reader cannot help feeling that this, too, is illusion, that the music at the close of Neil's life is arbitrarily imposed, like a final symphonic arrangement on a movie sound track.

As a study of isolation, of man's alienation even from himself, of loneliness and despair, *Music at the Close* is somberly effective. As a portrait of prairie society, it is a fascinating document. It does not have the brooding power of other prairie novels—*As for Me and My House* or *Grain*, for example, both of which came before it—but it provides far more detail of the everyday lives of people who lived through the troubled twenties and the dirty thirties. *Home Is the Stranger* provides a fitting postwar sequel and might well be read in tandem with this novel for a more comprehensive picture of the region that owes so much to McCourt for providing it with definition.

THOMAS McCULLOCH

The Stepsure Letters. Serially, in the *Acadian Recorder*: Halifax, December 22, 1821-May 11, 1822 (critics and rebuttals to March 1823). Book published as **Letters of Mephibosheth Stepsure**. Halifax: Blackadar, 1862. Toronto: McClelland and Stewart; New Canadian Library, 1960. Pages: 149. Paperback.

This slim volume anticipates a major trend in Canadian humour and much in the Canadian experience and personality. The book explores our Presbyterian side, at its most delightfully self-righteous, chuckling in amusement at its own audacity and smiling benignly at accepting its innate superiority. Stepsure's wit and wisdom have been largely overshadowed by Thomas Haliburton's more gregarious Sam Slick, with his wise saws and cunning ways. The vehicle of Haliburton's Tory cant appeared fifteen years later, in emulation of McCulloch, and caught the public imagination abroad, thus making its author a celebrity at home. Yet the author of *The Stepsure Letters* was a worthy public man. He published two novels, *William* and *Melville*, in 1824 and 1826 respectively, and three volumes of thought on religious subjects, whose titles are a tale in themselves–*Popery Condemned*, *Popery Again Condemned*, and *Calvinism*. He was an important Presbyterian educator in early Nova Scotian life, a man of letters, of science, of philosophy, and–for which we are ever in his debt–of bemused social conscience.

The letters from Mephibosheth Stepsure to readers in Halifax of the *Acadian Recorder* were published serially as reports from a country correspondent. Yet they show a consistency and continuity unusual in the genre. Each builds on its predecessors like chapters in a novel. Through his persona, Stepsure, the author sometimes alters the course of his narrative to deal with critics or expound on the progress of his undertaking. Thus we have the curious anomaly of fiction being aware of its own effect.

Unlike Sam Slick, Stepsure does not ramble around the province; he stays determinedly close to home. That is one of his prime maxims for a good life–stay home. Even the town he lives near offers no end of opportunity for wasted industry and insincere society. Like Stephen Leacock, McCulloch defines a single small-town community, while poking gleeful fun at its follies. The difference, though, is that McCulloch knows with a certainty how its inhabitants could be much improved, while Leacock contents himself with the deflation of hypocrisies and pretensions. McCulloch is closer, perhaps, to Robertson Davies in the Salterton trilogy, sharing with Davies a love of the *bon mot*, relish in the rapier thrust of a satiric jest, taking pleasure in the display of authorial charm, impious wit, and the sure knowledge of what is right and good and true.

The humour of these letters is inseparable from the austere message they convey. Through a variety of devices, McCulloch delivers his meaning. Names that amuse drive home lessons to be learned. There are the publicans, Tipple and Soakem, the gamesters, Trump and Cribbage; there are the parson, Mr. Drone; the sheriff, Holdfast; and Ledger, the merchant. There is humour in the situations, some of them isolated and others strung out through the narrative. The pig called Mammoth, stuck in the butter churn while his owners are off traipsing, scores a few good laughs, and the official autopsy on the body of a stranger performed by Pat O'Rafferty, because Pat had had experience in Newfoundland splitting codfish, works well–particularly when the operation discloses that the poor victim died of stuffing himself with cabbages stolen from the sheriff, who was boiling them down for pigs' slop. The sheriff's perennial guests, with their cards and grog, provide an example of what befalls those who stray from hard work and simple ways. There is much humour, too, in the voice of Stepsure himself, who is droll and sarcastic by turns. And each letter contains two or three scenarios that are meant to amuse while providing instructive examples of what happens to those who err. The story of Bill Scamp is typical: Bill is too smart for his own good and rises in the world on wit instead of work; he becomes rich, but overextends himself, and loses all–to Stepsure's son-in-law, a reward for the latter's prudence and industry.

As Stepsure offers them, the rules of life are really quite simple: stay near home; work hard, slow, and steady; avoid drink and cards and idle talk; attend to the soul, and bear in mind Parson Drone's favourite admonition that what cannot be cured must be endured; rest sure in the knowledge that property and prosperity are the rewards of virtue. How is it possible for such sombre advice to be the source of humour? Perhaps the most important device in the letters, which redeems them from self-righteousness, is Stepsure's lameness. As a cripple, he is scorned by society; even after he acquires wealth, he is denied position. Pride is balanced by pathos. There is a touch of irony in everything he says. The middle letters are the story of his rise from a "white nigger," a foundling sold at public auction, through the stages of his success, to his status as a man of property. His humble origins and his deformity lend him a curious humility, even when he is being preposterously pompous. Humour, too, accrues from the good spirits and gentle affection of the author. There is little of the rancour here that is found in the *Clockmaker* stories; only the droll, ironic bemusement of a tolerant man, who knows with certainty that he is in the right.

COLIN McDOUGALL

Execution. Toronto: Macmillan, 1958. Toronto:
Macmillan; Laurentian Library, 1967. Pages: 233.
Paperback.

Nowhere in fiction or documentary reportage has there been anything to equal McDougall's description of the Allied attack on
the Adolf Hitler Line at Montecassino: the carnage and stupidity
and heroism leave the reader brutalized, angry, and overwhelmingly sad. This is the appalling reality of combat, which bears
only the most tenuous relationship to other areas of human experience. In the long battle sequences leading up to Montecassino,
McDougall chronicles the movement of Canadian shock-troops
from their landing in Sicily through a series of skirmishes and
major offensives, in which the reader learns much about the techniques of modern warfare from the awesome perspective of the
front line. The reader learns to accept the absurdities of arbitrary
slaughter and the calculated sacrifice of life for tactical objectives.
Still, there can be no preparation for Montecassino.

This is a war novel, an authentic document of that terrible separate reality. Quite literally, it is a vision from beyond, delivered
by someone who has crossed over and returned. McDougall relates
the inexorable push of the Allies through Italy with a sure understanding of military procedures. He uses the specialized vocabulary of warfare with little explanation; yet the meaning is conveyed. The variety of weaponry ceases to be confusing when we
witness what it can do to the human body; abbreviated communications of the military become clear when we see their outcome;
there is a logic to everything, and that logic has nothing to do
with reason or morality.

McDougall is as adept at conveying the human responses to
war as at documenting the strategic details. The novel follows
the lives and, when necessary, records the deaths of a cluster of
Canadians, ranging in the chain of command from Brigadier
Kildare, through Major Barzin, Lieutenant Adam, Padre Doorn,
Sergeant-Major Mitchell, down to a variety of enlisted men. At
the centre is Adam, by the end a major with a distinguished service record. Most of the men under his command die and are
replaced; a few above him die. Death, the reduction of living men

to shattered flesh, surrounds him. Survival is a matter of efficiency, but also of luck.

The narrative moves rapidly in the combat sequences; between the conflicts, it meanders slowly, focusing on a man, a situation, a relationship. There is little of the world back home–thoughts of Canada and family are irrelevant in a place where hope can only drag a man down and make him more vulnerable. McDougall does not idealize these men, nor does he develop their characters; nor does he give them complex interior lives–there is not time for that, except on their brief periods of leave. Then, there is a little romance, a bit of spontaneous adventure, nothing more. Yet we know these men, for we see them as they see one another. When they die, we are sickened and move on.

John Adam provides the narrative centre, and he is the most fully realized character. The novel is episodic. The episodes are contained by parenthetical incidents that sum up everything that passes between them. Early in the novel, two ingratiating Italian deserters are pointlessly shot–because that is the standing order. In the end, an uncomprehending innocent, Private Jones, is shot by a Canadian firing squad–because that is the prescribed procedure. With bitter reluctance, Lieutenant Adam participates in both executions, and in countless executions in between, all except Montecassino–which he views after the battle, when the bodies of his men are littered in layers where they fell, with not even enough room for each to fall upon a separate piece of earth.

Nowhere in *Execution* is the writing less than competent. In the battle sequences, it is brilliant–a mixture of dispassionate detail and humane response. Some of the non-combat sequences seem a bit contrived, the language a bit awkward. It is as if they are filling in time until the action starts again–for, despite the horror, there is also a fascination with war, a certain exhilaration that McDougall tries neither to deny nor to justify. Nor does he make moral judgements–rather, the moral structure of the novel builds upon civilized responses he assumes are universal. War is appalling and absurd, but never does McDougall imply that it is not sometimes necessary, nor that it does not possess an awesome beauty and logic of its own.

EDWARD MEADE

Remember Me. London: Faber & Faber, 1946. Toronto: McClelland and Stewart, 1965. Pages: 238. Paperback.

This novel is a meshing together of two distinctly separate accounts of war. On the one hand, it is an historical document of the Second World War, recording with dispassionate thoroughness conditions and events as they occur in prose that has the severity of an academic treatise. The extent of Meade's vision is arbitrarily limited by the experience of his protagonist. It ranges from analyses of Allied strategy to explorations of the English character during the Blitz, to a panoramic view of aerial dogfights, all with an aplomb that an historian might envy. On the other hand, it is the memoir-like chronicle of a Canadian corporal, Bob O'Rourke, from the time he leaves his wife at the train station in the prairies, through four interminable years of waiting as the Allied forces build up strength in England, through D-Day, and on, until his death in the summer of 1944 in a French field. The prose in these personal parts is much more casual (although a bit stilted at times) and considerably more effusive than it is in the documentary sections. Curiously, the two accounts bleed into each other to make this a compelling novel of the world at war.

There is another voice in the novel, like a pastel thread woven through a sombre tweed, and that is the voice of patriotism. Germans are not thought of with ironic fondness: they are the Hun, Hitler's criminals up against George. The British are a credit to the human species; the average Englishman is an object, to Meade, of profound, if bemused, respect. It is the Canadians and Canada, however, who earn his highest praise. Unabashedly, he sings of his northern land, and in these fragments it is brought most vividly home that he is actually *writing* this novel during the war. Other war novels more effectively bring combat to life on the page, but none so well depicts the haunting thoughts of home and country that gave strength to Canadians during the long wait overseas, even while imposing on them an unbearable sadness. There are some fine paragraphs in praise of Canada that, in a peace-time context, might seem sentimental or forced, but that evoke a side of the war not usually remembered.

As a creative writer, Meade is at his best in the long descriptions of London under attack. Seldom has either the awesome destruction of the Blitz or the calm resolve of the people been rendered with such authenticity. He is excellent, also, in capturing the waste of those long, slow years of rebuilding, between the humiliation of Dunkirk – after which Hitler might readily have overrun England – and the shock of D-Day, when the greatest armada in history landed once more in Normandy. During those four years, England, as Meade describes it, became a land under military occupation, in which every aspect of life related to the war effort, while a million fighting men and their support equipment assembled for the invasion of Europe.

O'Rourke, Meade's protagonist, is an odd creation, for there is little that is extraordinary about him. Yet he easily carries the narrative burden. Even when things are most dreary in the waiting years, he manages to sustain the reader's interest. It is not because of anything that happens to him, for little does. Nor is it for his perceptions of the war, or of himself, for he is not a self-conscious man, nor is he much given to words. Yet he feels deeply and is both introspective and observant. Clearly the author identifies closely with his protagonist, yet he seems to use O'Rourke as a means of objectifying his own feelings, making him a Canadian everyman rather than an alter ego.

Meade writes from within the context of war, not in reflection after it is over, and that gives the novel's most documentary aspects a dramatic immediacy. His novel is a determinedly Canadian document, even in its most personal revelations of character and incident. Corporal O'Rourke may be an authorial persona, but he is meant to represent the country at large and the sacrifice the country made towards victory. His death, however, does not signify extinction of a Canadian ideal: in this book, rather, it is its quiet elevation to immortality. *Remember Me* will seem dated to most contemporary readers, but oddly enough this characteristic is the source of its lingering power.

JOHN METCALF

Going Down Slow. Toronto: McClelland and Stewart, 1972. Pages: 177.

This is a very funny novel. It is also a devastating commentary on our society and a curiously touching account of personal failure. The opening chapters delight with high comedy, but gradually the comedy becomes muted, drowned out by splendid invective, which, in turn, gives way to bombast–which is replaced by solemn mock-tragedy, beneath which there is a trace of genuine pathos. Unfortunately, we are not used to such sophisticated manipulations of genre and response; and that perhaps accounts for the novel's relative obscurity.

The main character in the novel is David Appleby, a perfect example of why Englishmen in this generation are liked so much better in their own country than in ours. At twenty-three, David has the self-assurance and cultural self-righteousness that make everything around him seem ridiculous or banal. He is a superb creation, pompous yet appealing, quite brilliant yet culturally myopic, a reckless idealist awash in egocentricity, an unregenerate bigot. He rails at Canadian primitivism, at how we spell "tire," at our flaccid history and sterile culture. He grouses about our lack of taste, of style, of sophistication. He is contemptuous of our cereal-box biculturalism. What standards England does not set, David sets on his own by fiat. If he likes a musician or a writer or a painter, that artist's work is marvellous. If he dislikes an artist, that artist is a bore, a fraud, an incompetent. His judgements are maliciously good-humoured, yet it is with some relief that we watch him slowly sink, if not into humility at least into anguished restraint. He is a randy, well-read, disorganized, supercilious young man, and gradually the New World and his own ineptness and arrogance get the best of him. Utterly deflated, he is a wretched figure at the end of the novel–one of us, though he would roundly deny it.

David teaches history and English at Merrymount High School in Montreal. David's greatest wit and invective are reserved for the "system" and the teachers it harbours. Anyone who has ever spent time inside a high school will recognize the stereotypes, and those who have taught will be unnerved by the accuracy of his barbs. (Metcalf has created a comic reality in which the world appears exactly as his protagonist judges it to be.) David lives with a friend who came over from England at the same time he did, two years earlier, but his friend has a sure grasp of the New World and leaves David breathlessly behind; bolstered only by an eroding sense of innate superiority. David also has a girlfriend, Susan Haddad, who happens to be a delinquent grade-eleven student at Merrymount. The relationship causes endless problems of romantic subterfuge, though none of moral probity – Susan is brilliant, and that is enough.

Metcalf is a master of the short-story idiom, that especially intense and lucid prose found in the very best short fiction that so often seems empty or superficial in the larger context of the novel. But in *Going Down Slow*, his prose works superbly. There is perhaps a superfluity of obscenities, a concession to the era in which the novel was written. There is a great deal of cranky erudition, of passionate eccentricity. And beneath the casually splenetic surface, there is evidence of superb narrative control. We are given brief glimpses into David's English past, long quotations from a bad writer or a good lyricist, but there is always a larger purpose, albeit skilfully integrated. *Going Down Slow* is a subtle novel as well as a gregarious one; it is deeply serious and uproariously amusing. It deserves much wider recognition.

General Ludd. Downsview: ECW Press, 1980.
Pages: 301.

General Ludd is possibly the finest comic novel ever published in Canada. Whether we have the sophistication to appreciate Metcalf's achievement remains to be seen. If his vision of our cultural vacuity is halfway accurate, he doesn't stand a chance.

The word "savage" must have been coined as a verb in anticipation of *General Ludd*. Through a range of emotion, from glee to despair, Metcalf savages everything in the contemporary world that does not measure up to his protagonist's outrageously biased expectations – and little does, except creative talent and genuine eccentricity. In emulation of the early-nineteenth-century Luddites, who struggled to stem the onslaught of progress, Jim Wells battles against all in our world that insults the sense and sensibility of reasonable men. He is doomed to failure. Yet there is triumph in the raucous voice of Wells's defeat – he flails at everything: television, functional illiteracy, fast-food outlets, ballpoint pens, and especially academic irrelevance of the kind our university English departments foster with such determination. No voice could be more appropriate for a comic vision in our present era. We have passed the age of the absurd, of black humour and comic depravity. In these times of cultural inanity, the only resort for the truly reactionary writer – and all comic writers are reactionaries, just as all satirists are ultimately visionaries – is vitriol. The smug savaging of a world beneath the hero's comprehension, wedded to the picaresque form of the traditional comic novel, has fostered a modern masterpiece.

In broad outline, the novel resembles *Going Down Slow*; the earlier work seems like a rehearsal, in street clothes, for the bizarre costume drama to follow. *General Ludd* is set in a university in the west end of Montreal; the protagonist has graduated from English teacher to poet-in-residence. Like David Appleby, Jim Wells is an overbearing snob, redeemed from pompous irrelevance by the extent of his suffering. The manically opinionated voice of both personalities is the same. The despair expressed at a world of rampant mediocrity is the same. Where the books differ most, and where *General Ludd* is better, is in the language. *General Ludd* is brilliantly written: the novel's nearly perfect use of language, its genuinely urbane demeanour, and the profound and sad humanity of its comic vision make it a truly superior work.

The narrative opens with a faculty reception at St. Xavier University to welcome Jim Wells, an award-winning Canadian poet. The story follows his quixotic, drunken meanderings through the academic year, punctuated by increasingly desperate parries at the indifferent windmills of an electronic society: the university, Montreal, Canada, the middle class, the Canada Council, and the Canadian publishing industry. His Dulcinea is a brilliant and endearingly unimaginative member of the faculty, Kathy Neilson. Inevitably, she betrays him, leaving him prisoner, at the novel's close, in the psychiatric ward of the very model of a major modern hospital.

The plot is linear, episodic, cumulative. Characterization ranges from the scathing caricature of members of the department to the uniquely grotesque Itzak Zemermann, author of the most execrable poetry since the expiration of Sarah Binks. There is a precarious balance, in the protagonist's life, between Zemermann and the truly talented John Caverly; between the ex-wife he has lost and Kathy, whom he genuinely loves; between city squalor and the calm of the country; between aggressive and anti-social eccentricity and immobilizing outrage; between eloquence and drunken incoherence. This balance, worked along the fulcrum of a picaresque structure, gives the novel a depth and dimension rare in comic fiction.

The most outstanding aspect of *General Ludd* is the language itself. Metcalf can be obscene, cruel, mocking, tender, irreverent, and hilarious by turns. He can make a single word explode with laughter; he can draw a sentence out into a sublime chuckle, or build paragraphs into scenes of devastating wit and comic wonder. He plays with words – not like a child playing, but like a virtuoso. He brings into casual usage words like "flensing" and "prinked," "vatic," "epicanthic," "staling," and "peculation." In railing against illiteracy he uses language with such loving precision that we share the tragedy of his losing stance and laugh with him contemptuously at the world that overwhelms us. He writes with urbanity, with generous allusions to writers from Lewis Carroll to H. Rider Haggard. With easy reference, he speaks of the worlds of music, art, and ideas. He draws syntax into an aggressive life of its own; he uses punctuation like a weapon and paragraphs as if they were poetic stanzas. His imagery is superb: "like paint from a brush uncurling and misting down through a jam-jar of fresh water." His love of words is contagious: he can speak of hames and pole straps and britchings with affection; he can speak with impatience of CB radios, which fill "with adolescent and constructed slang the appalling prospect of silence." Occasionally, language betrays Metcalf in his use of Britishisms, which are quite jarring as expressions of his Canadian protagonist's mind – words like "crumpet," "knickers," "sodding," "twaddle." Otherwise Jim Wells stands valiantly, pathetically on his own, a ludicrous eccentric at the centre of a vision that is at once hilarious and chilling.

JOHN MILLS

Skevington's Daughter. Ottawa: Oberon, 1978.
Pages: 195.

Mills is the most impressive minor novelist working in Canada
today. His first two novels, *The Land of Is* and *The October Men*,
show a sophisticated comic flair that owes far more to Sterne than
to Leacock, while *Skevington's Daughter*, his third and best, owes
even less to the Canadian comic tradition, which depends so much
on ironic wit, romance, and at least covert affirmation of the good
and true. Mills is decidedly out of the Canadian mainstream – by
choice, undoubtedly. His concerns are literary and personal, not
social and moralistic. His object is to delight by impressing, not to
distract or instruct. Formally, he is as inventive as Kroetsch, and
he has as bizarre a comic style as Leo Simpson. Yet lacking their
commitment to a humane purpose that the reader can share, he
is somewhat less an artist than either.

Skevington's Daughter is an epistolary novel. The letters are
gathered by a character, John Mills, who shares the biography of
his author, John Mills. The declared purpose is to arouse public
interest in a subsequent book by Mills about the nineteenth-
century travel writer, Francis Skevington, and his daughter, Stella.
However, Mills (the character) confesses to making up Skevington
and Stella. He refuses to allow, though, that they do not exist.
They are real because they are imagined.

Stella Skevington's letters, written aboard a ship in Mexico in
1840 to a friend back in England, are outrageous. Her father is a
gentleman traveller whose writings form part of the travel literature upon which Simon Motley, of Chester University in twentieth-
century Ontario, has built his modest career. Stella describes in
euphemistic detail her seduction of her father and their many
mutual conquests before she arranges his demise. All this fascinates Motley, whose colleague, Harry Peasemarsh, is also a
Skevington devotee, and dearly covets the letters, not for their
value as travel literature but for their influence on the so-called
Tidewater poets. Through the struggle between Peasemarsh and
Motley in the early 1970s, Mills (the author) offers a rather conventional parody of faculty politics. More off-beat is the woman
whose affections they share, Linda Crippen, an MA student whose

former male lover is a murderous psychopath and whose female lover converts a Mountie to the radical left before she herself succumbs to astrology.

Courageously, Mills (the author) opens with a long letter from Linda, filled with the ephemeral cant and jargon of the late sixties. Mills (the character) proclaims her a representative of her times (which, being a parody, she isn't; she is closer to being an artifact). Stella Skevington, in contrast, comes alive precisely because she is an artifact. She, Mills (the author) makes us accept, must represent the other side, the bawdy suppressed side, of Victorian gentility. The less realistic Mills (the author) is, the more he convinces.

In the epistolary format, there must be at least implicit justification for letter writing. And, while the purpose for gathering the letters arises out of the fiction, most of them seem written in a vacuum. This impression results from a kind of one-way correspondence, in which the addressee often remains unknown to the reader. Nevertheless, the author is adroit in his use of diction to convey characteristics of time and place and personality. Further, each letter is a reality in itself; the novel moves from one level of invention to another with effective ease to exploit the comic possibilities of their juxtaposition. The whole send-up of the Tidewater poets, for example, depends on the academic perspective of the authorial persona, Mills, who admits to inventing them – and himself appears ridiculous for making such a claim, so convincing are they. Similarly, Stella's letters would not be half so engaging were they not arranged within a design that includes Linda Crippen's accounts of offhand contemporary debauchery.

Skevington's Daughter is fraught with cleverness. The novel's serious purpose seems to be to combine an exploration of imaginative realities with a display of caustic wit and linguistic versatility. As either humour or satire, it is undermined by a nihilistic or amoral posture. It is limited by an air of self-satisfaction that verges on condescension; but it is a novel important for its accomplished technique, well worth reading as a study in the craft.

W.O. MITCHELL

Who Has Seen the Wind. Toronto: Macmillan, 1947.
Toronto: Seal, 1982. Pages: 293. Paperback.

W.O. Mitchell is an authentic Canadian "character," a raconteur
who can charm an auditorium full of school-children and warm
the frozen vitals of their most cynical teachers. At the same time
he can draw critics into line to pronounce upon the aesthetic quality
and profound significance of his performance. His stories of Jake
and the Kid lured many a radio listener to the town of Crocus,
Saskatchewan, where innocence consisted of being decent, and
experience was a matter of perception. Mitchell is a natural storyteller whose humane inquiries into knowledge and the ways of
the world amuse and quietly probe, until the conscience that
appears open to us miraculously turns out to be our own. He is a
humourist in the largest sense of the word, for although his stories
and novels often contain hardship and death, his vision is ultimately comic, informed not by divine but by human charity, by
an irrepressible affection for life. Some consider him a happy
nihilist, whistling in the dark. It is more appropriate to see him
as a whistler, thoughtfully absorbed in his diversion, despite the
darkness all around him.

Who Has Seen the Wind has been widely celebrated as a Canadian classic. With Twain's *Huckleberry Finn* and Golding's *Lord
of the Flies*, it shares that curious quality of being a children's
book written for adults. In Golding's novel, the purpose is overt:
theme and symbol nearly overwhelm the narrative. In Twain's
novel, meaning remains obscured beneath layers of comic intrigue,
understood fully only through critical analysis. Mitchell's *Who
Has Seen the Wind* follows a middle course. The serious intent of
the novel is inseparable from young Brian O'Connal's quest for
knowledge; at the same time, Mitchell reinforces the shared
pursuit of reader and protagonist with symbols, imagery, and
motifs drawn from the small town and the surrounding prairie.
Mitchell has made of the Canadian setting a convincing environment in which to search for God and the meaning of life, and in
which to discover the uncertainty of both.

The novel follows Brian's progress from age four to age twelve.
It does not always present the precise behaviour or thought pat-

tern appropriate to Brian's years. Sometimes, the author loads too heavy a metaphysical burden on young Brian's shoulders, too much consciousness of the ineffable for his limited frame to bear. Generally, however, Brian is a fine creation – at once a personable small-town boy between the wars and an archetypal searcher for order amid the chaos of human experience.

During the course of the novel, Brian struggles to comprehend the rare spiritual elation, like wind on the back of his neck, that he has sometimes felt. He must cope with death: his dog Jappy is killed; a gopher is cruelly tortured; his friend Fat loses his rabbits; his father dies, and his grandmother dies. He learns to cope with life's imperfections and anomalies: hypocrisy, a two-headed calf, Saint Sammy in his piano-case hovel. Through it all, Brian's tenacious yearning for enlightenment never flags. He learns from the young Ben, whose transcendent continuity with the prairie thrills Brian. He learns from conversations between his school principal and the shoemaker, who open a larger world of the mind and imagination for him. As Brian grows, the town gains definition – the reader's experience of it is simultaneous with Brian's own, even though Mitchell allows the narrative point of view to take in much that Brian knows only indirectly.

In some ways, the town represents the whole human community from a Canadian perspective. The vicious Mrs. Abercrombie and the school board; the Wongs – the China Kids; their father's suicide; the Reverend Powelly and his zealots; old Mrs. O'Connal's memories: together they stand for all Canadian small towns, small towns everywhere. It is the surrounding prairie that allows Mitchell to isolate the town and make it both unique and universal. The prairie provides the spiritual source in the novel. It stretches limitlessly; it brings the wind, the touch of God. It offers solitude and renewal. It is the place of death and the source of life. In the beautiful closing passages of the novel, it merges the finite, the growing, the animate, with infinity.

Mitchell is capable of great lyric passages, which transform the natural world into a realm of the imagination. Sometimes, however, the purpose of his descriptions is so transparent that they become merely illustrations and seem imposed on the narrative rather than part of it. Mitchell's characterization is so effective that it risks becoming caricature, as it does in the Jake and the Kid stories and in his novel *The Kite*. Saint Sammy is a fascinating enigma, but too much the classic grotesque. Brian's Uncle Sean is almost too obviously the rambunctious salt of the earth. The Bens are overly imbued with thematic significance. Mrs. Abercrombie is extravagantly hypocritical – and so on. Still, as aspects of Brian's quest, the characters serve an archetypal function and, individually, are enormously entertaining. Mitchell's novel is exciting and ambitious, touching and quite profound. For this novel alone he deserves a primary place in Canadian letters.

Jake and the Kid (1961). *See* Canadian Novels for Young Readers.

The Vanishing Point. Toronto: Macmillan, 1973. Toronto: Seal, 1983. Pages: 325. Paperback.

Despite serious themes and sombre reflections, Mitchell's irrepressible humour dominates this, his best work. After the public acclaim for *Who Has Seen the Wind*, Mitchell settled into the role of wise old rustic for a generation. With *The Vanishing Point, Since Daisy Creek*, and then *How I Spent My Summer Holidays*, his life seems to have caught up with his image.

A vanishing point is the theoretical merging of parallel lines to provide three-dimensional perspective on a two-dimensional plane, or the end of diminishing images in a sequence of mirror reflections. The vanishing point provides the controlling metaphor of the novel: things only seem to come together as they are diminished, whether they are parallel races of people or unlikely lovers. Unity lies in the reconciliation of diversity, not in its elimination. The Stony Indians of the Paradise Valley Reserve, where Carlyle Sinclair works as a teacher, maintain their differences from the surrounding white world with a naïve integrity that threatens them with extinction before assimilation. That is their special triumph, and the philosophical basis of Mitchell's novel.

In the tradition of the comic novel, there are marvellous digressions throughout *The Vanishing Point*. Whole chapters are assigned quite arbitrarily to a retrospective of Carlyle Sinclair's early life, including such episodes as how he burned himself at six while using a magic lantern to project a giant image of his penis against the wall; or how at the age of eleven he sold lingerie on the edge of town to Miss Rossdance and her girls. Some of the digressions, such as the presentation of Officer Dan's Safety Corral on Calgary television, have little to do with the plot. Others seem appropriate but gratuitous, like the brief story of Heally Richards's early life, which accounts for his preeminence as a faith healer. Several of the digressions, however, are inseparable from the central narrative. One long account by Archie Nicotine could stand on its own as a classic comic routine about the lack of communication between Indians and whites, and yet it arises perfectly out of the continuing story. In fact, Archie is never on stage without being hilarious, touching, proud, commanding, shifty, obsequious, and always in control of the scene. He is Mitchell's finest creation.

The form of the novel is quite simple; its genius lies in the telling. Set almost entirely in Calgary or on the Stony Reserve, it never strays too far from the central protagonist, Carlyle Sinclair. There are three parts to the novel. In the first, thirty-six-year-old Sinclair has been on the reserve for nine years, an established intruder, tolerated, even respected, but still treated warily. With exuberant affection and great compassion, Mitchell portrays contemporary Indian life, moving about from the degrading hovel in an alley where Gloria Catface plies her whore's trade, with her brother as pimp, up into Storm and Misty country beyond the reserve, where the Indian is utterly at home, or into the homes across the Beulah bridge where people with names like Lefthand, Snow, Ear, and Nicotine live out what is left of the old ways. Only Victoria Rider is different. She was recognized as a special child by Sinclair, when he first arrived. In the present time of the novel she has run away from the Calgary hospital where he has located her in nurses' training. Meanwhile, her old grandfather, Esau, is dying, and Archie wants the travelling charismatic, Heally Richards, to cure him.

The second part of the novel begins with Sinclair's arrival at Paradise and follows his progress among the Indians, particularly focusing on Victoria, in whom Carlyle sees aspects of both his dead wife and his dead unborn daughter. In the final section, Heally fails to resurrect Esau; Archie brings the pregnant Victoria back to Paradise; Carlyle painfully reassesses himself and, at last, talks to the Indians on their own terms, refusing to distort them in the white man's mirror any more, refusing to draw them towards the vanishing point. He and Victoria take up together, and the River Beulah again flows with a roar.

Mitchell does not bury his symbols and allusions in narrative obscurity. The reader is not meant to search for deeper meaning. It is all there, readily accessible. The novel gains resonance in the striking fusion of thoughtful and distressing themes with ebullient good humour, a mixture of verbal slapstick and subtle wit. *The Vanishing Point* is an account of Carlyle Sinclair's education, his struggle towards individual integrity; it is the story of Indians whose survival is precariously determined by their inability to adapt; it is an angry indictment of a whole civilization. The complexity and ambiguity essential to art do not lie in the novel's themes, or in its form, but in the compassion and understanding of its narrative voice, in the commitment of the containing vision to the ultimate goodness of humanity, despite horrors of our own creation.

SUSANNA MOODIE

Roughing It in the Bush: or, Life in Canada. London: Bentley, 1852. 2 volumes. Toronto: McClelland and Stewart; New Canadian Library, 1962. Pages: 240. Paperback.

In this fine narrative account of early settlement in southeastern Ontario, the line between fact and fiction is indistinguishable. Moodie uses the form of the journal-memoir but draws from the conventions of the novel to create a work of imaginative prose that cannot be classified exclusively either as document or as art. It is, rather, a pleasing combination of both. For a century, *Roughing It in the Bush* was treated as an ingenuous and somewhat quirky personal account, a British gentlewoman's record of the harsh and beautiful wilderness and its frontier society, not unlike Anna Jameson's *Winter Studies and Summer Rambles* or Catherine Parr Traill's *The Backwoods of Canada*. However, recent critics have come to recognize Moodie's skill in creating a work that has both wholeness of vision and an organic unity. Today, *Roughing It in the Bush* may safely be called a novel–one with strong elements of sentimental romance, which echo an established literary tradition, but also one with characteristics that anticipate the non-fiction or documentary novels so prominent in contemporary Canadian literature.

The narrative line running through the novel is quite pronounced, even though much of the work is episodic or discursive. Written in the first person, it tells of the period from 1832 to 1839 in the lives of Susanna Moodie and her husband, Dunbar, as they emigrate to Canada and are slowly brought to ruin, out of which they salvage little more than the very pride that brought them to their fall. They are not equipped, either emotionally or by the experience of their class, to cope with the demands of the frontier. Those less well-bred, who have less refinement and more realistic expectations, fare much better. The Moodies retreat to life in the clearing and a government sinecure in Belleville.

Susanna Moodie, the narrator, dominates. Her husband is a pale creation, and even such engaging set-piece figures as Brian the still-hunter and Malcolm, the little stumpy man, while skilfully drawn, remain in Moodie's shadow. It is her story. But she and the author are not one and the same. Moodie the author treats the character Susanna Moodie with considerable irony, often inflating her pretensions to the point of the ridiculous, or deflating her expectations to arouse the reader's sympathy. Moodie the author shapes Susanna Moodie's story into a sort of epic quest for assimilation and allows triumph in her protagonist's failure. The author effectively arranges scenes of drama and domesticity in counterpoint, to test in a Canadian context the values and habits of the British world the Moodies have left behind. She manages, simultaneously, to be critical of the old, yet sceptical of the new.

No one could read the opening chapter of *Roughing It in the Bush*, with its convincing use of dialogue and characterization, and its emotional dynamism, without realizing that it has some of the qualities of a novel. Unfortunately, because the modern reprint has excised large chunks of the work for economy, emphasis seems more on the procedures of settlement than on narrative and thematic development: and, indeed, Moodie writes persuasive accounts of logging bees and bartering, of primitive conditions and the techniques of survival. As a document of immigrant hardship, *Roughing It in the Bush* is outstanding, a major benchmark in our socio-cultural history. As a work of art, it is structurally flawed, self-indulgent, overwritten–nevertheless, it is as art that Moodie's achievement ultimately endures.

BRIAN MOORE

The Lonely Passion of Judith Hearne. Boston: Little, Brown, 1955. Pages: 253. *Judith Hearne*. Toronto: McClelland and Stewart; New Canadian Library, 1964. Paperback.

The only thing truly Canadian about Moore is his passport. Between his early life in Ireland and his later retreat to California he lived in Canada long enough to pick up citizenship and some acute perceptions of Canadian society. He is included here for the same reason that Graham Greene or Margaret Laurence might be included among African writers. His experience as an outsider among us has been beautifully shaped into the predominant form and theme of his fiction.

Moore has always walked the precarious line between art and commercial fiction. His recent novel, *The Doctor's Wife*, leans to the latter, with gratuitous and explicit sex, superficial characterization, and a plot echoing Harlequin romances. Still, his prose is nearly flawless. There is nothing spectacular about it; it is almost transparent, so right and easy is his use of language, syntax, diction, and subtle imagery. In his best works, when he tries more to move than to please, to illuminate rather than to entertain, his prose perfectly matches the rhythm and nuance of the unfolding narrative. Such is the case in his first and quite possibly best novel, *The Lonely Passion of Judith Hearne*.

Like many of Moore's novels, *Judith Hearne* is the moving portrait of a single, isolated personality, a character imprisoned by, and victim of, her own self-awareness. Moore's protagonists are often women. It is perhaps his outside perspective on their experience that allows him to define their dissociated personalities, cut off not only from others but from their own best inner resources. This is an area of their beings that he, like they themselves, can only divine from the surface evidence of their lives.

Judith is a spinster in her early forties who lives alone in a roominghouse in postwar Belfast with pictures of the Sacred Heart and her dead aunt D'Arcy and a perpetual bottle of cheap whisky to help her through the bad times. With compassion and insight, Moore describes Judith's solitude. She is a sad figure, and yet, as the object of Moore's ironic wit, she gains comic dignity. Her sense of martyrdom and melodrama, her incapacitating humility before God, make her almost pathetic, were it not that such concepts of herself issue from a fiery pride that is also the source of her strength of character, her indomitable will, her final rebellion against society and God, and her eventual reconciliation with the fallen world.

Judith's relations with people are soul depleting. Her old drinking friend, Edie, lies in Earnscliff Home, an institution for indigent women. Her Sunday friends, the O'Neills, indulge her with their hospitality, despite the nuisance caused by her stolid presence. Her lover, James Madden, wants only a business partner to help him Americanize Ireland. Fat Bernard and his doting mother, her landlady, oppress her. The Church offers only empty ritual and an indifferent God. All she has to help her cope with doubt and despair is her pride, and her bottle.

When she falls, it is a spectacular event. She gets drunk in the best hotel in Belfast, defying her own sense of frugality and propriety, and then she assaults the tabernacle on the church altar, certain finally that her prayers were always unheard. Having burned all bridges behind her, Judith finds ambivalent salvation in the anaesthesia of acceptance. Moore leaves her a cheerful ward of the Earnscliff Home.

The crisp clarity of Moore's prose gains dimension by his perfect rendering of spoken language, whether in dialogue or in the ruminations of the mind of Judith Hearne. The visual quality of his imagery and of events themselves contributes to the powerful sense of immediacy in the novel. Judith's life has an insistent presence in the reader's mind. The reader remains outside her experience, but intimately, urgently involved with it. What happens to her matters, and to Moore's lasting credit, her demented revolt is a triumph. The reader shares her rage and hurt and exultation.

The Luck of Ginger Coffey. Boston: Little, Brown, 1960. Toronto: McClelland and Stewart; New Canadian Library, 1972. Markham: Penguin, 1977. Pages: 201.
Paperback.

Ginger Coffey is a lovely novel. Typical of Moore's fiction, there are no great stylistic flourishes, no soaring flights of eloquence to animate the novel's main character. Ginger is too down-to-earth, too real and ordinary, to sustain such pyrotechnics. But he is one of the most endearing, enduring, roguish immigrants ever to grace our literary shores. The overwhelming struggle to reconcile his dreams with Canadian reality is a tragicomic vision of every new Canadian's experience here.

With his wife, Veronica, and their daughter, Paulie, Ginger Coffey, a Dubliner in his early middle age with great aspirations and no money at all, settles in Montreal to make his fortune. Gently ironic, Moore describes the progress of Ginger's assimilation. Ginger is a comic hero, reaching always beyond his attainment. Rejected as a neophyte executive, he tries journalism and ends up a proofreader; he makes deliveries for a diaper service on the side. His marriage teeters towards failure. His wife's apparent lover is a cartoonist, a feckless caricature, in Ginger's eyes, of what a man should be. Yet Ginger cannot fulfil the requirements, either, and he sinks deeper and deeper into comic despair – comic, because Moore never allows his hero the humility to be pathetic, nor sufficient understanding to be tragic. What he does give Ginger is personal integrity. Ginger is put on trial for urinating in a public place, for which he receives a six-month suspended sentence. His wife recognizes his integrity as the one great source of strength in his personality and later pleads for a reconciliation. In renewing his marriage, Ginger at last accepts the world the way it is; and Moore celebrates the survival not of the fittest, but of those who fit – a bittersweet resolution at best.

The novel is not a social satire, but a comic anatomy of society. Moore details the North American social experience with caustic wit. Against the dreams and the myths falls the reality. The petty, mean, drab lives of a variety of sharply defined secondary characters, like the grizzled proofreader, Old Billy, or the iron-pumping Warren K. Wilson, stand in revealing contrast to Ginger's vision of luck and plenty. In accord with his main character's personality, and to reinforce the narrative perspective from an alien point of view, Moore's language in this novel is tinged with more Irish than he employs in his Irish novels. Paradoxically, this is his most Canadian work – not only because of the content but because here alone he confronts the dissociation of immigrant experience, responding to Canada not just as background material but as a condition inseparable from his protagonist's personality.

I Am Mary Dunne. Toronto: McClelland and Stewart,
1968. Toronto: McClelland and Stewart; New Canadian
Library, 1976. Pages: 217. Markham: Penguin, 1977.
Paperback.

I Am Mary Dunne is a work of exceptional insight into both personality and society; it is fine, also, in the subtle tonalities of language, the almost imperceptible affectations of style, the sheer clarity of narrative purpose, as the story of Mary's day unfolds in an aura of suppressed hysteria, and the story of her fragmented life lies gradually exposed before her. The containing form of the novel is Mary's conscious reconstruction of the day just passed, while she lies in bed beside her third husband, Terrance Lavery, a successful British playwright with whom she lives in New York. That morning, disoriented in part by premenstrual anxiety, she forgot her name at the hairdresser's. In going over the events that followed – her lunch with an old and vicious acquaintance from her Montreal days (when she was married to Hatfield Bell); her dinner with an obnoxious former suitor from the days after she broke up with her first husband, Jimmy Phelan, in Toronto – she builds a chronological account of her life, which has enough continuity and consistency that she ultimately recognizes in herself a whole personality. She is still and always has been Mary Dunne from Butchersville, Nova Scotia.

Moore does not pretend to use stream-of-consciousness technique, and yet the action takes place entirely in Mary's ruminating mind. In tones ranging from analytic to confessional, she recounts the harrowing quest for her identity. She has been Mary and Maria, Mary Dunne, Mary Phelan, Mary Bell, Mary Lavery. She sinks into the Juarez Dooms, her term for the feelings of depletion she experienced following her Mexican divorce from Hat Bell, who she now discovers has committed suicide. She debates with her Mad Self, as she calls her fanatic irrational side. She exults in her love for Terrance, riles at her luncheon with Janice Sloan, who helped undermine her marriage to Hat, cringes at the obnoxious mewling of her ex-suitor Ernie Truelove. In a *tour de force*, Moore chronicles Mary's halting exploration of herself without intruding to make connections or define her progress. In the end there is not triumph but a quiet acceptance that, behind her many guises, there is a whole woman, that all the roles are contained by the personality who played them.

Moore is superb at detailing the isolation of the individual, separated by consciousness of self from the surrounding world. His characters have few inner resources besides pride and no deeper life of the soul or psyche to sustain them in their solitary condition. Moore is greatly concerned with spiritual poverty and psychological dissociation, but these concerns are manifest in his characters' anxieties and in their ultimate integrity. In the fallen world, honesty towards oneself becomes the only saving grace. While he is prolific and acclaimed–his novel *The Great Victorian Collection* won a Governor General's Award as did *The Luck of Ginger Coffey*–most of his fiction falls outside the purview of Canadian literature. The four novels discussed here, including *Black Robe*, have been included as representatives of his best work.

Black Robe. Toronto: McClelland and Stewart, 1985. Markham: Penguin, 1987. Pages: 246. Paperback.

This is a disconcerting novel, strange and curiously eccentric. It is either a terrible novel by a writer of world stature, or a very good novel. Critical opinion seems irreconcilably divided. I side with the latter–*Black Robe* seems to me a fine achievement, a splendid read. But I also recognize why others find it exploitative and/or awkward.

As the title implies, this novel is determinedly Canadian. Without rekindling the argument about when is a Canadian not Canadian, I feel it is important to draw Brian Moore back into the fold, at least for this one book. Most of his seventeen novels to date establish him as a citizen of the larger world, almost a man without a country, without a particularized sensibility. But *Black Robe* belongs with *The Temptations of Big Bear, Beautiful Losers*, and *Burning Water* as much as it does with the works of Graham Greene. This is not an attempt to bring Moore, the naturalized expatriate, to ground in the less aerie or exalted world of Canadian literature. There is much to recommend his writing in comparison to the best, anywhere. Rather, it is acknowledgement that, while he may have a wide reach, he also has a firm grasp on the particular realities of his sometime adopted home.

A brief explanation is perhaps in order to account for my placing *Black Robe* among such an unlikely gathering of novels as the three named above. It would be hard to imagine a more disparate group, yet what these novels have in common is quite striking. All of them, including Moore's, explode conventional concepts of historicity, demolish the conventions of historical reconstruction. Rudy Wiebe's *The Temptations of Big Bear* superimposes the past over the present: his vision of the Plains Cree at home on the prairie displaces, with a haunting irony, the prairie of wheat pools and curling rinks. Leonard Cohen's *Beautiful Losers* restores life to a seventeenth-century Iroquois "saint" with manic vulgarity; her world is wrenched into startling collision with our own through the sheer force and bravado of Cohen's hallucinatory style. George Bowering's *Burning Water* is a more self-conscious attack on historicity: through brilliant deployment of bathos, those arbitrary structures of language and perspective, by which we maintain the death of the past, are collapsed. What happens is what happened: history is now, and the past is what we make of it. Eighteenth-century Indians speak in twentieth-century vernacular because that's where we are, reading Bowering, and that's where he is, writing.

Moore's novel relates to all three. There is a postmodern contemporaneity about his seventeenth-century characters, especially the Algonkins, the Huron, and the Iroquois. He translates their reality for us with the same eccentric and arbitrary authority that he applies to their language. They speak with casual obscenity, but according to a rigid social grammar which, for instance, demands that an insult, no matter how vile, accompanied by laughter, no matter how forced, is acceptable – and yet the mildest slur, said plainly, is beyond countenance. His Indians speak in the gutter slang of our times, yet curiously, ironically, this reinforces the vast discrepancies between their world and our own, and of course between their world and that of the Jesuit "black robes" who travelled heroically, vainly, and ignorantly among them, martyrs to an utterly alien and unaccommodating European theology/theocracy.

At times in Moore's novel the reader seems to have slipped into a longhouse orgy conceived by Cohen, then to have fallen into the esoteric absurdity of an Indian conversation devised by Bowering, only to become lost among people dreamed into being by Wiebe, for whom the values and behaviour of our world are incomprehensible. Not that Moore's novel is derivative. It is not. He draws extensively from authentic sources, having researched his novel in the Jesuit *Relations*, letters by missionaries sent back to their superiors in France. But there are many types of authenticity, and Moore has opted for the morally authentic rather than for documentary verisimilitude. In a highly idiosyncratic way, he explores the confrontation between worlds that seem to occupy different dimensions of reality, and, within the heart and consciousness of Paul Laforgue, s.j., between knowledge (learned in Europe and held as principles of faith) and experience (while living with people the French called Les Sauvages, and witnessing often without comprehension the brutality and the profound affections of their precarious lives). In broad terms, Moore shows a fascination with the inevitable destruction of a people who, in taking the values of an alien culture, cease to be themselves. Although the virtual annihilation of the Hurons is beyond the scope of his narrative, it is certainly presaged throughout. On a more intimate level, Moore explores the troubled conscience of Father Laforgue as he sinks deeper and deeper into the centre of this dark continent, en route to his posting at Lake Huron in the fall of 1635, and deeper into himself, a man both enhanced by his convictions and, pathetically, their victim.

Black Robe is written in an almost excessively accessible idiom, replete with contemporary obscenity, absurdity, and wit. It deals with a tortured soul, tells a bicultural love story, offers a grotesque torture scene, many episodes charged with suspense, and a fair portion of high good humour. It is a serious and amusing novel, disturbing, provocative, and entertaining all at once. Responses to it, inevitably, are ambivalent. Not Moore's best novel, it is probably his most unusual – one of the most unusual in contemporary writing. It is certainly worthwhile to read within the exemplary canon of a major writer, as an exemplary work of Canadian literature, and as a strange and curious work in its own right.

ANGUS MOWAT

Carrying Place. Toronto: Saunders, 1944. Pages: 318.

Never has a Canadian novelist captured the feel of small-boat sailing with such passionate authority as does Angus Mowat in *Carrying Place*. Oddly enough, this novel is a brooding romance of the land, an island farm off Prince Edward County near Picton, Ontario, and a story of fatal love; it is not primarily about sailing, at all. Yet three episodes on the water, two in Lake Ontario and one off the Devon coast, are of crucial importance, structurally, thematically, and in terms of narrative development. In these passages the writing soars; with perfect use of that special language of small boats and the sea, Mowat shares the overwhelming thrill of grace and power in awesome harmony that only sailing can yield. So effective is his writing, then, that the narrative recedes and, when each time it abruptly returns, it seems an unnatural intrusion. And that is precisely what the author would seem to intend.

Carrying Place explores the impact on a man's life of love shared with a woman who is wilful, at best, and possibly quite evil. Certainly the effect of Mona Crozier on Eric Dalton extends from early childhood through both their lives, and is profoundly destructive. During four generations, their two families have farmed side by side on the island of Carrying Place, which they share, and there has been bad feeling between them from the beginning, when a Crozier usurped the title of half the land. The marriage of Mona and Eric would once again unite the divided island under the Dalton name; but this is too much by far, in a romance such as this, for love and nature to bear. They both marry others; and, as if they were cursed, they continue through their lives to hurt and haunt one another until at last they bring about each other's death. Two world wars seem an appropriate setting for enacting their mutual torment.

The First World War, in particular, looms large through the narrative. Yet the deceit of his lover leaves more enduring scars on Eric than his wounds from battle. In the end, the Second World War consumes him, quite literally, after he has killed Mona when their International 14 spills in a Lake Ontario storm and he drowns her to save his wife. With the deaths of Eric and Mona, the Dalton estate and the whole of Carrying Place pass from the family:

the cycle begun with Eric's great grandfather's dream of a farming dynasty ends in the wreckage and the twisted morality of an obsessive love. The natural element of these ill-fated lovers, so bound in their lives to the land, is the water, the inland sea, that resolves their troubles by ending them forever.

Mowat develops powerful themes with the sureness of a master storyteller, and yet his novel is sometimes in irons, as it were. The voice and point of view waver uncertainly as he tries to catch each breath of possible meaning, as he tries to evade the squalls of melodrama that skitter across the narrative, as he struggles to get a hold on the moral implications of his story. *Carrying Place* is an ambitious novel and, for the most part, its serious intentions are subtly developed. Mowat shows an intriguing command of narrative time, as he draws discontinuous episodes into a coherent and entertaining whole. His use of language is never less than competent, and in the sailing passages and in the intimately detailed descriptions of Prince Edward County it is superb. His achievement has been overshadowed by the phenomenal success of his son Farley's documentary books, but Angus Mowat deserves to be remembered and read. He was possibly the best of a whole generation of accomplished amateurs between the wars who took the writing of popular fiction seriously, and wrote serious popular novels of enduring merit.

ALICE MUNRO

Lives of Girls and Women. Toronto: McGraw-Hill
Ryerson, 1971. Scarborough: New American Library,
1974. Pages: 211. Paperback.

While *Lives of Girls and Women* has attracted negative attention for its honest treatment of female sexuality, it is one of the most highly regarded novels ever to have appeared in Canada. It is certainly one of the most enjoyable and rewarding to read.

Alice Munro's prose has the crystal clarity of an autumn day as remembered from the depths of winter by an open fire. There are levels of irony in her writing that mingle the warmth of nostalgia with lucid memories of what has been lost. She evokes uncanny feelings of empathy with her protagonists, yet never are they less than unique. Her collections of short stories, *Dance of the Happy Shades, Something I've Been Meaning to Tell You, The Moons of Jupiter,* and *The Progress of Love,* contain some of the most subtly wrought fiction in the English language. Yet it is her longer works, *Lives of Girls and Women* and *Who Do You Think You Are?* (published in England as *The Beggar Maid),* that constitute her major contribution to Canadian literature. While not of better quality than her short stories, they have had more impact on the developing trend in Canada of what might be called hyper-realism or super-realism, and on the public appreciation of this trend. If any one work could be said to typify the best aspects of Canadian fiction in this generation, *Lives of Girls and Women* would have to be it.

Munro combines exquisite clarity of vision, in which realism is elevated and intensified, with clarity of diction; she creates an unforgettable account of a girl's growing into womanhood in a small Canadian town. There are neither great dramatic events nor profound insights, and yet Munro writes with such truth and conviction that Del Jordan will always remain one of the major figures in our literature. (Jubilee, patterned after Munro's hometown of Wingham, has become one of our most memorable fictional communities.)

Lives of Girls and Women is a modest novel of affirmation, a portrait of the artist, a recollection of the lost past, a celebration of honest individuality, a document of small-town life during the forties, an unassuming work of art of the highest quality. It is also a novel of large, if elusive, themes. Critics generally find it a difficult work to discuss, for Munro's style is virtually transparent and her themes are fully integrated into the narrative. It is a novel that, curiously, evokes a highly subjective response: even the most austere academic cannot help but identify with its protagonist. Del follows a universal pattern in the phases of her growing up; only the details are her own.

Much of the novel's form derives from Del's evolving sexuality. There is an episodic quality as Munro illuminates Del's experiences from early consciousness of her separate physical being (brought about by a confrontation with a dead cow and then her dead uncle), to an exuberantly passionate affair with Garnet

French during her final year in high school. In between there are silly flirtations, romantic imaginings, grasping caresses, and a hilariously awkward scene of failed experimentation. All this provides Munro with a context within which to explore broader themes: Del's coming to terms with being female in a world of rapidly changing values, Del's coping with the sense of being different and yet unexceptional, her increasing awareness of her own sensitivity and separateness from the world around her, her need to share and love yet still be free. Gradually, the reader realizes that Del's story is a portrait of the artist as a girl and young woman, as well as an enormously engaging account of growing up. Little is mentioned of her developing sensibility, although Del's fascination with words is evident from the beginning; but from a distance one can see Munro using the novel to develop a particular aesthetic (in this respect "Epilogue: The Photographer" is most revealing). In any case, the mature Del who recalls the phases of her growing up has effectively become the artist her story intends her to be.

Well on in the novel, Del's mother proclaims to her the follies and pitfalls of the conventional woman's lot and admonishes her to fight domination by men in a sexist society. However, Del's mother is jaundiced, she abhors being female. It falls to Del, in the next generation, to reconcile freedom with pride, to take control and responsibility for her own life, without denying herself as a woman. Munro's novel depicts the phases of Del's advance into full consciousness. She is not concerned with the development of Del's character and sensibility–these are given from the beginning–but with Del's growing awareness and acceptance of herself. It is a novel of liberation and of maturation.

Here, as in her other fiction, Munro shows consummate control of the narrative point of view to achieve dimensions of significance that words themselves do not always imply. By having Del relate her account from an adult perspective, Munro creates an ironic distance between voice and event, which adds to the sense of loss. At the same time it effectively undermines the tendency towards sentimentality inherent in the autobiographical format. Always, we are aware of two Del Jordans–the girl growing up and the woman recollecting her past. And always, we know that these two are one and the same person. Thus, while we observe Del Jordan observing in retrospect her own struggle towards maturity, we also share in that struggle. It is an experience to remember, as immediate as if it were our own – which, in a sense, it is.

Who Do You Think You Are? Toronto: Macmillan, 1978. Scarborough: New American Library, 1979.
Pages: 210. Paperback.

Who Do You Think You Are? Both plaintive and assertive: the title tells the tale. This is a novel as ingenuously unaffected and enigmatic as a saint's confession. Munro's achievement in telling the story of a woman's struggle towards independence and a separate peace rivals *Lives of Girls and Women* for the impact of its content and surpasses it in form and technique. Rose, the protagonist, is neither a rebel nor a dissenter, but personal integrity and her indelible sense of the past draw her towards a self-reliance that she does not entirely want and that she copes with only tentatively at best. She is not heroic, nor is she the suffering victim. Like Del Jordan, she is more aware of herself than most people, and that makes all the difference. From a feminist perspective she is perhaps too pliant and uncertain. Social reactionaries will undoubtedly find her self-indulgent and uppity. However, neither would deny that she is a woman the reader can know, as if she were real and not an imaginative creation.

Munro's prose is transparent, as perfect as air. We breathe it in without being aware of it, and it sustains us. In all her fiction, the language "feels" right – the right word inevitably in the right place. It is not laden with lateral meanings or contorted with stylistic flourishes, yet there is always a rich allusiveness and quiet beauty. She is probably the best stylist writing in Canada today. She is certainly, in her prose, the most lucid and congenial.

Who Do You Think You Are? is offered by the publisher as a collection of linked stories – as if the genesis of individual chapters should determine the form of the whole. Most were published separately and may easily have been written with no conscious attempt at shaping a larger context. Munro has never claimed to understand fully, on a rational plane, what it is she does with her art – and in this case, her art suffers a demeaning label because the publisher has not recognized her achievement. There is nothing inferior about a collection of "linked" stories, but when the term is inappropriate it diminishes the work described. It suggests that there is not an organic wholeness, an aesthetic, thematic, dramatic dynamic coherence. The label denies form.

Each chapter of *Who Do You Think You Are?* has an internal integrity of its own and is complete in itself–the way a well-turned paragraph is, or a perfect image. But together the chapters make up a fiction infinitely larger than the sum of its parts. Each chapter tells of a phase in the protagonist's life, starting when she was a girl living behind a store in West Hanratty, Ontario, with a violent father and Flo, her acerbic, enduring stepmother. Succeeding chapters describe her leaving home, marrying well, establishing a career, leaving, falling in love, leaving, losing, returning home to visit, and gradually assimilating her past and the passage of time, the burdens of change.

Munro does not delve deeply into motivation or the dark recesses of the psyche, but she does trace the patterns of consciousness in Rose's mind with exquisite clarity; that is, she illuminates how Rose sees herself but leaves the reasons for her behaviour implicit in the text. The perspective is multiple: Rose is aware of herself in the present action, but she also reflects on the present from some time in the future, beyond the narrative perimeter. She *also* seems to reflect on the known future from the vantage of the present or past. Time and consciousness together provide a narrative design in which the separate segments are integral facets, indispensible to the whole.

In the first chapter, "Royal Beatings," Rose anticipates events in the last, when her stepmother is institutionalized. In the last chapter she draws the bittersweet memories of her childhood into a thoughtful present. Rose does not write her own story: this is not the protagonist's own account of herself. Rose is less in the autobiographical mode than Del Jordan; her voice is more distanced from that of her creator. Rose is a more mature creation.

bp nichol

Still. Vancouver: Pulp Press, 1983. Pages: 70. Paperback.

Still is a small exquisite novel, as enigmatic and illuminating as the finest cameo. Ignore the trivializing hype that surrounds its origin as fifth winner of the Pulp Press International 3-Day Novel-Writing Contest. Ignore the author's reputation as the leading avant-garde Canadian poet of his generation – this leads to expectations that distort his novel's genuine achievement. And ignore the novel's obscurity – in both senses, as a work that is largely unknown and, inwardly, within the text. That few people know of it is no measure of its worth. That it teases on the edge of incomprehension is a major source of its haunting brilliance.

While *Still* brings to mind the work of Alain Robbe-Grillet more than that of nichol's Canadian contemporaries, it is very much a novel of its own time and place. The juxtaposition of pure dialogue with passages of pure description at first seems more akin to postwar French experimentalism than to anything written by Timothy Findley or Audrey Thomas. But the conversation between the lovers at what might be the end of a long-standing affair reveals personalities and a relationship teeming with the self-aggrandizing anxieties that are, if not exclusively Canadian, utterly consistent with experience in a Canadian context. Although they speak quite naturally, they do so without reference to anything outside their own awareness of each other. We do not get to know anything *about* them, but we do know them! Each is a coherent and knowable personality. From the way they articulate themselves, we know gender, age, class, and predominant characteristics. And in the descriptive passages, which it seems relate to the speaking couple only through shared presence in a common text, we recognize a physical lived-in world continuous with our own, consistent in every detail with what we know from experience to be tangible and therefore real. Lovingly described, this house and landscape are people-occupied although, paradoxically, there are no people present in the description. Only the text itself brings people and place together, which grounds the speaking couple in a specific environment.

There are two people talking. One is a woman. One is a man. We know this by the way they talk. By syntactical nuance. By subtle assumptions and prerogatives in their discourse. The male outweighs the female as a centre of dialectical interest. The female holds her own; she is a presence, she is important. But she is not as important a presence as the male, her partner. Even though she has been touched recently by a tragedy that seems to have left him largely unaffected, she is not so close to the narrative centre as he is. Tensions and momentum build around him more than her. In the beginning they discuss their end. In the end they agree to go on exactly as they have been. Somehow, this seems for him a triumph – and, for her, an acceptable compromise.

That is the story. They talk. And interspersed between moments of the tersest dialogue imaginable are beautifully detailed descriptions of a house, inside and out. Overlapping visions of the grounds and environs gradually give way to a room-by-room tour of the interior. Words are a camera: nichol moves with meticulous care through his scene, sometimes zooming in for a close-up, sometimes panning across a wall, sometimes angling a shot for intentional distortion, sometimes withdrawing to a neutral distance and at other times forcing an intimacy on the reader by such proximity to artifact that one feels implicated in a violation of some sort. This is a lived-in place, yet never do we encounter there a living soul. Sometimes the scene is timeless, or takes in whole seasons, and at other times we see a table set, a toilet roll half gone; and we are haunted by the apparent absence of inhabitants.

Yet context – that is, in this case, the text itself – forces characters and setting together. It is almost betrayal when, in the closing lines of the novel, the author unites them in a single sentence. Until that point, it is the reader alone, in reading of both, who puts the people into place. Their explicit merging seems a minor failure of nerve on nichol's part. This, however, is an insignificant flaw in what I take to be one of the best experimental novels ever published in Canada.

Still is arguably a modernist experiment, not postmodern. In some ways, it is remarkably old-fashioned. The seemingly disembodied dialogue may strike the reader as absurd at first, because there is no context, there are no referents, but in fact it is linear, coherent, and, far from being absurd, quite touching. The descriptive passages may overlap somewhat arbitrarily and may seem obsessively detailed, but, while disconnected from the couple on a narrative level, they provide a clear and telling complement to their conversation, an objective correlative to the emotional plexus in which they find themselves. To appreciate this novel, it is not a question of penetrating narrative pyrotechnics or resolving anomalies in narrative design: it is simply a matter of reading carefully what is there. nichol has created an unusual and profound work of fiction, the likes of which one is unlikely to encounter again or elsewhere.

FREDERICK NIVEN

The Flying Years. London: Collins, 1935. Toronto: McClelland and Stewart, 1974. Pages: 253. Paperback.

As the title anticipates, there is such a rush of time and history here that the reader is left breathless, trying to cope with continual loss and renewal. Niven believes in progress and has found, in the radically foreshortened history of the Canadian West, a perfect correlation for his belief. Within the sixty years of a man's life, the town of Calgary grows from frontier outpost to sophisticated city. The change has been at terrible cost, but on the whole, the author thinks, it is a good thing. Indians have been contained; the buffalo slaughtered; wars far away have drained off the lifeblood of a generation; rail lines, the telephone, and grand hotels have been installed. Calgary has become a bustling centre of human activity poised between the timeless prairie and the timeless mountains. An old man, Angus Munro, sits in the Palliser Hotel at the novel's close, his mind a sanctuary for all that he has lived through since leaving Scotland at sixteen. He fades into timelessness, his story over.

There is little plot in *The Flying Years* but a great deal of incident. Niven does not arrange events for narrative effect, but allows them to accumulate in orderly sequence, like the phases of a man's life. Angus Munro is driven off the land in Scotland with his family in 1856, and he finds refuge in Canada. After several years back in Scotland again, working in a bookstore in Edinburgh, he returns to the Canadian West. After a variety of colourful jobs, he settles as an Indian agent in what is now Alberta. Munro's involvement with the Cree extends beyond learning their language, for he takes an Indian woman, Minota, as his wife, and they have a son. Minota dies of measles, a white man's disease, and Munro is then free to marry his beloved Fiona, someone "of his own race." His Indian son remains unacknowledged. His white son dies, a victim of the First World War. Niven applauds his character's sympathetic understanding of the Indians but does not easily forgive him his prejudices.

The story of Angus Munro and his family and his acquisitive friend, Sam Lovat-Douglas, and of the Indians Munro works with, provides a focal centre for Niven's chronicle of western Canadian history. The human story is told in leaps and bounds, however, and there is barely time for response before a new sequence has begun. Seldom does the reader become intimately concerned with the characters, but the life of the region comes alive in the imagination. And Niven is sophisticated enough to keep the larger historical, cultural, and political worlds within reach. In this, *The Flying Years* is quite unlike other prairie novels, which are, almost invariably, insular, and sometimes provincial.

Niven was prolific and popular, but not what might be called a "literary" writer. This novel, however, is elevated by the profound sympathy shown for the Indians and for its deep understanding of the rapidly changing conditions of the West as they affect individual lives. Niven's prose is competent, but not the stuff of fine art. His sense of time and history are superb; his sense of place translates into a convincing imaginative reality. There is little to fault in *The Flying Years*, for it strives to be no more than an edifying entertainment. There is limited drama in it, little psychological insight, little thematic or emotional ambiguity, little complexity. It is a novel that, despite its title, never soars.

HOWARD O'HAGAN

Tay John. New York: Laidlaw & Laidlaw, 1939. Toronto: McClelland and Stewart; New Canadian Library, 1974. Pages: 264. Paperback.

Tay John is the remarkable work of a naïve visionary: O'Hagan is a creative writer as primitive, or "natural," as any published in Canada this century. His unconventional novel reminds one vaguely of a painting on which Marc Chagall and Grandma Moses have collaborated. He mixes myth with metaphor, realism with surrealism, the authentic with the preposterous, in a novel quite unlike any other. There is a touching sincerity about the novel, even when it most offends the sensibility with its awkwardness of form and style, or the rational mind with its refusal to accept that different realities, the visionary and the actual, are mutually exclusive. *Tay John* draws heavily on western Indian mythology, with a strong infusion of the Christian, but it is entirely a new creation, one fortunately undisciplined by convention or rationality.

Tay John has three parts. The first is primarily the stuff of legend, rising occasionally, with archetypal echoes, to myth. The second, in which the narrator of the rest of the novel is introduced in the third person, hovers between yarn and documentary. The third gradually reverts to myth, but it is myth as hearsay this time. The progression of the novel is not circular; rather it moves towards completion. In the beginning, Tay John emerges from the womb of a dead woman who is buried in the earth. At the end, he slips back into the earth; he seems to disappear down into the snow with the corpse of the woman he loves.

Tay John is the offspring of a fundamentalist zealot, Red Rorty, who rapes a Shuswap woman and is grotesquely executed for his crime. His beard is set on fire, and a stone is placed in his mouth to absorb the agony, or to muffle the screams. The child, an Indian with blond hair (Tête Jaune), seems the answer to the tribe's messiah myth, and when he matures he leads them to Yellowhead Lake in the Rockies, a promised land. Prevented from taking a betrothed woman for himself, however, he deserts the tribe (he is more a failed Moses than a fallen Christ). This story is told in simple, direct language that suggests literal translations of Indian tales. Tay John wanders, learns white ways, becomes a cowboy, then a guide. He is accused of rape, then vindicated. Again he wanders. These events are related in the folksy voice of an old remittance man, Jack Denham, who continues Tay John's story in part three. Tay John turns up at a project, not unlike Jasper Park Lodge, which is being developed by one Alf Dobble. Tay John becomes enchanted with the beautiful courtesan he is meant to guide, Ardith Aeriola. She is also an object of the perverse passion of Father Thomas Rorty (Red's brother and Tay John's uncle), who, in a terrible fit of spiritual pride, emulates Christ by crucifying himself. Tay John rescues Ardith from Dobble's scornful attack; Ardith is pregnant and dying. The two beautiful outcasts journey off into the mountain snow.

This novel rewards the reader with a welter of motifs related to truth and beauty, suffering and salvation, Christianity and Amerindian legend. It mixes archetypes and ordinary people in a most unusual way. The unpretentious realism of the descriptive passages, the quiet evocative beauty of its mythic element, and its homespun social vision all contribute to the novel's quality as a work of substance. However, its naïveté, its unsophisticated prose, and its melodramatic story call that quality into question. Ultimately, the primary virtue of *Tay John* would appear to be in its idiosyncrasies rather than its inherent achievement as either art or vision.

MICHAEL ONDAATJE

Coming Through Slaughter. Toronto: Anansi, 1976.
Don Mills: General; New Press Canadian Classics, 1982.
Pages: 156. Paperback.

Coming Through Slaughter is not really about Buddy Bolden and his cornet and jazz and New Orleans early this century. It is about Michael Ondaatje: Bolden just provides the facts, the mythology of his style and times. Always, it is the narrator's story – whoever speaks, whatever the radical shift in narrative perspective, it is the artist's soul that is being offered up. Ondaatje is inseparable from the telling of his protagonist's story. The reader thinks he is reading an oblique and allusive document – and he is, but it is a document on Ondaatje's secret self, not of Bolden's mean and tragic life.

In Canadian literature, where experimental fiction is relatively rare, this work stands out as an exotic anomaly. It is, on the surface, a modest endeavour. Through a medley of interview fragments, authentic records of the time, recollections real and imagined, shards of poetry, occasional lyric wisps, witnessed events, opaque references, sharp, cruel images, and evocative details, Ondaatje presents his vision of Bolden. What holds it all together is jazz rather than the conventions of prose fiction. Form is not skeletal, but fluid and alive, like blood flowing in the reader's veins. Form is at the same time fractious, like the erratic but disciplined flow of blood spilling from a gaping wound.

Ondaatje as poet has developed an awesome subtext for his own life and times, less metaphor than subjective correlative. As an elusively confessional poem, his novel achieves a disconcerting magnitude, a vision of spiritual desolation. The whole builds to his final statement where he is all three: Bolden, and Bolden's witness, and himself alone:

> I sit with this room. With the grey walls that darken into corner. And one window with teeth in it. Sit so still you can hear your hair rustle in your shirt. Look away from the window when clouds and other things go by. Thirty-one years old. There are no prizes.

Coming Through Slaughter offers a brisk series of cameos and vignettes which show Bolden and his various allies in vivid detail, yet more spectral than real. The characters populate graphic scenes of violence and poignancy, but they are not realized as dramatic individuals in their own right. The point of view shifts radically and abruptly, but a voice and viewpoint, which remain apart from the present action, predominate. The language is precise and evocative. Ondaatje's prose is informed with the directness, the intensity, and the ambiguity of good music and rare poetry. At times, words and images speak so directly to the reader that mind is circumvented altogether. It is then that the novel as poem comes into its own.

In the meticulous presentation of period and place, Ondaatje creates a dream-vision derivative of black, jazz-age Louisiana. There never was such a place nor were there such people, except in the imagination (though the prototypes are in evidence in photographs and documentary records). To laud this novel for its authenticity is to miss the point entirely, reducing Ondaatje's grand aesthetic design to a miniature reproduction.

Michael Ondaatje is a poet of considerable reputation, whose work has taken on an increasingly prose-like quality, on the surface at least. In *The Collected Works of Billy the Kid*, he explores the possibilities of mixed media on the printed page. *Running in the Family* fictionalizes personal anecdote and family history, simply by their exceptionally articulate presentation in an artful arrangement. In *Coming Through Slaughter* (Slaughter is a town in Louisiana) he mixes media and genres. It is this novel's capacity to act as a vehicle for disciplined but eccentric craftsmanship, for a mordantly exacting imagination and an aesthetic flair for the bizarre, that elevates it into the realm of first-rate art.

As *The Double Hook* is the dominant experimental novel of the fifties in Canada, and *Five Legs* or possibly *Beautiful Losers*, of the sixties, *Coming Through Slaughter* rivals *Blown Figures* as the leading experimental novel of the seventies.

MARTHA OSTENSO

Wild Geese. Toronto: McClelland and Stewart, 1925.
Toronto: McClelland and Stewart; New Canadian Library, 1961. Pages: 239. Paperback.

With its combination of gothic perversity and penetrating insight, *Wild Geese* received a major American literary award when it first appeared, and it still makes compelling reading. Set on a farm in northern Manitoba, Ostenso's story echoes Scandinavian sagas and portrays immigrant hardship, but it is essentially a psychological romance.

Caleb Gare is a fascinating misanthrope who keeps his family in a state of terrible suppression. He blackmails his wife with the threat of revealing to her illegitimate son his humble origin. This story is balanced against the love affair of the son with Lind Archer, a visiting teacher to their remote locale. Lind is both observer and catalyst; her presence helps to undermine the tyrannical authority of Caleb. The moral fulcrum between the two stories is the magnificent Jude, Caleb's indomitable youngest daughter and Lind's friend and confidante. Jude is the natural woman, earth child and earth mother at the same time. Like her father, she rejects the mores of the civilized world, but she rejects his mores as well. Jude conceives, while Lind retreats to the city with plans for marital bliss. Jude's pregnancy is a triumph. Through her, the whole family is set free. In the end, Caleb perishes; appropriately, he is pursued by fire and, literally, drowns in the earth.

Ostenso's prose is authentic and exciting, although occasionally a bit forced or awkward. *Wild Geese* is unexceptional in form, but the narrative movement is compelling, almost too compelling at times. Like Grove, Ostenso discovered and exploited the possibilities of the family farm as an appropriate setting for a story seething with passion, fraught with the machinations of power. The natural world seems to be representative of her characters' interior conditions, and yet in part, paradoxically, the cause of them. It is in this reciprocity between nature and psyche that *Wild Geese* achieves the dramatic power that makes it still an impressive novel to read.

A fascinating end-note to *Wild Geese* is the question of its authorship. According to Peter E. Rider, in an introduction to the University of Toronto Press reprint of Douglas Durkin's 1923 novel, *The Magpie*, Durkin and Ostenso wrote *Wild Geese* together. However, in order to submit it for the Dodd Mead first-novel prize of $13,500, which it won, Durkin's name had to be omitted, since he had been published previously. Rider presents a convincing argument and notes the further extensive collaboration between the two authors over the forty years they lived together.

SIR GILBERT PARKER

The Seats of the Mighty. London: Methuen, 1896.
Toronto: McClelland and Stewart; New Canadian Library,
1971. Pages: 376. Paperback.

Parker was born in Camden East, Canada West, now known as the home of *Harrowsmith* magazine. He lived much of his life in England, serving in the British House of Commons, where he became a member of the Privy Council. His affinity for Britain and Tory imperialism plays a significant part in *The Seats of the Mighty*. This is a novel of minor achievement by any measure, yet great fun to read and an important indicator of Victorian taste and values.

The Seats of the Mighty could best be read in tandem with William Kirby's *The Golden Dog*, a much better novel from an aesthetic and an historical viewpoint. Both novels envision the last phase of the *ancien régime*, before the fall of New France, from a Victorian perspective. Kirby's novel honours history and exploits it; Parker's plays with it. In *The Seats of the Mighty*, he presents, at a safe distance, a range of historical figures from Washington to La Pompadour, from Bigot and Montcalm to Wolfe and Bonnie Prince Charlie. Not content with name-dropping to attain an aura of authenticity, he involves Wolfe *et al.* in incredible plots. At the centre of these machinations is his anachronistic English hero, Captain Robert Moray.

The novel purports to be Moray's story and is based loosely on the actual memoirs of a Captain Robert Stobo. Parker takes as much licence here, though, as he does with history in general – in conformity with the conventions of historical romance. His fiction shows relatively little interest in cultural authenticity, little sympathy for the people of Quebec and their situation on the eve of the Conquest. Instead, Quebec provides an exotic context within which to exercise the sterling virtues of his protagonist, a modest hero who turns the course of world history.

In the first part of the novel, Moray is a captive of the French. While on parole, he has fallen in love with Alixe Duvarney. After a period in prison Moray escapes and, in the second part of the novel, journeys down river to join General Wolfe. In the third phase of his adventure, he returns to Quebec in disguise; eventually, he leads Wolfe up the secret path to the Plains of Abraham, where a skirmish with Montcalm's troops is followed by Moray's reconciliation with Alixe. He is led to her refuge by the scarlet figure who had once been the Intendant Bigot's mistress, Caroline.

Bigot, the hobnailed courtier, is a presence throughout the novel; his coarse debauchery embodies all that is corrupt in New France. Alixe represents all that is good, and after scintillating adventures, she is appropriately united with the English hero. First, though, she is courted by both Moray and the devastatingly attractive and treacherous Doltaire. In disguise, she visits Moray in jail just before his execution (which Doltaire stops). Later she dances wildly, again in disguise, for Bigot and his cronies in a flourish of erotic innocence. Alixe has by far the most fun of anyone in the novel. Moray is somewhat insipid and invested with too much Victorian virtue; Doltaire is the most vital character but, being La Pompadour's emissary and Moray's rival, he is doomed by his author to die ignominiously.

It is difficult to discuss *The Seats of the Mighty* with academic gravity, for the book is meant as an entertainment. And it is an enormously successful entertainment, one of the best of its type. Parker manipulates plot and character with free-wheeling abandon. He writes in the first person with a naïve enthusiasm that is engaging even when Moray is most a prig. He displays a cheerful British chauvinism at the expense of both Quebec and Catholicism; he makes bigotry seem no more than an innocuous diversion. As a source of historical truths, or of insight into the human condition, this novel is impoverished. As a documentary on the popular sensibility of the Victorian empire, it is superb.

THOMAS RADDALL

His Majesty's Yankees. Toronto: McClelland and Stewart, 1942. Toronto: McClelland and Stewart; New Canadian Library, 1977. Pages: 409. Paperback.

Thomas Raddall is one of our finest storytellers. *His Majesty's Yankees* is his first and best historical novel. In a sweeping tale that blends high romance with discerning political and social commentary, Raddall explores Nova Scotia's involvement in the American Revolution. It is an unusual perspective, told with an enthusiasm for historical realities that makes it unforgettable reading. The reader does not have to be a fan of costume romances, for this novel has little in common with such ephemera. It abounds with swashbuckling intrigue and adventure, but these have never stood in the way of a good story.

Raddall's protagonist, young David Strang, sides initially with the rebel forces. Yankee practicality prevents aid from reaching the Bluenose dissidents, but it is finally the piratical exploits of the New Englanders that convert many, David among them, into staunch Loyalists. An additional motivation is provided by the king's power, and sustained by geography.

The story allows Raddall to explore history, rather than merely to have history provide the material for his story. The richness of *His Majesty's Yankees* arises from minute detail melded to great events. Raddall has researched every aspect of his characters' lives and times—or he is an utterly convincing liar. He writes facts with a vivid edge of authenticity and moves among them with easy familiarity, taking his readers with him.

Rare is the historical novel that measures up to this one as either art or entertainment. It is an old-fashioned novel, told from a point of view that honours old-fashioned virtues; and without being prissy or reactionary it assumes the reader shares the same values. The past is not brought forward; rather the reader is taken comfortably back into the past.

The prose is clear and precise. Narrative threads weave complex patterns but are always vividly discernible. Mood is handled with firm authority: the more exuberant the romance, the firmer the control. Raddall is a realist, an historian, a storyteller. He maintains objectivity and balance throughout, showing the colours of both sides in the rebellion, and the thousand shades between. Simultaneously, he explores the emotional complexities of a young man growing up, along with the personalities and relationships of those he loves and lives for. And, not least, he describes Nova Scotia as a place so real you can smell in his prose the sea at the tide's turn and hear the gulls in the wind.

The Nymph and the Lamp. Toronto: McClelland and Stewart, 1950. Toronto: McClelland and Stewart; New Canadian Library, 1965. Pages: 333. Paperback.

The Nymph and the Lamp is a story of love, but, even more, the story of a woman growing into the full dimensions of her own personality, a woman taking possession of herself. Isabel Jardine is a fine protagonist, sensitively portrayed. At the beginning of the novel she is colourless and ineffectual, drifting along. By the end she is a dynamic woman, filled with hope for the future and with the love she bears for a difficult man. It is not love that liberates her, but self-knowledge. Isabel's transition is accomplished in a manner that is not only convincing and engaging, but seemingly inevitable.

Matt Carney is a huge, solitary man in charge of the wireless station on a sand-bar island off the coast of Nova Scotia, much like Sable Island with its sand dunes and wild horses. He and Isabel have a tawdry affair in Halifax–his first–and he takes her back with him to his post. They gradually come to love each other, but then, as her affection deepens, he pulls away. Her isolation is magnified by the strange island setting. She turns to Skane,

Carney's brooding friend. Wounded, quite literally, she leaves. Her strength of character reinforced, she prospers. Discovering it was Carney's impending blindness that caused him to grow distant, she returns.

As in his historical fiction, Raddall moves perilously close to sentimental romance. What keeps him from slipping into sentimentality and contrivance are the firm hold he maintains on the psychology of his characters' lives and his realization of the solid earth on which they stand. The island setting haunts the reader's imagination, so convincing is Raddall's description of it, and so convincing is the significance it plays in his characters' experience. Image and symbol merge in this novel quite brilliantly, as do characters and place. The effect is romance, realistically conveyed.

DAVID ADAMS RICHARDS

Blood Ties. Ottawa: Oberon, 1976. Toronto: McClelland and Stewart; New Canadian Library, 1985. Pages: 278.
Paperback.

There is no easy way into this novel, the best to come out of the Maritimes in this generation (rivalled, perhaps, only by Richards's own 1985 novel, *The Road to the Stilt House*). Yet everything is laid out on the surface, ready to be seen on the most casual reading. Richards's first novel, *The Coming of Winter*, was justly celebrated – as a first novel. *Blood Ties* stands as a mature work, although the author was still in his early twenties when he wrote it. He has a style that is uncompromising, a vision of incomparable integrity, and an aesthetic sense that is as austere and moving as waves in a limitless ocean. He writes what I can only describe as "literal realism"; intuitively akin to Maritime painters like Pratt and Forrestall, recording the minutiae on the surface of hidden depths – not at all like either Colville or Blackwood, with their narrative allusions to meaning. There is no one in Canada today who writes like David Richards, nor has there ever been.

A disciplined artist, Richards refuses to give in to the reader's need to understand relationships and identities, to be, in effect, superior to the reality portrayed. He describes what characters do and say, never what they feel; only occasionally, when they are aware of it themselves, does he describe what they think. Yet their feelings come through as we watch their lives, for we see all the confused ambiguity of our own experience. Characters are identified incidentally, and their relationships to one another emerge as they interact. We must attend closely to them, to sort them out, as if we were strangers in their midst, which we are. In long, slow stretches and brief bursts of excitement, personalities become clear and emotions are laid open before us. What we learn is far beyond the capacity of these inarticulate, reticent people to reveal themselves.

Even the setting is vague, yet the details are as specific as blades of grass in a field. There is a river. Down river, a town. A mine. A factory. Fishing. Salt water. A high school. Here, a few houses, barns, fields, bush. And a highway. Slowly, what must be New Brunswick around the mouth of the Miramichi becomes a coherent world. The outside world seems hardly to intrude. If dates in 1967 and 1968 were not given to the three sections, then only the seasons and the cars would seem to set the time. And yet this is not so, for the values, the language, and the relationships suggest impositions of a specific outside world. Radio, television, movies are never mentioned, but their influence is obvious on family life, in the breakdown of authority, particularly of the Church, in the departures from the community, and in the changing traditions.

Blood Ties can be a frustrating novel to read. For pages, the reader may be uncertain whose life is being recorded in such detail, as pronouns are often the only labels characters have. In the dialogue, there is the interminable repetition of the inarticulate in conversation. Over and over, key phrases and expressive epithets are repeated, until talk becomes a kind of litany, revealing and concealing things quite apart from what is being said. Richards has perfect control of the violent and often obscene idiom of a specific locale. Not once does he hint at what the characters might really mean, or really feel. He shows them, in literal reality, as they appear to be. It is highly effective art, for the reader is limited only by his own imagination. As scenes accumulate, the reader's imagination forms a story of a cluster of people and their relationships, which is far more like the ragtag open-ended world of ordinary experience than of art–but it is intensified, focused, and manipulated so that, in spite of the confusions, the experience has been special, lasting, and coherent, in the way only art can be.

Road to the Stilt House. Ottawa: Oberon, 1985.
Pages: 171.

It is hard to imagine a novel more depressing than this. It is a fine novel, but distressing to read. Richards seems to write in monosyllables, in terse and enigmatic little sentences that repeat themselves apparently at random. He writes with precision and imagination about lives so mean and unregenerate they seem less than human. There is nothing valiant about them, nothing ennobling. These are people whose will has gone. There is the smell of poverty about them, and of failure and ignorance. They are at the bottom, filthy, indolent, and ugly. They live in a house on stilts, on a road going nowhere. There are hornets in the walls. There is nothing to redeem their lives and only sleep and bickering to get them by. "Today will be another day." "One day follows another." Variants of this occur throughout. No one rises above the stench and torpor to give a good goddamn.

So dismal is this world, set somewhere in the back end of New Brunswick (as the narrative describes it, presumably in the area of Richards's native Miramichi), that we hardly notice the difference between Arnold's perception of it and the external narrator's, even though Arnold is a deeply disturbed simple-minded social deviant. Those last few modifiers are, of course, delivered from a middle-class perspective–and the independent narrative voice that alternates through most of the novel with Arnold's is decidedly not middle class. It is a voice in harmony with the squalid lives it exposes to us. Taken together, the voices of this novel provide an illumination of one world for access to it by another. The third voice, which takes over in Part II of the narrative, belongs to Arnold's cousin Norman, who in his aspirations to upward mobility mediates between the two worlds while being ill at ease in both.

So dismal is this narrative world we hardly realize just how disturbed Arnold really is. At first his idiosyncrasies appear consistent with his environment and those around him. If he has slashed his belly with a knife, if he talks to the road, if he rails at the unfairness of it all (at the social worker, poverty, Canada, whatever) and threatens to get even, these seem plausible responses to the conditions of his life. Richards does not help us differentiate between Arnold and his world. He makes it difficult for us. The language of the narrative is Arnold's language; the perceptions, the level of comprehension, are apparently Arnold's. Only gradually do we come to recognize that Arnold, perhaps more aptly known as Seaweed, is truly an aberrant and demented soul. Ironically, the cues are not subtle. When his girlfriend, Trenda, leaves him, for example, because words are as beyond him as rational coping, he clenches his jaws until blood spurts from his gums, until several blackened teeth pop to the floor. He slaps his sickly mother, kicks in the television, refuses to take down the Christmas tree, kicks holes in the walls, pokes his cousin Norman in the guts with a stick. He toadies and bullies and sulks and rages. But he is surrounded by such coarseness, such squalor, stupidity, and violence, that nothing much of his erratic mean behaviour stands out from the apparent norm.

His little brother Randy is a bully, a pathetic Cub Scout aspirant bullied by his troop leader. His mother Mabel is sick and listens to the CBC; her boyfriend Harry endlessly repeats the story of his wife's miserable death; Harry's mother Sadie is a bully. They all talk dirty, eat poorly, watch television, wait for welfare and the welfare worker, Juliet, who moves casually among them, seeing to such amenities as food and fuel, and occasionally they talk with the priest, Billy, who is a maundering alcoholic. And then there is Norman, who lives next door, who made Arnold's Trenda pregnant, and who takes night courses and sometimes works. And there is Jerry, who murdered a Norwegian sailor, robs crypts, beats on Arnold viciously, marries Trenda, and eventually, in a prison break with Arnold, murders Arnold, after taking his clothes, and leaves his naked body in the snow.

Arnold is 5'2", and apologetic for being so small. He is inarticulate, surrounded by the inarticulate. He, alone, recognizes this limitation or, at least, rages against it. He is scrawny, a decrepit young man with stumps of blackened teeth, and with no hair on his chest or belly—for which he apologizes and feels great shame. As the novel progresses, a metamorphosis in Arnold's appearance occurs, which more than anything he says or thinks or does (for his saying/thinking/doing are severely limited) shows him slipping through eccentricity into madness and beyond, into the inevitable reach of death. When we first know him, he wears the same filthy red pants everywhere. In the end, after his mother and brother are dead, even before he burns the house to the ground, incinerating Harry, he takes to wearing filthy leather pants, a leather vest, a red neckerchief, and goes around with his head shaven and oily and his meagre tattoos flashing–a sinister runt of a man, frightening and pathetic.

Why read a novel of such wretchedness? Why pursue this meagre man through misery to his pointless end? Surely not to exercise that perverse pleasure of the middle class, embarrassment for privilege that we slyly construe as penance. If there is no redeeming factor within the narrative, wherein lies the worth of reading it? The answer lies in art. Why read Gogol? Why read Faulkner? Not because their visions are elevating but because they are so finely rendered. What their fiction does see, we also see, and not only with the eyes of our imagination but in the heart and the soul as well. That is the achievement of their art, to make us do so.

Richards does not compromise. His language is raw, direct, sparse, and demanding. Paradoxically, the more simple and direct his language is in this novel, the more difficult it is to grasp and the more complexity it conveys. I do not know of anyone in English, apart from Faulkner, who so brilliantly gives a voice to the inarticulate and access to such restricted consciousness. (I am thinking less of the damaged mind of Benjy in *The Sound and the Fury* than of the limited minds of the characters in *As I Lay Dying* or *Sanctuary*.) The syntax and word choice in *Road to the Stilt House* are severe. There is a painful absence of imagery, except in the twisted association of unexpected verbs and nouns. Less is more. An entire paragraph consists of the following: "To make you suffer in houses with boot marks and stabbed walls." And another paragraph reads: " 'The television crawled all over me day and night, and it was time to do something about it.' " Arnold says this to the priest, explaining why he kicked it in. And the following, with the economy of a paranoid Hemingway, delivers everything:

"I'd better not fight again," he said.
His body shook. The day passed minute by minute.

Passed, and went away.
Harry.
Sadie.
Mabel.
Randy.
He said this over and over again, wondering what to do.
Craig.
Juliet.
He said their names with his tongue, always watching for the
   night.
Billy the priest.
"I'm going to get angry," he said.
No-one answered.
They slept away from the cold as best they could.
Alone with their little beds.
"I'll go out and start trouble," he said.
"When?" Harry said.
"Tomorrow – after breakfast – I'll get even."
"With who," Sadie said. She robbed him of his dignity.
"With everyone."

It is difficult to imagine prose more elliptical and precise, a situation more obliquely said or more direct. Richards writes with such
integrity, in ways sanctioned, it would seem, not by precedent or
convention but by an utter conviction in the truth of what he does,
that the genius of his art makes of abject misery a vision of the
human condition that excites and appalls with stunning force.
Road to the Stilt House, possibly for what it does not say, and for
how it does not say these things, is bound to endure.

MAJOR JOHN RICHARDSON

Wacousta: or, The Prophecy; a Tale of the Canadas.
London: Cadell, 1832. 3 volumes. Toronto: McClelland
and Stewart; New Canadian Library, 1967. Pages: 268.
Paperback.

Richardson's *Wacousta* is at the centre of the Canadian tradition.
Judged against Walter Scott's historical romances or James Feni-

more Cooper's frontier romances, *Wacousta* is wondrously complex and enigmatic. Judged from a present perspective, within the tradition it so roundly represents, it is of major importance.

The book was written by a soldier and military historian who grew up in the immediate area of the novel's action and heard stories of the Ottawa uprising under Pontiac–literally at his grandmother's knee. *Wacousta* has a gothic authenticity about it that permeates some of our best writing. The story-lines are complex. It is a revenge tragedy playing out themes of false love, dubious honour, and enduring passion, against a frontier setting that engenders monumental antipathies–order against chaos; natural against unnatural; justice against mercy; sentiment against reason against emotion against will; the demonic against the civilized ways of society; the demonic against the natural order of things. If all this were contained clearly in a narrative design that rallied one set of values against another, the novel might simply be interesting. But Richardson does not allow easy assumptions to rest unchallenged. Which represents order, the Indians or the garrison? Who is demonic, the crazed Wacousta or the austere colonel? Which is natural, imported or indigenous society? Where is the chaos? Where the order? Do we despise the hero? Cheer the villain? Which is which? The novel reverberates with ambiguities, all recognizable in more recent Canadian fiction. It sustains a variety of conflicting interpretations. It is more than interesting; it is enthralling, haunting, and of major significance in anticipating themes and forms that permeate the Canadian tradition.

Twenty-four years before the present action of the novel, Wacousta, then a British gentleman, lost the ethereal Clara Beverley to De Haldimar. Sinking towards dementia through a series of identities, as a Scots renegade, then as a French officer with Montcalm, he eventually becomes second to Pontiac among the Ottawa Indians. De Haldimar, now a widower, rises to become commanding officer at Fort Detroit. The opportunity thus presented for revenge stirs Wacousta to terrible action. Ultimately, Michilimakinac falls and the besieged garrison at Detroit barely endures. All the principals die except one, De Haldimar's oldest son.

De Haldimar's three children dominate the narrative, although Wacousta himself supplies most of the action. Frederick is handsome and manly: he sustains relationships with both an Indian girl and his first cousin. Charles is effeminate and effete; he sustains relationships with the even more effete Sir Everard Valletort and with his own sister, Clara, a dead ringer for their deceased mother (whom Charles is also said to resemble). Clara is abducted by Wacousta, who seeks from her both solace and revenge. She draws his affection away from Ellen Holloway, whose husband has been wrongly executed by De Haldimar, earning Ellen's curse upon the De Haldimar family.

Jacobean complexities mount; contrivance and improbability reign supreme; identities explode, implode, are transformed. The grotesque, the morbid, the sordid, the fiendishly demonic work through the novel with infectious energy. This is high frontier romance at its best: gothic, ironic, exciting, and, under it all, quite profound.

Richardson's language tumbles forward in full, rich effusion. In a marvellous way it is explicit and ambiguous at the same time. Occasionally the images seem garish and incidents melodramatic, but always the effect remains under firm narrative control. The novel is not meant to be a meditation. It is a rousing entertainment, reaching many levels of response, more, almost certainly, than the author himself intended.

The Canadian Brothers: or The Prophecy Fulfilled; a Tale of the Late American War. Montreal: Armour & Ramsay, 1840. 2 volumes. Toronto: University of Toronto Press; Reprint Library, 1976. 2 volumes. Pages: 220 and 227.

Although not in the same league as *Wacousta*, this novel is still worth reading as a fine example of its type, and for the romantic insights it offers into Canadian history. *The Canadian Brothers* is something of a delayed sequel to *Wacousta*. What it lacks is *Wacousta*'s fortunate combination of story and style; and themes that pit man against nature, order against chaos, morality against either convention or anarchy. As a romanticized distortion of Canada's American War of 1812, this is an important document. As a story of intrigue, adventure, and murder, it is immensely diverting. As a literate and leisurely forum for a variety of ideas on warfare, imperialism, and the frontier, it has a civilized charm seldom encountered in the genre. And for the inordinate coincidences, contrivances, and confessions necessary for it to bear out the curse of *Wacousta*, it is an engaging failure.

Richardson himself fought in the War of 1812; at the age of fifteen, he served as an ensign with the 41st Regiment under General Brock. He saw Tecumseh; he participated in the defeat of Detroit and witnessed bloody battles in which Indians fought valiantly and viciously for both sides. He was captured in 1813 and held prisoner in Ohio and Kentucky. Years later he wrote a reputable history of the war. The distortions of the novel, then, are clearly for narrative purposes. Richardson knew very well that truth as it may be conveyed in art cannot be sacrificed to mere facts. *The Canadian Brothers* rings with authenticity, even when, on the narrative level, it appears most contrived.

The two Grantham brothers, descendants of the character Frederick De Haldimar in *Wacousta*, live much as Richardson himself had lived. Yet their fate leads them into gothic tragedy. Gerald falls in love with Matilda Montgomerie, an American descended from Wacousta and Ellen Holloway, whose curse resounds from the earlier book. Love leads Gerald, on Matilda's urging, to murder an American colonel (Richardson drew this part of the plot from a true case). Dishonoured, Gerald returns home and inadvertently kills his brother before dying himself–the prophetic curse fulfilled.

Even more than *Wacousta* did, this novel has suffered bowdlerizing from edition to edition, particularly under the influence of an American market. The new University of Toronto Press reprint appears to match the original Montreal edition. Scholars interested in *Wacousta* are advised to seek out an authentic earliest edition, although the general reader will undoubtedly prefer the condensed (and somewhat distorted) version presently available.

MORDECAI RICHLER

Son of a Smaller Hero. London: Deutsch, 1955. Toronto:
McClelland and Stewart; New Canadian Library, 1965.
Pages: 208. Paperback.

Mordecai Richler is one of the best-known Canadian novelists of
his generation. Primarily through his efforts in film and as a cultural pundit, he has maintained a high profile during the increasingly long periods between his novels. In the fifties and sixties he
was a dominant voice in Canadian letters, albeit a voice from self-
imposed exile. Since it first appeared in 1959, *The Apprenticeship of Duddy Kravitz* has had an enthusiastic following, and while
time has thrown a pall over the inventive absurdities of *The Incomparable Atuk* and *Cocksure*, *Duddy Kravitz* still thrives in Canadian literature courses everywhere. Richler's canon seems built
around this novel, so that *Son of a Smaller Hero* can be said to
anticipate it, and both *St. Urbain's Horseman* and *Joshua Then
and Now* can be called sequels. (Even *The Acrobats* and *A Choice
of Enemies* seem tentative explorations of themes and style that
Duddy Kravitz masters with such aplomb.) While this diminishes
none of them, it does reflect the movement towards consolidation,
in Richler's career, rather than towards growth or development.

Richler has gradually brought the two tendencies in his narrative approach—satire and social realism—into a single acerbic
vision, but he continues to use the same materials in his fiction in
essentially the same ways. The area around St. Urbain Street
and The Main in Montreal, an immigrant Jewish ghetto, has
become celebrated as Richler territory in a plethora of stories,
novels, books of essays, film, articles, and lectures. His fiction has
become somewhat predictable: *Joshua Then and Now*, published
in 1980, is totally professional, but few readers who are familiar
with Richler's work will be surprised by it. There is an uneasy
sense that they have been there before.

Never has the St. Urbain Street milieu received such sensitive
and thorough treatment as in Richler's second novel, and the first
in which he attempted to confront and exorcise the worlds that
made him. *Son of a Smaller Hero* has been overshadowed by the
more abrasively flamboyant qualities of *Duddy Kravitz* and its
successors, but is none the less a thoughtfully provocative and

engaging work of fiction. It is Richler's most unassuming novel, and his most personal, related with the determined sincerity of a conventional portrait of the artist. It compensates for a certain lack of psychological insight by encompassing more in theme and subject than the genre demands. As the protagonist struggles towards personal independence, we are given a convincing picture of the cultural, social, and familial conditions out of which his emergent sensibility is formed. At times, the novel verges on being a document of social realism as it articulates a world that Richler never quite breaks away from in his subsequent fiction, though he subjects it to a variety of splenetic revisions.

Noah Adler grows up in a working-class Jewish immigrant environment, amid ambiguous polarities: his young life is largely defined by the ironies of opposing relationships. The most important of these relationships is with his grandfather, Melech, the source of family strength, their link with the past and the stern embodiment of their Jewish heritage. Melech is the scourge of the family's conscience. But Noah discovers that, as a young man, Melech had been in love with a gentile girl in Lodz and had given her up. Noah pities the old man for the vehemence of his faith. Noah's father, Wolf, is Melech's opposite, an oafish, petty man given to recording his time spent on the toilet and the number of steps he has taken across the family coalyard. Wolf dies a public hero, apparently trying to rescue a copy of the Torah from a fire; actually he was after Melech's cashbox. Noah's mother, Leah, is a proud, demanding woman who nearly suffocates him with her possessiveness, until finally his lover, Miriam, a married gentile, sets him free; always there are extremes, and never is the choice between them clear.

Richler maintains a somewhat sardonic and highly critical perspective throughout the narrative, but he also shows great sympathy both for his protagonist's plight and for the terms of its origin. Little is given directly of Noah's character—he is intelligent, determined, essentially well-intentioned but with an edge of ruthlessness—while a great deal emerges about his situation. Ultimately, he must turn away from all that he loves, all that has made him, to be himself. Despite his mother's threat of imminent death, should he go, Noah leaves for England. Before going, though, he turns to his old *zeyda*, Melech, for benediction. His departure is not an attempt to escape; it is an attempt to resolve the dualities and discrepancies impinging on his life. This is not so much a novel of leaving home as of adjusting to what is left of home within the protagonist as he matures.

Richler describes the course of his character's consciousness in prose that is thoroughly competent, not at all flashy (as in his later, more absurdist writing), nor resolutely polished (as in his last two novels). The tone is muted without being dull. There is wit in this novel, and a measure of satire, but social realism and the struggle for personal definition and freedom predominate. It may not be Richler's best, but its genuine emotional integrity and enduring appeal have yet to be surpassed in the Richler canon.

The Apprenticeship of Duddy Kravitz. Toronto: Deutsch, 1959. Toronto: McClelland and Stewart; New Canadian Library, 1969. Pages: 377. Paperback.

Many elements of *Son of a Smaller Hero* are in this novel, but here they serve entirely different functions. Again we have the imposing relationship between a young man and his grandfather, the strong influence of a weak father, the Jewish immigrant section of Montreal around St. Urbain Street, the abrasive intercourse between Jews and the surrounding gentile world (both French and English), the young man's affair with a gentile girl. Yet this novel is an inversion of *Smaller Hero* in mood and intent. *The Apprenticeship of Duddy Kravitz* is tough, unrelenting, and sometimes hilarious social satire. Duddy is an anti-hero who gets what he sets out to get and does not have the insight to realize that that is not what he wants or needs after all. It is a novel filled with moral lessons, with judgements that are heavy with irony, and cruel, diverting, and clever. For all that, it has no consistent moral vision, no ethical centre, no sympathetic voice either containing it or emerging from within. Yet as a picaresque social satire, it is extremely effective. Duddy Kravitz is an unforgettable creation.

Richler has made Duddy a self-parodying stereotype, the young Jew-on-the-make, yet he allows his character a certain dimension of humanity. If we never quite feel sorry for Duddy – for instance when his father blatantly favours Duddy's older brother – we at least understand his hurt, enough to cheer despite better judgement when he rallies to new heights of devious achievement, as he invariably does. One of Richler's chief strengths in this novel is that he always keeps our response ambivalent, so that we are uncomfortably unsure of which side of the satire we are on.

Duddy Kravitz wants land. He has interpreted admonitions of his grandfather to mean that with land comes identity, dignity, power. While the novel traces Duddy's progress out of high school and through several adventures, it is this drive for land that dominates the narrative. Throughout his affair with a Québécois girl, Yvette, he plots to buy farmland north of Montreal, using Yvette as a front. To raise money, he takes up movie-making. Richler offers a hilarious spoof of cinematic pretensions with "Happy Bar Mitzvah, Bernie!" Duddy also swindles money out of Virgil, a crippled epileptic. He even scores against Jerry Dingleman, the Boy Wonder, a hood much admired by Duddy's taxi-driving father, Max. In the end, Duddy gets all the land he wants, but without Yvette, and without the respect of his grandfather; he has only the shrill, misguided admiration of Max.

This novel is widely known and much admired, although it arouses curiously contradictory responses. As with the best of satire, it is a sternly moral book, nowhere more so than when it is most humorous. Richler toys with absurdity and the bizarre, which he later exploits in *The Incomparable Atuk* and *Cocksure*, but generally he keeps to the conventions of social realism. His prose style is slick and sure, never pretentious or forced. Symbolism is entirely integrated. The imagery is reserved, although surprisingly lyrical on occasion. Richler can evoke the urban scene with knowing sensitivity. The whole novel is convincing, without being believable. Not until *St. Urbain's Horseman* does he recapture some of that quality of heart that makes *Son of a Smaller Hero* the more enduring achievement.

St. Urbain's Horseman. Toronto: McClelland and Stewart, 1971. Toronto: McClelland and Stewart; New Canadian Library, 1985. Pages: 467. Paperback.

St. Urbain's Horseman is an ambitious novel in which Richler reconciles aggressive satire with a sensitive chronicle of personal need. It is a work of major importance, although it is not completely a success. There is dazzling clarity and wit to Richler's prose, which is sufficient to skewer the mind and imagination of even the most recalcitrant reader. There are some wickedly hilarious episodes and some very touching ones. But the structure is arbitrary. Form does not arise inevitably from within the novel, but is imposed; chronology is a matter of convenience rather than necessity. This might have been a major flaw had Richler not tied the whole together by a present-action sequence in which the protagonist, Jake Hersh, must face a more-or-less trumped-up charge at London's Old Bailey. The impact of such an event on his sedentary domestic and professional situation forces him – or, rather, the author – into a confessional review of Jake's life. In the process, all the sources that have had an effect upon his identity – Jewish, Canadian, masculine, artistic – are critically assessed and they are all found wanting. The humour is in the assessment: the pathos and the bitterness are in the need to assess.

Jake Hersh is outraged by the past and future of the Jewish people. Living comfortably in London with his gentile wife and their children, he is haunted by images of the Holocaust and by the docility of history. As a film director who was recently paid not to direct a film and as a hopelessly faithful husband, he cannot qualify, even in his fantasies, as a radical or dissident. So he rails at the iniquities and inequities of society, and at his own moral impotence.

Into this vacuum of conscience, the absolutely loathsome Harry Stein insinuates himself. Harry is a true loser, as gross and disreputable a character as one is likely to find in realistic fiction. Inevitably, since he and Jake oddly complement each other, they become associates – and through Harry's offices, Jake is charged with aiding and abetting sodomy.

In extended flashback sequences, Jake's origins in the St. Urbain Street ghetto are described. Duddy Kravitz was a friend, but it is not Duddy's world Jake occupies: Richler's tone here is not savage mockery but bittersweet nostalgia. Jake, like Noah Adler in *Son of a Smaller Hero*, is deeply marked by his family, his class, and his Jewish heritage, all of which he yearns desperately to transcend – not to repudiate, but not to perpetuate, either. In London, he acquires all the illusions necessary to subdue his origins. However, the better things are for him, the more in control he is of his life, the worse he feels.

From the time he was a child, Jake's interior world had been dominated by his cousin Joey Hersh, the avenging Horseman. Even from the vantage of his London study, Jake imagines Joey, whom he has not seen in a generation, wreaking vengeance for his people against their enemies. Jake is obsessed with Joey. The Horseman is his surrogate conscience; one day he will destroy even the infamous Nazi, Dr. Mengele. When, finally, after his trial, Jake hears of Joey's death, he is crushed, then rises phoenix-like with the realization that the Horseman is within. Bolstered by Duddy, the vulgar hustler from whose exuberance as a survivor Jake takes perverse pride, Jake at least tentatively reconciles his many selves. For all its anger, hurt, and humour, *St. Urbain's Horseman* is ultimately a novel of personal affirmation.

Joshua Then and Now. Toronto: McClelland and
Stewart, 1980. Toronto: Seal, 1981. Pages: 435.
Paperback.

There is much to enjoy and admire in this novel, and a few things to abhor. As a *magnum opus*, a summing up of all that he has done before, it is Richler's best work. As a vehicle for his bitchy wit, it is superb. Among Canadian writers, only John Metcalf surpasses Richler in the art of the vitriolic diatribe against the mediocrities of contemporary society. Metcalf's bitterness is, however, nicely balanced by a well-honed sense of irony, a grace lacking in Richler's work. Well-phrased as Richler's barbs may be – and few can outdo him in the literacy of his invective – they seem the expression of a bilious character rather than a moral or ethical vision. His protagonist, Joshua Shapiro, is not a picaresque hero, but an overbearing, self-satisfied boor. Only in the closing phase of the novel does Joshua generate any sympathy, and then it is through disconcertingly forced pathos. By then, though, Richler has taken some nice shots at just about everyone. We have been amused – somewhat battered by the drubbing, but amused.

In Metcalf's *General Ludd*, we learn what is wrong with the world. In *Joshua Then and Now*, we discover what Joshua dislikes about it. Richler's novel turns fiction into a rhetorical device. It is virtually impossible to separate the narrative voice from the author's personality. It is not so much that Richler intrudes; he refuses ever to conceal his presence, much less refine himself out of existence. He speaks directly to his readers, and remains between us and his fiction–not as a medium or mediator, but as intentional creator. It is his world Joshua inhabits; he speaks with Richler's voice; articulates Richler's opinions and passions; Joshua represents Richler in a narrative context of marvellous contrivance.

It is in contrivance that Richler excels. He repeatedly resorts to the cliff-hanger mode of suspense, where the author builds up to a climax, then withdraws; he radically shifts venue, to leave his readers yearning for more, if only to resolve their frustration. By magnificent orchestration of time in the novel, he makes an outmoded technique contemporary. He uses a B-grade cinematic device: in a context of a man's whole life, all forty-seven years of it, cutaways from one age to another, from man to boy or youth or younger man, allow Richler to convey both the erratic diversity and the startling consistency of Joshua's experience of himself in the world. What might have been structural incoherence works as a brilliant formal metaphor for the protagonist's life.

Like *St. Urbain's Horseman*, this novel opens with an obscure problem of moral compromise. Josh is not up on a morals charge, but he is in disgrace for apparent homosexual indiscretions. (We know immediately that he is actually straight.) He is a forty-seven-year-old successful Jewish writer, a Canadian with homes in Montreal and the Eastern Townships; he has a beautiful gentile wife and a senator for a father-in-law; his mother is a stripper, his father irascible. He had a deprived childhood, a protracted, bohemian adolescence; he has a penchant for drinking with "the boys," a penchant for fidelity, and a load of hang-ups about all of the above. The plot does not develop, any more than the characters do; both are revealed at the author's discretion; bit by bit, Richler reveals why Josh's wife is in the hospital, why Josh is such an unpleasant personality, why Josh is obsessed with Ibiza, why his brother-in-law is a cad, why his friends are failures, his enemies and adversaries despicably narrow–and, almost inevitably, how Josh came to be wearing black lace panties when the neighbourhood cop stopped in to talk.

It all adds up to a man's life. Almost an essay at times, occasionally a satire, a confession, a romance, a memoir, this novel fuses genres and moods into a unified work of singular importance. It is highly original in form, and yet inseparable in content from Richler's other work; a mature pastiche of everything he has done before. Sometimes its abrasiveness seems ingratiatingly forced, almost obsequious; sometimes the moral assumptions become merely posturing; sometimes the reader tires of the author's immediacy and wishes he would leave us alone with his fiction. Yet, when all is done, this is as satisfying a novel to read as any in recent years. It deserves the status of a quality best-seller on the international market.

CHARLES G. D. ROBERTS

The Heart of the Ancient Wood. New York: Lippincott, 1900. Toronto: McClelland and Stewart; New Canadian Library, 1974. Pages: 276. Paperback.

From a present perspective, this novel could almost be dismissed as little more than a curiosity by a prolific writer of animal stories, unreadable novels in both romantic and realistic modes (apart from the estimable *In the Morning of Time*, a speculative projection into the primeval past), and much poetry, some of which rightfully endures as the best of its time. What sets this work apart is the extent to which it exemplifies a perennial theme in Canadian writing: the conflict between natural and moral law, between intuitive and civilized behaviour, between the wilderness and society. Roberts puts a fine romantic twist on the dilemma, but gives it a meagre resolution. He writes prose that is often clumsy and overripe, but it is prose that sometimes soars with naïve eloquence as it takes in the natural scene.

The narrative situation has the simplicity of a fable, though Roberts clearly means it to be more in the nature of a moral inquiry. A girl and her mother move to a farm cleared in the primeval wilderness of northern New Brunswick; there the girl, significantly named Miranda, grows to womanhood with an uncanny affinity for the wild animals and little knowledge of the ways of society. Miranda befriends what Roberts awkwardly calls "the furtive folk"; they, in turn, fall under a sort of spell she invokes, which protects her even from panthers and bears and prevents them all from killing within her ken, though that is their natural way. A woodsman, Young Dave, falls in love with Miranda and, although she feels nature stirring inside her, she refuses him, as he is a threat to her enchanted world. The time comes for her to choose between Dave and an old she-bear, who has been her constant, loving companion through the years. Without hesitating, Miranda takes up a rifle and kills the bear for the protection of her own kind. (She saves Dave because he is human, because together they will propagate the species.)

Despite the romantic notions of the plot, the anthropomorphic assumptions about animal behaviour, the sentimental language, and the wooden dialogue, there is much about the novel that is worthy. Roberts has a remarkable knowledge of the flora and fauna of his native province. Seldom have animals, birds, and even fish received so sympathetic and authoritative a treatment. And Roberts understands fully the harsh ways of nature, the continual cycle of life and death that wastes nothing on sympathy or remorse.

In this cycle lies the one supreme irony of the novel, which lifts it well beyond the trivial. For all her closeness to the natural world, Miranda does not comprehend the importance of death to survival. She lives in a romantic cocoon, where all creatures are in harmony, but as Roberts knows, natural harmony is not, in reality, a friendly relationship but one of predators and prey in precarious balance. Miranda's lover, then, is more a part of the real world of nature than she, for he hunts as a way of life. Eventually, Miranda's romantic illusions are shattered; with Dave's promise to take her back into society of her own kind, Roberts closes the story.

There are allusions to injustices of another sort throughout the novel, for both Miranda and her mother wear flashes of scarlet, a signal of the mother's unfair rejection by a hostile society. It is against the hypocrisy of the scarlet emblem that Roberts works out his fable about the reality and illusion of natural justice. Humane sentiment in close juxtaposition with restrained scenes of natural brutality yield a sophisticated moral conundrum not at all typical of the wild-animal genre. Coupled with the implications of Miranda's outcast state, this sets the reader to weightier considerations than might have been anticipated.

CHARLES G.D. ROBERTS

In the Morning of Time. London: Dent, 1925.
Pages: 192.

In the Morning of Time is the last and best and most unusual of Roberts's novels. It displays all the faults of his earlier fiction: the minor discrepancies of voice and point of view found in the animal stories, and the more significant violations of narrative consistency found in his popular romances. These, fortunately, it subsumes with a dynamic and awesome portrayal of primordial violence. Not unlike the better known *Quest for Fire*, it is a speculative exploration of Darwinian pre-history, where evolution is dramatically foreshortened by the simple expedient of narrative selectivity. Millions of years are crammed into a single episodic sequence. So long as animals remain in the foreground, even when they are somewhat improbably monstrous, Roberts is surprisingly convincing. When near-humans and then humans enter the scene, however, and are given arbitrary names like A-ya and Grôm and made to act out episodes in the descent of man, the effect sometimes falters. Still, scientific speculation as to our origins, an imagination caught up by the spectacle of natural violence, prose and plot suggesting the *Boy's Own Annual*– all these combine to make this novel a splendid artifact of earlier taste, and as exciting now as it ever was.

Roberts wades through pre-history with anthropocentric abandon. Even the novel's title, *In the Morning of Time*, insists on the primacy of our perspective in the present, outside a temporal purview that accounts for the discovery of fire, of the bow and arrow, of sex, love, cooking, and early ideas of racial and gender supremacy without deference to chronological imperatives. The narrative demands of a good story take precedence over logical possibility. Fine: it is the prerogative of the storyteller to remake reality and certainly to defy Darwin, Freud, and Claude Levi-Strauss, all at one go. But in doing so, he must provide a plausible alternative, especially if he is working in a realistic or quasi-realistic mode, as Roberts is. If only through the sheer power of imagery and syntax, he must create an aura of authenticity, without which his fiction will seem perpetually on the verge of collapse. That is this novel's principal problem, at least for the adult reader today. In compensation there is the raw primal vitality in a tale that demands we take the whole of animate history on this planet as a single coherent myth. Logic and chronology, in this context, are virtually irrelevant.

In the Morning of Time is marvellously structured, though perhaps more by accident than design. It begins with a prologue in two phases, each centring on a duel to the death of leviathans doomed to extinction. The first ends with the ignominious death of the victor; the second, between a late dinosaur and an early mammal, with the triumph of a man-ape, the cunning witness of their struggle. Then the action leaps ahead to early homo sapiens, when there were other man-like species still around, and the rest of the novel fabricates a pattern of social evolution and survival at once absurd and fascinating, simplistic and highly entertaining.

Roberts's reputation does not rest on this novel, nor even on his fiction, but on his poetry. His animal stories are certainly among the best written in their time and they have an enduring place in our literary history. A few of his poems remain as powerfully effective now as they ever were–especially "Tantramar Revisited" and some of the earlier sonnets. There is a tendency in his poetry and, ironically, in the best of his fiction for Roberts to intrude between the reader and text as a mediator, explaining what we are to get from his art, and why. When such violations are kept in check, however, as they are for the most part throughout *In the Morning of Time*, the stillness afforded by his absence, in the midst of furious activity, elevates his prose to the level of poetry. It is particularly for these interludes that one returns to this novel for subsequent readings–for despite the reservations I have suggested, it is a work to be read more than once, with great pleasure if not always with complete satisfaction.

THEODORE GOODRIDGE ROBERTS

The Harbour Master. London: Street and Smith, 1911. Toronto: McClelland and Stewart; New Canadian Library, 1968. Pages: 164.

In his introduction to the reprint edition of this novel, Desmond Pacey has made some extravagant claims for its quality, even though it is nothing more than an old-fashioned adventure yarn, one of nearly three dozen the author churned out in a productive career. That he was a poet of some note, brother of Sir Charles G.D. Roberts, cousin of Bliss Carman, father of the painter Goodridge Roberts, and a worthy gentleman of letters does not improve the literary merit of Roberts's fiction. *The Harbour Master* falls into that broad category of romantic adventure stories popular around the turn of the century, the best of which have no loftier aim than to excite and entertain. All the literary devices their authors can muster are put to this end. *The Harbour Master* is above the level of pulp fiction, but it never aspires to art.

What separates this novel from most such romances are the author's sure knowledge of his Newfoundland setting and his superb command of the unusual idiom of the people. The characters, Black Dennis Nowlan in particular, seem to derive their personalities from the setting, and the plot from beginning to end depends on the hard conditions of outport life. Only in the primitive and impoverished isolation of Chance Along, up south from St. John's, down north of Cape Race, could such events develop and be so resolved. There is an aura of authenticity about Roberts's presentation of Newfoundland, though it is more the special truth of a ballad than the dry facts of a documentary.

In the days of the sailing ships, Nowlan takes command of his small harbour village as if it were a ship and he the fierce and indomitable skipper; he organizes his men to plunder wrecks with an evil efficiency. Scavenging from wrecks was as acceptable as drawing fish from the sea, but Nowlan is not content with food stuffs and flotsam; he sets his men after gold and gems and is not above thieving and trickery to get them, though he stops short of murder (albeit, he and his men do sit idly beside a huge pile of driftwood waiting for a wreck to occur – a wreck that might easily have been prevented had they set the driftwood ablaze instead of saving it to use for light while they plundered). Nowlan is a hard master, fighting whoever balks at his command, but he is a fair man, and clever. All his judgement, however, leaves him when he saves a beautiful singer from the sea and determines to make her love him. She despises his uncouth advances, and he keeps her a virtual prisoner until a gentleman sailor from "up-along," the outside world, comes to the rescue. With the fearless aid of fair-minded Mary Kavanagh, a local girl in love with Nowlan, the sailor liberates both the singer and an invaluable bit of jewellery, and leaves Mary to marry her contrite harbour master.

Roberts writes uncluttered, disarmingly simple prose; he has a good ear for dialect and the cadences of life in the outports, and a refined eye for details to enhance a scene, whether of horror (such as the sudden appearance of a floating corpse) or of action (as in any of the numberless fights). The novel is brimming with contrivance and coincidence and awkward expressions of romantic emotion. Nevertheless, it moves along at a furious pace with a cheerful amorality, which makes it a delight to read. It is a superficial yarn, a good example of its type, and a fine factual fiction about a Newfoundland that never really was.

HEATHER ROBERTSON

Willie: A Romance. Toronto: James Lorimer, 1983. Don Mills: General, 1984. Pages: 464. Paperback.

Willie: A Romance is the first of a presumed trilogy, volume one of *The King Years*. Volume two, entitled *Lily: A Rhapsody in Red*, appeared in 1986. *Willie* won awards when it first came out. It deserved them. It is an inspired book of gossip. What more could be asked of a novel that romps through the recent historical past as if history were an open book and a closed world. The "historical past" has little in common with the actual past of lived-in time, which was surely as confusing and amorphous as the present. Rather, it is a time conceived in the imagination of the author, when everyone who was anyone knew everyone else, and everything connected, everything proceeded with a kind of manic determinism to make what happened happen. Never in the history of Canadian fiction has there been a novel to match this one for gossipy name-dropping and sheer unadulterated exploitation of historical inevitability. The larger plot is already known; many of the characters are documentary caricatures, familiar at least to history buffs. All that is left for the author is to add embellishments, to generate atmosphere, and to spin out a few lies.

I do not mean to suggest that *Willie* is without narrative design or written in haphazard prose. Robertson is articulate and very clever. She has devised an entertainment at once grand and intimate and seldom fails to amuse with the efficacy of her writing, the audacity of her vision. It would be hard not to like *Willie*, though not impossible–some readers will inevitably demand more of fiction than gossipy historical speculation of the quasi sort. But it is well done and, as with all such passing things, like fireworks on Parliament Hill, it can be greatly enjoyed for its momentary splendour.

The title character is, of course, William Lyon Mackenzie King. Of course. So much of this novel is delivered in an "of course" mode. Robertson plays on reader recognition to an amazing extreme: she has no shame. Charlie Whitton will, of course, grow into fiesty Charlotte Whitton, Ottawa's most noteworthy mayor. Harry will, of course, become Sir Harry Oakes. If there is a meeting of feminists/suffragettes, then of course Nellie McClung will be in attendance and her attendance duly noted for posterity. If there is a poetry reading, then Wilfred Campbell will read. If Red Emma Goldman's name can be slipped in, then of course it will be. Even Dr. John McRae is met, in passing, though his poem, "In Flanders Fields," is mercifully not recited. And Pauline Johnson and Florence Nightingale. And Laurier and a hundred other politicos. And at the centre, of course, is Lily Coolican of Renfrew, Lily of the Ottawa Valley. Ah, but Lily is invention, pure invention. She is seamstress, sawyer, secretary, photographer, and personage; and (of course) she is the eventual secret wife of WLMK. You see what Robertson does? In spite of your certain knowledge to the contrary, you accept the fantasy right along with the facts and artifacts as being all of a piece. Through the sheer exuberant power of Robertson's imagination, you take whatever she delivers as the truth and automatically dismiss its relevance to actuality. No one could read this novel and seriously think to gain new understanding of the Canadian past, political or otherwise. One does not listen to gossip in expectation of discovering great insights or receiving profound revelations.

Historical romance, like the roman à clef, may exploit reader recognition for fullest impact. But when well done, works of both genres stand on their own, apart from actuality. *Willie*, however, though being both, would flounder if the reader did not recognize the voluminous allusions to events and personalities outside the text. It is not self-contained but rather is an elaborate and ingeniously contrived gloss on what the author assumes we already know.

I do not mean to suggest that *Willie* is not in some ways a very serious novel. The plot itself is fascinating, and, in the process of chronicling Lily's adventures in high and low places, Robertson creates atmosphere quite brilliantly. Sometimes it is the atmosphere of privilege and bourgeois decadence, as in the passages describing Lily's employment on the staff of the Governor General's daughter, Princess Patricia. Sometimes it is the atmosphere of *noblesse oblige*, run riot, as in passages devoted to John D. Rockefeller, Jr. Sometimes it is the atmosphere of politics and of a country at war. The war passages, in fact, are the most convincing in the novel. Lily's true love, Talbot Papineau, writes her often from the Front and his letters are chilling. Politics is less well served. Laurier, for example, is rendered a cream puff, without any indication given of what genius might have elevated him to power; and Mackenzie King, who lusts for, loves, and finally marries Lily, only to refuse her his bed and board, while suitably neurotic and ambitious, is given little that might account for his political success. And sometimes it is an atmosphere of bigotry, of class and racial hatred, of economic exploitation.

Robertson has serious interests. Her novel is concerned with serious themes. But all is far outweighed by her fiction's obsessive headlong drive to entertain. It does that, but at what cost? The characters do not come alive. Situations seem invariably contrived. There is no depth to the narrative, no suggestion of ambiguity or ambivalence. All the world is as it is rendered here, and despite an innovative lack of restraint as to point of view and continuity and other such conventions, *Willie* is a very conservative novel in the formal sense. It belongs in the John O'Hara school of writing. We could have wished for something more from a writer as committed, talented, and intelligent as Robertson has shown herself to be. *Lily* follows a similar course, however, and the third novel in the trilogy promises to be the same – and many readers would be disappointed if it were not.

LEON ROOKE

Fat Woman. Toronto: General, 1980. Pages: 174. Don
Mills: General; New Press Canadian Classics, 1982.
Paperback.

Fat Woman reads like a character sketch that grew and grew,
until it burst the confines of a short story, the restraints of a novella,
to become a novel virtually by default. Rooke does not give us
Ella Mae Hopkins's story so much as he gives us, quite simply,
Ella Mae. She is the title character: fat woman, without an article.
Generic. And yet she is highly individualized, a very special person,
painfully distinct from the world around her. She is the embodiment of obesity, and one of the most fully realized and complex
characters the reader is likely to encounter anywhere in fiction.

There is no doubt that Ella Mae Hopkins is fiction. She is not
real. She does not rise beyond the text. Ella Mae is a literary
creation. Like the cur in *Shakespeare's Dog*, which won Rooke
the Governor General's Award, she is a one-man show, alive in
the pages of her own context and inseparable from them. This is
not a criticism but an acknowledgement of a particular kind of
achievement on the part of her author. Think of Hal Holbrook
doing Mark Twain, John Drainie doing Stephen Leacock. This is
Leon Rooke doing Ella Mae Hopkins.

Who is she and how does he do her so well? She is a poor, fat,
stupid woman in early middle age. She was born into poverty and
grew up as a miserable object of ridicule and abuse. For solace
she clings to her fundamentalist notions of God and righteousness,
to her romantically idealized notions of her husband Edward, and
to an innate sense of dignity and self-worth that seemingly nothing can shake, not even Edward, nor even God, when both turn
against her in the end, apparently for her own good. Ella Mae is
not intelligent, but she has a vivid imagination. She imagines
Edward a paragon, she imagines for herself a stomach serpent,
she imagines for God very specific sentiments and behaviour that
accord directly with her own emotional state at the time.

It is grit and pride, then, and the grotesque images of herself
that she conjures and endures, that give Ella Mae the strength as
a character to command our attention despite her wilful gullibility,
slovenly behaviour, and dull wit. She is a figure of remarkable

pathos. The author makes us care, because she lives to the fullest within the constraints he has imposed on her. She suffers for being fat and persists in gluttony until the closing pages. She sees Edward for the skinflint weasel that he is, yet with all the powers of her imagination engaged to the purpose she insists on idealizing him nearly to the point of idolatry. She practically hangs on every word of a radio right-winger and of her fundamentalist preacher, and she rails in her mind against her skinny disreputable neighbours. She loves her young sons and endures their insults, sometimes in an agony of grief. She schemes, remembers, dreams, all with the furious energy of a person wholly alive to herself, no matter how unhappy such awareness makes her. When in the end she literally loses control of her life, as Edward tries to protect her from herself, we share her sense of loss as almost a tragedy.

Rooke writes in a vernacular that seems inseparable from his protagonist's personality. Slipping casually in and out of Ella Mae's mind but never straying far from her perspective, he uses a colloquial English that is highly regional and yet, for me at least, impossible to pinpoint. It is Ella Mae Hopkins, using the language of wherever it is she lives–somewhere in North America, but, curiously, although well-described, nowhere in particular. The small-town environment is realized in detail, from freight yard to Dairy Queen, but it refuses to be situated in an identifiable region. Like the language, like Ella Mae herself, the locale is simultaneously specific and a generalization.

This paradoxical quality to the novel lends it an almost fairy-tale aura (albeit one more akin to the Brothers Grimm than, say, Hans Christian Anderson). It flows as seamlessly as a tale, following a single character through the course of one special day. There are, in fact, no chapter divisions. The whole is told in the past tense, framed by brief segments in the present, which has the effect of making the narrative immediate and yet distances it from everyday life. Ella Mae lives in a sort of enchanted world, where the illusions necessary for her survival are carefully nurtured, though as much through ignorance as understanding, and this world on this day quite suddenly collapses. In the end, her house, which has been her refuge, closes around her as a prison with a grotesque sort of moral inevitability, in consequence of her gluttony. As with all good fairy tales, there is a great deal of ambivalence here: just as eating provided the heroine surcease from the sorrows of her obesity, so, too, the cure may prove worse than the cause. Is this a story in which love triumphs, at the expense of life, or in which life prevails, despite the illusions of love? Or do life and love conjoin in Edward's desperate act of confinement; or are life and love both as illusory as Edward's worth? Or as substantial as Ella Mae? It is difficult to say – but well worth reading to the point of such wonderment. *Fat Woman* is a fine experience for any reader who is willing to believe there is life there, within the pages of a given text. Most of us are.

SINCLAIR ROSS

As for Me and My House. New York: Reynal, 1941.
Toronto: McClelland and Stewart; New Canadian Library,
1970. Pages: 165. Paperback.

It is not surprising that one of our best novels is one of the most subtle. There is a particular fascination in Canada for what cannot readily be apprehended. At the same time, however, *As for Me and My House* is one of the most powerful and moving novels in the whole of our literature. Characters and lives, inseparable from the elements surrounding them, yet somehow responsible for their own appalling conditions, speak to and for us profoundly.

Ross tells a simple, eloquent story of the love that binds two people, Philip Bentley and his wife, irrevocably in a state of intense frustration and mutual torment. Philip is a minister, an agnostic, the victim of conscience; he is an artist with limited imagination; a man burdened with inarticulable anxiety; an unbending and proud man. Mrs. Bentley is as wilful; isolated by pride and sensibility from her husband and the community; craving Philip's affection, existing in desperate loneliness; a musician once. Together, they prey upon each other's solitude.

Ross brings the Bentleys to Philip's new parish in Horizon, Saskatchewan, during the Depression. It is one in a series of posts Philip has held. They settle in, earning only enough to sustain their impoverishment. In the false-front setting, with the elements and isolation relentlessly impinging, they struggle merely to endure. A boy, Steve, is taken in to satisfy Philip's yearning for a son, a yearning born of his own fatherless childhood and also of his need to relate to someone without pressure or guilt. Mrs. Bentley has an admirer, whose attentions inflame Philip. Paul's refuge is words, as Philip's is art, and his wife's is music – refuge in each case, rather than a mode of communication or transcendence. Ultimately, the Bentleys lose the boy. They adopt Philip's bastard child, whose mother, Judith, a young parishioner and the only character in the novel with the potential to break free of the town's tight grip, dies in childbirth. Relationships echo and re-echo. Mrs. Bentley sets aside enough money for them to leave – but whether the cycle Ross has described leads to renewal or to repetition is undetermined in the novel.

Mrs. Bentley – she has no other name – narrates, recording their lives in a journal. From her perspective, we see Philip endlessly closing himself into his study, while she remains alone, outside. Season after season, we follow Mrs. Bentley on her walks along the railroad tracks, which lead her away from town into the prairie horizon. Observations and judgements are hers; all that she tells us is coloured by her pride, her personality, her isolation. She records Philip's story, but it is she, more than he, who is revealed.

It is important to realize that Mrs. Bentley is an unreliable narrator. It is easy to fall in with her, for she is sincere and sensitive and articulate. But she is quite often wrong, particularly in her assessment of Philip's needs or motives but also in her understanding of her own; and she is unable to acknowledge her errors, even when they become painfully apparent.

The ambiguities resulting from Ross's brilliant use of narrative voice are lent solidity (without resolution) by his meticulous orchestration of natural imagery. Mrs. Bentley is perceptive in matters of the outside world, in direct contrast to her wrongheadedness over matters within. The prairie wind, the dust, the cold, the beating sun, all reinforce the oppressive reality in which she lives. Ross is careful, however, to avoid pathetic fallacy; at most, his characters' interior worlds and their external conditions coincide. From this coincidence, though, issue the disturbing ironies that permeate the novel.

The prose style of the novel is spare but powerful. Only in his short stories, some of the finest in the language (gathered under the titles *The Lamp at Noon and Other Stories* and *The Race and Other Stories*), does Ross's use of precise allusive language approach the genius of *As for Me and My House*. In his most recent novel, *Sawbones Memorial*, he shows the same haunting use of the ambiguous voice, or, in this case, voices. But as he does not root the conflicting human dimensions of his fiction as solidly in the setting, there is not the same resonant complexity. *As for Me and My House* stands alone as a singular work of art, one of the very best in our own, or any other, tradition.

JANE RULE

The Young in One Another's Arms. New York:
Doubleday, 1977. Toronto: Totem, 1978. Pages: 204.
Paperback.

There is a slick professional quality to Jane Rule's fiction, combined with an ambiguous sort of roughness that suggests mildly cynical mistrust of its own polish. Her first novel, *Desert of the Heart*, could easily have been a conventional romance in the guise of realism, were it not for the tentatively off-beat subject matter. *The Young in One Another's Arms*, while more complex and demanding, barely escapes sentimentality and romantic contrivance. It is, broadly speaking, a realistic novel although it mounts an effective campaign against the more dreary conventions of realistic fiction. Rule so obviously remains in control of narrative reality that her novel redefines the genre. She reveals herself working, with Brechtian candour, around the novel's perimeters. Somewhat reminiscent of older novels, which addressed the reader directly as "Dear Reader," but without the cloying familiarity, she editorializes on characters and events, turning sardonic attitude into atmosphere, until the reader is almost convinced the world is exactly as she sees it.

The novel is divided roughly into two, according to locale. There is Vancouver city life and the country life on Galiano Island, with a transitional phase of anxiety and violence between. While related in the authorial third-person voice, the centre of consciousness throughout stays close to Ruth Wheeler, a feisty, one-armed fifty-year-old boarding-house den mother to a half dozen young misfits and an elderly in-law. The first half of the novel is disarmingly conventional, as Rule introduces a stock set of characters. Gradually, however, the atmosphere among them intensifies with the imminent threat of the house's demolition to make way for a bridge approach, and with the unscheduled visit of Hal, Ruth's aggressively obnoxious husband. An aura of sexuality grows with the interdependence of the boarders; they cling together as a sort of incestuous and arbitrary family, bound by mutual abhorrence of middle-class society. The turning point occurs when the innocuous, simple-minded Willard has his head blown off while he is trying to save the house. Ruth, her invalid mother-in-law, Clara, and an awkward *ménage à trois*, along with an irrepressible black homosexual who calls himself Boyd Wonder, move to Galiano and open a café and do all sorts of beneficial things for the locals that suggest nothing so much as a practical application of sixties rhetoric. They win, they lose; they lose, they win; and the novel ends.

This is a novel of diverse themes. None of them can be comfortably abstracted from context, so successfully are they integrated with the fiction and with each other. This is, in fact, a novel of the post-sixties; the war in Vietnam draws to a dull halt in the background, and Canada's occasional betrayal of draft dodgers is scathingly condemned. Idealists and anarchists are confronted by reality, and reality wins – but instead of losing, Rule's characters adapt. In many ways, this is an American novel, merely set in Canada. At one time Rule betrays her perspective as an outsider when she uneasily identifies the *Georgia Strait* as "the local underground paper." It is a novel about sexual politics, with a great deal said or shown about male and female conditions in contemporary society. It is also – and in this it is a very Canadian novel – an account of the need for community. It is a stirring plea for love and compassion and mutual support, for helping one another through the bad parts, to the good parts ahead. As philosophy, it is perhaps simplistic; as a work of fiction, it is highly effective in arousing and sustaining the reader's involvement with the characters' lives.

Contract with the World. New York: Harcourt Brace
Jovanovich, 1980. Pages: 339.

Jane Rule takes even greater risks in this novel through subtleties of style and form than by her forthright treatment of sexuality or her defiantly intellectual explorations of creativity and the
creative consciousness. As the chronicle of a decade in the lives of
a group of friends during the seventies, *Contract with the World*
adheres to the conventions of a genre: each of six characters in
turn presents a segment of shared reality from his or her perspective; taken together, the accounts of their interpenetrating
lives provide a microcosmic vision of the contemporary urban
world and of Vancouver, in particular. The fact that much of the
experience they share is sexual, or even that it is homosexual,
does not in these times constitute excessive risk. Those readers
offended by Rule's explicit and humane treatment of sexuality
need not read what she writes, although they are the ones who
should. The fact that her characters talk a great deal about life
and art may put the success of her novel in jeopardy; but ideas
are so well integrated into the characters' experience of themselves that the narrative is never bogged down by the spectacle of
people thinking. It is because of her sophisticated manipulation
of diverse but apparently objective realities that Rule runs the
greatest risk, that of being misunderstood. Yet, this is what makes
her novel such a remarkable achievement.

Not only does the voice of *Contract with the World* change, subtly,
in accordance with whichever personality dominates a narrative
section; but the truth itself seems to adapt, and the author never
intrudes to say that this is only the way things seem, from that
particular perspective. Thus, while cynicism seems the most viable
approach to life from Mike Trasco's point of view, from that of
Joseph Rabinowitz a benign nihilism seems the only appropriate
response. The world is aggressive and hostile when we share
Carlotta's perception of it; dumbly nurturing from Alma's point
of view; silly and cruel from Allen's; and the source of infinite
stimulus from Roxanne's. The reality of each of the main characters, in turn, is represented as authentic.

Jane Rule's fiction is never merely an exercise in craft or an
expression of sensibility, although she is a superb and sensitive
craftsman. She has things to say and, more important, things to

talk about. In *Contract with the World*, the main characters articulate, in their lives and relationships as well as in their discussions and ruminations, an intelligent consideration of aesthetic and sexual experience. For Joseph, passively heterosexual, words are a psychotic effluent, literally pouring out of him during emotional breakdown. His macho friend Mike is an anti-dilettante, anti-utilitarian sculptor who gives up art to sell house-trailers in Arizona after his wife Alma rejects him for Roxanne, an exotic waif wholly committed to the sounds of the real world happening. Alma tries writing, and fails. Her friend Carlotta makes pictures of their mutual friends as a form of psychological exorcism and makes love to both Mike and Roxanne, but refuses Alma, who finds a measure of fulfilment, however, selling international artworks in an inflated market. Another of the group, Allen, takes prize photographs until he is compromised with some boys in Toronto; as a consequence, his touchingly fey young friend Pierre kills himself, and Allen begins to create art with a camera. Through all this, the characters discuss themselves and each other and discuss art, its uses and abuses. Often, ironically, they represent the opposite of what they profess. Their affinity is not just a narrative device – rooming houses serve the purpose of drawing characters together in both *Desert of the Heart* and *The Young in One Another's Arms* – but their need, it seems, to expose to each other their vulnerabilities. They seem drawn together, even when they are bitterly antagonistic, because that is what they want, not merely what the author wants.

Contract with the World is not a novel of social vision, nor is it a psychological novel, nor, ultimately, a novel of ideas. It is a novel of feeling and insight. The characters are not representatives of sexual or creative types. They live their sexuality, through a decade from their mid-twenties to their mid-thirties; and they use art to come to terms with themselves in the larger world or to keep themselves insulated from its ambiguities and terrors. They change, they endure, and Rule observes them, illuminating in the process their personalities and their experience. She is far less concerned with motivation or morality than with the conditions of being. If that sounds like an esoteric abstraction, in context it is not. *Contract with the World* is an engaging and provocative novel.

PAUL ST. PIERRE

Breaking Smith's Quarter Horse. Toronto: Ryerson
Press, 1966. Vancouver: Douglas & McIntyre, 1984.
Pages: 164. Paperback.

This novel is the equivalent in prose of a poem by Robert Service,
one of the songs of a sourdough, not a rhyme of the Red Cross
man. It might share the awkward and aggressive social conscience
of the latter, but it is essentially the qualities of the former that
make it memorable. It is highly evocative in mood of another world,
where the code of the North holds sway over the lives of men. It is
evocative in detail, as well, but in the way of a tale, not as a realistic
fiction – we do not participate in Smith's life deep in the British
Columbia interior any more than we feel the cold with Sam McGee.
Our emotional response is derived from what we think about Smith
and his world, not how we feel. We are intrigued and entertained,
but we are no more involved here with actual human experience
than we are in the stories of Dan McGrew and the lady, Lou. Like
Service, St. Pierre uses the devices of art with dexterity and aplomb
to amuse rather than to move his readers. There is no depth, no
ambiguity or dimension, no essential fusion of thought and feeling,
of illusion and reality. But the tale is told so well, for what it is,
that we thrill to the telling.

Smith is a "character," the last of a breed. He ranches in the
Namko Country on the Chilcotin Plateau, just an ordinary sort of
man, his author says, not believing it for a minute. He is married
to the long-suffering Norah, with whom he has sons Sherwood,
Roosevelt, Exeter, and John. You almost expect to hear that Smith
is too manly to have daughters. He is a self-contained and satisfied man, despite the hardships of his life, perhaps because of them.
He is an Audie Murphy sort of cowboy (does anyone remember
Audie Murphy?). He lives comfortably with the prospect of failure
and loss that threatens the collapse of his dream – which seems to
be, essentially, to survive. He is a man of few words and a strong
will. He is admired by the Indians in the area, who are people of
fewer words, for the most part, and stronger will, and inscrutable
ways, or ways that would seem inscrutable but for the profound
sympathy in which they are held by Smith and his author.

Smith has a quarter horse he wants broken in the Indian way.

He is convinced it will be the best cutting horse on the Chilcotin Plateau if it is broken right. He pays an ancient Indian, Ol Antoine, to do the job, to gentle the horse, breathe in its nostrils, spit into its face, and whisper and talk to it until it understands. Only the Indian can make a cutting horse of such a maverick stud, a great cutting horse, according to Smith. The novel is the story of Smith's will against Ol Antoine's, Smith's ambition against the Indian's capacity for procrastination. Interfering in procedures is the trial of Gabriel Jimmyboy for murder, two hundred miles away at Williams Lake. Both Smith and Ol Antoine are involved. Smith ends up in jail, the victim of his own pride. Ol Antoine becomes a hero of sorts and inspires the release of Gabriel Jimmyboy by restating the speech of Chief Joseph to his people in Montana, generations ago, to lay down their arms and fight no more. Compassion wins the day and the murderer is acquitted. And a year later, Ol Antoine still has not talked to the horse; Smith breaks it, bucking him out in the usual way. There is nothing special about that horse, after all.

Clearly, this is more a tale, a yarn, a fireside story, than it is a novel in the formal sense. St. Pierre spins out his account of life in the interior, of ranching, Indians, hardship and hard work, shifting values and strong personalities, with an offhand eloquence. Sometimes he becomes so engrossed in his own narrative that he disappears into the colourful language and quaint colloquialisms. At other times he is so editorially obtrusive that the fiction fades— in the midst of a courtroom drama, he pauses to discuss the taxpayers' meagre contribution to Indian education in the 1930s (the novel is set in the 1950s, or possibly the early 60s). Yet for all the inconsistencies of voice and point of view, *Breaking Smith's Quarter Horse* works well in part because of the author's intrusive personality. When he jokes that the Williams Lake courthouse compares to Vancouver's, the way the Pacific Great Eastern Railway compares to the CPR, not as long but just as wide, or quotes the B.C. Evidence Act as to the status of aboriginal veracity, we realize that this is a storyteller talking; the telling is what is important.

You feel good, reading Paul St. Pierre. I am not entirely sure this is a compliment: he is writing of loss as much as of strength. But there is no question, and it's the same with Service, that you feel damned good hearing the way he tells about it.

LAURA GOODMAN SALVERSON

The Viking Heart. Toronto: McClelland and Stewart,
1923. Toronto: McClelland and Stewart; New Canadian
Library, 1975. Pages: 326. Paperback.

This novel is an epic of Icelandic immigrants to Manitoba, who
slowly become Canadian while losing none of the characteristics
of their ancient Norse heritage. From the early sagas of her people,
which are so much an integral part of their culture, Salverson
apparently learned to cut across genre boundaries, for her novel
contains strong elements of romance and occasionally melodrama,
as well as documentary realism, genealogical history, and moral
discourse. This was her first published novel, and while lofty purpose and naïve energy make it her best, it is by no means a polished work. Yet neither were the old sagas, which in her earnest
way she emulates.

Salverson clearly means *The Viking Heart* to be a song of her
people. The plot includes four generations of Icelanders in Canada and covers a period from the mid-1870s well into the First
World War, but there is a resounding echo throughout of the ancestral past. Her characters speak with ease about a thousand years
of Icelandic history, and about how the Norse once ventured over
the world and mingled their blood with Normans and Anglo-
Saxons, making them, too, proud and strong. It is almost as if she
were saying to British Canadians: "Look, we are all one people,"
and at the same time, saying, "We are the best among you." ("We"
is quite appropriate, here, for the narrative voice is clearly of Icelandic immigrant stock.) But the novel is also a song of Canada,
for Salverson is also Canadian, and it extols Canada's bounty and
beauty with chauvinistic fervour. Reconciliation of the two realities
does not come easily. This is a song ultimately of the goodness of
struggle and of victory over despair.

While the point of view of the novel moves about rather haphazardly, it does not stay long away from Borga Lindal and her
husband, Bjorn. It is Borga, as a young girl, whom we see driven
from Iceland by the volcano that claims her brother's life; and it
is she whose son Thor dies as a Canadian medical officer in the
Great War – a sacrifice that Borga comes to accept with pride as
the seal on her family's Canadian identity. Between these two

events, Salverson traces the history of several families from their mud hovels to homesteads to prosperous farms or life in the city. She follows the children of that first generation as they grow and mature, fall in love, marry and have children, or die. Borga's daughter Ninna is disowned for heartless coquetry; Elizabeth becomes a fashion designer and marries Balder Fjalsted, who becomes a great musician; Tomi Johnson brings a French bride home from the front; Margaret Hafstein goes off to medical school. The reader follows their stories from the time their parents meet; and no matter how romantic or contrived their lives may appear, the reader becomes thoroughly involved with them. Rare will be the reader who does not respond to Borga's grief at the memorial service for Thor and who does not, at least momentarily, applaud her courage.

As with a true saga, *The Viking Heart* offers a little of everything, unified by the epic intent of the whole. Thus there are recitations of family lore and beautifully detailed descriptions of domestic life. There are scenes of intense drama, such as the agonizing birth of Thor, who is brought forth with silver serving spoons used as forceps. There is the appalling humour of Ninna taking over a young doctor's office so that he has no idea what has hit him. There is the horror of Loki Fjalsted forcing his wife to help him kill and bleed a calf, which drives her insane, and the pathos, years later, of her regaining her senses while Loki lies dead with his head cradled in her lap. There are passages in praise of God and even more in praise of the Icelandic character. There are a few admonitions for social reform and some on moral behaviour and civic responsibility. The reader who does not insist on sophisticated prose and subtle design will come away satisfied. Naïve enthusiasm, great emotional range, and a wealth of authentic historical detail are all fused into a moving, unified whole by the sheer force of authorial will.

CAROL SHIELDS

Small Ceremonies. Toronto: McGraw-Hill Ryerson, 1976. Toronto: Totem, 1978. Pages: 179. Paperback.

This novel is as subtle as a wisp of perfume in a crowded room. Much of the sustaining interest through the narrative depends on Carol Shields's deft perceptions and crisp wit applied to the trivia of domestic life. Themes emerge softly but deliberately; a narrative structure takes shape in the reader's mind. Nothing is rushed or forced. The novel relates, in confessional tones, a year in Judith Gill's life, minus the summer–summers are free time. Gradually an awareness grows of the way that things are inter-related. From the midst of their intricate density, Judith observes the world around her, and is kept apart from it.

Judith is preoccupied with the small ceremonies of family life. These provide her a context, an identity; they give her substance. At the same time, she is quietly overwhelmed by them, uneasy without being desperate. At forty, she feels that somehow things are not as they should be; life is not quite enough. She watches through autumn, winter, and spring; she records and watches– herself; her husband, a Milton specialist teaching university in an unnamed Ontario city; her daughter, turning seventeen; her son, secretive, twelve, in love with a pen-pal he has never seen; her friends; their friends; colleagues; acquaintances. She writes. For a while she worked at fiction, but now she is writing a biog-raphy, her third, this one about Susanna Moodie. While she records the moving present, she fills in details of her life in random flashbacks. There is nothing terrible or tragic; merely wearing, time-consuming. And Judith has vitality and wit enough to have endured with personality intact. Through the course of the year things change, things stay the same–she is sustained by the minutiae, wryly observed, of domestic continuity.

Within this context, which grows in density and intensity, Shields reveals more and more of her central themes, which impose a narrative form on all that precedes. As she says, in retrospect anything can have shape and meaning. But her method is not casual: *Small Ceremonies* is exquisitely crafted fiction.

The main themes develop around concepts of ambivalence. Art is redemptive, ennobling. It is also derivative, a mode of escape or self-delusion. Judith's biographies work in both ways. So do Furlong Eberhardt's novels, which are redolent with the "Canadian consciousness." So, too, with Judith's son's chain of letters and her husband's woven tapestry explicating themes in *Paradise Lost*. And so, too, with John Spalding, the failed author who was their absentee landlord during a sabbatical in Birmingham and whose plot Judith borrowed for her failed novel, before Furlong stole it from her for his celebrated one. Spalding then finally has a success, with a novel about Judith and family, whom he has never met but has put together from domestic remnants of their stay at his place in England. And, of course, Susanna Moodie, as ambivalent a personality as our world of letters has given us, helps to weave all these bits together.

With even more sophisticated intricacy, the ambivalent reality of contemporary woman is theme; becomes plot. Above all, Shields has written a novel about women. Women watch, record, nurture. But they also aspire and struggle. If their aims are diffuse, that is because society has made them so; and if diverse, that is because individuality among women, at the level of aspiration and achievement, has become acceptable; indeed, it is mandatory.

Still, this is not a polemical novel. It is realism, wherein all factors contribute to its effect as art. The quietly innovative style, the simple precision of language, the occasional striking, even disconcerting, image – all work towards the same end, to convey Judith Gill's unsettling experience of herself.

The year following the publication of *Small Ceremonies* saw the appearance of *The Box Garden*, a sequel of equal calibre, similar technique, but a somewhat different perspective. The two novels complement one another perfectly. *The Box Garden* develops around the personality of Charleen Forrest, Judith Gill's divorced sister who is a poet living in Vancouver. Charleen comes home to attend their mother's wedding in Scarborough, with her orthodontist-lover, Eugene, in tow. Shields writes from inside Charleen's personality with as much wit, insight, poetry, cynicism, and humane warmth as she conveyed in Judith's story, showing with stunning effectiveness how two such different people can share so many vital concerns; showing, also, how two such people, similar in origin and development, can have such different lives. The two characters really should be experienced together – the two books read as parts of the same larger novel.

LEO SIMPSON

Arkwright. Toronto: Macmillan, 1971. Pages: 442.

This first novel is comic, moving, and profound, a dazzling combination. It is also chaotic and occasionally prolix. The intricate mosaic of subplots, digressions, and parables consistently engages the reader's interest, but the many levels of reality simultaneously being exposed, or created, tend to become confused–a three-dimensional mosaic. The resultant vertigo, however, is part of the novel's apparent intent: it is meant to distort basic assumptions and leave the reader unsettled but at the same time delightfully amused. Simpson combines high, or rather deep, moral purpose with a wicked sense of the hilarious and the absurd.

Sprawling and baroque as *Arkwright* is, its development is never haphazard. At the centre is the personal and comic quest of Addison Arkwright, who searches for an identity he can comfortably live with. To give purpose to his life, he becomes the biographer of his powerful misanthropic uncle Casper–a device that allows Simpson scope for broad social satire. Through Casper, Addison becomes involved in the Elmtree sect, a bizarre parody of organized religion, which is based in Toronto and devoted to failure. There are also grotesquely ironic, inanely improbable, and outrageously perverse aspects to the narrative action that are held together by the beguiling ingenuousness of Addison's personality.

On a realistic level, the novel tells a story of love and contains a touching account of Arkwright's struggle for custody of his daughter, Jens. On an entirely different level, Simpson jokes, jibes, puns in scattered directions. The overall effect exhausts the reader long before the resources of the novel are depleted.

Simpson's second novel, *The Peacock Papers*, is verbally more restrained, and yet more bizarre, stretching improbability into the profoundly absurd. It is a modern battle of the books, in which a small-town reader becomes the vanquished champion of literacy. Jeffrey Anchyr finds himself allied with the novelist Thomas Love Peacock (formerly deceased) and a prattling pedant (his passion is the dispossessed Cumrum Indians, who return to avenge their artifactuality), in a fight to the death defending the town library against McLuhanite forces of modernity. As in the first novel, Simpson never falters when it comes to the essentially conservative values his fiction upholds. But then the best of humour never does. Reality cannot be ridiculed without the assumption of basic truths.

Simpson's subsequent novel, *Kowalski's Last Chance*, is set in the same area as *The Peacock Papers*, which is patterned roughly after Peterborough and its environs. While this work contains brilliant flashes of humour and evidence of the same almost austere social conscience that contributes to the bizarre twists of his earlier work, the two strains do not mesh. Instead of using the comic to expose hypocritical and sinister aspects of society, Simpson seems to be offering it as an alternative. The effect is of whistling in the dark; or believing in leprechauns because logic demands respite from the reality we normally endure. Kowalski himself is an agreeable innocent, too much so, perhaps, in a corrupt world. He has not the advantages of Jeffrey Anchyr and Addison Arkwright–he is not himself a fallen man.

JOSEF ŠKVORECKÝ

The Engineer of Human Souls. Toronto: Lester & Orpen Dennys, 1984. Pages: 571. Tr. Paul Wilson (*Pribéh inzenyra a lidskych dusi.*
Toronto: Sixty-Eight Publishers, 1977).

"And why are you telling it?"
"For the joy, the grief and the sadness of life and death."
This brief exchange sums up both the intentions and the achievement of Josef Škvorecký's sprawling novel of the human condition as witnessed from a mid-twentieth-century cosmopolitan perspective. *The Engineer of Human Souls* is vast in scope and yet intimate in the details it conveys of separate lives. By the conflation of narrative time, so that events separated by nearly forty years are simultaneous in the reader's mind, Škvorecký makes the sweep of history, for all its grandeur and indifference, an immediate context for individual experience. His characters live within history, not on its surface. Despite the episodic nature of the novel, Škvorecký is not bound by conventions of sequentiality. The past is no more distant than the present. Time is spatial,

and within it he displays a panoply of human experience as wide and rich as one is likely to encounter anywhere.

The Engineer of Human Souls is determinedly Czech. It is also very Canadian. The principal narrator, Daniel Smiricky, teaches English at Edenvale College, just west of Toronto. It is 1976. He is a writer; he writes novels in Czech. His seminar on the novel in English provides this novel with its most obvious structural device: each of its seven parts is told under the aegis of a major writer–all but the last, which is under the authority of one H.P. Lovecraft. Smiricky left Czechoslovakia in 1968, when the Soviets crushed the Dubcek regime. His friends are mostly exiles and émigrés from the same place, from the same time, from different times. Their Toronto in the 1970s is a hotbed of political gossip, nostalgia, paranoia, and pleasure. Canada is an opiate: what they cannot forget, they remember in relative comfort. Smiricky's Toronto is innocent, ignorant, indifferent. He cannot reconcile his knowledge of what has been, the successive tyrannies of fascism and communism that overwhelmed his homeland, with his present experience, where he is indulged and at ease. Yet he forgives himself his present comfort with an ingenuous bewilderment that makes him simultaneously a bit obnoxious and quite endearing.

Seeping into his present consciousness and present life, like water through layers of cheesecloth, are myriad episodes from his past. The narrative slowly builds and accumulates, cutting from the 1940s to the 1970s, cutting from one week in Toronto to another, from one account of Daniel's youth in Kostelec, his hometown, to another. In the beginning it seems almost glib–the rather facile free-association of random fragments drawn, perhaps, from the author's own life, imposed on his hapless, pleasant, and pliant persona within the text. Gradually, however, narrative cross-references pool; Daniel's life and world gather dimension and depth. Amidst the innocent absurdities of academic life in Canada, against a background of literary discussion at once trivial and profound, among a motley crew of Czech émigrés in a Toronto context to which they condescend, which they do not always comprehend, and for which they are grateful, Škvorecký delivers episodic glimpses of life in a totalitarian state, of growing up amidst barbarous oppression, of coming to maturity against a strange montage of fear and privation, of sharing lusts, adventures, and comic relief with fellow Czechs of the same age. As the narrative develops, a thick and complex world lies revealed before us, in which individual experience is inseparable from history itself, yet each person is pathetically alone.

The Engineer of Human Souls is a novel teeming with activity. As Daniel notes, somewhat soulfully, his life is very full. There is no one atmosphere or generic mood to hold it all together, only his personality, which sometimes gets swallowed up in the onrush of episodic fragments. Seminars in Edenvale give way to scenes of piecework in a Messerschmitt factory in Kostelec, which open onto a dinner party off Eglinton Avenue, or a yacht scene off Toronto Island, or the viewing of Leni Riefenstahl's film *Triumph of the Will* in Rosedale (for its feminist statement, despite its Nazi sympathies). These in turn bleed into other snippets from the past: Danny's love for the factory girl, Nadia, which leads him into a rather inept act of sabotage; ribald washroom chatter off the assembly line; Danny's love for Marie, unrequited; his love for Irena; his writing; his tenor sax. In the present, his lust requited with the wife of a crippled compatriot, and eventually with a student, Irene, thirty years his junior, his life seems an absurd parody of the past. There are no more atrocities, nor are there the hilarious, absurd, and touching times. There is no more abject terror or indolent fear, but there is no more genuine affection either, no more love or passion.

This is a great, huge, enigmatic novel. It is a vision of tyranny and horror from the inside looking out as well as from the outside looking in. From the inside, we see the ordinariness of life amidst oppression, and ordinary emotions and relationships become heroic in contrast to the ideological extremes of the left as well as the right. From the outside, we share in the pathos of those for whom time and circumstance provide the balm of indifference: to forget the past is, perhaps, to lose oneself.

There is room only for irony in a world such as ours, committed through sheer good fortune and historical naïveté to the dead centre, ideologically and culturally as well. This is the Canada Škvorecký envisions for us, a world so far from tyranny and atrocity that such things seem only an awkward residue within the lives of a few latecomers among us, and this will wash away in due course. His novel is sad and by turns hilarious and horrific, poignant and sometimes satiric, sometimes a burlesque, sometimes ironic, and often filled with such genuine sentiments that the reader feels privileged to have shared Škvorecký's vision for a while – privileged, and quite disturbed.

Until *The Engineer of Human Souls* (an expression apparently coined by Stalin to describe writers and here used ironically), I had not thought of Josef Škvorecký as a Canadian writer. He has lived and worked in Toronto for nearly twenty years but his novels are published first in Czech and then appear in English as rerouted missives from the Eastern Bloc. His Canadian connection has seemed almost incidental. It appeared grasping on our part to include him in a tradition to which he seemed indifferent. The greater his international reputation, the more unseemly it became to take him as our own: the best we could do was provide an amenable context for the clandestine and heroic activities of a cultural refugee. But with this novel his perspective has shifted somewhat, he has become a Canadian writer in spite of himself, and his earlier novels that anticipated this one are drawn retroactively into the Canadian sphere. In unprecedented acknowledgement of his Canadianness, he was given the Governor General's Award for fiction in English, for Paul Wilson's translation of *The Engineer of Human Souls* from the Czech original.

ELIZABETH SMART

By Grand Central Station I Sat Down and Wept.
London: Editions Poetry, 1945. Markham: Deneau, 1982.
Pages: 128. Paperback.

This is a love story unique in the telling. Elizabeth Smart has written a brilliant and difficult prose poem, which is all the more remarkable for being so little known. *By Grand Central Station I Sat Down and Wept* conveys the frantic intensity and nearly hysterical lucidity of a young woman overwhelmed by love. Often the reader is baffled, unsure of what is happening, but never is the emotional pitch in doubt. The truth of feeling dominates empirical reality: things are as they seem.

For the novel to sustain a cumulative poetic effect it should be read in one sitting. To do so, however, is an exhausting experience, in part because the reader's impulse to discover the novel's shape and meaning must continually be suppressed. The story conforms to the logic of love rather than of reason. In part, too, it is wearying because sensibility takes a battering from the collision of different realities. The reader is meant to experience the novel rather than understand it.

The writer-narrator is a single voice. There is no persona speaking to us here. A woman herself, from within, speaks directly to us, within. What we perceive is not her world, not even her perception of the world, but rather what her perception evokes in her imagination. The language, images, allusions all are poetic, yet the novel is prose. It has the associative leaps of poetry, but not the music. It shows the disregard of prose for the medium of print: a poem acknowledges the page on which it is written, by the posture of its lines, the shape of its spaces, the texture even of the dark letters clustered on the passive white.

The story, insofar as it is revealed, is quite simple. A woman of twenty hosts a writer and his wife on the California coast during a summer. She is to type his manuscript, but instead they fall in love. The wife apparently dies – although whether through suicide, accident, murder, or only in the lovers' imagination, is unclear. The lovers travel east; they are jailed in Arizona, then released. The narrator journeys home to Ottawa for family sanction, approval of her love. She leaves, disappointed. The lovers endure the sordid conditions of a New York hotel. He kills love with his pity for her. She kills love with jealousy of the wife who seems to haunt them. The narrator is pregnant; the wife's child was lost. The narrator returns to California, as if to rediscover love. Bereft, she returns to New York, perhaps to lose her child, to weep and to ruminate on the love that is gone.

In this framework are hung sensitive and moving passages that celebrate the pain and loneliness, the power and ecstasy of love. Spare and vivid imagery drawn from the natural world, from classical and biblical mythologies, and from everyday life co-exist in a condition of tremendous excitation. Time and space collapse in allusions fused by the speaker's passion and take on a new shape and meaning. The speaker yearns for the exact metaphor for each elusive instant of her love, to make it at once precise and universal, personal and transcendent. She welds ephemeral and abstract words to words so rich and certain that her world is precisely and yet obliquely rendered, as if seen through a tear drop.

Smart has given us a fresh and awesome vision of the conditions of love. The setting of her novel is the Second World War, which often, as here, seems to provide the measure of love, to be a determinant in its course. Sometimes love is monumentally more important than several million deaths, and sometimes it is the victim of no more than a message of death from far away. Love, the body, war seem inseparable. Love also parallels the life of the soul. Its ecstasy is transcendent; it invites martyrdom. Love is spiritual, and the spirit of one transported by it is often in torment, often soaring, never at rest. This stunning novel explores love as a separate reality; nothing in itself, yet able to take everything into its domain.

After three decades of relative silence, Smart published another novel, *The Assumption of Rogues and Rascals*, which is stylistically, thematically, and to some extent in content a sequel to *By Grand Central Station*. It lacks the passionate intensity of the first, as well as its inspired disregard for narrative proprieties, and for that it is a lesser work. Perhaps it would have been impossible for Smart, as a mature writer, to replicate the vital and reckless originality born out of her youth, without the attempt seeming derivative.

RAY SMITH

Lord Nelson Tavern. Toronto: McClelland and Stewart,
1974. Toronto: McClelland and Stewart; New Canadian
Library, 1981. Pages: 160. Paperback.

The most notable aspect of *Lord Nelson Tavern* is its delightful shattering of the conventions of narrative time and chronology. With an absurd logic of its own, Smith's novel records its characters' lives as they age, not progressively, but regressively through the years–they grow older but their time context remains perpetually the same. They are students together in Halifax, the postwar generation. As the novel advances, they become another generation, and then another–their memories include the war, then pre-war and the Depression. But their perspective remains the 1960s. Gould and Rachel go around together, then marry;

Rachel has Ti-Paulo's child, Sarah, who matures to thirteen and seduces Paleologue the poet, sleeps around, ages to thirty-three; and it always remains the mid-sixties. It is a truly innovative device, allowing Smith an unusual perspective for characterization and social commentary – neither of which concerns him very much. At heart, *Lord Nelson Tavern* is a conservative contemporary novel with a radically experimental twist that makes it stand out among its peers.

The plot consists of the intermingled stories of a group of undergraduates as they mature through forty some years or die along the way or fade into the margin. The characters themselves are stereotypes, yet each comes remarkably to life as an individual, although, curiously, without breaking out of his or her limited reality. Grilse remains the lack-lustre adventurer, who cannot articulate the excitement of his life and therefore becomes nothing; Naseby is nasty, luring people into his company with his capacity to bring out their worst. Eventually, he is killed by Sarah's careless indifference, as he rapes her. There are also Ti-Paulo, the short, long-suffering painter; and Nora Noon, the sad sleep-about who never seems to be in focus but becomes a great artist; Francesca, so beautiful and rich that her personality is irrelevant, and her lover Dimitri, who is also perfect, and as empty; Paleologue, who becomes a successful poet, and Gussie, his equally successful actress wife; the domesticated Gould and Rachel. Their stories bump up against each other and sometimes merge. They relate their lives to each other, sometimes revealing truths, but more often hiding them – and the sad thing is that what they do not say does not exist. In the end, their stories only add up to a confused collection of stories. That is the point: there is nothing more, so that must be enough.

Smith has a zany sense of humour, and his novel is filled with absurdities, but under it all, this is a realistic novel. He writes with flair and a gift for anecdote. The reader cares for his characters, perhaps in part because they are stereotypes and therefore founded on truths of the ordinary world, and in part because they are invested with a vulnerability, which is viewed with compassion. Smith writes as a redeemed nihilist. This is the way things might be – but they might also be otherwise.

ROBERT J.C. STEAD

Grain. Toronto: McClelland and Stewart, 1926. Toronto: McClelland and Stewart; New Canadian Library, 1963. Pages: 207. Paperback.

Grain is the sleeper of Canadian fiction, a classic example of prairie realism with more authentic details of the agrarian life than all the works of Grove put together, with a more coherent social vision of the West than any of McCourt's novels, and with an even more complete coincidence of land and personality than *Wild Geese*. It is a singular achievement, but largely unread, except by *aficionados* of the prairie genre. It holds up through time, however, and will be increasingly regarded as a major novel in the Canadian literary tradition. It is, as critics are fond of saying, a flawed novel – but it is still a fine work.

Stead was a popularizer of prairie motifs. His other novels and his poetry and journalism were designed simply to entertain. Even *Grain*, in its opening chapters, comes perilously close to pulp before it finds its stride. Once the pace is set, however, the serious themes, the prairie setting, and the marvellous inchoate character of Gander Stake impose restraint on Stead's romantic enthusiasms.

Gander is a memorable creation. The novel begins with his birth in 1896 in rural Manitoba and follows his awkward, inarticulate, and often satisfying struggle with life until immediately after the First World War, when he leaves the farm for Winnipeg. He is not very bright; he is slow to develop social and sexual awareness, but well meaning and strong willed. The action of the novel revolves around this ordinary hero, a boy, then a man, with conviction and loyalties far in excess of his understanding of them.

Gander and the prairie setting are inseparable. Upon close consideration, however, it becomes clear that Gander is attached more to the procedures of farm life than to the natural world itself. Gander takes on a man's work at ten years of age and grows up to be a steam-thresher engineer. The land is valuable to him. He loves it for what it can be made to do, but otherwise, except in memories of his boyhood, he accepts it without question or curiosity. It is simply the larger aspect of his being.

Gander's refusal to fight in the war, his devotion to his childhood sweetheart, Jo Burge, his commitment to the machinery of farming, all embody themes of pride and honour and personal integrity, which ultimately lead to a bitter resolution. Stead does not work out his themes abstractly; they are integrated fully into the narrative. For example, Jo's brother is killed in the war; thus comes an insuperable barrier between her and Gander, the inarticulate pacifist; Jo marries a wasting veteran; there is nothing left between the lovers but an impossible love. Gander's childhood is made pleasant, in part, because his older brother, a wastrel, leaves home. In the end, his brother's son returns with an uncle, Cal, who marries Gander's sister – and a suffocating cycle is completed.

Gander is simple, but not a fool. He is a pacifist, but not a coward – he throws himself against the thresher belt to save a life. He is not, in the end, a hopeless fugitive – he goes off to the city to be with Jerry Chansley, a city girl. He is not a man of nature: he is a farmer, a man of machines and the land. The farm, Stead argues with conviction, is not, as romantics and naturalists would have it, a place where man and nature merge. It is where they co-exist. With unerring realism, Stead shows the farm as a workaday world that, despite the details of its differences, is not unlike any other.

Stead writes clear and unpretentious prose, allowing the characters and the action to speak directly to the reader without the benefit or the intrusion of a narrator or an authorial mediator. The story seems to tell itself. There is a good deal of humour in the novel, most of which comes from how the characters see themselves. Human warmth permeates, but Stead never descends to bathos or sentimentality. *Grain* is prairie realism at its best, a work that has benefited from the retrospective mellowing effect of age.

ARTHUR STRINGER

The Prairie Mother. Toronto: McClelland and Stewart, 1920. Pages: 359.

With children called Dinkie and Pee-Wee and Poppsy and a husband called Dinky-Dunk, the narrator of this novel begins at a

distinct disadvantage, which is not enhanced by her being under
ether in a labour room as she opens the narrative. By chapter
two, Tabby McKail, otherwise known as "Gee-Gee," "Babushka,"
and "Lady-Bird," is home at Casa Grande, "the second-best house
within thirty miles of Buckhorn, with glass door-knobs and a laun-
dry chute, and a brood to rear, and a hard-working husband to
cook for," not to mention a "sullen-eyed breed" called Iroquois
Annie and Old Whinnie, the hired man, to be bossed, and Bobs,
the collie, to be loved, and herself to be rallied out of post-partum
depression and a morbid concern for her "lord and master," who
is out of sorts – and rightly so, having to endure in a world of so
much treacle. It is positively bizarre that anyone ever read beyond
the first ten pages of this novel. But read they did: in his time,
Stringer was a very popular writer, with *The Prairie Mother, The
Prairie Wife, The Prairie Child*, and many other novels to his credit.
Of more importance to us now, he was an improbable precursor of
the prairie realists, naturalists, and postmoderns.

It is not worth recounting the story: enough said that all works
out in the end. Dinky-Dunk proves himself, though a temporary
failure, an honourable man; and Gee-Gee is shown to be a weak
and cunning woman. Despite authorial ineptitude, there are
redeeming features to this novel. Stringer was obviously familiar with the procedures of prairie life early in this century and
casually includes descriptions of scenery and society that have
an unpretentious air of authenticity about them. When he forgets
to be amusing and drops the paraphernalia of his tedious plot,
brief glimpses of prairie life come through with disarming clarity.
In spite of himself, he provides a portrait of the Canadian West
during a most significant period of transition, immediately following the First World War. It was then that the pioneer era, with
its emphasis on work and the worth of the individual, gave way
to the new age of technology and commerce, when a man could be
crushed by machines and foreclosures as well as by the elemental
world he perennially struggled to subdue. It is the beginning of a
period that less than a decade later Grove and Stead documented
with infinitely greater authority, followed by McCourt and Ross,
then Wiebe and Kroetsch.

Sometimes a truly bad novel can provide insight into works of
far greater merit. Thus it is with *The Prairie Mother*, itself an
arbitrary representative of Stringer's prairie fiction. If for nothing else, it is worth reading to experience possibly the worst exam-

ple of a transexual point of view in the history of literature. If women really saw as Stringer has them see, they would have been extinct ages ago, victims of their own vacuity, and the best of men would reproduce geometrically, like crystals, through adhesion of virtue upon virtue.

PETER SUCH

Riverrun. Toronto: Clarke, Irwin, 1973. Toronto: Irwin, 1982. Pages: 145. Paperback.

This novel transcribes the obscenity of genocide onto the nerve ends of our conscience. Peter Such writes with a nearly mystical sense for the Beothuk of Newfoundland, who were extinguished entirely; he focuses on the brief period between 1818 and 1823 when there were but a few stragglers left, and their end was inevitable. *Riverrun* is a strangely lyrical threnody. It reaches us from depths that usually are touched only by the rarest poetry.

Yet *Riverrun* reads easily, without poetry's ambiguities, with only its capacity for profound understanding and sympathy. It is a prose vision of the way things were, in which spare and eloquent language, strikingly simple words and images and syntax all draw the reader into the last days of the Beothuk, from several perspectives. The sounds of the novel's prose echo the cries of the people as, bewildered, they vanish.

In the first section, Nonosabasut – say the names out loud; get the feel of their cadenced syllables – Nonosabasut dreams of his people's return to strength. But he is young, and no one is left to tell the stories that link them with their past or define their modes of survival. He is killed. His wife, Demasduit, is taken away. In the second section, in the white man's community, she becomes Mary March. She dies. Her corpse is returned: many of the whites regret the imminent extinction of the Beothuk. Shawnadithit, who is Nonosabasut's niece, becomes the last of her people. It is an awesome burden, described in the third and final section. She dies, June 6, 1829, in captivity, and her grave in St. John's has been lost.

Riverrun does not pretend to be an historical document. It is much more than that. Peter Such transcends facts and time to merge our experience with his characters' experiences. We live their essential truth; their tragedy comes to us not as drama but as a terrible vacuum within us. The author displays–or, rather, demands–moral consciousness in this fiction; he calls the reader to accept responsibility, not guilt. He assumes we share in the suffering as well.

Such's first novel, *Fallout*, while flawed in comparison, explores the implications of the Elliot Lake uranium bust in the fifties. As in *Riverrun*, Such approaches the social drama from oblique personal angles that reveal a great deal about his characters' lives without presuming to define their historical situation. As in *Riverrun*, he sings praise of the small human decencies in the face of grave upheaval that are the redeeming quality of the species. In both novels, he maintains such command of simple language that his prose is almost transparent. Even in his recent work, a spy thriller called *The Dolphin's Wake*, his prose maintains the same lucid, haunting quality. In this case, though, the language gives atmospheric dimension to the intrigue and adventure, without any broader implications. *Riverrun* remains his most accomplished work.

SUSAN SWAN

The Biggest Modern Woman of the World. Toronto: Lester & Orpen Dennys, 1983. Pages: 340. Paperback.

Anna Swan was a giantess. It seems absurd to use a feminine diminutive to describe the real-life giant from Nova Scotia, but that is how she was known, and it is as a giantess that her author, Susan Swan, brings her back to life in fiction. The real Anna died in 1888, at forty-two. Being fiction, Swan's Swan transcends chronology, as she does mortality, to live in the reader's imagination as a vital, ongoing presence, one of the most vivid and fully realized characters a reader is likely to encounter among words anywhere.

Anna Swan was a freak. This novel is her biography. The Biggest Modern Woman of the World was the name given her by P.T. Barnum when she performed at his American Museum on Broadway in the 1880s. It is the title she uses to describe herself, to distinguish herself from the normals, in Susan Swan's account of her life. Anna is a freak, but she is also a very normal human being. Due to her immense proportions, she is the object of curiosity, derision, and unconscionable cruelty. Despite assumptions to the contrary, she is subject to distress and humiliation, to a range of emotional responses as broad and deep as felt by anyone, whether aroused by stupid urchins who bait her, or Queen Victoria and her feckless son, who wickedly insult her. Anna is strong of character, intelligent and proud. She is also ambitious, romantic, and naïve. She is not, as her author creates her in *The Biggest Modern Woman of the World*, larger than life; she is not heroically conceived or rendered as a living myth. But she is "as large as life"–authentic, convincing, engaging, a wholly believable personality about whom we are made to care with a surprising sense of intimacy and compassion.

This novel is what might be called "documentary fiction." In the protagonist's words, it is a "Real Time Spiel in which all the diaries, testimonials, and devices that I've inserted to entertain you" constitute the presentation of her life as a performance. There is tragedy, comedy, romance, pathos, and irony–by turns, and sometimes simultaneously. The design of the narrative is determined by its biographical function. Anna's story provides the novel's shape or structure, upon which the author arranges a marvellously diverse array of documentary material (almost all of it invention, based on research) in order to transform a bit of arcane history into monumental fiction and a fictional monument to the bigger half of the Tallest Couple in the World.

Anna's story is a pastiche told in many voices. The author remains always sufficiently in control, through the force of her colourful and lucid prose, that the many points of view and modes of speech all seem a reflection of the central character's presence in the fiction, and in the world. Swan's prose is such that, no matter who speaks, there is continuity of vision, with Anna at the centre. What we experience, as readers, is not a sort of narrative cacophony due to the piecemeal construction of Anna's story but a strong feeling for the richness of her life.

Shortly before her death, the author's Anna describes herself: "I was born to be measured and I do not fit in anywhere." The facts of the real Anna Swan are that she grew to 7' 6½" and weighed between 350 and 500 lbs. Or she was 7' 11½", as she sometimes claimed. Or 8' 1", as Barnum described her. She was married to The Kentucky Giant, Martin Van Buren Bates, who was several inches shorter. She loved Angus McAskill, another Nova Scotian, who was an inch taller. (Did the actual Swan love McAskill? The "real" Swan does, in the fictional present.) She has two children, one stillborn and one, measuring thirty inches at birth, who lives only two days. The father of her children, who is not her husband, is eventually cut in half in an accident. Until then he was of normal height, a huckster and promoter and, at his death, a clown. Anna makes her living as a giantess. She and Martin retire to a house built specially to accommodate their size, in Ohio, where she dies.

Susan Swan divides her story into four parts. In the first, Anna grows up in Nova Scotia amidst poverty and ignorance. She loses her virginity to an icicle; visits New York; returns to teacher's college in Truro, where she is made to sit in the corridor so as not to distract her fellow student-teachers. The second part follows Anna's adventures in New York among the freaks and human oddities associated with Barnum and the normals who, for the most part, are contemptible. There she consummates her affair with Angus, becomes refined and sophisticated, and meets her future husband. In the third, she travels to Europe, meets the Queen, marries Martin, and makes love with her manager, Judge Hiram Percival Ingalls, otherwise known as Apollo. In the final section of the novel, time is foreshortened: she moves to Ohio, in and out of retirement, has a few domestic adventures and a crisis wherein she thinks she is shrinking, only to find herself Apollo's dupe. And then she dies.

It is a most unusual biography – as, of course, might be expected since it is, in fact, a very inventive novel. It is a story told with gusto, with passion and sensitivity. I am not sure what Susan Swan could do with fiction, if she did not have as large and vulnerable and promising a subject to deal with as the Nova Scotia giantess. Certainly Swan is a very good writer, but in this novel one cannot help but feel the character of the protagonist dominates and virtually determines the quality of her context. That is illusion, I realize – a measure of the author's achievement. Still, it is interesting to speculate about what Susan Swan will accomplish without Anna Swan to help her along.

SCOTT SYMONS

Combat Journal for Place d'Armes; A Personal Narrative. Toronto: McClelland and Stewart, 1967. 1978. Pages: 279. Paperback.

Scott Symons's best book, called *Heritage*, is about furniture, beautifully photographed by John de Visser. *Place d'Armes* is not as good as the insistent authorial voice apparently thinks it is; but it is a provocative novel, worth consideration on a number of counts. For its explicit treatment of male homosexuality, it merits a singular place in our literature. Symons attempts to convey homosexual eroticism, and nearly succeeds in bringing it off, but for a certain archaic awkwardness in the language. As an attempt to telescope narrative realities, story within story within story, the novel is highly sophisticated, although not original. Encumbered by dreary typographical aids, it is an obnoxiously coy, arch, bitter, angry, painful, and chaotic account of three weeks in a character's life, and an intriguing work of art.

Hugh Anderson leaves the conventions of Toronto and family life for a brief, frantic period of residence in Montreal, near Place d'Armes. He keeps a combat journal, as he calls it, for his assault on the depths of reality. It is a notebook in which he monitors himself and prepares for a novel in which Andrew, his character, writes a diary for a novelette – in which he creates someone called Hugh Anderson. Thus, the man who yearns for completion through creativity becomes, himself, created. It is an indirect approach to fullness of being.

Montreal is a major character in the novel, portrayed in as fragmented a fashion as the multiple protagonist. Place d'Armes, in particular, with its dark secrets and extravagant demeanour, its decadent residue of history and commerce, acts as far more than setting or context. It is a dynamic foil for Hugh-Andrew-Hugh's personality in its chaotic struggle; ultimately the place both consumes and liberates him.

Exactly what drives Hugh Anderson, or what he is searching for, is never made explicit; we know only that his struggle represents a movement from non-meaning to meaning. Yet Symons manages to make it all quite immediate and palpable through the rather exotic indulgences of his prose style. Probably even more effective are the relentless tone of the flagellant that he maintains throughout and the ambiguity as to whether it is spiritual or sexual ecstasy such abasement induces. Also providing narrative coherence are the strong social attitudes of the authorial voice–Tory romantic, wallowing smugly between decadence and idealism. This voice fuses all the characters into one: it provides the novel's only real substance, and its ephemerality as well.

After a lengthy silence, Scott Symons came out with a new novel in 1985, which he acknowledges to have taken over a decade to live and write. *Helmet of Flesh* is very long. It is described in the dust-jacket copy as "one of the grand achievements of modern fiction." It is not.

JUDITH TERRY

Miss Abigail's Part; or Version and Diversion.
Toronto: Macmillan, 1986. Pages: 328.

I did not want to like this novel. Novels written "in the style of" and "after the manner of" make me very nervous. That this one was well reviewed gave me no particular assurance. Reviewers like to be amused at the expense of literature. And a novel written as a "complement" to the "divine" Jane Austen's *Mansfield Park* seemed more than tolerance of a dilettante's enthusiasm could bear. Another author had already tried, in *Sanditon*, to complete an Austen project, and with considerable success–if imitation can be deemed a genuine achievement. But here was a novel that promised to add dimensions to Jane Austen's world, to enhance, enlarge, and make it more accessible to modern readers!

Once into it, I emerged only to answer the obligatory calls of daily life. The fact is, *Miss Abigail's Part* is not only great good fun but a fine novel itself. Granted it owes much to Austen, the way Tom Stoppard's *Rosencrantz and Guildenstern Are Dead* owes much to Shakespeare and Jean Rhys's *Wide Sargasso Sea* to Charlotte Bronte. Without the original there would be no complement. That is not to say these are sequels, copies, or revisions. Rather, Stoppard, Rhys, and Terry create not only from imagination and their own particular experience but from another world as well, the structured and coherent reality of someone else's fictional creation. Austen is the inspiration behind *Miss Abigail's Part*, but of more importance, her writing provides the author a point of departure for plot, character, atmosphere, sentiment, and social setting–surely another author's work is valid, put to such use. And in Terry's hands, Austen is well-used, indeed.

The reader unfamiliar with *Mansfield Park* need worry not at all about being ignorant of characters and events in Terry's fiction, for it stands entirely independent of its principal source. Yet an extra measure of delight will undoubtedly be drawn by those who know Sotherton and Mansfield estates, the Rushworths, Bertrams, Crawfords, and Miss Fanny Price, the various hangers-on and functionaries, such featured episodes as that associated, for instance, with the locked wall-gate at Sotherton or the abandoned theatrical at Mansfield.

Terry plays the late twentieth-century expectations of her readers against the proprieties of early nineteenth-century sensibility. Without violating the illusions of gentility gleaned from Austen, in the first half of her novel, Terry still allows her characters to tumble in the grass, in the boathouse, and in bed. They discuss civil rights, democratic principles, and agrarian as well as political revolution. They do so, always, in the most refined style, described in elevated language worthy of Austen and in the most restrained good taste–albeit, on occasion passion makes the prose sing quite lyrically. Thus, while setting us at ease in Austen's world, Terry shows much more of it than Austen ever cared to admit. Then, in the second half of the novel, Austen's world is turned upside down, so to speak, its underside exposed.

In *Miss Abigail's Part*, Jane Hartwell relates her own story. The first half of her narrative is set mostly at Mansfield Park where Jane works in service as a lady's maid. Her adventures there are muted by her position, especially since the affairs of her so-called betters are so trivial and she must remain largely unseen and certainly unacknowledged in the background. This does not prevent her from being nearly raped by Tom Bertram and neatly seduced by Henry Crawford. But, on the whole, her adventures in the first half of the book are ones of sentiment and spirited response. She observes with a keen eye and comments without equivocation, according to the dictates of a personality by nature well-turned towards free expression and democratic ideals.

The first half of the novel is a sort of gathering force from which the second springs. Quite suddenly, with Jane leaving Mansfield Park both proud and in disgrace, Austen's world is left behind–or, rather, drawn into startling confrontation with another world it parallels without ever touching. On the road and in the city, Terry offers a maelstrom of revolutionists, King's men, thieves, prostitutes, characters of Hogarthian eccentricity; violence, vengeance, and debauchery. There are a grotesque rape scene in the midst of a thieves' den decorated with the decadent booty of their trade (an episode from which Jane recovers with remarkable celerity), a cattle stampede through the streets of London, little acts of loyalty and affection, an absurd duel. Through all the muck of urban squalor, Jane Hartwell rises to become Miss Abigail, first lady (or nearly so) of British Theatre, and in all good time the wife of a Lord brought into the narrative at the last moment–by way of confounding expectations shaped by conventional romance, such as Austen might provide.

The curious thing about the sudden shift from country life to city, from passive life to active and from propriety to controlled chaos, is that it seems in Terry's hands inevitable. In the first half of her novel she subtly undermines Austen's genteel world so that when it cracks open we are not surprised to see spill out a ribald teeming clatter suggesting on the one hand Henry Fielding and, on the other, Charles Dickens. What started as the recollections of a newly risen Lady becomes, as the novel unfolds and the narrator warms to her more recent adventures and successes, the chronicle of a survivor. Jane Hartwell passes from Austen heroine through phases as a female Tom Jones, then Oliver Twist, and finally Moll Flanders, with a bit of Fanny Hill thrown in, and is left at the novel's end still young enough, and free, to enjoy life's triumph. After a version of Austen, a splendid diversion indeed.

AUDREY THOMAS

Mrs. Blood. New York: Bobbs-Merrill, 1970. Vancouver,
Talonbooks, 1975. Pages: 220. Paperback.

Mrs. Blood is a muted scream of protest against the indignity of
mortal flesh. Or stifled, perhaps, rather than muted, as the protagonist bears the insult on her body of an interminable pregnancy complicated by massive hemorrhaging. She is white in West
Africa; a North American from New York State, via Vancouver.
Her husband is English, a professor. She is educated, liberated,
well travelled, well read, a woman of her times. Her body belongs
only to her – the ultimate illusion. Her awareness, increased
through this assault from within, has led only to self-consciousness,
not sensitivity, and to a morbid obsession with her past, particularly a passionate but demeaning affair before she was married.
She bleeds, she endures; Mrs. Blood, Mrs. Thing, as she sees herself.
In the end, the child is lost.

With unrelenting directness, Thomas describes the physical
details of her unnamed character's condition. The character's body
provides her own most tangible reality. Her past and present
worlds appear fragmentarily, from oblique angles, vivid but not
solid, shapes without form. Her husband, Jason, her children, Mary
and Nicholas, her steward, Joseph, and her neighbours in the European compound exist only in her perception of them. She views
them from a hospital bed, then from her home, while convalescing;
always they are threatening, draining, insubstantial. The girlfriend she travelled Europe with, her days of independence in
Vancouver, her lovers (one in particular), the past shaped by her
sexuality, the past that made her passive, frightened, the past
when she asserted herself, all are evoked by her physical misery.
Worlds of childhood, of summer work in an insane asylum, of
in-laws and old friends, of domesticity, of newspapers, all collide
in the anxiety sustained by her traitorous body.

Thomas ties everything into an amorphous whole with subtle
skill. There is little plot, no story-line; remembered episodes emerge
as tableaux without movement. Details are filled in, echo each
other, relate to other details of other episodes. Different ocean
voyages, for instance – with her friend, her husband; to England,
to Africa; with the children – seem to merge, yet remain distinct.

They are not unrelated to the child within her, struggling in treacherous amniotic fluid to survive. Twice she has witnessed death at sea. Things occur, she knows, in threes. Thomas makes the novel move by mood, by the sense of urgent necessity for completion–for the pregnancy to terminate, for symbols and images to resolve into coherence, into definition.

Mrs. Blood is an unusual novel. The prose style conveys the controlled hysteria of the narrator, balanced against her need for almost ruthless exposure of herself. We are her intimates, kept at a distance. Thomas shows considerable courage and originality in distortions of time and sequence, and in word play and shifting perspectives, in order to convey her character's dissociated condition. In this, the cultural and emotional dissociation of a cosmopolitan American-Canadian becomes painfully evident. Thomas writes of a woman's body with revolutionary candour and without sentimentality or bravado. She portrays Africa from the naïve, disoriented point of view of an outsider–humility unusual in Canadian novels about Africa, of which there are a considerable number. It is a bleak view, powerfully defined, relieved by glimmerings of defiance, however anguished or stifled.

"Munchmeyer" and "Prospero on the Island".
Indianapolis: Bobbs-Merrill, 1971. Pages: 157.

These two novellas were published under one cover for good reason. From the reader's fixed perspective, they are as inseparable as a mirror and the image it contains. Each has a reality of its own, yet it is in the illusion of their unity that their full impact is felt. Thomas is a prolific writer and has been more experimental in other works, particularly the novel *Blown Figures*. Nowhere, however, has she matched these novellas either for effective balance of a formal dichotomy, or fine subtlety of language.

Munchmeyer is a perpetual graduate student who escapes the realities of wife and children by pretending to work on a novel in his basement refuge. Left alone, he transforms into the third-person centre of an acid fantasy in which he is chased through an empty department store by a mysterious cult of homosexuals. His trip begins and ends on a Stanley Park beach with a dream creation, his Miracle Girl, who is ultimately indifferent to him.

He does finally become a writer, an outgrowth of the fake and fantasy Munchmeyers. This version of himself, however, is no better at sorting out real from unreal. He ends up reduced to being only a figure of his landlady's erotic invention, a man who cannot even create himself.

"Munchmeyer" is a sad and complex metaphor for the vacuous realities met in contemporary experience, formed through a completely convincing male persona. "Prospero on the Island" is its calm and gentle and seemingly uncomplicated inversion. The central consciousness is Miranda Archer, who has come to an island off the British Columbia coast with only her youngest child and a Canada Council grant, to write a novel about a character called Munchmeyer. Her Prospero is an art professor on sabbatical. Her love for him is highly charged; it is never consummated, yet it is life-giving rather than frustrating, and by it she is put more directly in touch with her own emotions. Her feelings for people, for life and art, are intensified and focused. However, only on the island is their love enchantment. Back in the University of British Columbia milieu, they will simply be separate people, each with a creative bent.

If the male half of Thomas's double vision suggests suffocation and fragmentation, the female offers an integrated sensibility in the making, and an invigorating air of expressed emotion. With admirable dexterity, Thomas exploits conventional gender stereotypes without seeming to endorse them. She is able to do this partly because her two main characters are aspects of the same circumscribing personality. Miranda is, and is meant to appear to be, an authorial persona. Munchmeyer is born out of her sensibility; he is her creation. But he is also Audrey Thomas's creation, as is Miranda, the yin and yang of a larger whole.

Blown Figures. Vancouver: Talonbooks, 1974.
Pages: 547. Paperback.

Blown Figures should have made Audrey Thomas a major literary presence in Canada. Yet she remains in relative obscurity. Perhaps the fault lies with her publishers, or in the determinedly experimental form and seemingly narcissistic content of her most effective work, or with our own provincialism. Perhaps it has something to do with the fierce anxieties of her protagonists or with her apparent lack of discretion or reticence. In her more recent novel, *Latakia*, a powerful and yet plaintive display of narrative rhetoric, form does not quite manage to contain the unrestrained emotion or to provide its objective equivalent. In *Songs My Mother Taught Me*, an earlier novel, narrative and emotional logic are similarly in conflict, and the effect is again that needs are being met outside the fictional reality – always a danger in "confessional" fiction. At her best, however, Audrey Thomas turns autobiographical illusion into fine art, albeit art that is highly discomforting to read. *Blown Figures* is the most disturbing work in her entire canon. It is the most innovative, formally, and the most successful – one of the major experimental novels in Canadian literature.

Much of the content in *Blown Figures* has appeared, with variations, in Thomas's other fiction. Africa provides the primary setting. There are ocean voyages, affairs in London, memories of Canada, the United States, the adult past. In content, it is almost a sequel to *Mrs. Blood*, for a woman here returns to Africa, driven by guilt and sorrow to search for and to account for the baby she lost, stillborn, when she lived in Accra some five years earlier. Back in Canada are her husband and two children. Ahead, through continued dissociation of reason and emotion fostered by her renewed African experience, is transcendence through madness, the merging of personality with an alien place. It is not an easy resolution for the narrative, or for Isobel, the protagonist, but it is the only one possible.

Blown Figures has at its centre an account of Isobel's journey from England by boat to Dakar, by train and taxi to Bamako in Mali, by bus to Accra in Ghana. On the boat she makes love with a young Dutchman. Across West Africa she accompanies an American woman absorbed with the problems of her fifth abortion. Time slips in a constant rhythm from the present into the past, with occasional loops while the narrative circles back to repeat brief episodes. At the same time, the narrative voice struggles to convey Isobel's experience of herself. Linear time provides a base for memory fragments: Isobel's past becomes a metaphor, in effect, for her distraught condition in the present.

What is most intriguing about this novel, and what makes it such a radically effective vision of a distressed personality, is the relationship between protagonist and narrator. The voice speaks, in the first person, of Isobel in the third. Isobel seems to be talking to herself, about herself, in the third-person voice, as she tries desperately to objectify, to artifactualize, herself through fictional representation (yet never quite believing it will work and so intruding to sneer at herself as a character and at her own inadequacy as a creator). Between character and creator there is a tremendous tension and an inviolate intimacy. The protagonist keeps drawing the narrator back to the narrative as though demanding the continuation of her story, and the narrative voice keeps drifting away into what seems to be their common past, as if searching out clues as to where next to take their story. The "I" speaker addresses a Miss Miller, who is never identified and who, as an arbitrary rhetorical device, provides disconcerting unity to the narrator's discursive account.

There is, of course, a larger consciousness containing both character and voice, a consciousness embodied by the novel as a whole and by its form in particular (not just thematic, dramatic, and rhetorical form, but its actual shape as a book, the arrangement of paper and print). *Blown Figures* is filled with blank spaces. Most chapters sooner or later break into scattered bits of trivia. Nursery rhymes, comic snippets, curiosities from the African press, examples of Africa the mystery and Africa the travesty, taunts directed at Isobel, at Miss Miller, at the world, memory fragments, dream fragments, all lie scattered across the tops of otherwise empty pages. The whiteness becomes overwhelming. The reader reads the emptiness–so attentively in fact that I, for one, turned each of the five blank pages at the end, one at a time, considering each in turn. Not since *Tristram Shandy* has the physical page been so effectively incorporated into narrative reality.

> *Intertidal Life*. Toronto: Stoddart, 1984. Toronto: General Paperbacks, 1986. Pages: 282. Paperback.

Audrey Thomas is a very good writer, but Audrey Thomas as a protagonist is sometimes tiresome and sometimes indiscreet. It is this combination that makes *Intertidal Life* an unnerving document–fictional in form but so close to life that the reader feels implicated in an unconscionable violation of privacy, despite assurances provided by the text itself that all is, in fact, fiction.

Thomas writes autobiographical fiction. Time and again in her novels and short stories the same main character and circumstances lie revealed before us, splayed in a variety of voices and disguises that do little to conceal their common source outside the text, in the author's life. Not that Thomas herself is an open book: it may or may not be that she lives her life to write about it. But that is how it seems – and *seems*, in fiction, is what is. Evident, as the reader moves from one of her novels to another and from story to story, is a consistency and continuity of *facts*, of characters and their backgrounds, of experiences, relationships, situations, and events, all of which belie invention. Names may change, details may vary, but essentially, despite radical variations in form, the source of material remains the same. Since formal variants disallow the possibility that all are parts of a single larger work, and since references and allusions are so often extraneous or virtually irrelevant to the narrative at hand, a common autobiographical source becomes the inescapable explanation for their presence.

This is not to say that good fiction cannot originate in actuality. Perhaps all good fiction does, at one remove or another. Malcolm Lowry, no less than Audrey Thomas, made art of his life. Clark Blaise, Michael Ondaatje, Alice Munro, John Glassco, all have drawn extensively from their own experience in the world to create their fictional realities. The fact that Thomas does not make the transformation complete, does not wholly reinvent herself, as Munro does, or allow invention to displace personality, as in the "memoirs" of Glassco and Ondaatje, but, rather, implicitly demands the reader's identification of the textual world with outside reality – this is her special, daring, unnerving, courageous, and foolhardy genius.

Where does the author's life leave off and the fiction take over? Where does the fiction end and our own experience draw apart from it? In truth, reading Thomas, especially *Intertidal Life*, it is impossible to know. In trying to define the elusiveness of postmodernism, I would point to the merging of consciousness within the text, here, of reader, character, and writer, as the best example of what postmodernism can do, without knowing quite what to call such an effect. It is not something one would encounter reading Margaret Laurence.

There is a paradoxical quality to one's response in reading *Intertidal Life* . So ingenuous is the voice, so unabashedly vulnerable does the protagonist-narrator allow herself to be, the reader feels privileged to share such intimacy. At the same time, her lack of restraint, her insistent openness, makes her account seem at times an indiscretion and the reader's presence there a violation. When I suggested above that Thomas could become tiresome within the text, I was perhaps implying that the reader becomes as much a participant in her character's life as she is, so much so that one sometimes feels moved to lose patience with her, to get fed up with the indelicacies of her sexuality, the indulgences of her emotions, the endless ruminations over her bereft condition in the world (but since she narrates, what else could one expect?). You want to tell her, okay now, enough words; stop writing about it, stop rewriting yourself. (This is where it becomes hard to tell the writer from her protagonist.) You want to say, let it go, let it be; don't write. And of course, your involvement makes you part of the text – if there were no words, you would not be there. Where would you be?

Intertidal Life does not develop a plot but, rather, explicates a situation. Alice Hoyle's husband of fourteen years, Peter, leaves her. It is the latter days of hippiedom. Peter leaves to find himself, but mostly to have a good time. He lives in their house in Vancouver. Alice lives in their cabin on Gabriola Island. Their three daughters, Hannah, Anne, and Flora, remain with her during the first year of their separation. Flora, the youngest, comes back seven years later to share, in 1979, the frame story that is meant to put the early days of Alice's estrangement in perspective. But since Alice still grieves for her dead marriage and the loss of her thoroughly uningenuous husband, well, *plus ça change*, etc. As the novel closes, Alice goes in for surgery – maybe *this* will make Peter return or at least suffer remorse for having left!

Through most of the novel, Alice describes herself coping, moping, making love, dealing with the loss of love, dealing with herself as a loser: insisting, it seems, that that is what she is. Used and abused; gentle and loving; painfully self-aware and pathetically self-absorbed; pathetically pliant. Peter comes back now and then, pretty much at his own convenience. She is grateful, hurt, and angry at herself with each encounter. Occasionally she is bitchy or defiant. Usually, she is "woman," whom society has shaped to forbear, bear children, and be alone. Her solitude, for she is so much lost within herself that her children and her friends seem hardly to penetrate, is the source of both her strength and of her suffering.

Much of the narrative is devoted to Alice's relationships, especially with other people on the island, almost all of them, despite her assertion to the contrary, her own age, variants of herself. There is Stella, whose legendary promiscuity does nothing to assuage her emptiness. Stella and Peter, for a while, are lovers. There is Raven. Alice and Raven are occasional lovers, although Alice is quite fond of Raven's friend, Selene. So is Raven. Selene and Raven are hippies, encamped at Coon Bay. Stella, her girlfriend Trudl, and her deaf boyfriend Harold live with Stella's dad. We do not get to know him. We do not get to know anyone very well. It is sad, how little these people know of each other. It is sad, how alone Alice is, among them.

Running through the novel as a leitmotif are manifestations of an obsession Alice seems to share with her author for the etymology and variant meanings of words. Dictionary excerpts intrude upon the narrative–apparently at random. Not so: in fact, a whole sub-text builds throughout the novel, built on the diverse usage of specific words, especially words related to gender. This is a novel about language and consciousness and the inseparability of the two. It is about the impositions of language on behaviour and response, the conditioning effect of language, the extent to which women's experience, especially, is determined by the linguistic realities we live within. It is a novel about words, and about being.

Thomas is a fine writer: she is alive within words. Sometimes they threaten to engulf and overwhelm her, so that she will sink among them like a stone through water, and language will close over so that from the surface there is nothing left of her at all. But the water has changed shape. As it recedes while you read, you will see in the tidal pools a finely articulated organism that looks just like a stone but is alive.

ARITHA VAN HERK

No Fixed Address: An Amorous Journey. Toronto:
McClelland and Stewart, 1986. Toronto: Seal, 1987.
Pages: 319. Paperback.

No Fixed Address closes with the image of an endless number of
panties, of every hue imaginable, being retrieved (by a "you"
persona) from along the side of a road that runs infinitely north,
to nowhere. There is really no accounting for this; it is not a situation that arises inevitably from the text. Memorable as it might
be, redolent with elusive significance, this image is imposed upon
the narrative. Van Herk's fiction is generally contrived, such that,
as we read, we have a sense of the writer at work, only an episode
or two ahead. She knows what she is doing, but so do we. She
works with assurance, and we follow because she writes well. We
follow, but we are not caught up in the narrative. Why are panties strewn along the roadside? We do not really care.

Aritha van Herk has a considerable following (in the broader
sense) among co-regionalists in Alberta, among certain feminists,
and, more especially, outside Canada, among readers for whom
English is a second language. Her work cannot be ignored, and if
it sometimes seems like Atwood without the big words or Kroetsch
without the balls, well, that does not diminish the extent of her
impact. I do not in fact believe her work is regional, except in the
most superficial sense. She names the geography with relentless
specificity, such as one finds in Old Testament accounts of Hebrew
migration and settlement; but there is nothing of the interchange
between interior and external realities, between landscape and
the psyche, between geography and the human condition, that
one finds in the diverse regionalism of Robert Kroetsch, Rudy
Wiebe, and Sheila Watson. Nor, despite its obvious explication of
reality from a female perspective, do I find her work especially
feminist. To write of women as aspiring men, to insist that women
can live successfully in the so-called man's world of pig-farming
or prospecting camps, or bus-driving, or commercial travelling,
begs the question. Superficially, van Herk may seem to challenge
the tyrannies of gender bias: but rather than breaking down the
barriers, the stereotypes, the inequities, her protagonists pass
through them. They claim their place in the world of men; but,
dammit, it is not a man's world. The assumption here is that men

are somehow in the right, and in their rightful place. Van Herk could learn from Munro, or Thomas, or even Atwood, that the aping of men is not triumph but capitulation. To rail at being a woman, as opposed to hating what society makes of being a woman, is not feminist but, rather, a denial of feminism. Yet, Aritha van Herk is hailed by some as a feminist and regionalist. And for the simplicity of her prose, the small words and terse syntax, she is celebrated for the disarming clarity of her style.

No Fixed Address is van Herk's third novel. It is her best. *The Tent Peg*, her second, is a carefully crafted and thoughtfully low-key study of "characters" caught up in a common "situation," a work camp in the far North. The protagonist at the centre is a woman who, despite her initial disguise as a man, is all "woman." (When writing about van Herk's work, it is difficult to avoid using parentheses and quotation marks to indicate variant meanings and special emphasis, a response invited by her tendency on the one hand to build her fiction on classical and biblical mythologies, and on the other to direct her readers toward archetypal "significance.") Her first novel, called *Judith*, could have been, with editing, quite excellent. It won a major prize from Seal Books and set a standard for following awards that has so far been transcended only by Janette Turner Hospital's *The Ivory Swing. Judith* is about a woman pig farmer, but that is like saying *Surfacing* is about a trip to the woods. It tries to be a fiesty, probing, and sensitive testament to one woman's capacity for life; and it nearly succeeds.

In *No Fixed Address*, we pursue a self-absorbed young woman with the improbable name of Arachne through an episodic narrative as flat and linear as a prairie highway – until, suddenly, two-thirds of the way through the novel, reality itself spins topsy-turvy, and the going gets rough, and reading is like careening over mountain roads, around precarious switch-backs, close to the edge, unsure of what lies ahead. In the first and larger part of the novel (each of the four sections is separately entitled "Notebook on a Missing Person"), Arachne traverses Alberta as if it were a map, selling panties to small-town general stores. She does not wear any herself (such are the sources and emblems of pride). She lives with a nice man in Calgary, a cartographer called Thomas Telfer (who makes her over from a working-class rebel to a middle-class reject). On the road, in what could be a parody were it not all taken so seriously by the author, she reverses the stereotype of the salesman on the make and makes love with anything that moves (so long as there is a man attached to it). In flashback sequences inter-filed through her odyssey of dreary towns and fleshly diversion (in which there seems little satisfaction, except with a man of almost ninety who does not seem entirely sure of what is happening to him), we learn of her childhood and of her growing up and of her early sex life. It was rough; she was tough; sex was not up to much.

When Thomas meets her, Arachne is driving a Vancouver city bus. When she leaves him in Calgary, after temporarily kidnapping the old man from a nursing home, she drives her inherited black 1959 Mercedes, Type 300, right out of the realistic world, from modernism into postmodernism. In weird and haunting sequences at the Banff Springs Hotel, along the road, on a ferry, on Vancouver Island, through the northern B.C. interior, and into oblivion, she robs, is robbed, buys half a defunct coal mine, murders, meets her doppelgänger, makes love with the ghost of a drowned flier, drives far northern highways with a carload of drunks–men, of course. She stumbles onto a geodetic survey marker with Thomas Telfer's initials on it; takes off with the men in a helicopter–which never, in the narrative, lands. All that remains of Arachne is a web of lines across the map, and panties, like the dry husks of dead flies, cast along the roadside. Arachne, the spider-named, has disappeared. The you-persona in italics who tries to find her, in brief parenthetical episodes that frame the novel, finds only the panties, no answers. They are not dead flies but multi-coloured, irrelevant souvenirs of a world that Arachne (perhaps equating underwear with conventional femininity, and lack of it with the apparent freedoms of conventional masculinity) has transcended. Interesting.

GUY VANDERHAEGHE

My Present Age. Toronto: Macmillan, 1984. Toronto: Seal, 1986. Pages: 241. Paperback.

Ed is thirty-one. He is a "character." He tells his own story in a kind of runaway manic fashion that nearly obscures his depressive condition. He speaks for himself: his author is perfectly contained within his personality, hidden behind his antic responses to a hostile world, his hostile responses to an indifferent world. Ed is an anti-hero. He is a slob, sly and caustic, exceptionally self-centred, and possessed of an imagination that cannot distinguish between literary reality and actual experience. He reads a lot, and seems to regard himself much of the time as a character in a novel.

He is, of course, a character in a novel. He is a kind of modern-day Don Quixote, railing against all the absurdities of his age. Vanderhaeghe even gives him a Sancho Panza, in the person of one Stanley Rubacek, who travels with him on his odyssey around the city, searching for his estranged and pregnant wife who does not want to be found (by him, at least). Vanderhaeghe gives him a world to live in worth railing against, a world in which the absurdities of contemporary life are placed in direct and clashing confrontation with a sensibility shaped by Classics Comics, by the classics of literature and Western thought, by an essentially contemplative and cowardly disposition. Burger Kings, Canadian Tire, and middle-class success, talk-show hosts who haunt and bully him, divorce lawyers with no appreciation of Balzac, middle-class decorum—these are the world; and it is against such vestiges of civilization that he mounts Rocinante and does battle, while, almost incidentally, pursuing Dulcinea hidden away in her motel. (Rocinante is a dying blue Fiat, eventually displaced by Stanley Rubacek's Grand Prix.)

Ed—his abrupt abbreviated name, as incomplete and assertive as his personality—has so much in common with Cervante's ancient Don, it is quite amazing how well the parallel is hidden. Vanderhaeghe is far too fine a writer to insist that we "get" the connection. But it is there, nonetheless, giving his novel marvellous dimension and resonance. We are given, in a prairie city in Canada, a man whose perceptions of reality are shaped by books, who is utterly out of step with his times, who pursues an absurd and touching quest, who is absurd and a delight, pathetic and mad, hero and anti-hero, all at once. Perhaps the boom and collapse of the sixties does not exactly parallel the age of romance on whose back Quixote rode. Perhaps to ridicule an age of irony leads more to tragedy than to laughter. But Vanderhaeghe does not attempt to make the parallel exact. He is not creating a parody of the original, he is echoing it.

It is important in reading this novel to differentiate between Ed's experience of the world and the world Ed is given by the author to experience. It is Ed who describes his disembodied adversary, the talk-show Beast who berates him over the airwaves, as "the kind of man who cups and conspicuously hitches up his genitals before taking a seat. He went to a radio arts academy in Oklahoma. He orders his wife to lose weight. He has turned his son into a bed-wetter and his daughter into a drum majorette." That is Ed, imagining. It is Vanderhaeghe, however, who allows that what Victoria's father likes to do best is "Cut the lawn and shoot air pistols in the basement." That is fact, born out by a shooting episode, hilariously described. It is important to recognize Ed's perception from objective, if sometimes bizarre, reality. Otherwise we cannot separate ourselves from Ed's world. And of course that is the point: if we cannot distance ourselves from that world, then we are deservedly the object of satiric derision. And, sadly, ironically, amused at being so.

Vanderhaeghe plays with English as Rodin might have played with plasticine–but without the solemnity. He is a master of the vernacular, of language as it is actually used and lived within by real people living in Saskatoon (or is it Regina?). It is the language of actuality, not literature: words written down in such a way as to capture that uncanny combination of spontaneity and cliché that characterizes the way living people speak. In a context so filled with literary references and allusions, the effect is a disconcerting reinforcement of the novel's principal thrust against the conflicting values and realities of our present age. Linguistic paradox becomes a sub-text for the paradox of contemporary life, and, as important, a correlative for the distorted sensibility of the novel's erstwhile protagonist.

Ed is not really a protagonist. He would like to be one, but he has difficulty getting out of bed. His functioning in the world seems largely a retaliatory tactic. He drinks a lot, washes seldom, eats Cocoa Puffs, and fulminates against the world in scathing asides. When he does rally to the point of action, his author floods the narrative with flashbacks, recollections, and reconstructions of the past, so that he seems a reincarnation of Leacock's retroactive Mr. Juggins, a man whose every forward step is followed by two to the rear. Between intention and action falls such a plethora of anecdotes and aphorisms that we lose track of just what it was Ed intended to do. The author does not, of course, and so there is progression of sorts. The plot, however, is slight. It is the character who fills the narrative, not what he does.

Ed has been separated from his wife for more than a year and lives alone in a grungy apartment. He has written a novel–and just as well, since for more than ten years he has been representing himself as a writer. He imagines all sorts of lives for himself, but it is the guise of writer he most often wears. His eventual novel is a Western, starring the redoubtable Sam Waters. Sam is an Ed persona as he might have been created by the combined talents of Nietzsche and Zane Grey.

Victoria calls Ed. They meet, he gives her a bad time, they part, he searches for her, finds her, she rejects him. He retreats into a kind of coherent madness, pathetically waiting for Victoria, who will never call. That is the plot. The story is so much more. Ed is the story. His thoughts and feelings and memories, his personality, his voice, his zany quarrel with the world: these are what *My Present Age* is all about.

Among Canadian novels, this one is most like Richard B. Wright's *The Weekend Man*, although more ambitious in scope and more sophisticated in its achievement. It is a busy novel, frenetic at times. Vanderhaeghe packs in so much literate and caustic wit, so many episodic tangents and narrative asides, that we sometimes lose track of just what a sad figure Ed really is–a fat feckless dropout (who has become a fat feckless reject) from a world not much worth being a part of. It is a bleak vision, redeemed only by the comic absurdity of a pathetic Ed, at the dead centre.

STEPHEN VIZINCZEY

In Praise of Older Women. Toronto: Contemporary Canada Press, 1965. Toronto: Seal, 1985. Pages: 203.
Paperback.

In the postscript to this novel, Vizinczey offers the most fitting label for his fiction: "realistic erotica." Erotic literature aspires to different ends than other writing and must be judged against different criteria. If it does not create an aura of sexual arousal, then its narrow goal has been missed. To this end, most erotica is written in confessional or fabulist or surrealistic modes. Realism demands responses generally inappropriate to the genre, related to morality, emotional maturity, and aesthetic integrity. When a writer does dare to write realistic erotica, he or she must discover a well-defined format within which to work – thus the memoir, or amorous recollections, which Vizinczey uses to such pleasing effect.

It is difficult to accuse either the character or his creator of sexism and exploitation when both are so acutely aware of the ironies of their separate pursuits. Vizinczey's aim is to create erotic fiction; Andras Vajda, his protagonist, wants to seduce women. Perhaps another statement in the postscript reveals the source of this irony: "the philanderer's life demonstrates the basic paradox of personal freedom . . . the libertine has always been as much pitied as envied." This, and the sly wit expressed a few pages previously, that "Sex is the bad news that we have no supernatural powers," suggest why what might have been rather silly is instead an urbane and witty book.

In Praise of Older Women is not a confessional novel. It is the memoir of a smug intellectual, who writes from the bemused perspective of early middle age (and an academic post at the University of Saskatchewan), in celebration of his own amorous adventures as a youth and young man. Andras, Andrea, Andrew, as he is variously named, becomes almost an ironic metaphor for the sparkling ephemerality of postwar Europe, set in relief against a lustreless background. Yet Vizinczey never strays far from his chronicle of seduction to develop such thematic possibilities – which would in all probability have dissipated the erotic effect of his novel. As Andras recounts his sexual history, from his earliest bottom-smacking in pre-war Hungary through to his lusty bouts with bored housewives as he completes his doctorate in philosophy at the University of Toronto, he provides commentary on the psychology of seduction, the advantages to young lovers of older women, and the nature of amorous love. If there is a covert suggestion that Andras is relating his story in self-justification – a certain morose quality occasionally creeps in – his declared purpose is to educate the reader, and for this he maintains a suitably arrogant front. Such ambiguity helps to elevate Vizinczey's novel above the merely sensational. Then, too, the refined prose style and the unquestionable intellect of the narrator both lend the novel an atmosphere of dignified superficiality.

But the novel is primarily a straightforward account of one seduction after another. Each is related in fond detail; the emphasis is on the yearning narrator and on the psychology of his conquest. Enough is given of the actual love-making to make these scenes the climax of each separate account. Before the inevitable parting is described, morals are drawn, and the narrator sets himself and the reader up for his next encounter. Just enough psychological insight and social background are given in each encounter so that they do not seem repetitive and yet avoid being case histories. Andras's first mistress (in this context, the term *mistress* seems more appropriate than *lover*) is Maya, a woman of experience. After her, there is a dazzling array – not so many, in reality, but when all else in the young man's life is made secondary, his conquests seem manifold. The Second World War, the Hungarian Revolution, Andras's flight as a refugee in 1956, all seem ephemeral relative to his sexuality.

Like most men who style themselves lovers, Andras is wholly egocentric. All else in the world is only a backdrop to his adventures with himself. Yet Vizinczey manages to work in several moving discussions on Hungarian nationalism, many acute observations about human nature and about society in Europe and Canada, many urbane witticisms, and abundant evidence of a melancholy, droll sense of humour. His protagonist seems the very embodiment of sentimental sophistication, a continental without any depth of character at all – possibly the ideal personality for a libertine.

Vizinczey's prose is curiously formal. This may, in part, be due to his Hungarian origin, but it is also due to the singleminded demands of the genre. *In Praise of Older Women* first appeared as a vanity publication, sponsored by the author. It has since sold several million copies and has been made into a humourless movie. For its intelligence, its irony, its facile sophistication, and its exploitative sensuality, I would judge it the best work of erotica publicly published in Canada to date – certainly the most successful.

SHEILA WATSON

The Double Hook. Toronto: McClelland and Stewart, 1959. Toronto: McClelland and Stewart; New Canadian Library, 1966. Pages: 134. Paperback.

This novel is outstanding in our literature; it is infinitely intriguing as a symbolist prose poem, and yet it manages to engage the imagination on a narrative level as well. Watson describes a spiritual metamorphosis in the lives of a community tucked among hills that are a surreal rendering of the Cariboo country in the British Columbia interior. In spare, allusive prose, she relates the movement among the community members towards an acceptance of the duality of their lives, recognition that their/our natural condition lies somewhere between the glory and the darkness, hope and fear, spirit and body. It is a common enough theme in our literature—see *Swamp Angel*, in particular—but nowhere is it articulated in so striking a fashion. Usually, fiction works from the concrete to the abstract, from the specific to the universal. But Watson works the other way. She conveys her vision of a moral universe not by story so much as by form and image, between which the narrative unfolds.

Three families, and Kip and Theophil, live in a small community surrounded by barren hills, under the dispensation of Coyote, who watches, unseen. In the beginning, an old woman, Mrs. Potter, dies at the hands of her son James. Even after her death the others see her fishing in the stream that runs through their lives. Their lives change: James's sister Greta burns up in their house, which she covets; Angel leaves her husband; Ara perceives God and death; James runs away and returns; Kip reaches for the glory and is blinded. In the end, a child is born to Lenchen, and James takes responsibility for them both. But Coyote has the last word: "I have set his feet on the sloping shoulders of the world."

The movement of the novel is from fear, which is divisive, to hope, which draws the community together. Images of desiccated anatomy permeate the book, particularly as applied to the landscape. These are associated with Coyote. Against them are set striking images of air, earth, fire, and water, universal elements, essence without form, each of which, as a symbol, sustains opposite meanings (water, for instance, can purify and quench, or it can drown). Amid the symbolism inherent in two extremes of imagery–body and essence–reality remains more or less constant. It is the characters' recognition that changes, as perceptions shift and as their lives move from fear towards hope.

The Double Hook is a demanding novel, yet it is not difficult to read. The prose is graphic and clear. Its symbolism is reinforced by the narrative flow, not contrived to accommodate it. The rich allusiveness of the novel, summoning to mind Indian, Celtic, biblical, and classical mythology, never intrudes. There is poetry not only in the nearly perfect imagery and rhythms of language, but also in the spaces between words and images, in the resonant ambiguities that Watson brilliantly invokes. It is a novel that can be enjoyed, as with the best of poetry, on a number of levels at the same time, without necessarily being understood. Somewhat difficult to classify, perhaps, Watson's novel is nonetheless a major work of art.

While *The Double Hook* is highly original, an interesting case can be made for the intimate connections between it and Jean Giono's *Colline*, published in France in 1929. Watson lived for a time in Paris, and almost certainly was aware of Giono's celebrated Pan trilogy, of which *Colline* was the first volume. Her novel follows his with exacting precision in details of plot, character, setting, imagery, poetic diction and syntax, the merging of several mythologies, the rich allusive symbolism. This note is not meant to diminish Watson's achievement (which, even allowing for the possible influence of Giono, is considerable), but rather to suggest new approaches to its critical assessment. *The Double Hook* remains of singular importance in the Canadian tradition.

RUDY WIEBE

Peace Shall Destroy Many. Toronto: McClelland and Stewart, 1962. Toronto: McClelland and Stewart; New Canadian Library, 1964. Pages: 240. Paperback.

This is Wiebe's first novel and the first of three with Mennonite motifs. While *The Blue Mountains of China* has greater scope, in terms of both geography and adventures of the human soul, it has not the coherent intensity of *Peace Shall Destroy Many*. It is discursive and polemical, albeit moving in places beyond anything else Wiebe has written. Published between these two novels, *The First and Vital Candle* has neither the range of its successor nor the intensity of its antecedent. Of the three, it is Wiebe's first novel that remains the highest achievement, though it, too, is eclipsed by the works to follow, particularly *The Temptations of Big Bear*.

Wiebe is a sombre and demanding writer. Although by no means humourless, his writing is informed by gravely serious intent. *Peace Shall Destroy Many* describes a Saskatchewan Mennonite community struggling to keep its separate peace, separate integrity, during the Second World War. The people of Wapiti sustain the conditions of exile, because exile alone keeps them from assimilation into a world that would overwhelm them–in this, their situation suggests that of world Jewry before the war. The Mennonite community accepts the domineering authority of a tyrannical leader in order to preserve its special quality as a people. Against the context of Hitler's Germany, this is a concept of disturbing implications. Wiebe is not modest in his ambitions.

At the narrative centre is young Thom Wiens, who is a member of the community and yet, by virtue of his reflective consciousness, stands somewhat apart from it. Ultimately, it is Thom who assumes moral responsibility for Wapiti after it is wrenched away from Deacon Block. Thom comes to realize that neither suppression nor isolation will halt community disintegration–only in aggressive love can God's peace be had in the fallen world.

Obviously, Wiebe's intent imposes a tremendous burden of responsibility upon him as a novelist. *Peace Shall Destroy Many* is art, however, before it is meaning. That is what lifts it out of the realm of denominational polemics or spiritual propaganda. Nor does Wiebe use doctrine as the source of plot complexity, as do writers like Hugh Hood and Morley Callaghan. Rather, the spiritual is a full dimension of his characters' reality.

Wiebe describes the sad struggle of his Mennonite people to keep their values alive. For some, such as Thom's father, who laments having left Russia, these values are only the remnants of a lost homeland. At the other extreme, in the schoolteacher's admiration for Nazi Germany, they have been miserably distorted. Against such loss, Deacon Block's moral righteousness binds the community together–but with such intensity that it threatens to destroy it. Finally, Thom, from a dramatic vantage atop the coffin of Block's daughter, perceives the tyranny of arbitrary authority and turns away from subservience towards responsibility and Christian love.

Many take *The Blue Mountains of China*, rather than *Peace Shall Destroy Many*, to be the best of Wiebe's early work. It is certainly the most ambitious. It is a vast epic of Mennonite migration on four continents over the better part of a century, and yet it has details of individual experience that are exquisitely moving. Wiebe's intent in this novel exceeds his grasp, however. In style and form, it is a daring leap ahead, yet it remains a busily textured but amorphous assemblage. The structure is complex and fragmented, anticipating the form of *The Temptations of Big Bear* ; but divergent perspectives, multiple voices, strained syntax in *Big Bear* contribute to the coherence of the whole, while here they mitigate against it. Language in *Blue Mountains* is the biggest problem. Gone is the lucidity of Wiebe's earlier writing, but not yet has he developed the disciplined prose complexity of the later works. Occasionally the language becomes virtually impenetrable–the words are English but their usage robs them of meaning. *The Blue Mountains of China* was undoubtedly an essential phase, aesthetically and perhaps spiritually, in Wiebe's development as a writer. *Peace Shall Destroy Many*, however, remains paramount among his earlier work, in part for its eloquent clarity of style and purpose.

The Temptations of Big Bear. Toronto: McClelland and Stewart, 1973. Toronto: McClelland and Stewart; New Canadian Library, 1976. Pages: 415. Paperback.

The Temptations of Big Bear is a great novel, so powerful and uncompromising that its possible flaws are irrelevant. It is great in vision and heart and understanding, and great in form, language, and narrative technique. It is not, however, an easy novel to read. One does not read Rudy Wiebe for diversion: his fiction demands rapt attention. In return, it gives depth and intensity of experience rivalled by few novels anywhere. It has an historical and ontological range seldom found in contemporary fiction.

In Wiebe's vision–of three hundred thousand square miles of prairie, of our history from 1876 to 1888 and, by implication, from primeval time to the present, of several thousand of people, chiefly the Cree, and of a few of them in particular and a few of the whites with whom they came into tentative and terminal contact–he achieves a quality of spiritual realism that somehow evaded him in his earlier Mennonite novels. *The Temptations of Big Bear* is not Christian allegory, however, nor is it rife with religious symbolism. The temptations of the title do not make Big Bear a Christlike figure; rather, the allusion shows the epic proportions of his situation. Here is a man torn by the struggle between power and spiritual integrity. On one extreme, many of his people, particularly the Worthy Young Men, urge him to lead them into battle. On another, his people's miserable condition demands that he make a treaty with the whites. Either way, he is the leader of his people. Yet, honest to the dictates of his own spirit, he can do neither. Neither pride nor propriety entice him to take action. He dies a lonely man, his people lost. There was no winning for him, except in death.

Big Bear provides the dominant voice and consciousness in the novel, but spiritual definition comes from Wiebe's vividly authentic portrayal of Indian life. With uncanny empathy, he shows Indians alive in a world where all things are continuous with one another, all things are holy. For such people, the concept of land ownership is more than difficult to grasp: it is absurd. Courts and laws are grotesque to a people unable to lie or use language for deceit. A soldier is incomprehensible to them: someone whose function is to kill, who has no responsibilities to hunt, to make love, to live. The train is equally incomprehensible, a *deus ex machina* not because it is a mysterious machine, but because it is an endless source of whites, supplies, soldiers. Wiebe shows Indians, not simple or weak, but baffled. Their reality is so entirely different, infused with spirit and necessity, that they have no chance for survival. To grasp his achievement is to realize the spiritual abyss between the two worlds, white and Indian.

For insight into how Wiebe accomplishes such authenticity while overcoming the limitations of fact and history, read his short story

"Where Is the Voice Coming From?" It is a marvellous explication of his visionary method. And it helps to show how he makes *The Temptations of Big Bear* work as an intimate coherent vision, despite its expansiveness and its variety of narrative forms and voices. *Big Bear* is a personal "meditation on the past"; the mind that conceives and conveys it all, the narrative consciousness that sustains the many voices and perspectives, remains constant, contains everything. It is a singular, multifarious, profound, and compassionate vision.

Big Bear is not historical fiction in any conventional sense. It is not a re-creation, but a form of transcendence. It shows us worlds beyond words or facts or time. It shows us ourselves. Nowhere, however, does Wiebe lay blame. The story of Big Bear and his people is not something we did to someone else. It is what we did to ourselves; what we have been through. It is not guilt but consciousness – and thus responsibility – that he imposes and demands. It is the presence of the past that is important. He makes it unforgettable.

The Scorched-Wood People. Toronto: McClelland and Stewart, 1977. Toronto: McClelland and Stewart; New Canadian Library, 1981. Pages: 351. Paperback.

Here Wiebe provides an entirely different perspective on the times and some of the places portrayed so well in *The Temptations of Big Bear*. Here again is the Northwest during the tumultuous years late in the last century when treaties were forced and rebellions surged and heroes raged, heroes who are now lost in the detritus of conventional history. The scorched-wood people, the Boil-brûlés or Métis, have as different a history from the Indians as from the whites; and Wiebe adopts different techniques for its telling. Personality and collective soul give way to the historical clash of wills and individual spirits. The reader stands in witness as Wiebe presents the Métis case. An epic consciousness tells the story, a Métis singer. He alone, of the whole community, can see beyond his own knowledge or experience. Pierre Falcon, like all epic poets, is irrelevant as a personality; but as an epic voice envisioning the course of his people's destiny, he is absolute. Critics or reviewers who have trouble with Wiebe's admittedly demanding prose have seen Falcon as a narrative flaw, a weakness, since as a person he could not see or know all that he relates. Much happens after he is historically dead. Wryly, he alludes to his own passing. He is not a person, though. He is a singer, an artist, the voice and consciousness of his people.

The prose is problematic. It takes twenty pages, perhaps, to adapt to Wiebe's use of language in this novel. It is difficult, but infinitely satisfying. His diction and syntax are unusual, arresting, sometimes provocative. Never are the words transparent, as is often the case in the best writing. Always we must attend the medium and transcend it. The language works, and quite brilliantly, if we submit to its demands. Take even the first page: analysed, it resonates. But it does not invite so much as it challenges. The challenge met, his prose evokes responses that do not separate into meaning or emotion, but accumulate towards vision.

The vision of Falcon is the story of his people. It is told through its heroes, principally Louis Riel and Gabriel Dumont. Others enter the story and leave, as narrative and historical necessity dictate; but it is these two, the statesman and the fighter, teacher and buffalo hunter, prophet and soldier, who embody the Métis in spirit and in flesh. Wiebe shows Riel and Dumont as great leaders of men as if he is answering some essential imperative to restore them as such to history: the one was hanged; the other later toured on exhibit with the Buffalo Bill Wild West Show.

As a study of two men against the historical complexity they helped to create, this is a powerfully affecting novel. Riel's messianic asceticism, at times not unrelated to dementia, and Dumont's uncomplicated faith and cunning earthiness come across in a blend of intimate detail against a striking sweep of history.

There is a peculiar and unsettling urgency to *The Scorched-Wood People*: where Big Bear and his Cree are grieved, here there is anger and the Métis are championed. The treachery of John A. Macdonald is vilified. There was not inevitability to the Métis' demise, as Wiebe describes things. It was a matter of political intent. He does not allow us to identify with the Métis, however profoundly we may sympathize – the loss is not ours but theirs. In that it tends to lay blame, this is a lesser novel than *The Temptations of Big Bear*. And it lacks the other's deep spirituality, despite its relentless concern with religion. It has not quite the same power to move us from within. The vision sometimes falters: the facts refuse always to sing. Still, Wiebe has given us two great fictions. Surely a third will come, for there must be a perspective from which the white man's vision of those times can be told, one with which Wiebe can reconcile his own radical view of history. In the meantime he has published a couple of relatively inconsequential novels, *The Mad Trapper* and *My Lovely Enemy*, which seem— and will, I hope, seem in retrospect–to be only a transitional phase in his movement towards the fulfilment or completion of his major prairie work. It may be odd to appraise a writer in terms of what is desired, but such critical indulgence seems justified by the brilliance of Wiebe's earlier achievement.

ETHEL WILSON

Hetty Dorval. Toronto: Macmillan, 1947. 1967.
Pages: 92. Paperback.

Wilson is a master at making the simple profound, and the profound quite straightforward and simple. *Hetty Dorval* is an entirely unpretentious and engaging novel in which the impact on a young girl's life of her encounters with a notorious woman of the world is assessed in retrospect by the girl as an adult narrator. In effect, Wilson relates two stories. She follows Frankie Burnaby's life from twelve through nineteen, describing its highlights in a steady progression. She also tells the story of Hetty Dorval, obliquely, in fragments, through the same period of time, up until the beginning of the Second World War, when Hetty disappears behind a Nazi wall of silence in Vienna with her latest paramour. Themes of innocence and experience intertwining create a quiet mixture of apparent naïveté and unassuming sophistication.

The novel opens in Lytton, British Columbia, a small town where the Thompson and Fraser rivers meet. It closes in London, with the threat of war in Europe looming on the near horizon. At twelve, Frankie rides the fifteen miles south from the family ranch into Lytton every week for school, then goes home for the weekends with her parents. She makes friends with a secretive and beautiful newcomer to Lytton, who lives in a log cottage at the edge of

town, a cottage that eventually becomes the scene of a Burnaby
family triumph. Knowing her own reputation, Hetty Dorval makes
her young friend promise to keep their occasional meetings secret.
Hetty does not want complications. When Frankie's parents discover her deceit, they feel betrayed. Hetty's potential for destruction is depleted, however, by the Burnabys' intelligence and firm
control of their own lives. Frankie's vulnerability is offset by the
strength of family affections.

Frankie goes away to school in Vancouver where she sees Hetty,
once, in a jewellery store. At sixteen, she and her mother sail to
England, and on shipboard they encounter Hetty, who throws herself on their mercy, pleading with them not to reveal anything
about her – she is on the verge of marrying a rather ancient peer
of the realm. Several years later, in London, when Frankie is
nineteen, Hetty again appears and threatens once more to hurt
those Frankie loves. Frankie responds, stronger now, it seems – but
haunted by the indelible image of Hetty Dorval in her life. Therein
lies the motive for her telling the story.

Hetty Dorval is an adventuress, with a reputation for having
left broken hearts, broken marriages, and broken lives strewn
behind her from Shanghai to Vancouver. Hetty appears utterly
self-concerned. She is beautiful and without conscience. That which
threatens to hurt her or complicate her life, she dismisses without thought. Wilson's novel purports to be Hetty's story, but always
we see her as she appears to the world, enigmatic, infinitely
enticing, soft but invulnerable, dangerous. The picture emerges
of Hetty preying on the innocence of the unwary. When Frankie
finally turns on her, it is with bitter determination, for Frankie
knows how insidious Hetty's power can be. It is this attraction
she feels for the damned that Frankie finally expels from her life,
and not the person who is beginning to age, to slip into self-parody,
soon to be swallowed up by the war.

Wilson's descriptions of the British Columbia interior are exquisite. Her images have a simple, graphic directness that suggests a real place, but at the same time a place somehow lost in
the narrator's childhood past. As Frankie grows older and moves
into the world of experience, first Vancouver, then England, then
Paris, the language becomes less precise, the images more diffuse,
more concerned with manners and affectations than with surrounding reality. Early in the narrative the language sometimes

betrays a childish delight that comes precariously close to sentimentality. But that is how Wilson gets across Frankie's naïve
trust, the innocence that makes her so open to corruption, to a
fascination with Hetty Dorval–and also indicates the warm, open,
uncomplicated nature that allows her, Frankie, to prevail in the
end. This novel has been neglected in favour of Wilson's *Swamp
Angel*, but it is a fine and subtle work, second to none.

***The Innocent Traveller*. Toronto: Macmillan, 1949.**
Toronto: McClelland and Stewart; New Canadian Library,
1982. Pages: 276. Paperback.

Technically, this is the most sophisticated of Wilson's novels; thematically it is the most diffuse. The unusual point of view effectively involves the reader in the life of Topaz Edgeworth as if she
were a shared relative. The narrative ranges with casual omniscience across the hundred-year span of the protagonist's life,
assuming a logically improbable intimacy that is, nonetheless,
convincing. The voice of the novel is gossipy, biased, enthralled
with its subject. Yet the speaker never steps forward; the point of
view never resolves into a coherent perspective. The structure of
the novel is equally evasive, yet surprisingly appropriate to the
content. In the first third of the novel, Topaz Edgeworth is very
much in evidence, clearly the centre of the narrative. The middle
section, however, sees her nearly lost from view in a welter of
relatives, in the peregrinations of a large and worldly family. In
the final part, through attrition it seems, Topaz rises once again
to the fore. From an irrepressible girl in Staffordshire to an irascible old woman in Vancouver, Topaz is the bane and delight of family
and friends; and when she finally does die, it seems that she might
never have been.

From the beginning–with Topaz under the dinner table toying
with Matthew Arnold's feet, while her father magisterially directs
the family's attention to conversation with their distinguished
guest–through to the end–when a centenarian Topaz discovers
her apparent paralysis on a city street is due to the importunate
descent of her white calico drawers–Wilson declares the importance of her protagonist is a matter of character, not incident or
achievement. Topaz achieves nothing in her life beyond an emo-

tionally fecund longevity. In her middle years, while others are marrying, working, raising families, emigrating, doing things, even dying, the perfectly pleasant, persistently talkative Topaz Edgeworth seems hardly a presence at all.

The pacing of the novel is carefully modulated to reinforce the protagonist's oddly poignant ephemerality. The language, the delicate choice of words and their precise disposition in context, carries with it an elegant simplicity exactly suited to the protagonist's personality. Even the occasional lapses, when diction becomes precious or coy, seem appropriate. The biggest problem in the novel comes of seeing Topaz Edgeworth as a protagonist at all. The reason for chronicling her life seems, through much of the novel, to lie outside the narrative, as if the author has a private purpose she is unwilling or, perhaps, unable to share. Topaz does not command attention by virtue of her own existence. That is quite possibly the point of Wilson's story, but it is an insufficient basis for a novel that owes form and substance to the delineation of character.

The Innocent Traveller is a delight to read, however, for the lovely gentle wit it displays and the shrewd observations it shares about society and individual behaviour. There is warmth and goodwill in the writing of this novel, not at all muted by the elusive eccentricities of the main character. There are precise and moving scenes of a Victorian childhood, and haunting descriptions of life in early Vancouver. There is superb humour scattered in flashes among the domestic details, and a wealth of allusive images that anticipate the naturalistic symbolism of Wilson's next and more successful work, *Swamp Angel*. There is much to be admired in this novel, and certainly much to be enjoyed. It is a very good novel by a writer whose other fiction shows her to be capable of even better.

Swamp Angel. Toronto: Macmillan, 1954. Toronto: McClelland and Stewart; New Canadian Library, 1962. Pages: 157. Paperback.

Swamp Angel begins with Maggie Lloyd deserting her second husband in Vancouver and follows her journey for refuge to the British Columbia interior past Kamloops. But it is a novel of discovery rather than flight. Characteristic of Wilson's writing, it is an uncomplicated story, quietly and simply told, in which there are implications of profound depth and complexity. It is a feminist novel, written at a time when the struggle for emancipation seemed more a personal than a social endeavour, and more metaphysical than psychological. Before Maggie can be at peace, she must learn to accept herself as a woman, a loving, life-sustaining, changing, dying human being. The course of her discovery provides the novel's narrative and symbolic design.

Maggie's second marriage was an attempt to turn away from the tragic deaths of her first husband, their daughter, and her father. Instead, it is a brutish reminder of her loss. Eventually tiring of Vardoe's demands, Maggie leaves. She travels to a place called Three Loon Lake, where she works at the Gunnarsens' lodge and attempts once again to seal over the past. Gradually, she learns to live with her ghosts and with the reality of death; she learns to accept responsibility not only for things but people; she learns to accept the essential ambivalence of life. No longer mother, wife, or daughter, she becomes a whole person, interdependent with the world.

Working in counterpoint with Maggie's life at Three Loon Lake is the account of her friend, Nell Severance, back in Vancouver. Nell is a wilful, cranky, fat old woman, a former juggler who has an omnivorous lust for life, and who shows uncanny insight into the souls of others. This ability allows her to manipulate people, usually to their advantage. She helps Vardoe cope with his self-pity over Maggie's desertion, for example, and sees him into an affair more in tune with his limited personality. And she sees her conventional daughter, Hilda, through to a satisfactory marriage, never revealing to Hilda her illegitimacy. The swamp angel, a revolver she had used in her juggling act and still keeps as a souvenir, is, in its ambivalence, an appropriate symbol of her life. When Nell anticipates her own death and sends the gun to Maggie at Three Loon Lake, it becomes for Maggie, too, a symbol of the ambivalence of life, of struggle and acceptance, essence and being, body and soul. Nell at one point asks for it back, but Maggie will not relinquish it, trusting the truth of Nell's original impulse. When Nell dies, Maggie throws the revolver into the lake. As a symbol, it has become redundant.

In a sense, Maggie's whole relationship with Nell is symbolic, for Nell is the natural life force, in wilful human form, that Maggie admires and finally comes to embody. In a similar manner, the

Chinese cab driver and his younger brother play symbolic roles; so does Mr. Cunningham, whom Maggie saves from drowning; so do both Haldar and Vera Gunnarsen, and their son Alan. Each represents some aspect of Maggie's struggle towards full consciousness of herself and the reconciliation of opposites within her. More explicit are such graphic scenes as when the eagle steals the osprey's catch, or when the fawn and the kitten play, or when Maggie swims, a seal and a god but not yet a woman, whole in herself. In such scenes, meaning and action are perfectly fused. So full is this novel, so naturally are its metaphysical intentions arranged in the narrative, that it seems almost a modest work. But it is not–either in intent or accomplishment. There is a brilliant, polished simplicity to Wilson's prose. *Swamp Angel* is a novel of refined character, powerful and touching to read.

ADELE WISEMAN

The Sacrifice. Toronto: Macmillan, 1956. Toronto: Macmillan; Laurentian Library, 1968.
Pages: 346. Paperback.

The Sacrifice overwhelms the reader with an aura of greatness that almost obscures the humility at its centre. Wiseman's commanding vision of a devout man's exile from God, parallelled by the travail of immigrant experience in the New World, moves the reader to profound compassion–the whole is an awesome epiphany.

As an example of immigrant fiction, *The Sacrifice* is without peer. The pattern of loss, isolation, struggle, and assimilation that marks the genre is here rendered with authenticity and dramatic intensity that makes all other such novels seem pale imitations. Perhaps because immigrant experience is not an end in itself, but the supporting structure upon which Wiseman builds a complex allegory of spiritual duress, the immigrant in this novel is universal, both an everyman and (as his name, Abraham, implies) our common source.

Abraham, Sarah, and their son Isaac settle into the Jewish section of an unnamed Winnipeg. They are isolated by language, by belief, and by custom from the Canadian world surrounding them, yet nurtured by the community close at hand. Wiseman describes life in the ghetto with penetrating insight and a great deal of affection. She portrays the distortion of ancient and Old World traditions, the distress between generations imposed by the New World, the clash of opposing cultures, and the terrible threat and appeal of assimilation. Were there no more to the novel than this, it would be a major document.

The spiritual dimension of the book is graphically defined on a narrative level. Abraham and Sarah fled pogroms in the Ukraine, one of which saw their sons Jacob and Moses murdered by Christians on Easter Sunday, during Passover. Abraham's hatred for God, following this sacrifice, gives way to piety; however, it is a false god he thence carries within him, a god of death who is in the image of his dead sons. Abraham expects so much of his surviving son that, when Isaac dies in rescuing the Torah from a fire, it is not an act of faith but a necessary sacrifice to his father's god. After he is widowed, Abraham becomes enthralled with the woman Laiah, whose barren promiscuity seems to embody seductive death; and whom he murders in a sacrifice to his own tortured concept of God—an act of exorcism that frees his dead sons at last and restores Abraham to the true God. From the asylum at the end of the narrative, he sends his grandson Moishe, or Moses, back down into the community, the ghetto of the chosen in the New World, with a message of brotherhood and love.

So rich and beautiful is Wiseman's prose that one is hardly aware of the complexity of her novel. Even when the biblical allusions are abundantly evident—as with characters' names, for example— the effect is to simplify the narrative rather than to draw elaborately significant parallels. Her novel does not attempt a retelling of the ancient stories in modern dress but provides a continuation of them, a testing of their implications. Knowing about the original Abraham, for instance, helps the reader understand Wiseman's Abraham, helps to resolve the mystery of Laiah's murder as his unconditional surrender to God. Other allusions are so subtly interwoven that the reader is hardly aware of their impact. Symbolism arises out of the narrative reality, rather than being imposed upon it. However, it is in the systematic foreshadowing of events and responses that Wiseman is most effective. Every aspect of her novel is meticulously orchestrated: everything that happens seems, in retrospect, to have been inevitable. Abraham's profession as a butcher, for example, is related time and again to ritual slaughter and sacred laws, on the one hand, and to the act of sacrifice, on the other.

Wiseman is not a prolific writer. Her only other novel, *Crackpot*, is admired by some for its oblique portrayal of a fat and innocent whore named Hoda. So much affection is expended on Hoda and so little on humanity, however, that the narrative collapses into a paroxysm of confused anger. Wiseman's reputation rests with *The Sacrifice*, which, in a mixture of dread and beauty, takes in the secret thoughts of a tormented soul, the experience of a displaced people, and the whole of man's relationship with God. *The Sacrifice* is not a modest work, but it has a spiritual humility as profoundly humbling as any in our literature.

RICHARD B. WRIGHT

The Weekend Man. Toronto: Macmillan, 1967. Toronto: Macmillan; Laurentian Library, 1977. Pages: 261. Paperback.

The Weekend Man is a well-written and thoughtful popular novel, filled with acerbic wit and cutting insights into the malaise of contemporary society. Most readers will find it a comic horror story, as easy to read now as when it came out a decade ago. Yet somehow it remains ephemeral, for Wes Wakeham, Wright's protagonist, is an ineffectual dissenter and no more substantial in the reader's mind than he is in the world he abjures. Wright has published five other novels: *In the Middle of a Life, Farthing's Fortunes, Final Things, The Teacher's Daughter,* and *Tourists*. Each attempts to counteract his tendency towards superficiality in a different way. *Farthing's Fortunes*, in particular, is a self-consciously literary work. In *The Weekend Man*, however, it is the surface of things that occupies his character's mind, and the apparent void beneath the surface that haunts him. While it is perhaps a limited novel, the limitations are appropriate to its intent.

In *The Weekend Man*, Wes Wakeham takes the reader into his confidence from the very beginning, sometimes using the familiar second-person voice, assuming our complicity with his views of the world, or at least our tolerance for them. In conspiratorial tones, he describes the last week before Christmas in the present tense. There is no reason for him to be talking, no motive for a confession or an accounting—it is an arbitrary point of view. Accepting that, the voice is superbly done. Wright never falters. Everything described is perfectly in keeping with Wes Wakeham's character, told as he sees it. Yet *The Weekend Man* is not, strictly speaking, a novel of character. Wes shows endearing quirks and predispositions as he remains valiantly indifferent to the meaningless world of suburban big business and struggles towards some modest understanding of his relations with others, but he never quite comes alive. His context is not realistic but sardonically didactic. He is an authorial attitude; the persona for an essay on individualism in a corporate age.

As entertainment, *The Weekend Man* is superb. Wright gives his protagonist a lifestyle loaded with ironies. Wes is married but separated; at thirty, neither young nor old; father of a son with Down's Syndrome; employee for a cultural business; a television watcher and an old movie snob; moderate in his vices as well as his virtues; a decent man out of step with his times, but too ordinary to do much about it except retreat into benign idiosyncrasy. He is vaguely resentful of his father's wartime memories, of his wife's middle-class vacuity, of his son's opaque view of the future. He is a victim of the holocaust of Wednesday, October 24, 1962, that did not happen (the day Kennedy's blockade of Cuba was challenged by the Russians and atomic war seemed imminent). Can there be any point to anything in a world that exists on borrowed time, yet is obsessed with plastic triviality? Wes Wakeham has no answer; neither does his author.

We are amused by this novel rather than disturbed and oddly reassured that someone else sees the shallowness around us as clearly as we do. The central motif of the novel, of consciousness poised indifferently between the past and the future, last weekend and next, offers an effective metaphor for the present age. Wright's ability to see that the determination of Wes Wakeham's breakfast menu by drawing lots actually limits Wes's power of choice, or that Wes's accidental success in publishing is as real as any corporate success can be, lends the whole work a sad aura of irony that no amount of comic flair can dispel. This ambiguity and the exceptional clarity of the prose style lift *The Weekend Man* well above the level of popular fiction, the conventions of which it exploits with disarming ease.

QUÉBÉCOIS NOVELS IN TRANSLATION

While the novels in this section were selected with the advice of several authorities in the field, the critical commentaries are my own responsibility entirely.

I have tried to provide a comprehensive selection of translated works but inevitably, due to practical considerations, certain works of distinction have been omitted. Other novels by authors included here and works by writers of note who are not represented are not necessarily of lesser merit. Rather, in my judgement they do not seem as relevant to an anglophone's appreciation of the Québécois novel, its traditions and its contemporary achievement. For this purpose, the novels I have discussed here are essential reading. (It should be noted that I have included in this section several novels by Canadian writers who are francophone but not Québécois. These novels, it seems to me, participate more in the Québécois tradition than in any other.)

HUBERT AQUIN

Prochain Episode. Toronto: McClelland and Stewart; New Canadian Library, 1972. Pages: 125. *Tr.* Penny Williams (*Prochain Episode*. Montréal: Cercle du Livre de France, 1965). Paperback.

Prochain Episode is a work of tortured genius, probably the best and most important novel to come out of the modern separatist movement. Aquin argues with passionate eloquence for violent revolution; he speaks rhapsodically for the beauty of blood, shed for the love of his betrayed and betraying mistress, the country of Quebec. Against this yearning is set the nearly overwhelming appeal of peace through suicide; reconciliation through death with two centuries of subjugation, escape from the humiliations of sustained defeat; if only there is enough resolve to support the act.

From his room in an institution (to which he has been taken from his Montreal jail cell for observation, where he was held as a suspected terrorist), the narrator rages against the enticements of suicide, and against the conditions that drive him to consider it. To occupy himself, to impose order on the chaos of his mind, to build a barrier between himself and despair, he determines to write a spy novel. His protagonist is a version of himself, at war with sinister forces in Switzerland; while he, in his Montreal cell, struggles to cope with his love for Quebec, the guilt he feels for her defeat, the bitterness for her degradation, the passion for her gift of life. All of this is transformed, in the narrator's novel, into the elusive blonde, K. The two narratives are interpenetrating; the man of violence in the cell and the man of intrigue in Switzerland share a single consciousness, and each provides an explication of the other's reality. The spy's inability to execute his mission and kill H. de Heutz, alias Carl von Ryndt, alias François-Marc de Saugy, provides the action of his story; paradoxically, that story embodies the cell-narrator's lack of action as a Quebec patriot. Both men are inept saboteurs and foolish lovers; they are mirror images of each other.

Which is the creator and which the created? Does the pen originate the spy or does the spy compel the pen, draw it across the page, make the writer write, make the writer, through writing, be? Aquin is fascinated by such paradoxes of process. His fiction is a disordered and incomplete context in which motive and desire, resolve and action, love and blood struggle towards coherence. His writing is complex and very beautiful. In his call to revolutionary violence, Aquin is sometimes intensely lyrical: he convinces through style as well as argument that blood spilled through love is a transcendent act–even while both his protagonists are unable to draw themselves into action. At other times, his evocations of despair are chilling in the extreme; suicide becomes a reasonable option. Through precise words ambiguously deployed, he generates excitement in the spy segments that carries over into the cell, and emotions in the cell that determine his spy's reality. In all, *Prochain Episode* is a disturbing novel about the souls of a troubled man and a troubled nation, both hovering between death and glory.

The Antiphonary. Don Mills: General; New Press
Canadian Classics, 1983. Pages: 196. *Tr.* Alan Brown
(*L'Antiphonaire.* Montréal: Cercle du Livre de France,
1969). Paperback.

It is far easier to describe what happens in *The Antiphonary* than
to say what the novel is about. As in much of Aquin's fiction, there
are two distinctly separable and yet interpenetrating realities.
The divisions between creation and being, appearance and meaning, are obscure; the maker and what is made, the creator and
what is created, are indeterminate; as elusive, in Aquin's fiction,
as form itself.

After a single chapter, the authorial voice is usurped. From the
second chapter until her death near the end of the novel, Christine Forestier apparently documents the progress of her troubled
consciousness. Her ruminative notes include the researched material she has gathered about the sixteenth century for a Ph.D. thesis in Medical Science; emerging sporadically from her notes is a
fabulous account of medieval chicanery, which takes on a reality
of its own. Out of Christine's work on Jule-César Beausang, a
disciple of Paracelsus, poor Renata Belmissieri struggles into reality as a fledgling smuggler. Belmissieri is murdered, and we witness Beausang's private death. A fallen priest, Leonico Chigi, who
emends Beausang's manuscripts for profit, has an affair with and
then murders a woman who has already murdered her husband,
an early printer of Beausang's manuscripts (which through all
this have been spirited from Italy through Switzerland to France
and, ultimately, into the hands–or mind–of Christine, a twentieth-
century North American).

Out of her imagination, coupled with the dry bones of factuality,
Christine creates a world every bit as real and vital as the world
her body inhabits–which is real enough. Her husband murders a
pharmacist who rapes Christine in San Diego; then he maims
her lover in Montreal, and dies in a car accident. Eventually
Christine, who is pregnant by the pharmacist, is drugged and
seduced by her lover's doctor; in the end, she kills herself. At this
point, the narrative is briefly taken over by Christine's lover's
wife, although the last words belong to the doctor (who has been
the lover of Christine's lover's wife). Love and death tumble over
each other in a grotesque display of existential paranoia. There is

no meaning but the lack of meaning, no reality but what the mind creates. Love and death are merely devices for coping, strategies to endure.

Hamlet's Twin. Toronto: McClelland and Stewart, 1979. Pages: 208. *Tr.* Sheila Fischman (*Neige noire*. Montréal: La Presse, 1974).

Occasionally I have gone back to reassess a writer's canon from which I had already selected representative work for the original edition of this book. Sometimes another evaluation has seemed called for by something I have read or heard or because a new work casts all that preceded it into a fresh light. In the case of *Hamlet's Twin*, however, only serendipity led me to retrieve a copy from a "remaindered" bin and re-read it – to discover with amazement that I had never read it in the first place. Published in French in 1974 under the more appropriate title of *Neige noire*, this was Aquin's final novel. How I missed it must go unaccountable; but I am convinced it is one of the best experimental novels ever written in Canada, one of the great novels of Quebec. The following is an act of contrition as well as of appreciation.

The central paradox of *Hamlet's Twin* is that everything contained is greater than that which contains it. This holds true for life, love, time, and especially, art. The novel contains the shooting script for a film about a man who will make a film of his own, from his own life, in which the struggle between fiction and truth will engulf the containing context, the novel itself. The reader, insists the narrative voice, is a viewer. The story as a whole is about time and the terror of human consciousness, told through a film-script format with marginal commentary that seems to circumvent the narrative itself and pass directly into the reader's mind. The reader thus becomes in some sense an invention of the writer and is contained by the novel, at the novel's centre. But he is also at home outside the text, containing, as part of his experience of the world, the innermost thoughts and fears of the writer writing.

In presenting a scripted story, Aquin tells us what we should see, rather than what we do see. He is free to comment on what effect each shot in the story should have on the viewer and how it should relate to other shots. This method allows him repeatedly to juxtapose shots and scenes without narrative explanation, which leaves us both bewildered and, paradoxically, enlightened. The linearity of film as an unbroken continuum allows significance to arise simply from sequential arrangement. Furthermore, in describing shots that must stand without words, he drifts into involved discussions about the implications of his images: words, to transcend the limitations of wordlessness; images, to transcend the limitations of words. And always, time exists as the medium of images and words, as their context and antithesis. All is in the present tense, passing from the future, unread and unseen, into the past as it is read and then, in the mind, seen. The present is merely an interface between the two, the past and the future. Time itself is an illusion. This is a novel, ultimately about time. It is a tragic novel.

Nicolas and Sylvie are lovers. After completing a role as Fortinbras in Shakespeare's *Hamlet*, Nicolas takes Sylvie to Norway on their wedding trip. She dies there and Nicolas returns to Montreal with her friend Eva as his lover, to script his life from the beginning of the novel until the end of the film. Scenes of splendid and of sordid eroticism punctuate the story. Allusions to Fortinbras as Hamlet's twin, to the play within a play, to Norway's history and, especially, Norway's geography slide in and out of the narrative. Brief snatches of dialogue provide a seemingly realistic base for the juxtaposition of lingering scenes shot through with rapid flashes, sometimes incongruous and sometimes complementary, of landscape and of lovemaking. Throughout, the authorial voice comments on his own responses to what is to be (is being) shown; gradually shifts into discussion with the viewer on art, life, the nature of cinematic "reality," and time and human consciousness; and, as the plot becomes increasingly macabre, sinks into a lethargic communion with the reader and retreats from the script, from time, from everything.

This novel is not pointedly Québécois. It addresses experience at once more intimate and more far-reaching than Aquin's earlier fiction. It is a novel to be read and re-read, until somewhere deep within it we find ourselves contained by his creation and the horrors he envisions life to be, in a world where commitment is illusion, art is a diversion, and love is only a prelude to despair. At that point we are on the outside looking in, containing.

PHILIPPE-JOSEPH AUBERT DE GASPÉ

Canadians of Old. Toronto: McClelland and Stewart, 1974. Pages: 364. *Tr.* Charles G.D. Roberts (*Les Anciens Canadiens*. Québec: Desbarets & Derbishire, 1863).

L'Influence d'un livre, written by a son of the same name who predeceased the senior Philippe Aubert de Gaspé, lays claim to being the first Québécois novel. But the father deserves credit as the earliest popularizer of Québécois historical romance. *Canadians of Old* was written when the author was in his seventies, and captures, in its romantic reflections on the past, not only an idealized vision of early French Canada but something of an old man's benevolent lament for his lost youth. Set in a period a full generation before the author was born, this novel represents a concerted attempt to capture, for posterity, a world that was rapidly fading from public memory.

Using plot and character as vehicles, the author delivers a rich panoply of life in Quebec in the middle of the eighteenth century. The story involves the son of a seigneur and an orphaned young Scot; the two become fast friends at school in Quebec but inevitably find themselves on opposing sides during the war of Conquest. They come together again as friends after the fighting stops, although Archie Cameron never does marry Jules d'Haberville's sister. Instead, in a ménage of symbolic possibilities, the lovers live together as brother and sister under the seigneurial roof where Jules and his English wife rear their family in happy comfort.

It is the happy times the author most wants to convey: his novel is an idyll of the past, a rousing romantic adventure, with intrigue, passion, danger, and honour exercised at every turn. It is also an epic of the road, for much of the novel takes place on a journey from seminary to seigneury. But most important, it is a document. Aubert de Gaspé begins and ends his account with himself in the text, speaking as a mediator between the reader and history. In these sections, he describes the past in the present tense. By allowing the "machinery" of his fiction to show, the immediacy of the past is emphasized, and yet its inaccessibility is confirmed.

Throughout the novel, the author shows remarkable range in

relating legends, songs, and superstitions of the Québécois people, in modes from pastoral to grotesque. He also describes, with a fondness for detail, the customs, sensibility, and experience of Quebec as he knows it must have been. In the original edition (and, oddly enough, reproduced untranslated in English editions), Aubert de Gaspé appended extensive notes. The notes act as a fascinating historical gloss on the romantic narrative, and affirm the author's documentary intentions. Inexplicably, and quite inexcusably, the cover of the New Canadian Library edition assigns full credit for the novel to its translator, Sir Charles G.D. Roberts. Philippe-Joseph Aubert de Gaspé's name does not appear on the book's front cover or spine, only in the back cover copy and on the title page.

YVES BEAUCHEMIN

The Alley Cat. Toronto: McClelland and Stewart, 1986. Pages: 450. *Tr.* Sheila Fischman (*Le Matou*. Montréal: Editions Québec/Amerique, 1981). Paperback.

This is a literary curiosity of protean proportions. Most of the major phases in the development of the novel are here exploited with such casual authority the reader is seldom distracted from the narrative at hand. Yet Beauchemin has managed to blend elements of the gothic and the picaresque from eighteenth-century fiction with panoramic social realism reminiscent of the nineteenth century and the myopic social determinism of early twentieth-century naturalism, all in a context teeming with the attitudes and absurdities of the present time. In following the adventures of Florent Boissonneault as he makes his way in the world, we plunge headlong through a sprawling account of contemporary life in Quebec, enthralled by the detail and gusto of Beauchemin's narrative vision so much that we never realize what a remarkable pastiche it really is. Unlike most postmodern writing, his novel does not exploit its generic eclecticism for wry or devastating commentary on the human condition. Rather, it uses the resources of literature to assert the viability of its own literariness–that is, it is a novel that intends to be taken as a novel, as a work of fiction.

Superficially, *The Alley Cat* seems almost naïve. It is a vision of the real world, yes, but the real world as seen through the medium of fiction, the real world translated through art into a coherent and meaningful context in which we as readers are invited to exercise our imaginations. The Montreal presented in this novel, the small Québécois town, the Florida compound are all authentic in virtually every detail. Yet they are populated with such a Dickensian cast of characters and caricatures that setting seems discontinuous with our world outside the narrative. Besides Boissonneault and his wife Elise, there are the malevolent Egon Ratablavasky, the five-year-old foul-mouthed alcoholic called Monsieur Emile, the eccentric chef, Aurélien Picquot, the Anglo-villain, Slipskin, the slimy journalist, Rosario Gladu, a dog called Virtue, and a cat called Breakfast. And dozens more. Some, such as the hero's parents, are unexceptional and some, like his cousin, Father Jeunehomme, the fanatical seeker after remnants of Gogol's *Dead Souls*, The Second Part, are quite off-the-wall.

The story itself would be a conventional account of a young man's rise from servile mediocrity to solvent satisfaction in a bourgeois world were it not for the quirky characters and incidents encountered along the way. With the aid of a benefactor who nearly destroys him, Florent Boissonneault goes from salesman to restaurateur to impoverishment to antiquarian entrepreneur and back to restaurateur. Some of his adventures are hilarious and some are harrowing; some are absurd and some provide sardonic commentary on contemporary life. Never, however, do we see inside the man, the character. This is not a novel of psychological analysis. Motivation and behaviour are governed by narrative necessity. Response is described, not shown. The milieu explored, the attitudes exposed, may be thoroughly in the wake of the Quiet Revolution, but the narrative itself is firmly rooted in earlier times, in conventions established by Balzac and Zola and Flaubert, all of whom figure in the story. Dickens is at least as important to Beauchemin's purpose as René Lévesque; Gogol is more of a presence than Gilles Vigneault. Quebec, itself, is gently satirized, while simultaneously much of our Western world is savaged. Literary models are whimsically parodied; fiction itself is wickedly exploited. *The Alley Cat* is not a great novel by any means, but reading it is a great experience.

VICTOR-LÉVY BEAULIEU

Jos Connaissant: A Novel. Toronto: Exile Editions,
1982. Pages: 171. *Tr.* Ray Chamberlain (*Jos Connaissant.*
Montréal: Editions du Jour, 1970.) Paperback.

While reading this novel I kept referring to the notes on the back
cover, more and more convinced my copy had been misbound. Can a
novel that displays unremitting fascination with death, decom-
position, putrescence, and filth, with worms, vermin, and excres-
cence, with misery, maiming, cruelty, and pain, can such a novel
really be described as a "gently ironic story of separation and
exile"? Can fiction displaying a diabolically morbid obsession
with genitals, with virtually every bodily orifice and the various
textures, discharges, and distensions of the same, especially in
acts of hetero- and homosexual incest, buggery, and self-manipu-
lation, real and imagined, can such be the fiction that "All Québec
has come to love"? This "story of Jos and his family" may indeed
have become "the immensely popular television program *Race
de Monde*," but only after suffering an utter transformation, one
must assume, from dung beetle or grave slug into a fake butterfly.

It is quite possible, in fact, to imagine extrapolating from the
text of *Jos Connaissant* a set of characters and relationships that
might sustain a television series–but only if the sordid, morbid,
and obsessively vile originating context is entirely expunged, and
in its place the world of poverty and ignorance is made quaint,
heart-warming, and humane. I can imagine that: the Plouffes in
Montreal (or as Beaulieu names it, Morial Mort). Although two of
the main characters are dead from the start, and another is a
corpse through much of the narrative, most of the characters are
quite memorable. Jos is a thirty-year-old quasi-mystic who lives
in an empty room, but for his books, a chaise longue, and his plaster
buddha. He works as a deliveryman for a supermarket. His first
affair is consummated at great length with Marie, an exotic dancer
turned waitress of thirty-nine. Jos is inordinately fond of his Mom,
about whom he has strong sexual feelings, derived from a combination of fantasy and childhood memories. He is not close to his
father, who has thrown him out to live on his own before the narrative begins. Everyone in Jos's life is a "character." There is the
filthy proprietor of the restaurant where Marie works; the writer-
brother with whom he shared early sexual encounters; the dere-

lict uncle; the friend who sliced his genitals off; the brother from
Paris; the frightened sister.

Childhood in Trois-Pistoles and life in Morial Mort are equally
infused with the vile detritus of unpleasant lives, and both are
contained by the sordid realities of life as a nasty imposition.
Beaulieu's world is not depraved; it is obsessive. Death, decrepi-
tude, the ubiquitous phallus, these are the measures of Jos's world,
of Beaulieu's vision. The writing itself is powerful, but the vision
is so oppressive that the flights of metaphor, the intensely complex and striking images, the capacity for words to reach from
the sewer to transcendent ecstasy are all but overwhelmed. *Jos
Connaissant* is no doubt an important contemporary novel, in
which a particular philosophical attitude is made graphically
manifest, but it is not a pleasant experience to read. It is quite an
unpleasant novel, and it remains so in the mind long after it has
been set aside.

GERARD BESSETTE

Not for Every Eye. Toronto: Exile, 1984. Pages: 98. *Tr.*
Glen Shortliffe (*Le Libraire*. Paris: Julliard, 1960).
Paperback.

Not for Every Eye is a spare and supple satire. It is not a realistic
novel, yet in its own wry way it is true to life, demanding emotional as well as intellectual response. Bessette's wit is piercing:
at times, as he exposes Québécois provincialism to ridicule, the
novel takes on a decidedly sinister cast. Yet the reader's guide
through this sardonic vision, by every civilized measure a corrupt and hollow man, provides a cheerful antidote.

Hervé Jodoin is utterly "laid back"–a man too filled with ennui
even to bother being bored, a man so literal-minded that the common discourse of those around him seems preposterous. He is an
improbable protagonist in any context other than satire: he is a
misanthrope, dour and indifferent, fastidious only in the arrangement of his own affairs, so that his life will demand as little as
humanly possible in the way of involvement, decision, or con-

scious response. The reader familiar with Melville will recognize in Jodoin the soul of Bartleby the scrivener, but without Bartleby's morbid countenance; Jodoin has the saving grace of indiscriminate cynicism in an ironic context. Indeed, irony is the watchword of the fiction. Sometimes the irony is Bessette's, and sometimes it is the means of his character's survival in a world that is forever impinging on his passion for disengagement.

Not for Every Eye is a brief novel, written in simple, direct style. It consists of Jodoin's diary entries; his proclaimed motive for writing is to fill up his Sunday time, when the beer parlour is closed and there is nothing else to do. Jodoin is guileless. He yawns in the reader's face; but by virtue of his radical indifference to us, he is entirely engaging as a narrator. His account tells of his coming from Montreal to Saint Joachim to work in Léon's Book Shop, not quite destitute but on the seedy side of respectable. He takes a room, where he sleeps; he spends seven hours a day, six days a week, in Trefflé's, the beer parlour, drinking twenty glasses of draft beer a session. His job gives him command over all the books in Léon's store; he sits on a stool and does his best to ignore co-workers in the toy, religious articles, and stationery departments. Customers only arouse his interest when he can unload such inappropriate works on them that their future patronage will almost certainly be denied.

The plot of the novel, such as it is, involves Léon's revelation to Jodoin of a *sanctum sanctorum*, where he keeps a special cache of books "not meant for every eye." These indexed works are to be sold with extreme discretion, and at inflated prices. Jodoin unfortunately releases a particularly noxious volume to a student, and suddenly M. Léon's bookstore is at the centre of a town scandal and a vicious power struggle between factions of the Church. The offending book, Voltaire's *Essay on Morals and Manners*, sparks treachery and intrigue – all of which is resolved by Hervé Jodoin who, taking blame for the offence himself, absconds with the storeroom of forbidden books to Montreal, where he sells his hoard for enough to live on for a while, in modest comfort. In a world of such provincialism, pettiness, and hypocrisy, Bessette's seedy misanthrope seems strangely, ironically, heroic.

MARIE-CLAIRE BLAIS

Mad Shadows. Toronto: McClelland and Stewart; New Canadian Library, 1971. Pages: 123. *Tr.* Merloyd Lawrence (*La Belle Bête*. Québec: Institut, 1959). Paperback.

Mad Shadows is the blueprint of a troubled psyche. Whether that psyche is the author's or her Quebec homeland's, or the psyche of an abstruse narrative persona, is quite irrelevant to the novel's impact. Blais conveys the bone-deep shock of a terrible nightmare, but her story follows the head-long logic of a cruel daydream. She has created a primitive, naïve, and profound work of gothic surrealism.

This was the author's first novel, written–apparently in fifteen days–when she was still in her teens; it betrays the obsessive rush and arrogance of adolescence in its imaginative excesses and conveys something approaching genius in its poetic restraints on image and diction. Blais describes absolutely nothing that is extraneous to the tale itself. Paradoxically, repetition provides the primary narrative technique. Characters, for example, are no more dramatically complex than figures in a folktale, yet by endlessly enumerating their predominant features, Blais lends them an aura of ghoulish profundity. Patrice is a beautiful idiot; his sister, Isabelle-Marie, is bitter and ugly. Their relationship is determined by these singular characteristics, which, in turn, are reinforced by their relationship. Their mother, Louise, is utterly fickle: she loves Patrice for his reflection of her own fading beauty and despises Isabelle-Marie for her reflected ugliness. She robs both her children of their souls. Over and over, Blais iterates their meagre personalities; with each repetition, she progresses the tale a step further. Louise develops a thread of blood across her cheek, which blossoms slowly into cancer. She marries her equal in vanity, a crippled dandy named Lanz, who is murdered by Patrice's jealousy. Isabelle-Marie marries a blind boy and begins to shed her ugliness; her husband gains his sight and, repelled by her image, turns her away with their ugly daughter. She returns to Louise and eventually plunges her brother's head in boiling water to make him grotesque as well. Louise sends both away–Isabelle-Marie for her crime and Patrice for his acquired ugliness–and rots alone on her vast farm estate until her daughter returns and burns her to death. At the end, Patrice also returns; he plunges into the lake in search of his beautiful reflection.

From beginning to end, the world surrounding these three characters represents another reality, strangely removed from the reality of Louise and her children. Louise's world is beyond reach and, like a sinister folk or fairy tale, ominously beyond rational meaning. Layers of interpretation can be sheared off the awkwardly perverse surface, and the mysteries beneath gape wider and deeper than ever. Blais has created the surreal image of a deformed soul, a tortured psyche, an image that can be explored but never resolved. Her novel is a perfect paradigm of Québécois society in a furious state of transition. *Mad Shadows* marks the bursting free of imagination festering under two centuries of sentimentality and social restraint. When it appeared it caused a furor, and for good reason. As the purging of an ancient wound, it was brutally painful; but it formed the necessary prelude to scar tissue, a healing of sorts.

A Season in the Life of Emmanuel. New York: Grosset
& Dunlap, 1969. Pages: 145. *Tr.* Derek Coltman (*Une
Saison dans la vie d'Emmanuel*. Montréal: Editions du
Jour, 1965).

In this novel, Blais turns away from the nightmare surrealism of *Mad Shadows*, but she continues to indulge an obsession with the morbid and the grotesque. The gothic impulse is infused with a portrayal of domesticity, and the effect is powerfully disconcerting. The external world is defined by ignorance and poverty; it is sociologically authentic. But the characters' perception of this world and the innovative arrangement of incident and point of view make it seem bizarre.

The predominant and overwhelming phenomenon in the life of the rural Québécois family into which Emmanuel is born, as the sixteenth child, is death. In this first winter of his existence, some time earlier this century, he bears uncomprehending witness to the macabre trivialization of mortality. His Grand-mère Antoinette, who is the focal centre of the family, relishes each funeral for the food and festivities; others in the family treat death with a range of emotions from indifference to bewildered anguish. One death in particular carries the structural weight of the novel, the death of the sensitive Jean-le-Maigre. His sister's movement from the convent to the mortification of fasting to the comforts of prostitution provides a major subplot. Scattered throughout the story are fragments of the mean and strangely heroic lives of Number Seven and Pomme (who loses most of a hand in a factory where he begins work at eleven years of age) and, in brief flashes, of their brothers and sisters, alive and dead, their parents, the ubiquitous Church that preys on their souls, and such inept social institutions as school and the reformatory. Mixed with the rural squalor of their lives is a fetid air of sexuality and a perverse drive for spiritual aggrandizement.

But there is more to the novel than a story of grim reality: Blais's casual morbidity, her oblique perspectives, and her poetic style combine to form an existential folktale rather than a social document. A curious mood of horror and ennui dominates the novel, perhaps reflecting the author's vision of Québécois society caught between a sordid past and her morbid projection for the future.

ROCH CARRIER

La Guerre, Yes Sir! Toronto: Anansi, 1970. Pages: 113. *Tr.* Sheila Fischman (*La Guerre, Yes Sir!* Montréal: Editions du Jour, 1968). Paperback.

Roch Carrier's fiction fibrillates with emotional intensity. His style, spare and direct, echoes the folktale in language, in technique, and in content. Yet there is an edge of urbanity to his work. Carrier is an author of sophisticated literary consciousness; curiously, his novels seem to be more popular in translation than in the original. This may be attributed, in part, to his effective exploitation of the stereotypes of Québécois society that are commonly upheld in English Canada. But his best novels carry about them an aura of authenticity that has more to do with the imagination than with social realism. *La Guerre, Yes Sir!* is the first volume of a triptych. Although differing considerably, the three novels expose the violent confrontation of opposing realities in the Québécois experience, French and English, Church and human nature, rural and urban, traditional and modern. *Floralie, Where Are You?* reaches deep into the allegorical depths of the soul; *Is It the Sun, Philibert?* is a cry of social despair.

La Guerre, Yes Sir! itself is a tale teeming with life; the story springs from the land itself. Unity is provided by time–one day in the Second World War–and place–a remote Québécois village incongruously called Bralington–and by the corpse of Corriveau, who is the dead centre of the novel's action and idea. Lying in his coffin, attended by a disinterested honour guard of *maudits anglais* at a wake in his parents' house, Corriveau embodies the death of an innocence that never really existed except in the Québécois imagination. Crowding against him in the narrative are the bizarre antics of the villagers–superstitious, ignorant, spiteful, loving, and insistently human. The war is an intrusion on their world, a violation, a contagion that Corriveau has brought home in his coffin.

As the novel opens, Joseph cuts off his hand to escape the draft (the hand is later used as a puck, then rescued by his wife, only to be tossed to the dog to gnaw on); and Amélie is forced, by the war, to support the love of two men. Still the war is distant until, with Corriveau and his entourage, an alien conflict becomes the immediate condition of the villagers' lives. In an atmosphere of earthiness and vulgarity, amidst cider and *tourtières*, Carrier moves the plot forward. Grotesque values of the past collapse; there is only moral and social confusion to take their place. The novel's folktale ambiance conveys both a lost heritage and a threatening future.

LAURE CONAN (MARIE-LOUISE-FÉLICITÉ ANGERS)

Angéline de Montbrun. Toronto: University of Toronto Press; Reprint Library, 1974. Pages: 169. *Tr.* Yves Brunelle ("Angéline de Montbrun," *La Revue Canadienne*, June 1881-August 1882, in 14 parts, 146 pages. *Angéline de Montbrun*, Québec: Leger Brousseau, 1884).

One of the great eccentric works of fiction in the Québécois tradition, *Angéline de Montbrun* gains depth and complexity with each era of interpretation. Devotion, piety, and Christian forbearance are cast in the sinister light of perversity throughout the novel; incest, masochism, morbid obsessions, and violent passions vie for the reader's attention in the narrative with Christian virtues. It is doubtful that the author intended such a mélange, or even that she fully appreciated the radical form of her novel.

The first half of the novel is epistolary. A series of letters, mostly between Maurice Darville and his sister Mina, relates the progress of Darville's love for the nearly perfect Angéline de Montbrun and Mina's unrequited affection for Angéline's widower father, Charles de Montbrun. Throughout this fairly conventional exchange, the father and daughter are upheld as paragons, whose devotion to each other suffers only the blight of being, perhaps, too intense. They are not only one in blood; they are one in appearance and outlook and even their souls are said to be in perfect harmony. The Darville siblings nevertheless become a part of de Montbrun family life at Valriant, on the Gaspé coast.

Abruptly, halfway through the novel, the sentimental narrative stops. In a few brief pages, Conan describes the death of the father, the disfigurement of the daughter, the end of the daughter's engagement to Darville, and the flight of the vivacious Mina to the Ursuline convent in Quebec (Mina becomes a ghoulish sacristan in the chapel where de Montbrun is buried). A quite different account begins to unfold, an account told primarily through diary entries written by Angéline, who has retreated from the world.

The second part of the novel reads like a mirror inversion of the first. Angéline mourns her dead father, laments the loss of her lover, savours the suffering her God makes her endure. God, her father, and her lover merge in her mind as one. In the great morbid passion of her diary entries, it is often difficult to distinguish agony from ecstasy, the fervidly sacred from the profane. Morbidity reigns supreme. By a striking use of flashbacks arranged out of sequence, Conan builds a chilling portrait of a psyche obsessed with death and of a love that only death will consummate. The psychological depths of the novel are astounding. In its formal aspects, in the light it casts into the darkest recesses of sexuality and desire, in the light it throws upon moral and spiritual passion, *Angéline de Montbrun* is radically ahead of its time.

RÉJEAN DUCHARME

The Swallower Swallowed. London: Hamish Hamilton, 1968. Pages: 237. *Tr*. Barbara Bray (*L'Avalée des avalés*. Paris: Gallimard, 1966).

There is no equivalent to this vision of reality from a child's perspective in English-Canadian literature, or perhaps anywhere. In Ducharme's novel, no attempt is made to replicate a child's consciousness through such stylistic effects as simplified vocabulary and syntax, ingenuous juxtaposition of images, or the coy articulation of complex ideas through a description of juvenile experience and response. Ducharme's Bernice Einberg is an entirely convincing nine-year-old, seen from the inside out, whose mind is parsed meticulously in words of staggering ambiguity, opacity, and erudition. In no way is she a child realistically presented, yet her reality – a moral and philosophical reality – is authentically conveyed. The words and concepts may not be hers, but they are appropriate equivalents of her perception of herself in the world.

Bernice is so absorbed with her own being that there is no room within her for the humane resolution of opposites through which people generally survive – rather, she lives at the convergence of opposites, where hate obliterates love and evil destroys goodness, where appearance and reality merge and become one. Consequently, while she is a moral monstrosity, she is also strangely benevolent from her own perspective.

Bernice is wilfully evil. But that evil is not the absence of good; nor is it the corruption of innocence. It is the function of her survival as an inviolate personality, utterly alone in the world. At nine, she murders her mother's cat; at eleven, she murders its replacement. While still in her mid-teens in Israel, she holds another living person up as a shield to absorb Arab bullets meant for her. She murders her imaginary alter-ego, whom she calls Constance Chlore, and mourns the loss for years, without re-creating her. Her father sends her away from home: she taunts him with more than six hundred passionately incestuous letters addressed to her brother, which she knows the father will intercept. She is a diabolical creation of her own love for herself and a brilliantly eccentric embodiment of Ducharme's evident fascination with moral dualities and the convergence of opposites.

The narrative admits only distorted perceptions of Bernice's surrounding milieu; the author moves her through three distinct environments, between ages nine and fifteen or sixteen. The first third of the novel is set at the family home, a converted abbey on an island in the St. Lawrence near Montreal, where Bernice lives with her brother, Christian (who is a Christian while she, by agreement her father's daughter, is Jewish), and with her parents (Dead Cat and Einberg). The second phase of the novel places her with materially successful and morally austere relatives in New York; the third takes her to the front in Israel. She survives.

There is no sense of narrative development in the novel, although a great deal happens; nor does Bernice herself develop, mature, or change. As a construction of her own consciousness, it is enough that she remains constant while the world changes. In language that is so heavily loaded with allusions that the words themselves sometimes burst free of definition, where ideas clamour towards coherence even while clashing in a cacophony of ambiguous meaning, Ducharme has created a novel of infinite fascination and singular importance.

JACQUES FERRON

Dr. Cotnoir. Montreal: Harvest House, 1973. Pages: 86.
Tr. Pierre Cloutier (*Cotnoir*. Montréal: Editions d'Orphée,
1962). Paperback.

The major source of appeal in this slight and celebrated novel is
its presumptuous naïveté. *Dr. Cotnoir* insists the reader attend to
the art of the fiction rather than become immersed in the illusion
of fictional reality. Ferron writes so that the telling and the tale
seem at odds with each other: the narrative stumbles through
inconsistencies of voice and point of view, through ragged-edged
reversals of temporal sequence, through language that is as much a
barrier as a medium, towards inconclusive completion. It is an
attempt to rework the novel form, to move it away from romance
and social realism so that it more accurately reflects the sensibility of the people.

　Dr. Cotnoir is an act of rebellion rather than of liberation; in
retrospect, it seems rooted still in the cultural history of its own
time. Little more than twenty years after its original publication, it
seems awkwardly dated, a necessary embarrassment. The plot
itself is timeless: there is a funeral, but not enough mourners
attend to make up a party of pallbearers. Cotnoir, the corpse, has
lived his working life in Longueuil, a middle-class extension of
Montreal, and practised among working-class clients in Ville
Jacques-Cartier. His wife, from France, has stayed indoors, and
will return to France when his estate is settled. A con-man attends
the funeral, as do two doctors, one of whom is the putative narrator,
and several businessmen. Outside, after the service, the idiot,
Emmanuel, cavorts, a man who was given freedom from the
"burden of solicitude" by the unorthodox dead doctor.

　The narrative dips backwards into the immediate past to account
for Emmanuel, to provide brief glimpses into Cotnoir at work, to
describe Cotnoir's passing and the arrival of the con-man, who
garners bounty for condolences rendered. In language that is
casually rhetorical, often colloquial, and sometimes improbably
arch, Ferron manipulates form and content into an illusion of
artlessness. It is an interesting achievement, a worthy precursor
to the art of Blais and Carrier and an engaging transition from
Lemelin and Roy.

ANTOINE GÉRIN-LAJOIE

Jean Rivard. Toronto: McClelland and Stewart; New
Canadian Library, 1977. Pages: 276. *Tr.* Vida Bruce (*Jean
Rivard*. Montréal: Rolland, 1874). Paperback.

Jean Rivard is at the centre of an agrarian myth that dominated
the Québécois imagination for more than a century. The book was
not the first *roman de la terre*; nor is it the best. But it is the most
unabashedly persuasive. *Jean Rivard* uses all the elements of the
romantic idiom to engage the reader's sympathies and every
polemical device possible to convince the reader of the validity
and virtue of its vision. Its impact as a work of art has been
negligible, but as popular propaganda it has affected the lives of
generations.

The prose in *Jean Rivard* is serviceable, at best, and the narrative control artless; and yet the work has an awkward air of
authenticity. Gérin-Lajoie relates an extravagantly romantic tale:
he chronicles Jean Rivard's advance from ambitious youth to prosperous maturity to honoured retirement. In 1843, at nineteen,
Jean begins clearing the land for his farm in the Eastern Townships. By the novel's close, he has had a township named after
him, been mayor of the town bearing his name, served admirably
in Parliament, and begun to reap the glories of a just old age – all
for having worked diligently on the land and for having honoured
God, the Catholic Church, the French people, and his family bonds.

It is almost impossible not to be cynical about such patently
propagandistic and exploitive themes. Yet the contemporary
reader's interest is held by the headlong drive of the narrative.
Brief, dramatic episodes of reward repaying industry and virtue
are separated by practical accounts of such activities as sugaring-off
and making potash; there are letters of woe from Jean's city friend,
a hapless lawyer named Gustave Charmenil; there are letters of
rectitude from the curé. The novel loses momentum near the end,
however, as Jean's turgid secrets of success and prolix words of
advice – which are meant to reinforce the object lessons of his
exemplary life – are detailed. It is an uninspiring novel to read
now, but an important novel to have read.

JACQUES GODBOUT

Knife on the Table. Toronto: McClelland and Stewart;
New Canadian Library, 1976. Pages: 128. *Tr.* Penny
Williams (*Le Couteau sur la table*. Paris: Les Editions du
Seuil, 1965). Paperback.

There is something so diffuse, and yet so precise, about this novel
that the reader feels disconcertingly lost in what seems to be
familiar territory. Conventional sources of coherence are to no
avail: verb tenses shift apparently at random; a decade passes
back and forth between the beginning and the end of a single
sentence; setting, starkly realized, shifts with the narrator's random thoughts. Neither theme nor form, time nor place, character
nor story, provides literal coherence. Yet each of the eighty-five
brief segments of the novel has an almost crystaline purity, and
out of the segments a story emerges rich in emotion and in symbolic significance.

Godbout is an accomplished illusionist, creating unity out of
disunity, meaning out of confusion. The narrator intersperses an
account of incidents in the fifties with details of his present life,
in the early sixties. The two eras seem interpenetrating. The narrator is without definition himself: he is unnamed, an embodiment,
it seems, of French North America. He struggles, in the fifties,
through a passionate affair with Patricia – wealthy, anglophone,
manipulative. Winter characterizes their relationship. A decade
later he is still intrigued by her, but he is emerging into spring.
In the fifties, he and Patricia both take lovers: she, an English
student from Westmount; he, a Québécoise called Madeleine
whose soul he seems to share. When Madeleine dies, the narrator
plunges into the life of America. With Patricia, he had previously
crossed Canada by train, a witness from the window of a Pullman
berth. After Madeleine, and a brief flurry with Madeleine's sister,
Monique, he travels the continent, working under different names
at different jobs, merging with the continent he travels. Finally,
in this new spring, he has come home. Before Patricia, he had
been in the Canadian Army. Now he thrills to the call of the
Québécois revolution. With all the choices that have apparently
been open to him, only now can he choose to be himself.

Godbout's nationalism is not a narrow claim for provincial

sovereignty. It is a vision of the French nation in America as the source of individual liberty for the Québécois people. He does not call for violence but, in the violent sexuality of his narrative passions, he anticipates it.

GERMAINE GUÈVREMONT

The Outlander. Toronto: McClelland and Stewart; New Canadian Library, 1978. Pages: 290. *Tr.* Eric Sutton (*Le Survenant*. Montréal: Beauchemin, 1945; *Marie-Didace*. Montréal: Beauchemin, 1947). Paperback.

Two novels are combined to make up the three-part work called in English *The Outlander*. These were preceded by a collection of stories or *paysanneries*, which act as a sort of prologue. Characters and locale in the collection, *En pleine terre*, are much the same as in *The Outlander* but their context lacks the sources of continuity in the latter that give it such eerie power. These sources include themes of change, the deterioration of old values and customs and habits; themes of timelessness, the solemn presence of unchanging nature, the patient forbearance of the land itself. They include a richness of detail as the narrative moves from sequence to sequence, so that a picture of remarkable clarity and authenticity gradually emerges. They include a prose style that combines rather cool eloquence with colloquial dialogue and a casual command of local idiom. Perhaps the most significant source of continuity in *The Outlander* is the presence of the Stranger in Monk's Inlet, a small community near Sorel on the St. Lawrence.

The Stranger is the enigmatic embodiment of the outside world. In touching their lives, he brings irrevocable change to all the people in the community, particularly to the Beauchemin family, with whom he stays for a while. The Beauchemins provide the focal centre of the narrative, and at their own centre is the father, Didace. The attractiveness of the Stranger intrudes on family life, bringing discord and enmity into the open. By the time the Stranger leaves, at the end of part one, Didace has fallen out with his only son and, an old man, he prepares to take a new wife, an

Acadian widow, into his home. Part two describes the intrusion of the Acadian woman, the flight and death of Didace's son, and the birth of his granddaughter, Marie-Didace. The third part chronicles the deaths of Didace and his second wife, and the first six years of Marie-Didace's life. The granddaughter has become heir to the family land, though as a female she cannot carry on the family name.

The author envisions great sadness ensuing from the corruption of old ways, yet the novel is not a lament; nor is it a warning. Rather, it is a somewhat ironic celebration of what has inevitably passed. In a haunting blend of naturalism and surrealism, mixing graphic descriptions with elusive, allusive possibilities of meaning, Guèvremont has created a beautiful document of other times.

JEAN-CHARLES HARVEY

Sackcloth for Banner. Toronto: Macmillan, 1938. Pages: 262. *Tr.* Lukin Barette (*Les Demi-Civilisés*. Montreal: Editions du Totem, 1934). Published also as: *Fear's Folly*. Ottawa: Carleton University Press, 1982. Pages: 178. *Tr.* John Glassco. Paperback.

The response to this novel in Quebec was vicious. A cardinal of the Church vilified Harvey, invoked a ban on the book and, in league with the "half-civilized" élite the novel exposes–including Premier Duplessis–forced the author out of his job as a newspaper editor and out of his subsequent job as a civil servant. In this, far more is revealed of Quebec in the 1930s than by Harvey in his fiction. The novel now seems awkward and naïve, a difficult work to take seriously. Its curious mixture of romance and rhetoric, of idealism and cynicism, of social realism and surrealism, is held together by little more than the author's sincerity and a certain melifluous cadence in his prose. As art, *Sackcloth for Banner* is negligible; as a document of its era it is rather inept. But for the responses it evoked, and for their implications in Québécois social and cultural history, it is of major importance.

The plot is simple enough, although it attempts complexity. Max Hubert tells his own story. (Inexplicably, the narrative shifts to the third person on two occasions, while the author brings in details that otherwise threaten to escape him.) Max moves from a St. Lawrence farm into Quebec City as a youth. As he matures he seeks a vocation, but the functions of priest, lawyer, professor, and journalist all prove empty. He falls in love with Dorothée Meunier, and her father gives Max the funds to edit his own journal. A terrible secret takes Dorothée away from Max and she eventually enters a convent. Meanwhile, Max founders, but he stands by his ideals as an editor while his journal collapses under him. He learns Dorothée's secret, but too late; she flees the convent to die of exposure in his arms.

Before this maudlin ending, Max journeys back to his childhood home where the very walls and artifacts wail for the loss he shares with his people of their hardy peasant past. At this point, Max has already articulated his interior debates with himself, a brief Québécois history, diatribes on twentieth-century religion, and assaults on the hollow elite, while espousing the primacy of free thought, explicating ideals of art and society, and, for good measure, explaining to the reader a number of his dreams. There is little formal coherence to all this: the romance does not provide an adequate structure to support the rhetoric, and neither social conscience nor the will to reform unify the discursiveness of the narrative. Harvey's achievement is not as a novelist but as a committed reformer, struggling to link an honoured past with a worthy future. Given its context in the history of ideas in Quebec, *Sackcloth for Banner* is a significant failure.

ANNE HÉBERT

The Silent Rooms. Toronto: Paperjacks, 1975. Pages: 167. *Tr.* Kathy Mezei (*Les Chambres de bois*. Paris: Editions du Seuil, 1958). Paperback.

The curiously desiccated prose in this novel creates the impression of a gothic fairy tale, terrifying and intriguing at the same time. *The Silent Rooms* is the first novel by one of Canada's major

poet-novelists and has been highly acclaimed for a variety of conflicting reasons. So pared is it of meaning or complexity, some
readers insist it must be a symbolist parable. Others find, in its
enigmatic simplicity, great insight into the human heart. Some
readers imagine an emotional lushness in its stylized imagery,
while others find depths of ambiguous allusion. For some, the novel
is ephemeral, a dream; for others, it is a vision of unwavering
authenticity. One thing is certain: this is not a realistic novel.
Hébert writes in a convention that considers social realism anti-
thetical to the writer's function: Hébert's novel does not reflect
reality–it creates reality. The author owes more to the folktale
than to the classics, but there is an elegance about this novel, a
sureness of style, that has little to do with the folk tradition. This
elegance, matched with the novel's singular directness, makes
The Silent Rooms a fascinating achievement.

The story–for the novel has neither the complexity nor the formal coherence of a plot–is in three parts. In the first, the daughter of a sullen widower in a mining town, charged with keeping
house for her father and her three sisters, meets a mysterious boy
who is the son of a tyrannical seigneur. These two, Catherine and
Michel, fall in love; in the second part, the lovers marry and live
in oppressive leisure in two rooms in an unnamed city. Michel's
sister, Lia, betrays their family inheritance and then moves in
with the stifled young couple. Lia's presence changes the gap
between husband and wife to a chasm, and eventually Catherine
becomes ill. The third section of the novel chronicles Catherine's
convalescence on the Mediterranean coast, her love affair with a
stranger, and her final rejection of the grotesque *ménage à trois*
with Michel and Lia. The whole is a fable of emancipation, of a
woman who transcends the roles of drudge and ornament to take
possession of herself. Beyond that it is–like a good fairy tale–
whatever the reader wants it to be.

Kamouraska. Don Mills: General; New Press Canadian
Classics, 1982. Pages: 250. *Tr.* Norman Shapiro.
(*Kamouraska*. Paris: Editions du Seuil, 1970). Paperback.

Hébert's unparallelled command of time and consciousness within
the narrative lifts this novel to the highest level of contemporary

achievement. *Kamouraska* is an overwhelmingly powerful post-modern romance set in the historical past. As an account of love and death it is conventional enough, and the characters are stock figures of nineteenth-century sentimental fiction, moved and motivated by the author's design more than by psychological inevitability or thematic need. It is not the story but the telling that is gripping and bizarre.

Hébert builds her fiction around an actual murder, in 1839, of the young squire of Kamouraska, Antoine Tassy, who was killed by his wife's lover. There is no fixed point of view in the novel, but the limit of narrative consciousness–the frame of reference for the reader in the frenetic accumulation of memory and dream, experienced and imagined realities–is the mind of Elizabeth D'Aulnières. At thirty-eight, Elizabeth has borne eleven children and is awaiting the death of her innocuous second husband, Jérôme Rolland, after an uneventful marriage of eighteen years. Within these perimeters, contained by Elizabeth's brooding presence, events of preceding years are related to one another retroactively, sequentially, even prophetically. Time and voice are not of the ruminating mind, but serve the author's larger vision of a life shaped by passion and ruled by domestic necessity.

Almost from the beginning, Hébert reveals the outcome of the trial for Antoine Tassy's murder. Elizabeth is released from prison after a few months; her maid, after a couple of years; and George Nelson, Elizabeth's lover, having fled to Vermont, is never brought to trial at all. Huge in the reader's mind is the question of how this woman came to such a crime, a woman who decades later awkwardly awaits the death of another husband; the same woman who, as a naïve girl of sixteen, married a fat libertine and had two children by him; an ordinarily unhappy young woman who draws her foreign doctor into a frenzied affair and has a child by him as well; a woman who throughout her life has been fussed over and indulged by spinster aunts, household help, children, a lover, and most of all, by herself.

Hébert makes Elizabeth an enthralling enigma, even though her crime of passion, its prelude and its consequences, are straightforward enough. In a swirl of rich, allusive prose and ragged narrative design, the author illuminates a life that is, in itself, merely sad, and makes of it a tragedy.

Héloïse. Don Mills: General; New Press Canadian Classics, 1983. Pages 101. *Tr.* Sheila Fischman (*Héloïse.* Paris: Editions du Seuil, 1980). Paperback.

Héloïse is breathtaking, a story of the macabre, bone-chilling and beautiful, told with the uncanny assurance of one entirely at home among the undead. Set in contemporary Paris, Hébert's tale conveys with haunting lyricism the imminence of unspeakable horrors. As with all of her writing that touches on the strange and unnatural, the reality of the narrative supplants our own, loosening our grasp on the safe and rational world outside the text. We are within the fiction as we read, and frightened there beyond the power of most such tales to move us. Time, which is the measure of life against the stillness of death, seems irresolute. Verb tenses dance indeterminately; syntactical logic is thrown askew. Héloïse and her dreadful cohort, Bottereau, disport themselves in the attire and attitudes of another era and yet seem as appropriate to the nether regions of Paris–the Métro, the derelict stations, the graves–as do Bernard and Christine (at least in the beginning) in the regions above. In a context of exquisite opacity that includes both worlds, there is a ghostly inevitability to their interpenetration, and ultimately to the conquest over time of timelessness, over life of the living dead.

The plot of *Héloïse* is unpretentious–straightforward, and paced with the sure quickness of a folktale. Just before his wedding, Bernard encounters a strange young woman on the Métro. She becomes an obsession: though he marries Christine, his every thought is dominated by the vampiric Héloïse. With his bride he moves into an antiquated apartment that oddly shapes their life together. It had been Héloïse's home, in generations past. Bernard pursues Héloïse through the depths of the Métro, eventually makes love with her, and nearly dies. His wife is raped and murdered by Bottereau, Héloïse's mentor. Bernard becomes one with the dead, deep in the earth under Paris.

Héloïse is horrifying and yet mesmerizing. From the beginning we recognize the lure of death and its perversity–and yet we pursue it through the narrative, as surely as Bernard pursues it through Paris and the psychic catacombs of his own mind. The end is inevitable: we read not to discover what happens but to know how. The real story–the real excitement, suspense, and horror–is in the telling. Hébert writes so well of the unnatural, the supernatural, the inexplicable, that the reader becomes virtually haunted by her words and her vision. *Héloïse* is a brief novel. Its meaning is blatant and, paradoxically, elusive–and what really is death, if not these? Its impact is overwhelming. *Héloïse* is a work of genius, not recommended for late-night reading.

LOUIS HÉMON

Maria Chapdelaine. Toronto: Macmillan, 1921.
Pages: 263. Toronto: Aquila, 1984. *Tr.* W.H. Blake (*Maria Chapdelaine*. Paris: Delagrave, 1916). Paperback.

Maria Chapdelaine is commonly regarded as a classic of Québécois literature, although it was written by a foreigner who spent less than two years in Canada (and had the misfortune to be killed in northern Ontario at the age of thirty-two). In his brief stay, Hémon absorbed much of the Québécois way of life and even more of its mythology; he transformed his knowledge into as haunting and charming a *roman de la terre* as was ever written. Sentimental by present standards, occasionally mawkish, and more than a little awkward in its wedding of documentary and romantic voices, *Maria Chapdelaine* still engages the reader's sympathies.

As an outsider, Hémon sustains an ironic detachment from his subject. He celebrates the life of Québécois pioneers who, three hundred years after their forbears settled in the New World, struggle to clear land in the primeval forests. He sees these people as humble, determined, industrious, and pious. He also sees their hardships and deprivations; and the sacrifices they make to remain a nation while surrounded by forces of annihilation. Much has been said of how Hémon has perpetuated the myth of the happy habitant, and indeed his portrait of life among the Québécois peasantry early in this century is filled with great warmth and charity. But his vision is ironic: these are not foolish rustics but struggling pioneers.

Maria's father has moved his family five times, and her mother has supported him with grudging tolerance. Maria herself has said prayers for her beloved's safety, a thousand *Aves* on Christmas Eve. But her beloved dies. Again and again, Hémon balances a romantic ideal with austere actuality. Eventually, Maria accepts the proposal of the man who appeals to her least of her three suitors. Her beloved, François Paradis, is dead; Lorenzo Surprenant's promise of prosperity in the United States seems too easy. Eutrope Gagnon's offer of a hard life clearing land – the life that killed Maria's mother, farming at the edge of extinction – wins her in the end. Hémon's story is a sombre and romantic paradigm, embodying Hémon's vision of Québécois survival. As the novel opens, Maria is described with her father outside the church at Peribonka in the Lake St. John region. From there the narrative follows them twelve miles up-river to their isolated homestead and chronicles the next year in the life of the Chapdelaine family. Maria's love and loss and eventual reconciliation with her lot provide the primary narrative movement. Her story is interspersed with detailed accounts of day-to-day life, of agrarian Québécois society, and of relations between clergy and community, family and the land. Perhaps not the inimitable work of genius publishers have claimed it to be, *Maria Chapdelaine* is undoubtedly a better work than recent critics have allowed, and certainly a very influential novel in the Québécois tradition.

ANDRÉ LANGEVIN

Dust over the City. Toronto: McClelland and Stewart; New Canadian Library, 1974. *Tr.* John Latrobe and Robert Gottlieb (*Poussière sur la ville*. Montréal: Cercle du Livre de France, 1953). Paperback.

The action in this novel extends over a full year, yet the fall and winter predominate. The bleakest seasons in the asbestos-mining town of Macklin (based on Thetford Mines, in the Eastern Townships) coincide with the drab and sordid condition of the characters' lives. The pall of asbestos dust, the warden of subterranean passages, and the nondescript community between, provide a complex metaphor embodying the relationship between a young doctor, Alain Dubois, and his wife, Madeleine.

Dubois narrates the story of their arrival in Macklin, the failure of their marriage, the disintegration of their separate personalities, and the town's gruesome victory over them. Dubois is a classic example of the unreliable narrator: he dissembles not only to the reader, but to himself. As he recounts the winter of their discontent, he assigns the quality of heroic rebelliousness to his wife's inconstancy and casts a tragic light over his own pathetic forbearance. Madeleine is utterly fickle–a characteristic that her husband dignifies with the label "pride." He is self-pitying, though he sees pity as an ennobling virtue. The inhabitants of the town seem to be a collective adversary; Macklin is a closed, self-righteous world, a moral vacuum. Even Dubois's old mentor, Doctor Lafleur, will not pass judgement on his situation; the old doctor refuses to become morally involved, leaving Dubois to grapple with the injustice of God by himself. The priest, a practical man, disdains happiness, particularly for others. The housekeeper offers only pleasantries, tolerance without understanding. Jim the taxi-driver remains aloof, his own person. In the suffocating world of Macklin, only Madeleine, in her husband's estimation, has the courage to demand personal fulfilment.

Within days of the young couple's arrival in town, Madeleine breaks local convention by appearing in Kouri's restaurant unescorted; before long, she is seen in public clinging to the arm of a young man of the town. Eventually, she brings her lover home, while Dubois drinks in his office downstairs and miserably continues his efforts to ingratiate himself with his errant wife. The town punishes them. Madeleine kills herself, yet Dubois refuses to leave. He will remain there to pity the whole community, as he has pitied his wife.

False pity and false pride are the dimensions of Alain Dubois's miserable existence. The illusion of free will, the illusion of social order and divine justice, are the themes that obsess the young doctor, and the themes Langevin's fiction explores with chilling cynicism. *Dust over the City* is one of the most important Québécois novels preceding the Quiet Revolution. It expresses much of the social and moral blight that demanded reform.

ROGER LEMELIN

The Plouffe Family. Toronto: McClelland and Stewart;
New Canadian Library, 1975. Pages: 383. *Tr.* Mary Finch
(*Les Plouffe*. Québec: Bélisle, 1948). Paperback.

Roger Lemelin's linked novels of Quebec's lower town mark a
revolution in Québécois society and in that society's perception of
itself. In the first, *The Town Below*, Lemelin chronicles the dehumanizing conditions of urban poverty, and in so doing he resolutely dispels any residual myth of the contented habitant as an
embodiment of French Canada. With an ironic blend of passion
and detachment, he constructs a realistic image of moral and social
corruption among the oppressed working class, and the doomed,
if sometimes valiant and pathetic, efforts of several individuals
to cope, even to rise above their lot. The third novel, *In Quest of
Splendour*, while essentially a novel of social realism, exchanges
the sardonic humour of the first for an attitude of romance and a
sharper focus. It portrays the struggle of a single character to transcend the conditions of his life. The most recent is *The Crime of
Ovide Plouffe*. The second novel, *The Plouffe Family*, is most
popular. It is more satiric than the other two and features what
is, by tradition, the primary unit in Québécois society: the family.

Lemelin's evident purpose in *The Plouffe Family* is to expose
the deficits of Québécois society; to criticize the exploitive collabora-
tion of Church and tradition and to arouse sympathy for the Plouffe
family, who are the engaging victims of both. At the same time,
Lemelin satirizes the human foibles of his characters; in the family relationships, he finds such behavioural absurdities that the
Plouffes seem at once ridiculous and inspired. Ovide is the pivotal character in the novel. But, despite his indulgent vitality, he
is no more attractive than the plodding Napoleon or the petulant
and irresolute Cécile. And all the family is dominated by the
mother, Josephine.

In league with the priest, Josephine bends the lives of her
children to her will with emotional blackmail. She is all that is
well-intentioned and suffocating in this French North American
nation, which Lemelin casually calls Laurentia. But with the coming of the Second World War, her authority begins to expire. The
Church betrays her in support of the English war (one of the great

set-pieces in the novel is Lemelin's description of the Sacred Heart procession in 1940 in protest against conscription, when the Cardinal urges the Québécois into the fight). Quebec folk traditions of family life dissipate, and Josephine's children belatedly grow up and begin to take on lives of their own. By 1945, the period of the Epilogue, the Plouffes and Quebec are caught up in a state of radical change. Lemelin's vision of Quebec on the verge of the Quiet Revolution anticipates history.

ANTONINE MAILLET

La Sagouine. Toronto: Simon & Pierre, 1986. Pages: 183. *Tr.* Luis de Céspedes (*La Sagouine*. Montréal: Leméac, 1971). Paperback.

La Sagouine is not a novel; it is a person. The text of this book is a monologue, delivered by a seventy-two-year-old Acadian scrubwoman in a theatrical presentation devised by Antonine Maillet. "La Sagouine" is more than a title character, and much more than a down-at-heels raconteur; she fills the stage, and the reader's mind, with her experience and personality. More than that, she speaks for and embodies her people, the impoverished and dispossessed of our society. She articulates lives of ignorance and deprivation with pathos but never self-pity, with a wry, cynical wit and bitterness born of pride. She accepts squalor as just, as what is due to her and her kind. Her acceptance makes her at once convincing—and a tragedy. She herself is not tragic, but her condition is.

In the course of telling her story, La Sagouine provides insight into appalling poverty—pancakes reheated for three meals a day, beans for a weekend treat; life in a tumbledown shanty; death by deprivation and disease. There is nothing romantic or rustic about the real poor. She accepts that only three of her nine children survived, because there is nothing else she can do. She accepts that Christmas is for others, and always has been, that standing in the church is no worse than what she deserves, that a shack large enough to do the washing inside in winter is beyond possibility. Somehow, deep in her Acadian past, she finds a source of pride. She does not speak for all Acadians, but for the impoverished and the dispossessed, for all those in this country who live a marginal existence.

Maillet describes La Sagouine's condition without sentimentality, without false affection, and without condescension. As La Sagouine talks to her bucket, to the audience, to the reader directly, Maillet illuminates a world that has no light of its own. True, there is an indomitable quality to the old scrub-woman, but this does not provide compensation. There is much to admire in the way La Sagouine's ignorance and wit come together to mock society, to deflate sophistication, and to ridicule pretension. But this alters nothing. In her life–through wars, the Depression, the struggle to make land and sea yield up enough for survival–La Sagouine has developed a wily will to endure. This she conveys in anecdotes, jokes, fragmented bits of reminiscence, one-liners, homilies, pronouncements, and righteous judgements–all of which is held together, given narrative form and vitality, by the old woman's personality.

Pélagie. Toronto: Doubleday, 1982. Pages: 251. *Tr.* Philip
Stratford (*Pélagie-La-Charrette*. Paris: Grasset and
Leméac, 1979). Paperback.

This novel is the song of Maillet's people, the song of *Acadie*. She sings names and memories as they have been shaped by time and adversity. Louis-à-Bélonie-à-Bélonie-à-Thadée-à-Bélonie-le-Vieux Maillet and Pélagie-the-Grouch, daughter of Pélagie-à-Madeleine-à-Pélagie-the-Cart, these two, and their cohorts around the hearth in 1880, bridge in names and stories the two centuries from the Great Disruption to the present, wherein Antonine-Maillet-the-storyteller sings her novel for us, holds the Acadian soul like a mirror before us. We see ourselves, as surely as if we were their direct heirs, in that generation of eighteenth-century refugees, eight generations before our own, six generations descendent from the original settlers out of France. Some of us, of course, are. And all of us, of course, are–for this is history, this song, part of our history as a people in Canada.

This is a true story, true in spirit and true in the telling. It takes place over the span of a decade, fifteen years after the brutal expulsion of the Acadians by the British in 1755. Pélagie, a young widow, leads a raggedy band of her compatriots home from Georgia, overland by oxen-cart–home by the back door, as they say, where they will resettle and for another hundred years will live in seclusion, afraid of being banished again, and for another hundred years after that will live on the edge of the society that displaced them. Until now: until the present, where they speak and sing of themselves and hold their own in the world again.

Along the route, Pélagie's caravan picks up remnants of their people, scattered throughout the continent. They lose some to death, to disease, to starvation. Some turn south for Louisiana; some disappear. Through ten winters and against incredible hardships, Pélagie drives her band with indomitable courage. Taking on the mantle of legend as she goes, she is accompanied by equally legendary companions: the feral child, Catoune, grown to womanhood; the club-footed midwife and healer, Celina; the giant, P'tite Goule; the cantankerous centenarian storyteller, Bélonie. And there are Landrys, Giroués, Cormiers, Maillets, LeBlancs, Robichauds, Belliveaus, Thibodeaus, Allains, and Bastaraches, Richards, and more. There are many names, many strains, to the Acadian caravan, the hope of a new *Acadie*. And intersecting the great overland trek as it passes through Charleston and Baltimore, Philadelphia (to coincide with independence celebrations for the birth of the new American republic) and Boston, are encounters with the four-masted ship of Pélagie's lover, Captain Broussard-called-Beausoleil, who himself becomes legend for carrying others of their countrymen home.

There are gripping and heroic tales of adventure along the route, interspersed with commentary by descendants of Pélagie and Bélonie a hundred years later, and the occasional comment by the "author," a hundred years after that, in the present. But what makes this novel a work of such genius is the hypnotic quality of the language as the narrative ranges from mythic to realistic, ironic to romantic. Maillet turns the litany of Acadian names into poetry; the people in exile, like the Hebrews in Genesis/Exodus, themselves become poetry. She writes with a richness of language, with repetition of key phrases like echoes, with images as exact and elusive as pride, with words that sing, and we read with exhilaration and are deeply moved by the experiences and the lives we are privileged to share.

Without stories there cannot be a people. Without language and imagination shaped by their struggle through history, there cannot be a people. In writing this beautiful and loving account, Maillet assures her people long life. Her literary achievement with *Pélagie* has been recognized by the Prix Goncourt. Her desire to avenge her ancestors has been accomplished with the fierce and affectionate energy she lavishes upon them. *Pélagie* is a fine tribute, and a fine gift to the people of Canada (for it is with stories such as this that we do become a "people").

ANDRÉ MAJOR

Man on the Run. Dunvegan: Quadrant, 1984. Pages: 114. *Tr.* David Lobdell (*Les Rescapes*. Montréal: Editions Quinze, 1976.) Paperback.

Man on the Run is the third in a series, following *The Scarecrows of Saint-Emmanuel* and *Inspector Therien*. It might as easily have been part three of a single work. While it stands alone, all three participate in a common if somewhat disjointed vision, with common characters and an elusive continuity of situation, mood, and motif. It is a bleak vision of contemporary Quebec, paradoxically related with a strong affection for the details of everyday life. Through the curiously disembodied quality of his prose Major has created a world that resembles actuality and yet is somehow quite separate from it, a world more akin to the folk myth than to ordinary experience.

Although *Man on the Run* is barely more than a hundred pages in length, it so deftly shades in the complexity of its characters' lives that it seems like a major opus. It is slow-moving and dense, without conventional transitions from one sub-plot or storyline to another, with no attempt to tie them together or sort them out. Rather than being put off, frustrated because we cannot get into this world, we are mesmerized by our condition as captive, unable to get out. On a gut level, we share the anxiety and gloom of these people in the novel. At the same time we are aware that the suffocating condition of their lives originates with themselves. Our response is disturbingly ambivalent: our admiration for the author's talent is coupled with our distress from the impact of his achievement.

Major's novel is dominated by a sinuous and sometimes sordid sensuality. There are at least four separate stories, all but one of which is concerned with unpleasant relations between the sexes. In one, Momo Boulanger, having escaped from prison and found, or perhaps caught, Inspector Therien frozen to death in a bear trap, kidnaps the pregnant Marie-Rose and holes up with her in a ghost town through the winter, after which she takes her infant and leaves him, a fugitive living by his wits alone in the wilderness. In another, Jerome Poirier becomes mayor of Saint-Emmanuel, then a member of the National Assembly, while his brother's wife entertains selected "clients" and strips at the hotel he owns. His own wife, who has left him, lives in the city where she has an affair with the ex-mayor before dumping him for a fling in Toronto. In yet another story, an old man rescues a woman from her dissolute husband, and she, after living with him for a while and watching him die, takes up with Calixa Boulanger, Momo's brother. And so it goes: brief narrative fragments, close descriptions of buildings and the landscape, of the textures and the touch of things, provide dimension and atmosphere. It is all quite sad, except perhaps for the muted affection of Calixa for the eventual woman of his life. It is a gloomy existential vision of a world that, rather disconcertingly, is separate from but intersects our own.

CLAIRE MARTIN
(CLAIRE FAUCHER)

Best Man. Ottawa: Oberon, 1983. Pages: 149. *Tr.* David Lobdell (*Doux-Amer*. Montréal: Le Cercle du Livre de France, 1960). Paperback.

Best Man is a most unusual love story. The perspective and personality of the narrator make it unusual. He is at the same time passionately involved, consumed by an obsessive love, and dispassionately objective, meticulously analytic about the whole protracted affair. *Best Man* is a story of love, loss, compromise, and reconciliation. It is told by a man who allows the most intimate details of his emotional life to lie revealed before us, yet he conveys such revelations with cool dispatch. We are intrigued, and we are unnerved, as we read of his willingness to suffer for love, if suffering is all he can retain of it rather than lose it entirely. We are disconcerted less by the pain he willingly endures than by his apparent understanding of his own behaviour. We share with him the extreme discomfort of being caught, suspended, and strung out between emotional and intellectual realities. This, surely, is the very experience of love.

The narrator lives in a somewhat disembodied world. External details are not important. Behaviour and response are everything. For ten years, he loves Gabrielle Lubin. He is a publisher; she, a writer. They do not live together. His devotion is met with quiet affection, with acceptance. Suddenly, she drops him. Her new lover quickly becomes her husband. His name is Michel Bullard. He uses her. He is eight years younger, only thirty-four. The narrator is devastated. He insinuates himself into their life, clinging desperately to remnants of the past, fragments of affection. The ecstasy of being in her presence yields within him sufficient compensation to let him bear the pain. Gradually, as Gabrielle's marital affair deteriorates, he finds himself more and more comfortable with his own sometimes extreme emotions. The tension of the narrative, and within the narrator, between thought and feeling is articulated episodically in the story of Gabrielle and Michel. When Gabrielle's love story is complete, when the cool self-willed Gabrielle has exhausted the limits of passion, she returns to the narrator. And he accepts her. Them. It is enough.

I am not sure that the narrator has a name. So inseparable is his consciousness of the world from his reader's own, it does not occur as a question, any more than it would to query one's own name while reading. He is aware and therefore is, as we are. This does not mean his personality is passive or indistinct, such that it is displaced by the reader's. What it means is that he is so well realized as a character, by virtue not of what he perceives and experiences, but of how, that while reading we only know the world as he knows it; our personality is displaced by his. Only the finest of writers could accomplish this. Claire Martin, even in translation, is a very fine, subtle, and powerful writer. It is a pity she is not more widely read.

JACQUES POULIN

The *Jimmy Trilogy*. Toronto: Anansi, 1979. Pages: 250.
Tr. Sheila Fischman. Paperback.

My Kingdom for a Horse (*Mon cheval pour un royaumen*. Montreal: Editions du Jour, 1967.) Pages: 9-58.

This brief novel is a fine introduction to the unusual narrative imagination of Jacques Poulin. He tells a story that demands our attention, although it is difficult to say just what the story is about. In this novel (and despite its brevity it seems a novel, not a novella), Pierre Delisle is a writer and in the opening and closing passages is apparently in jail, talking to a confessor, or, more likely, in a hospital run by nuns, talking to a psychiatrist. The bulk of the novel is his account of the recent past, by which he intends to explain his present situation. Obsessed with what he calls his carapace, his protective/imprisoning shell, he carries on a desultory *ménage à trois* with Nathalie and the philosopher-turned-caleche-driver-turned-suicide, Simon. He becomes involved in a terrorist plot and is wounded when he plants a bomb by a statue on the Plains of Abraham. He ruminates a good deal, especially about his carapace and about being some kind of zouave (literally, a soldier; these two words, zouave and carapace, are repeated and repeated in this and the other novels until the reader is driven nearly to distraction). He is an intellectual and, by his own admission, capable of feeling little. His story is not quite what I have described, for nothing in it is as substantial or coherent as the above suggests. Reality is much more ephemeral, as Poulin renders it; meaning and significance are much more elusive than paraphrase might imply. To read such fiction is to be lost among tangibles, to find oneself a spectre in the palpable world contained by the text.

Jimmy (*Jimmy*. Montreal: Editions du Jour, 1969.)
Pages: 59-156.

Jimmy is about an eleven-year-old boy who calls himself after world driving champion Jimmy Clark and prides himself on being "the biggest liar in the whole city of Québec." Most of the novel is set at the family cottage on the banks of the St. Lawrence, and in the fragmented imaginary world of the self-professed young expert on stories, racing cars, helicopters, boats, and much else besides. His mother is recovering from a miscarriage. His father is a psychiatrist who spends most of his time in the attic writing a book on Hemingway. His special friend is the old Commodore in the next cottage. His closest companion is a cat. He is a child of his times: alive in a world shaped by television, by an oblique understanding of adult experience, and by his own irrepressible imagination. Poulin's rendition of childhood is curiously poignant, with an underlying element of terror.

The Heart of the Blue Whale. (*Le Coeur de la baleine bleue.* Montreal: Editions du Jour, 1971.) Pages: 157-250.

And then. And then you read the third novel of the trilogy, and inexplicably the three collapse and become one. The connections among them are tenuous, surreal. There is a caleche driver called Simon here; he is a character in death's dream kingdom, calling the narrator to him. There is Charlie the Blue Whale, the young girl whose heart beats in the narrator's chest after a transplant and whom he dreams a relationship with and almost loves. There is Jimmy at the cottage, Jimmy the character in the writer-narrator's newest work of fiction. The narrator's name is Noel. His wife's is Elise, or Eglise. The man she leaves Noel for is a hockey player called Bill. Noel's doctor is Grondon; the old waitress is Marie. The setting is Quebec City. The distance between Noel and his imagined world disappears; between Poulin and his fiction, between us and Poulin's novel. It all makes sense on some level we cannot quite grasp—and dare not, lest it collapse into meaninglessness.

After reading these novels, originally published with two years between each, I cannot decide whether I have been genuinely engaged or merely manipulated into thinking so. It does not really matter, since the end is the same. I have been caught up, as a reader, in a psycho-realistic world that conforms to some other conception/perception of reality than my own or what I might, outside the text, think feasible. I have been made to care, beyond understanding; made to respond, when the rational impulse is to

reject. I have been drawn into what Roch Carrier calls in his introduction to *The Jimmy Trilogy* "a serious game between reader
and writer." It is an experience I would not for the world have
missed.

RINGUET
(PHILIPPE PANNETON)

Thirty Acres. Toronto: McClelland and Stewart; New
Canadian Library, 1960. Pages: 249. *Tr.* Dorothea and
Felix Walter (*Trente arpents*. Paris: Flammarion, 1938).
Paperback.

Thirty Acres is possibly the single most important novel in the
Québécois tradition. As with most revolutionary phenomena, it
is a turning-in upon the traditions that preceded it, as well as a
breaking away from those traditions. Ringuet's novel incorporates
major elements of the *roman de la terre*, the principal fictional
expression of Québécois life until that time. But *Thirty Acres* is
insistently realistic, hard-edged, and ironic. The virtues celebrated
in *Maria Chapdelaine* have their counterparts in vice and folly in
Ringuet's vision of the ancestral farm, the family, and the parish
church.

The novel portrays the cycles of Euchariste Moisan's life, measuring it out in protracted seasons, and draws tragedy and pathos
out of the fertile soil of a Quebec farm. The land itself remains
the same but times change, and time changes. Man's pride,
which gives him dominion over family and farm, precedes his fall.
Euchariste inherits thirty acres on the north shore of the St. Lawrence at age twenty-three. He marries, fathers a dozen children,
guides his farm through years of prosperity, and is supplanted by
his own offspring. He finishes his days as a night watchman in a
garage in the United States, living with a younger son's hostile
family and surrounded by an unknown language and an alien
lifestyle. His commitment to progress as a young man fills him
with pride in his own achievements; but gradually that commitment gives way, through a series of defeats and the passage of

time, to a crabbed conservatism, and to his eventual displacement from the land. It is a tragic reversal; the exercise of traditional virtues, and defiance against traditional restraints, leads to a period of prosperity – and then to ignominious deprivation.

It might be argued that Moisan's downfall is through *hubris*, the consequence of his own personality. But Ringuet makes it clear that Euchariste Moisan is a character formed by the traditions and conditions of his rural Québécois society, and that even at his most rebellious, his behaviour is consistent with traditional values. *Thirty Acres* is a disturbing account, written in prose that is both precise and richly allusive. Ringuet's style is timeless: the novel could as easily have been written a century ago or yesterday, but for its unrelenting irony and insistent realism.

GABRIELLE ROY

The Tin Flute. Toronto: McClelland and Stewart; New
Canadian Library, 1981. Pages: 384. *Tr.* Alan Brown
(*Bonheur d'occasion*. Montréal: Editions Pascal, 1945).
Paperback.

Gabrielle Roy's first novel is also her most celebrated. She is a major writer in both English and French Canada, and her books are as highly appraised and appreciated in translation as in the original. *The Tin Flute* is a Canadian classic, and its author a writer of world stature. There is little formal innovation in this particular novel; instead, Roy combines a precise and unambiguous style, uncomplicated linear plot development, a conventional third-person omniscient point of view, and a discrete but engaged voice to serve as a balance for the radical specificity of detail that makes her book seem such an authentic portrait of an economic and spiritual slum. The novel is set in pre-war Saint-Henri, in Montreal, and evokes conditions that everywhere signify poverty and ignorance.

With great compassion, Roy describes the life of young Florentine Lacasse and her family; the narrative grows around Florentine's pathetic yearning to rise above her bleak situation.

Against the story of Rose-Anna, the loving mother of twelve; Azarius, the dreamer-father; Florentine's dying brother, Daniel; and the impoverished life of the family, Roy describes Florentine's grasping need for Jean Lévesque, by whom she becomes pregnant, and the touching love of Emmanuel Létourneau, who marries her. Florentine is a vain and shallow product of her world; her life holds the promise only of a squalid future. She does not even have the memory of a happy rural past, now inaccessible, that taunts her mother—the idyllic past of the oppressed urban Québécois that perhaps never really was.

In a world of such poverty there seems no room for hope or dreams. Only with the coming of the Second World War does the cycle of despair promise to break. Its bleakness offset by compassion, *The Tin Flute* sensitively conveys a vision of soul-depleting conditions and of ordinary personalities struggling to cope, to survive.

Where Nests the Water Hen. Toronto: McClelland and Stewart; New Canadian Library, 1970. Pages: 160. *Tr*. Harry L. Binsse (*La Petite Poule d'eau*. Montréal: Beauchemin, 1950). Paperback.

In some respects, Gabrielle Roy's work is out of keeping with modern Quebec literature. Perhaps betraying her own origins as a Franco-Manitoban, her books are readily aligned with the English-Canadian sensibility. This is as true of her urbane and heavily ironic novels like *The Tin Flute, The Cashier*, and *Windflower* as of her more gentle works like *Where Nests the Water Hen* and *Street of Riches*. By discussing only her first two full-length works, I do not mean to suggest that only these are important. She continued for a generation to be prolific and proficient. But as evidence of her great breadth of vision and understanding, one need go no further.

While *The Tin Flute* is a sombre social document, *Where Nests the Water Hen* is a novel of joy and hope and unity in the face of oppressive geographical and social isolation; it is also the story of sadness, of loss, and of resignation in the face of time and change. Ultimately it is a simple story of life endured and life embraced, told with warmth and compassion. Part one tells of Luzina Tousignant's annual pilgrimage from her island home, on the Little Water Hen in northern Manitoba, through Portage de Près to Rorketon and thence to Sainte Rose du Lac to have another child. It is a complete story in itself, yet it anticipates the second part of the novel. This part is devoted to the school that the Tousignants build behind their house; it tells of Luzina's dreams and the forbearance of Hippolyte, her husband, and of the frustrations and ambitions of the children. Through government aid, a series of teachers come to the school in consecutive summers: the beautiful young Mademoiselle Côté, the pathetically embittered Miss O'Rorke, and the indolent Armand Dubreuil. Then no more come. But these three strangers are enough to stir the imaginations of the Tousignant children: one by one they leave home. Edmond becomes a doctor, Josephine a teacher. There is great sadness in telling of their loss into the world.

Part three provides another dimension of the story. It is an account of Father Joseph-Marie, who journeys to the Tousignants' for a visit. His mission along the way, his love, simplicity, and intelligence, his worldliness and naïveté, his good humour and ambition, all make him an ideal foil for the Tousignants; he is a representative of the Canada beyond the Little Water Hen. In its separate parts, this novel appears to be simple in theme and structure; yet consideration reveals it to be a rich and complex work by one of Canada's most accomplished novelists.

FELIX-ANTOINE SAVARD

Master of the River. Montreal: Harvest House, 1976.
Pages: 135. *Tr.* Richard Howard (*Menaud,*
maître-draveur. Montréal: Editions Fides, 1964).
Paperback.

Savard's novel celebrates the French-Canadian race with all the force and naïve authenticity of an epic folk poem. At the same time, Savard laments the waning strength of the people and their diminished sovereignty over their ancestral lands. In a simple story, he describes lost glory: the past is elevated to the level of myth and forebears to the stature of heroes. For three hundred years, the French in Canada have been lords of the land they tilled and masters of the forest wilderness. But as the twentieth century closes around them, English-speaking outsiders buy up timber leases and limit access to the lands. In his lament, Savard's language is simple yet ornate, like liturgical prose; it is filled with uncomplicated images of the natural world, as if it were the outward expression of the French-Canadian soul.

Savard has created a haunting threnody. Yet it is a warning, too, of what is yet to come, and a strident call to arms. Scattered through the narrative like sporadic echoes of doom are references to Louis Hémon's *Maria Chapdelaine*. Savard accepts the earlier novel's romantic vision as authentic; he documents, in equally romantic and far more poetic terms, the failure of the "folk" to stand fast against the encroachments of the outside world. His protagonist, Menaud, is a widower with two grown children. Menaud agonizes over his generation's betrayal of the past and pins his hopes on his children. But his son dies in a log jam, and his daughter becomes engaged to a scoundrel bent on selling out to the English. Then the man his daughter truly loves, young Alexis Tremblay, offers to become Menaud's ally. Menaud rises above his personal tragedy to fight the tragedy threatening his people. Together, the young man and the old man foment revolution. But the indifference of the people leads to failure, and Menaud goes mad. In the end, Alexis and Marie are united on a spot of land enclosed by the English outsiders. *Master of the River* is a bitter vision of loss and betrayal; paradoxically, it is a call for pride and self-possession, a rallying cry for a people threatened with extinction.

YVES THERIAULT

Agaguk. Toronto: Ryerson, 1967. Pages: 229. *Tr.* Miriam Chapin (*Agaguk*. Paris: Grasset, 1958). Paperback.

It is hard to imagine a more authentic representation of Eskimo life than this powerful novel, set in the tundra wilderness of the eastern Arctic during the late 1930s. The third-person narrative voice shifts deftly from documentary omniscience to a casual, intimate knowledge of the characters' lives. Never does Theriault pretend to be other than an outsider, but his knowledge is thorough and comfortably integrated with the dramatic action. Uncannily, the reader seems to experience Eskimo reality without quite understanding it.

The novel describes the struggle of a young hunter, Agaguk, and his wife, Iriook, to survive on their own away from the tribal village. In the wilderness, they gradually and painfully rework age-old customs of behaviour to suit private necessity. Although Agaguk and Iriook do not realize it, their lives ring the changes from primitive to modern as they struggle, against inhuman traditions, to keep what is best of the old, and as they fight against exploitive civilization to gain what is best of the white man's world. Although the novel is filled with moral implication, Theriault does not judge – or, rather, his judgements are never simplistic, for he recognizes that morality is a relative thing. The time of absolute authority – of chief over tribe, of man over woman, of strong over weak – is passing. Cruelty and cunning might once have been necessary, but they no longer serve the Eskimo needs.

Theriault chronicles the struggles between Agaguk and Iriook; between the humans and the unforgiving environment; between the two rebels and the other members of the tribe. Set against the story of Agaguk is a tale of murder and intrigue in the village where Agaguk's father is chief. Thematic and dramatic dimensions of the novel work in perfect harmony. Leaving his father's village, Agaguk is literally turning away from the tyrannical past. He fights a renegade wolf to protect his son, and his features are mutilated; thus his old identity is literally obscured. In letting his infant daughter live, he anticipates a new era. Theriault has so richly endowed his fiction with layers of meaning and allusion that it might be read as an allegory of modern Quebec, or of the new woman, or of Western civilization, or of moral relativism. But above all it is a moving account of Eskimos in their own harsh and beautiful land.

MICHEL TREMBLAY

Thérèse and Pierrette and the Little Hanging Angel.
Toronto: McClelland and Stewart, 1984. Pages: 262.
Tr. Sheila Fischman (*Thérèse et Pierrette a l'école des Saints-Anges*. Montréal: Les Editions Leméac, 1980).
Paperback.

In this novel, Michel Tremblay comes across as a gentle genius of the commonplace. As he did in his celebrated 1968 play, *Les Belles Soeurs*, he illuminates the working-class world of Montreal tenements, Québécois Catholicism, and stifled aspirations, all with deep affection tempered by sardonic wit. This is a slow novel to read–not because it drags but because Tremblay refuses to be hurried in his lavish descriptions of the little experiences felt by ordinary people in the course of their ordinary lives. He invests the everyday with a kind of narrative magic, as if here, for this time only, these people and the incidents of their lives will be given the spotlight–so let all of their foibles, their meanness, their insularity, and the warmth of their world be exposed to the glare. He is a writer of great understanding, however, but limited insight. He knows intimately the restrictions that religion, poverty, and ignorance impose on the lives of his characters, but he seems either insensitive or uninterested in the more profound implications of these, in terms of sensibility, Québécois society, or the world at large. Neither the subtleties nor the larger significance of human behaviour seem to interest him nearly so much as the surface of things.

Thérèse and Pierrette and the Little Hanging Angel has many subplots but no principal narrative focus. It is set in a working-class parish of Montreal called Saint Stanislas-de-Kostka, mostly in and around the Ecole des Saints-Anges, where for a week in June, 1942, all attention is directed toward mounting the procession for the annual Corpus Christi celebration. Sister Sainte-Catherine, in charge of preparations, is locked in a terrible battle with the principal, Mother Benoîte des Anges, who is, in turn, involved in a variety of power struggles within the Church community. Despite animosities, the spirited Sister Sainte-Catherine once again gets the procession rolling, drawing on her Grade Six girls, especially the trio known as Thérèse-n-Pierrette (Simone, the unnamed third, whose harelip has been surgically repaired before the novel opens, is the weakest, and ends up playing the "hanging angel" to Pierrette's Virgin and Thérèse's St. Bernadette). Simone's brother has a crush on Pierrette; and the neighbourhood Lothario has a potentially dangerous obsession with Thérèse–this is perhaps the most sinister element in the novel. Certain nuns have crushes on other nuns; many of them pair off in awkward parodies of romantic love. Thérèse's little brother Marcel has an invisible talking cat called Duplessis and visits an invisible family next door. Simone's father is crabby; her mother is proud. And so it goes. Details accumulate. The picture becomes more and more intricate. Everything is curiously the same size and has the same importance: there is no perspective, no shading toward the centre, no variation of pace or texture. Tremblay's parish of Saint Stanislas-de-Kostka is like one of those popular paintings of city life that, for its lack of focus and perspective, reminds one vaguely of wallpaper.

Yet the pastels have shadows: behind the smiles, tears; behind the snarls, sadness. This is no ordinary cityscape but a meticulously rendered panorama of the human comedy against a backdrop of war, poverty, and spiritual privation. People here are mean, small, nasty, and often ignorant. Yet, for all of that, they are the object of the author's affection, which we as readers are privileged to share.

PIERRE TURGEON

The First Person. Ottawa: Oberon, 1982. Pages: 79.
Tr. David Lobdell (*La Premiére personne*. Montréal:
Editions Quinze, 1981).

Postmodernism in Canadian or Québécois novels is usually a matter of form, but this novel articulates the extremes of postmodernism as a philosophy. Apart from the sustained disjunction of narrative fragments, which creates the impression of a narrator uninterested in the procedures of narrative, the form of this novel is quite arbitrary and conventional. As might be expected, the narrator displays an obsessive concern with language and the relationship between words and personal being. There are violations of genre and generic effect, as elements of confessional fiction clash with bits of a detective romance and eruptive smatterings of contemplative fiction, social realism, macabre psychological exposition, and sordid mean-street naturalism. There is nothing particularly innovative about such formal erraticism, especially when it is contained within a rigid narrative structure that is slavishly coherent in terms of time and space; and it is only mildly disconcerting to read a narrative voice that seems to lose track of itself. However, it is a weird and unusual experience in a Canadian novel to encounter postmodernism as a philosophy, a view of the world as an absurd, amoral, degenerate, and irredeemable context in which the charade of human existence is played out.

Appropriately, perhaps, Turgeon has set his novel mostly in Los Angeles. From Quebec to California is a journey from entombment to the land of the living dead. The narrator deserts his job as a computer operator one hundred feet underground, below rue Parthenais in Montreal, leaves his wife and their two children (with whom he shares a mutual indifference), and absconds to California with utterly no feelings of remorse whatsoever, with only a new identity, fabricated through the computer, as a detective named Marc Fréchette. (The name is taken from the lead actor in Antonioni's film *Zabriskie Point*, who subsequently died an absurd and pathetic/bathetic death in prison–possibly the victim of murder.) As a wholly synthetic product of the television age, the narrator locates himself at the heart of the displaced American heartland. California is the centre of mindless violence and mindless sex, of life as a consumer product, of a world with highways and heroin as the perimeters of experience, with hockey as a surreal equivalent for reality and artificial ice as a fitting spot beneath which to bury the dead. This is a world of such imagined brutality that bodies crushed by onrushing traffic are dismembered and pulverized out of existence. It is a world of such grotesque brutality that parts of a woman's corpse frozen into the ice of a hockey rink protrude above the surface, inviting the narrator to kiss ice over frozen lips. It is the world of Forest Lawn and Hollywood and dismal nightclubs, corrupt detectives, sleazy relationships. It is an entirely appropriate context for a Québécois dreamer who has no soul, no identity, no self except what an exploration of words and syntactical patterns might yield up to him, should he ever try to discover rather than evade himself.

A sordid urgency pervades this novel, paradoxically combined with enervating disinterestedness. Fragments of nearly incoherent speculation on the relations between mathematics and psychology, language and the nature of existence, are scattered virtually at random throughout the narrative. As the narrator connects with Carly, whose husband hires him to find her, and has an affair with her at her lover's home while he, a goaltender, is on tour, bits and pieces of utterly purposeless violence and scathing epithets punctuate the story and awkwardly force its progress toward completion. It is not a pleasant world that by the inherent fascination for moral absurdity we as readers are forced to share.

The First Person is representative of a phenomenon of the 1980s, in which the contemporary culture of Quebec seems intent on assimilating the North American world – not *being* assimilated – and transforming it into the authentic experience of Quebec. Ironically, this brings Turgeon more into line with mainstream writers of English Canada, writers like Atwood and Ondaatje, in whose work the metamorphosis of American experience into Canadian reality is of major consequence. This does not, of course, make him less Québécois. Nor does the constrained vision of his compatriots as "a people of no passion and no destiny" mean he is not one of them. He is.

CANADIAN NOVELS FOR
YOUNG READERS

The novels in this section have been selected on the basis of their enduring appeal to young readers. Some are genuine works of literary art; others are popular fiction directed towards a limited readership. Several novels in the main section of this book, such as *The Harbour Master, The Incredible Journey*, and *Lords of the North*, might have been included here, but for one reason or another demanded more detailed consideration. Conversely, a few of the novels here, like *Hold Fast, The King's Daughter*, and *What's the Matter, Girl?* might easily sustain more elaborate critical response. Rather than separating the novels into formal categories, I have simply suggested what I feel is the most appropriate age range in each case. This information is contained in square brackets at the end of the bibliographical note for each entry. I am indebted for assistance throughout this section to my daughters Julie and Laura Moss, without whose patience and enthusiasm, curiosity and lively intelligence, this part of the *Reader's Guide* would never have been written. (For the *Second Edition* I have been on my own: Julie and Laura are now more at home with adult literature. I miss their advice here but benefited from it a great deal in writing the new entries for the main section.)

ELIZABETH BROCHMANN

What's the Matter, Girl? New York: Harper & Row,
1980. Pages: 121. [15 up]

This is a beautiful and moving novel. It is not a children's book, but it is not quite an adult novel either. *What's the Matter, Girl?* is the sensitive account of a thirteen-year-old's coming of age in a fallen world. It is told in the present tense, with numerous flashbacks, from the limited perspective of young Anna Swales as she awaits the return of her beloved Uncle Arion from Hitler's war;

and then it follows for a brief time her devastated response to the imbecilic state in which the war has left him.

This is a tough and bitter time for the young protagonist, related in language that is simple and sometimes raw, in detail that is sometimes chilling. It is a time of moral confusion, as Anna considers the letters Arion wrote her from the Front, letters of horrific conditions and monstrous behaviour written to her on Vancouver Island, near Port Salish, in the heart of a large and ordinarily eccentric family. It is a time of sexual confusion, as Anna struggles to understand her overwhelming affection for her soldier-uncle, only a few years older than herself. And it becomes a time of disillusionment when Arion finally appears–the collapse of childhood; the end of innocence.

All of this is related from a point of view that makes the harsh realities of the adult world seem a violent intrusion. There is a directness that one finds in the best of writing for young readers; and there is not that double vision essential to adult fiction of growing up, in which the images of childhood are played against the mature sensibility of a narrating voice or authorial vision. In this novel the narrator is a child, caught up in the immediacy of her own experience, and her context is created as an extension of her experience rather than as an objective world in itself. As a work of adult fiction, *What's the Matter, Girl?* might be considered somewhat simplistic and might seem to lack dimension. Yet these same characteristics make it accessible, and fascinating, to young readers who are sufficiently mature to cope with disturbing insights into the complexity of the human condition.

MORLEY CALLAGHAN

Luke Baldwin's Vow. Philadelphia: Winston, 1948.
Richmond Hill: Scholastic-TAB, 1975. Pages: 187.
Paperback. [11–14]

Still in his pre-teens, Luke Baldwin is orphaned and left in the charge of his Aunt Helen and Uncle Henry, who live in Collingwood on Georgian Bay. Henry Baldwin is a rational, practical man. Through the course of the novel, Luke tries to follow his dying father's admonitions to learn from his uncle, but finds Henry a man without imagination whose emotional life is sorely diminished by his "good sense." Uncle Henry manages his mill business successfully and earns Luke's respect but has little understanding of people or affection for them. Ironically, what Luke learns from him is to protect himself from the practical people of the world. Callaghan builds his narrative around the relationship between Luke and the old dog he finds at his aunt and uncle's, a collie called Dan. In several fantasy interludes and a detailed account of their shared activities, the author conveys the strength and vitality of their relationship–and its impracticality. Deciding the old dog is useless, Uncle Henry condemns him to death. In a highly dramatic rescue episode, Luke retrieves old Dan from the river bottom, and on the advice of an elderly neighbour bargains with his uncle for Dan's life with money he will make rounding up cattle in the evenings. His uncle accepts the offer. Luke vows thereafter to be wary of practical people, and the reader is left with the strong feeling that the most important things in life are not necessarily related to hard work and good sense. Callaghan is one of our most celebrated novelists. His precise style and fast pacing are ideally suited to fiction for young readers. *Luke Baldwin's Vow* remains an intriguing and thought-provoking novel.

CATHERINE ANTHONY CLARK

The Golden Pine Cone. Toronto: Macmillan, 1950.
Pages: 182. [11–14]

Bren and Lucy find a golden earring in the shape of a pine cone near their log home in the British Columbia interior, and that is the beginning of their strange, fantastical adventures. The earring was stolen from the spirit Tekontha, and if the wicked Nasookin finds it Tekontha will not be able to protect the country from his mischief. Possession of the pine cone has transported Bren and Lucy into this Other World, while still leaving them in touch with their own. With Ooshka, their dog (who can talk, in the enchanted world, just as the other animals can talk), Bren and Lucy set out on a quest to the valley of Tekontha to return her magic earring and to preserve her benevolent power. Along the way, weird and exciting encounters with a monstrous snake, a kind old mammoth beast, Squareheads and Ice People, the Wild Woman, Head Goose, Frogskins, Fungus Man, and myriad other creatures precede the children's inevitable success. Clark spins out a fascinating and sometimes diffuse tale of fantasy and adventure. Her prose is a trifle archaic and her human characters are curiously less convincing than her imaginary ones, at least to the contemporary reader; but on the whole, this novel deserves recognition and appreciation as an offbeat children's classic.

LYN COOK

The Bells on Finland Street. Toronto: Macmillan, 1950. 1978. Pages: 197. [11–14]

The bells ring through fairyland when someone smiles, according to a Finnish legend, and sometimes they can be heard even in the ordinary world. Lyn Cook makes them peal on Finland Street in Sudbury, where her ten-year-old protagonist, Elin, triumphs over poverty and prejudice. Adults who have not lost the knack of guileless response will shudder with pleasure as they follow Elin's story; children will be charmed by its innocent sentimentality. Elin Laukka, an immigrant girl, yearns to take figure-skating lessons with her friends. Because her father earns so little as a miner, Elin has to work for a kindly neighbourhood grocer to pay for the skates and lessons. All goes well – until her father has an accident at work. Elin must pay the property taxes on their home and forgo her dream. But then her grandfather, visiting from Finland, buys her a pair of skates and teaches her to skate himself. By the annual Carnival she is good enough to join her friends representing Finland in the pageant; and she dreams of some day skating for Canada in Finland. Elin's triumph is a suitably uplifting close to a warm story packed full of lofty ideals and numerous rhetorical commentaries–about Canada, about the hardships of immigrant experience, about democracy, Sudbury, nickel, Finland, and familial bonds. Curiously, the pedagogical intent of the novel, although softened by its emotional richness, betrays a flaw that many contemporary readers will find disconcerting: Cook seems unaware of social injustice–epitomized by an impoverished family trying to survive on Inco wages–or of sexism–implicit in her insistence on gender stereotypes–or of the haunting pathos of finding beauty in clouds of sulphur, pride in glowing mounds of slag. Despite its social naïveté, however, *The Bells on Finland Street* is a delightful novel. There is inspiration aplenty to compensate for its occasional lapses of conscience.

MONIQUE CORRIVEAU

The Wapiti. Toronto: Macmillan, 1968. Pages: 188.
Tr. J.M. L'Heureux (*Le Wapiti*. Québec: Les Editions
Jeunesse, 1964). [13 up]

This enthralling historical romance opens in 1656 and follows, for a decade, the exploits of a most remarkable youth. In the course of describing Matthew Rousseau's adventures in New France and among the mighty Seskanoo Indians to the west (a fictional composite), Corriveau reveals a plenitude of documentary knowledge about the people and customs of the period. She writes with authority about everything from the seventeenth-century architecture of Quebec City to the various Indian methods of making snowshoes. But, what is most important, all her details are fully integrated into the narrative; they are presented in terms of Matthew's experiences rather than as background information. Corriveau is particularly perceptive in illuminating the psychological differences between the Indians and the French. When Matthew is kidnapped by Iroquois and adopted by a Seskanoo chief, after he has fled Quebec for a murder he did not commit, the author has ample opportunity to describe Indian life. The Seskanoo have had no previous direct contact with whites. Through strength of character, through luck, and by understanding the primitive wisdom of his hosts, Matthew soon earns their highest respect. When the whole of New France is threatened by an Indian massacre, and the French prove reluctant to being saved, Matthew courageously barters his good reputation among the Indians, and his life, for peace throughout the colony. What more could any reader of historical romance demand? Matthew is no ordinary hero. Grown from a foundling draper's apprentice of fifteen to a mighty woodsman, sensitive artist, imaginative cartographer, and citizen of the wilderness, he will captivate almost any reader's imagination. Real life among the Indians and the French in Canada's earliest days comes alive in *The Wapiti*, and at the novel's centre is one of the most dynamic and engaging protagonists our fiction has produced.

MARY ALICE AND JOHN DOWNIE

Honor Bound. Toronto: Oxford, 1971. 1980. Pages: 192. Paperback. [13 up]

Honor Bound is among the very best historical novels for young readers to come out of English Canada. In prose that is eminently readable and often quite lyrical, it describes the saga of a United Empire Loyalist family who flee Philadelphia after the American Revolution to settle on rugged farmland just west of what is now Kingston. Through the Avery family, the authors provide the Loyalist view of a period dominated in the Canadian imagination by American folklore and tradition: loyalty to the king is admirable; republican democracy is, in practice, tyranny of the majority. It is a refreshing perspective. All members of the Avery family are important to the narrative during their perilous journey northwards through Albany and Oswego to Cataraqui and then to their land grant. But once they are settled, it is thirteen-year-old Miles who dominates the story. Miles and Sam Trick and their thieving friend Alf Brown have a variety of adventures among the Indians and in the wilderness; their escapades culminate in a hair-raising race down the St. Lawrence to prevent

Miles's sister, Honor, from embarking for England in despair over the apparent demise of her family. The Downies skilfully blend intrigue and excitement with a rich assortment of detail about pioneer life in Ontario. Characterization is first-rate: the main characters come alive and the secondary ones are suitably outlined. And there are enough twists of plot and shiftings of fortune to maintain the reader's rapt attention. *Honor Bound* is excellent fiction, and can be enjoyed by readers of all ages.

BRIAN DOYLE

Angel Square. Vancouver: Groundwood/Douglas & McIntyre, 1984. Pages: 127. Paperback. [11–15]

It is hard to imagine a novel delivering more to the young reader than *Angel Square*. It is funny and fast-paced; it is teeming with sentimentality, disguised but not obscured by the street-wise toughness of its young protagonist. It is a mystery, eventually solved; and it is a story of entrepreneurial achievement, as Tommy makes enough money for Christmas through part-time jobs at a synagogue, a Catholic and a Protestant church, and at Woolworths. It is an effervescent sociological document: the intimate portrait of a place, Ottawa's Lowertown, and a time, December of 1945. The story has romance–Tommy, in Grade Five, courts the girl he thinks of as "the lovely Margot Lane" by sending cards for every occasion, all signed with his alias, The Shadow, until in the end she penetrates his subterfuge and they talk. Most of all, this is an account of the determinedly irrepressible imagination of a boy in no hurry to grow up, who loves and sometimes envies his retarded sister, who has a best Jewish friend, a best French friend, and a best Catholic friend (a Jew, a Pea Soup, and a Dogan–he is "nothing" himself), and who relates to the world mostly as Lamont Cranston, The Shadow, whose companion in the radio series is, of course, the lovely Margot Lane.

It is a relief to read a novel for young readers that deals with the world as perceived by the young (albeit nostalgically recalled by the mature writer) without in any way suggesting that this is merely an incomplete version of adult reality. *Angel Square* is not, even by implication, about growing up. It is about being a kid. Although set a generation ago and filled with allusions to bygone radio programs, outmoded cap-gun fights, old movies, and all sorts of esoteric details of a specific place in another era, it is beautifully written to be entirely accessible to the contemporary reader. (You can read Doyle out loud the way you read Mark Twain, though superficially they are not alike.) His other books display the same enthusiasm for the rhythms of language and the complexities of being alive: *Hey Dad!*, *You Can Pick Me Up at Peggy's Cove*, and *Up to Low* are well worth reading. *Angel Square*, however, is very special, his *Huckleberry Finn*. Perhaps the serious themes of racial, ethnic, and religious tolerance, love and loyalty, courage and determination, in balance with lively motifs of adventure, excitement, good-humoured brawling, and high-spirited play, make it so, or perhaps it is the rich and rolling prose. Whatever! *Angel Square* is a very special novel.

MABEL DUNHAM

Kristli's Trees. Toronto: McClelland and Stewart, 1947. 1974. Pages: 198. [10–13]

Kristli's Trees is a warm and richly textured account of a Mennonite farm boy in his eighth year. Kristli Eby lives in Waterloo County with his father and mother and sisters, and shares with the family and their Mennonite neighbours a strong sense of the past. His ancestors came up from "Pennsylfawny" after the American Revolution in Conestoga wagons. Kristli listens to tales of the old times from his Groszgroszdoddy, Samuel Eby, whose own Groszgroszdoddy came to Canada as the first Mennonite bishop in the area, and whose great-grandfather, in turn, had come to the New World from Switzerland. Kristli's sense of roots is reinforced by his father's ritual: each year, Mr. Eby plants a maple sapling on Kristli's birthday. Through the course of the novel, Kristli discovers that goodness and being different are, for a Mennonite, closely related–that roots are the source of both identity and moral strength. But Dunham does not preach: she illustrates. The Ebys are described, in simple but detailed language, as real people; Kristli's adventures – on the farm, when he is swept away in the river, at the great Brubacher Reunion, with his rascally cousin Mannie, at a huge after-church dinner – are all related with loving enthusiasm. The author clearly delights in the Pennsylvania Dutch dialect of her characters and holds their lifestyle in deep affection.

SARAH ELLIS

The Baby Project. Vancouver: Groundwood/Douglas & McIntyre, 1986. Pages: 144. Paperback. [11–15]

This is a problem book, a coming-to-terms-with-the-real-world book. It is much better than most. It is not at all didactic – it is very well written, with convincing characters in a credible family-life situation. While it displays a clear bias in many of its attitudes and values, especially related to gender, it does not discount more conservative alternatives. While Mum is a dynamic engineer and Dad is a dreamer, a house-husband, and a sometimes taxi-driver, the narrative does not suggest that this is the only or even the best way for things to be; only that this is how things sometimes are. Moreover, there is no answer, no resolution to the central problem of the novel, the death of an infant; there is neither compensation suggested nor an attempt at explanation. Rather, there is a compassionate and honest portrayal of the family, of eleven-year-old Jessica, her older brothers, her parents, and a few of their friends and relations, as they come to accept the crib-death of baby Lucie. It is a novel of acceptance, or reconciliation to loss and to grief and to change. Fortunately, it is written in such a way as to provide the young reader reassurance, not to instill fear.

The narrative develops around Jessica and much of the book describes the world of an eleven-year-old in North Vancouver from her own perspective, focusing especially on a school project she and her mildly eccentric friend Margaret work on about babies. Conveniently, coinciding with their research, Jessica's thirty-eight-year-old mother announces that she is pregnant. The anticipation of Lucie's birth, and Jessica's intimate involvement with the process through her project, create a tremendous context of warmth and understanding. When, only a few weeks after she is born, Lucie dies, Jessica is devastated. Briefly, the family seems to collapse.

The tragedy itself is presented in a muted and slightly oblique fashion, as it might be experienced by a child of Jessica's age. The reader is spared grisly details but not the surrounding sadness. Then the author describes, in a quite beautiful series of sparing but compassionate sequences, how each person affected comes to terms with his or her own feelings, how each copes separately with grief and comes together with the others, as time goes by. Sarah Ellis writes in a direct and simple prose, with an uncanny command of adolescent and familial language that more flamboyant writers might well admire and emulate.

GREY OWL (GEORGE STANSFIELD BELANEY/WA-SHA-QUON-ASIN)

The Adventures of Sajo and Her Beaver People.
London: Dickson, 1935. Published as *Sajo and the Beaver People*. Toronto: Macmillan; Laurentian Library, 1977. Pages: 187. Paperback. [10–13]

Can there be a storyteller, anywhere, more disarming than the legendary Grey Owl? In telling the tale of two Ojibway children and their beaver friends in the Canadian North, the author breaks every rule of good narration except the most important: he holds the reader's attention. Chattily, he moves in and out of his account, affirming aspects of the story from his own experience, explaining animal behaviour and Indian customs, openly inviting the reader to share his company and participate in the realities described. Grey Owl is not a good writer, nor a particularly astute student of nature, though there was a time when he was thought to be both. He writes with ingenuous affectation and with an air of inscrutable authority that are quite mesmerizing. His account of Big Feather's gift of two beaver kittens to his motherless children, Sajo and Shapian, of their subsequent adventures together, of how one of the beavers ends up in a city zoo, and of the beaver's rescue, has continued to enchant readers for almost half a century. Grey Owl's notes on the wilderness, with accompanying (rather clumsy) sketches, have the uncomplicated charm of lore in a Boy Scout manual; the excitement with which he writes of a murderous otter, a forest fire, Indian children in the city, a beaver reunion when the kittens are set free, is contagious. As a writer of fiction–and everything he wrote, especially his autobiographical writing, is in some sense fiction–Grey Owl was and remains a genuine, accomplished primitive.

RODERICK HAIG-BROWN

Starbuck Valley Winter. New York: Morrow, 1943.
Toronto: Science Research Associates, 1968.
Pages: 280. [13 up]

Roderick Haig-Brown writes with authority about the western Canadian wilderness. His works on sport fishing are renowned; his works for young readers remain among the best ever written. *Starbuck Valley Winter* narrates the adventures of sixteen-year-old Don Morgan during a winter in the British Columbia bush, where Don tries to make enough money by trapping to buy his own fishing boat in the spring. Accompanied by a problematical friend, Tubby Miller, Don struggles to make the wilderness yield. His efforts are ultimately reinforced by the mysterious Lee Jetson, who turns out to be far less menacing than the boys had thought. In the end, loaded with skins for sale and bounty, Don gets his boat. Haig-Brown describes the practical procedures of hunting and trapping in fascinating detail. Because Don is a novice, there is ample narrative justification for recounting the lore and methods of bush life. Because the hero is daring and capable, there is a plentiful source in the novel for excitement. Through Don's adolescent enthusiasm and determination, the author shares his own profound understanding of both the human and the natural worlds.

In prose that is elegant and yet easy to read, he draws his readers into experiences that may not normally be to their taste and makes those experiences thoroughly interesting. He instils in the reader a respect for nature and for those close to it, who live in its debt.

CHRISTIE HARRIS

Raven's Cry. Toronto: McClelland and Stewart, 1966. 1973. Pages: 193. Paperback. [13 up]

In less than two hundred pages, Christie Harris relates the dramatized history of a people, from their proud and affluent sovereignty over the Pacific Northwest to their eventual demise. In 1775, when the novel opens, ten thousand Haida flourished in the Queen Charlotte Islands area. By 1900, fewer than six hundred Haida were left; they lived in scattered settlements and their society and culture had been reduced to remnants. In the 1960s, when the novel ends, only the legacy of their art remains, and an ethnic pride that barely conceals the tragedy of genocide. Artlessly, but in prose that is very readable and filled with fascinating bits of historical information, Harris chronicles the Haida story. She focuses on a series of chiefs, all bearing the name Edinsa. Following a pattern of matrilineal succession, each Edinsa witnesses the further debasement of his people–from the first sighting of whites in a "flying canoe" to the demeaning twentieth-century anthropological reconstructions of their past. Harris writes history as if it were fiction, employing the narrative devices of dialogue, characterization, and dramatic incident with abandon, to create an enthralling vista across historical time. And she writes fiction as if it were history: she provides documentary details in abundance and lends substance to her narrative by employing dates, references to personalities and events, and a self-conscious air of authorial objectivity. The effect, although occasionally confusing, is often quite splendid. *Raven's Cry* is accessible as a document because the reader is moved by the narrative; it is moving because its wealth of documentary information is so dramatically accessible.

JOHN F. HAYES

Flaming Prairie. Toronto: Copp Clark, 1965.
Pages: 313. [12–15]

Flaming Prairie is only one in a remarkable series of historical novels by John F. Hayes in which the author brings an authentic vision of the Canadian past into dramatic life. This one describes the events of the Métis Rebellion in the Canadian Northwest during the spring of 1885. While Hayes superbly exploits the narrative possibilities of history, he remains true to the documentary facts. His hero, a sixteen-year-old orphan from Kingston named Jeff Carson, is pure fiction; but his description of the fighting at Duck Lake, at Batoche, and in the surrounding Saskatchewan countryside, his conception of the main characters, Crozier, Middleton, Dumont, and Riel, and of many of the minor ones, are all adapted from real accounts of the time. Hayes skilfully develops the adventures of his young protagonist within the context of actual events; the reader comes away from the novel with a comprehensive grasp of what happened, and why. The contemporary reader might be suspicious of the excessive good qualities assigned to the whites and annoyed by the mild condescension shown early in the novel towards the Métis. Yet Hayes determinedly draws attention to the legitimate grievances that generated the rebellion, and demands of his reader sympathy and respect for the Métis cause. What young readers will likely enjoy most are the spine-chilling heroics of Jeff and his friend Charlie; what they will most remember is the Hayes version of an extremely dynamic episode in Canadian history.

MARSHA HEWITT AND CLAIRE MACKAY

One Proud Summer. Toronto: Women's Educational
Press, 1981. Pages: 160. Paperback. [12 up]

This book is a remarkable hybrid: a novel, document, tract, inspirational polemic. It tells the story of striking mill workers in
Valleyfield, Quebec, during the summer of 1946. Against the combined forces of a powerful company, a reactionary Church, and
provincial police under the direct orders of Le Chef, Maurice
Duplessis, a bitterly fought strike lasting nearly one hundred days
brought about the formation of a legitimate union and the beginning of social reform for workers in one of the most exploitive
industries in the country. Québécois workers endured intolerable
conditions and this novel focuses on their struggle against anglophone management, whose power rested securely on the authority of church and state. Women were especially exploited in the
textile industry, and the authors develop their narrative around
a particular cluster of women. Children were gruesomely abused
by the system: the novel's principal protagonist is thirteen-year-
old Lucie Laplante. Inevitably, then, *One Proud Summer* is fiercely
biased toward labour, feminism, and the legitimate aspirations
for dignity and social equality of the Québécois working class.

It is also a ripping good story, related with a tough sort of tenderness and eloquence that lifts it at times to the finest level of
literature. Occasionally, sentiment gives way to sentimentality
and contrivance; occasionally, the authors try too hard to sustain
access for the young reader to complex social history through the
use of jarring teenage banter; and, occasionally, "message" obscures meaning. However, the novel's high moral purpose, reinforced by documentary photographs and a bibliography, is for the
most part admirably served by fine writing, a strong narrative
line, and the galvanic force of the authors' own convictions. I
learned as I read this novel and I was deeply moved by it. I cannot
imagine other readers, of any age, not being likewise enthralled.

(See also Claire Mackay, *The Minerva Program.*)

JAMES HOUSTON

Frozen Fire. Toronto: McClelland and Stewart, 1977.
Pages: 149. Markham: Penguin, 1979. Paperback. [12–15]

Houston is one of those rare novelists who writes with equal profi-
ciency for young readers or adults. *Frozen Fire*, like his many other
works, is set in the Canadian Arctic; like the others, it draws both
drama and substance from the author's comfortable familiarity
with the far North. In this novel, thirteen-year-old Matthew Morgan travels from Arizona to Frobisher on Baffin Island, after his
mother dies, to be with his father, a geologist whose dreams of
riches seem always to exceed his grasp. Houston describes life in
the isolated community on Frobisher Bay, particularly Eskimo
life, from Matthew's point of view. The inside of a plywood Eskimo
home, the battered snowmobiles, the dissipation and the quiet
dignity of his friend Kayak's family – all make a deep impression
on Matt, and on the reader. Not until Ross Morgan and his helicopter pilot are lost, however, does the real drama begin – and
then it builds with unrelenting intensity. Matthew and Kayak
set out by snowmobile to search on their own for the missing men.
Seventy-five miles away, across the Bay, they run out of gas. Their
struggle for survival includes encounters with wild animals, a
pair of mysterious recluses, their own naïveté, and, mostly, the
cold, the wind, and the snow. The boys learn from each other, suffer together, and become virtually brothers. Eventually, adrift on
an ice pan that is perilously diminishing with the spring break-up,
they accept death together – only to be rescued at the last minute,
through their own ingenuity and a good bit of luck. *Frozen Fire* is
a gripping tale, direct, powerful, satisfying to read on every count.

MONICA HUGHES

The Tomorrow City. London: Hamish Hamilton, 1978. London: Methuen, 1982. Pages: 137. [12–15]

In a prolific burst of creativity during the last several years, Monica Hughes has published works about the Klondike Gold Rush and West Coast Indians as well as in the area of her greatest strength, science fiction. In *Beyond the Dark River* she enlivens the "sf" with young Hutterite and Indian protagonists in a western Canadian setting, while in *Keeper of the Isis Light* she moves the narrative action to another world entirely. *The Tomorrow City* is set apparently in mid-Atlantic, in a city of the future that has been given over to the charge of a mighty computer, Cinencom or C-Three, which has been programmed to create the perfect urban environment. Unfortunately, the computer arranges to dispose of old people as well as old buildings, recluses along with refuse. Before long, the population of the city is brainwashed into believing "C-Three knows best." Fortunately, Caro Henderson and her friend David resist C-Three's power (the primary medium of which is television) and, in an involved and exciting plot, eliminate the electronic menace–although not before Caro is blinded, nor before the author has delivered a snappy diatribe against technological anarchy. Hughes writes a clear, brittle prose ideally suited to the speculative nature of her best work. She gives free rein to the reader's imagination through provocative and frighteningly prophetic concepts, which she develops with a flair for the ominous and the bizarre. *The Tomorrow City* is skilfully devised to have a lasting impact on the conscience as well as the consciousness of its young readers.

GORDON KORMAN

Who Is Bugs Potter? Richmond Hill: Scholastic-TAB, 1980. Pages: 179. Paperback. [10–14]

This is fiction for the non-reader; fast food for the mind. Korman is a very young writer and quite prolific. By the time he graduated from university he had nearly a dozen titles to his credit, many of them in multiple reprint. From the first, in *This Can't Be Happening at Macdonald Hall!*, he has displayed an uncanny knack for marketable narrative. His writing is smooth, fast paced, as empty of significance as the average television serial–and as popular. I have been taken to task even by quite sophisticated young readers for leaving Korman out of the first edition of this book. They seldom recall anything of the story or the characters, but they clearly remember their own pleasure in reading him. That, surely, is worth something. Reading Korman will do the proficient reader no harm and may just possibly help to bring the poor reader along.

It is easy to see how kids from ten to fourteen get caught up in the high-spirited and improbable antics of a fifteen-year-old, especially one as eccentric as Bugs Potter. Bugs is a rock-and-roll drummer from Winnipeg who, apparently by some curious administrative glitch, ends up in Toronto as part of the Canadian High School Orchestra, comprising a hundred of the best young musicians in the country. During their ten days of rehearsal, the musicians are immersed in the cultural life of Toronto–all, that is, except Bugs Potter and his reluctant sidekick and roommate, Adam Webb. These two sneak off to rock clubs at night, where Bugs creates a monstrous sensation as mystery guest drummer with various bands. He also schemes to meet the gorgeous BiBi Lanay, film star, fake European, and owner of the fabulous–and jinxed–Falusi Emerald, which, of course, is eagerly coveted by two amusingly inept thieves. And so it goes. Bugs takes the Toronto scene by storm, but in the end returns to Winnipeg. The emerald is safe. BiBi is safe. Adam, the reader's representative within the text, feels strangely privileged to have been involved with Bugs Potter. I did not; but then, I am not a McDonald's enthusiast, either.

JEAN LITTLE

From Anna. Toronto: Fitzhenry & Whiteside, 1972. 1977.
Pages: 201. Paperback. [10–13]

Jean Little writes fully developed novels for young readers, with rounded characters, plots that are provocative and relatively intricate, and themes that captivate both heart and mind. *From*

Anna is a serious novel, yet there are times when the reader will laugh aloud. It is filled with warmth and compassion, yet there are fear, anger, bitterness, and frustration expressed throughout. It is a complex work, and yet accessible even to very young readers. In part it is accessible because everyone will identify with the title character, Anna Solden, for everyone at times feels awkward, ignorant, unloved. The novel opens in Frankfurt in 1933. Under the impress of rising fanaticism in Germany, Anna, her brothers and sisters, and her parents move to Toronto. Once in Canada, it is discovered that the nine-year-old immigrant girl is extremely short-sighted. At a special school, Anna gradually develops confidence and learns perfect English, and eventually wins the affection and grudging respect of her rather insensitive siblings. The novel closes with a Christmas scene that is charged with emotion: by then, Anna has triumphed over her handicap, which is as much psychological and social as it is physical. She has become proud, in the best sense of the word, and, not without a special importance of its own, a Canadian. Jean Little has complete command of the children's literature genre: everything in this novel is exactly appropriate to the young readers it was written for. Few will read it without being moved, enlightened, and well entertained.

JANET LUNN

Double Spell. Toronto: Peter Martin, 1968. 1981. Pages: 134. Toronto: Irwin, 1983. Paperback. [11–14]

Double Spell is a superb example of what I would call supernatural realism. It is not fantasy–the imaginative creation of other worlds–nor is it speculative fiction, which demands the suspension of disbelief. Right from the beginning, this novel sets out to convince the young reader that the highly improbable might possibly, just possibly, occur. With intriguing contrariness, logical procedures within the narrative yield increasingly illogical conclusions, until at last reason gives way, in a triumph of the creative imagination, to a splendid acceptance of mystery and wonder. Twelve-year-old twins, Jane and Elizabeth Hubbard, come across an ancient doll that seems to impel them, through shared dreams, disjointed memory fragments, and haunting visions from other times, to resolve the enigma of its origins and its apparent powers. As the twins plod through Toronto streets and Toronto history, trying to make sense of their strange adventure, their personalities seem to change. As the haunting builds, practical Jane becomes enthralled – until, in the end, she is nearly destroyed by the past which, as the twins discover, is their own, their actual heritage. Lunn has written a sophisticated thriller, in which the psychology and the mystique of twins play a large part, and the domestic details of life in the city provide an engaging background. *Double Spell* is scary, and good, exciting fun; a well-written mind-opener.

CLAIRE MACKAY

The Minerva Program. Toronto: James Lorimer, 1984.
Pages: 178. Paperback. [11–15]

Claire Mackay is a good writer, a very good writer. Her prose is clear, direct, engaging, and her command of easy-going and enthralling narrative is superb. *The Minerva Program* is what we used to call (and it sounds archaic now) "a good read." It certainly has dimensions of social significance, but messages, such as they are, are entirely integrated with story and character. Minerva Wright is a grade-seven student in Toronto who, in the course of learning about computers at school, inadvertently uncovers a fraud and finds herself barred from access to school equipment. Then, in the course of the novel, she schemes to clear her name. But Mackay's book is really about people: about their problems with themselves, their friends, the computer age, and their inner-city environment. It is also about the joys and frustrations of friendship, family, imagination, and the inner self.

Mackay has a good grasp on the complexities of adolescence. Minerva's story is in the Nancy Drew tradition, albeit updated to include video arcades and punk styles, but Minerva herself has the fullness of character we expect to find in the best of adult fiction. Yet she remains remarkably accessible for the young reader, whose world her author seems to know so well. Mackay writes with warmth and wit. Sometimes this novel is very funny. The Toronto setting and the working-class milieu are used effectively to create mood but also to develop plot and character and, more significantly, to develop themes of considerable social relevance. As in the novel *One Proud Summer*, which Mackay wrote with Marsha Hewitt, there is a marked working-class/feminist bias. Never does this novel preach, however. It merely asserts the validity of women's experience and the experience of ordinary working people, whether teachers, cashiers, or cooks. And it asserts the validity of a young girl's experience and imagination in the contemporary world. That Minerva is black is a rather gratuitous measure, for there are no special insights in the novel pertaining to black experience, but perhaps *that* is the point.

(See also Marsha Hewitt and Claire Mackay, *One Proud Summer*.)

KEVIN MAJOR

Hold Fast. Toronto: Clarke, Irwin, 1978. Pages: 170. Paperback. [13 up]

Kevin Major is a Newfoundlander, and among the best Canadian writers of his generation. In the last few years, with only three novels, he has established himself as a figure of singular importance in our literature. *Hold Fast, Far from Shore*, and *Thirty-Six Exposures* are for younger readers, but refuse to bear the epithet "second-rank." In fact, Major defies many of the conventions of so-called children's literature. Characters swear in his novels, and break the law; people drink and have sexual experiences and sexual anxieties; people die and others grieve or are defiant. In prose that is exact and vivid, an equivalent in words to super-realism on the artist's canvas, the author describes life from an adolescent Newfoundlander's perspective. He has a superb command of outport dialect; he has a refined and highly engaging sense of narrative style, one that is uncannily appropriate to his narrator's personality. In *Hold Fast*, fourteen-year-old Michael recounts his own story with cheeky wit and irrepressible bravado. Newly orphaned, he has to cope with his parents' funeral and the responsibility he feels for his younger brother, Brent; he has to confront his own anxiety at having to leave the village of Marten to live hundreds of miles away with relatives in St. Albert. Adolescent pride and fierce strength of character combine to make his life in the city oppressive; after a few months, he runs away. With his cousin Curtis in tow, after intriguing adventures along the road, he returns to his brother, his Aunt Flo, and his dying grandfather at home. It is a simple, honest story, with implications, even for very young readers, that are profound and complex. *Hold Fast* is a fine novel, a genuine work of literature in its own right.

MARKOOSIE

Harpoon of the Hunter. Montreal: McGill-Queen's
Press, 1970. Pages: 81. Paperback. [12 up]

To include this among novels for young readers does not mean that it is a children's book. It can be read and understood by readers as young as twelve, and *should* be read by them for gripping insights into an experienced world entirely different from their own. But it can also be read, and should be read, by adults–who, perhaps, could benefit from a stark reminder of the extent to which they may have lost perspective and proportion.

Markoosie is an Inuit charter pilot, who originally wrote *Harpoon of the Hunter* in his own language, then translated it into English. In keeping with the oral tradition from which it springs, it is addressed to the community; the community includes all who are old enough to listen, old enough to hear. But it also participates in a literary tradition extending through the sagas of medieval Europe to the northern fictions of Farley Mowat and James Houston, Yves Theriault and Gabrielle Roy.

Harpoon of the Hunter is without question a literary work, rather than a cultural artifact or anthropological document. It relates a story of hardship, violence, stoic endurance, and death. It tells of a people whose existence is inseparable from the harsh and frozen land in which they live, who are as much a part of the land as the snow and the ice, and as much its adversary as they are of the polar bear and the musk ox and the other creatures with which they share the fight for survival. Markoosie provides an intimate portrait of his people, with attention to details that only an Inuit could know or would think to focus on. Nor does he portray his people as being without fear, or grief, or affection, as they so often are by even the most sympathetic of outside observers. That they cope and carry on, despite the most terrible adversity, does not mean they do not suffer.

Markoosie's narrative is built around a sixteen-year-old youth called Kamik, but it cuts away from him and back, time and again, shifting tense as it does so even when the action is occurring simultaneously. As we follow Kamik on the hunt for a rabid polar bear, we also witness the worries in his small community that lead those left behind to send for help even before the hunters have run into trouble. Kamik's father is killed by a different bear; a search party is mounted under Angootik from nearby Kikitajoak, a larger, more prosperous community across a treacherous channel of moving ice. Kamik's seven companions are mauled and dismembered before Kamik manages to kill the rabid bear and set out alone for home. Angootik's party closes in, finds the remains of Kamik's father, finds the remains of his companions. Kamik is rescued. The survivors of his small settlement agree to return with their rescuers to Kikitajoak. Crossing the channel ice, Angootik, his daughter, who has become Kamik's betrothed, and Kamik's mother slip through the ice. Kamik refuses help: he drifts to sea and embraces his own death. Out of this simply and powerfully told account of the struggle for survival we draw a strange reassurance. Individuals die, but life goes on. The People endure.

SUSANNE MARTEL

The King's Daughter. Vancouver: Groundwood/Douglas
& McIntyre, 1980. Pages: 211. *Tr.* David Homel (*Jeanne,
fille du roy*. Montréal: Editions Fides, 1974). Paperback.
[13 up]

The King's Daughter is a beautifully written novel, already a classic in French; it is destined to become a classic in the English-Canadian tradition as well. Mature readers will find it a thoroughly engaging work of historical fiction. It is not a child's novel so much as an exciting and sensitive narrative that is wonderfully accessible even to the very young. It is difficult to imagine someone not being captivated by *The King's Daughter*. The character of eighteen-year-old Jeanne Chatel is strongly developed, and her adventures as a "daughter" of Louis XIV, an orphan girl sent to New France in the 1670s as a bride for one of the early woodsmen, are action-packed. A wealth of detail about life in the colony is delivered not as background information but as the very texture of Jeanne's experiences. The hardship and danger, including murderous attacks by Iroquois, are related as exciting elements in Jeanne's romantic quest to belong. Her love for a proud and difficult husband and the winning of both his affection and his respect are inseparable from her coming to terms with the New World. Jeanne is a romantic heroine the reader will take to heart: self-reliant, resourceful, headstrong, and determinedly optimistic. Her creator, Susanne Martel, has given us a vividly authentic picture of early Canada, an engaging story of universal appeal – and a protagonist who lives in the imagination long after the novel has been left behind. *The King's Daughter* is popular fiction at its very best.

LESLIE McFARLANE
(aka FRANKLIN W. DIXON)

The Last of the Great Picnics. Toronto: McClelland and
Stewart, 1965. 1974. Pages: 99. [10–13]

This low-key and pleasing novel has a strong regional flavour.
McFarlane describes life on a family farm in the Ottawa Valley
with casual authority and relates events of one particular day,
July first, 1887, with infectious enthusiasm. The narrative, told
in the third person, portrays the world from the perspectives of
David and Janet Graham. The author does not emphasize traditional gender roles, but neither does he deny them: David, at
eleven, is the older and is somewhat more the centre of the narrative action. The two children travel with their Uncle Ogden to
the Dominion Day celebrations in Perth. An encounter on the
way with a shaved-headed bully erupts at the picnic near a huge
hot-air balloon from which, later, a man descends to the earth in
a series of red, white, and blue parachutes. This is not before David
and Janet have been plucked from the mud to share a carriage
with the venerable Sir John A. Macdonald. The old Prime Minister recalls the great picnics of the past, which he credits with restor-
ing him to office in 1876–picnics in Uxbridge and Orangeville
and Belleville, drawing as many as fifteen thousand. Before the
whole crowd, David and Janet return with Sir John A. to the picnic,
and then return home, grandly satisfied. For David, a shroud has
been lifted away from history; McFarlane likewise makes history
come alive for the young readers of his novel.

W.O. MITCHELL

Jake and the Kid. Toronto: Macmillan, 1961. Toronto:
Seal, 1982. Pages: 184. Paperback. [11–14]

Young readers familiar with *Who Has Seen the Wind*, Mitchell's
classic novel about the metaphysical struggles of childhood in a
prairie town, may be surprised by *Jake and the Kid*. The stories

in this book are related by the Kid himself in a kind of juvenile dialect that, although a bit stilted, effectively conveys the naïve enthusiasms and sense of wonder of a boy growing up. There is no sustaining plot, but the distinguishing features of character and setting remain constant. (Impossibly so, in fact; the time of the stories varies from the 1940s through to 1955 and yet nothing ages or changes – appropriately, perhaps, in an idyll of youth and innocence such as this.) Crocus, Saskatchewan, gradually comes into definition as details accumulate from episode to episode. Repeat Golightly, the barber, appears and reappears; Miss Henchbaw, the teacher and Jake's adversary for possession of the Kid's imagination, becomes more and more obstreperous and, curiously, more humane. It is Jake, however, who most unifies the book. Jake is the hired man who keeps things going while the Kid's father is overseas at war. Jake tells tall tales, mostly about himself, and gives sound advice, mostly to the Kid. The two of them, Jake and the Kid, make a memorable pair. Their context, adapted from radio and television episodes, has little of the emotional and dramatic intensity of *Who Has Seen the Wind*, and lacks its high seriousness, which, to his lasting credit, Mitchell made accessible to young readers. Still, *Jake and the Kid* is satisfying entertainment, the work of a master storyteller.

L.M. MONTGOMERY

Anne of Green Gables. New York: Grosset & Dunlap, 1908. Toronto: Seal, 1981. Pages: 309. Paperback. [12–15]

Anne Shirley is our most famous orphan. In a children's literature where being an orphan seems almost a prerequisite for main-character status, Anne stands out. It is the excesses in her character that have made her a popular favourite around the world for three-quarters of a century: she is irrepressibly imaginative and optimistic; she is charmingly loquacious and dramatically sensitive; she is determinedly lovable. A red-haired, green-eyed, freckle-faced foundling of eleven, she appears at Avonlea on Prince Edward Island by mistake – Matthew and his sister Marilla

Cuthbert had specifically asked the orphanage to send them a boy. But Anne quickly works her way into their hearts, as she does into the reader's, and the house of Green Gables soon comes alive with its newest resident. Before long, the whole area around Avonlea is transformed: Barry's pond becomes the Lake of Shining Waters; ordinary people become kindred spirits. Anne's enthusiasms light up her surroundings, and her appalling histrionics give them a special vitality. Although contemporary readers might find Anne's world a little sweet, it has the undeniable appeal of an idyll. Prince Edward Island becomes a place of enchantment and the procedures of growing up seem a bittersweet dream. Not all is idyllic, of course: Anne battles her way through school with her rival, Gilbert Blythe; she suffers several humiliations and endures the death of her beloved Matthew. She determines, finally, to stay on in Avonlea with Marilla and teach, rather than go off to college. It is a sacrifice at once self-searching and noble, typical of Anne throughout the novel. Montgomery wrote many other works for young readers – some would say even her adult writing is more suitable for young readers – but none has caught and held public affection like this, her first.

FARLEY MOWAT

Lost in the Barrens. Boston: Little, Brown, 1956.
Toronto: McClelland and Stewart, 1977. 1980. Pages: 244.
Paperback. [11–14]

Mowat is one of our most popular writers, and one of the most prolific. He is known primarily for personal narratives, like *The Dog Who Wouldn't Be*, and for impassioned pleas for endangered animals and peoples, like *Never Cry Wolf, A Whale for the Killing*, and *People of the Deer*. But his novels have been for young readers, and the most successful of these is *Lost in the Barrens*. Mowat is not a subtle storyteller, but he has a sure sense of his materials. In his account of seventeen-year-old Jamie Macnair and his Cree friend, Awasin, Mowat not only relates what happens to them but provides a detailed explanation of how they cope.

After reading this novel, the reader could start a fire without matches, catch fish and game with rudimentary gear, even build a log cabin, including the fireplace, with only a hatchet. Intriguing details are provided into Cree, Chipeweyan, and Eskimo life, and into the ways of the wilderness, nearly a thousand miles north of Winnipeg. Jamie and Awasin are uncomplicated characters who manage admirably with the perils they have brought upon themselves (aided by numerous examples of authorial coincidence and a great deal of authorial goodwill). They happily survive their ordeal against wild animals and the elements to animate a sequel, *The Curse of the Viking Grave.*

RUTH NICHOLS

A Walk Out of the World. Toronto: Longmans, 1969.
Pages: 192. [10–13]

Readers should be prepared for strange and delightful happenings when reading fiction by Ruth Nichols. She has a fantastical imagination, unrestrained by logic or practicality, and refreshingly free of the need to instruct or uplift. There is an enthralling naïveté about the worlds she creates; a sinister beauty; magical charm. In this novel, written while she was still in her teens, two children transcend their mundane, sterile life in what might well be Vancouver and, in a different dimension of time, participate in a world of enchantment that seems more naturally their home than the one they have left behind. Judith and Tobit become Lady and Sir, then Princess and Prince. Among Water Folk and dwarfs with green hair and the underground people of the winter forest, across Whispering Plains and the Black River, they struggle to liberate the White City from the wicked Hagérrak, and restore it to the lovely five-hundred-year-old Lady Iorwen. Princess Judith fulfils her destiny, as a child of the House of the Wanderer, by compelling the ancient usurper to take his own life. Judith and Tobit, at home merely children, in this enchanted world are "real" people. Judith in particular thrills at their adventures and wistfully, when they are home again, remembers the special places and creatures known, of all the people in the ordinary world, only to her and her brother. Nichols's writing has the knack of making it all seem plausible and impossible at the same time, as only the very best speculative fiction can do.

JACK O'BRIEN

Silver Chief, Dog of the North. New York: Holt, Rinehart and Winston, 1933. 1966. Pages: 218. [10–14]

This book may not, in fact, be Canadian but it is read as if it were. This and the other Silver Chief novels are set in the Canadian North, somewhere west of Hudson Bay. They draw on the author's undeniable knowledge of northern experience and play on prejudice that at the time of writing might have been held as truth. Since they are in most school libraries and many public libraries throughout Canada and are taken by young readers to be Canadian, I have felt it important to discuss them here–specifically, the first in the series–as a warning against misinformation and blatant bigotry. This would not be an issue were the Silver Chief novels not on the whole so well written and widely received.

In this novel, the wolf-dog is born and matures in the wilderness and after his mother is killed by Indians runs free until captured by Sergeant Jim Thorpe of the Royal Northwest Mounted Police, a truly noble example of young manhood who is said to traverse the arctic wastes in resplendent scarlet uniform, on horseback whenever possible but otherwise by dog-sled. Some of this is silly (the Indians cannot capture Silver Chief but the white man, Thorpe, snares and tames him quite easily), but the descriptions of animal ferocity are compelling and the passionate bond between Thorpe and the dog is presented in a moving way. Their adventure together, capturing the renegade halfbreed Laval and bringing him to justice, is related in gripping prose that excites great fear and wonder. The outcome of their ordeal in the frozen wilderness is somewhat forced but reasonably convincing.

Most young readers, as they have for several generations, will find this story entirely engrossing. But they will also, unfortunately, come to accept that Indians are generally vicious and surly, that wolves stalk and kill humans (Farley Mowat and *Never Cry Wolf* to the contrary), and that the might of authority, as wielded by the Mounties, is an absolute right. They will also leave the text convinced, perhaps, that halfbreeds are genetically defective, a mixture of "Indian, French, and Lord knows what" whose fused blood has developed "a strain of cunning and cruelty that submerged any good qualities of either race." Such ignorant condescension runs through the narrative – and yet these are exciting, convincing books. Perhaps reading them will provide young readers the opportunity to learn about such aberrant attitudes and, with guidance, to reject them.

JAMES REANEY

The Boy with an R in His Hand. Toronto: Macmillan, 1965. Erin: Porcupine's Quill, 1984. Pages: 101. Paperback. [10–13]

While the narrative adventures in this novel appeal directly to the interests of younger readers, there is much about it that will especially amuse adults. Reaney creates devastating caricatures of some of the leading Tory personalities in muddy York, circa 1825. Names vaguely familiar in history, at least to Torontonians, take on corporeal form: Bishop Strachan appears as a sinister prig; the Lieutenant-Governor and his entourage seem stupidly pretentious; names like Jarvis and Lyons and Allan dart furtively through the pages. Only the Reformer, William Lyon Mackenzie, editor of the *Colonial Advocate*, earns the author's wholehearted endorsement. Reaney has fun playing with tidbits of historical information and gossip, but it is the story of young Alec and Joel Buchanan that animates the narrative. Apparently orphaned in the Red River Settlement, the boys are forced to come east to live with their mean and prosperous (and Tory) uncle. Alec is a proud and cheeky boy, filled with moral righteousness, and a natural, in Reaney's scheme of things, to apprentice with Mr. Mackenzie in his print shop. In the end, after Tory hoodlums riotously demolish Mackenzie's press, the boys' lost father is restored to them and they leave Canada with him for home in Scotland–though not before Reaney has regaled his readers with a plenitude of information about early printing. Reaney is a fine writer and easy to read, although occasionally he slips in archaic words and syntax that seem at best gratuitous. Still, he shares his enthusiasms with great generosity of spirit and style.

MARSHALL SAUNDERS

Beautiful Joe. Toronto: Baptist Book Room, 1894.
Toronto: McClelland and Stewart, 1986. Pages: 266.
Paperback. [12–15]

Beautiful Joe has been a Canadian favourite for nearly a century. Beautiful Joe is an ironically named mongrel dog who was mutilated by his first owner: he had his ears and tail chopped off because he showed spunk when he was a puppy. Rescued and brought to live with the Morris family, he enjoys the next twelve years in great style and tells his own story from the vantage of a comfortable old age. While adults may find a dog as narrator in a quasi-realistic novel somewhat disconcerting, it is a device that effectively draws young readers into the heart of the story. Joe's account of himself moves rapidly through anecdotes that will engage, with their excesses of sentimentality and violence, almost any imagination, young or old. Each of the many brief chapters, while describing Joe's adventures with the Morris children or their other pets or other animals, in the coastal town of Fairport or on vacation at a family farm, contributes to the same end: moral instruction through highly charged entertainment. Saunders writes of cruelty, suffering, and violent death in a display of unrestrained Victorian rhetoric, as she makes a plea for kindness to animals and love among all the creatures of the world.

ERNEST THOMPSON SETON

Two Little Savages: Being the Adventures of Two Boys Who Lived as Indians and What They Learned. With Over Two Hundred Drawings. Toronto: William Briggs, 1903. Pages: 552. [10 up]

One of the great memories of my childhood is listening to my father read aloud from Seton's *Wild Animals I Have Known*. I did not encounter *Two Little Savages* until nearly forty years later. When I read it now I am immediately taken back to a time when, as they say, the world was young. Much of this novel's impact on the adult reader is undoubtedly due to nostalgia. I do not know if it will evoke such genuine wonder in the young reader of today as it would have in the past. Seton's planet Earth, with its animals and Indians and woodcraft, is a long way from the Star Wars world that enthralls contemporary minds. Still, it would be worth digging this book out of the dusty corner of an older library and giving it a try. Seton creates a special sort of magic that just might still work.

In contrast to Catharine Parr Traill (see below), who records her naturalist observations as esoteric asides, Seton makes knowledge of the natural world a part of the adventure–he not only conveys his enthusiasm for plants, birds, animals, and the lore of the wilderness, he instills this enthusiasm in his young reader's imagination. His margins are teeming with sketches and diagrams: a drawing of an Indian pipe lies across the page from scratchings labelled wonderfully as the "Trail of a Snapper"; a pile of stones drawn to indicate the Indian sign for "We camped here because one of us was sick" is across from the full-page illustration of an extensive vocabulary in stones, twigs, grass, smoke, and blazes on the sides of trees. A step-by-step explanation of how to assemble rubbing-sticks to make a fire, accompanied by detailed diagrams, is inserted alongside an intriguing narrative account of Indian fire-making. (The emulation of Indians is the highest achievement to which a non-Indian may aspire.) There is also a detailed description of how to make an Indian war bonnet, including drawings of which feather signifies having taken an enemy scalp and which stands for having slapped his face. What young adventurer could resist such a book!?

This treasure trove provides access to information on everything from Indian bands to bobolinks, taxidermy to willow withes for tying teepee poles, catnip tea to worm measuring (!). Holding it all together in a sprawling narrative context is Seton's account of Yan, a pioneer boy in mid-nineteenth-century Ontario who is determined to become an Indian in knowledge and deed, if not in fact. His story consists of countless subplots in which he and his friends imitate the Indians in earnest but high-spirited play in the wilderness on the edge of settlement. It is a "Boys' story" in which girls and women seem hardly to exist; thus, it might be accused of being sexist, but through omission and not, as in Traill's novel, by reinforcing divisive gender stereotypes. Despite its length, the time when it was written, and the rather condescending title, this novel is still very readable, never talks down to its readers, idealizes but never patronizes the Indian, and could challenge, I think, imaginations not yet wholly given over to intergalactic cataclysm.

BARBARA SMUCKER

Underground to Canada. Toronto: Clarke, Irwin, 1977.
Pages: 157. Markham: Penguin, 1978. Paperback. [13 up]

Despite a certain amount of romantic contrivance, this is one of the best novels about slavery I have encountered. Smucker conveys the cruelties and gross indignities endured by blacks in the American South with the authority of an eyewitness, although her knowledge of their condition comes from extensive research and her profound sympathy for fellow humans. In describing the escape from slavery of a few heroic individuals, Smucker does nothing to diminish its horrors. With prose of singular purity and precision she describes life in the South from the slaves' point of view. Her main character is a spirited twelve-year-old, June Lilly (or Julilly), who is taken from her mother in Virginia and transported to a Mississippi plantation where the work is onerous and conditions are deplorable. The younger children eat gruel from troughs; the whip is the only incentive to sustain productivity; the field-workers live like animals. Smucker's point is not that all slaves were always miserable, but that slavery itself is an unconscionable abomination. Then a Canadian visitor to the plantation secretly arranges for the escape of Julilly, her friend Liza, who has been crippled by beatings, and two others. The frightening flight to freedom on the Underground Railway sweeps the reader into the action and sustains a heightened sense of involvement rare in the best of fiction. As Julilly and her friends walk by night across Mississippi, Tennessee, Kentucky, and Ohio to Canada, they encounter people of charity and courage who aid them, mostly Mennonites and Quakers and a few freed blacks. Many of these characters are drawn from history. The fugitives are pursued right to Lake Erie – they are worth five hundred dollars each, expensive livestock. In the end, Julilly rejoins her mother in St. Catharines, Ontario, where they will have to cope with prejudice and poverty but where they are free at last. This is a sensitive and moving novel, filled with dramatic action, intense emotion, and a great deal of information.

CATHARINE PARR TRAILL

Canadian Crusoes: A Tale of the Rice Lake Plains.
London: A. Hall, Virtue, 1852. Scholarly Edition: Centre
for Editing Early Canadian Texts. Ottawa: Carleton
University Press, 1986. Ed. Rupert Schieder. Pages: 324.
Paperback. [14 up]

It would take a dedicated young reader to penetrate the scholarly paraphernalia accompanying this edition and get into the narrative itself. Once there, only the most intrepid will persist through the first fifty pages or so of miserably bad writing to get to the heart of the tale. Not surprisingly, this Canadian "classic for children" had been out of print since 1923. It is a plodding and laborious piece of fiction, condescending, contrived, and overwritten. It is doubtful that many contemporary readers will find it worth the effort. Yet this is, perhaps, a shame: once Traill reaches a certain point in her narrative, the story and characters, and her profound affection for the natural world take over and the latter part of the novel is quite engaging. The forced vocabulary, patronizing tone, gender stereotyping, and obsessively correct descriptions of flora, fauna, and terrain gradually give way to an account of three youngsters–Catharine, who is twelve at the beginning of their story, and her brother Hector and cousin Louis, both fourteen–and the rescued Mohawk girl, Indiana, who are lost for two years in the wilderness north of Peterborough, Ontario (and never more than eight miles from home).

To say their story is engaging is not to suggest that it is exciting. Generally, Traill is more concerned with inculcating moral lessons or pinpointing exact locations in terms of boundaries at the time of writing. (The adventure itself takes place in the late eighteenth century. Current inhabitants of the region might be intrigued by Traill's mid-nineteenth-century estimation of what their countryside was like, then.) There are several quite gripping encounters with sympathetically portrayed and yet ferocious Indians, and there is a forest fire that rather fizzles. On the whole, the source of greatest interest for young readers of Traill's novel will be the same as that for scholars, the same that marks her non-fiction accounts of lasting importance: she conveys an infectious enthusiasm for her adopted home; she is a keen and tireless recorder of the natural world in Canada and fully aware of its vulnerability in the face of progress. We share her sense of impending loss and, too, her excitement at the prospects of a civilized agrarian future. Through her writing, we have come to think of Traill as the embodiment of the pioneering Canadian spirit. Some of this spirit she conveys in *Canadian Crusoes*, though perhaps not so much as she intended.

JAN TRUSS

Jasmin. Vancouver: Groundwood/Douglas & McIntyre, 1982. Pages: 196. Paperback. [12–15]

Jasmin Marie Antoinette Stalke lives with her parents and her seven brothers and sisters, including retarded albino Leroy and baby Honey Angelina, in a log home in the foothills of Alberta.

There are three rooms in the house: two downstairs and a steep-sided attic for the children. Beginning first thing in the morning the television blares, and continues until everyone but the father has gone to bed at night. There is an outhouse and the immediate landscape teems with derelict machinery, car wrecks, and the other detritus of careless encounters with civilization. These are poor and ignorant people, without imagination, without aspirations, and, despite a rough affection for one another, without much sensitivity to the personal well-being of others or the conventions of society.

The oldest child amidst this squalor and sloth, Jasmin is confronted by her imminent failure of grade six, haunted by her failure, somehow, as a person. She has virtually no sense of self-worth. Yet the family depends on her: she washes the dishes, minds Leroy, keeps things from sinking into a torpor of indifference. Her reward for being oldest is a bed by the single window in the attic. No one expects her to think or feel or be anything. Her teachers expect nothing; her family only that she fit in, do her chores, be there. And so, on a clear spring night she leaves.

The novel is mostly about her running away. Jasmin is resourceful and imaginative, despite her background, but eventually she deteriorates, becoming almost animal-like. Delirious, she is rescued by a young couple who recognize her as a special person, sensitive, creative, and, behind the firmly set chin, frightened. They become her friends. Meanwhile, her retarded brother, who followed her into the bush, has also degenerated into an animal state in isolation; but whereas this is ultimately liberating for Jasmin, it is a catastrophe for Leroy. Things work out in the end, conditionally, for everyone. The conclusion, however, should not be misread: there is a gritty toughness to this novel, an insistence on the stark realities of social and economic deprivation, of psychological deprivation, that will move the reader, regardless of age or gender, to think carefully about such things. The writing style is aimed at the adolescent, and only occasionally, as when the author tries to fill the mouths of her characters with poor grammar, does it betray its adult origin. On the whole, this is a very fine novel, written specifically for young readers. It is immensely powerful, moving, and illuminating—a superb fiction.

The illustration on the cover of this novel, a painting by Margaret Farrell Bruno, is remarkable. Usually I do not comment in this book on such ancillary things; but Bruno so beautifully captures the strength and bewilderment, the wary sensitivity, the haunted, dreaming anxiety of Jasmin's character, that it is virtually a novel on its own. It is a work of art to wonder at, to be moved by, and to assimilate into one's own experience of oneself–a superb portrait.

DAVID WALKER

Pirate Rock. Toronto: Collins, 1969. Richmond Hill: Scholastic-TAB, 1974. Pages: 227. [12–15]

As its title implies, this is a novel of high adventure. Set in the Bay of Fundy, where Maine and New Brunswick meet, *Pirate Rock* relates the escapades of two brothers in their early teens whose reckless curiosity ensnares them in a web of kidnapping and espionage. Nelson and Keith Kelly take summer jobs manning the speedboat of a wealthy Montrealer (Becker, a former Nazi who spent time after the war in a Russian work camp, where he was co-opted to the communist cause). The boys become suspicious about things around the Becker estate. They are joined in their detective work by Becker's step-daughter, Kim, who is at least as daring, but inhibited in sharing the adventure by her relationship to the principal villain. After action-packed pages of intrigue and excitement, and a budding romance between Kim and Keith, the boys save a kidnapped American scientist, dispose of Becker and, with the aid of the RCMP, smash an international spy ring. This is the stuff of daydreams and Walker tells his tale exceedingly well. His intimate knowledge and effective use of the Maritime locale give the novel a depth and intensity not often found in thrillers. Walker writes popular fiction–the "Geordie" books were long-time best-sellers. His children's novels display the polish and the pacing of a professional's work and reverberate with the insights into adolescence and adventure of a humane and gifted raconteur.

SCOTT YOUNG

Scrubs on Skates. Boston: Little, Brown. 1952. Toronto:
McClelland and Stewart, 1985. Pages: 233.
Paperback. [12–14]

This novel is a souvenir from the past. I distinctly remember reading it in 1952, when I was twelve. In all honesty, I remembered
absolutely nothing about it when I sat down to read it again thirty-
some years later. This is not the same novel it was–I know this
not because it all came back to me as I read, but because it is
strewn rather haphazardly with references to the mid-1980s. The
effect of updating is disconcerting, since the social setting of the
novel is early postwar (that is, World War II). To find Lech Walesa
and Wayne Gretzky mentioned in a context of forties talk and
bobby socks is apt to throw the adult reader somewhat askew.
Many may be annoyed by unpleasant echoes of another era: girls
and women play supporting roles, at best; the French boy gets
kidded about his accent; the Indian kid is called Chief; Pete's sister is going to study psychology "to be a good wife"; the big Polish
kid, Bill Spunska, makes good through sheer grit. But all this
can be ignored when the puck is on the ice. For many, *Scrubs on
Skates* will seem fresh, fascinating, and only a bit otherworldly
as it works play by play through a series of high school hockey
games in a timeless Winnipeg. The plot, in which Pete Gordon
becomes reconciled to being the best player on the league's weakest team, provides Scott Young with a framework in which to
develop a number of conventional ploys to pull the heart-strings
but also allows him to create games on paper that have such a
ring of authenticity, and such narrative authority, that one almost
hears Foster Hewitt calling shots.

Two other hockey novels by Scott Young have been issued in
reprint along with this one, the three being offered as a trilogy.
Boy on Defence follows the young Polish player, Bill Spunska, into
the city championship. *A Boy at the Leafs' Camp* tests Bill's mettle
among the pros–and finds him (and there must be a joke here
somewhere) ready for the Olympic team but not quite up to Leafs'
calibre. In all three, Young carefully explains the game and

clarifies terminology in game context. Had I read more carefully, way back then, I might have learned a lot more about hockey than I ever got to know playing PeeWee. Finally, I understand what "icing the puck" means.

APPENDIX A

Selections in Chronological Order

1769   *The History of Emily Montague* (Brooke)

1821-22 "The Stepsure Letters" (McCulloch; serially)

1824   *St. Ursula's Convent* (Hart)

1831   *Bogle Corbet* (Galt)

1832   *Wacousta* (Richardson)

1836   *The Clockmaker* (Haliburton)

1840   *The Canadian Brothers* (Richardson)

1843   *Belinda* (Holmes)

1849   *The Old Judge* (Haliburton)

1852   *Roughing It in the Bush* (Moodie)
        Canadian Crusoes (Traill)

1862   *Letters of Mephibosheth Stepsure* (McCulloch)

1863   *Les Anciens Canadiens* (Aubert de Gaspé)

1864   *Antoinette de Mirecourt* (Leprohon)

1870   *The Lady of the Ice* (De Mille)

1874   *Jean Rivard: le défricheur* (Gérin-Lajoie)

1876   *Kate Danton* (Fleming)
        Jean Rivard: économiste (Gérin-Lajoie)

1877   *The Golden Dog* (Kirby)

1884   *Angéline de Montbrun* (Conan)

1888   *A Strange Manuscript Found in a Copper Cylinder* (De Mille)

1893   *What Necessity Knows* (Dougall)

1894   *Beautiful Joe* (Saunders)

1896   *The Seats of the Mighty* (Parker)

1899   *The Curé of St. Philippe* (Grey)

1900   *Lords of the North* (Laut)
        The Heart of the Ancient Wood (C.G.D. Roberts)

1901   *The Man from Glengarry* (Connor)

1903   *Two Little Savages* (Seton)

CHRONOLOGY

1904	*The Imperialist* (Duncan)
1908	*The Measure of the Rule* (Barr) *My Lady of the Snows* (Brown) *Sowing Seeds in Danny* (McClung) *Anne of Green Gables* (Montgomery)
1911	*Nonsense Novels* (Leacock) *The Harbour Master* (T. Roberts)
1912	*Sunshine Sketches of a Little Town* (Leacock)
1916	*Maria Chapdelaine* (Hémon)
1920	*The Prairie Mother* (Stringer)
1922	*Over Prairie Trails* (Grove)
1923	*The Magpie* (Durkin) *The Viking Heart* (Salverson)
1925	*Settlers of the Marsh* (Grove) *Wild Geese* (Ostenso) *In the Morning of Time* (C.G.D. Roberts)
1926	*Grain* (Stead)
1927	*Jalna* (de la Roche) *A Search for America* (Grove)
1928	*Rockbound* (Day)
1929	*White Narcissus* (Knister)
1930	*Generals Die in Bed* (Harrison)
1933	*Fruits of the Earth* (Grove) *Silver Chief* (O'Brien)
1934	*Such Is My Beloved* (Callaghan) *Les Demi-civilisés* (Harvey)
1935	*They Shall Inherit the Earth* (Callaghan) *The Adventures of Sajo and Her Beaver People* (Grey Owl) *The Flying Years* (Niven)
1936	*Think of the Earth* (Brooker)
1937	*More Joy in Heaven* (Callaghan) *God's Sparrows* (Child)
1938	*Trente arpents* (Ringuet)
1939	*Tay John* (O'Hagan)
1941	*Barometer Rising* (MacLennan) *As for Me and My House* (Ross)

1942   *His Majesty's Yankees* (Raddall)

1943   *Starbuck Valley Winter* (Haig-Brown)

1944   *Earth and High Heaven* (Graham)
        The Master of the Mill (Grove)
        Carrying Place (A. Mowat)

1945   *Le Survenant* (Guèvremont)
        Two Solitudes (MacLennan)
        Bonheur d'occasion (Roy)
        By Grand Central Station I Sat Down and Wept (Smart)

1946   *Remember Me* (Meade)

1947   *Kristli's Trees* (Dunham)
        Marie-Didace (Guèvremont)
        Sarah Binks (Hiebert)
        Under the Volcano (Lowry)
        Music at the Close (McCourt)
        Who Has Seen the Wind (Mitchell)
        Hetty Dorval (Wilson)

1948   *Luke Baldwin's Vow* (Callaghan)
        Les Plouffe (Lemelin)

1949   *Turvey* (Birney)
        Storm Below (Garner)
        The Innocent Traveller (Wilson)

1950   *The Golden Pine Cone* (Clark)
        The Bells on Finland Street (Cook)
        Cabbagetown (Garner)
        The Nymph and the Lamp (Raddall)
        La Petite Poule d'eau (Roy)

1951   *The Loved and the Lost* (Callaghan)
        Tempest-Tost (Davies)
        The Second Scroll (Klein)
        Each Man's Son (MacLennan)

1952   *The Mountain and the Valley* (Buckler)
        Scrubs on Skates (Young)

1953   *Poussière sur la ville* (Langevin)

1954   *The Channel Shore* (Bruce)
        Mist on the River (Evans)
        The English Governess (Glassco; first version)
        Swamp Angel (Wilson)

1955   *The Last of the Curlews* (Bodsworth)
        The Lonely Passion of Judith Hearne (Moore)
        Son of a Smaller Hero (Richler)

CHRONOLOGY

1956   *Lost in the Barrens* (F. Mowat)
        The Sacrifice (Wiseman)

1957   "Its Image in the Mirror" (Gallant)
        Under the Ribs of Death (Marlyn)

1958   *Les Chambres de bois* (Hébert)
        Execution (McDougall)
        Agaguk (Theriault)

1959   *La Belle Bête* (Blais)
        Green Water, Green Sky (Gallant)
        The Watch that Ends the Night (MacLennan)
        The Apprenticeship of Duddy Kravitz (Richler)
        The Double Hook (Watson)

1960   *Le Libraire* (Bessette)
        A Candle to Light the Sun (Blondal)
        Doux-Amer (Martin)
        The Luck of Ginger Coffey (Moore)

1961   *The Incredible Journey* (Burnford)
        Jake and the Kid (Mitchell)

1962   *Four Days* (Buell)
        The Kissing Man (Elliott)
        Cotnoir (Ferron)
        Silence on the Shore (Garner)
        Peace Shall Destroy Many (Wiebe)

1964   *Le Wapiti* (Corriveau)
        Sunburst (Gotlieb)
        White Figure, White Ground (Hood)
        The Betrayal (Kreisel)
        The Stone Angel (Laurence)
        The Deserter (Le Pan)
        Menaud, maître-draveur (Savard)

1965   *Prochain épisode* (Aquin)
        Une Saison dans la vie d'Emmanuel (Blais)
        Le Couteau sur la table (Godbout)
        Flaming Prairie (Hayes)
        The Last of the Great Picnics (McFarlane)
        The Boy with an R in His Hand (Reaney)
        In Praise of Older Women (Vizinczey)

1966   *Beautiful Losers* (L. Cohen)
        L'Avalée des avalés (Ducharme)
        Raven's Cry (Harris)
        A Jest of God (Laurence)
        Breaking Smith's Quarter Horse (St. Pierre)

1967   *The Sparrow's Fall* (Bodsworth)
       Mirror on the Floor (Bowering)
       Mon cheval pour un royaume (Poulin)
       Combat Journal for Place d'Armes (Symons)

1968   *La Guerre, Yes Sir!* (Carrier)
       Double Spell (Lunn)
       I Am Mary Dunne (Moore)

1969   *L'Antiphonaire* (Aquin)
       The Edible Woman (Atwood)
       Five Legs (Gibson)
       The Studhorse Man (Kroetsch)
       The Fire-Dwellers (Laurence)
       A Walk out of the World (Nichols)
       Jimmy (Poulin)
       Pirate Rock (Walker)

1970   *Jos Connaissant* (Beaulieu)
       Fifth Business (Davies)
       A Fairly Good Time (Gallant)
       The New Ancestors (Godfrey)
       Kamouraska (Hébert)
       House of Hate (Janes)
       A Bird in the House (Laurence)
       From a Seaside Town (Levine)
       Harpoon of the Hunter (Markoosie)
       Mrs. Blood (Thomas)
       The Weekend Man (Wright)

1971   *Communion* (Gibson)
       The White Dawn (Houston)
       La Sagouine (Maillet)
       Lives of Girls and Women (Munro)
       Le Coeur de la baleine bleue (Poulin)
       St. Urbain's Horseman (Richler)
       Arkwright (Simpson)
       "Munchmeyer" and "Prospero on the Island" (Thomas)
       Honor Bound (Downie)

1972   *Surfacing* (Atwood)
       Scann (Harlow)
       You Can't Get There from Here (Hood)
       White Eskimo (Horwood)
       From Anna (Little)
       Going Down Slow (Metcalf)

1973   *The Book of Eve* (Beresford-Howe)
       Storm of Fortune (Clarke)
       The Pegnitz Junction (Gallant)

Gone Indian (Kroetsch)
The Vanishing Point (Mitchell)
Riverrun (Such)
The Temptations of Big Bear (Wiebe)

1974   *Neige noire* (Aquin)
The Disinherited (M. Cohen)
The Diviners (Laurence)
Jeanne, fille du roy (Martel)
Lord Nelson Tavern (Smith)
Blown Figures (Thomas)

1975   *Wooden Hunters* (M. Cohen)
World of Wonders (Davies)
The Candy Factory (Fraser)
The Swing in the Garden (Hood)
Badlands (Kroetsch)

1976   *Lady Oracle* (Atwood)
Bear (Engel)
Harriet Marwood, Governess (Glassco)
The Glass Knight (Helwig)
Les Rescapes (Major)
Coming Through Slaughter (Ondaatje)
Blood Ties (Richards)
Small Ceremonies (Shields)

1977   *A Short Sad Book* (Bowering)
The Wars (Findley)
The Invention of the World (Hodgins)
A New Athens (Hood)
Frozen Fire (Houston)
The Young in One Another's Arms (Rule)
Underground to Canada (Smucker)
The Scorched-Wood People (Wiebe)

1978   *Abra* (Barfoot)
The Glassy Sea (Engel)
The Tomorrow City (Hughes)
Hold Fast (Major)
Skevington's Daughter (Mills)
Who Do You Think You Are? (Munro)

1979   *Lunar Attractions* (Blaise)
The Sweet Second Summer of Kitty Malone (M. Cohen)
The Resurrection of Joseph Bourne (Hodgins)
Reservoir Ravine (Hood)
Pélagie-La-Charrette (Maillet)

1980   *Burning Water* (Bowering)
What's the Matter, Girl? (Brochmann)
Nightmare Tales (Freiberg)

Héloïse (Hébert)
Who Is Bugs Potter? (Korman)
General Ludd (Metcalf)
Joshua Then and Now (Richler)
Fat Woman (Rooke)
Contract with the World (Rule)
Thérèse et Pierrette à l'école des Saints-Anges (Tremblay)

1981 *Le Matou* (Beauchemin)
The Rebel Angels (Davies)
Lunatic Villas (Engel)
Famous Last Words (Findley)
One Proud Summer (Hewitt & Mackay)
Black and White Keys (Hood)
Obasan (Kogawa)
La Première personne (Turgeon)

1982 *Dancing in the Dark* (Barfoot)
The Ivory Swing (Hospital)
Shoeless Joe (Kinsella)
Jasmin (Truss)

1983 *A Time for Judas* (Callaghan)
The Spanish Doctor (M. Cohen)
Tolerable Levels of Violence (Collins)
Alibi (Kroetsch)
Still (nichol)
The Biggest Modern Woman of the World (Swan)

1984 *Angel Square* (Doyle)
Not Wanted on the Voyage (Findley)
The Scenic Art (Hood)
Penumbra (Kerslake)
The Minerva Program (Mackay)
Willie: A Romance (Robertson)
The Engineer of Human Souls (Škvorecký)
Intertidal Life (Thomas)
My Present Age (Vanderhaeghe)

1985 *The Handmaid's Tale* (Atwood)
What's Bred in the Bone (Davies)
Borderline (Hospital)
Black Robe (Moore)
Road to the Stilt House (Richards)

1986 *Nadine* (M. Cohen)
The Baby Project (Ellis)
The Telling of Lies (Findley)
The Motor Boys in Ottawa (Hood)
Miss Abigail's Part (Terry)
No Fixed Address (van Herk)

Selections By Primary Setting

(Where appropriate, selections are listed under more than one heading; listings are chronological.)

THE MARITIMES AND NEWFOUNDLAND

"The Stepsure Letters" (McCulloch; 1821-22)
The Clockmaker (Haliburton; 1836)
The Old Judge (Haliburton; 1849)
Beautiful Joe (Saunders; 1894)
The Heart of the Ancient Wood (C.G.D. Roberts; 1900)
Anne of Green Gables (Montgomery; 1908)
The Harbour Master (T. Roberts; 1911)
Rockbound (Day; 1928)
Barometer Rising (MacLennan; 1941)
His Majesty's Yankees (Raddall; 1942)
The Nymph and the Lamp (Raddall; 1950)
Each Man's Son (MacLennan; 1951)
The Mountain and the Valley (Buckler; 1952)
The Channel Shore (Bruce; 1954)
White Figure, White Ground (Hood; 1964)
Pirate Rock (Walker; 1969)
House of Hate (Janes; 1970)
La Sagouine (Maillet; 1971)
White Eskimo (Horwood; 1972)
Riverrun (Such; 1973)
Lord Nelson Tavern (Smith; 1974)
Blood Ties (Richards; 1976)
Hold Fast (Major; 1978)
Pélagie-La-Charrette (Maillet; 1979)
Nightmare Tales (Freiberg; 1980)
The Biggest Modern Woman of the World (Swan; 1983)
Penumbra (Kerslake; 1984)
Road to the Stilt House (Richards; 1985)

QUEBEC

The History of Emily Montague (Brooke; 1769)
St. Ursula's Convent (Hart; 1824)
Les Anciens Canadiens (Aubert de Gaspé; 1863)
Antoinette de Mirecourt (Leprohon; 1864)
The Lady of the Ice (De Mille; 1870)
Jean Rivard: le défricheur (Gérin-Lajoie; 1874)
Kate Danton (Fleming; 1876)
Jean Rivard: économiste (Gérin-Lajoie; 1876)

The Golden Dog (Kirby; 1877)
Angéline de Montbrun (Conan; 1884)
What Necessity Knows (Dougall; 1893)
The Seats of the Mighty (Parker; 1896)
The Curé of St. Philippe (Grey; 1899)
Maria Chapdelaine (Hémon; 1916)
Les Demi-civilisés (Harvey; 1934)
Trente arpents (Ringuet; 1938)
Earth and High Heaven (Graham; 1944)
Le Survenant (Guèvremont; 1945)
Two Solitudes (MacLennan; 1945)
Bonheur d'occasion (Roy; 1945)
Marie-Didace (Guèvremont; 1947)
Les Plouffe (Lemelin; 1948)
The Loved and the Lost (Callaghan; 1951)
Poussière sur la ville (Langevin; 1953)
Son of a Smaller Hero (Richler; 1955)
"Its Image on the Mirror" (Gallant; 1957)
Les Chambres de bois (Hébert; 1958)
La Belle Bête (Blais; 1959)
The Watch that Ends the Night (MacLennan; 1959)
The Apprenticeship of Duddy Kravitz (Richler; 1959)
Le Libraire (Bessette; 1960)
Doux-Amer (Martin; 1960)
The Luck of Ginger Coffey (Moore; 1960)
Four Days (Buell; 1962)
Cotnoir (Ferron; 1962)
Le Wapiti (Corriveau; 1964)
Menaud, maître-draveur (Savard; 1964)
Prochain épisode (Aquin; 1965)
Une Saison dans la vie d'Emmanuel (Blais; 1965)
Le Couteau sur la table (Godbout; 1965)
Beautiful Losers (Cohen; 1966)
L'Avalée des avalés (Ducharme; 1966)
Mon cheval pour un royaume (Poulin; 1967)
Combat Journal for Place d'Armes (Symons; 1967)
La Guerre, Yes Sir! (Carrier; 1968)
L'Antiphonaire (Aquin; 1969)
Jimmy (Poulin; 1969)
Jos Connaissant (Beaulieu; 1970)
Kamouraska (Hébert; 1970)
La Coeur de la baleine bleue (Poulin; 1971)
St. Urbain's Horseman (Richler; 1971)
Surfacing (Atwood; 1972)
Going Down Slow (Metcalf; 1972)
The Book of Eve (Beresford-Howe; 1973)
Neige noire (Aquin; 1974)

PRIMARY SETTING

Jeanne, fille du roy (Martel; 1974)
Les Rescapes (Major; 1976)
General Ludd (Metcalf; 1980)
Joshua Then and Now (Richler; 1980)
Thérèse et Pierrette (Tremblay; 1980)
Le Matou (Beauchemin; 1981)
One Proud Summer (Hewitt & Mackay; 1981)
La Première personne (Turgeon; 1981)
Borderline (Hospital; 1985)

ONTARIO

Bogle Corbet (Galt; 1831)
Wacousta (Richardson; 1832)
The Canadian Brothers (Richardson; 1840)
Belinda (Holmes; 1843)
Canadian Crusoes (Traill; 1852)
Roughing It in the Bush (Moodie; 1852)
The Man from Glengarry (Connor; 1901)
Two Little Savages (Seton; 1903)
The Imperialist (Duncan; 1904)
The Measure of the Rule (Barr; 1908)
My Lady of the Snows (Brown; 1908)
Sunshine Sketches of a Little Town (Leacock; 1912)
Jalna (de la Roche; 1927)
White Narcissus (Knister; 1929)
Such Is My Beloved (Callaghan; 1934)
They Shall Inherit the Earth (Callaghan; 1935)
More Joy in Heaven (Callaghan; 1937)
God's Sparrows (Child; 1937)
The Master of the Mill (Grove; 1944)
Carrying Place (A. Mowat; 1944)
Kristli's Trees (Dunham; 1947)
Luke Baldwin's Vow (Callaghan; 1948)
The Bells on Finland Street (Cook; 1950)
Cabbagetown (Garner; 1950)
Tempest-Tost (Davies; 1951)
The Incredible Journey (Burnford; 1961)
The Kissing Man (Elliott; 1962)
Silence on the Shore (Garner; 1962)
The Last of the Great Picnics (McFarlane; 1965)
The Boy with an R in His Hand (Reaney; 1965)
Double Spell (Lunn; 1968)
The Edible Woman (Atwood; 1969)
Five Legs (Gibson; 1969)
Fifth Business (Davies; 1970)
The Weekend Man (Wright; 1970)

Communion (Gibson; 1971)
Lives of Girls and Women (Munro; 1971)
Arkwright (Simpson; 1971)
Honor Bound (Downie; 1971)
From Anna (Little; 1972)
Storm of Fortune (Clarke; 1973)
The Disinherited (M. Cohen; 1974)
The Diviners (Laurence; 1974)
World of Wonders (Davies; 1975)
The Candy Factory (Fraser; 1975)
The Swing in the Garden (Hood; 1975)
Lady Oracle (Atwood; 1976)
Bear (Engel; 1976)
The Glass Knight (Helwig; 1976)
Small Ceremonies (Shields; 1976)
A New Athens (Hood; 1977)
Abra (Barfoot; 1978)
The Glassy Sea (Engel; 1978)
Who Do You Think You Are? (Munro; 1978)
The Sweet Second Summer of Kitty Malone (M. Cohen; 1979)
Reservoir Ravine (Hood; 1979)
Who Is Bugs Potter? (Korman; 1980)
The Rebel Angels (Davies; 1981)
Lunatic Villas (Engel; 1981)
Dancing in the Dark (Barfoot; 1982)
Tolerable Levels of Violence (Collins; 1983)
Still (nichol; 1983)
Angel Square (Doyle; 1984)
The Minerva Program (Mackay; 1984)
Willie: A Romance (Robertson; 1984)
The Engineer of Human Souls (Škvorecký, 1984)
What's Bred in the Bone (Davies; 1985)
Black Robe (Moore; 1985)
Nadine (M. Cohen; 1986)

THE PRAIRIES/THE WEST

Lords of the North (Laut; 1900)
Sowing Seeds in Danny (McClung; 1908)
The Prairie Mother (Stringer; 1920)
Over Prairie Trails (Grove; 1922)
The Magpie (Durkin; 1923)
The Viking Heart (Salverson; 1923)
Settlers of the Marsh (Grove; 1925)
Wild Geese (Ostenso; 1925)
Grain (Stead; 1926)
Fruits of the Earth (Grove; 1933)

The Adventures of Sajo and Her Beaver People (Grey Owl; 1935)
The Flying Years (Niven; 1935)
Think of the Earth (Brooker; 1936)
Tay John (O'Hagan; 1939)
As for Me and My House (Ross; 1941)
Sarah Binks (Hiebert; 1947)
Music at the Close (McCourt; 1947)
Who Has Seen the Wind (Mitchell; 1947)
La Petite Poule d'eau (Roy; 1950)
Scrubs on Skates (Young; 1952)
The Sacrifice (Wiseman; 1956)
Under the Ribs of Death (Marlyn; 1957)
A Candle to Light the Sun (Blondal; 1960)
Jake and the Kid (Mitchell; 1961)
Peace Shall Destroy Many (Wiebe; 1962)
The Betrayal (Kreisel; 1964)
The Stone Angel (Laurence; 1964)
Flaming Prairie (Hayes; 1965)
A Jest of God (Laurence; 1966)
The Studhorse Man (Kroetsch; 1969)
A Bird in the House (Laurence; 1970)
Gone Indian (Kroetsch; 1973)
The Vanishing Point (Mitchell; 1973)
The Temptations of Big Bear (Wiebe; 1973)
The Diviners (Laurence; 1974)
Badlands (Kroetsch; 1975)
The Scorched-Wood People (Wiebe; 1977)
Obasan (Kogawa; 1981)
Jasmin (Truss; 1982)
Alibi (Kroetsch; 1983)
My Present Age (Vanderhaeghe; 1984)
No Fixed Address (van Herk; 1986)

BRITISH COLUMBIA

Starbuck Valley Winter (Haig-Brown; 1943)
Hetty Dorval (Wilson; 1947)
The Innocent Traveller (Wilson; 1949)
The Golden Pine Cone (Clark; 1950)
Mist on the River (Evans; 1954)
Swamp Angel (Wilson; 1954)
The Double Hook (Watson; 1959)
Raven's Cry (Harris; 1966)
Breaking Smith's Quarter Horse (St. Pierre; 1966)
Mirror on the Floor (Bowering; 1967)
The Fire-Dwellers (Laurence; 1969)
A Walk out of the World (Nichols; 1969)

"Munchmeyer" and "Prospero on the Island" (Thomas; 1971)
Scann (Harlow; 1972)
Wooden Hunters (M. Cohen; 1975)
A Short Sad Book (Bowering; 1977)
The Invention of the World (Hodgins; 1977)
The Young in One Another's Arms (Rule; 1977)
Skevington's Daughter (Mills; 1978)
The Resurrection of Joseph Bourne (Hodgins; 1979)
Burning Water (Bowering; 1980)
What's the Matter, Girl? (Brochmann; 1980)
Contract with the World (Rule; 1980)
Obasan (Kogawa; 1981)
Intertidal Life (Thomas; 1984)
The Baby Project (Ellis; 1986)
No Fixed Address (van Herk; 1986)

THE NORTH

Silver Chief (O'Brien; 1933)
Lost in the Barrens (F. Mowat; 1956)
Agaguk (Theriault; 1958)
The Incredible Journey (Burnford; 1961)
The Sparrow's Fall (Bodsworth; 1967)
Harpoon of the Hunter (Markoosie; 1970)
The White Dawn (Houston; 1971)
White Eskimo (Horwood; 1972)
Frozen Fire (Houston; 1977)
No Fixed Address (van Herk; 1986)

OTHER

(Many of the following are set in Canada as well as the
other places designated)

St. Ursula's Convent (Hart; 1824. England)
A Strange Manuscript Found in a Copper Cylinder (De Mille; 1888.
Antarctic/Fantasy)
Nonsense Novels (Leacock; 1911. Various)
In the Morning of Time (Roberts; 1925. Pre-History)
A Search for America (Grove; 1927. United States)
Generals Die in Bed (Harrison; 1930. Europe)
God's Sparrows (Child; 1937. Europe)
By Grand Central Station I Sat Down and Wept (Smart; 1945. United States)
Remember Me (Meade; 1946. England/Europe)
Under the Volcano (Lowry; 1947. Mexico)
Turvey (Birney; 1949. Europe)
Storm Below (Garner; 1949. North Atlantic)

The Innocent Traveller (Wilson; 1949. England)
The Second Scroll (Klein; 1951. Europe/North Africa/Israel)
The English Governess (Glassco; 1954. England/France)
The Last of the Curlews (Bodsworth; 1955. Western Hemisphere)
The Lonely Passion of Judith Hearne (Moore; 1955. Ireland)
Les Chambres de bois (Hébert; 1958. France)
Execution (McDougall; 1958. Italy)
Green Water, Green Sky (Gallant; 1959. France)
Sunburst (Gotlieb; 1964. United States/Fantasy)
The Deserter (Le Pan; 1964. England/Europe)
Prochain épisode (Aquin; 1965. Switzerland)
In Praise of Older Women (Vizinczey; 1965. Europe)
L'Avalées des avalés (Ducharme; 1966. United States/Israel)
I Am Mary Dunne (Moore; 1968. United States)
L'Antiphonaire (Aquin; 1969. United States/Europe)
A Fairly Good Time (Gallant; 1970. France)
The New Ancestors (Godfrey; 1970. Africa)
From a Seaside Town (Levine; 1970. England)
Mrs. Blood (Thomas; 1970. Africa)
St. Urbain's Horseman (Richler; 1971. England/Europe)
You Can't Get There from Here (Hood; 1972. Africa/Fantasy)
From Anna (Little; 1972. Germany)
The Pegnitz Junction (Gallant; 1973. France/Germany)
Neige noire (Aquin; 1974. Norway)
Blown Figures (Thomas; 1974. Africa)
World of Wonders (Davies; 1975. Europe)
Coming Through Slaughter (Ondaatje; 1976. United States)
The Wars (Findley; 1977. England/Europe)
The Invention of the World (Hodgins; 1977. Ireland)
Underground to Canada (Smucker; 1977. United States)
The Tomorrow City (Hughes; 1978. Fantasy)
Skevington's Daughter (Mills; 1978. Mexico)
Lunar Attractions (Blaise; 1979. United States)
Pélagie-La-Charrette (Maillet; 1979. United States)
Burning Water (Bowering; 1980. Various)
Héloïse (Hébert; 1980. France)
Fat Woman (Rooke; 1980. United States)
Famous Last Words (Findley; 1981. Europe)
La Première personne (Turgeon; 1981. United States)
The Ivory Swing (Hospital; 1982. India)
Shoeless Joe (Kinsella; 1982. United States)
A Time for Judas (Callaghan; 1983. Palestine)
The Spanish Doctor (M. Cohen; 1983. Europe)
Alibi (Kroetsch; 1984. Wales/Europe)
The Biggest Modern Woman of the World (Swan; 1984, United States)
Not Wanted on the Voyage (Findley; 1984. Mt. Ararat)
The Engineer of Human Souls (Škvorecký; 1984. Czechoslovakia)

The Handmaid's Tale (Atwood; 1985. United States)
What's Bred in the Bone (Davies; 1985. England/Europe)
Borderline (Hospital; 1985. United States)
Nadine (M. Cohen; 1986. Europe/Israel)
The Telling of Lies (Findley; 1986. United States)
Miss Abigail's Part (Terry; 1986. England)

Winners of the Governor General's Award for Fiction

1936   *Think of the Earth* (Bertram Brooker)

1937   *The Dark Weaver* (Laura Goodman Salverson)

1938   *Swiss Sonata* (Gwethalyn Graham)

1939   *The Champlain Road* (Franklin D. McDowell)

1940   *Thirty Acres* (Ringuet. Translation of *Trente arpents*)

1941   *Three Came to Ville Marie* (Alan Sullivan)

1942   *Little Man* (G. Herbert Sallans)

1943   *The Pied Piper of Dipper Creek* (Thomas Raddall)

1944   *Earth and High Heaven* (Gwethalyn Graham)

1945   *Two Solitudes* (Hugh MacLennan)

1946   *Continental Revue* (Winifred Bambrick)

1947   *The Tin Flute* (Gabrielle Roy. Translation of *Bonheur d'occasion*)

1948   *The Precipice* (Hugh MacLennan)

1949   *Mr. Ames Against Time* (Philip Child)

1950   *The Outlander* (Germaine Guèvremont. Translation of *Le Survenant* and *Marie-Didace*)

1951   *The Loved and the Lost* (Morley Callaghan)

1952   *The Pillar* (David Walker)

1953   *Digby* (David Walker)

1954   *The Fall of a Titan* (Igor Gouzenko)

1955   *The Sixth of June* (Lionel Shapiro)

1956   *The Sacrifice* (Adele Wiseman)

1957   *Street of Riches* (Gabrielle Roy. Translation of *Rue Deschambault*)

1958   *Execution* (Colin McDougall)

1959   *Malgré tout, la joie* (André Giroux)
       The Watch that Ends the Night (Hugh MacLennan)

GOVERNOR GENERAL'S AWARD WINNERS

1960   *The Luck of Ginger Coffey* (Brian Moore)

1961   *Hear Us O Lord from Heaven Thy Dwelling Place* (Malcolm Lowry)
Ashini (Yves Thériault)

1962   *Running to Paradise* (Kildare Dobbs)
Contes du pays incertain (Jacques Ferron)

1963   *Hugh Garner's Best Stories* (Hugh Garner)

1964   *The Deserter* (Douglas Le Pan)
Les Terres sèches (Jean-Paul Pinsonneault)

1965   *L'incubation* (Gérard Bessette)

1966   *A Jest of God* (Margaret Laurence)
La Joue droite (Claire Martin)

1967   *Salut Galarneau* (Jacques Godbout)

1968   *Trou de mémoire* (Hubert Aquin)
Manuscrits de Pauline Archange (Marie-Claire Blais)
Dance of the Happy Shades (Alice Munro)
Cocksure (Mordecai Richler)

1969   *The Studhorse Man* (Robert Kroetsch)
Une Forêt pour Zoé (Louise Maheux-Forcier)

1970   *La Femme de Loth* (Monique Bosco)
The New Ancestors (Dave Godfrey)

1971   *Le Cycle* (Gérard Bessette)
St. Urbain's Horseman (Mordecai Richler)

1972   *The Manticore* (Robertson Davies)
Don l'Orignal (Antonine Maillet)

1973   *L'Hiver de force* (Réjean Ducharme)
The Temptations of Big Bear (Rudy Wiebe)

1974   *Don Quichotte de la démanche* (Victor-Lévy Beaulieu)
The Diviners (Margaret Laurence)

1975   *Les Enfants du sabbat* (Anne Hébert)
The Great Victorian Collection (Brian Moore)

1976   *Bear* (Marian Engel)
Les Rescapés (André Major)

1977   *The Wars* (Timothy Findley)
Ces Enfants de ma vie (Gabrielle Roy)

1978   *Who Do You Think You Are?* (Alice Munro)
Les Grandes Marées (Jacques Poulin)

1979   *The Resurrection of Joseph Bourne* (Jack Hodgins)
Le Sourd dans la ville (Marie-Claire Blais)

1980   *Burning Water* (George Bowering)
        La Première Personne (Pierre Turgeon)

1981   *Home Truths* (Mavis Gallant)
        La Province lunaire (Denys Chabot)

1982   *Man Descending* (Guy Vanderhaeghe)
        Le Cercle des arènes (Roger Fournier)

1983   *Shakespeare's Dog* (Leon Rooke)
        Laura Laur (Suzanne Jacob)

1984   *The Engineer of Human Souls* (Josef Škvorecký)
        Agonie (Jacques Brault)

1985   *The Handmaid's Tale* (Margaret Atwood)
        Lucie on un midi en novembre (Fernand Ouellette)

A Canadian Novel Short List

The following will give the reader a minimal claim to familiarity with the mainstream of Canadian fiction. These are not necessarily our best novels, nor even the best of their authors' works, but they represent the central tradition, as seen from a contemporary perspective. Seven Québécois novels available in English translation are included.

The History of Emily Montague (Brooke; 1769)
Wacousta (Richardson; 1832)
Roughing It in the Bush (Moodie; 1852)
The Imperialist (Duncan; 1904)
Sunshine Sketches of a Little Town (Leacock; 1912)
Maria Chapdelaine (Hémon; 1916)
Settlers of the Marsh (Grove; 1925)
Wild Geese (Ostenso; 1925)
Such Is My Beloved (Callaghan; 1934)
Trente arpents (Ringuet; 1938. *Thirty Acres*)
As For Me and My House (Ross; 1941)
Two Solitudes (MacLennan; 1945)
Bonheur d'occasion (Roy; 1945. *The Tin Flute*)
Who Has Seen the Wind (Mitchell; 1947)
The Mountain and the Valley (Buckler; 1952)
Swamp Angel (Wilson; 1954)
The Sacrifice (Wiseman; 1956)
La Belle Bête (Blais; 1959. *Mad Shadows*)
The Apprenticeship of Duddy Kravitz (Richler; 1959)
The Double Hook (Watson; 1959)
The Stone Angel (Laurence; 1964)
Prochain épisode (Aquin; 1965)
The Studhorse Man (Kroetsch; 1969)
Fifth Business (Davies; 1970)

Kamouraska (Hébert; 1970)
Lives of Girls and Women (Munro; 1971)
Surfacing (Atwood; 1972)
The Temptations of Big Bear (Wiebe; 1973)
The Disinherited (M. Cohen; 1974)
Blown Figures (Thomas; 1974)
The Invention of the World (Hodgins; 1977)
The Glassy Sea (Engel; 1978)
Pélagie-La-Charrette (Maillet; 1979)
Burning Water (Bowering; 1980)
Not Wanted on the Voyage (Findley; 1984)
Road to the Stilt House (Richards; 1985)
Borderline (Hospital; 1985)

Canadian Poet-Novelists Included in This Book

(Many novelists write poetry, but it seems a Canadian phenomenon that so many of our writers are equally accomplished in both genres.)

Margaret Atwood	A.M. Klein
Earle Birney	Raymond Knister
George Bowering	Joy Kogawa
Charles Bruce	Robert Kroetsch
Leonard Cohen	Douglas Le Pan
James De Mille	bp nichol
Stanley Freiberg	Michael Ondaatje
John Glassco	Charles G.D. Roberts
Anne Hébert	Elizabeth Smart
Susan Kerslake	

APPENDIX B

The following lists are simply suggestions, meant as a guide to novels most appropriate to the reader's particular interest. Groupings are arranged more or less in a sequence, from selections based on form or type to selections based on dominant themes or motifs. Lists are arranged chronologically; Québécois novels, according to their original date of publication in French. Novels for Young Readers are designated *YR*.

Experimental or Avant-garde Novels
Angéline de Montbrun (Conan; 1884)
Tay John (O'Hagan; 1939)
By Grand Central Station I Sat Down and Wept (Smart; 1945)
The Second Scroll (Klein; 1951)
"Its Image on the Mirror" (Gallant; 1957)
Les Chambres de bois (Hébert; 1958)
La Belle Bête (Blais; 1959)
The Double Hook (Watson; 1959)
The Kissing Man (Elliott; 1962)
The Deserter (Le Pan; 1964)
Prochain épisode (Aquin; 1965)
Le Couteau sur la table (Godbout; 1965)
Beautiful Losers (L. Cohen; 1966)
L'Avalée des avalés (Ducharme; 1966)
Mon cheval pour un royaume (Poulin; 1967)
Combat Journal for Place d'Armes (Symons; 1967)
L'Antiphonaire (Aquin; 1969)
Five Legs (Gibson; 1969)
Jimmy (Poulin; 1969)
The New Ancestors (Godfrey; 1970)
Kamouraska (Hébert; 1970)
Communion (Gibson; 1971)
Le Coeur de la baleine bleue (Poulin; 1971)
"Munchmeyer" and "Prospero on the Island" (Thomas; 1971)
Surfacing (Atwood; 1972)
Scann (Harlow; 1972)
The Pegnitz Junction (Gallant; 1973)
Gone Indian (Kroetsch; 1973)
Riverrun (Such; 1973)
Neige noire (Aquin; 1974)
Lord Nelson Tavern (Smith; 1974)
Blown Figures (Thomas; 1974)
Coming Through Slaughter (Ondaatje; 1976)
A Short Sad Book (Bowering; 1977)
Skevington's Daughter (Mills; 1978)

The Resurrection of Joseph Bourne (Hodgins; 1979)
Burning Water (Bowering; 1980)
Héloïse (Hébert; 1980)
La Première personne (Turgeon; 1981)
Shoeless Joe (Kinsella; 1982)
Still (nichol; 1983)
Not Wanted on the Voyage (Findley; 1984)
Penumbra (Kerslake; 1984)
Borderline (Hospital; 1985)

Visionary/Quasi-Visionary Novels

Think of the Earth (Brooker; 1936)
Tay John (O'Hagan; 1939)
The Second Scroll (Klein; 1951)
The Double Hook (Watson; 1959)
The Deserter (Le Pan; 1964)
Beautiful Losers (L. Cohen; 1966)
Riverrun (Such; 1973)
The Temptations of Big Bear (Wiebe; 1973)
Héloïse (Hébert; 1980)
Not Wanted on the Voyage (Findley; 1984)
The Handmaid's Tale (Atwood; 1985)

Novels with a Significant Spiritual Dimension

What Necessity Knows (Dougall; 1893)
Such Is My Beloved (Callaghan; 1934)
Who Has Seen the Wind (Mitchell; 1947)
The Sacrifice (Wiseman; 1956)
The Watch that Ends the Night (MacLennan; 1959)
Peace Shall Destroy Many (Wiebe; 1962)
White Figure, White Ground (Hood; 1964)
The Sparrow's Fall (Bodsworth; 1967)
Fifth Business (Davies; 1970)
Communion (Gibson; 1971)
Arkwright (Simpson; 1971)
The Glassy Sea (Engel; 1978)
The Resurrection of Joseph Bourne (Hodgins; 1979)

Novels with a Moral Vision or Significant Moral Concern

"The Stepsure Letters" (McCulloch; 1821-22)
The Old Judge (Haliburton; 1849)
A Strange Manuscript Found in a Copper Cylinder (De Mille; 1888)
Sowing Seeds in Danny (McClung; 1908)

The Magpie (Durkin; 1923)
Les Demi-civilisés (Harvey; 1934)
They Shall Inherit the Earth (Callaghan; 1935)
More Joy in Heaven (Callaghan; 1937)
God's Sparrows (Child; 1937)
Hetty Dorval (Wilson; 1947)
Turvey (Birney; 1949)
The Loved and the Lost (Callaghan; 1951)
Poussière sur la ville (Langevin; 1953)
Mist on the River (Evans; 1954)
The Last of the Curlews (Bodsworth; 1955)
Son of a Smaller Hero (Richler; 1955)
Execution (McDougall; 1958)
Agaguk (Theriault; 1958)
The Apprenticeship of Duddy Kravitz (Richler; 1959)
Le Libraire (Bessette; 1960)
Four Days (Buell; 1962)
The Betrayal (Kreisel; 1964)
Une Saison dans la vie d'Emmanuel (Blais; 1965)
L'Avalée des avalés (Ducharme; 1966)
L'Antiphonaire (Aquin; 1969)
The New Ancestors (Godfrey; 1970)
St. Urbain's Horseman (Richler; 1971)
Arkwright (Simpson; 1971)
Scann (Harlow; 1972)
You Can't Get There from Here (Hood; 1972)
The Pegnitz Junction (Gallant; 1973)
The Vanishing Point (Mitchell; 1973)
Wooden Hunters (M. Cohen; 1975)
The Candy Factory (Fraser; 1975)
The Wars (Findley; 1977)
The Young in One Another's Arms (Rule; 1977)
Underground to Canada (Smucker; 1977. *YR*)
The Scorched-Wood People (Wiebe; 1977)
General Ludd (Metcalf; 1980)
Joshua Then and Now (Richler; 1980)
Contract with the World (Rule; 1980)
Obasan (Kogawa; 1981)
The Ivory Swing (Hospital; 1982)
The Spanish Doctor (M. Cohen; 1983)
Tolerable Levels of Violence (Collins; 1983)
Not Wanted on the Voyage (Findley; 1984)
The Handmaid's Tale (Atwood; 1985)
Borderline (Hospital; 1985)
Black Robe (Moore; 1985)
Road to the Stilt House (Richards; 1985)
Nadine (M. Cohen; 1986)

SELECTION CATEGORIES

The Novel of Ideas

A Strange Manuscript Found in a Copper Cylinder (De Mille; 1888)
The Magpie (Durkin; 1923)
The Betrayal (Kreisel; 1964)
You Can't Get There from Here (Hood; 1972)
A Short Sad Book (Bowering; 1977)
Tolerable Levels of Violence (Collins; 1983)

Didactic Novels

"The Stepsure Letters" (McCulloch; 1821-22)
Bogle Corbet (Galt; 1831)
The Clockmaker (Haliburton; 1836)
Canadian Crusoes (Traill; 1852. *YR*)
Jean Rivard: le défricheur (Gérin-Lajoie; 1874)
Jean Rivard: économiste (Gérin-Lajoie; 1876)
The Heart of the Ancient Wood (C.G.D. Roberts; 1900)
Two Little Savages (Seton; 1903. *YR*)
In the Morning of Time (C.G.D. Roberts; 1925)
A Search for America (Grove; 1927)
Earth and High Heaven (Graham; 1944)
The Master of the Mill (Grove; 1944)
The Last of the Curlews (Bodsworth; 1955)
Under the Ribs of Death (Marlyn; 1957)
Menaud, maître-draveur (Savard; 1964)
White Eskimo (Horwood; 1972)
The Vanishing Point (Mitchell; 1973)
Wooden Hunters (M. Cohen; 1975)
Underground to Canada (Smucker; 1977. *YR*)
The Scorched-Wood People (Wiebe; 1977)
Pélagie-La-Charrette (Maillet; 1979)
General Ludd (Metcalf; 1980)
One Proud Summer (Hewitt & Mackay; 1981. *YR*)
Obasan (Kogawa; 1981)
Tolerable Levels of Violence (Collins; 1983)
The Handmaid's Tale (Atwood; 1985)
The Baby Project (Ellis; 1986. *YR*)

War Novels

The Canadian Brothers (Richardson; 1840. 1812-14)
Generals Die in Bed (Harrison; 1930. World War I)
God's Sparrows (Child; 1937. World War I)
Remember Me (Meade; 1946. World War II)
Turvey (Birney; 1949. World War II)
Storm Below (Garner; 1949. World War II)
Execution (McDougall; 1958. World War II)
The Deserter (Le Pan; 1964. World War II)

The Wars (Findley; 1977. World War I)
Famous Last Words (Findley; 1981. World War II)
Obasan (Kogawa; 1981. World War II)
The Engineer of Human Souls (Škvorecký; 1984. World War II)

Historical Novels

St. Ursula's Convent (Hart; 1824)
Wacousta (Richardson; 1832)
Canadian Crusoes (Traill; 1952. *YR*)
Les Anciens Canadiens (Aubert de Gaspé; 1863)
Antoinette de Mirecourt (Leprohon; 1864)
The Lady of the Ice (De Mille; 1870)
The Golden Dog (Kirby; 1877)
The Seats of the Mighty (Parker; 1896)
Lords of the North (Laut; 1900)
His Majesty's Yankees (Raddall; 1942)
Le Wapiti (Corriveau; 1964. *YR*)
Flaming Prairie (Hayes; 1965. *YR*)
The Boy with an R in His Hand (Reaney; 1965. *YR*)
Raven's Cry (Harris; 1966. *YR*)
Kamouraska (Hébert; 1970)
Riverrun (Such; 1973)
The Temptations of Big Bear (Wiebe; 1973)
Jeanne, fille du roy (Martel; 1974. *YR*)
Badlands (Kroetsch; 1975)
Underground to Canada (Smucker; 1977. *YR*)
The Scorched-Wood People (Wiebe; 1977)
Pélagie-La-Charrette (Maillet; 1979)
Burning Water (Bowering; 1980)
Famous Last Words (Findley; 1981)
One Proud Summer (Hewitt & Mackay; 1981. *YR*)
Obasan (Kogawa; 1981)
A Time for Judas (Callaghan; 1983)
The Spanish Doctor (M. Cohen; 1983)
The Biggest Modern Woman of the World (Swan; 1983)
Willie: A Romance (Robertson; 1984)
Black Robe (Moore; 1985)
Miss Abigail's Part (Terry; 1986)

Psychological Novels: Analytic or Behavioural

By Grand Central Station I Sat Down and Wept (Smart; 1945)
Under the Volcano (Lowry; 1947)
The Mountain and the Valley (Buckler; 1952)
"Its Image on the Mirror" (Gallant; 1957)
Green Water, Green Sky (Gallant; 1959)
Doux-Amer (Martin; 1960)

SELECTION CATEGORIES

The Deserter (Le Pan; 1964)
Prochain épisode (Aquin; 1965)
L'Avalée des avalés (Ducharme; 1966)
Mon cheval pour une royaume (Poulin; 1967)
Combat Journal for Place d'Armes (Symons; 1967)
Jimmy (Poulin; 1969)
Fifth Business (Davies; 1970)
Kamouraska (Hebert; 1970)
From a Seaside Town (Levine; 1970)
Mrs. Blood (Thomas; 1970)
Lives of Girls and Women (Munro; 1971)
Le Coeur de la baleine bleue (Poulin; 1971)
Surfacing (Atwood; 1972)
The Pegnitz Junction (Gallant; 1973)
Neige noire (Aquin; 1974)
The Diviners (Laurence; 1974)
Blown Figures (Thomas; 1974)
Small Ceremonies (Shields; 1976)
The Wars (Findley; 1977)
Abra (Barfoot; 1978)
The Glassy Sea (Engel; 1978)
Who Do You Think You Are? (Munro; 1978)
Héloïse (Hébert; 1980)
Fat Woman (Rooke; 1980)
What's the Matter, Girl (Brochmann; 1980)
Lunatic Villas (Engel; 1981)
Obasan (Kogawa; 1981)
La Première personne (Turgeon; 1981)
Dancing in the Dark (Barfoot; 1982)
The Ivory Swing (Hospital; 1982)
Jasmin (Truss; 1982. *YR*)
Alibi (Kroetsch; 1983)
Still (nichol; 1983)
The Biggest Modern Woman of the World (Swan; 1983)
Penumbra (Kerslake; 1984)
The Engineer of Human Souls (Škvorecký; 1984)
Intertidal Life (Thomas; 1984)
My Present Age (Vanderhaeghe; 1984)
What's Bred in the Bone (Davies; 1985)
Borderline (Hospital; 1985)
Road to the Stilt House (Richards; 1985)
Nadine (M. Cohen; 1986)

Love Stories

The History of Emily Montague (Brooke; 1769)
St. Ursula's Convent (Hart; 1824)
Antoinette de Mirecourt (Leprohon; 1864)

The Lady of the Ice (De Mille; 1870)
Kate Danton (Fleming; 1876)
Angéline de Montbrun (Conan; 1884)
Settlers of the Marsh (Grove; 1925)
Jalna (de la Roche; 1927)
Earth and High Heaven (Graham; 1944)
Carrying Place (A. Mowat; 1944)
By Grand Central Station I Sat Down and Wept (Smart; 1945)
The Nymph and the Lamp (Raddall; 1950)
The Loved and the Lost (Callaghan; 1951)
The English Governess (Glassco; 1954. S&M)
Les Chambres de bois (Hébert; 1958)
Doux-Amer (Martin; 1960)
Mirror on the Floor (Bowering; 1967)
Kamouraska (Hébert; 1970)
"Prospero on the Island" (Thomas; 1971)
The Pegnitz Junction (Gallant; 1973)
Jeanne, fille du roy (Martel; 1974. *YR*)
Bear (Engel; 1976. With a bear)
The Glass Knight (Helwig; 1976)
The Sweet Second Summer of Kitty Malone (M. Cohen; 1979)
Héloïse (Hébert; 1980)
Willie: A Romance (Robertson; 1984)

Erotica

The English Governess (Glassco; 1954. Final version: *Harriet Marwood, Governess*, 1976)
In Praise of Older Women (Vizinczey; 1965)
Neige noire (Aquin; 1974)
No Fixed Address (van Herk; 1986)

Adventure Novels

The Seats of the Mighty (Parker; 1896)
Lords of the North (Laut; 1900)
Two Little Savages (Seton; 1903. *YR*)
The Harbour Master (T. Roberts; 1911)
Silver Chief (O'Brien; 1933. *YR*)
His Majesty's Yankees (Raddall; 1942)
Starbuck Valley Winter (Haig-Brown; 1943. *YR*)
The Golden Pine Cone (Clark; 1950. *YR*)
Scrubs on Skates (Young; 1952. *YR*)
Lost in the Barrens (F. Mowat; 1956. *YR*)
The Incredible Journey (Burnford; 1961)
Four Days (Buell; 1962)
Flaming Prairie (Hayes; 1965. *YR*)
Breaking Smith's Quarter Horse (St. Pierre; 1966)

A Walk out of the World (Nichols; 1969. *YR*)
Pirate Rock (Walker; 1969. *YR*)
Harpoon of the Hunter (Markoosie; 1970. *YR*)
White Eskimo (Horwood; 1972)
Frozen Fire (Houston; 1977. YR)
Who Is Bugs Potter? (Korman; 1980. *YR*)
La Première personne (Turgeon; 1981)
Shoeless Joe (Kinsella; 1982)
Jasmin (Truss; 1982. *YR*)
Angel Square (Doyle; 1984. *YR*)
The Minerva Program (Mackay; 1984. *YR*)
Black Robe (Moore; 1985)
The Telling of Lies (Findley; 1986)
Miss Abigail's Part (Terry; 1986)

Animal Stories

Beautiful Joe (Saunders; 1894. *YR*)
The Heart of the Ancient Wood (C.G.D. Roberts; 1900)
In the Morning of Time (C.G.D. Roberts; 1925)
Silver Chief (O'Brien; 1933. *YR*)
The Adventures of Sajo and Her Beaver People (Grey Owl; 1935. *YR*)
The Last of the Curlews (Bodsworth; 1955)
The Incredible Journey (Burnford; 1961)
Bear (Engel; 1976)

Speculative Fiction/Science Fiction

A Strange Manuscript Found in a Copper Cylinder (De Mille; 1888)
In the Morning of Time (C.G.D. Roberts; 1925)
Sunburst (Gotlieb; 1964)
A Walk out of the World (Nichols; 1969. *YR*)
The Tomorrow City (Hughes; 1978. *YR*)
Famous Last Words (Findley; 1981)
Shoeless Joe (Kinsella; 1982)
A Time for Judas (Callaghan; 1983)
Tolerable Levels of Violence (Collins; 1983)
Not Wanted on the Voyage (Findley; 1984)
The Handmaid's Tale (Atwood; 1985)

The Fantastic/The Supernatural/The Mythic

The Heart of the Ancient Wood (C.G.D. Roberts; 1900)
Tay John (O'Hagan; 1939)
Le Survenant (Guèvremont; 1945)
Marie-Didace (Guèvremont; 1947)
The Golden Pine Cone (Clark; 1950. *YR*)
The Double Hook (Watson; 1959)
L'Antiphonaire (Aquin; 1969)

"Munchmeyer" (Thomas; 1971)
Scann (Harlow; 1972)
Gone Indian (Kroetsch; 1973)
Lord Nelson Tavern (Smith; 1974)
The Candy Factory (Fraser; 1975)
The Invention of the World (Hodgins; 1977)
The Resurrection of Joseph Bourne (Hodgins; 1979)
Héloïse (Hébert; 1980)
Not Wanted on the Voyage (Findley; 1984)
Borderline (Hospital; 1985)

Horror and the Bizarre

Wacousta (Richardson; 1832)
Angéline de Montbrun (Conan; 1884)
Think of the Earth (Brooker; 1936)
The English Governess (Glassco; 1954)
La Belle Bête (Blais; 1958)
Beautiful Losers (L. Cohen; 1966)
L'Avalée des avalés (Ducharme; 1966)
Kamouraska (Hébert; 1970)
Communion (Gibson; 1971)
Surfacing (Atwood; 1972)
Scann (Harlow; 1972)
You Can't Get There from Here (Hood; 1972)
The Candy Factory (Fraser; 1975)
Bear (Engel; 1976)
The Wars (Findley; 1977)
Burning Water (Bowering; 1980)
Nightmare Tales (Freiberg; 1980)
Héloïse (Hébert; 1980)
Rebel Angels (Davies; 1981)
Tolerable Levels of Violence (Collins; 1983)
The Handmaid's Tale (Atwood; 1985)

Satire/Humour/Wit/Irony

"The Stepsure Letters" (McCulloch; 1821-22)
The Clockmaker (Haliburton; 1836)
Belinda (Holmes; 1843)
The Old Judge (Haliburton; 1849)
A Strange Manuscript Found in a Copper Cylinder (De Mille; 1888)
The Measure of the Rule (Barr; 1908)
Sowing Seeds in Danny (McClung; 1908)
Nonsense Novels (Leacock; 1911)
Sunshine Sketches of a Little Town (Leacock; 1912)
Sarah Binks (Hiebert; 1947)
Les Plouffe (Lemelin; 1948)

Turvey (Birney; 1949)
Tempest-Tost (Davies; 1951)
The Apprenticeship of Duddy Kravitz (Richler; 1959)
Le Libraire (Bessette; 1960)
The Luck of Ginger Coffey (Moore; 1960)
Jake and the Kid (Mitchell; 1961. *YR*)
Beautiful Losers (L. Cohen; 1966)
La Guerre, Yes Sir! (Carrier; 1968)
The Edible Woman (Atwood; 1969)
The Studhorse Man (Kroetsch; 1969)
The Weekend Man (Wright; 1970)
La Sagouine (Maillet; 1971)
Arkwright (Simpson; 1971)
You Can't Get There from Here (Hood; 1972)
Going Down Slow (Metcalf; 1972)
Gone Indian (Kroetsch; 1973)
Badlands (Kroetsch; 1975)
Lady Oracle (Atwood; 1976)
A Short Sad Book (Bowering; 1977)
Skevington's Daughter (Mills; 1978)
The Resurrection of Joseph Bourne (Hodgins; 1979)
Burning Water (Bowering; 1980)
General Ludd (Metcalf; 1980)
Le Matou (Beauchemin; 1981)
The Rebel Angels (Davies; 1981)
Shoeless Joe (Kinsella; 1982)
Alibi (Kroetsch; 1983)
Angel Square (Doyle; 1984. *YR*)
Not Wanted on the Voyage (Findley; 1984)
The Engineer of Human Souls (Škvorecký; 1984)
My Present Age (Vanderhaeghe; 1984)
Miss Abigail's Part (Terry; 1986)

Social Criticism/Commentary

The History of Emily Montague (Brooke; 1769)
"The Stepsure Letters" (McCulloch; 1821-22)
The Clockmaker (Haliburton; 1836)
The Old Judge (Haliburton; 1849)
A Strange Manuscript Found in a Copper Cylinder (De Mille; 1888)
What Necessity Knows (Dougall; 1893)
The Curé of St. Philippe (Grey; 1899)
The Imperialist (Duncan; 1904)
Sowing Seeds in Danny (McClung; 1908)
Sunshine Sketches of a Little Town (Leacock; 1912)
The Magpie (Durkin; 1923)
A Search for America (Grove; 1927)
Les Demi-civilisés (Harvey; 1934)

Trente arpents (Ringuet; 1938)
Earth and High Heaven (Graham; 1944)
The Master of the Mill (Grove; 1944)
Bonheur d'occasion (Roy; 1945)
Les Plouffe (Lemelin; 1948)
Cabbagetown (Garner; 1950)
Tempest-Tost (Davies; 1951)
Poussière sur la ville (Langevin; 1953)
Mist on the River (Evans; 1954)
The Apprenticeship of Duddy Kravitz (Richler; 1959)
Le Libraire (Bessette; 1960)
The Deserter (Le Pan; 1964)
Menaud, maître-draveur (Savard; 1964)
Prochain épisode (Aquin; 1965)
Une Saison dans la vie d'Emmanuel (Blais; 1965)
Le Couteau sur la table (Godbout; 1965)
Beautiful Losers (L. Cohen; 1966)
The Edible Woman (Atwood; 1969)
Jos Connaissant (Beaulieu; 1970)
The Weekend Man (Wright; 1970)
Communion (Gibson; 1971)
"Munchmeyer" (Thomas; 1971)
Storm of Fortune (Clarke; 1973)
Wooden Hunters (M. Cohen; 1975)
The Candy Factory (Fraser; 1975)
Lady Oracle (Atwood; 1976)
Les Rescapes (Major; 1976)
A Short Sad Book (Bowering; 1977)
The Young in One Another's Arms (Rule; 1977)
The Glassy Sea (Engel; 1978)
General Ludd (Metcalf; 1980)
Thérese et Pierrette (Tremblay; 1980)
Le Matou (Beauchemin; 1981)
One Proud Summer (Hewitt & Mackay; 1981)
The Spanish Doctor (M. Cohen; 1983)
Tolerable Levels of Violence (Collins; 1983)
The Engineer of Human Souls (Škvorecký; 1984)
The Handmaid's Tale (Atwood; 1985)
Borderline (Hospital; 1985)
Road to the Stilt House (Richards; 1985)
Nadine (M. Cohen; 1986)
Miss Abigail's Part (Terry; 1986)

SELECTION CATEGORIES

Regional Novels

(Included below are only those novels that truly define a locale as a specific region of the imagination.)

The Old Judge (Haliburton; 1849. Nova Scotia)
Canadian Crusoes (Traill; 1852. *YR* . Southeastern Ontario)
Jean Rivard: le défricheur (Gérin-Lajoie; 1874. Eastern Townships)
Jean Rivard; économiste (Gérin-Lajoie; 1876. Eastern Townships)
What Necessity Knows (Dougall; 1893. Eastern Townships)
The Man from Glengarry (Connor; 1901. Ottawa Valley)
Maria Chapdelaine (Hémon; 1916. Lac St. Jean)
The Viking Heart (Salverson; 1923. Manitoba)
Rockbound (Day; 1929. Nova Scotia)
Fruits of the Earth (Grove; 1933. Prairies)
Trente arpents (Ringuet; 1938. St. Lawrence)
As for Me and My House (Ross; 1941. Prairies)
Carrying Place (A. Mowat; 1944. Southeastern Ontario)
Le Survenant (Guèvremont; 1945. St. Lawrence)
Marie-Didace (Guèvremont; 1947. St. Lawrence)
Music at the Close (McCourt; 1947. Prairies)
Who Has Seen the Wind (Mitchell; 1947. Prairies)
The Nymph and the Lamp (Raddall; 1950. Nova Scotia; Sable Island)
La Petite Poule d'eau (Roy; 1950. Northern Manitoba)
Each Man's Son (MacLennan; 1951. Cape Breton)
The Mountain and the Valley (Buckler; 1952. Annapolis Valley)
The Channel Shore (Bruce; 1954. Nova Scotia)
Swamp Angel (Wilson; 1954. British Columbia; Interior)
Agaguk (Theriault; 1958. Arctic)
The Double Hook (Watson; 1959. British Columbia; Interior)
The Kissing Man (Elliott; 1962. Southwestern Ontario)
Menaud, maître-draveur (Savard; 1964. Quebec; rural)
Breaking Smith's Quarter Horse (St. Pierre; 1966. British Columbia; Interior)
La Guerre, Yes Sir! (Carrier; 1968. Quebec; rural)
Five Legs (Gibson; 1969. Southwestern Ontario)
The Studhorse Man (Kroetsch; 1969. Alberta)
Harpoon of the Hunter (Markoosie; 1970. *YR*. The North)
The White Dawn (Houston; 1971. Arctic)
Lives of Girls and Women (Munro; 1971. Southwestern Ontario)
Scann (Harlow; 1972. British Columbia; Interior)
The Temptations of Big Bear (Wiebe; 1973. Prairies)
The Disinherited (M. Cohen; 1974. Southeastern Ontario)
The Diviners (Laurence; 1974. Prairies)
Les Rescapes (Major; 1976. Quebec)
Blood Ties (Richards; 1976. New Brunswick; Miramichi)
The Invention of the World (Hodgins; 1977. Vancouver Island)

A New Athens (Hood; 1977. Southeastern Ontario)
The Sweet Second Summer of Kitty Malone (M. Cohen; 1979. Southeastern Ontario)
The Resurrection of Joseph Bourne (Hodgins; 1979. Vancouver Island)
Nightmare Tales (Freiberg; 1980. Annapolis Valley)
Jasmin (Truss; 1982. *YR*. Alberta)
Penumbra (Kerslake; 1984. Maritimes)
Intertidal Life (Thomas; 1984. Gulf Islands)
Road to the Stilt House (Richards; 1985. Maritimes)

Indians/Inuit/Métis

The History of Emily Montague (Brooke; 1769)
Wacousta (Richardson; 1832)
The Canadian Brothers (Richardson; 1840)
Canadian Crusoes (Traill; 1852. *YR*)
Lords of the North (Laut; 1900)
Two Little Savages (Seton; 1903. *YR*)
Silver Chief (O'Brien; 1933. *YR*)
The Adventures of Sajo and Her Beaver People (Grey Owl; 1935. *YR*)
The Flying Years (Niven; 1935)
Tay John (O'Hagan; 1939)
Mist on the River (Evans; 1954)
Lost in the Barrens (F. Mowat; 1956. *YR*)
Agaguk (Theriault; 1958)
Le Wapiti (Corriveau; 1964. *YR*)
Flaming Prairie (Hayes; 1965. *YR*)
Beautiful Losers (L. Cohen; 1966)
Raven's Cry (Harris; 1966. *YR*)
Breaking Smith's Quarter Horse (St. Pierre; 1966)
The Sparrow's Fall (Bodsworth; 1967)
Harpoon of the Hunter (Markoosie; 1970. *YR*)
The White Dawn (Houston; 1971)
White Eskimo (Horwood; 1972)
Gone Indian (Kroetsch; 1973)
The Vanishing Point (Mitchell; 1973)
Riverrun (Such; 1973)
The Temptations of Big Bear (Wiebe; 1973)
The Diviners (Laurence; 1974)
Jeanne, fille du roy (Martel; 1974. *YR*)
Wooden Hunters (M. Cohen; 1975)
Frozen Fire (Houston; 1977. *YR*)
The Scorched-Wood People (Wiebe; 1977)
Burning Water (Bowering; 1980)
Black Robe (Moore; 1985)

SELECTION CATEGORIES

Wilderness/The Frontier

Bogle Corbet (Galt; 1831)
Wacousta (Richardson; 1832)
The Canadian Brothers (Richardson; 1840)
Roughing It in the Bush (Moodie; 1852)
Canadian Crusoes (Traill; 1852. *YR*)
Jean Rivard: le défricheur (Gérin-Lajoie; 1874)
Lords of the North (Laut; 1900)
The Heart of the Ancient Wood (C.G.D. Roberts; 1900)
Two Little Savages (Seton; 1903. *YR*)
Maria Chapdelaine (Hémon; 1916)
The Viking Heart (Salverson; 1923)
Settlers of the Marsh (Grove; 1925)
Silver Chief (O'Brien; 1933. *YR*)
The Flying Years (Niven; 1935)
Starbuck Valley Winter (Haig-Brown; 1943. *YR*)
La Petite Poule d'eau (Roy; 1950)
Lost in the Barrens (F. Mowat; 1956. *YR*)
The Incredible Journey (Burnford; 1961)
Le Wapiti (Corriveau; 1964. *YR*)
Flaming Prairie (Hayes; 1965. *YR*)
Breaking Smith's Quarter Horse (St. Pierre; 1966)
The Sparrow's Fall (Bodsworth; 1967)
Harpoon of the Hunter (Markoosie; 1970. *YR*)
Surfacing (Atwood; 1972)
Scann (Harlow; 1972)
Jeanne, fille du roy (Martel; 1974. *YR*)
Frozen Fire (Houston; 1977. *YR*)
Black Robe (Moore; 1985)

The Family Farm

Jean Rivard: le défricheur (Gérin-Lajoie; 1874)
Maria Chapdelaine (Hémon; 1916)
The Prairie Mother (Stringer; 1920)
Settlers of the Marsh (Grove; 1925)
Wild Geese (Ostenso; 1925)
Grain (Stead; 1926)
Fruits of the Earth (Grove; 1933)
Trente arpents (Ringuet; 1938)
Music at the Close (McCourt; 1947)
La Petite Poule d'eau (Roy; 1950)
The Mountain and the Valley (Buckler; 1952)
The Disinherited (M. Cohen; 1974)

Rural/The Country Life

Belinda (Holmes; 1843)
Kate Danton (Fleming; 1876)
The Man from Glengarry (Connor; 1901)
Anne of Green Gables (Montgomery; 1908. *YR*)
Over Prairie Trails (Grove; 1922)
Jalna (de la Roche; 1927)
White Narcissus (Knister; 1929)
Carrying Place (A. Mowat; 1944)
Le Survenant (Guèvremont; 1945)
Kristli's Trees (Dunham; 1947. *YR*)
Marie-Didace (Guèvremont; 1947)
Luke Baldwin's Vow (Callaghan; 1948. *YR*)
The Channel Shore (Bruce; 1954)
La Belle Bête (Blais; 1959)
Peace Shall Destroy Many (Wiebe; 1962)
Menaud: maître-draveur (Savard; 1964)
The Last of the Great Picnics (McFarlane; 1965. *YR*)
The Studhorse Man (Kroetsch; 1969)
Kamouraska (Hébert; 1970)
Blood Ties (Richards; 1976)
Abra (Barfoot; 1978)
The Sweet Second Summer of Kitty Malone (M. Cohen; 1979)
Jasmin (Truss; 1982. *YR*)
Road to the Stilt House (Richards; 1985)

The Small Town

"The Stepsure Letters" (McCulloch; 1821-22)
Bogle Corbet (Galt; 1831)
What Necessity Knows (Dougall; 1893)
The Curé of St. Philippe (Grey; 1899)
The Imperialist (Duncan; 1904)
Sowing Seeds in Danny (McClung; 1908)
Sunshine Sketches of a Little Town (Leacock; 1912)
Think of the Earth (Brooker; 1936)
As for Me and My House (Ross; 1941)
Who Has Seen the Wind (Mitchell; 1947)
Tempest-Tost (Davies; 1951)
Poussière sur la ville (Langevin; 1953)
The Double Hook (Watson; 1959)
Le Libraire (Bessette; 1960)
A Candle to Light the Sun (Blondal; 1960)
The Kissing Man (Elliott; 1962)
A Jest of God (Laurence; 1966)

Lives of Girls and Women (Munro; 1971)
Scann (Harlow; 1972)
The Glass Knight (Helwig; 1976)
Les Rescapes (Major; 1976)
The Resurrection of Joseph Bourne (Hodgins; 1979)

Urban Experience

The Old Judge (Haliburton; 1849. Halifax)
Antoinette de Mirecourt (Leprohon; 1864. Montreal)
The Measure of the Rule (Barr; 1908. Toronto)
My Lady of the Snows (Brown; 1908. Ottawa)
The Magpie (Durkin; 1923. Winnipeg)
Such Is My Beloved (Callaghan; 1934. Toronto)
Les Demi-civilisés (Harvey; 1934. Quebec)
They Shall Inherit the Earth (Callaghan; 1935. Toronto)
More Joy in Heaven (Callaghan; 1937. Toronto)
Barometer Rising (MacLennan; 1941. Halifax)
Earth and High Heaven (Graham; 1944. Montreal)
Bonheur d'occasion (Roy; 1945. Montreal)
Les Plouffe (Lemelin; 1948. Quebec)
The Innocent Traveller (Wilson; 1949. Vancouver)
Cabbagetown (Garner; 1950. Toronto)
The Loved and the Lost (Callaghan; 1951. Montreal)
The Lonely Passion of Judith Hearne (Moore; 1955. Belfast)
Son of a Smaller Hero (Richler; 1955. Montreal)
The Sacrifice (Wiseman; 1956. Winnipeg)
Under the Ribs of Death (Marlyn; 1957. Winnipeg)
The Watch that Ends the Night (MacLennan; 1959. Montreal)
The Apprenticeship of Duddy Kravitz (Richler; 1959. Montreal)
The Luck of Ginger Coffey (Moore; 1960. Montreal)
Silence on the Shore (Garner; 1962. Toronto)
The Deserter (Le Pan; 1964. London)
Prochain épisode (Aquin; 1965. Montreal)
Le Couteau sur la table (Godbout; 1965. Montreal)
The Boy with an R in His Hand (Reaney; 1965. Toronto. *YR*)
Beautiful Losers (L. Cohen; 1966. Montreal)
Mirror on the Floor (Bowering; 1967. Vancouver)
Combat Journal for Place d'Armes (Symons; 1967. Montreal)
Double Spell (Lunn; 1968. Toronto. *YR*)
I Am Mary Dunne (Moore; 1968. New York)
The Edible Woman (Atwood; 1969. Toronto)
The Fire-Dwellers (Laurence; 1969. Vancouver)
Jos Connaissant (Beaulieu; 1970. Montreal)
A Fairly Good Time (Gallant; 1970. Paris)
The Weekend Man (Wright; 1970. Toronto)
St. Urbain's Horseman (Richler; 1971. Montreal)
"Munchmeyer" (Thomas; 1971. Vancouver)
From Anna (Little; 1972. Toronto. *YR*)

Going Down Slow (Metcalf; 1972. Montreal)
The Book of Eve (Beresford-Howe; 1973. Montreal)
Storm of Fortune (Clarke; 1973. Toronto)
Lord Nelson Tavern (Smith; 1974. Halifax)
The Candy Factory (Fraser; 1975. Toronto)
The Young in One Another's Arms (Rule; 1977. Vancouver)
Lunar Attractions (Blaise; 1979. U.S. Midwest)
Héloïse (Hébert; 1980. Paris)
General Ludd (Metcalf; 1980. Montreal)
Contract with the World (Rule; 1980. Vancouver)
Thérèse et Pierrette (Tremblay; 1980. Montreal)
Le Matou (Beauchemin; 1981. Montreal)
The Rebel Angels (Davies; 1981. Toronto)
Lunatic Villas (Engel; 1981. Toronto)
La Première personne (Turgeon; 1981. Los Angeles)
Angel Square (Doyle; 1984. Ottawa. *YR*)
The Minerva Program (Mackay; 1984. Toronto. *YR*)
My Present Age (Vanderhaeghe; 1984. Saskatoon)

Immigrant/Emigrant Experience

Bogle Corbet (Galt; 1831. English/Scottish)
Roughing It in the Bush (Moodie; 1852. English)
The Viking Heart (Salverson; 1923. Icelandic)
Settlers of the Marsh (Grove; 1925. Swedish)
A Search for America (Grove; 1927. Swedish/Scottish)
The Flying Years (Niven; 1935. Scottish)
The Innocent Traveller (Wilson; 1949. English)
Son of a Smaller Hero (Richler; 1955. Jewish-Polish)
The Sacrifice (Wiseman; 1956. Jewish-Ukrainian)
Under the Ribs of Death (Marlyn; 1957. Hungarian)
The Luck of Ginger Coffey (Moore; 1960. Irish)
Peace Shall Destroy Many (Wiebe; 1962. Mennonite-Ukrainian)
In Praise of Older Women (Vizinczey; 1965. Hungarian)
Honor Bound (Downie; 1971. American. *YR*)
From Anna (Little; 1972. German. *YR*)
Going Down Slow (Metcalf; 1972. English)
Storm of Fortune (Clarke; 1973. Barbadian)
Jeanne, fille du roy (Martel; 1974. French. *YR*)
Underground to Canada (Smucker; 1977. Black-American. *YR*)

Politics

The History of Emily Montague (Brooke; 1769)
Jean Rivard: économiste (Gérin-Lajoie; 1876)
The Curé of St. Philippe (Grey; 1899)
The Imperialist (Duncan; 1904)
My Lady of the Snows (Brown; 1908)
Sunshine Sketches of a Little Town (Leacock; 1912)

The Magpie (Durkin; 1923)
The Master of the Mill (Grove; 1944)
Two Solitudes (MacLennan; 1945)
Cabbagetown (Garner; 1950)
The Watch that Ends the Night (MacLennan; 1959)
Prochain épisode (Aquin; 1965)
The Last of the Great Picnics (McFarlane; 1965 *YR*)
The New Ancestors (Godfrey; 1970)
You Can't Get There from Here (Hood; 1972)
The Scorched-Wood People (Wiebe; 1977)
Famous Last Words (Findley; 1981)
Willie: A Romance (Robertson; 1983)

Sexual Politics

(Novels in which conflict arises from the impositions of gender stereotyping.)

The History of Emily Montague (Brooke; 1769)
Belinda (Holmes; 1843)
Antoinette de Mirecourt (Leprohon; 1864)
The Lady of the Ice (De Mille; 1870)
What Necessity Knows (Dougall; 1893)
Settlers of the Marsh (Grove; 1925)
Wild Geese (Ostenso; 1925)
As for Me and My House (Ross; 1941)
Carrying Place (A. Mowat; 1944)
The Loved and the Lost (Callaghan; 1951)
Poussière sur la ville (Langevin; 1953)
The Channel Shore (Bruce; 1954)
Swamp Angel (Wilson; 1954)
"Its Image on the Mirror" (Gallant; 1957)
Green Water, Green Sky (Gallant; 1959)
Doux-Amer (Martin; 1960)
The Stone Angel (Laurence; 1964)
Le Couteau sur la table (Godbout; 1965)
Beautiful Losers (L. Cohen; 1966)
Combat Journal for Place d'Armes (Symons; 1967)
I Am Mary Dunne (Moore; 1968)
L'Antiphonaire (Aquin; 1969)
The Edible Woman (Atwood; 1969)
The Fire-Dwellers (Laurence; 1969)
A Fairly Good Time (Gallant; 1970)
The New Ancestors (Godfrey; 1970)
From a Seaside Town (Levine; 1970)
Mrs. Blood (Thomas; 1970)
Lives of Girls and Women (Munro; 1971)
Le Coeur de la baleine bleue (Poulin; 1971)
"Munchmeyer" and "Prospero on the Island" (Thomas; 1971)

Surfacing (Atwood; 1972)
The Book of Eve (Beresford-Howe; 1973)
Storm of Fortune (Clarke; 1973)
The Pegnitz Junction (Gallant; 1973)
Neige noire (Aquin; 1974)
The Diviners (Laurence; 1974)
Jeanne, fille du roy (Martel; 1974. *YR*)
Blown Figures (Thomas; 1974)
Wooden Hunters (M. Cohen; 1975)
The Candy Factory (Fraser; 1975)
The Glass Knight (Helwig; 1976)
Small Ceremonies (Shields; 1976)
The Wars (Findley; 1977)
The Young in One Another's Arms (Rule; 1977)
The Glassy Sea (Engel; 1978)
Who Do You Think You Are? (Munro; 1978)
The Sweet Second Summer of Kitty Malone (M. Cohen; 1979)
Fat Woman (Rooke; 1980)
Contract with the World (Rule; 1980)
The Rebel Angels (Davies; 1981)
Lunatic Villas (Engel; 1981)
Dancing in the Dark (Barfoot; 1982)
The Ivory Swing (Hospital; 1982)
Alibi (Kroetsch; 1983)
Still (nichol; 1983)
Not Wanted on the Voyage (Findley; 1984)
Intertidal Life (Thomas; 1984)
My Present Age (Vanderhaeghe; 1984)
The Handmaid's Tale (Atwood; 1985)
Borderline (Hospital; 1985)
Miss Abigail's Part (Terry; 1986)
No Fixed Address (van Herk; 1986)

Homosexuality
Beautiful Losers (L. Cohen; 1966)
Combat Journal for Place d'Armes (Symons; 1967)
World of Wonders (Davies; 1975)
The Wars (Findley; 1977)
The Young in One Another's Arms (Rule; 1977)
Lunar Attractions (Blaise; 1979)
Burning Water (Bowering; 1980)
Joshua Then and Now (Richler; 1980)
Contract with the World (Rule; 1980)

Feminism
The History of Emily Montague (Brooke; 1769)
What Necessity Knows (Dougall; 1893)
Sowing Seeds in Danny (McClung; 1908)

SELECTION CATEGORIES

The Magpie (Durkin; 1923)
The Nymph and the Lamp (Raddall; 1950)
Swamp Angel (Wilson; 1954)
The Stone Angel (Laurence; 1964)
I Am Mary Dunne (Moore; 1968)
The Edible Woman (Atwood; 1969)
The Fire-Dwellers (Laurence; 1969)
A Fairly Good Time (Gallant; 1970)
Mrs. Blood (Thomas; 1970)
Lives of Girls and Women (Munro; 1971)
"Munchmeyer" and "Prospero on the Island" (Thomas; 1971)
Surfacing (Atwood; 1972)
The Book of Eve (Beresford-Howe; 1973)
The Pegnitz Junction (Gallant; 1973)
The Diviners (Laurence; 1974)
Jeanne, fille du roy (Martel; 1974. *YR*)
Blown Figures (Thomas; 1974)
Bear (Engel; 1976)
The Glass Knight (Helwig; 1976)
Small Ceremonies (Shields; 1976)
The Young in One Another's Arms (Rule; 1977)
Abra (Barfoot; 1978)
The Glassy Sea (Engel; 1978)
Who Do You Think You Are? (Munro; 1978)
Contract with the World (Rule; 1980)
Lunatic Villas (Engel; 1981)
One Proud Summer (Hewitt & Mackay; 1981. *YR*)
Dancing in the Dark (Barfoot; 1982)
The Ivory Swing (Hospital; 1982)
The Biggest Modern Woman of the World (Swan; 1983)
Intertidal Life (Engel; 1984)
The Minerva Program (Mackay; 1984. *YR*)
The Handmaid's Tale (Atwood; 1985)
Borderline (Hospital; 1985)
No Fixed Address (van Herk; 1986)

Growing Up
Anne of Green Gables (Montgomery; 1908. *YR*)
God's Sparrows (Child; 1937)
Who Has Seen the Wind (Mitchell; 1947)
The Mountain and the Valley (Buckler; 1952)
Green Water, Green Sky (Gallant; 1959)
A Candle to Light the Sun (Blondal; 1960)
L'Avalée des avalés (Ducharme; 1966)
Jimmy (Poulin; 1969)
A Bird in the House (Laurence; 1970)
The Swing in the Garden (Hood; 1975)

Lunar Attractions (Blaise; 1979)
Thérèse et Pierrette (Tremblay; 1980)
What's the Matter, Girl? (Brochmann; 1980. *YR*)
Jasmin (Truss; 1982. *YR*)
Penumbra (Kerslake; 1984)
The Baby Project (Ellis; 1986. *YR*)

Family Life
The Imperialist (Duncan; 1904)
Maria Chapdelaine (Hémon; 1916)
The Prairie Mother (Stringer; 1920)
The Viking Heart (Salverson; 1923)
Jalna (de la Roche; 1927)
Fruits of the Earth (Grove; 1933)
God's Sparrows (Child; 1937)
Trente arpents (Ringuet; 1938)
The Master of the Mill (Grove; 1944)
Bonheur d'occasion (Roy; 1945)
Les Plouffe (Lemelin; 1948)
The Innocent Traveller (Wilson; 1949)
La Petite Poule d'eau (Roy; 1950)
The Mountain and the Valley (Buckler; 1952)
The Channel Shore (Bruce; 1954)
The Sacrifice (Wiseman; 1956)
La Belle Bête (Blais; 1959)
Une Saison dans la vie d'Emmanuel (Blais; 1965)
House of Hate (Janes; 1970)
A Bird in the House (Laurence; 1970)
Honor Bound (Downie; 1971. *YR*)
The Disinherited (M. Cohen; 1974)
The Swing in the Garden (Hood; 1975)
Blood Ties (Richards; 1976)
Small Ceremonies (Shields; 1976)
A New Athens (Hood; 1977)
Reservoir Ravine (Hood; 1979)
What's the Matter, Girl? (Brochmann; 1980. *YR*)
Road to the Stilt House (Richards; 1985)
The Baby Project (Ellis; 1986. *YR*)

Growing Old/Being Old
The Flying Years (Niven; 1935)
Trente arpents (Ringuet; 1938)
The Master of the Mill (Grove; 1944)
The Innocent Traveller (Wilson; 1949)
The Stone Angel (Laurence; 1964)
La Sagouine (Maillet; 1971)
The Book of Eve (Beresford-Howe; 1973)

Index

Bold-face numbers indicate main entry.

INDEX

INDEX

INDEX

INDEX